Annual of Scientific Discovery
by David Ames Wells

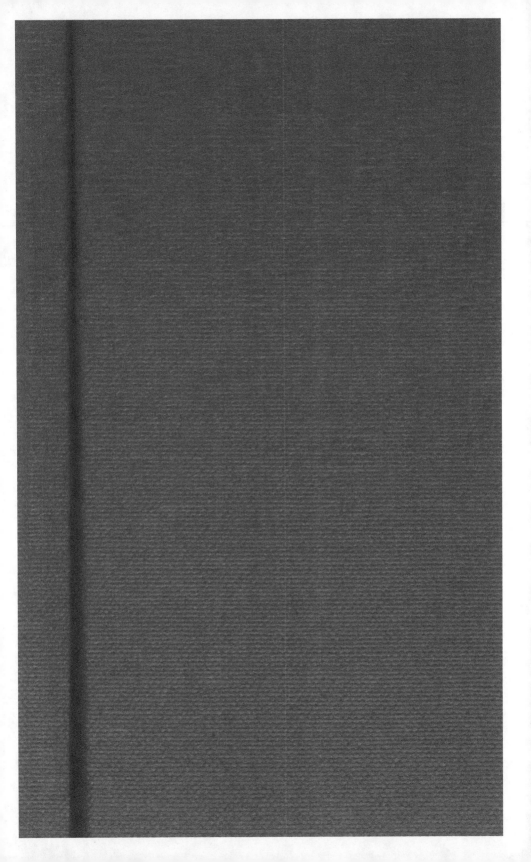

The Annual of Scientific Discovery

FOR 1865.

PUBLISHED BY GOULD AND LINCOLN, BOSTON.

In issuing the ANNUAL OF SCIENTIFIC DISCOVERY FOR 1865, the publishers would take occasion to direct special attention to the character and object of this long-established and popular work.

The Annual is published near the commencement of every year, presenting a compact, carefully arranged, and easily accessible summary of all the important new facts and theories in every department of science and the industrial arts, which have been announced to the world during the preceding twelve months, — the statements being made in as popular language as the subjects will admit. The boundaries of every department of science are now enlarging so rapidly, that the publication of a yearly *résumé* of progress has long been felt by students and specialists to be an indispensable necessity, — no other so ready and convenient method of "*posting up*" being available.

But there are in addition a very large number of intelligent persons in this country who, without the time or opportunity to devote themselves to any special study or reading, nevertheless desire to become acquainted with the truths of science, and with what is going on in the scientific world. To these the *Annual of Scientific Discovery* especially addresses itself; and although its circulation has been large, we feel assured that the character and object of the work needs only to be made more fully known to insure for it even a much wider circulation.

Appreciated, however, as the Annual has been in previous years by large numbers not only of the intelligent American people, but also the English, its publication at the present time seems more needful and opportune than ever before. The high prices which have prevailed for the last two years, and the preoccupation of the attention of the people with the incidents of a great war, have terminated the existence of some American journals, accustomed to report the details of scientific progress, and have diminished the circulation or fullness of many others. The high rates of foreign exchange have also caused the discontinuance of subscrip-

(1)

tions to many European scientific journals, which formerly circulated very largely in this country; and have thus cut off another source of popular information.

Under these circumstances, therefore, it will be seen that this is almost the only medium in the United States through which the reports of recent scientific progress, at home and abroad, are promptly rendered accessible to the public, — an assertion which is strikingly illustrated by the fact, that the present volume contains the first detailed account, published on this side of the Atlantic, of the remarkable discoveries effected during the past year, through the agency of Spectrum Analysis.

Among other noticeable features of the present volume, is a complete *résumé* of the recent discoveries respecting the " pre-historic man," and the antiquity of the human race; a report of Tyndall's recent investigations in relation to light and heat; photo-sculpture; Draper's speculations on the transition of matter; recent improvements in war implements and constructions; on the cultivation of fish; production of sexes at will; utilization of sewage; production of petroleum; use of steam expansively, &c. &c.

The full Series of the Annual of Scientific Discovery now numbers *sixteen volumes*. They constitute a most complete Encyclopedia of scientific and practical knowledge; and in the language of the N. Y. *Times*, " Condense a greater quantity of sterling matter than any other set of books in the world!" The series has furthermore this advantage over any Encyclopedia, inasmuch as it chronicles the *failures* as well as the *achievements* in science; and a record of the first is equally indispensable with the last, to all who desire to know what has been attempted or speculated upon by the pioneers of invention and discovery, as well as what has been realized.

The Series contains fine steel engravings of Professors, — Agassiz, Silliman, Hitchcock, Wyman, Mitchel, Joseph Henry, A. D. Bache, H. D. Rogers, Dr. A. A. Gould, Isaac Lea, Esq., Richard M. Hoe, Esq., Capt. J. Ericsson, Admiral Dahlgren, Gen. Gilmore, &c.

Price per Volume, 12mo, Cloth, ... 1 75
Price per complete Set, 16 Volumes, uniform style, with neat,
    substantial box, ... 28 00

ANNUAL

OF

SCIENTIFIC DISCOVERY:

OR,

YEAR-BOOK OF FACTS IN SCIENCE AND ART

FOR 1865.

EXHIBITING THE

MOST IMPORTANT DISCOVERIES AND IMPROVEMENTS

IN

MECHANICS, USEFUL ARTS, NATURAL PHILOSOPHY, CHEMISTRY, ASTRONOMY, GEOLOGY, ZOOLOGY, BOTANY, MINERALOGY, METEOROLOGY, GEOGRAPHY, ANTIQUITIES, ETC.

TOGETHER WITH

NOTES ON THE PROGRESS OF SCIENCE DURING THE YEAR 1864; A LIST OF RECENT SCIENTIFIC PUBLICATIONS; OBITUARIES OF EMINENT SCIENTIFIC MEN, ETC.

EDITED BY

DAVID A. WELLS, A.M., M.D.,

AUTHOR OF PRINCIPLES OF NATURAL PHILOSOPHY, PRINCIPLES OF CHEMISTRY, FIRST PRINCIPLES OF GEOLOGY, ETC.

BOSTON:
GOULD AND LINCOLN.
59 WASHINGTON STREET.
NEW YORK: SHELDON AND COMPANY.
CINCINNATI: GEORGE S. BLANCHARD.
LONDON: TRUBNER & CO.
1865.

NOTES BY THE EDITOR

PROGRESS OF SCIENCE FOR THE YEAR 1864.

THE most noticeable events in the history of the progress of science for the year 1864, have been, first and foremost, the remarkable discoveries made by Messrs. Huggins and Miller, of England, through the process of "spectrum analysis;" and the great additional light that has been thrown upon the subject of the "antiquity of the human race," and the contemporaneous existence of man with certain of the extinct animals. Other matters of prominent interest are the continued development of the business of obtaining and utilizing petroleum; the continued investigations of Tyndall and others in respect to the properties of light and heat; the application of photography to sculpture and topography; the investigations in respect to the use of steam expansively; sewage utilization; meat preservation and packing, and fish culture; and the results of unremitting experimentation in all that relates to military and naval warfare. An exceedingly interesting and suggestive paper will also be found in this volume, by Prof. Draper, in relation to the "Transitions of Matter."

The discoveries of Messrs. Huggins and Miller, and especially of the first-named investigator, in respect to the nebulæ, have been truly characterized by English authority as by far the most wonderful and interesting that have ever been recorded in the whole history of science; and cannot fail to excite the most intense interest. The nebulæ which Mr. Huggins has observed, are six of the so-called "planetary nebulæ," and an equal number of nebulæ with a more or less distinctly bright luminous centre. The intent of the inquiry has been, What is the condition of this nebulous matter? Is it highly gaseous, expanded to an enormous area in space? or is its luminosity caused, as some have considered, by myriads of solid masses comi-

5

into collision, and thus that their heat and light are revealed by the telescope? Mr. Huggins's observations go to show that in some, at least, of these nebulæ there is no solid matter at all. Herschel has stated that the mass of one of these planetary nebulæ, if distant from us as far as 61 Cygni, would fill a space equal in diameter to seven times that of the orbit of Neptune; and hence, were it not that the light was concentrated nearly into a single line, its examination would not be practicable. In the light of these nebulæ, as is shown elsewhere, there is nothing to indicate, as in the case of the sun, a solid luminous globe, behind the luminous photosphere, but the light from them is such as is characteristic of gaseity. When a star occurred in, or was associated with, the nebulæ, a very feeble continuous spectrum was observed. To understand fully the researches which have led to Mr. Huggins's conclusions, the reader would do well to refer to the explanations of the process of spectrum analysis as detailed in the volumes of the *Annual of Scientific Discovery* for 1862, '63, and '64; there being at the present time no continuous and complete published record of these investigations.   .

The 34th annual meeting of the British Association for the Advancement of Science, was held at Bath, England, and was very largely attended by British and foreign scientists. The annual address of the President, Sir Chas. Lyell (republished *in full* in this volume), was, in the main, a popular discussion of the most recent geological results and theories, and cannot fail to be read with interest.

At this meeting a Committee of the Association, consisting of Lord Wrottesley, Sir W. Armstrong, the Astronomer Royal, the Master of the Mint, Prof. Leon Levi, Mr. W. Ewart (Chairman of a similar committee in the House of Commons), and other distinguished gentlemen, reported in favor of adopting the metric system (of weights and measures) of France, and the report was unanimously adopted, yet with some discussion as to whether the unit should be the French meter or not. Among the recommendations of the Committee, were the following: —

That it is desirable, in the interests of science, to adopt a decimal system of weights and measures. That in furtherance of this proposal it is desirable, from its scientific capabilities, to adopt the metric system. That it be recommended to the Government, in all cases in which statistical documents issued by them relate to questions of international interest, to give the metric equivalents to English weights and measures. That in communications respecting weights and measures, presented to foreign countries which have adopted the metric system, equivalents in the metric system be given for the ordinary English expressions for length, capacity, bulk, and weight. That it be recommended to the authors of scientific communications, in all cases where the expense or labor involved would not be too great, to give the metric equivalents of the weights and measures mentioned. That treatises explaining the metric system, with diagrams, should be forthwith laid before the public. That works on arithmetic should contain metric tables of weights and measures, with suitable exercises on those tables ; and that inspectors of schools should examine candidates for pupil-teachers in the metric system. That in reports made to the British Association, degrees of heat and cold be given according to both the Centigrade and Fahrenheit thermometers ; and that the scales of thermometers constructed for scientific purposes be divided both according to the Centigrade and Fahrenheit scales ; and that barometric scales be divided into fractions of the meter, as well as into those of the foot and inch.

In the discussion which followed the presentation of the report of the Committee, Sir John Bowring stated that at the recent Postal Congress at Paris, at which 16 governments in Europe and America were represented, a resolution was unanimously adopted that the metric system should be universally adopted for postal communication, and that if adopted as a principle, it would afford the greatest possible facility for the settlement of accounts and intercommunication generally. The second fact was this, that in China, where there were agglomerated no less than 400,000,000 of human beings, the decimal system universally prevailed, and he had never heard of a boy of seven years who made a mistake in any account. He had even heard savages say that the decimal and metric system must have come from God. They found it the greatest blessing, because, having their ten fingers, they always carried with them the means of settling their accounts.

A deputation from the chemical section of the Association, through Prof. Williamson, bore testimony to the results of the experience of chemists in their use of the metric system in operations of daily occurrence, and stated that working chemists, with very few exceptions, were in the habit of using the metric system in almost all their experimental operations, and that they derived from it an advantage which nothing could induce them to sacrifice or exchange for that absence of system which at present prevailed in England. Profs. Owen and Hoffman gave it as their opinion that the discordancy in the systems of weights and measures of different countries is so great, and so much time and labor is required to convert the weights and measures of one country into their equivalents of a foreign system, that practically the knowledge of one nation was a sealed book to the scientific men of others. And as to the facility with which the system could be learned, Prof. Levi, the eminent statistical and politico-economic writer, stated "that a boy could make the same progress in arithmetic taught according to the metric system in ten months as would, according to the existing method, take him two years and ten months to accomplish."

The Old and the New Systems of Education.—A year or two since a Parliamentary Commission was appointed in England, to inquire into the management of certain leading colleges and schools, and especially in regard to the studies pursued and the instruction given therein. In prosecuting these investigations, the Commission were naturally led to devote considerable attention to the relations and intrinsic worth of the two great educational methods of the present day, —the linguistic and the scientific,—and for the purpose of obtaining the requisite information, they invited the testimony of many of the most prominent educators in the kingdom. The testimony of these gentlemen is given in the Appendix of the Report of the Commission recently published, and from it, we derive the following interesting summary. The grounds taken by the advocates of an extended classical education, are well represented in the following answer given by the Rev. F. Temple, master of the famous Rugby School, in reply to a question of the Commission : —

Question—"As in your judgment the opinion of a first-rate scientific man, who is not a first-rate man in classical attainments, depreciatory of the disciplinary value of classical attainments, is not of very high value, so would you think that the opinion of a first-rate classical scholar not having the same rank scientifically and tending to depreciate the disciplinary value of scientific attainment was also not of very great value?"

Answer—"No; I do not think it would be in the same degree at all, because it is essentially a part of the one kind of study to know human nature, and it is not a part of the other. The one is naturally led to the study of man, and to the study, therefore, of what is good for the discipline of the mind; the other has not studied man, but things, and it is not his business to know what is good for the discipline of the mind. The study of the philosophy of the question comes properly within the sphere of one man's science, but not properly within the sphere of the other man's science."

Among the scientists whose testimony was taken, were Profs. Faraday, Owen, Sir Charles Lyell, Dr. Carpenter (the well-known author of several works on anatomy, physiology, and the microscope), and others. Their testimony is clear, decided, and very convincing. Differing on some minor points, they united in asserting that the sin of the public schools is, that although the great majority of boys do not go to the universities, yet the requirements of those who do go to the universities in fact regulate the system. Dr. Carpenter, in arguing that even mathematics is no substitute for the physical sciences, remarked : —

"Mathematical training exercises the mind most strenuously in a very narrow groove, so to speak. It starts with axioms which have nothing to do with external phenomena, but which the mind finds in itself; and the whole science of mathematics may be evolved out of the original axioms which the mind finds in itself. * * * Now it is the essence of scientific training that the mind finds the object of its study in the external world; and it appears to me that a training which leaves out of view the relation of man to external nature, is a very defective one, and that the faculties which bring his intelligence into relation with the phenomena of the external world are subjects for education and discipline equally important with the faculties by which he exercises his reason purely upon abstraction. * * * I may add, that having given considerable attention to the refuted phenomena of mesmerism, electrobiology, spiritualism, etc., I have had occasion to observe that the *want of scientific habits of mind* is the source of a vast amount of prevalent misconception as to what constitutes adequate proof of the marvels reported by witnesses neither untruthful nor unintelligent as to ordinary matters. I could mention striking instances of misconception in men of high literary cultivation, or high mathematical attainments; whilst I have met with no one who had undergone the discipline of an adequate course of scientific study, who has not at once recognized the fallacies in such testimony when they have been pointed out to him."

Sir Charles Lyell considered that the principle of limiting education to the languages and the mathematics is a direct injury to many men. A large portion of those who would have shown a strong taste for the sciences, are forced into one line, and after they leave their colleges they neglect branches they have been taught, and so cultivate neither the one nor the other. I have known men quite late in life, who have forgotten all the Latin and Greek which they spent their early years in acquiring, hit upon geology or some other branch, and all at once their energies have been awakened, and you have been astonished to see how they came out. They would have taken that line long before, and done good work in it, had they been taught the elements of it at school. *Question.* So there was a mental waste in their youth? *Answer.* Quite so.

The following is an extract from Prof. Faraday's testimony.

"Up to this very day there come to me persons of good education, men and women quite fit for all that you expect from education; they come to me, and they talk to me, about things that belong to natural science; about mesmerism, table-turning, flying through the air, about the laws of gravity; they come to me to ask me questions, and they insist against me, who think I know a little of these laws, that I am wrong and they are right, in a manner which shows how little the ordinary course of education has taught such minds. Let them study natural things, and they will get a very different idea from that which they have obtained by that education. It happens up to this day. I do not wonder at those who have not been educated at all, but such as I refer to, say to me, ' I have felt it, and done it, and seen it, and though I have not flown through the air, I believe it.' ' Persons who have been fully educated according to the present system, come with the same propositions as the untaught and stronger ones, because they have a stronger conviction that they are right. They are ignorant of their ignorance at the end of all that education. It happens even with men who are excellent mathematicians. * * * Who are the men whose powers are really developed? Who are they who have made the electric telegraph, the steam engine, and the railroad? Are they the men who have been taught Latin and Greek? Were the Stephensons such? These men had that knowledge which habitually had been neglected and pushed down below. It has only been those who, having a special inclination for this kind of knowledge, have forced themselves out of that ignorance by an education and into a life of their own."

The language of the other gentlemen consulted was of the same tenor, and equally urgent for a change in the dominant system. They showed that the physical sciences might be safely studied before the languages are commenced; that they might be pursued hand in hand with the languages without crowding and with a gain of time. And they especially insisted that no nation in this day can safely continue a system of education which ignores the study of natural laws and the physical constitution of the globe.

In a recent series of lectures published by Prof. Max Muller on the " Science of Language," this distinguished linguistic authority thus speaks of the usefulness of the study of modern languages in throwing light upon the laws of language : —

" The importance of the modern languages for a true insight into the nature of language, and for a true appreciation of the principles which govern the growth of ancient languages, has never been sufficiently appreciated. Because a study of the ancient languages has always been confined to a small minority, and because it is generally supposed that it is easier to learn a modern than an ancient tongue, people have become accustomed to look upon the so-called classical languages,—Sanskrit, Greek, and Latin,—as vehicles of thought more pure and perfect than the spoken or so-called vulgar dialects of Europe. We are not speaking at present of the literature of Greece, or Rome, or ancient India, as compared with the literature of England, France, Germany, and Italy. We speak only of language, of the roots and words, the declensions, conjugations, and constructions peculiar to each dialect; and with regard to these it must be admitted that the modern stand on a perfect equality with the ancient languages. Can it be supposed that we, who are always advancing in art, in science, in philosophy, and religion, should have allowed language, the most powerful instrument of the mind, to fall from its pristine purity, to lose its vigor and nobility, and to become a mere jargon? Language, though it changes continually, does by no means continually decay; or at all events, what we are wont to call decay and corruption in the history of language is in truth nothing but the necessary condition of its life. Before the tribunal of the Science of Language, the difference between ancient and modern languages vanishes. As in botany, aged trees are not placed in a different class from young trees, it would be against all the principles of scientific classification to distinguish between old and young languages. We must study the tree as a whole, from the time when the seed is placed in the soil to the time when it bears fruit; and we must study language in the same manner as a whole, tracing its life uninterruptedly from the simplest roots to the most complex derivatives. He who can see in modern languages nothing but corruption or anomaly, understands but little of the true nature of language. If the ancient languages throw light on the origin of the modern dialects, many secrets in the nature of the dead languages can only be explained by the evidence of the living dialects. Apart from all other considerations, modern languages help us to establish, by evidence which cannot be questioned, the leading principles of the science of language. They are to the student of language what the tertiary, or even more recent, formations are to the geologist.

"In the modern romance dialects, we have before our eyes a more complete and distinct picture or repetition of the origin and growth of language than anywhere else in the whole history of human speech. We can watch the Latin from the time of the first Scipionic inscription (283 B. C.) to the time when we meet with the first traces of Neo-Latin speech in Italy, Spain, and France. We can then follow for 1,000 years the later history of modern Latin, in its six distinct dialects, all possessing a rich and well-authenticated literature. If certain forms of grammar are doubtful in French, they receive light from the collateral evidence which is to be found in Italian or Spanish. If the origin of a word is obscure in Italian, we have only to look to French and Spanish, and we shall generally receive some useful hints to guide us in our researches. Where, except in these modern dialects, can we expect to find a perfectly certain standard by which to measure the possible changes which words may undergo both in form and meaning without losing their identity? We can here silence all objections by facts, and we can force conviction by tracing, step by step, every change of sound and sense from Latin to French; whereas when we have to deal with Greek and Latin and Sanskrit, we can only use the soft pressure of inductive reasoning."

At the anniversary meeting of the Royal Society (Eng.), the President, Gen. Sabine, stated that the great work which has been going on for some years under the auspices of the Society, viz: that of preparing a Catalogue of the titles of all the papers and articles contained in all the leading scientific *Transactions* and *Journals* for the present century, was in the process of completion. The number of titles of papers already copied exceeds 180,000, and the copying is to be brought down to 1863 inclusive.

A manuscript catalogue in 82 volumes, with more to follow, containing the titles of the several works in chronological order, is placed for use in the Royal Society's Library. The next step will be a printed catalogue of the whole number of titles, arranged alphabetically according to authors' names, accompanied by an alphabetical index of subjects; and in this way there will be offered to scientific inquirers in all parts of the world an easy means of reference to all the important scientific subjects published during 63 years of the present century,—a century the most active and fruitful in scientific results since the world began.

The cost of printing this great catalogue will be generously assumed by the British Government. A certain number of copies will be presented to scientific institutions and public libraries in all parts of the world; and the remainder of the edition will be offered for sale at the cost of printing and paper only.

No Science of History. — Mr. Froude, the well-known English historian, in a recent lecture before the Royal Institution, on the Science of History took the ground, that there can be no such thing as a science of history, because of the impossibility of educing the laws of human motives and actions, as in physical science the laws of natural phenomena are educed by observation, and that which will be, can be predicted from what has been. "Whether the end be seventy years hence, or seven hundred," said the lecturer, in his peroration, "be the close of the mortal history of humanity as far distant in the future, as its shadowy beginnings seem now to lie behind us — this only we may foretell with confidence, — that the riddle of man's nature will remain unsolved. There will be that in him yet which physical laws will fail to explain, — that something, whatever it may be, in himself and in the world, which science cannot fathom, and which suggests the unknown possibilities of his origin and his destiny.

Interesting Sanitary Memoranda. — The following Sanitary facts are worthy of note. When Mr. Edwin Chadwick, about twenty years ago, raised in Great Britain the question of Sanitary reform, and persisted in keeping it before the public until steps were taken to carry out measures for drainage, sewerage, water supply and other essential works, he asserted that by adoption of the proposed improvement, a diminution of one third in the number of deaths in a town or a district might be confidently looked for. It seemed a bold prediction, but it has been more than verified; for in all the British towns which have accepted and accomplished sanitary reforms, it is found that the diminution in the number of deaths is one half. In other words, instead of thirty deaths in every 1,000 of the population, the number is now not more than fifteen, and in some instances even less than fifteen. "Many," says the editor of *Chambers's Journal*, "will be able to identify for themselves towns in which such satisfactory results have been obtained. There is no doubt about the matter, for it is as clearly demonstrated by comparison of a drained section of a town with the undrained part as by town with town. Hence we see that if sanitary reform were carried out over the whole kingdom, there would be a saving of one-half in the rate of mortality to be added to the usual increase of population by births, which at the next census in 1871 would tell with striking effect in the tables of increase. With a gain so large as this, emigration need not be dreaded, nor plague and pestilence apart, should fears be entertained as to the sanitary amelioration of the country at large. Though undrained and ill-watered towns are still numerous, there is a growing tendency towards improvement, which cannot fail to be recognized in all future records of the population of the realm."

Animal Mechanics. — A curious and valuable contribution to science has been recently made by Rev. S. Haughton of Dublin, in a paper detailing certain experiments, — on the mechanical force of the muscles, their duration when in operation, and their value, — the whole investigation, considering the vague nature of the subject, having evidently been prosecuted with a most wonderful degree of skill and minuteness. Prof. Haughton lays down the two following principles or rather postulates as he terms thus: —

1st. The amount of work done by a given muscle in a given time is proportional to its weight, that is the number of muscular fibres in its construction.

2d. The mean lengths of the different muscles employed at each point are proportional to the perpendicular let fall from the center of motion of the joint upon the direction in which the muscles act.

He considers that the 2d postulate is supported by these three considerations: (1) The distance through which the point of application of a muscle is moved by its contraction, is proportional to the mean length of the muscle. (2) It is geometrically evident that the perpendiculars let fall on the directions of the muscles, are proportional to the spaces moved through by their points of application. (3) The Divine contriver of the joint has made a perfect mechanism, and therefore employs a minimum expenditure of force.

Natural Selection. — Mr. Wallace, the English Naturalist, in a paper recently read before the Anthropological Society, arrives at the following conclusions, which help to account for the variation and transmutation of species: (1.) Peculiarities of every kind are more or less hereditary. (2.) The offspring of every animal vary more or less in all parts of their organization. (3.) The universe in which these animals live is not absolutely invariable. (4.) The animals in any country (those at least which are not dying out) must at each successive period be brought into harmony with the surrounding conditions. These are all the elements required for change of form and structure in animals, keeping exact pace with changes of whatever nature in the surrounding universe. Such changes must be slow, for the changes in the universe must be very slow; but just as these slow changes become important, when we look at results, after long periods of action, as we do when we perceive the alterations of the earth's surface during geological epochs: so the parallel changes in animal form become more and more striking, according as the time they have been going on is great, as we see when we compare our living animals with those which we disentomb from each successively older geological formation.

ANNUAL OF SCIENTIFIC DISCOVERY.

MECHANICS AND USEFUL ARTS.

PROPOSED GREAT IRON BRIDGE.

A GIGANTIC iron girder bridge, surpassing in dimensions the great Britannia Bridge over the Menai Straits, is proposed to be constructed across the Firth of Forth, about 17 miles from Edinburgh, Scotland. Its length will be 3,887 yards, or more than two miles, with four spans of 500 feet each, over the navigable channel.

The clear height of the bridge in the channel will be 195 ft. at high water of spring tides, thus giving ample height beneath for the tallest vessels. The frame of the girders over the widest spans will be about 70 feet, giving a total visible elevation of 195 ft. for the distance of nearly half a mile, the height diminishing at the ends of the bridge as the spans become reduced in width. Taking the submerged part of the work, the height will be 25 ft. of foundation below the silt bottom, 50 ft. of depth of water at ebb spring tides, and 18 ft. of fluctuation of tides, making in all 285 ft. in height of work to be executed. The middle piers will be of stone to the height of ten feet above high water at spring tides, and the rest of the structure will be of malleable iron. The dimensions of the Britannia Bridge may be stated by way of contrast: Span, 460 ft.; height, 104 ft.; depth of tube, 30 ft. The cost of the bridge is estimated at between £500,000 and £600,000.

How a Chain Suspension Bridge is constructed. — Most people understand how a stone bridge is erected, but the way in which the chains of a suspension bridge are got across appears to puzzle many. It is needless to say that the very modern invention of a suspension bridge is only a bridge formed of powerful chains, buried in the ground at their ends, and then built link by link over high towers, the chains being of sufficient strength to support the road and foot-

15

way afterwards to be hung from them.   The chains, or rather jointed iron bars, as they really are, are built together by joining side-
ways a series of flat iron bars, or parts of links, — ten and eleven
bars, an odd and even number, alternately composing one link; and
the bridge having one, two, or three chains of numerous links at
each side, according to the weight it is built to carry and the distance it has to cross.   The first thing done is to get the anchorage
of the shore-ends of the chains at each side.   This, in some of the
great suspension bridges, is done by taking down the links no less
than 75 ft. deep into the heart of the limestone rocks, and then building them in with solid masonry.   The series of bars composing the
links are then embedded at each side, and from these moorings first
a thin rope is passed over the towers and across to the other side,
then a thick rope is conveyed along the thin, and lastly a wire rope
along the thick one.   With two wire ropes thus got across, a cradle
is slung between them, and the workmen can then go on placing and
bolting together as they take a single bar or plank of iron of each
link in the chain.   The wire ropes are strong enough to support
their weight till they are joined in the middle, and thenceforth they
support themselves.   It is then simply a question of the cradle traveling to and fro till all the bars of each link have been added on
every additional bar, making the whole work stronger.

THE MT. CENIS TUNNEL.

At a recent meeting of the Institution of Civil Engineers, London,
Mr. Sopwith, in a paper on the progress of this great work, said,
that, at the average rate of two metres per day, from June 30,
1864, six years and seven months would be required for the completion of the tunnel.   An immense advantage had been gained in the
rate of execution by the use of the boring-machines of M. Sommeil-
ler's system, so that the above period would suffice for what would
otherwise have occupied twenty-six years and three months by hand
labor, at the rate of 1,665 feet per day at each end, the average progress before the use of the machinery.   These machines did not
weigh more than 600 weight, and could pierce a hole about one
and a quarter inch diameter, and three feet deep, into a rock in
twenty minutes.   It would occupy a couple of workmen two hours to
do so much.   The machine consists of two parts : one, a cylinder for
propelling the borer against the rock ; the second, a rotary engine
for working the valve of the striking cylinder, turning the borer on
its axis at each successive stroke, and advancing or withdrawing the
cylinder, striking as occasion requires.   It gives 250 blows per minute.   The effective pressure on the piston in striking was 216
pounds.   Compressed air was used to drive the machinery and supply fresh air to the workmen.   It was used at a pressure of five atmospheres above atmospheric pressure, and was conveyed to the
front of the advanced gallery by a pipe.   Holes were bored in the
front by the machine, which was then withdrawn, and a gang of men
charged the holes with gunpowder and fired them; another set of
men removed the *debris*.

SIR JOHN HERSCHEL ON THE FRENCH AND ENGLISH STANDARDS OF MEASUREMENT.

The following is the substance of a letter communicated during the past year to the *London Times* by Sir John Herschel, in reference to the proposed introduction of the French metrical system into Great Britain in place of the present English standard of measure. The letter is especially noteworthy for the reason that its celebrated author places himself in opposition to the general current of public opinion on the subject.

After stating that he considers the change on purely scientific grounds to be a retrograde rather than an advance movement, he proceeds to give the following as his reasons: " Whatever be the historical origin of our standard of weight, capacity, and length, as a matter of fact our British system refers itself with quite as much arithmetical simplicity, through the medium of the inch, to the length of the earth's polar axis (a unit common to all nations), as the French does through that of the metre to the elliptic quadrant of a meridian passing through Paris (a unit peculiar to France). It does so as regards our actual legal standards of weight and capacity with much more precision than the French system, and as regards that of length, (with a correction which, if legalized, would be absolutely imperceptible, from the smallness of its amount, in any transaction of life, and which can be applied, *currente calamo*, almost without calculation to any statement of lengths,) with even still greater, and indeed with all but mathematical exactness.

If the earth's polar axis be conceived divided into five hundred million inches, and a foot to be taken to consist of twelve such inches, then one hundred of our actual legal imperial half-pints by measure, or one thousand of our actual imperial ounces by weight, of distilled water at our actual standard temperature of 62° Fahr. will fill a hollow cube having one such foot as its side. The amount of error in either case is only one part in eight thousand.

The theoretical French metre is one ten-millionth part of the elliptic quadrant above mentioned ; the theoretical litre is one-thousandth of a cubic metre ; and the theoretical gramme, one millionth part of a cubic metre of distilled water at 32° Fahr. The actual error of the French legal, or standard litre or gramme, or the deviation of these standards as they actually exist, from their true theoretical value, is one part in 2730, and is consequently relatively nearly three times as great as the error in our standards of capacity and weight when referred to the earth's polar axis as their theoretical origin in the manner above stated.

Our actual imperial measures of length deviate, it is true, by more than this amount from their theoretical values so defined ; that is to say, by one part in one thousand ; so that a correction of one exact thousandth part subtracted from the stated amount of any length in imperial measures suffices to reduce it to its equivalent in such units as correspond to similar aliquots of the polar axis : a correction performed if needed, as already remarked, *instanter* and *currente calamo* requiring no tables and almost no calculation. So corrected, the outstanding error is only one part in 64,000. The actual legal metre in

2*

use in France is, however, not immaculate in this respect, its amount of error being one part in 6400, which is ten times that which our British measures so corrected would exhibit.

If it were worth while to legalize so trifling an alteration (and an act passed rendering permissive the decimalization of our own system, it would be necessary to do so as a means of bringing the national units of length, weight, and capacity into exact decimal correspondence), no mortal would be aware, practically speaking, that any change had been made in our mile, yard, foot, or inch. I have in common use two foot-rules, bought at respectable shops, and neither the worse for wear, which differ by more than the amount of change required. In addition to North America, which employs the British system of weights and measures, British commerce extends to Russia, British India, and Australia, all of them superior in area, and the last two, at least, of equal importance, commercially speaking, with the totality of the metricized nations. The Russian sagene is an exact multiple of the English foot (imperial). The *hath* (the legal measure of length in British India) is 18 imperial inches. The Australian system is identical with our own. Taking into consideration this immense preponderance, both in area, in population, and in commerce, we are not only justified in taking our stand against this innovation, but entitled to inquire, if uniformity be insisted on, why, with an equally good theoretical basis (to say the least), the majority is called upon to give way to the minority.

MINUTE MAGNITUDES.

Mr. Whitworth, the celebrated English mechanician, lays down two achievements as being those whereupon the excellence of all machines mainly depends, — namely, how to produce a flat surface, and how to measure small distances and quantities accurately. The plain flat surfaces of iron or steel which used to satisfy engineers a few years ago, would now be regarded as alternations of ridges, grooves, lumps, and holes ; while the thicknesses of wires, plates, and sheets, which could once be measured to the hundreth of an inch or so, can now be measured by —— But let us explain this matter a little.

When we turn a screw once round, in a nut or hole fitted to receive it, we at the same time push it forward to a distance equal to one thread of the screw ; consequently, if the screw be turned only one tenth round, it advances only one tenth of the distance between one thread and another ; consequently, again, if there were a hundred threads to the inch, and the screw were turned only one one hundredth part of a circumference, it would advance only one ten thousandth part of an inch forward. All this is well known to persons accustomed to tools and machinery ; but Mr. Whitworth's merit consists in showing how to attain the actual results in a degree hardly conceivable. A few years ago, he contrived an apparatus which would detect the difference between the length of two bars, even if it were so minute as one-millionth part of an inch ! There was a screw with ten threads to an inch ; there was a tangent-screw wheel with 400 teeth in its circumference, and a graduated circle with 250 divisions ; these parts were so connected that a movement equal to one division of the circle was equal to 10 x 400 x 250= 1,000,000, —that is, equal to an advance of the screw through a space of only one-millionth of an inch. This micrometer was placed at one end of a frame, on which the bar to be measured was temporarily placed. When a small piece of metal with its opposite surfaces parallel, and exquisitely true, is placed between the bar and the micrometer, the latter is screwed up until the small piece of metal (called the contact-piece) is just nipped and held between them; then, if the screw be brought back merely one-millionth of an inch, the contact-piece is loosened and falls. Although the eye does not detect it, the machine does veritably measure this infinitesimal quantity. As Sir Emerson Tennent says, in his *Story of the Guns:* "So nice is the adjustment, that, in using it, an inch of steel can be held to be an inch only so long as the thermometer stands at 62° Fahrenheit, the slightest excess of temperature producing an appreciable elongation. And the standard yard, a square bar of steel, when placed in the machine, is so expanded by the slightest touch of the finger, as to show an appreciable lengthening even under the influence of the infinitesimal amount of heat thus imparted! Mr. Whitworth, like other inventors, earns more honor than profit by such exquisite contrivances as these; but his profit begins when he applies the same principle in his workshop to produce articles in general demand. The result is seen in many ways. Some years ago, there was a difficulty in working metals to one-twentieth of an inch; but the one-thousandth of an inch is now worked as accurately as the one-twentieth was then." In making the exquisite details of the Whitworth rifle, or in shaping and adjusting the separate pieces, the workmen have come to regard the ten-thousandth part of an inch (one-hundredth part of one-hundredth of an inch) as a quantity within their cognizance, and on which their credit as good workmen may depend. In the course of his elaborate experiments on rifling, hexagonal bores, conoidal bullets, and so forth, Mr. Whitworth made a cylinder 0·5770 inches, internal diameter, a rod 0·5770 inches thick; and another rod 0·5769 inches thick; the one rod fitted tightly into the cylinder when both were clean and dry; the other rod passed quite loosely into it; and yet the two rods differed in thickness only by the ten-thousandth part of an inch. In short, "a little," to the last generation, would, by our present mechanicians, be easily divided into a hundred parts.

To produce minute results, instead of merely measuring them when produced by others, is the purpose of many beautiful contrivances. Photography is now one of the agents for effecting this. There are little photographic pictures, not larger than a pin's head, containing multitudes of portaits of distinguished persons; a focalizing apparatus produced them, and a microscope is necessary to render them visible.

At the great International Exhibition of 1862, many persons glanced at the beautiful micrographical machine constructed by Mr. Peters, the London banker; but the glance told little, except to those who were previously somewhat versed in the subject. Most attractive were the wonderful bits of writing on glass which had been effected by the machine, and which could only be rendered visible by the aid of powerful microscopes. Mr. Peters, as an amateur man of science, invented the machine, and some time afterwards presented it to the Microscopial Society, by whom it was exhibited at the great International gathering. Suppose that a metal bar is suspended vertically, by a fulcrum or point exactly in the middle; if the bar is swung to and fro, the top will describe a curve exactly like, in size and form, that described by the lower end, but opposite in direction. If the lower end is twice as far distant from the fulcrum as the upper, and if the bar be swung to and fro, the lower end will describe a curve or arc just twice as long as that described by the upper, though similar in shape. If, on the other hand, the lower end of the bar be nearer to the fulcrum than the upper; and if the ratio of distances be (say) ten to one, then the upper end will describe an arc ten times as large as the lower, though of course reversed in direction. And so on in any other ratio. Now, let there be a blunt tracer at one end of the bar, and a pencil at the other; if we write, or draw, or trace any figure with the tracer, the pencil may be made to copy the figure on a piece of paper, — enlarged if the tracer be nearer to the fulcrum than the pencil, diminished if otherwise. Here we have the first germ of Mr. Peters's micrograph; a writing in moderately-sized characters, reproduced in smaller dimensions by this kind of pantagraph. In the first machine which he made, the fulcrum was a hundred and twenty-five times nearer to one end of the bar than to the other; and the pencil-copy was to the tracing in the ratio of one to 125 in size. But notable as was this power of diminution, Mr. Peters hit upon an expedient that enabled him to eclipse it in an astonishing degree. Instead of causing the short arm of his bar or lever to carry a pencil or graver, he caused it to move the *long* arm of another but much smaller lever; thus obtaining the product of the two diminutions multiplied into each other, instead of the diminution due to a simple lever. In his large lever, he made the fulcrum 125 times nearer to the short than to the long end; in his smaller, the ratio was 50 to one; and as the short arm of the first acted upon the long arm of the second, the two ratios were multiplied, insomuch that the copy-writing was 6250 times smaller than the original tracing. Suppose, for example, that the tracer ruled parallel lines one-tenth of an inch apart; then the pencil would rule lines 1-62,500th of an inch apart; and any writing, drawing, or device would be reduced in similar ratio. The next achievement of Mr. Peters was so to construct the exquisite details of his machine that he could vary the power of diminution at pleasure, from a ratio of one to 110 up to a ratio of one to 6250. Considering that no kind of pencil could draw such minutely approximate lines on paper, he employed diamond to scratch on glass. The bits of diamond called "turned points" are found better for this purpose than "splinters." The long end of the lever, which is downwards, carries a tracer, with which any design or writing is traced. The upper end carries a small piece of glass, carefully adjusted; over the glass is mounted a diamond pointing downwards, which remains stationary while the glass moves under it. Delicate mechanism is connected with the diamond, by means of which it may be raised or lowered, and also pressed with greater or less force upon the glass; and so effective are these contrivances, that the thick and thin strokes of ordinary writing can be faithfully transferred to the minute copy on glass.

THE SIZE OF A DROP OF LIQUID.

The size of a drop of liquid is often spoken of as a definite quantity. In a paper on this subject by Mr. Tate, in the *Philosophical Magazine*, it is shown that not only the size but the weight varies with the diameter of the tube, and the density, temperature, and chemical composition of the liquid itself. He gives the results of experiments which show that,—1. Other things being the same, the weight of a drop of liquid is proportional to the diameter of the tube in which it is formed. 2. With regard to capillarity, the weight of the drop is in proportion to the weight of water which would be raised in that tube by capillary action. 3. The augmentations of weight are in proportion to the diameter of the surfaces on which the drops are formed. 4. The weight of a drop is diminished by an augmentation of temperature. 5. Independent of density, the chemical composition of a liquid affects the weight of its drop in a remarkable manner. 6. In different solutions of common salt and other natural salts, the augmentation in the weight of the drop is in proportion to the weight of dry salt in solution. The foregoing principles are supported by tabulated statements.

THE FRACTION 3,14159.

The celebrated interminable fraction 3·14159..., which the mathematician calls π, is the ratio of the circumference to the diameter. But it is thousands of things besides. It is constantly turning up in mathematics: and if arithmetic and algebra had been studied without geometry, π must have come in somehow, though at what stage or under what name must have depended upon the casualties of algebraical invention. As it is, our trigonometry being founded on the circle, π first appears as the ratio stated. If, for instance, a deep study of probable fluctuation from the average had preceded geometry, π might have emerged as a number perfectly indispensable in such problems as – What is the chance of the number of aces lying between a million $+x$, and a million $-x$, when six million of throws are made with a die? I have not gone into any detail of all those cases in which the paradoxer finds out, by his unassisted acumen, that results of mathematical investigation *cannot be:* in fact, this discovery is only an accompaniment, though a necessary one, of his paradoxical statement of that which *must be.* Logicians are beginning to see that the notion of *horse* is inseparably connected with that of *non-horse:* that the first without the second would be no notion at all. And it is clear that the positive affirmation of that which contradicts mathematical demonstration, cannot but be accompanied by a declaration, mostly overtly made, that demonstration is false. If the mathematician were interested in punishing this indiscretion, he could make his denier ridiculous by inventing asserted results which would completely take him in.

More than thirty years ago I had a friend, now long gone, who was a mathematician, but not of the higher branches: he was, *inter alia*, thoroughly up in all that relates to mortality, life assurance, &c. One day, explaining to him how it should be ascertained what the chance is of the survivors of a large number of persons now alive dy-

ing between given limits of numbers at the end of a certain time, I
came, of course, upon the introduction of π, which I could only describe as the ratio of the circumference of a circle to its diameter.
"Oh, my dear friend! that must be a delusion; what can the circle
have to do with the numbers alive at the end of a given time?"— "I
cannot demonstrate it to you; but it is demonstrated."— "Oh!
stuff! I think you can prove anything with your differential calculus: figment, depend upon it." I said no more; but, a few days afterwards, I went to him and very gravely told him that I had discovered the law of human mortality in the Carlisle Table, of which he
thought very highly. I told him that the law was involved in this
circumstance. Take the table of expectation of life, choose any
age, take its expectation and make the nearest integer a new age, do
the same with that, and so on; begin at what age you like, you are
sure to end at the place where the age past is equal, or most nearly
equal, to the expectation to come. "You don't mean that this always happens?"— "Try it." He did try, again and again; and
found it as I said. "This is, indeed, a curious thing; this *is* a discovery." I might have sent him about trumpeting the law of life:
but I contented myself with informing him that the same thing would
happen with any table whatsoever, in which the first column goes up
and the second goes down; and that if a proficient in the higher
mathematics chose to palm a figment upon him, he could do without
the circle: *à corsaire, corsaire et demi*, the French proverb says.—
Prof. De Morgan, London Athenœum.

STRAIGHT EDGES AND FLAT SURFACES.

At the recent meeting of the British Association, Mr. James Williams read a paper on the "Flexibility of Iron," from which we extract the following interesting passage:—

"It is a common saying, 'rigid as a bar of iron,' and but few
persons are aware how very flexible iron, as well as other metal is.
Many builders in introducing cast and wrought girders, or beams to
support enormous weights, are of opinion that such beams are strong
enough to what they call 'bear any weight without bending,' and
are much surprised to be told by a mechanician that these same
girders, however stiff they may appear, will not even bear their own
weight without considerable deflexion. Many good working mechanicians even are quite unaware of the extreme subtlety of the
metal they are operating on. It is only that class of mechanics who
are engaged in scraping up valve faces, slide lathes, and similar
tools, and, above all, attempting to make 'flat surfaces' and 'straight
edges,' that can comprehend in a fair way the trying difficulty of
keeping such works true after they have once got them so. In the
engineers' workshop, where straight bars of metal are used for the
purpose of testing the work under process of manufacture, it is necessary to keep at least three bars of surfaces of each kind for the purpose of testing each other, for it has often been known that a straight
edge, got up with all the care and accuracy possible, true to-day will
be bent to-morrow; indeed, the very handling of it while in use is
quite sufficient to distort to such a degree that the workman frequently has to put it by awhile until it comes to the natural temperature of

the room he works in, the partial heat of the hands alone being sufficient to render it useless for its object. In getting up straight edges and flat surfaces, if two only are used to test each other, it is all but a certainty that one will be hollow and the other rounding, but by using three we are enabled to discover this defect."

MACHINERY vs. MAN-POWER.

Mr. T. A. McIntyre, of Albany, communicates to the *Scientific American* the following notice of some rapid work which recently came under his observation in a planing mill of that city. He says: "The proprietors received orders one morning to tongue and groove 4,000 boards. The demand being urgent, they put their machines to their highest speed. Noticing the remarkable speed with which the boards went through one of the machines, I thought I would time it, and found that 19 boards passed through in two minutes, this would be 570 in an hour, and 6,270 in a day (11 hours being the mill day). A man at a liberal estimate, could not put in a tongue and groove and plane more than four boards an hour; so that this machine, with one man feeding and two men taking away, did as much work as 142 men."

STEEL SHIPS.

"Two large ships, built of steel plates, were recently launched in the Mersey. Though some small vessels have been built of the same material, this is the first instance in which steel has been used for ocean ships. The steel now manufactured for shipbuilding purposes is said to have an advantage over iron, in being more ductile and malleable, as well as stronger and lighter. These qualities bring with them, it is also said, greater economy in building and increased capacity, both most important considerations. Mr. Jones, one of the builders, states that in the *Formby*, one of the newly launched vessels, of 1,276 tons burden, the weight of steel used is 500 tons, whereas, if she had been constructed of iron, 800 tons of that metal would have been required. In a vessel like the *Warrior*, he declared that by using steel greater strength might be obtained with a saving of one half in the weight of metal. Mr. Reed, constructor of the Navy, made a special journey from London to attend the launch and examine the ships. He remarked, that merchant ships can be built to test a principle, when war ships cannot, as the former can be examined and repaired annually, while the latter are sent abroad for periods of three or four years. He perfectly agreed with what had been said of the importance of steel for the construction of small ships, and stated that the Government took great interest in the question of employing steel as a material for ship-building."—*Journal of the Society of Arts.*

ENGINES WITHOUT BED-PLATES.

On the engines of the two great iron-clad vessels constructed during the past year by Capt. Ericsson, the *Puritan* and *Dictator*, there is a novelty which warrants attention. They have neither bed-plates nor frames, properly speaking. The duty borne by these details usually found in other engines, is transferred to light but rigid wrought-iron kelsons, or bulkheads, running athwart-ships. The entire machinery is upheld and retained in place by these kelsons; girders they are in reality, for while they carry the engines they also form a chord to the arc of the ship's bottom and materially strengthen the hull. The absence of bed plates dispenses with at least forty tuns of iron, in round numbers; for these details and their appendages would, with engines of the usual construction, weigh that amount, while the absence of heavy cast-iron frames is also a source of great advantage. This is particularly the case in a vessel-of-war, where every pound of extra weight.is a positive injury, increasing the draft, the load, and adding to the labor of the ship in a sea-way. The cylinders are bolted directly to the wrought-iron kelsons mentioned previously, and the power exerted within them is transferred to a short rock-shaft, supported on vertical pillow-blocks, bolted and braced firmly to the same kelsons: beyond this arrangement there is no other. Cumbrous and heavy frames which interfere with a thorough inspection of and access to the machinery, and massive bed-plates, are both wanting, and the other details of the engines are equally sound from an engineering point of view. — *Scientific American.*

ON THE MARINE ENGINES OF THE U. S. NAVY.

In the Report of the Secretary of the Navy, communicated to Congress December, 1864, the following interesting statements are made respecting the use, construction, and improvement of the steam machinery of the United States Navy. The Secretary says: —

As our navy has become not only exclusively a steam navy, but a very large one, with an enormous consumption of coal and great expenditure for the construction and repair of machinery, it becomes a matter of the first consequence that only the best machinery be obtained for it. This problem is one of very difficult, costly, and slow solution. The great maritime countries of England and France have not yet solved it, either in the commercial or war marine, and at this hour the best authorities do not agree upon it. So many conditions enter into the problem that, as prominence is given more or less to one or the other, different conclusions are reached. It is evident that the question is purely a practical one; it can only be answered by extensive experience and accurate observations. Mindful of the importance of this matter, the Department, notwithstanding the great pressure upon its resources by the war, has kept it in view and promoted by every means the acquisition of the necessary information. The proportions of hulls have been varied with a view to determine the relative development of speed in proportion to given power; machinery has been constructed upon different types and systems, and the Department has encouraged all offers from citizens, as well as from its own officers, to build new machinery that gave promise of improvement. The navy at this moment contains marine machinery on an extensive scale of every kind; their results are in its log-books, from which can be determined their various merits, both for general service and for particular applications.

In the wooden vessels of the navy nearly every variety and type of engine, of valve-gear, of rate of expansion, of surface condenser, of screw propeller, and of boilers, have been thoroughly tested; but the results thus far show that the machinery designed by the Steam Engineering Bureau of the Department has not been surpassed, perhaps not equaled, by any of its competitors, while in many cases their results have been greatly below it.

In its iron-clads, the Department has experimented by the construction of different classes and sizes, both in wood and iron, propelled by one screw and by two screws, working independently of each other. In its most recent constructions, of the *Miantonomoh* class, a wooden vessel designed by the naval constructors, and built at the navy-yards, with Ericsson turrets, and machinery designed by the Bureau of Steam Engineering, a high rate of speed, perfect ventilation, impregnability, and the enormous battery of four 15-inch guns, have been combined in a vessel of the moderate size of 1,564 tons, drawing only twelve feet of water. These vessels are free from the disadvantage of fouling, which so greatly reduces the speed of iron ones.

Others of this type, but of increased tonnage, are in process of construction, to have still higher speed, and be adapted to coast service.

In the steamers bought from the commercial marine of the country, and in the captured blockade runners, now adapted for naval service, are to be found every variety of machinery, both screw and paddle-wheel, constructed either in this country or Great Britain. So far as the exigencies of the war would permit, the different types of machinery have been submitted to careful experiment to ascertain their relative merits. Nearly every variety of boiler and of expansive gear, of rate of expansion, and of saturated and superheated steam, has been made the subject of accurate experiment, and it is believed that the files of the Department contain the latest and most reliable information on these subjects.

Nearly all the kinds of coal of the seaboard States have been the subject of careful experiment, with a view to ascertain their comparative value for naval purposes. A board of engineers has also experimented with petroleum as a substitute for coal in naval steamers.

As opinion appears to have settled upon the horizontal and the vertical tubular boilers, as the only ones proper for naval service, the Department has one of each kind manufactured according to designs furnished by a board of nine engineers, employed in the principal private steam-engine manufacturing establishments of the country, and by the Bureau of Steam Engineering, for the purpose of accurate experiments, to determine their respective merits. These experiments will be of the most elaborate nature, and will, it is presumed, enable a choice to be made. They are now in progress.

A commission of nine, on practical engineering, has been appointed by the Department, consisting of three from the Academy of Science, three from the Franklin Institute, and three on the part of the Department, — all eminent in physical science, — to devise the proper apparatus, and make the necessary experiments therewith, to ascertain by practical results the economy of using steam with different degrees of expansion. These experiments, which are now in progress, will

3

be as elaborate and as complete as it is possible to make them. And under the practical conditions of steam engineering, it is believed they will indisputably set at rest the amount of gain to be obtained from using steam with different measures of expansion, and also determine the relative merits of different kinds of valve-gear, steam pressure, etc., besides settling many incidental questions of great importance.

ON THE ECONOMY OF WORKING STEAM EXPANSIVELY.

Steam engineers and scientists generally, have, it is well known, been greatly interested of late in regard to the question of the economy of using steam expansively; and during the winter of 1860–61, a series of experiments were made by Mr. Isherwood, Chief Engineer of the U. S. Navy, under the auspices of the Government, with a view of testing the question. These experiments were reported in the *Annual of Scientific Discovery* for 1862, p. 25: and in the succeeding article we give the English opinion of them as expressed in one of the leading British Scientific journals. Some two years ago, Congress appropriated the sum of $20,000 for the further prosecution of this investigation, and Mr. Horatio Allen of New York City, and Mr. Isherwood of the Navy were appointed Commissioners to conduct the experiments. Committees representing the American Institute of New York, and the Franklin Institute of Philadelphia, were also appointed, by request from these associations, to attend and counsel concerning the experiment. The result of the investigations as far as they have been made public, have been furnished us by Dr. Warren Rowell, Chairman of the Committee on the part of the American Institute. In a recent letter to the editor, he says : " An engine was constructed in accordance with the suggestions of the best practical and theoretical engineers in the country. The engine frame was made large enough to take in seven or eight different diameters of cylinders in succession, and to use steam of the same pressure and the same quantity in each cylinder, the same amount of work in each instance being put on the engine. The comparison that has been made, is this. The first cylinder tried used one cubic foot of steam when the piston had performed twenty-one twenty-fourths of the stroke : this cylinder was then taken out of the frame of the engine, and a cylinder put in its place that held a cubic foot of steam when the piston had performed sixteen twenty-fourths of the stroke ; and the Committee found that there was not a '*pound's* difference' in the consumption of either fuel or water in a 72 hours' experiment. This result was quite unexpected, because it was thought by the Commissioners and others, that if there was any possible expansive force to be obtained, it would be between two thirds and seven eighths of the stroke."

Another set of experiments, bearing on the same subject, are also now in the course of induction by Messrs. Hecker, Watermann, Rowell, and others in New York, the results of which have not as yet been fully made public ; but copying from the columns of the *Scientific American*, we will endeavor to state what is and ought to be ascertained. In a series of experiments made by the above-named gentlemen in 1860, it was found that when the steam was cut off at one quarter of the stroke in an unjacketed cylinder, 66 per cent of the steam formed in the boiler was condensed in the cylinder; and when both the cylinder and valve-chest were immersed in steam of the boiler temperature, 30 per cent of the steam was condensed in the cylinder. The process by which this large amount of condensation takes place is supposed to be this. When the steam is cut off and begins to expand, a portion of its heat is consumed in the performance of work; or, if the expression is preferred, it is cooled by expanding. This cooling causes a portion of the steam to be condensed into water, which is deposited in a fine dew all over the inner surface of the cylinder. It will be borne in mind that this condensation takes place under pressure. There is not heat enough in the cylinder to keep all of the water evaporated under the pressure that is actually exerted. When the piston has finished its stroke the exhaust port is opened, and the pressure upon the water clinging to the interior surface of the cylinder—the pressure that held it in the liquid state—is removed, and this water immediately flashes into steam. In this change a portion of the heat required to convert the steam into water is absorbed from the walls of the cylinder, thus cooling the walls, and preparing them to repeat the process of condensation at the next stroke.

The proof of this condensation is found in the indicator cards, where the line of pressure falls below, not merely the curve of the Marriotte law, but also below this curve when corrected for the heat consumed in the performance of work. And that the same process takes place in engines generally may be learned by a careful examination of the numerous cards taken from those engines.

It will be observed that the condensation takes place on the steam side of the piston and thus diminishes the working pressure, while the re-evaporation occurs when the exhaust port is open, and when the steam formed in the cylinder, if it exerts any pressure at all, exerts a back pressure on the piston. Thus the condensation and the re-evaporation are both injurious in their operation.

It is manifest that if the inner surface of the walls of the cylinder could be kept sufficiently heated, no water could be deposited upon them, and thus this process of condensation and re-evaporation would be prevented. The plan devised by Mr. Waterman to keep the inner surface of the cylinder hot, is to make the walls very thin, and to surround them with steam of the boiler temperature. In the experimental engine the walls are of steel one-tenth of an inch in thickness, and the engine is being tried first with hot steam around the cylinder, and then under the same conditions with only a jacket of confined air.

Should the fact of the large condensation above referred to, be established, it will prove a very important matter in the construction and working of engines.

STEAM ENGINE ECONOMY.

" A patent case has been recently tried at Washington, U. S., which has elicited certain statements so remarkable in their bearing on the system of steam engine construction adopted of late in the American Navy, that we cannot pass it without notice. The case in question is simple enough in itself. A Mr. Mattingly, of Washington, sued a steamboat company for a share of the savings effected by a peculiar form of cut-off valve, the patent right in which he held, and had sold to the company, taking a share of the savings effected as the pecuniary consideration. The defence set up was singular enough.   The complainant asserted, and as he believed, proved that the saving in fuel amounted to over 30 per cent; and he demanded a verdict in accordance with his statement.   The defendants, however, called Mr. Benjamin Isherwood, the Chief Engineer of the U. S. Navy, to prove not only that the particular cut-off which afforded the *casus belli* could not possibly effect the alleged saving; but that the only possible saving which could be effected by that, or any other cut-off, amounted at the maximum to 18 per cent, and that therefore a saving of 30 per cent was a physical impossibility.   This statement is startling enough; but Chief Engineer Isherwood does his work thoroughly, and he proceeded to strengthen his evidence by swearing that no one believed his ' new discovery' to be true until 1860, and that since then, all the new marine engines for the navy were built and building upon it.   It is nothing new to us to learn that American engines generally are constructed without much regard to the strict principles which can alone secure economy.   The indicator and its use are almost unknown in the States.   This little instrument affords the only known means of ascertaining the exact duty performed by steam within a cylinder; and in its absence we can only form a vague idea of the really useful effect produced by the combustion of fuel.   A constant habit of observation and a thorough practical acquaintance with a large number of steam engines of different constructions, working under varying conditions, can alone give that knowledge which will permit us to build engines capable of doing a large duty with little coal.   This knowledge is tolerably well diffused throughout the workshops of Great Britain; the young engineer being generally afforded every opportunity for testing the actual performance of engines by the aid of the indicator.   More can be learned in this way in half an hour, than can be derived from theoretical instruction, however good, in a year; and we cannot expect men who are almost, or altogether unacquainted with the nature and properties of the instrument, to turn out first-class engines.   It is very probable that we shall be accused of attaching an undue importance to so small a thing.   Those who have studied the subject will take a different view of the matter, and will, without doubt, indorse a statement which will bear repetition, namely, that without the use of the indicator there can be no real knowledge of what does or does not constitute a good engine.   Until its use extends in America, we do not look for much improvement in steam engineering.   Although our Western friends are somewhat lax in their practice elsewhere, we did not expect that their navy would afford such precedents as Mr. Isherwood's evidence indicates; evidence, too, which comes upon us with all the force which can be conferred by an oath, and all the strength which can be derived from the high position of the swearer.   Mr. Isherwood has, we fear, led many a feeble mind astray.   The engineers of Washington possess a great deal of common sense; however, Mr. Mattingly's friends sent to New York for Mr. Dickinson, an adept in engineering, and a man learned in the law as well, — a combination of professional attainments all too rare in England.   Mr. Dickinson's powers of cross-examination threw new light on the subject, from which it appears that the 'red tape-ism' is all-powerful in the Naval Department of President Lincoln's administration. To a final suggestion that the question should be fairly put to the test on the river Potomac, in presence of judge and jury, the defendants turned a deaf ear. The experiment was made, notwithstanding, on board the steamship *Collyer*; when it turned out that with 600 pounds of coal an hour, she could run at the rate of 27 revolutions a minute with expansion, and that but 20 a minute could be got without expansion, and with 700 pounds an hour. This evidence was deemed so conclusive, that a verdict was at once given for the complainant. It is not difficult to imagine what English engineers will think of all this. Mr. Isherwood's evidence is so opposed to all theory and all practice, that, did he hold a different position, or were he less talented, his word would simply be passed over with a smile, or perchance, a hearty laugh. The value of expansion, prop-erly carried out, is pretty well understood among us; and it would be unfair to deny that many American engineers attach a proper im-portance to the principle as well. When the Chief Engineer of a great navy, gives utterance to sentiments and opinions so widely op-posed to those held by other experts, a natural curiosity is experi-enced to know where he got them. We will try and enlighten our readers.

In the early part of the year 1860, the United States Navy De-partment, in the plenitude of its wisdom, deemed it right that certain experiments should be made to determine the relative econ-omy of using steam with different measures of expansion. Not content with the evidence afforded them by the practical operations of the Cornish pumping engine, the locomotives on the New York railroads, or the marine engines in use on the rivers and seas of the Western Continent, the gentlemen of the Department resolved on instituting thorough experimental research into the whole subject; and with this object in view they appointed Chief Engineer Isherwood, and three other engineers, as a committee, to make the experiments. As very valuable results were anticipated, it is natural to suppose, that more than one engine was reported on : that the best engines in the navy would be selected, and the necessary data derived from the performance of the engines tried, at sea, under the ordinary condi-tions of working, first, and subsequently, under such extraordinary conditions as seem best adapted to the attainment of the end in view. Such a conclusion is not more natural than erroneous. But one steam-er, the *Michigan*, was selected. At the time of the experiments, February 1860, she was out of commission, frozen up in Lake Erie; the hull had been recently repaired, and the old boilers replaced with new ones, constructed on Martin's patent, with vertical water tubes, instead of horizontal flues over the furnaces. The engines were two in number, of a form not much known in England : the cylinders, 36 inches in diameter, and having a stroke of eight feet lying in an inclined position and at an angle of 28 degrees with the keel. Not content with confining the experiment to the narrow basis afforded by a single steamboat, Mr. Isherwood and his col-leagues still further restricted it, by retaining only one of the two cylinders in use : the other being uncoupled from the crank-shaft

3*

and put out of communication with the boilers. The valves were of the ordinary double beat poppet kind, habitually used in American paddle engines. The steam valves were made to act as expansion valves, by means of an arrangement known as "Sickles's cut-off." The distance between the boiler and engine was 25 feet: and the total length of the steampipe over 17 inches in diameter, exposed to the refrigerating influence of the atmosphere, was 30 feet; and the pipes being set on a slight incline, the water of condensation naturally found its way into the cylinder. The steam pipes were clothed with felt and wood lagging. The heads of the cylinders, the valve chest, and the long nozzles, peculiar to this form of engine, were without covering of any kind. It is needless to enter into any minute detail of the experiments. We have already alluded to Mr. Isherwood's talents, and he spared no trouble to obtain exact results from the engine under trial. The vessel was moored fast, the ice cut away from about the floats, and the whole power of the engine exerted in paddling the water backwards. Each experiment lasted 72 consecutive hours, during which the engine was neither slowed nor stopped; with the steam cut off at eleven-twelfths of the stroke, the consumption of coal amounted to 4·847 pounds per hour: cut-off at seven-tenths to 4·324 pounds; at four-ninths to 3·725 pounds, at three-tenths to 3·677 pounds; at one-fourth to 3·428 pounds; at one-sixth to 3·81 pounds; and at four-fifths to 4·281 pounds. From these results we find, that the gain by expansion is decided up to a cut-off at one-fourth of the stroke, and that there is no advantage to be derived from expansion afterwards, *with the particular engine under consideration.* The results perfectly satisfied Mr. Isherwood. He prepared a very elaborate report, — a model of its kind, — in the course of which he attempts with much plausibility to upset Mariote's law as applied to the expansion of steam, and laid it before the Secretary of the Navy. As a result, it now appears, from the Washington investigation, that the engines for the American Navy have been, almost from that day forth, constructed without any regard to the carrying out of the principles of expansion. The crop thus sown will be reaped erelong in diminished speed, and in increased coal bills.

If the engine of the *Michigan* had been specially designed to prove that the advantages of expansion were a delusion, it could not possibly have been better adapted to the end. Mr. Isherwood is a careful, and, we presume, a conscientious experimenter, but all his conclusions in this case are vitiated by being drawn from false premises. He has recently published a large and handsome volume, a large portion of which is taken up with a detailed account of these experiments, and their analysis. It required little penetration to see where the author has lamentably failed to make out a case. No provision whatever, either by superheating or otherwise, was made to prevent condensation in the cylinder of the *Michigan's* engine. The length of the stroke was eight feet, the number of double strokes per minute, with the steam at full pressure, was a little over 20; with the steam cut off at one-fourth rather less than 14. The steam had to traverse some 30 feet of steam pipe, lightly clothed, in an atmosphere only raised above 29° by the heat abstracted from the engines and boilers, to be subsequently isolated for a space of three or four seconds at a time, within a cylinder lagged, it is true, at the sides, but wholly exposed to the atmosphere at the ends. The cylinder was three feet in diameter, the area of each lid was over seven square feet. It requires no very abstruse calculation to point out the value of this area as a refrigerator during each tedious stroke. Then we have the valve chests and nozzles all aiding the same work. Nor is this all. Mr. Isherwood, on his own showing, proves that the loss due to clearance and nozzle space in the *Michigan's* engine, amounted to a positive reduction of average pressure equal to 12 per cent when the steam was cut off at one-sixth of the stroke, and to nearly eight per cent when the cut-off took place at one-fourth of the stroke. Some men are mentally so constituted that they only regard any fact from one point of view. Instead of gathering from his experience that it was advisable that clearance of all kinds should be reduced to a lower limit than that found in the particular engine experimented on, Mr. Isherwood, with a strange perversity, takes this very loss of pressure as evidence that expansion is wasteful in practice and should not be employed. Our readers can form their own estimate of the value of conclusions so arrived at.

It is doubtful if the history of nations can show a more astounding instance of folly in a case where the safety of the country was involved, and that country actually at war, than that presented by the recent proceeding of the Bureau of American Marine. On the evidence afforded by a series of experiments on a single engine in an old and small steamer on an inland lake, conducted by four engineers, far removed from supervision of any kind; the engine being, on the showing of those most interested in proving the reverse, totally unsuited in every respect for the application of expansion, — the piston moving at but 176 ft. per minute, and the steam not superheated in the slightest degree, — those in authority have determined, in their wisdom, to set aside all the teaching of the last fifty years. They have wilfully shut their eyes to the work of improvement going on daily in England and France, and have, with a temerity almost without parallel, staked the future of a great navy and enormous sum of money on the truthfulness of a single obscure experiment, bearing but a remote analogy in its conditions to those under which steam should properly be employed. It is as though the American engineering world had retrograded the third part of a century. We shall expect, next, to have war steamers denounced, and the old liner pronounced just the thing to defend the interests of the people, or push on a war of aggression on distant shores.

Americans are very clever. They have taught us many new things. This time, in the attempt to teach the world something new, they have overshot the mark, and only repeated an old story in our ears, — the story of human folly." — *From the London Mechanic's Magazine*, Jan. 1864.

IMPROVEMENTS IN STEAM BOILERS.

At the last meeting of the British Association, Mr. Zerah Colburn, the well-known American engineer, read a paper, giving a *résumé* of the latest information and improvements concerning steam boilers;

and describing in particular a form of boiler invented by Mr. Joseph Harrison of Philadelphia. We give the substance of this paper under its several heads : —

Evaporation to Surface.—The rate at which heat may be transmitted through an iron boiler plate, without injury to its substance, has never been precisely ascertained. About 70,000 units of heat per hour, equal to the evaporation in that time of one cubic foot of water from 60°, is believed to be the utmost per square foot of plate of ordinary thickness. But in order to approximately apply the *whole* heat of a furnace to the purposes of evaporation, a much larger area of heating surface, per unit of work done is requisite. Watt fixed the proportion of one square yard of heating surface per cubic foot of water evaporated per hour, and this has been sanctioned by modern practice. But the average depth, or, in other words, the thickness of the stratum, of water thus boiled away is only one and one-third inches per hour, one forty-fifth-inch per minute, or one twenty-seven thousandth inch per second, over the whole heating surface. From ten to twelve seconds are thus occupied in vaporizing a *couche* of water, no thicker than a single leaf of the paper upon which books are commonly printed. If, in proportion to the evaporation, an insufficient extent of heating surface be provided, there is not only a direct waste of heat, — the products of combustion escaping at a temperature corresponding, perhaps, to that of incandescent iron, — but the furnace plates may be burnt. Notwithstanding the active convection of heat in water, an intense flame directed against the sides or roof of a boiler furnace, will, in time, crack or blister the iron. It is not certain that this result occurs from the inability of the metal to transmit the heat, for it is more likely that, under vigorous vaporization, the gravity of the liquid water (and it is its gravity only that brings it to the heating surfaces) is insufficient to bear down effectively against the rising volumes of steam. If, by powerful mechanical means, the water could be constantly maintained in contact with the heating surfaces, it is possible that the rate of evaporation upon a given area could be increased without injury to the plate. In the hardening of anvil faces and of steel dies, the requisite rapidity of cooling is obtained, not merely by immersion in water, but by its forcible descent, in a strong jet, upon the heated metal.

External heating Surface.—Under the conditions, however, of ordinary practice, no restriction of the heating surface is permissible. This surface is sometimes that of the exterior only of the boiler, but it is more usual, and on most accounts preferable, to dispose it internally by means of fire boxes, flues, or tubes. The external surface of a boiler can only be increased by increasing its length or its diameter, or by increasing both of these together. Plain cylindrical boilers 90 feet, and in one or two instances 104 feet in length, have been employed, but even apart from any consideration of the great amount of space which they occupy, they are mechanically objectionable, and they are now no longer made. In increasing the external surface of a boiler by enlarging its diameter, it is weakened exactly in proportion to the increase. the bursting pressure, for a given thickness of plates, being inversely as the diameter. The danger attending the presence of a large quantity of heated water in a boiler is now well understood, and, such as it is, it increases as the square of the diameter, so that, in a boiler of a given length, the elements of weakness and danger are collectively related to the cube of the diameter. External heating surface may be provided for in a number of smaller vessels, as in the retort boilers by Mr. Dunn, but these are of the water-tube family, which, heretofore, has been found subject to choking with the solid matter deposited by the water.

Internal heating Surface. — Next are the boilers with internal heating surfaces. Internal fire tubes were in use in steam boilers in the last century, and they were applied within a cylindrical barrel by the Cornish engineers, among whom was Trevithick, who employed both the straight flue and the return flue, and who made the fireplace within the flue. The Cornish boiler, in this form was improved by Mr. Fairbairn and the late Mr. Hetherington, who added another fire tube, thus making the two-flued boiler now so extensively employed in Lancashire. The two flues, although somewhat smaller than the single flue, afforded a greater extent of heating surface, besides securing increased regularity in firing. The principle of subdividing the flame and heated products of combustion, so as to obtain greatly increased heating surface within a barrel of given diameter, was fully carried out in the multitubular boiler invented by Neville, of London, in 1826, employed by Seguin, in France, in 1828, and subsequently in the Liverpool and Manchester locomotives, from which it has been handed down to the present practice of engineers. Not since Watt's time, however, has the evaporative power of a square foot of heating surface been increased, the improvement in the plan of steam boilers being that, chiefly, of inclosing a greater extent of surface within a given space. The heating surface, in the boilers of the Great Eastern steamship, is equal to the entire area of her vast main deck; that in the Adriatic measures more than three-fourths of an acre, while the Warrior and the Black Prince have, in their boilers, 2,500 square yards of surface of tubes, the aggregate length of which is more than five and one-half miles.

Objections to Multitubular Boilers. — But it is only where, as in steamships and in locomotive engines, the dimensions and weight of boilers must be the least possible, that the multitubular arrangement is even to be tolerated. It is costly and subject to rapid decay. In steamships, especially, the life of multitubular boilers is comparatively short. The boilers in her Majesty's vessels of war are found to last but from five to seven years; those of the West Indian Royal mailships last, according to Mr. Pitcher, of Northfield, six years only, and those of the Dover and Calais packets, taking the testimony of the former mail contractor, Mr. Churchward, need to be renewed every three and a half or four years. On land, multitubular boilers, working under constant strain, and, in most cases, as constantly concentrating a saturated solution of sulphate of lime, are nearly out of the question for the purpose of manufactories, although there are instances of their employment, even in spinning mills. A boiler rated at 40 nominal horse-power will ordinarily evaporate 60 cubic feet of water per hour, or upwards of 100 tuns of water per week of 60 hours. And feed water containing as much as 40 grains of solid matter, per gallon, is often regarded as very good, not only when the inorganic impurity consists of the deliquescent salts of soda, but even when it is neither more nor less than an obdurate carbonate or sulphate of lime.   Whatever the solid matter contained in the water may be, it is never carried over with the steam, but is left behind in the evaporating apparatus, and 100 tuns of the water, fed in a single week to a boiler in the manufacturing districts, commonly contains a hundred weight or more of dissolved gypsum or marble, and of which all that is not held in solution is deposited in a calcareous lining upon the internal metallic surfaces.   This fact will explain why not only water tube, but multifire tube boilers cannot be economically employed under the ordinary circumstances of steam generation.   The consideration of deposit or scaling, as well as that of workmanship, imposes a limit to the subdivision of heating surface among a great number of small tubes.

Objections to Wrought-Iron Spheres. — In ordinary boiler making the geometrical advantage of the sphere cannot be turned to account. It cannot be produced economically in plate iron, nor if made in plate iron, could it be advantageously applied in a steam boiler.   The hollow sphere has this property, to wit : with a given thickness of metal it has twice the strength of a hollow cylinder of the same diameter.   This is upon the assumption (which is correct where the cylinder is of a length greater than its own diameter), that the ends of the cylinder offer no resistance to a bursting pressure exerted against the circumference. Under over-pressure, a closed cylinder would take the shape of a barrel, and if of homogeneous material and structure, it would burst at the middle of its length, and in the direction of the circumference. The circumference of a sphere of a diameter of 1 being always 3·14159, the sum of the length of the two sides of a cylinder of the same diameter, and having a plane of rupture of the same area, is 1·5708, or exactly half as much.   And not only are the boiler-heads of no service in resisting the strain in the direction of the circumference of the cylinder, and not only are they weak in themselves, except when of a hemispherical form, or when well stayed, but, furthermore, the whole pressure against them is exerted to produce a strain on the sides of the cylinder in the direction of its length, and where there is no through stay-rod between the opposite heads this strain is necessarily equal to one-half of that exerted in the direction of the circumference.

Weakness of ordinary Boilers. — The bursting pressure of steam-boilers is commonly calculated from the average tensile strength of wrought-iron plates.   This strength is very variable however, and it would be more logical to take the minimum.   The most extensive series of experiments upon the strength of iron plates is that made by Mr. Kirkaldy for Messrs. Napier, of Glasgow.   The number of samples of each description of iron tested was not large, yet the tensile strength ranged between very wide limits.   That of Yorkshire iron varied between 62,544 lbs. per square inch and 40,541 lbs., both specimens being from the same makers.   Staffordshire plates varied between 60,985 lbs., and 35,007 lbs., and Lanarkshire plates between 57,659 lbs. and 32,450 lbs.   The conclusion cannot be resisted that engineers are frequently dealing with boiler plates of a tensile strength not greater than from 16 to 18 tuns per square inch, notwithstanding that the average strength may be 22 tuns, and the maximum 27 tuns. And the loss of this strength in punching the rivet holes is not merely that of the iron cut out, but the punch is found to sensibly injure that which remains.   Mr. Fairbairn's well-known and frequently verified ratio of 56 to 100, as the strength of a single riveted joint to that of the unpunched plate, must be always admitted in calculations of the strength of riveted boilers.   The 40-horse Lancashire boiler, seven feet in diameter, will thus be often found to have an ultimate strength not greater, when new, than that corresponding to a pressure of from 210 lbs. to 235 lbs. per square inch.   This, however, is without taking account of the strain exerted longitudinally upon the shell of the boiler by the pressure on the ends, and it is upon the assumption, which is hardly tenable, that the boiler heads, and especially the flues, are of the same strength as the cylindrical body or shell.   Without the angle-iron strengthening recommended by Mr. Fairbairn, the collapsing pressure of the flues of large boilers was found, in that gentleman's experiments, to be sometimes as little as 87 lbs. per square inch.   The strain resulting from the circumferential and longitudinal components, in the outer shell, is one-eighth greater than that calculable for the circumference alone, so that, even if the heads and flues were stayed to the strength of the shell, this would correspond to a pressure of but from 190 lbs. to 210 lbs., instead of 210 lbs. to 235 lbs., as just supposed.   But these estimates are for the strength of the boiler when new.

Corrosion the great Destroyer. — In the experience of the officers of the Manchester Boiler Association, with from 1,300 to 1,600 boilers always under their care, one boiler out of every seven, and, in some years, as in 1862, nearly one of every four became defective by corrosion alone, while of every eight boilers examined in the course of a year seven are found to be defective in some respects.   Thus, in 1862, with 1,376 boilers under inspection, 85 positively dangerous, and 987 objectionable defects were discovered, 37 dangerous and 270 objectionable cases of corrosion alone having been reported.   As a boiler malady, corrosion corresponds in its comparative frequency and fatality to the great destroyer of human life, — consumption.   It is the one great disease.   It is frequently internal, in consequence of the presence of acid in the water; but it is still oftener external, and it is most insidious and certain wherever there is the least leakage of steam into the brick-work setting.   Condensed steam, or distilled water, is an active solvent of iron, as well as of lead, and peaty water, which, so far as *inorganic* matter is concerned, is very pure, and distilled water from surface condensers, and, indeed, any water that is quite soft is known to eat rapidly into the substance of the boiler in which it is used. A trickling, however slight, of condensed steam, down the outside of a boiler, will infallibly cause corrosion, and to this was directly traced a large number of the 47 boiler explosions which occurred in the United Kingdom in 1863.

Cast Iron not corroded. — Corrosion is most rapid where the iron is comparatively pure, as in the best Yorkshire and Staffordshire plates.   The presence, however, of a small proportion of carbon, as in steel, or especially of silver and carbon, as in cast-iron, renders

it nearly indestructible. The experience even with kitchen uten-
sils demonstrates this; but it is more satisfactory to observe the
fact in engineering operations on the great scale. When Nelson
first introduced the hot-blast, he employed wrought-iron heating
stoves, and although only 300° Fahr. was at first fixed upon for the
temperature of the blast, the stoves were rapidly destroyed. It need
hardly be mentioned that a wrought-iron gas retort would be worthless, where cast iron answers well, being inferior only to fire clay.
It is the same with forge tuyeres, cast iron lasting indefinitely.
Since superheated steam began to be generally employed, much difficulty has been experienced from the rapid corrosion of the superheaters. The Peninsular and Oriental Company's engineers have been
compelled to adopt copper, instead of plate iron, heating surfaces for
this purpose. Messrs. Richardson &. Sons, of Hartlepool, have, on
the other hand, adopted cast iron, and their superheaters of this material show no corrosion whatever, after four years' use. The sulphurous fumes from locomotive engines rapidly corrode the plate iron
station roofs, while the cast-iron girders and cornices remain unaffected. Cast-iron bridges are indestructible by rusting, while large
quantities of iron scales are being removed from wrought-iron
bridges, including the Conway and Britannia tubes. From abundant
experience with cast-iron steam boilers and the tubes of cast-iron
heating apparatus, it may be taken as settled, that where the thickness is moderate, cast iron may be thus employed without the possibility of corrosion.

Strength of Cast Iron. — The tensile strength of cast iron varies
between 5 tuns and 15 tuns per square inch. Considered as a material for boilers only, the minimum strength should be regarded exactly, as from 16 tuns to 18 tuns has been taken for wrought-iron
plates. Cast-iron boilers eight feet in diameter and of great length,
were at one time made, but these were manifestly objectionable.
The spherical form of moderate diameter, is preferable; and whatever is the bursting strength of a riveted wrought-iron cylinder, that
of a cast-iron sphere of the same diameter and the same thickness of
metal, will be the same. The plate iron, of a strength of 18 tuns per
square inch, is virtually weakened to 10 tuns by the loss in riveting,
and, as the hollow sphere is twice stronger than the hollow cylinder
of the same diameter and thickness, the cast iron, having no joints,
becomes equal in this comparison to the wrought plate. If we could
always count upon the maximum strength of iron, to wit, 27 tuns per
square inch for wrought, and 15 tuns for cast, a 14 feet cast-iron
sphere would have the same strength to resist bursting as the seven
feet cylinder of the Lancashire 40-horse boiler, supposing the same
thickness of metal in each case.

No Scale in Harrison Boilers. — But there is no occasion to make
a boiler as a single large sphere, for it is now ascertained from extensive experience that hollow cast-iron spheres of small diameter, do
not retain the solid matter deposited by the water. Small water
tubes, and indeed all small water spaces in ordinary boilers, always
choke with deposit when the feed water contains lime; but cast-iron
boiler spheres, although they may be temporarily coated internally
with scale, are found to part with this whenever they are emptied of

water. This fact is the most striking discovery that has been made in boiler engineering. It removes the fatal defect of small subdivided water spaces, which can now be employed with the certainty of their remaining constantly clear of deposit. This discovery has been made in the use of a cast-iron boiler invented by Mr. Hamson of Philadelphia, and which is constructed as follows: Any number of cast-iron hollow spheres are employed, whose dimensions are eight inches in external diameter, and three-eighths of an inch thick, communicating with each other through open necks, and being held together by internal tie bolts. A number of these spheres are arranged in the form of a rectangular slab; and several of these slabs, set side by side, and connected together, form the boiler, about two-thirds of the whole number of spheres being filled with water, while the remainder serve as steam room. The bursting strength of these spheres corresponds to a pressure of upwards of 1,500 pounds per square inch, as verified by repeated experiment, being, therefore, from six to seven times greater than that of the ordinary Lancashire boilers of large size. The evaporative power, as in all other boilers, depends upon the extent and ratio of the grate area and heating surface; but in practice from seven and a half to eight pounds of water are evaporated, per pound of coal in a cast-iron boiler, which, for each tun of its own weight, supplies steam equal to ten indicated horse-power. The joints between the spheres are made by special machinery, securing the utmost accuracy of fitting, and there is no leakage, either of water or steam. The spheres occupied as steam space, are screened by fire bricks from the direct action of the heat; but enough is allowed to reach them to secure complete drying, and if desired, any degree of superheating of the steam. The slabs into which each series of spheres is assembled, are placed in an inclined position, which secures the thorough calculation of the water. The whole quantity of water carried in a 40-horse boiler, is three tuns, the boiler weighing 13 tuns, and presenting 1,000 square feet of water-heating, and 500 square feet of steam-drying surface. In Manchester, with the feed-water taken from the Irwell, or from the canal, a hard scale is soon formed in the ordinary boilers; but in the cast-iron boiler a succession of thin scales of extreme hardness are found to form upon and to become detached of themselves from the inner surfaces of the water spheres. These scales are blown out with the water at the end of the week, and only small quantities can be discovered when purposely sought for.

A pint of loose scales and dirt is the most that has yet been found in a careful internal examination, after nine months daily work. None of the iron is removed with the scale, the weight of the spheres after three years' service, being the same as when new. In America, Mr. Harrison's cast-iron boiler has been worked for six years.

The self-scaling action, which has been found to be the same in all cases where the boiler has been worked, can only be explained by conjectures.

STEEL BOILERS.

Important experiments have recently been made in Prussia with steel boilers. Two boilers, each 30 feet long and 4 feet in diameter, without flues, were placed side by side. One was made of steel plates one-fourth

4

of an inch thick, the other of iron plates 0·414 of an inch in thickness. The steel boiler was tested by hydraulic pressure up to 195 pounds per square inch. Both boilers were worked for about a year and a half under 65 pound pressure. At the end of that time there was less scale in the steel than in the iron boiler. The steel boiler generated 25 per cent more steam and evaporated an average of 11·66 cubic feet of water per hour; the iron evaporated 9·37 cubic feet. The quantity of coal consumed per 12 hours was 2,706 for the steel, and 2,972 for the iron boiler. The plates of the steel boiler directly over the fire were found to be uninjured while those of the other were worn out. The advantages of the steel boiler are strength, lightness, rapidity of evaporation, durability under heat, the securing of more perfect riveting, and comparative freedom from scale.

NEW MECHANICAL ACTION OF STEAM.

In a recent English invention it is claimed "that the expansive force of the steam is made to act equally on two pistons, and force them apart with the power due to the area of the pistons and the pressure of the steam, and that the force thus exerted on two pistons is united and conveyed to the crank shaft; whereas, in steam engines of the usual construction, with a piston working in a cylinder, *half the force exerted is always acting on one of the ends of the cylinder.*"

NEW CALORIC ENGINE.

A new caloric engine, invented by Mr. Roper of Boston, Mass. has the following peculiarities. It is designed to be used where small power is required; and the main novelty about it is, that it does not use, upon the piston, common air heated, but only the products of combustion. The air to supply oxygen for the combustion of anthracite coal is pumped in; the carbon is burned rapidly and completely, under pressure, and the resulting carbonic acid gas and uncombined nitrogen gas from the air, are passed from the generator to the piston, which is in the form of a hollow plunger, so arranged that it is packed and fitted only at the top, where there is the least heat. In this way the common difficulty of lubricating a hot cylinder and piston is obviated. The generator of heat is surrounded with firebrick or soapstone, which prevents the iron from being burnt. The engine is single acting,—that is, the power is applied to the piston moving in one direction, during which movement the air to feed the fire is pumped in; the momentum acquired at the same time, by a balance or fly-wheel, is used to carry the piston back to its original position.

ON OUR FUTURE LOCOMOTION.

"It would be presumptuous to augur that steam locomotives and their trains will erelong fail to meet the demands of society; but it would be much more so to conclude that they comprise the perfection of mechanical resource, and are to be the *ne plus ultra* of land traveling for all time to come. In nature nothing is born or matured at once; and in art nothing springs complete from human brains. Inventions, like plants, are designed to grow until they are ripe; and when all is got out of them that can be, to give place to others. When one has fulfilled its promise in the front ranks of civilization, it is to fall back until it reaches the hindermost. Ages may elapse before this is done, or can be done while barbarism endures. Flint implements continued in use through ages of bronze; and iron has not yet reached all savage tribes. That the rapid transit of men and merchandise is an important, and destined to become a leading element in civilization, no one can doubt who observes its influence on the social, political, commercial, and intellectual world. If it stands still, progress in other departments must be arrested. Whatever may be the extreme limits to speed, there is little risk in asserting that the present mean rate will in time be deemed intolerably slow. It is not every one that is now satisfied with it, and the number is not small who wish it were doubled.

When faith in progress becomes general, improvements in the arts will become common. The more there is of it, the less of that depressing unbelief which meets new projects, sometimes with derision, always with suspicion, and against which valuable novelties have to struggle into life. Preferring to rest satisfied with things as they are, it is doubtless ready to ask what possibility there is of any marked advance in traveling by steam? and where the necessity for it? The very objections to mail coaches in the last century, which were to pass over roads good and bad, night and day, at the incredible average rate of ten miles an hour; to the first steamboats, also, which, if they did not threaten to upset and break the limbs of their passengers, would subject them to the double risk of being scalded to death, or blown piecemeal into the air. Had the leap from ten miles by horses, to fifty by steam, been attempted at once, it would have staggered the boldest, and probably have brought public execration on the proposer; but nothing of the kind can take place. By the law of progress, improvements are gradual, never precipitate.

The timid would not now willingly be among the first to travel at the rate of 80 or 100 miles an hour, if they even had little fear of its taking away their breath. The feeling is a natural one, and therefore to be respected, although it has no rational foundation. It is chiefly ascribable to ignorance of the fact that the highest speed no more affects our bodily organs, than the lowest.

Passengers in the cabin of a ship flying before the wind, have no more sensation of going forward, than when she is lying at anchor. A balloon rushing upward, or in a lateral direction, appears to the aeronauts stationary and motionless. In night rail trains we walk to and fro, sit and sleep, unconscious of progression as in a parlor or bedroom. In daytime it is the same if we close our eyes to objects outside. Jolts from obstructions and irregularities of roads, with changes of direction and diversities of speed, tell us we are moving. In a perfect system of travel, there could be no sense of motion at all, whether the rate was one mile an hour, or a hundred, or five hundred. And even that is a snail's pace when we look, and we ought often to look, beyond our petty doings to those of the Great Engineer. Our earth is one of a line of passenger cars that conveys us through space at a mean velocity of 68,000 miles an hour, without disturbing a loose brick on a chimney, or displacing a grain of dust, proclaiming the fact that uniformity of motion is equivalent to rest, and suggesting that as with time and eternity, heat and cold, light and darkness, attraction and repulsion, &c., rest and motion are one.   Hence, if the time should ever come, when 1,000 miles an hour can be done, old ladies and children will be no more inconvenienced than now, and in all probability not near as much." — *Journal Franklin Institute.*

THE PNEUMATIC RAILWAY.

In former numbers of the *Annual of Scientific Discovery* (see vol. for 1864, p. 21), we have described the workings of the so-called " Pneumatic Despatch" as used in London and elsewhere.   During the past year the directors of the Crystal Palace, near London, have constructed upon the same principle a pneumatic railway, consisting of a brickwork tunnel, or tube, about 600 yards long, 10 ft. high, and 9 ft. wide.   This tube, which is capable of admitting an ordinary size railway carriage, is laid with a single line of rails, fitted with opening and closing valves at either extremity, and supplied with all the other requisite apparatus for propelling passenger trains on the pneumatic principle.

The object of laying down this experimental line was to afford, both to the scientific world and the traveling public, a practical demonstration of the applicability to passenger traffic of the motive power already employed by the Pneumatic Despatch Company in the conveyance of letters and parcels.

The trial trips recently made with this railway are reported as perfectly successful, and are thus described in the *London Times*, of August 20, 1864 : The pneumatic principle of propulsion is very simple. It has been likened to the action of a pea-shooter, — a rough kind of comparison, perhaps, yet one sufficiently accurate as a popular illustration. The tunnel may be taken to represent the pea-shooter, and the train the pea, which is driven along in one direction by a strong blast of air, and drawn back again in the opposite direction by the exhaustion of the air in front of it.   The train may be said, in fact, to be blown through the tube on the down journey, and sucked through it on the return journey.   It must not, however, be supposed that the passengers are deposited at their destination with a sudden jerk, as the simile we have used might seem to imply.   Such an inconvenience is entirely obviated by the mechanical arrangements employed.   The motion is throughout smooth, easy, and agreeable, and the stoppages are effected gently and gradually.   Indeed, when it is considered that the curve in the tunnel is unusually sharp, being of eight chains radius, and that the gradients are as high as one in fifteen, it is surprising that the motion should be so much steadier and pleasanter than ordinary railway traveling.   The journey of 600 yards was performed either way in about 50 seconds, with an atmospheric pressure of only two and one half ounces to the square inch ; but a higher rate of speed, if desirable, can easily be obtained consistently with safety.   Indeed, one great incidental advantage of this species of locomotion is that it excludes all risk of the collisions occasionally attendant on railway traveling ; for it is plain that no two trains could ever run full tilt against each other where all the propelling force is expended in one direction at one time.   The worst mishap which it is said could well happen is that, owing to some sudden failure in the machinery, the train might be abruptly brought to a dead stop in the middle of the tunnel, when the passengers would have to alight from the carriages and grope their way as best they could out of the tube. Such a predicament certainly would not be enviable, but it might be more ludicrous than dangerous.

The train used consisted of one very long, roomy, and comfortable carriage, resembling an elongated omnibus, and capable of accommodating some 30 or 35 passengers. Passengers enter this carriage at either end, and the entrances are closed with sliding glass doors. Fixed behind the carriage there is a framework of the same form, and nearly the same dimensions, as the sectional area of the tunnel; and attached to the outer edge of this frame is a fringe of bristles forming a thick brush. As the carriage moves along through the tunnel the brush comes into close contact with the arched brickwork, so as to prevent the escape of the air. With this elastic collar round it, the carriage forms a close fitting piston, against which the propulsive force is directed. The motive power is supplied in this: At the departure station a large fan-wheel, with an iron disc, concave in surface and 22 feet in diameter, is made to revolve by the aid of a small stationary engine at such speed as may be required, the pressure of the air increasing, of course, according to the rapidity of the revolutions, and thus generating the force necessary to send the heavy carriage up a steeper incline than is to be found upon any existing railway. The disc gyrates in an iron case resembling that of a huge paddlewheel; and from its broad periphery the particles of air stream off in strong currents. When driving the air into the upper end of the tunnel to propel the down-train fresh quantities rush to the surface of the disc to supply the partial vacuum thus created; and on the other hand, when the disc is exhausting the air in the tunnel with the view of drawing back the up-train, the air rushes out like an artificial hurricane from the escaped valves of the disc case, making the adjacent trees shake like reeds and almost blowing off his feet any incautious spectator who approaches too near it.

When the down journey is to be performed the breaks are taken off the wheels and the carriage moves by its own momentum into the mouth of the tube, passing in its course over a deep air-well in the floor, covered with an iron grating. Up this opening a gust of wind is sent by the disc, when a valve, formed by a pair of iron doors, hung like lock-gates, immediately closes firmly over the entrance of the tunnel, confining the increasing atmospheric pressure between the valve and the rear of the carriage. The force being thus brought to bear upon the end of the train, the latter, shut up within the tube, glides smoothly along towards its destination, the revolving disc keeping up the motive power until it reaches the steep incline, whence its own momentum again suffices to carry it the rest of the distance. The return journey, as above indicated, is affected by the aid of the exhausting process. At a given signal a valve is opened, and the disc-wheel set to work in withdrawing the air from the tube. Near the upper end of the tube there is a large aperture, or side-vault, which forms the throat through which the air is, so to speak, exhaled, the iron doors at the upper terminus still being kept shut. In a second or two the train posted at the lower terminus, yielding to the exhausting process going on in its front, and urged by the ordinary pressure of the atmosphere from behind, moves off on its upward journey and rapidly ascending the incline approaches the iron gates, which fly open to receive it, and it emerges at once into daylight. Such is the mode in which the system works, and it seems capable of being adapted to railway communication within the metropolis and other large towns, or wherever tunnelled lines with steep gradients exist. The chief obstacles encountered in practically working the atmospheric railway, introduced some 15 years ago, are considered to have been effectually overcome by the present modification of the principle. Under the former system the tube was of very small size, and fixed upon the ground; a longitudinal or continuous valve opening at the top, along which a rod, connecting the piston with the carriages passed, and the valve closing behind the rod as it moved onwards. The amount of atmospheric pressure required to be exerted where the area of the tube was so small was enormous, being from seven to ten pounds per square inch; whereas under the present system the pressure is only two and one-half ounces per square inch; and, moreover, the great leakage and waste of power which rendered the old atmosphere system so costly in working are here in great measure avoided. It need hardly be added that the worst drawbacks to traveling through tunnels — viz: the smoke and sulphureous vapors emitted from the locomotive, and the close, unwholesome atmosphere of the tunnels themselves — are in this case got rid of. Every train, in fact, carries its own supply of fresh air along with it, and also expels the foul air before it.

Improved Pneumatic Despatch.— Mr. C. A. Varley, of Liverpool, has invented an improved apparatus for the transmission of parcels on the pneumatic principle. The novelty of the invention consists in the use of compressed air as a motive power for the propulsion of carriages in one direction, while a vacuum is created for their transmission in the other. In the old plan, the pressure used was limited to that of the atmosphere,— 15 pounds to the square inch,— but by the new system, any amount of pressure can be obtained by the use of compressed air.

The London Engineer thus describes the application of Mr. Varley's invention by one of the telegraph companies in Liverpool, for the transmission of written despatches from one office to another, a distance of about 300 yards. It says: " In the cells beneath the central office of the company in Castle Street, is an engine usually worked at about one horse-power, though much more force can be gained if necessary. This engine works a double air-pump, which removes the air from one chamber and forces it into another. The chambers are called the ' exhaust ' and the ' compressed air ' chambers, and are connected by pipes and valves with the apparatus in the room on the first floor. If a message has to be sent, it is placed in a little round flannel bag made to fit loosely into the tube. A valve is then opened in connection with the compressed air chamber; the compressed air, which is kept at 11 pounds on the square inch, rushes into the tube, and the bag is urged with immense rapidity to its destination. On its arrival there the signal is given on an electric bell, the valve stopped, and the operator is ready to receive the return message. The signal is given on the electric bell, and the valve and all outer communications at the operator's end closed. A communication is then opened with the exhaust chamber, and the air, rushing from the far end to supply the vacuum, brings the little bag along with it. On its arrival a spring is touched, the valve falls, and the air rushes in. The operator is then able to open the case and take out the message. The average speed of these tubes, which are one and one half inches diameter, is about 40 miles per hour, so that any number of messages may be sent or received from the exchange in 17 seconds."

IMPROVED RAILWAY CAR TRUCKS.

In car trucks, as generally constructed, the wheels are made fast to the axles. It follows that they must be of equal size, and pass over tracks of equal length at the same time, or there must be a sliding or jumping motion given to one of them equal to the difference in the size of the wheels, or the length of the track. But practically, the wheels cannot be made or kept of the same size while in use, nor can the tracks on the right and left of the cars be of the same length, except while running in a straight line; the consequence must be that a grinding, sliding, and jumping motion is nearly constant. The result of these irregularities and inequalities is to rapidly destroy both the wheels, axles, and rails; also, to weaken the cars.

An estimate of the amount of this sliding and jumping, which occurs every day on extensive roads, will astonish every one who has not investigated the subject. Suppose the wheels upon the opposite ends of the axle in a rigid truck differ in their circumference the amount of one-fourth of an inch. At every revolution the lesser wheel must be brought up to equal the larger by a jump or slide. This difficulty is rather increased in passing curves. These objections attending the use of a " rigid truck " are sought to be overcome by Mr. Walter Youmans, Lansingburg, N. Y., in an invention, the fundamental principles of which are comprised in making the wheels turn on adjustable axles, and in so adjusting the axles as to keep them always at right angles to the truck. By this improvement it is claimed, that all sliding and jumping of the wheels is obviated; for turning independently of each other, each wheel is kept in its proper position, without causing any strain upon its fellow.

A considerable gain in the power of the locomotive is obtained, by being relieved of the necessity of turning every axle in the train with every revolution of the wheels, at a leverage of about 16 inches from the centre of motion. This improvement seems to have great merit, and will doubtless find its way into universal use.

Railway Car for different Gauges. — The following is an invention of Mr. Tisdale, of Boston, by means of which a car can be made to conform to two different gauges of railway tracks. The wheels are made to move upon the axle back and forwards by flanges, running between two rails placed on each side of the truck, so forming a groove, one end of which is set to four feet eight and one-half inch gauge, the other to five feet six inch; by moving the car back or forwards in the groove, the wheels open or close together on the axle; when they have come to the desired gauge they are fixed firmly and very simply by clutch boxes and wedges, which turn round by hand and lock with a slide key. When this is done the car is ready for use.

IRON MASTS.

The *Achilles*, one of the new iron-clads of the British Navy, has been fitted with iron masts. Of these the mainmast weighs no less than 21 tuns 12 cwt.; its length being 121 feet 9 inches, diameter three feet four inches, and length of head from hounds 20 feet. Each mast is formed of three curved plates half an inch in thickness, which form the skin or outside shell of each, the joint where the vertical edges of the plates meet being so formed that the outsides of the masts show no ridges. Under each of the vertical joints three strong tie-irons are placed to which are riveted the plates forming the mast; the rivets on the outside being countersunk or let in flush, the exterior of the mast consequently presenting a round and perfectly smooth surface. Experience has shown that iron masts last much longer than wooden, that they are lighter and stronger, serve as valuable ventilators, and are also better conductors of electricity. If they are shot away and fall overboard they will immediately sink, instead of floating alongside and fouling the screw, as is the case with wooden masts.

Enormous Iron Plate. — Messrs. John Brown & Co., of the Atlas Works, Sheffield, England, have succeeded in rolling an iron plate, six feet by seven feet and thirteen and a half inches thick. The idea of manufacturing so enormous a plate originated, we believe, with Captain Inglis, of the Royal Engineers, with a view of ascertaining if it would be desirable to protect casemates with such a powerful covering.

THE STRENGTH OF WROUGHT-IRON GIRDERS.

The strength of wrought-iron girders has been critically examined by Mr. Wm. Fairbairn, F.R.S. He says from his experiment it is evident that wrought-iron girders of ordinary construction are not safe when submitted to violent disturbances equivalent to one-third the weight that would break them. They, however, exhibit wonderful tenacity when subjected to the same treatment with one-fourth the load; and assuming, therefore, that an iron girder bridge will bear with this load 12,000,000 changes without injury, it is clear that it would require 328 years, at the rate of 100 changes per day before its security was affected. It would, however, be dangerous to risk a load of one-third the breaking weight upon bridges of this description, as, according to the last experiment, the beam broke with 313,000 changes; or a period of eight years, at the same rate as before, would be sufficient to break it. It is more than probable that the beam had been injured by the previous 3,000,000 changes to which it had been subjected; and, assuming this to be true, it would follow that the beam was undergoing a gradual deterioration which must some time, however remote, have terminated in fracture.

WELDING BY HYDRAULIC PRESSURE.

"Experiments have lately been made at Paris by M. Duportail, engineer, to ascertain whether iron might be welded by hydraulic pressure instead of by the sledge-hammer. The latter, indeed, has not a sufficient impetus to reach the very core of the metal, while continuous pressure acts indefinitely to any depth. In the experiments alluded to M. Duportail caused two iron bars, one and one-half inches in diameter, and heated to the welding point, to be placed between the piston and the top of an hydraulic press. The bars were welded together by this means with extraordinary ease, the iron being, as it were, kneaded together, and bulged out at the sides under the pressure. The action

of the press was suspended when the part welded was brought down to the thickness of the bars. After cooling, the welded part was cut through to examine the inside, which was found perfectly compact. To try it, one of the halves was placed under a forge-hammer weighing 1,800 kil., and it was not until the third stroke that the welding was discovered."

Alluding to the above, the *London Artisan* says :—

A highly ingenious form of hydraulic press for forging metals was also patented some time since by Mr. Bessemer. Its construction was as follows :—

An ordinary ram of a hydraulic press is in communication through a pipe with the usual force-pump plunger, driven with a crank on a shaft provided with a heavy fly-wheel. The barrel, in which is working the plunger, is unprovided with valves, and is continued as a simple pipe till it communicates with the cylinder of the press. The water between the plunger of this kind of pipe and the ram thus acts as a communicator of motion between the two, and they rise and fall through distances varying respectively as the areas of the plungers. It will be seen that the heavy fly-wheel does the principal work in compressing; for as soon as the rams — the propelling plunger and the driven plunger — meet with resistance, the inertia of the heavy fly-wheel at once comes into play. We do not know whether this invention has been found successful in practice; and a yet more recent patent of Mr. Bessemer embodies the plan of supporting the bearings of the bottom roll of mills for rolling armor plates on a hydraulic ram. This ram is in communication with water pressure, which can be let on or off, as required, by means of a valve. In case the armor plate being rolled should stick — as often takes place — the water below the ram is let out, with the result of relieving the plate from pressure.

It is scarcely possible to over-estimate the importance of the application of the hydraulic press for forging purposes, and it may be ranked almost as high in the scale of practical improvements in working iron as the introduction of the rolling mill, and at least as high as the introduction of the steam hammer. It would seem to fit in with the recent inventions, giving us a command over the production of steel in large masses, affording, as it does, means of working a substance of much more delicate manipulation than even wrought iron. Nor does the use of the hydraulic press seem to be confined to working of iron and steel in an incandescent state, as is evidenced in the remarkable production of steel tubes drawn cold by hydraulic pressure.

NEW PLAN FOR THE PRODUCTION OF CAST STEEL FROM PIG IRON.

M. Cazanave, a French inventor, has recently devised the following new plan for producing cast steel directly from pig iron.

The foundation of this new method is the influence of steam on a thin stream of pig iron. If we take an iron tube of a certain diameter with sides of the necessary strength, form a ring out of it, and fix on its circumference towards the centre three or more tubes, we have a tube ring with three or more radii. The radius is made fast to the tubular pipe; the ends of these tubes, which are open, do not quite reach to the centre of the ring, and have, therefore, between the ends an empty space, in which the pig iron is allowed to flow in a stream of a certain strength. The stream let into the boiler from the tubular pipe flows out of the openings of the three tubes, and operates directly upon the pig iron. It is said that the oxygen of the steam oxidizes the carbon of the pig iron, the silicium, a portion of the sulphur, phosphorus, and other impurities in the pig iron ; the hydrogen combines with the carbon, sulphur, phosphorus, arsenic, and other bodies, with which it forms combinations of hydrogen. The carbonized and purified metal falls into a crucible or other vessel placed immediately under the apparatus. The metal obtained contains impurities, and must, therefore, be smelted in crucibles in a blast or reverberatory furnace. This is the essential part of the process ; the simplicity of the method and the cheapness of the product are evident.

"Now arise the questions : Is it possible to obtain steel in large quantities by this method ; will it be of the same quality as the small quantity obtained on trial ; and, if it is possible, at what price can it be obtained ?

"In answer to these questions, Cazanave asserts that by his method steel can be obtained in great quantities, not inferior to the best steel, and proportionately cheaper : for his best quality steel can be obtained for £18 per tun. This is difficult to believe, but the inventor affirms that it is so, and at the same time warrants the excellent quality of his steel. In the present method of obtaining steel, good iron must be used, which is cemented, and the cemented iron, that is, the steel is smelted in crucibles. By Cazanave's method cementation of the iron is avoided, so that the cast steel may be obtained in unlimited quantities. If this new method turns out practicable, it will be possible to work up the whole daily production of a blast-furnace into steel. For this only the apparatus is required, which is not very costly, and which would be erected near the blast-furnace and stream of pig iron. The stream would be divided into rays of the necessary strength, and each one directed into an apparatus. By Bessemer's process about ten tuns of steel are obtained per day at Sheffield ; while by Cazanave's method 60 and 70 tuns per day could be obtained, and a blast-furnace is being erected at Charleroi which will produce about 74 tuns per day! The samples of steel furnished by this new process are reported to be very good."—*Colliery Guardian, Eng.*

Absorption of Carbon by Iron. — Mr. Caron, in a paper read before the British Association at its last meeting, stated that recent experiments made by him, showed that iron may be made to absorb any quantity of carbon by means of its oxide. Thus a gramme of oxide of iron, being subjected to reduction in hydrogen, yielded seven-tenths of a gramme of pure iron. This, after being heated for an hour in oxide of carbon, weighed nearly a gramme ; after another hour of the same process, its weight rose to a gramme and a half ; after a third hour, to two grammes ; and so, until it reached the weight of three grammes after the sixth time. Nearly the whole of this increase of weight is owing to the absorption of carbon, the rest being a very small proportion of oxygen.

REDUCTION OF CAST IRON BY SUPERHEATED STEAM.

The following account of some highly interesting experiments on the decarbonization of cast iron by superheated steam, is reported to the *Scientific American* by the experimenters, Messrs. Duffield and Hart of Detroit, Michigan.

They state that during the past year they commenced a series of experiments upon the action of superheated steam upon the quality of iron, with the following points in view : —

1st. To see whether superheated steam could be used in the place of air, for the decarbonization of the iron.

2d. If the chemical interchange would set in between the hydrogen of the superheated steam and the sulphur, in combination with the iron, to form sulphuretted hydrogen gas, thus freeing the iron from such a deleterious substance, and correct perfectly what is technically known as red shortness.

3d. To see if the oxygen, if liberated, would unite with the carbon in the iron, producing an intense combustion as much increased in intensity, as the ratio of oxygen to the hydrogen in steam exceeds the ratio of oxygen to hydrogen in the atmosphere, the latter principle being involved in the Bessemer or pneumatic method of making steel. If the superheated steam process was successful, it would do away with the blowing engine, as the pressure would be derived direct from the boiler, thus economizing the expense of the engine, and the cost for attendance, &c.

As this matter was solely theoretical, and we could not say how it would act until fairly tried, apparatus was devised for testing the matter thoroughly by experiment. This consisted of a coil 34 feet long, ⅜ pipe, coiled within a foot circle. Around this was built a furnace, where a bright red heat could be brought upon every portion of the coil, by means of charcoal ; the furnace was connected with the main boiler in the laboratory, by a pipe, in such a way that the condensed steam would not have to traverse the coil. From the coil the pipe led to a Sefstroms furnace driven by a fan, containing a crucible holding a sufficient quantity of molten cast iron, combined with a large proportion of sulphur. Into this, while in a liquid state, with steam at a temperature of 1,200° Fahr., the tuyere at the end of the steam pipe, transmitting the superheated steam, was lowered into the metal. We were disappointed that the molten iron did not evolve gases, and burst into vivid combustion. We were aware that ordinary steam cooled the metal, and therefore was inapplicable for use in the temperature of iron ; but we had hoped this might be due to the ordinary aqueous vapor carried forward in the swift mechanical current of the steam, and thought if we could deprive the steam of its moisture, — that is, make a perfectly dry steam, — that this objection would cease. Such proved to be by our experiments a false deduction, for so soon as steam was introduced, the molten metal passed into a semi-fluid and then a solid state. When the steam was first brought in contact with the metal, the iron had the appearance of boiling and was rapidly chilled. As no vivid combustion set in, we considered that it was due entirely to the mechanical displacement under the force of steam. We read in text-books that iron at a red heat decomposes water. We have not succeeded in proving this decomposition to be to such an extent as would render it available in the arts, for so quickly cooled is the iron that the decomposition is so small as to be nearly imperceptible.

We could reasonably infer, if the superheated steam was decomposed by contact with the molten iron, that an oxy-hydrogen mixture on a grand scale would be formed, and a small volcano, generating an intense heat, be created. In order to modify this intensity, ordinary steam could have been introduced along with the superheated steam, then the heat generated would be under the control of the operator. We tried melting the iron under the flame of the oxy-hydrogen blow-pipe; a bead was formed, which was metallic iron encased in a shell of oxide of iron. Here there is another point to be viewed, viz: the iron in the mixed gases is rapidly oxidized, and loss of metal to a great extent incurred. Unfortunately for the iron manufacturers, the play of affinities between the elements of steam and iron, with its impurity, are in the wrong direction; combustion is not accelerated, chemical decompositions do not set in, from the fact that the temperature is rapidly lowered, for reasons already given. Since making the above experiments, information relative to the patent lately taken out by Mr. Parry, of England, on this subject, has reached us. His method is to introduce steam as well as air into the molten iron. The steam is introduced until the metal is brought to a semi-fluid consistency, and then shut off, and air forced through, which again increases the temperature, these alternate exposures of the molten metal conducing to desulphurize and purify the metal. From the experiments we have already detailed, we are forced to conclude that the superheated steam claimed by Mr. Parry to purify the metal, has had attributed to it the benefits derived from the air blown through; and he has unwittingly placed to the credit of the steam, what should have been credited to air. With all the facts we have learned from other sources, added to those we have derived from practical experiment, we are of the opinion that, as yet, the pneumatic or Bessemer process is superior as regards economy, practical working, and ease with which it is managed. We are also led to the firm conviction, deduced from our experiments, that the role played by superheated steam, is a mere imaginary one; it does not desulphurize to any extent, or to one half the rapidity that the pneumatic process does; but, in fact, if any chemical action takes place, it is the oxidation of the metal.

These results are submitted, and are not intended to cast a blight on future experiments, but to show that steam or superheated steam does not play such an important part in the iron manufacture as many have supposed.

THE PRESERVATION OF METALS.

The preservation of copper and iron in the sea has been made the subject of long research by M. Becquerel, who has submitted a memoir to the Academy of Sciences at Paris. The causes of the injury (mechanical, physical, and chemical) influence all the chemical actions and tend to the production of electricity by means of isolated voltaic pairs. After considering the important experiments of Davy and others in regard to copper sheathing, M. Becquerel describes the careful method which he adopted in order to determine the amount of

electric action required to decompose a milligramme of water, and to ascertain the electric state of all the parts of a protected metal; and thus to find the laws on which a system of protection might be based. In order to conduct these experiments on a large scale, the Imperial Minister of the Marine placed at M. Becquerel's disposal all the means desired, with the assistance of the most eminent naval engineers in the port of Toulon. The result of these experiments show, with regard to copper, that, as on every metallic surface, there circulates by the intermediate liquid which wets it, currents producing electro-chemical decomposition; if we wish to preserve a surface so as to avoid these deposits we must arm the surface with an electro-motive power equal to that point at which these deposits become insensible. For this purpose laminæ of iron and zinc have been employed. Laminæ of copper, armed with iron, and laminæ of iron protected by zinc, present similar effects, with the difference that the sphere of electric activity is less, where the extent depends on the difference between the electro-motive forces of the protecting and protected metal. Whenever the iron is covered with several coats of white lead it is preserved so long as the paint remains; but when it is once removed, either by friction or the slow dissolving action of the sea, the metal is attacked in various parts; those which have lost the paint become negative and the local alterations are gradually disseminated. M. Becquerel trusts that the means proposed will be found to be successful in preserving vessels from the action of sea-water and from the attachment of marine animals.

In a subsequent communication to the Academy, M. Becquerel made some additional statements relative to his researches. He stated that he had considered that he had demonstrated that when one of the extremities of a bar of iron or steel is placed in salt water, in contact with a bar of zinc, the surface of which is a hundred times less, the intensity of the currents derived from the surface of the protected metal, which results from the oxidation of the zinc, diminishes in proportion as it becomes more and more distant from the points of contact of the two metals; so that protection takes place at considerable distances. In fresh water the effects are very different. The derived currents, which are the cause of the preservation of the iron as well as the electro-motive force, lose their power. They, however, still retain sufficient to preserve from oxidation large surfaces of iron formed of pieces superposed on each other, or juxtaposed and armed with zinc or a suitable alloy. In conclusion, M. Becquerel asserts that if iron or steel be placed in either fresh or salt water, so that the curve of the intensities of the electro-motive force derived from contact with zinc shall never meet the right line of the iron, the iron is protected. The process is also adapted to the preservation of iron water-pipes in wet earth.

The Protection of Iron Bridges from Oxidation. — A new iron bridge of the Thames at London is to be protected from oxidation by a new process patented by Messrs. Morewood & Co., and is alike important from the great cost which will be incurred, and the testing of a rather abstruse chemical formula for the preservation of iron from oxidation and decay. The process is as follows: "The iron is to be thoroughly cleaned and heated to the requisite temperature in a furnace planned by the inventors. When this temperature is attained, it is to be plunged into a bath of prussite of potash and chloride of potassium, in a molten state, so that when the iron is withdrawn it may easily part with the surplus of the aforesaid chemicals, which should run off like oil. The iron is then to be dipped into boiling water, containing a certain proportion of cyanide of potassium; from thence it is removed to a bath for a final washing, and set up on end to dry. All the processes are to be carried on under cover, and before exposure to the atmosphere the iron is to be coated with an asphaltum paint twice, at given intervals; and again it is to receive two coats after fixing. Of course all the necessary planing, drilling, and fitting is to be done preparatory to the indurating. The time the iron is to remain in the bath will vary from one to five minutes, according to the weight of the metal to be operated upon. The elaborate character of the process to which the contractor is rigidly bound, will account for the large sum to be expended in carrying out this part of the work; £4 per tun is allowed to the contractor for the induration and painting; Messrs. Morewood will receive from the contractors 5s. per tun as their royalty, which it is estimated will be £1,000. Thus £16,000 is to be spent in this effort to prevent oxidation, no greater proof of which, in its damaging results, can be offered than the case of the cleaning of the oxide (or rust) from the Menai Bridge, from which has lately been removed above 40 tuns of oxide of iron." — *London Mechanics' Magazine.*

Prevention of Rust on Iron. — Many a valuable hint is to be obtained from an intelligent practical laboring man, which may lead the philosopher into a train of ideas that may, perhaps, result in discoveries or inventions of great importance. When bricklayers leave off work for a day or two, as from Saturday to Monday, they push their trowel in and out of the moist mortar, so that the bright steel may be smeared all over with a film of it, and find this plan an effectual remedy against rust. In Wren's *Parentalia*, there is a passage bearing upon this subject: "In taking out iron cramps and ties from stonework, at least 400 years old, which were so bedded in mortar that all air was perfectly excluded, the iron appeared as fresh as from the forge." In the victualling department at Plymouth, some years ago, I observed a man lime-whiting the inside of some iron tanks, previously to their being filled with water for the service of the crew and passengers during a voyage: this was to prevent the iron rust affecting the water. In London, I have also recently seen men, with a tub of lime-whiting and a mop, smearing the inside of large waterpipes, as security against rust. Oxygen, which is the main cause of rust, is abundant in the composition of both water and the atmosphere; and that quicklime has an astonishing affinity for it is evinced in the homely practice of preserving polished steel or iron goods, such as fire-irons, fenders, and the fronts of "bright stoves," when not in use, a little powdered lime beaten upon them out of a muslin bag being found sufficient to prevent their rusting. Another instance, very different and far more delicate, bearing upon the same principles: the manufacturers of needles, watch-springs, cutlery, &c. generally introduce a small packet of quicklime in the same box or parcel with polished steel goods, as security from rust, before sending it to a distant customer, or stowing it away for future use. These cases are extremely curious, because, as a general rule, bright steel or iron has a most powerful affinity for oxygen; consequently it is

very readily acted upon by damp, and is rusted in a short time, either by decomposing the water and obtaining oxygen from that source, or direct from the atmosphere. It is not absolutely essential that the quicklime should be in actual contact with the metal, but if somewhere near, as in the case of the parcel of lime packed up with the needles or watchsprings, the bright metal will remain a long while without the least alteration in its appearance; the lime (which is already an oxide of calcium), either receiving an additional dose of oxygen, or being converted into a carbonate of lime.—*Mr. C. H. Smith, in Builder.*

New Process for coating Metals.—At a recent meeting of the French Academy, a communication was read by M. Weil, "On New Processes for Covering Metals with Firmly Adherent and Bright Layers of other Metals." The method consists in dipping the metal to be coated in a saline solution of the metal to be deposited, rendered distinctly alkaline with potash or soda, and mixed with some organic matter, such as tartaric acid or glycerine. At the same time, it is necessary in some cases to set up a weak voltaic current by keeping a piece of zinc or lead in contact with the metal. In this way the author obtains a firm layer of copper, or iron and steel, and procures various and beautiful effects according to the thickness of the copper deposited. Silver, nickel, and other metlas can be applied in the same way. The process, it will be seen, is susceptible of numerous applications. A curious fact mentioned is that a clean surface of copper may be coated with zinc by placing the two metals in contact, in a solution of caustic soda or potash. In the cold the deposit of zinc takes place slowly, but at 100° it is effected rapidly.

ON THE PRESERVATION OF WOOD.

The following composition is recommended to protect the bottom of posts, palings, and tubs set in the earth: 40 parts of chalk are added to 50 parts of resin, and four parts of linseed oil, melted together in an iron pot. One part of native oxide of copper is then added, and one part of sulphuric acid is cautiously stirred in. The mixture is applied hot with a strong brush, and forms, when dry, a varnish as hard as stone. — *London Chemical News.*

Preservative Action of Sulphate of Copper on Wood. — The experiments of M. König have demonstrated that the sulphate of copper deprives wood of the nitrogenous matter which acts as a ferment, this matter being found in the solution of the copper. At the same time a combination of resin and copper is formed, which closes up the pores of the wood and preserves it from the action of the air. The wood, however, is still susceptible of decomposition, in consequence of the variations of temperature and humidity. M. Weltz, while occupied with the solution of the last questions, has arrived at the following conclusions: He has remarked that the wood gradually blackens as the layers of metallic copper are produced on it. The sulphate of copper is fixed in the wood: this salt decomposes itself into metallic copper and sulphuric acid. The latter chars the wood, and it is through this layer of charcoal, the preserving agency of which has been so often remarked, that the wood is enabled to resist the action

...dity. M. Weltz's ideas are confirmed by the following fact: ...south of Spain there exists an ancient copper-mine (Mina de ...onto), which dates from the first years of the Christian era. The ...odwork which sustains the galleries, is still in a perfect state of preservation. It is charred, a circumstance which is explained by the quantity of crystallized sulphate of copper and of metallic copper in regulus which covers it. The wood has remained exposed nearly 18 centuries to the action of the atmosphere and its humidity, having been charred by the sulphate of copper while depositing metallic copper on its surface. — *Repertoire de Chimie.*

NEW METHODS FOR PRESERVING MEATS, FRUITS, VEGETABLES, &c.

At a recent industrial exhibition at St. Petersburg, the following mode of preserving fruits, invented by the *maître d'hotel* of the Grand Duke Nicholas, attracted great attention. Quicklime is slacked in water, into which four or five drops of creosote for each quart of water have been mixed: the lime must be neither too much nor too little slacked; there is a certain knack which practice alone can teach. Take a box and lay in its bottom a bed of the slacked lime, above this spread a layer of the materials to be preserved; at the four angles and elsewhere lay packages of powdered charcoal; then make another bed of the lime, followed by another layer of the fruit. When the box is full put on the lid, and close it air-tight. Thus preserved, the fruits will last a whole year.—*Cosmos.*

A new process for preserving uncooked meat, recently brought out in Europe, is to extract the atmospheric air by means of a vacuum, and then to admit nitrogen or azote. This permeates the substance of the flesh, and prevents the putrefactive changes which would otherwise ensue.

Pagliari Process for Preserving Meat. — A new process for preserving meat, proposed by M. Pagliari, has been reported to the Academy of Sciences by M. Pasteur. It consists in enclosing the meat in a layer of benzoin and alum, a mixture at once anti-hygrometric and antiseptic. The meat thus enclosed and abandoned to the air loses the greater part of the liquids which, by their tendency to decompose, contribute most actively to putrefaction. In the office of the Academy were deposited a leg of mutton and several other pieces of meat, which had been sent from Italy. The mutton had lost much of its freshness and gave out a little odor; but a fine piece of beef did not give the least sign of alteration and seemed to preserve its original freshness.

Morgan's Plan of Preserving Meat.—The following plan of preserving meat has also been devised by Prof. Morgan, Professor of Anatomy in the Royal College of Surgeons, Ireland, and by him is explained in a recent number of the (Dublin) Agricultural Review. In this paper, after arguing that salted meats cause scurvy and other diseases, in consequence of the phosphoric acid and other substances being removed by solution in the brine, he says:—

"I shall first detail the *modus operandi* of my process. The animal is killed in the usual manner by a blow on the head, causing instantaneous death. It is then turned on the back, the chest opened, the bag of pericardium, containing the heart, opened. The right side of the heart, into which all the venous or returning blood enters, is seen distended; the ear or right auricular tip, as most convenient, is opened, or its tip cut off, or an incision made into the right ventricle; another also directly into the left. The animal is turned on the side to let the blood run out. A pipe, furnished with a stop-cock and coupling at the outer end, is now introduced into the incision made in the left ventricle, and makes its way at once into the aorta. The fingers holding a piece of stout cord, are now passed round the aorta, close to the heart (including at the same time the pulmonary artery) and the cord is tied strongly over both, so that the pipe is fixed in the aorta firmly. To the outer end a coupling, connected with an India-rubber or other tube, ¾ of an inch in diameter, 18 to 20 feet long, joins this to a vessel or tank elevated to the hight of the length of the tube; brine of ordinary strength, with a little saltpetre dissolved in it, is let on; it directly (under 15 seconds in most cases) rushes out at the incision made either in the right auricle or ventricle before mentioned. About five gallons will suffice. This clears the smaller vessels for the next stage, which is the essential one. The brine so used can be recovered if desired, by adding a little old brine and heating. The materials to be ultimately used are now put into the tank, taking care that they are strained, and a stout clip or clamp is put on the incision in the right side of the heart. The fluid is then turned on, and directly makes its way to the right side, as before; but its exit being now prevented, and its admission into the smaller vessels being secured by the first process of clearing these vessels, as mentioned, the fluid, by the pressure and capillary attraction of minute vessels and muscular fiber, percolates through every particle of the animal, and can be seen at the moment diffusing itself in any part, by making incisions in the hide, horn, bone, and flesh, or any other parts. The quantity I use is about one gallon of brine to the cwt., a quarter to half a pound of nitre, two pounds of sugar, a little spice, sauce, etc., to taste; also half an ounce of the monophosphoric acid, which, having the power of coagulating albumen, and forming a compound with it, retains this very desirable element in the flesh, and gives an extra supply of phosphoric acid, which is, of course at present denied the sailor, as above stated. The use of boiling brine in the second stage I also advocate, as it coagulates the albumen, or gives a set (as it is called by cooks) to the meat. It is needless to remark that the entire animal is cured almost instantaneously.

"I would now draw attention to the further treatment of the flesh referring to—1st, the method scientifically used; 2d, the advantages attained; 3d, the mechanical advantages; if we now consider the first part of the process complete.

"The animal is in a few hours cut up into the eight-pound pieces required by the navy, and is ready for casking in the usual way, or in dry salt (all expense of preparing being done away), or for drying by being transferred to a drying-house (as in the specimens for inspection). It is obvious that it loses none of those materials abstracted by the present method of salting, so that the meat is absolutely perfect, as in fresh meat without water, having, as I hold, the additional advantages of salt, which the weight of authority is in favor of rather than against, and of sugar, now issued to the navy, along with the lemon juice; the use of sugar Liebig shows plainly is for the formation of lactic acid (which, as mentioned

5*

before, he has found abstracted by the brine), and a most essential compound, not only of muscle juice, but of gastric juice as well as an important respiratory food. I would suggest the use of 'saeur kraut,' or some other vegetable product containing lactic acid, or lactic acid itself. Sugar is in an economic point of view, specially advantageous, as it is about two-thirds the price of meat, or less, while it improves the flavor and keeps soft the flesh, aiding also in the preservation."

ON THE PRESERVATION OF MEAT.

The following is an abstract of a lecture on the above subject recently given before the Society of Arts, London, by Prof. Crace Calvert.

Preserving Meat by Cold. — A low temperature is most favorable to the preservation of flesh and other animal substances, and under that condition it will not enter into putrefaction, the best proof of which is that elephants in a perfect state of preservation have been found in Siberia buried in ice, where they have doubtless existed for many thousands of years.

Preserving Meat and Vegetables by Drying. — A high state of desiccation or dryness also contributes powerfully to the prevention of decay. Thus in Buenos Ayres and Monte Video meat is cut into thin slices, covered with maize flour, dried in the sun, and it is consumed largely, under the name of tasago or charke, by the inhabitants of the interior, and also by the black population in Brazil and the West Indies. Further, dried meat reduced to powder is used by travelers in Tartary and adjacent countries. A remarkable instance of the preservation of animal matter by extreme desiccation is related by Dr. Wefer, who states that in 1787, during a journey in Peru, he found on the borders of the sea many hundreds of corpses slightly buried in the sand, which, though they had evidently remained there for two or three centuries, were perfectly dry and free from putrefaction. I will also mention in this connection the process of M. M. Masson & Gannal, for the preservation of vegetables, which consists in submitting the vegetables for a few minutes to the action of high-pressure steam (70 pounds to the square inch), then drying them by air heated to 100°; when, after compression by hydraulic pressure, they are made into tablets for sale. When required for use it is only necessary to place the tablets for five hours in cold water, when the vegetable substances swell out to their former size and appearance, and are ready for cooking.

By excluding the Air. — As the presence of oxygen or air is an essential condition of putrefaction, the consequence is that many methods have been invented to exclude that agent, or rather the sporules or germs of cryptogamic plants or animals, which are the true ferments or microscopic source of fermentation and putrefaction. Permit me to describe concisely some of the methods proposed; and I believe that one of the best processes for excluding air was that invented by Appert, in 1854. It consists in introducing the meat or other animal substance, with some water, into vessels which are nearly closed; these are then placed in a large boiler with salt (which raises the boiling point of the liquor), and the contents of the vessels are kept boiling for about an hour, so as to exclude all air, and destroy, by the high temperature, all the sporules or germs of putrefaction they may contain, when they are hermetically closed. M. Appert has improved this process in placing the prepared vessels in a closed boiler, by which means he raises the temperature (by pressure) to 234°, effecting thus the same purpose more rapidly and economically. To give you an idea of the extent of this trade, I may state that M. Appert prepared over 500,000 pounds of meat for the French army in the Crimea. I am aware that many modifications have been applied to this process, but I shall only mention that of Mr. G. McAll, who adds to the previous principle of preservation a small quantity of sulphate of soda, well known to be a powerful antiseptic.

The preservation of animal and vegetable substances by the exclusion of air and cryptogamic sporules is also effected by other methods than those above described; for instance, they are embedded in oil, or in glycerine, or in saccharine sirups.

It has also been proposed to protect animal matters by covering their external surfaces with coatings impermeable to air. Two of the most recent are the following: M. Pelletier has proposed to cover the animal matter with a layer of gum, then immerse it in acetate of alumina, and, lastly, in a solution of gelatine, allowing the whole to dry on the surface of the animal matter. The characteristic of this method is the use of acetate of alumina, which is not only a powerful antiseptic, but also forms an insoluble compound with gelatine, thus protecting the animal matter from external injury. M. Pagliari has lately introduced a method which is stated to give very good results. It consists in boiling benzoin resin in a solution of alum, immersing the animal matter in the solution, and driving off the excess of moisture by a current of hot air, which leaves the above antiseptics on the animal matter.

By Smoke and Carbolic Acid.—It is scarcely necessary to mention the old method of using smoke arising from the combustion of various kinds of wood, except to state that in this case it is the creosote and pyroligneous acids which are the preservative agents. The preservation of animal matter by a very similar action is effected by the use of carbolic acid, a product obtained from coal tar. It is much to be regretted that this substance, which is the most powerful antiseptic known, cannot be made available for the preservation of food, but there can be no doubt that, for the preservation of organic substances intended for use in arts and manufactures, no cheaper or more effective material can be found. For example, I have ascertained that one part of carbolic acid added to five thousand parts of a strong solution of glue will keep it perfectly sweet for at least two years, and probably for an indefinite period. Also, if hides or skins are immersed for 24 hours in a solution of one part of carbolic acid to 50 of water, and then dried in the air, they will remain quite sweet. In fact, hides and bones so prepared have been safely imported from Monte Video. From these facts, and many others with which I am acquainted, I firmly believe that this substance is destined within a few years to be largely used as an antiseptic and disinfectant.

By Salt and Heat.—I need hardly speak of the power of chloride of sodium, or common salt, in preserving animal matters, and it is highly probable that the process of Mr. Morgan of Dublin (described in the preceding article, *Ed.*) is likely to be of great service. At

the last London International Exhibition, Messrs. Jones and Tre-
vethick displayed some meat, fowls, and game preserved by the
following process, which received the approbation of the jurors.
Meat is placed in a tin canister, which is then hermetically closed,
with the exception of two small apertures in the lid. It is then
plunged into a vessel containing water, and after the air has been
exhausted through one aperture by means of an air pump, sulphurous acid gas is admitted through the second aperture and the alternate action of exhausting the air and replenishing the sulphurous
acid gas is kept up until the whole of the air has been removed. The
sulphurous acid gas, in its turn, is exhausted, and nitrogen admitted.
The two apertures are then soldered up, and the operation is completed.

IMPROVEMENTS IN BEEF PACKING.

Some important improvements in beef and pork packing have recently been introduced by Messrs. A. E. Kent & Co. of Chicago.
Hitherto the cutting of beef for market into mess, extra mess, prime
mess, India mess, etc., has been done by hand,—by single man power,—
but recently Messrs. Kent & Co. have introduced into their establishment circular saws and steam power. Two large saws have been
erected which are driven by steam, and these saws are made to do the
work of upwards of 20 men with handsaws, and in a much neater and
better manner than formerly. The application of circular saws in cutting beef has been experimented with repeatedly by others, but it has
never met with success until now. The great difficulty to be overcome was the clogging of the saws with the meat, so that no power
could be applied that would make them work smoothly and regularly.
Thanks, however, to Yankee ingenuity, this has been overcome. Besides the main table on which the saws are placed, a false table has
been erected, running on rollers, so constructed that when the saw
passes through the quarter of beef, the divisions of the table gradually
spread, and this keeps the meat from interfering with the progress of
the saw. The invention is very simple, but none the less valuable because of its simplicity. A whole quarter of beef is placed on this false
table, which is pushed against the saw, and, as the sawing proceeds,
the table gradually spreads, so that the only part of the saw which is
touched with the meat is the edge.

To test the labor-saving qualities of this improvement, the product
of ten head of oxen was placed on the table, to be cut into mess beef;
the manager took his watch in his hand, and gave the order to start.
Away went the saws whirring, and quarter after quarter of the beef
disappeared after having been cut into small pieces; and in exactly
six minutes from the time of starting, the whole ten head of oxen were
cut! Now, this was all done with two saws and six men, who fed
them and took off the pieces as they were cut. At this rate, these
two saws and six men could cut up 1,000 head in ten hours. This
shows the capacity of the improvement when fully tested. But with
ordinary running, the two saws and six men can more easily cut 500
beeves per day, than could 15 men 200 per day by the old handsaw
process.

Here then is a saving of more than one-half the labor, and about
two-thirds of the time usually employed, and also a great improve-

meat in the manner of cutting. When offering mess for sale the inspectors are particular in seeing that the pieces are cut square and smooth. If they are not, they are rejected and branded inferior. This damages the sale, and the owner incurs a loss thereby. By the application of these saws, every piece is cut alike,—there are no haggled pieces, no ragged edges,—every piece is cut smooth, and clean, and square. In this respect alone, not to speak of the labor saved, the invention is a highly valuable one. — *Scientific American.*

UTILIZATION OF BRINE.

At a recent meeting of the Glasgow Philosophical Society, Mr. A. Whitelaw read a paper giving an account of a process discovered by him for utilizing the brine of salted meat by means of the process of dialysis. When fresh meat, he said, had been sprinkled with salt for a few days, it was found swimming in brine. Fresh meat contained more than ¾ of its weight of water, which was retained in it as in a sponge. But flesh had not the power to retain brine to that extent, and in similar circumstances it absorbed only about half as much saturated brine as of water, so that, under the action of salt, flesh allowed a portion of its water to flow out. This expelled water, as might naturally be expected, was saturated with the soluble nutritive ingredients of the flesh; it was, in fact, juice of flesh,—soup, with all its valuable and restorative properties. In the large curing establishments of this city very considerable quantities of this brine were produced and thrown away as useless. This was the material to which Mr. Whitelaw has applied the process of dialysis, and he thought with success, for the removal of the salts of the brine, and for the production, at a cheap rate, of pure fresh extract of meat. His process he stated as follows: The brine, after being filtered to free it from any particles of flesh or other mechanical impurities it might contain, was then subjected to the operation of dialysis. The vessels or bags in which he conducted the operation might be made of various materials and of many shapes; but whatever might be their material or shape, he called them "dialysers." Such an apparatus as the following would be found to answer the purpose: A square vat made of a frame-work of iron filled up with sheets of skin or parchment paper in such a way as to be water-tight, and strengthened, if necessary, by stays or straps of metal. The sides, ends, and bottom being composed of this soft dialysing material, exposed a great surface to the action of the water contained in an outer vat, in which the dialyser was placed. He found a series of ox-bladders fitted with stop-cocks, or gutta-percha mouth-tubes, and plugs, and hung on rods stretching across and into vats of water, a very cheap and effective arrangement. He could also employ skins of animals either as open bags or closed, and fitted with stop-cocks or bags of double cloth, with a layer of soft gelatine interspersed between them. Other arrangements would readily suggest themselves, and might be adopted according to circumstances. But supposing the bladder arrangement was taken, which he thought would be found practically the best, being cheap, easily managed, and exposing a great surface to the dialytic action. The bladders were filled with the filtered brine by means of fillers, and hung in rows on poles across, and suspended into vats of water. The water in those vats was renewed once a day, or oftener if required, and he found that actually at the end of the third or fourth day, according to the size of the bladders employed, almost all the common salt and nitre of the brine had been removed, and that the liquid contained in the bladders was pure juice of flesh in a fresh and wholesome condition. The juice, as obtained from the "dialysers," might now be employed in making rich soups without any further preparation, or it might be concentrated by evaporation to the state of solid extract of meat. Mr. Whitelaw, at this stage, requested a friend present to heat a portion of the juice of flesh so as to produce a soup, and he asked the members to taste it and experience the result.   He also had prepared more carefully a soup from the brine, to which he directed attention. (Both were found to be very palatable.)   The brine used, he continued, was from one of the most respectable curing-houses in Glasgow, and was perfectly pure and wholesome.   The liquid from the dialysers might be treated in several ways.   It might be evaporated in an enamelled vessel to a more or less concentrated state, or to dryness, and in these various conditions packed in tins or jars for sale.   It might be concentrated at a temperature of 120°, by means of a vacuum pan or form.   Again, the more or less concentrated liquid might be used along with flour used in the manufacture of meat biscuits.   The products he had named were all highly nutritive, portable, and admirably adapted for the use of hospitals, for an army in the field, and for ships' stores.   The dialysis of brine might be conducted in salt water, so as to remove the greater portion of its salt, and the process completed in a small quantity of fresh rain, or other water.   In this way ships at sea might economize their brine, and so restore to the meat in a great measure the nutritive power that it had lost in the process of salting.   Thus, then, Mr. Whitelaw said, he obtained an extract of flesh at a cheap rate, from a hitherto waste material.   Two gallons of brine yielded one pound of solid extract, containing the coagulated albumen and coloring matter.   For the production of the same directly from meat something like 20 pounds of lean beef would be required.   The quantity of brine annually wasted was very great.   He believed he was considerably under the truth when he said that in Glasgow alone 60,000 gallons were thrown away yearly.   If they estimated one gallon as equal to seven pounds of meat in soup-producing power, then this was equal to a yearly waste of 187 tons of meat without bone.   Estimating the meat as worth sixpence per pound, this amounted to a loss of £10,472.   In this way the waste over the country must, he said, be very great.

As an appendix to this notice Mr. Whitelaw also detailed a method, applicable to ships at sea, by which the quality of the meat supplied to the men may be much improved and their food varied.

The salt meat is placed in a dialytic bag made of untanned skin, or other suitable material, and the bag filled nearly, but not quite, full of brine from the beef barrel.   The dialyser is then placed in sea water, and the process allowed to go on for several days, till the meat and brine are sufficiently fresh for use, or till the brine in the dialytic bag is within one or two degrees of Twadde's hydrometer of the same strength of sea water.   In this way, as the brine becomes freed from salt, the beef, which, by the action of salt, has been contracted, gives its salt to the brine in the bag, and so the process goes on, the beef expanding like a sponge, and gradually taking up a great part of the natural juice that it had previously lost in the salting process. In this way no loss of juice is sustained by steeping, and the brine left in the bags, after a nightly dialysis in fresh water, can be used for soup.

Thoroughly salted beef, without bone, takes up nearly one-third its weight of juice, and this absorption takes place gradually as the strength of the brine in the dialyser becomes reduced.

Meat thus treated — being, in fact, fresh meat — may be cooked in a variety of ways that are obviously not available for salt meat; and so the food of sailors, and consequently their health, may be improved.

INDUSTRY OF MANURES.

Mr. A. W. Hoffman, the well-known English Chemist, as a Juror of the great London Exhibition of 1862, has recently published a report under the above title, from which we make the following extracts.

After alluding to the great impulse given to the cause of sanitary reform in Great Britain by the sudden outburst of the cholera in that country, in 1836, he calls attention to the controversy which took place among the various authorities respecting the proper size and form of drains to be used in connection with dwelling-houses.

Small circular stoneware tubes were recommended by one party; large brick flat-bottomed sewers by the other. The tubular system happily proved to be the cheapest as well as the best; and its advocates, after a ten years' struggle, finally carried the day. Whole towns are now drained through 12-inch pipes, which would formerly have been deemed of scant dimension for the drainage of a single mansion.

The application of the manurial streams from urban drains to irrigate farm lands was also warmly advocated by the sanitary reformers, but as warmly declared impracticable by several leading engineers, whose views upon that part of the question prevailed.

The second invasion of Asiatic cholera, in 1849, gave a new impulse to the abolition of cesspools; and the value of tubular drains, of small size and rapid scour, for their replacement, had by that time obtained very general recognition. But the leading engineers of England, while admitting, theoretically, the value of sewage to fertilize land, still denied the soundness and economy of the mechanical arrangements proposed by the sanitary reformers for its distribution. On an engineering question, public opinion (not unnaturally) sided at the outset with the engineers. The new system has had, therefore, to encounter a professional opposition, all the more formidable for being thoroughly conscientious. Probably that opposition, with the controversy it has engendered, and, above all, the *experiments* to which it has given rise, constitutes a wholesome ordeal to test the soundness of the new plan, and to bring about the correction of such weak points as it may present. But, in the meantime, the application of town sewage to farm lands on an extensive national scale, has stood, and still stands, adjourned.

Hence the present condition, obviously transitional, of the great manufacturing and commercial towns of England; hence the insufferable pollution of her streams and rivers; hence that prodigious squandering of the elements of human blood, for which she is so bitterly reproached by Liebig.

But steam-power, which has imposed on the British laborer a struggle for existence, by reason of free trade competition, brings him also the means of issuing victorious from the encounter. Why may not the steam-urged plowshare pass to and fro through the field, as the steam-driven shuttle passes through the fabric in the loom?

If pure water can be pumped by steam-power at an infinitesimal cost *into* a town for its supply, why may not the very same water, enriched with the *ejecta* of the population, and so converted into a powerful manure, be also pumped *out* of the town by steam-power, and applied to maintain the fertility of the land? In a word, why may not husbandry rise, in its turn, from the rank of a *handicraft* to that of a *manufacture;* the farm be organized and worked like a factory; and food, like every other commodity, be at length produced by *steam-power*?

These questions are now in every mouth; and the agricultural revolution they imply appears to be, at this moment, in course of accomplishment by the English people.

Already, on many an English farm, the characteristic tall factory-chimney is seen rising among the trees; the steam-engine is heard panting below; and the rapid thrashing-wheel, with its noisy revolutions, supersedes the laborer's tardy flail. Already, at somewhat fewer points, the farm-locomotive stands smoking in the field, winding to and fro, round anchored windlass, the slender rope of steel which draws the rapid plowshare through the soil; thus furrowed twice as deep, and thrice as fast, as formerly by man and horse; and thus economically enriched with proportionately increased supplies of atmospheric plant-food.

And lastly, already, at still rarer intervals, the subterranean pipes for sewage-irrigation ramify beneath the fields, precisely as the pipes for water distribution ramify beneath the streets of the adjacent town; the propelling power being, in both cases, that of steam.

These innovations are, doubtless, still experimental; and, like all innovations, they are vaunted by some with premature zeal as perfect, while others, with pardonable scepticism, decry them as utterly impracticable. Truth for the present seems to lie between these extremes. The steam plow, though answering well in large and level fields with favorable soils, still requires adaptation to less easy conditions of tillage. The tubular irrigating system is still liable to the sudden influx of storm-waters, overburdening, and often overmastering the steam-pumps so as seriously to interefere with the economy of the distributive operation. But inventive research and practical experiment are rapidly proceeding side by side, and every year, not to say every month, sees some fresh truth elicited, some previous "impossibility" achieved.

Utilization of Urban Ejecta as Manure. — The separation of surface-water from sewage is, by a certain number, confidently relied on to solve the problem of sewage utilization, in conformity with Mr. F: O. Ward's formula, — "*the rain-fall to the river, the sewage to the soil.*" Others are of opinion that sewage, even when diluted by admixture with rain-swollen brooks, may be economically pumped on the land.

A third party believed gravitation to be the only economical distributive power for sewage, and open gutters contoured along the undulating ground the only channel suited for its conveyance.

On these mechanical questions the Reporter, as a chemist, has of course no opinion to offer. But, that the reckless squandering of town sewage to the sea, if continued on its present prodigious scale, *must*, in a few generations, justify the worst forebodings of Liebig, and that the same steam-power which has induced the evil can alone supply the remedy, the Reporter confidently believes.

And here, perhaps, is the place to interpose a few remarks, in most respectful deprecation of the support which Liebig, in several of his works, and more especially in his latest publication, affords to the cesspool system of urban defecation. He devotes an entire chapter (the seventh) to a description of the movable cesspools, or casks upon wheels, employed in the soldiers' barracks, in several garrison towns of Baden to receive and carry away the whole of the ejecta, fluid and solid. He states the average cost of these cesspool-carts to be between £9 and £10 apiece; their term of duration about five years; and their maintenance-charge about 15 per cent of their first cost. He adds that the sale of the manure collected and conveyed away in these carts, from several garrisons, numbering in all 8,000 men, brings in an annually increasing sum; the receipts having risen from £285 in 1852 to £680 in 1858, and the tendency of the price being upward still. Upon this system he bestows encomiums, made weighty by his illustrious name and eminent authority. "Sandy wastes," he says, "more particularly in the vicinity of Bastadt and Carlsruhe, have thus been turned into cornfields of great fertility. And he adds that "there might thus be established a perfect circulation of the conditions of life, which would provide 8,000 men with bread year after year, without in the least reducing the productiveness of the fields on which the corn is grown." He further devotes much space in his Appendix to a report upon Japanese husbandry, addressed to the Minister of Agriculture at Berlin, by Dr. H. Maron, and containing a detailed account of the Japanese method of urban defecation, which is also accomplished by a system of movable cesspools, lifted out and carried through the open streets by hand.

The Japanese, Dr. Maron states, use open privies, not constructed as in Germany, in some remote corner of the yard, but forming an essential part of the interior of their dwellings. The aperture is level with the ground, and beneath it is set a bucket or earthen pot for removal, when full, by human hands. The Coolies thus employed are to be met, he tells us, of an evening, marching in long strings along all the roads leading out of the Japanese towns, each Coolie bearing two buckets or earthen pots of night-soil for conveyance to the neighboring farm. Caravans of pack-horses, similarly laden, are sent, he states, 200 or 300 miles into the interior; and canal-boats leave each town daily as regularly as the mail, each loaded by Coolies with high-piled buckets of the precious stuff, the effluvia of which, it is admitted, render the task of conducting these barges "a species of martyrdom."

It is precisely from this degrading and loathsome kind of drudgery that England is now resolutely bent on emancipating mankind; while yet restoring to the land quite as faithfully as the Japanese, the fer-

6

tilizing residua of human food. It is precisely against what may be
termed "the martyrdom of stench," and the still fiercer martyrdoms of
blood-pollution and loathsome pestilence which stench engenders,
that the English Sanitary Reformers protest and struggle with all their
force. The organization of the so-called "continuous tubular circulating system," by which, with the aid of steam-power, the healthy and
ceaseless interchange of pure water and manurial liquor between town
and country is now sought to be achieved, seems destined to constitute the mechanical complement of the great chemico-physiological
truths promulgated by Liebig. It is not, however, pretended by the
warmest advocates of this system, that it can be accomplished by a
single generation. It is admitted, on the contrary, that the complete
tubularization of the farms of Europe must be a task as gradual as the
complete drain and water-pipeage of her towns, or as the universal extension of her railway and electric communications. But as the magnitude of such a project may be, for many minds the very pivot on
which their judgment of it, favorable or adverse, may turn, the *Reporter*
quotes here, from a speech of Mr. F. O. Ward (in 1855), some remarks bearing on this point.

"It is argued," said the speaker, after adverting to the cost of the
requisite pipeage. — "it is argued from this vast expenditure and
widely extended range of distribution that the plan is impracticable.
But I think this resembles the arguments urged against gas-lighting at
the outset. 'What!' it was said in the old days of oil-lamps, to
the daring innovators who proposed gas-lighting, 'do you seriously
ask us to tear up all the streets of our towns, and lay down thousands
of miles of subterranean arteries, to circulate a subtle vapor through
every street and into every house, to do, at a cost of millions upon
millions, what our lamps and candles already do sufficiently well?'
Such was the language used; and the proposal of gas-lighting was
regarded at the outset, by the majority of mankind, as the wildest
and most visionary hallucination. But when Murdoch's factory had
been illuminated with gas, the whole problem was virtually solved;
and when the first line of gas-lights burned along Pall Mall, the illumination of all the towns of Europe became merely a question of
time. Just so, when the first farm was successfully laid down with
irrigating tubes for the distribution of liquid manure, there ceased to
be any argument about the cost and quantity of pipeage for this purpose. Nor should we be deterred from grappling with the sewage
problem by contemplating the vast magnitude of the results which it
it will lead in the course of time,—of generations perhaps,—when the
whole subsoil of Europe will probably be piped for the distribution of
liquid manure, just as all Flanders is already honeycombed with tanks
for its storage.

CONSUMPTION OF WATER.

A man is generally supposed to require about one-half gallon of
water per day for drinking, cooking, &c.; and about four gallons
more for washing, bathing, and other purposes; a family of five heads
will require about nine gallons per day. In Paris, the consumption
of this liquid is officially stated to be $4\frac{1}{2}$ gallons for every man per
day; $16\frac{1}{2}$ for every horse; nine for a two-wheeled carriage; and $16\frac{1}{2}$

for a four wheeled, per day; 92 gallons for every square yard of garden, per annum; 66 gallons for a bath, per day; and one-fifth gallon for every square yard of public road, per day. The consumption in Madrid, according to the report of the directors of the Canal de Isabella, 2d Company, is 5¾ gallons for every man per diem; 21½ for every horse; 14½ for every two-wheeled carriage; 21½ for every four-wheeled carriage, per diem; 12 gallons for every square yard of garden. The following is the consumption in gallons of water per day, and individual, in the chief towns of Europe and America. Rome, 243; New York, 125; Marseilles, 103½; Besançon, 54; Dijon, 41; Bordeaux, 37½; Hamburg, 28; Genoa, 26½; Madrid, 26; Glasgow, 25; London, 24; Lyons, 19; Manchester, 18; Brussels, 17½; Monaco, 17; Toulouse, 16½; Geneva, 16½; Narbonne, 16; Philadelphia, 15½; Paris, 15; Grenoble, 14½; Montpellier, 13; Nantes, 13; Clermont, 12; Edinburgh, 11; Havre, 10; Angouleme, 9; Liverpool, 6; Metz, 5½; St. Etienne, 5½; Altona, 5½; Constantinople, 4½; Rio de Janeiro, 2. This statement only comprises the quantity of water supplied by aqueducts; those yielded by wells and other means, are not easy to ascertain. — *London Artisan.*

ON THE MANUFACTURE OF MAPLE SUGAR IN THE NORTHERN UNITED STATES.

The following is a report of a paper recently read before the Polytechnic Association of New York, by Mr. S. D. Tillman:—

The amount of maple sugar made in the United States in the year 1860 was, in round numbers, 39,000,000 pounds. The product of 1864, stimulated by the high price of cane sugar, was probably far in excess of that of 1860, or of any former year. A comparative estimate of the quantity of sap gathered, and sugar manufactured, may be made from the statement lately sent to me by a very intelligent member of the Shaker Community, at Canterbury, N. H. This Society have three maple groves; in one, 1,150 trees were tapped on the 1st of March last, a few hundred of the holes were reamed out on the 1st of April, and on the 16th of April the spiles were all withdrawn. The whole quantity of sap gathered from these trees was 618 barrels. The other two groves contain about 600 tapped trees each, making the whole number 2,350. The amount of sugar made from 618 barrels, or 19,776 gallons of sap, is 4,000 pounds; about one pound for five gallons of molasses is made generally from the sap of the latest run, which is so changed in its character that it will not properly granulate. In one camp the sap is boiled in a series of cast-iron pans, all connected at the bottom by a pipe. Thus the sweeter part of the sap runs out at the bottom, as fast as the fresh sap is allowed to run in. The process is completed in another pan. In one camp the cast-iron pans have been taken out and copper pans substituted; four of them are eight feet long and two feet wide, and six or eight inches deep. The sirup pan into which the sweeter liquid from the other pans flows, is four feet long, two feet wide and eight inches deep. These pans are above and at the side of each other, so that the sap from the bottom of the first pan runs into the top of the second, and so on through the series, the whole being governed by faucets. In this series about two barrels of sap can be boiled down per hour.

At my suggestion, the correspondent, Mr. Blinn, tested the strength of the sap drawn at various hights of the tree, the highest being taken at 15 feet, and the result proved that the sap increases in sweetness, slightly, with increase of hight.   The sweetest sap tested was 3° by the Baumé hydrometer. - The position of the tree was found to affect the strength of the sap ; in trees near watercourses the saccharine quality was extremely diluted.   Sap from the root of a tree stood at 4° Baumé.   The first flow of sap being the best, it occurred to me that it might be increased by being allowed to pass into vacuum.   I requested that a small India-rubber bag, from which the air had been driven, should be attached to a spile, or a vessel from which the air had been exhausted by means of an air-pump.   The still more simple plan was proposed of placing a little water in a tin can, and after heating it until the steam had driven out the air, closing it, and attaching it by an air-tight connection with the spile.   The first and last plans were tried, and with complete success.   With the steam can, in which the steam was condensed when the can was withdrawn from the flame, the quantity caught in twelve minutes was four fluid ounces ; the quantity which ran from the same spile in the usual way in the same time was 1¾ ounces, — the increase of flow being about 114 per cent.   Subsequent trials gave always over 100 per cent increase.   The Community at Canterbury have made some sirup from the sap of several varieties of the birch ; also from that of the oil-nut or butternut tree, but they have not succeeded in granulating it.

The flow of the sap in the maple is influenced by the weather to a great degree.   The most abundant flow is just after there has been a white frost at night.   A humid state of the atmosphere is considered preferable to a clear and cloudless day.   At Canterbury, a northwest wind is considered the most propitious ; a southeast next best ; east, medium.   The winds from all other points of the compass are less favorable, while a breeze from the south destroys all hope.   An occasional rain during the sugar season is beneficial ; if the fall of water is very abundant, the flow of sap is greatly increased immediately after, but its sweetness is much diminished.

CARBONIZATION OF ILLUMINATING GAS.

The London *Artisan* says: "The advantages resulting to gas consumers from the carburization of the gas supplied by the companies has now become generally recognized, and the apparatus for effecting the thorough mixture of the benzole or naphtha vapor with the gas has now been so simplified, that whatever objections may formerly have existed have been entirely removed, so that it may be hoped that Dr. Knapp's observation, as to the discovery being of benefit to individuals only, will no longer apply.   Referring to naphthalized gas (as it may here be mentioned that the carburization is always effected with mineral naphtha, benzole, or some other material not widely different from them), Dr. Knapp, in his well-known *Technology*, observed that 'the illuminating power of gas is very much increased by the presence of volatile hydrocarbons, and many years ago Mr. Lowe introduced, or rather proposed, a plan for saturating inferior qualities, or ordinary coal gas, with naphtha, or the spirit distilled from coal-tar, and thus augmenting its illuminating power nearly one-half.   The remarkable increase of light, however, produced by naphthalized gas frightened the gas companies, who foresaw nothing but ruin in the diminished quantity of gas which would necessarily be consumed for the production of an equal amount of light. Cold water was consequently thrown upon the project, and the invention has only been of benefit to individuals, and not to the public at large, which might have been the case had it been introduced upon a large scale.' Since this opinion was expressed other inventors have been more successful than Mr. Lowe, and there is no reason why the benefits of a rich, pure, and economical light should not be generally diffused. The *Artisan* then speaks of an invention known as Woodward's gas carbonizer, as giving all the results that could be desired. In this apparatus the gas is made to pass over the surface of benzole or mineral naphtha, receiving its vapor and obtaining a vastly increased illuminating power. It is claimed that in passing over the surface of the fluid the gas comes into contact only with the amount necessary for its purification, so that the vitality of the spirit is retained until it is all consumed. Dr. Muspratt has reported very favorably upon the invention, and photometric experiments have proved that, taking gas at 4s. 6d. per 1,000 cubic feet, there is a saving of more than one-third, the same amount of light being obtained for 2s. 11d."

PRACTICAL ICE-MAKING MACHINE.

At the recent meeting of the British Association, Mr. A. C. Kirk gave the following description of a machine invented by him for the artificial production of ice. The machine in question was constructed for Messrs. Young & Co., and superseded another machine used for cooling parafine oil. This latter, Mr. K. said, proving too small for the increasing size of the work, and the use of a material so volatile, inflammable, expensive, and in all respects so dangerous as ether, being a serious drawback, I was requested, in the beginning of 1862, to try if some efficient substitute could not be found. Atmospheric air being the substitute which at once suggested itself to me as not only safe but inexpensive, I commenced a series of experiments, which at last resulted in a small model, by which I was able to freeze mercury. A large machine was immediately proceeded with, which worked so satisfactorily that the use of the ether machine was discontinued, and this year at the works a more powerful one has been erected, capable, if applied to such a purpose, of making three tuns of ice in twenty-four hours. I shall now proceed to describe the nature of this machine, which, it will be seen, is allied to the air-engine in the same manner as the ether machine is to the steam-engine. If we enclose a quantity of air in a strong vessel, into the top of which we fix a common air-syringe, and force the piston downwards by hand, we shall compress the enclosed air, which, by the power so spent, will be heated; and if we now cool the whole apparatus down to its original temperature, and allow the air to force the piston gradually back, the air by the effort will be cooled; but inasmuch as the cooled air will not occupy the same space as the air originally did, the piston will not return to the point at which it was when we commenced, and thus less power will be given out during the expansion of the air than was spent in its compression. It is not necessary that the air be at the atmospheric pressure: if air of greater density be employed, the cool-

6*

ing power of the machine will be increased. We have thus got an elementary cooling machine, and as before, power is spent in working it. To render this a practicable machine, the first thing necessary is to perform the compressing or heating operation, and the expansion or cooling operation in separate compartments; the one surrounded by water to abstract the heat generated, and the other surrounded by the substance to be cooled, or from which heat is to be taken. The one compartment being thus very cold and the other comparatively warm, the next thing is to provide means by which the air can be continually transferred from one to the other, without carrying heat from the hot compartment to the cold. Thus, if the temperature of the hot compartment be 70° and that of the cold zero, the air must enter the cold compartment preparatory to expansion at a temperature as nearly zero as possible, and in returning to the hot compartment must enter it preparatory to compression, at a temperature as nearly 70° as possible. That beautiful invention of Stirling, the regenerator, or respirator, as it is sometimes called, composed ordinarily of a large quantity of wire gauze, through which the air passes, enables us to accomplish this very perfectly. When the machine is fairly agoing, the layers of gauze next the cool compartment become as cold as the compartment itself, and those next the hot compartment as hot, while the layers between those shade off through the intermediate grades of temperature. Thus the air in passing from the hot to the cold compartment, warms the gauze and is itself cooled, and the cold air in returning is gradually warmed, cooling the gauze in its course; and although the air is continually being passed backwards and forwards from the hot compartment to the cold, and *vice versa*, no heat is conveyed by it from the hot end to warm the cold and interfere with the cooling power of the air during expansion. By the help of the diagrams, Mr. Kirk then explained the arrangements by which this was carried out. He concluded by saying that the advantages attending the use of this machine were, that no expensive or dangerous fluid was employed, involving risk of fire or suffocation to the attendants; that the cooling power might be reduced to any extent when required, the consumption of motive power being similarly reduced; and that cupped leather packings might be employed, which gave so little trouble that in the first machine one worked for four months without being touched. He further stated that the cost of the machine, without boilers, was £700.

Mr. Young said he was able to say that the machine was all that was ever expected. Former machines they had used always kept them in a state of bodily terror, and once they had a slight fire; but by using this new machine there was no longer any cause for fear. The machine was an extraordinary success. It went on day and night, without intermission and without trouble. With one tun of coal, costing 4s., they could produce one tun of ice. He was glad to be able to give his testimony to the perfect working of the machine. (Applause.) All manufacturers must hail such a chemical invention.

HOW TO SETTLE SHIFTING SANDS.

The Landes in the Gulf of Gascony are composed of loose drifting sand, which in 1789 covered 300 square miles. M. Bremontier, of the then Administration of Forests in France, set himself to fix this mercurial surface, and the means he used were planting it with the pinaster. In a report of his proceedings, which he published, he compared this sandy tract to a billowy sea, — it offered nothing to the eye but a monotonous repetition of white wavy billocks perfectly destitute of vegetation. When violent storms of wind occurred, the surface of these downs was entirely changed; what were hills had become valleys, and valleys hills. The sand on these occasions was often blown into the interior of the country, actually covering cultivated fields, villages, and even entire forests. This was done so gradually, in a shower of particles as fine as the sand used for hour-glasses, that nothing was destroyed. The sand gradually rose among the crops, as if they were inundated with water, and the herbage and the tops of trees appeared quite green and healthy, even to the moment of their being submerged. On this moving and shifting sea, M. Bremontier sowed seeds of the common broom, mixed with those of the pinaster; commencing on the side next the sea, or on that from which the wind generally prevailed, and sowing in narrow zones, in a direction at right angles to that of the wind. The first zone was protected by a line of hurdles, and after it was established it protected the second, as the second did the third, and so on. To prevent the seed being blown away before it had germinated and become firmly rooted, he protected it by various ingenious modes, such as hurdles and thatching, and he had at last the gratification, after conquering many difficulties, of seeing his first zones firmly established. The rest was then comparatively easy; and by degrees the tree covered the whole of these sandy downs, not only providing the interior country with a barrier against the incursion of the sands, but turning the downs themselves from a desolate waste into a source of productive industry. Although the timber is of little value, the manufacture of tar, turpentine, and other resinous products furnishes sufficient occupation for the inhabitants who are thinly scattered over large spaces. Among the efforts of man to control the elements and the powers of nature, the conquest of the Landes from the desolation of the desert is entitled to a place beside the recovery of Holland from the empire of the sea.

FLOW OF WATER THROUGH IRREGULAR TUBES.

At a recent meeting of the N. Y. Polytechnic Association, Mr. J. B. Root explained an experiment made by him in relation to the flow of water through irregular tubes. He constructed a tube of tin 30 inches long, and 2¼ inches in diameter. Within this tube were soldered 11 diaphragms or discs, at regular distances from each other. In each circular disc, there was a hole ⅜ of an inch in diameter, the center of which was the center of the disc. Half-way from each disc the tube was perforated on the upper side by a very small hole. One end of this tube was inserted into a bulkhead about nine feet below the surface of the water. The object of this apparatus was to measure the retardation of the water, in passing through the discs, by means of the height of the jets sent through the small holes on the top of the tube. The jet from the first hole was about two feet high; the next jet was lower, and so on to the last hole, from which the water barely oozed out. The rate in decrease in height was directly as the number of discs inserted — that is, the water after passing ten discs, gave a jet only one-ninth as high as after passing one.

The Chairman remarked that the principle of retardation, here illustrated, had been applied to the pistons of pumps, by cutting around the piston a series of grooves close to each other, thus forming what is called a water packing. It was said, however, not to work as well as was at first expected. Not long since a case occurred at the Jersey City Water Works relating to the subject now under discussion. It became necessary to lay down, under the Hackensack River, for the distance of 1,000 feet, another main pipe of 36 inches internal diameter. Mayor Cleveland of Jersey City, then a Water Commissioner, made some important experiments to prove that water was greatly retarded wherever turned from a right line, even if the pipe be enlarged on the curves.

Mr. Dixon said the proposition was to lay under the river a pipe which would adjust itself to the bottom by means of from 14 to 18 movable joints. The position of the pipes, on either side of a joint, may be illustrated by supposing two common clay smoking pipes to be laid down in opposite directions, so that the mouths of their bowls would come together; these being fastened by a collar, they would be free to move up or down, and thus such pipes would adjust themselves to the bed of the river. Mr. Cleveland objected to this plan on the ground that the pipes so laid would not deliver the quantity required, because the curves would impede the flow of the water. In order to remedy this, the contractor proposed to enlarge the pipe at the curves, from 36 to 46 inches in diameter, the pipe being brought down to its original size between each curve. This proposition was approved by several prominent engineers. Mr. Cleveland objected to these enlargements; he believed they would increase rather than diminish the evil complained of. In order to demonstrate his statement, he made the following experiments: First, he constructed a straight pipe of lead, 36 inches long and one and a half inches internal diameter; second, he made another pipe extending the same distance, and containing two curves, so as to carry the water in a direction perpendicular to its first course, then again in first course, thus turning two right angles. The diameter of the ends of the pipe was 1½ inches, and that of the curved part was 1 11-12 inches. Parallel lines drawn through the center of the two ends were just 2½ inches apart. Third, he constructed another pipe containing four curves, the two curves, additional to those in the second pipe, were to bring the water back, so that its entrance and discharge were in the same right line. The curves in the third pipe, were of the same diameter with those in the second pipe. The pipe between each two curves, as well as at each end, was 1½ inches in diameter. These pipes were constructed with the greatest care; the curves were fitted in halves over wooden forms, and soldered on the outside, the inside being made so smooth as to leave no crease at the joints. A tank of water was prepared 5 feet 2⅝ inches in diameter at the top, and two feet deep. A hole was made on the side at the bottom, into which each of the pipes was in turn fitted. The object being to discharge precisely the same quantity of water through each pipe, two marks were made on the inside of the tank, the upper one being the height of the water at the commencement of the discharge, and the lower one the height at the close. The pipe on being inserted was closed at the end, by clay placed on by hand, which could be instantly removed on the signal being given ; and instantly restored when the surface of the water in the tank had reached the lower mark. The experiments of discharging through the several tubes were made with great care, and afterward repeated, to verify their accuracy, and the following is the result : —

The same quantity of water passed

Through the straight pipe in 218 seconds.

Through the one joint pipe in 314 seconds.

Through the two joint pipe in 371 seconds.

From this it appears that the increased time required for the flow through the second pipe was over 40 per cent, and for the third pipe over 70 per cent. These experiments decided the question and the proposed plan was abandoned.

A NEW APPLICATION OF THE SLAKING OF QUICKLIME.

A novel application of the slaking of quicklime has been proposed by Dr. John Davy, in the *Edinburgh New Philosophical Journal*. It is well known that as soon as water is added to and absorbed by well-burnt lime fresh from the kiln, an immediate union takes place, the mass becoming broken up and falling into powder, with the production of much heat and steam. This does not take place when the lime has been exposed to the action of the air for two or three days, during which the lime generally absorbs a little water. With respect to these phenomena, Dr. Davy records the result of several experiments which showed the explosive power of the lime when placed in holes or receivers and treated with water, or with solutions of common salt, carbonate of ammonia, &c. We have no space for the details which led Dr. Davy to suggest the application of the explosive force of lime to the blasting of rocks and similar purposes, but give an account of two of his experiments. A boring was made in a block of sandstone about fifteen inches deep and two inches in diameter; this was filled with small pieces of quicklime, and the hole was closed by a plug of wood. No rending ensued, although the hydrate was formed. The elastic expansive force was not superior to the resistance, and the steam was condensed. A second experiment was made, substituting for the boring in a rock a strong earthenware jar capable of holding about a quart. It was similarly charged, and tightly corked, the cork bound down firmly with a cord. After about 15 minutes an explosion took place, with a report like a pistol. The jar was broken in several pieces, and some of them were projected many yards from the spot. Now as coal is not nearly so resisting as sandstone, and as its boring is easily effected, Dr. Davy expresses the hope that the experiment may be repeated in a colliery. It is easily made, at a cost not worth mentioning, is attended with no serious danger, and, should it be successful, it may conduce to the saving of many valuable lives.

UTILIZATION OF WASTE PRODUCTS.

At a recent meeting of the New York Polytechnic Association, Prof. Joy, of Columbia College, enumerated the following as among the instances where attention to the utilization of waste material was desirable : —

Waste Vulcanized Rubber. —There seems to be a want of some ready method of devulcanizing old India rubber. Several patents have been issued for this purpose, but the fact that there is no demand for worn-out articles of India rubber, would lead us to conclude that this material is not utilized to any great extent.

Slag from Iron Furnaces. — At Mantsel, Germany, Prof. Joy recently observed the following plan for using the slag of the furnaces. The slag is formed into molds of about a cubic foot each, and distributed to workmen. Each man takes his share of the blocks in an iron wheelbarrow and wheels them home, when they still contain heat enough to cook the meal for the family. After they are cooled these rectangular blocks are an excellent material for building walls.

(At the last meeting of the British Association Dr. Paul stated that he had succeeded in blowing the slag into a state of very fine division by sending steam or air into it just as it flowed from the blast furnace in a liquid state. It was thus blown into a substance resembling wood in appearance. This substance.was taken and ground into dust, mixed with lime, subjected to a powerful pressure, and made into bricks, of which he exhibited some examples. These bricks required no fire. After being pressed they were allowed to dry, and could be used at once, the influence of the atmosphere producing a slow kind of hardening.) — *Editor.*

Zinc wasted in galvanizing Iron. — A large portion of the zinc used for coating iron is evaporated and lost. Plans for preventing this loss are worthy of the attention of inventors. The whole history of zinc is that of a waste product. . It was first found in chimneys where ores of other metals were being smelted and people were thus led to seek for it in its own ores.

Waste from Gas-works. — Constant progress has been made in the utilization of the waste substances produced in the manufacture of illuminating gas. At one time the companies paid persons for carting away the lime used for purifying the gas. The lime absorbs bisulphide of carbon, sulphuretted hydrogen and sulphur, coming from the distillation of the coal, and when exposed for a long time to the atmosphere it absorbs oxygen and becomes the sulphate of lime or plaster. This is now understood by a sufficient number of farmers to make a demand for the waste lime at a moderate price.

Mr. Cleland, the Director of the Liverpool Gas Works, states that he has largely reduced the cost of purifying gas by using oxide of iron, and saving the sulphur and ammonia. The material from the purifiers is heated to about 1,000° Fahrenheit in a close iron retort. A portion of the sulphur combines chemically with the iron, while the balance is distilled over. As soon as the sulphur ceases to come over, the contents of the retort are drawn and moistened, and in this state exposed to the action of the atmosphere. The oxidation is rapid, and the mass glows until frequently wet and stirred. In a few weeks a sulphate of iron is produced, containing 30 to 40 per cent sulphuric acid. The salt is decomposed by passing the vapor of ammonia from the waste waters of the hydraulic mains through it. In this way sulphate of ammonia and an oxide of iron are obtained. The oxide of iron can be used again. The sulphate of ammonia is purified by crystallization. Mr. Cleland says that he has obtained 100 tuns of sulphur in this way.

Preparation of Sal Ammoniac. — About two per cent of ammoniacal gas water goes over with the tarry products and is collected at the end of the hydraulic main in cisterns. This was formerly a waste product; it is now saved, and the greater portion of sal ammoniac of commerce is prepared from it. In London alone 840,000 tuns of coal are consumed every year in the manufacture of gas. This yields about 37,000,000 lbs. of gas water. The water is subjected to distillation in two retorts, the first of which is heated directly by the fire, and the second by the latent heat of the steam from the first. The steam and gas are passed through a worm to be condensed, and flow into a large leaden tank containing muriatic acid. Uncondensable gases pass out of the tank and are conducted through the fire where the sulphuretted hydrogen is consumed, into the chimney. The muriatic acid is saturated to neutrality, and requires very little further treatment for the formation of beautiful white crystals of sal ammoniac. This sal ammoniac is the starting-point in the manufacture of the salts of ammonia, and can now be obtained in great abundance by the above method.

Oil and Fat from Refuse oily Cotton, Waste, &c.—Edward Tonybee digests the refuse material in about half its weight of concentrated sulphuric acid contained in leaden vessels and warmed by steam. They are thus dissolved and the fat separated. After standing the fatty acids collect on the top, and can be removed and further purified by distillation. To the residual solution sufficient finely divided phosphate of lime is added to neutralize the sulphuric acid, and a valuable compost containing phosphates and nitrogenous matter obtained.

There is a great waste in our woolen manufactories of a valuable substance; that is, the oil of the wool. When wool has been thoroughly cleansed, it is found to have lost thirty, forty, or in some cases as high as sixty per cent of its weight, and the most of this is oil,—an excellent oil for some purposes, and especially for soap. There is an establishment in England that takes wool to cleanse for the oil, making no other charge for the work.

The oil can be extracted by means of the bisulphide of carbon, which is a cheap article. It is also used for extracting oil from the rape seed instead of pressing the seed. It is also used for extracting the alkaloids and the essential oils of plants. It has been stated that it leaves no odor.

NEW PLAN FOR UTILIZING SCRAP TIN.

A new method of utilizing Scrap tin plate in the reduction of sulphuretted lead ore, has been devised by Prof. Everett of New York. The theory of the reduction of sulphuretted lead ore by iron is based upon the fact of the great affinity of iron at a high heat for sulphur. The metallic lead is set free by the sulphur leaving the ore and uniting with the iron forming the sulphide of iron. By the use of scrap tin plate the iron process is carried to its highest state of perfection, because the tinned iron plate is made of the very best wrought iron. Furthermore, a saving is made of all the tin upon the scraps, which for many purposes, improves the quality of the lead; but it is easily separated if desired. Another advantage arises from the thinness of these scraps; they present so much surface that part of the iron is oxidized, and makes an excellent flux, thus saving the addition of an artificial flux and reducing the time required for smelting very materially. The waste product used in this process has until now been thrown away.

NEW USE FOR INFUSORIAL DEPOSITS.

"In the lakes of Sweden there are vast layers of iron oxide almost exclusively built up by animalcules. This kind of iron-stone is called lake-ore. In winter the Swedish peasant, who has but little to do in that season, makes holes in the ice of a lake, and with a long pole brings up mud, &c. until he comes upon an iron bank. A kind of sieve is then let down to extract the ore. One man can raise in this manner about one tun per diem. Besides the excellent polishing material furnished by these infusorial deposits, Liebig has recently drawn attention to another application of which they are susceptible. His observations were made upon an infusorial deposit which constitutes the under soil of the commons or plains of Lüneburg, in Germany; and he has shown that these microscopic remains, as well as those taken from several other localities, can be very easily converted into *silicate of potash* or *silicate of soda*, sometimes known as '*soluble glass*.' It was first ascertained by analysis that this infusorial earth contained 87 per cent of pure silica. The following method was then adopted to convert it into silicate of soda: 148 pounds of calcined carbonate of soda are dissolved in five times their weight of boiling water; to this is added a milk of lime, prepared with 84 pounds of quicklime. After boiling the mixture for ten minutes or a quarter of an hour, the alkaline liquid, which now contains caustic soda, is decanted off from the insoluble carbonate of lime, and evaporated in an iron vessel, until it has acquired a specific gravity of 1·15. At this moment 240 pounds of the infusorial earth is added. The latter dissolves rapidly in the alkaline solution, and leaves scarcely any residue. If by any accident a smaller quantity of infusorial earth than that prescribed be taken, the soluble glass obtained is too alkaline and very deliquescent."

SILK NATURALLY DYED.

Some experiments of an interesting character have recently been made in Italy, with a view of causing the silkworm to produce silk ready dyed. On this point we know that when certain coloring matters extracted from the vegetable kingdom are mixed with the food of animals they are absorbed without decomposition and color the bones and tissues of the body. Starting from this fact, Messrs. Barri and Alessandrini, in Italy, sprinkled certain organic coloring matters over the mulberry leaves on which the silkworms were feeding. M. Roulin, in France, employed in the same way the coloring matter known as *chica.* These attempts have met with partial success only, up to the present time. Colored cocoons were however thus produced several times. Some observers assert, however, that the silk was not really secreted in a colored state, but that the coloring matter sprinkled on the leaves merely adhered to the body of the grub and colored the cocoon mechanically during its construction. This appears to be the reason why the colored silk that was obtained in these experiments was neither uniform in tint nor of a good color. Others, however, still persist in a contrary opinion. M. Roulin commenced his experiments by sprinkling *indigo* over the mulberry leaves, and obtained *blue cocoons*; he then experimented with *chica*, a fine red dye extracted from the *Bignonia chica*, which the Indians of Oronoco employ to dye their skin, and obtained cocoons of a red color with a tolerably uniform tint, and of a permanent dye. He still continues these investigations, hoping to obtain silk ready dyed of all kinds of colors.

ARTIFICIAL CULTURE OF OYSTERS.

The plan of M. Coste, of France, for propagating oysters, which under the auspices of the French Government is now in most successful operation, is substantially as follows : M. Coste gets fresh oysters for propagation from the open sea ; he turns to advantage those that are rejected by the trade ; and, lastly, he collects the myriads of embryo oysters which, at each spawning season, issue from the valves of the oyster, and which are now lost to commerce for want of some contrivance to prevent their escape and inevitable destruction. Every oyster produces from one to two million of young ; out of these not more than ten or twelve attach themselves to their parent's shell ; all the rest are dispersed, perish in the mud, or are devoured by fish ! Now if bundles made of the branches of trees, fagots of brushwood, or any similar objects, be let down and secured to the oyster banks by weights, the young oysters will, on issuing from the parent's valves, attach themselves to these fagots, and may, on attaining perfect growth, be taken up with the branches and transported to places where it is desirable to establish new oyster-beds. A model plan for breeding oysters may be seen in the lake of Fusaro, in Italy, where mussels and oysters are *cultivated* with much success,— *where almost the entire quantity of spawn is developed without loss.*

One of the beds of oysters thus prepared by M. Coste, at the mouth of the river Auray, in France, yielded the first year after it was matured, over 20,000,000 of good merchantable oysters.

ON SOME OF THE SOURCES AVAILABLE FOR THE SUPPLY OF POTASH.

Three or four years ago MM. Maumené and Rogelet patented in England a method for obtaining potash from *Suint*, the name given by the French to a compound of potash and some organic acids, which is excreted in the sweat of sheep and found on the wool. This compound is easily soluble in water, and is obtained from the wool by simple washing ; the solution may then be evaporated, and the potash obtained by calcination and lixiviation. *Suint* forms about 15 per cent of the weight of the raw fleece, and yields 33 per cent of potash, so it is easy to see that if all the scourings of all the wool produced was worked up, the supply of alkali from this source alone would be very considerable. MM. Maumené and Rogelet have, in fact, calculated that the washings of the raw fleeces from the 47,000-000 of sheep in France would produce nitrate of potassium enough to charge 1,870,000,000 cartridges, which is no doubt the most useful application of the product they can conceive.

Another small source of potash is beet-root juice. This is of no great interest to English readers, but we may mention that when the liquor remaining after the fermentation and distillation of beet-root molasses is boiled down, incinerated, and the charred mass lixiviated, a considerable amount of potash salts is obtained. The molasses contains from 10 to 12 per cent of its weight of salts, more than half of which are alkaline.

The home sources to which English manufactures have to look for their potassium compounds are sea-weeds and the primitive rocks. The first of these sources has long been worked, and the industry is well understood. Nevertheless, the methods employed for obtaining the salts have been found capable of much improvement, which it has received at the hands of Mr. E. C. Standford and others. Sea-water, we should remark, may always be looked to as a source of potash, but this is of the less importance to us in consequence of our sources of common salt.

The account of M. Balard's process, with the modifications introduced by M. Merle, for separating the saline constituents of sea-water, will be perused with interest by all scientific readers. Sea-water is first concentrated to 28° Baumé (or 1·24 sp. gr.), at which degree four-fifths of the chloride of sodium is deposited. There remain in solution with the other chloride of sodium, sulphate of magnesium, and chlorides of potassium and magnesium. M. Merle now avails himself of M. Carre's refrigerating machine. The mother liquor, a little diluted, is made to pass in a continuous stream through refrigerating vessels constructed on M. Carre's principle, by which the liquor is cooled to —18° C. At this temperature a double decomposition takes place between the sulphate of magnesium and chloride of sodium, sulphate of sodium being deposited, and the chlorides of magnesium, sodium, and potassium passing away in the solution. To separate these chlorides the solution is then boiled down to 36° B., at which nearly the whole of the chloride of sodium is deposited in a fine powder. The hot liquor from this is next run off into shallow coolers, when the whole of the potash is deposited in the form of a double chloride of potassium and magnesium, from which the magnesium salt is removed by washing the mass with half its weight of water. In this way ¾ of the chloride of potassium are obtained in a tolerable state of purity. Our readers will see that no account is here taken of the bromides and iodides, which, indeed, are thrown away with the chloride of magnesium.

The small amount of potassium salt in proportion to the sodium compounds obtained from sea-water will of course limit this industry to those countries in which the latter compounds have a higher relative value than in England. We may look with much more interest to our mineral sources of potassium in the primitive rocks. Many of our readers no doubt have some acquaintance with a process for estimating the alkalies in felspathic rocks, which consists in calcining the mineral with a mixture of fluorspar and carbonate of lime, and washing out the alkalies which have become carbonated in the calcination. The great objection to this as an analytical process is that the calcination must be repeated two or three times in order to be certain of removing the whole of the alkalies, all of which may, however, be removed in a single washing. It is this process which

Mr. F. O. Ward and Captain Wynants have utilized, and so far perfected as to make it available for the production of potash on a manufacturing scale. The felspar is ground to a fine powder, and then mixed with finely-powdered fluorspar. To these chalk and hydrate of lime are added, and the mixture, moistened with water, is made up into balls. These are exposed to a yellowish-red heat for several hours, by which they are converted into a sort of porous frit. On subsequent lixiviation with hot water this frit yields the whole of the alkali previously existing in the felspar. The alkaline lye of course contains some silica and alumina, but these are easily removed by the addition of a little lime, and then the filtered liquor has only to be boiled down in order to obtain a product very much resembling American potashes.

Simple as this process appears, it has only been made practically available after an enormous number of experiments, both on a large and small scale. The best proportions of materials, the best temperature, and the best mode of applying the heat, had each to be determined, and could only be arrived at after great labor and expense. All these points, however, appear to be settled, and we may now look to the industrial application of the process to furnish us with an abundance of potash.—*London Chemical Gazette.*

SUMMARY OF INDUSTRIAL NOVELTIES.

New Plan for Mural Decoration. — M. Balze of Paris has recently brought out a new plan of painting in enamel on a large scale, intended to supersede mosaic, fresco, and other methods of mural decoration. The plan seems to be neither more nor less than the method of the Dutch tile-painters of the sixteenth and seventeenth centuries, by means of which they produced pictures, sometimes of considerable size, upon white tiles. The methods seem identical; thus, white tiles, — such as are used on the continent to surround kitchen fireplaces, and the like, — are placed upon the floor and numbered, according to their positions, so as to admit of rearrangement. Upon the ground thus displayed, the artist, with a full brush, paints his picture, the tiles are rebaked, and the work, where it requires it, retouched. The tiles may then be placed upon a wall, and the work is done. The result is a durable picture, wholly of the artist's own production, on any scale, comparatively inexpensive, unaffected by a foul atmosphere such as that of London, which may be cleaned with a birch-broom, and be as brilliant in color as we need to have it. Although this plan is by no means a novelty in Art, or even in domestic decoration, it suggests what might well be done in situations where great refinement of ornament is not required.

Factitious Blocks of Wood. — A patent has been taken out by G. Colomb, of Aigle, Switzerland, for making ornamental blocks of wood as follows : He takes the shavings of soft pine or other wood, and dyes them different colors, then packs them together so as to form a truss, which is put into a frame and dipped into a solution of warm glue; it is then subjected to severe pressure and formed into a block, after which it is dried with a current of hot air in a warm room. Such blocks of wood may be cut and used for ornamental purposes, as substitutes for high-priced natural woods that are employed for cabinet work.

Improved Loom. — At a recent meeting of the N. Y. Polytechnic Association, Mr. Overton described a new loom in successful operation, in which the ordinary beater was dispensed with. A motion is produced in which the shuttle is carried backward and forward by a circular beater placed between each thread, so that the transverse thread, forming the woof or filling, is pressed up by a spring as fast as the shuttle moves. The objection to the ordinary loom is the concussion made by the beater. These concussions are so great that where many looms are placed in one building they have the effect of a concentrated blow, thus shaking the whole structure. Buildings containing weaving apparatus must therefore be made with unusually strong foundations and heavy walls. The object of the new invention is to remedy the effect of the beater, which presses the filling only after the shuttle has passed beyond the warp, by a beater which operates continuously with the shuttle, thus accomplishing by a series of pressures what was formerly done by a blow.

Weimer's Self-instructing Scale for Pianos. — This consists of a number of blocks, so formed that they may be readily placed against the key-board of a piano : resting on the keys without interfering with the action of the latter. On the blocks are painted lines representing a musical staff, with notes, each of which represents the key directly beneath it, the letter or name of the note being painted directly below the latter, so that the scholar, as he strikes a key, may see at once its name and the position on the staff of the note designating it.

Improved File. — An improved file, recently invented by R. D. Dodge of Iowa, is made up of a number of small steel cutters, — in shape parallelograms, — which are all slipped over a central bar, and there confined by a sliding shank, and a screw-handle. These cutters are simply flat pieces of steel with oblong holes in them, the edges being beveled off so as to form a cutting edge. The object is to produce a file that can be easily sharpened when dull, that will be more durable than an ordinary file, and one that will work more efficiently for special purposes than files of the usual construction.

When the handle is unscrewed, the shank can be slipped off, and the cutters removed and sharpened on an emery wheel or grindstone, thus obviating the necessity of re-cutting, as is done with other files. — *Scientific American.*

Artificial Ivory. — The following method of producing an artificial ivory is published by M. Ghistain of Paris. Take 60 per cent of the powder of marine plants, 15 per cent of glue, and an equal quantity of coal tar; boil till thoroughly mixed; dry in an oven at a temperature of 300° Fahr. till it becomes plastic. The compound will assume the appearance of ivory by heating it in an aqueous solution of caustic potash, and letting it macerate for several hours in diluted sulphuric acid; after which subject it to the action of chlorine or chloride of lime, repeating the operation till it becomes perfectly white.

New Applications of Aluminum. — R. Pinkney, of London — a manufacturer of metallic pens — has applied for a patent for pens made of aluminum and copper alloys, as a substitute for those made of steel and gold. He states that an alloy composed of 95 per cent aluminum is of a fine gold color; and another composed of 7½ per cent of copper is of a beautiful green color. Aluminum bronze is very ductile, and is suitable for undergoing the rolling and hammering operations through which steel and gold pass in the making of pens.

Aluminum Bronze Powders and Leaf.—A patent has also been taken out by J. Erwood, of London, for manufacturing powders of aluminum bronze to take the place of common bronze powders, and Dutch metal leaf, to be applied to paper-hangings, gildings, &c. Aluminum bronze is composed of 90 parts copper and 10 of aluminum, and is of a beautiful yellow color. It is rolled, annealed, and beaten until it becomes as thin as foil or leaf, in which condition it can be used for common gilding. To reduce it to powder the foil is stamped and ground in the same manner that common bronze powders are reduced from tin and brass.

Hermetical Barrels for Petroleum. — It is well known that crude and refined oils, from their great permeability, readily penetrate through all wooden barrels or packages hitherto used, so that their loss from leakage and evaporation has been a large per cent, amounting to millions of dollars annually. To prevent this, metallic barrels, metal-lined barrels, etc., have been substituted, but without fully attaining the desired end. Mr. L. S. Robbins, of New York city, claims that he has discovered that by first coating a barrel with drying linseed oil, which answers to the cuticle of a tree, and then treating the wood of the barrel from the inside with a strong solution of potash,—that each barrel so treated will take up about 18 pounds of water, which from the oil coating on the outside can never evaporate, nor can the oil pass through, thus making it essentially and positively a hermetical package. — *Scientific American.*

New Maritime Sounding Apparatus.—M. Gouezel has invented an apparatus in which the suspension line is dispensed with. It consists of a rod of iron, furnished with nippers at the extremity, which supports a cylindrical weight capable of being detached from the rod; above the weight a float of hollow metal is fixed, which contains a small clock so arranged as to stop by concussion; a bell is also attached, and above the whole a signal. The time of dropping the apparatus is noted; on striking the bottom the clock is stopped, and the float is detached and rises to the surface; the depth is calculated from the time of the descent. The objection to long lines in deep-sea soundings, which are bent by under-currents, seems to be obviated by this invention.

A Preparation for Preserving Leather.—We translate, from the *Gerber Courier*, a receipt for a preparation which is said to insure great durability to leather, and to make it very pliable and soft. It consists of four articles, tallow, soap, rosin, and water. These ingredients are prepared as follows: 21 parts of tallow are melted in a vessel, three parts of rosin added, and the two when melted mixed well together. In another vessel seven parts of good washing soap are dissolved in 70 parts of pure rain water. After it is dissolved and the mass heated to the boiling point we add the part prepared before, let it boil once more gently, and the preparation is ready for use. It is especially adapted to boots, harness leather, and belting. — *Shoe and Leather Reporter.*

7*

A New Adhesive Gum. — M. Stahl recommends a new process for the consolidation of friable fossils and other articles liable to break. Hitherto, in order to give sufficient solidity to such fossils preserved in museums, they used to be dipped into glue. Pieces thus prepared with due care acquire sufficient hardness to allow of their being handled at lectures, and will keep a long time, provided they are not exposed to damp. But in the case of fossils containing salts, glue loses all its power, and in such cases no attempt has been made to consolidate them. Pieces treated with glue do not admit of good plaster casts being taken of them. The glue, swelling under the wet plaster, either splits the model or raises up the pieces of the mould; or, if there is too little glue to effect this, a chemical action takes place by which the surface of the plaster, in contact with the model is decomposed, and the finer details are thus obliterated.

M. Stahl obviates these inconveniences as follows : —

He takes four parts of common rosin, and as many of spermaceti, which he melts and mixes together. While the mixture is boiling, he applies it with a brush on the surface of the fossil, which becomes hard as soon as it is cold, when casts may immediately be taken of it. In the case of brittle but compact substances, spermaceti alone will do. When the fossil is still sticking in the earth, and there is danger of breaking it in getting it out, the mixture may be applied; but as it gets cold on the surface and makes a kind of crust, M. Stahl then passes a ball of cotton steeped in burning spirits of wine over it; the crust immediately melts, and is absorbed by the fossil.

Rattan Splints. — These splints have been invented and used in England for the treatment of fractures and other injuries where the use of such appliances is indicated. They are constructed of from four to seven pieces of cane cut of equal length and fixed parallel to each other by means of copper wires passing through the sides at given distances. The advantages of these splints are their lightness and flexibility, admitting air between the rods, and thus favoring the functions of the skin.

Large Lithograph. — The largest lithograph ever worked from a single stone has been shown in Paris, during the past year. It was a life-sized picture of Napoleon III., and the print measured upwards of six feet high by three broad. The stone was eight feet by four, and uniformly excellent in all qualities desirable for lithographic purposes.

Reproduction of Pencil Drawings. — Some time since, M. Villanis, an officer in the Russian service, observed that if a sheet of paper on which a plan or any drawing or writing has been executed with pencil, be moistened with acidulated water, and afterward inked, the pencil marks alone will take the ink, and the whole drawing may then be transferred to metal or stone. Captain Sytenko, director of the photographic service of the staff at St. Petersburg, has introduced very ingenious modifications into this process, and contrived a portable military press, by means of which it does not require more than ten minutes to effect the transfer of the drawing upon a zinc plate or lithographic stone.

USE OF ZINC FOR COINAGE.

The French Government having recently proposed to lower the standard of its silver coinage, on account of the increasing scarcity of silver, and the continued disappearance of the old silver coinage from circulation, authorized M. Peligot, chemist to the mint, to make experiments to ascertain how far the introduction of some zinc, or the complete substitution of zinc for copper as an alloy in the coins in question, would affect their appearance and durability. M. Peligot has in accordance with his instructions, therefore, recently reported to the French Academy, that his experiments undoubtedly show that alloys of silver and zinc possess considerable physical advantages over the corresponding alloys of silver and copper, while they are of course sensibly cheaper, since the market price of copper is more than four times that of zinc.

An alloy of silver and zinc, in the proportions of 165 zinc to 835 silver he found to be appreciably whiter than the corresponding alloy of copper and silver, while it is also "remarkably malleable" and "perfectly homogeneous when rolled." He experimented also on alloys of silver and zinc in atomic proportions, and found that both an alloy of one equivalent (or 108 parts by weight) of silver with one equivalent (or 32 parts by weight) of zinc, and an alloy of two equivalents (or 216 parts) of silver with one equivalent (32 parts) of zinc, are readily malleable, while alloys containing either two equivalents of zinc to one of silver, or three equivalents of zinc to two of silver are too brittle to be rolled. All the alloys of silver and zinc upon which he experimented are more fusible, more sonorous, and more elastic than alloys, in the same proportions, of silver and copper; and when those of them which are malleable have had their malleability impaired by hammering, it can be readily restored by simple heating. Moreover, the zinc alloys have over the copper alloy the very great advantage of no verdigris being formed by the contact with them of acid liquors and the equally great advantage of not being nearly so readily discolored by sulphuretted hydrogen, or other sulphur-compounds. M. Peligot, indeed, states that an alloy of 800 parts silver with 200 parts zinc will preserve its whiteness unimpaired in a solution of a polysulphide in which the standard alloy of silver and copper would soon become quite black.

Zinc would thus certainly seem to be better adapted than copper to alloy silver with, for coinage; while some of the alloys of silver and zinc above mentioned—especially that of 800 parts silver with 200 parts zinc—should be worth the attention of silversmiths, and other producers of ornamental metal work.

IMPROVEMENTS IN ENGRAVING.

In the process of engraving metallic plates by etching with acids there has been one obstacle to perfect work which we have regarded as insurmountable. As heretofore practiced, this process consisted in covering the plate with a thin coating of wax; which was attended with difficulties almost insurmountable. But these difficulties have been completely overcome by a French invention which is one of the most beautiful that has ever been made in this delicate art. The inventor is Monsieur E. Vial, of Paris, and the following is a description of his process: A drawing is made with a greasy ink on a steel plate, and the plate is then plunged into a saturated solution of sulphate of copper containing 10 per cent of nitric acid. By the action of the steel the copper is reduced from the sulphate, and all portions of the steel plate not protected by the ink are instantly covered with a coating of metallic copper, which protects the steel from the action of the nitric acid. The acid soaks away the ink, and dissolves the steel, forming channels beneath the lines. But as the acid soaks away the ink it is followed by the copper solution, and a coating of metallic copper is deposited within the lines, protecting them from the further action of the acid. As the copper is deposited first at the edges of the lines, all action of the acids upon the sides of the channels is prevented, and as the acid continues its work longest towards the middle of the line, the channels are made of " V " form, which is precisely the form desired by the engraver.

In the old method it was necessary to remove the plate from the bath as soon as the finest lines were etched, and to cover these parts with wax to prevent the further action of the acid; and the plate required to be removed as many times as there were variations of shade in the engraving. But by M. Vial's process the copper is deposited first in the finest lines, while the action of the acid continues longest in those which are widest. Thus the depth of the engraving is proportioned exactly to the breadth and thickness of the ink-mark, and this by a single immersion of the plate in the bath. The process occupies but five minutes. The copper is removed by ammonia before the plate is used for printing.

Old engravings may be reproduced by this process by transferring the picture to the steel plate, or the design may be first drawn upon paper and then transferred.

Additional Improvements. — Some curious experiments in engraving, executed before the Emperor of France, by M. Dulos, are thus described in *Galignani's Messenger.* A sheet of copper, drawn on with lithographic ink, is subjected to the voltaic pile, by which it receives a deposit of iron on those parts not covered by the ink. The ink is then removed by means of benzine, and the sheet is then in the state of an engraved copper-plate, — that is, the design is sunk into the plate, and the deposit of iron constitutes the lights. The plate is now dipped into a bath of cyanide of silver, under the action of the galvanic current. Silver is deposited on the copper and not on the iron. The plate is then taken out, and mercury poured upon it. Now, since mercury exercises no action on iron, it can only attack the silver which has filled up the lines originally made with lithographic ink. Hence, where those lines are, we now see mercury standing up in relief. Plaster of Paris is now poured over the plate in this condition, and thereby an impression is obtained in which the reliefs made by the mercury are reproduced hollow. (Why the ink was removed, or silver deposited in this case, is not clearly stated.) By the aid of the pile, copper may be deposited on this impression, and the hollows will then come out again in relief. One thus obtains not only a plate which may be printed from, but a matrix which will give an indefinite number of plates. For topographic engraving, the sheet of copper, after being drawn upon, receives a coating of silver, which only goes upon the metal, leaving the lithographic ink untouched. The ink is removed as before by benzine. The surfaces which are thus laid bare are oxidized and mercury is again poured on the plate. This metal recoils from the oxidized lines, and collects on the silver, making reliefs where lights ought to be. An impression in plaster is obtained as before, and the electro-chemical plate which is to be used for the printing has the lines of the drawing in relief as required.

IDEOGRAPHY.

Sir W. Armstrong, at the British Association for 1863, in his inaugural address, expressed surprise and regret that, notwithstanding the many improvements of modern times in the communication of intelligence and thought, our present mode of writing is not more free from imperfection than was that in use centuries ago. What he desires is a set of symbols which will enable us to communicate with each other more rapidly, and at the same time more distinctly, by writing. Don De Mas, Spanish Ambassador at the Court of China, has also recently entered upon an investigation of this general subject, and has published a work with the following title: "Ideography: a Dissertation on the Possibility and Facility of Forming a General System of Writing, by means of which all Nations may understand each other without knowing each other's language." The aim of the author is to introduce a medium of communication which may be to all nations something like what the Latin language once was to the learned in all parts of western Europe, and what written Chinese is at the present day to the inhabitants of the various provinces of China, Japan, Cochin China, and Tonquin, where languages are spoken so different in sound that those who speak them cannot understand each other in conversation, though they can carry on discussions — as our author has repeatedly witnessed — with pencil and paper. He considers it ridiculous to doubt the possibility of our doing in Europe what five hundred millions of Asiatics so far inferior to us are doing every day. Even granting this it does not prove the possibility, still less the facility, as he maintains, of inventing and bringing into general use a completely new written language. He himself abandons the idea of attempting to create a universal spoken language, both on account of the difficulty of the task, and the impossibility of securing the general adoption of the language, even if it were made ready to hand. It appears to us that these two fatal objections apply with scarcely less force to his present effort. He has certainly proved the possibility of constructing a system of written communication capable of use, to a certain extent, because he has actually accomplished the feat, so far as to express the first hundred and fifty lines of Virgil's Æneid in his proposed language. But he is greatly mistaken if he thinks he has proved the facility of the task. Even to understand what he has done is no easy matter, and the labor of doing it must have been immense. None can comprehend, still less acquire, his system of writing, who are not well versed in language, and acquainted with, at least, the elements of logic. We leave our readers to judge whether this in itself is not sufficient to prove the hopeless impracticability of the scheme. Comparatively few will ever be able, and still fewer willing, to make any use of it.

We may just state that the method proposed consists in employing musical notes in different positions on the staff to represent radical notions, with sundry strokes, curves and dots, to indicate the various modifications of these ideas; so that a page of the new writing presents very much the same appearance as a page of printed music. The symbols denote not sounds, but ideas; and the language is therefore a representation of thought, not of speech,—in fact, a very elaborate and complicated system of hieroglyphics. It is scarcely necessary to say we regard the work rather as an ingenious curiosity than as of any practical value. — *London Athenæum.*

INTERESTING ILLUSTRATIONS OF THE FORCE OF GUNPOWDER.

In the town of Erith, England, on the 1st of October, 1864, 150,000 pounds of gunpowder were accidentally exploded, causing a report heard at the distance of over 90 miles, and a shock which people living 25 miles away thought to be the effect of an earthquake. The gunpowder was contained in two barges, and a large and a small magazine.

As this is one of the greatest explosions of powder (over 70 tons) which has ever happened at one time, it is a matter of no little interest to note the results of the occurrence. Fortunately the loss of life was small, 12 killed and 20 wounded; but the damage to property was very great.

At more than two miles from the spot not only were doors and windows smashed in, but houses were partially destroyed. One residence was injured to the amount of $5,000. 100 yards of river embankment were blown away; fortunately the tide was low and the damage was repaired with great celerity, else a large and populous region would have been submerged. A watchman at Gravesend, some miles off, one of the very few who saw from a distance the great catastrophe, as well as heard the awful thunder and felt the shock, says: "On turning round I saw as it were a pillar of fire rising to the clouds, which it appeared to strike, and then spread out like a huge fan, presenting a most beautiful and grand spectacle."

The destruction of houses and other material near the scene of explosion was of course complete. One report says: "The buildings that lately covered some acres are heaps of tumbled earth and bricks and massive fragments of timber; beams of half a ton's weight have been blown like feathers across the adjacent fields." The property destroyed in the surrounding district is estimated at $5,000,000. A clock in a house seven miles away was stopped by the explosion. At Woolwich, four miles from the magazines, a shower of letters, invoices, and other papers fell, shortly after the explosion, and an examination of these first informed the people there of the scene of the accident. Persons at that place report: "Immediately after the calamity an immense pillar of smoke rose from the spot high into the air, thick, black, and palpable, with a huge spreading top, and about a quarter of an hour elapsed before it died away."

In and near Erith, two or three miles from the magazines, for some minutes after the explosion, "the earth heaved and trembled." Men were thrown violently from their beds; scarcely a house in the place had a pane of glass left whole. At Woolwich, four miles distant, door and window frames and sashes were smashed in, portions of ceiling and wall shaken down, many persons were violently thrown out of their beds, and several persons were injured.

At Chatham, 25 miles distant, the windows in the great workshops were violently shaken, and doors were forced open.

At Deptford, four or five miles off, 150 gaslights in a large factory were blown out at once. The same thing occurred at a police station in Whitechapel, London. The people of Soham, 80 miles from Erith, heard a noise resembling thunder, and felt a shock which they attributed to an earthquake. The sound of the tremendous report spread even further, for it was supposed to be distant thunder at a place 94 miles away. In the Crystal Palace in London, some doors were violently forced open, and paintings knocked down from the walls.

The most remarkable effect of the explosion was upon animals in the large region around. The mortality among canary birds for miles around was very great; they dropped from their perches and died of fright, or of the concussion. Parrots were badly frightened, and dropped from their perches to the bottoms of their cages, refusing to speak for some hours. Dogs, cats and other animals manifested symptoms of the greatest alarm. For many miles from Erith the cattle in the fields, at first struck dumb and motionless at the stunning report, presently set off in the wildest excitement, racing around the enclosures, and could not be quieted for some hours. All the churches for 15 miles around, and most of them for 20 miles, have suffered by broken windows and cracked walls.

Such were some of the phenomena of this terrible explosion.

A writer in the *London Times* thus speculates on the probable effect of the explosion of 2,000 tons of powder, the amount stored in the government magazines at Purfleet, 16 miles from London :—

2,000 tons of powder would occupy 75,000 cubic feet of space, or equal to a pile 100 feet long, 40 feet wide and 20 feet high, quite the size of an ordinary parish church. As powder, at the moment of its explosion, exerts an elastic force of 1,000 times the pressure of the atmosphere (15,000 pounds to the square inch), the ignition of this quantity would instantaneously liberate a force equal to 14,000,000 tons. As the vibrations of force radiate equally in all directions, like those of light and heat, it necessarily follows that its intensity diminishes in proportion as the circle of its radiation increases in diameter. Thus, taking the direct distance from London to Purfleet as 16 miles, an explosion at the latter magazine would, by the time it reached town, be distributed over 10,000,000,000 square yards of surface, and, therefore, the mechanical effect of the shock to the houses in London would be a little over 31 pounds per square yard of surface, or 220 pounds on the front of an ordinary average dwelling-house. This would be augmented to a slight extent from the fact that the power of the shock would not radiate downward in consequence of the earth, and would react in other directions.

The quantity of powder exploded at Erith on the occasion of the late catastrophe was 104,000 pounds, or 1,733 cubic feet; this, probably, produced a force of 800,000 tons, and this, radiating to London, was spread over a space of 5,600,000,000 square yards, and reduced its effective force on the houses of the metropolis to about six ounces per square yard. It may seem surprising to many that this small force should have been so distinctly felt; but when it is remembered that a very few pounds exerted in banging a door will give rise to a very severe feeling of concussion in most houses, the surprise will cease. The pressure which would be exerted upon the houses of the metropolis by an explosion at Purfleet, of three pounds or four pounds per square yard, would probably be sufficient to break most windows facing in its direction, and houses would feel the shock very severely; for, though the pressure would not be more than that specified above, the wave of force arising from such a quantity of powder would be of great duration.

IMPROVEMENTS IN THE SCIENCE OF WARFARE.

The Ship of the Future, — *impregnable and unconquerable.* — The London *Mechanics' Magazine,* in the following interesting sketch, gives some hints as to what will be required for effective harbor defence, and what can be done to make a coast line impregnable to an enemy. It says :—

"Let us take a plunge into the future, and describe the ship or gunboat which can best defend our shores. She will possess three paramount qualifications : Firstly, she will carry guns capable of playing havoc with any ship from distant ports able to live in such seas as she would have to encounter in order to reach our coast; secondly, our ship of the future will steam fast enough to run alongside any foe at her pleasure, or to retreat, when that very objectionable step is dictated by the necessity for drawing the foe into a region where she can be properly attacked; and, thirdly, she will be so heavily armored that an enemy's shot shall fall harmless from her sides.

These characteristics can only be obtained at the expense of many of those qualities the possession of which can alone render a man-of-war fit for foreign service; and this is well, because the right ship is certain to remain in the right place only when there is no other place to which she can go. Let us treat of her armament, in the first instance.

As regards sub-marine artillery, many recent experiments prove conclusively that the discharge of the heaviest ordnance beneath the water level, is not only practicable, but that the effect of the missiles so discharged is terribly destructive at short ranges. Our future ship will carry two 20-ton muzzle-loading guns; we imagine that guns of the Blakely or Parrott class will be found most suitable. These guns will habitually use conically-fronted elongated shells, and heavy charges of powder. On board, two or more " wells " will be constructed, or rather two water-tight compartments into which the sea can be admitted, or from which it can be excluded at pleasure.

For six feet or thereabouts, above the water-line the ship — about 250 feet long — will be very heavily plated, the plating at that height terminating in a shot-proof deck. Two inches of iron on six inches of teak and strong deck beams will go far to make this deck all that is required, as shot must always strike at a very obtuse angle. A second deck will be provided at or about the water-line, and into the intervening space the guns will be raised in order that they may be loaded, while they will be submerged in the water, in order that they may be discharged, from five to seven feet below the water-level. Perhaps a somewhat different arrangement may be adopted; in any case, however, the guns must be capable of doing damage below the water-level.

Light wooden top-sides may be provided for the comfort of the crew, and, perhaps, to deceive an enemy as to the real character of the ship with which we would have to cope. A light draught of water will be indispensable; 12 feet may be taken as a maximum, perhaps, beyond which it will not be prudent to go, as a ship of this class must be able to run close in shore. As a consequence of the breadth, say 30 feet proportional to her length, our ship will have a very flat floor. Her plating must be brought down far below the water-line. As little armor will be carried above that level, there is apparently no reason why the hull should not possess ample buoyancy to support any reasonable weight which can be suspended from its sides in this way. Masts and sails will be out of place.

The utility of this gunboat, for such she will be virtually, notwithstanding her size, will absolutely primarily depend on great speed. With such a moderate draught of water as 12 feet no single screw would be sufficient to confer this qualification; and for this reason, and some other considerations connected with facility for manœuvering, it becomes expedient that two propellers should be employed. These propellers, then, will be driven by independent engines of great power, direct acting, and capable of running at a very high velocity.

As the ship is not intended to proceed further out to sea than 50 or 60 miles, or to take any cruise which would occupy more than three days at most, nearly all the space on the lower deck from one end to the other will be available for engines, boilers, and coal; and because 300 tons of this last will always be enough to take on board at one time, an enormous amount of boiler room will be available. The engines will be constructed to work expansively under ordinary circumstances, with ½ or ¼ boiler-power; when going into action the funnels may be lowered, and blowers fitted in the engine-room will, even then, with ease, burn 50 pounds of coal per square foot of grate.

As the hull to be driven will be long and sharp, a speed may, under such conditions, be maintained — the engines being worked at full power, and the steam full stroke — for four or five hours at a time, such as no sea-going ship ever equalled. In moderate weather as much as 21 knots may be realized. As the engines will only be called on to make such an extraordinary exertion at rare intervals, and as plenty of time will always be found to make repairs in port, where such ships will spend much of their time, there is little danger of a breakdown, and the machinery can always be kept in first-rate order.

Stores, water, every consideration save armament, will give way to the attainment of excessive speed for comparatively short periods,— a speed which it is impossible to realize under any other conditions,— a speed which will convert these coast defence ships into sea-eagles, making their swoop where and when they please close to our shores;

8

destroying, sinking, burning, yet affording no tangible object of attack to an enemy, whose ships they can pursue, overtake, fly from, elude, with an ease and certainty which finds no parallel, save in the career of the great destroyer of all things—Death.

Their mode of attack will be very simple,—each ship will run alongside a foe as quickly as possible; while in pursuit, short as that pursuit will be, her guns may be used above water with effect, perhaps; at all events, they may be used. It will be no easy matter to prevent our ship of the future running alongside any ordinary iron-clad frigate. It may be equally impossible for her, being alongside, to remain there ten seconds; but these ten seconds are sufficient to discharge two 20-ton guns below the water level, below that six or seven feet of submerged plating which we find on the sides of the Warrior or the Black Prince. We have but to turn to the last Ordnance Report to learn what ensues. The largest ship afloat will go down, or become water-logged and helpless, in five minutes after a hole four feet square, is knocked in her bottom; and at a range of 50 feet a 10-ton gun would smash in this hole in thin skin plates, with ease, in much less than ten seconds. In her turn, our ship will set submarine ordnance at naught, because she can carry plating where no frigate or liner can,—far under water. Above it, from her insignificant height, she would afford a very small mark, not easily hit, while the peculiar conditions under which she would be used, and the exceptional nature of the service on which she would be employed; the absence of heavy stores, rigging and masts; the small number of her guns; the trifling weight of coals to be carried, &c. would leave a margin of buoyancy great enough to permit enormously heavy plates being carried above water, plates thick enough, at least, to render their pounding a very thankless task.

It is needless to say that such a ship as we have sketched, more dimly and slightly than we could wish, will be utterly unsuitable for long voyages; she must perforce remain at home. It is absurd to sacrifice speed and armor in order that frigates may carry coal for ten days and provisions for three months,—that they may be fitted for foreign service, in fact,—and then to compel them to remain at home to perform duties for which they are to a certain extent incapacitated by the presence of things which, however useful and necessary on a voyage to China or India, are at once unnecessary and out of place on board a ship intended specially for coast defence.

On the Structure of Ships of War. — In a discussion at the last meeting of the British Association on the construction of iron-clads, &c. Admiral Belcher, R. N., submitted the following remarks: He thought that our ships of-war needed no more protection than would keep their hulls safely floating, with such protection for those fighting the guns as might be deemed sufficient to keep off shells and musketry, suffering heavy shot to pass freely through instead of causing spiral showers of splinters such as resulted from the destruction of the late targets at Shoeburyness. The present paper, therefore, dealt with a mode of construction adequate for contending with ordinary batteries, and also permitting external planking, and consequently the old copper sheating below water. It had been so generally assumed that no thickness of armor-plate could be employed which could resist our new monster ordnance that his attention had been directed to meet the difficulty half way, by protecting the mere vital shell of the lower hull, so as to defy the ordinary assault of any ordinary gun-bearing vessel which should not by its accumulated weight or mass of matter render defence impossib.e. It was important, therefore, that such a tonnage should be provided as should, as in the case of the *Warrior* class, be capable of floating the contemplated armament independent of the forward and after compartments, which might be assumed as mere assistant means of flotation, and to be so fitted with cellular divisions below the level of flotation as to render injury to those parts below the reach of shot of very trifling importance.

Assuming that an iron spherical shot of thirteen inches was the missile to be dreaded, the question to be considered was not exactly what flat plate of iron was to resist it,—for the authorities stated that no reasonable thickness, even up to 12 inches, would withstand the impact. Looking, however, only to the floating carcass of the ship, and disregarding the ports until we had an impregnable stage on which to place guns, then we should be at liberty to increase the thickness to any amount. His proposition was to construct the ship on the customary plan of close iron ribs, but filling up the interstices between the iron with condensed teak. Assuming that we constructed a vessel with 36 inches depth of rib at the vulnerable portions which shot could reach, which would probably involve 12 vertical feet of her side,—say eight feet below water and four feet above,—we should then have a vessel of stronger framework than any now built, building, or in contemplation. Then assuming that these iron ribs presented two inches at the exterior, tapering in 36 inches to one inside, placed six inches asunder, and filled in with compressed timber or other matter, we should have per cubic yard of bulwark 3,412.125 pounds, that of the *Warrior* being 3,123 pounds, showing only a difference of about 290 pounds to the cubic yard.

It was yet to be determined, by actual experiment, whether that resistance would offer the protection sought. Perhaps it would not, but as he proposed to add a six-inch planking outside, he considered that the comparative danger with our present iron-clads would be reduced to *nil*, or at least to something which would satisfy the seamen. On a previous occasion he had alluded to paper as an opposing medium. In 1816, at Algiers, a ream of foolscap, end on, resisted a 68-pound shot from a 27-feet gun, at 76 yards; and in 1854, he proposed to the Admiralty to construct movable battery rafts of brown paper, but the design was not carried out. · Lately, he learned from a newspaper that, ten years after his proposal, it was found that paper of one inch thickness was fired at and not quite penetrated, while a similar shot went quite through ten inches of good oak. In conclusion, he would observe that condensed millboard weighed less than oak or teak, and, interposed in the manner he had suggested, might form a target which would set even the largest ordnance at defiance.

— *Ericsson on the Construction of Impregnable Armor.*—The following is an extract of a letter recently addressed to the Secretary of the Navy on the above subject by Mr. Ericsson: "The English have failed in producing an armor capable of resisting projectiles of great speed and weight. Solid blocks of wrought iron, of the best quality, one foot in thickness, have been split under the impact of the projectile. The enormous dynamic force lodged in the shot, compared with the inadequate cohesive force of the metal at the place struck, together with the incompressible nature of the material, furnishes a ready explanation of the cause of the fractures which have resulted from heavy charges of powder at short ranges with the solid English targets.

"Having attentively studied the subject, and demonstrated satisfactorily the cause of the unexpected destruction of the enormous solid targets, the expedient at once suggested itself to the writer, of applying a *laminated* protection in order to exhaust the *vis viva* of the shot, by degrees, before reaching the solid blocks intended as the real armor. The peculiar feature of the laminated protection is evidently that each successive lamina, or plate, may be split without affecting the next; forming, as it does, a separate body placed at a measurable distance from the neighboring plate. Not so with a solid projectile; a split or crack of sufficient width must inevitably — owing to the incompressible nature of the material — run through the entire substance. Hence the destruction of the enormous blocks of wrought iron tested in England.

"The condition of my 15-inch target, recently tested by Captain Dahlgren, at the Washington Navy Yard, proves incontestably that, by interposing a laminated protection, armor may be made absolutely impregnable. Not only are the 5-inch wrought slab and the backing of 4-inch plating — together nine inches — completely uninjured; but there remain also in the centre of the indentation made by the shot, more than two inches thickness of the outer plating. The absolute protection thus afforded by the 6-inch thick plate lining to the 5-inch wrought slabs of the 15-inch target, placed close to the muzzle (34 yards) of an 11-inch Dahlgren gun, fired with 30 pounds of powder, proves conclusively that the side armor of the *Puritan* and *Dictator* will be impregnable. This side armor, it will be remembered, is composed of 6-inch plating, under which is inserted the longitudinal wrought-iron slabs (stringers), backed by the 4-feet thickness of oak, firmly attached to the side of the ship without the employment of the objectionable through-bolts employed in the *Warrior* and other European iron-clads."

Resistance of Iron Plates to Heavy Shot. — Mr. Scott Russell, from the result of the various experiments that have been made by the British Government, deduces the following thicknesses of iron-plates as proof against shots of various weights. For the present: the 4½-inch plate against the 68-pounder; 6½-inch plate against the 136-pounder; 7½-inch against the 200-pounder; and 8½-inch against the 270-pounder. For the future: the 10-inch plate against the 400-pounder; 11-inch against the 500-pounder; and 12-inch against the 600-pounder. These results, Mr. Russel states, are entitled to our full confidence, as the experiments at Shoeburyness fully bear them out.

New Experience with Iron-clad Vessels in Action. — Some additional experience in the value and working of iron-clad vessels in warfare, has been gained during the past year from a conflict which took place in the Bay of Mobile, between a formidable iron-clad Confederate ram — the *Tennessee* — and a fleet of wooden vessels of war and monitors, under the command of Admiral Farragut of the

U. S. Navy;—the conflict resulting in the surrender of the Confederate vessel.

The ram in question was some two years in building, and no pains or expense were spared to render her impregnable. A committee of U. S. naval officers appointed to examine her subsequent to her capture, reported as follows:—

"The hull of the vessel appeared to be exceedingly strongly built in every part, the material being oak and yellow pine, with iron fastenings. Length from stern to stern on deck, 209 feet; greatest breadth of beam on deck, 48 feet; mean average draught of water, about 14 feet. The deck is covered fore and aft with wrought-iron plates two inches thick. The sides of the vessel are protected by an overhang, sponsoned, and covered with two layers of 2-inch wrought iron. The sides of the vessel below the deck are about eight feet in thickness. The prow is provided with a ram or beak, which projects about two feet under water and is covered with wrought-iron plates.

"The casemate of the vessel is very strongly built. It is 78 feet eight inches long and 28 feet nine inches wide inside, — the sides of the vessel extending 10 feet from it on either side at the greatest breadth of beam. The framing consists of heavy yellow pine beams, 13 inches thick, and placed close together vertically, the inside planking of yellow pine, 5½ inches thick, laid horizontally, and outside of this horizontal planking there is a layer of oak timber four inches thick, bolted on vertically, upon which the iron plating is secured. The plating or armor of the casemate forward is six inches thick, consisting of three two-inch iron plates of about six inches wide each, and abaft, and on the sides, five inches thick, consisting of two two-inch thick and one one-inch thick iron plates of the same width. The yellow pine framing of the casemate is planked over inside with 2½-inch oak timber laid on diagonally.

"The whole of the armor plating is fastened with through bolts 1¼ inches in diameter, with washers and nuts inside. The casemate is covered on top with wrought-iron gratings, composed of bars two inches thick and six inches wide, laid flat, and supported on wooden beams 12 inches square, and about five feet distant from each other."

The armament of the *Tennessee* consisted of six rifled guns—two of 7-inch caliber and four of 6¾-inch,—all of the Brooks pattern. Her ports were closed with shutters of 5-inch iron. These were attached at the centre of one of their sides by a pivot on which they revolved by means of a cog-wheel inside, and turned out of the way outside when her ports were opened. The projectiles used were 95 and 110-pound solid shot. Her draught of water was 14 feet eight inches; her engines, two in number, high pressure, driving a geared propeller; and her complement of men and officers 187.

The U. S. fleet under the command of Com. Farragut, consisted of several vessels of the class of the *Hartford*, and several monitors. At the commencement of the conflict the rebel Admiral, with great courage, plunged his iron-mailed vessel into the midst of his enemy's fleet, with a view of crushing the wooden vessels one after another, like the performance of the *Merrimac* in the James River in 1862. But Admiral Farragut had other intentions. He signalled for his fleet to gather around him, and a combined butting of the *Tennessee*

8*

was made by several vessels.   This, however, seems to have produced
no effect except in preventing her from destroying any of the Federal
vessels.   The monitors then closed upon her, and after some firing
she surrendered.   The causes of the surrender were, 1st. The wound-
ing of her commander and the demoralization of the crew.   2d. The
uselessness of three guns, which could not be used on account of the
jamming of two port covers and the loss of a third.   3d. The carrying
away of the rudder chains, by which the vessel became partially unman-
ageable.

The report of the Board of officers above referred to, concerning
the injuries received by the *Tennessee*, is as follows :—

"The injuries to the casemate of the *Tennessee* from shot is very
considerable.   On its after-side nearly all the plating is started, one
bolt·driven in, several nuts knocked off inside, gun-carriage of the
after pivot-gun damaged, and the steering-rod or chain cut near that
gun.   There are unmistakable marks on the after part of the casemate of not less than nine 11-inch solid shot having struck within
the space of a few square feet, in the immediate vicinity of that port.
On the port side of the casemate the armor is also badly damaged.
On that side, nearly amidships of the casemate, and between the two
broadside guns a 15-inch solid shot knocked a hole through the
armor, and backing, leaving on the inside an undetached mass of oak
and pine splinters, about three-by-four feet, and projecting inside of
the casemate about two feet from the side. This is the only shot that
penetrated the wooden backing of the casemate, although there are
numerous places on the inside giving evidence of the effect of the shot.

"There are visible between 40 and 50 indentations and marks
of shot on the hull, deck, and casemate, varying from very severe to
slight—nine of the deepest indentations on the after part of the
casemate evidently being 11-inch shot, and the marks of about 30
of other calibers on different parts of the vessel.   There are also a
few other marks, being, however, merely scratches or slight indentations of the plating.   The smoke-stack was shot away, although it
is not improbable that the severe ramming the vessel had previously
received, facilitated its fall.   There were no external visible marks or
evidences, however, of injury inflicted upon the hull of the *Tennessee*
by this ramming."

It would thus appear, that the armor of this vessel, although injured, was nevertheless sufficient to withstand without serious detriment all the steel shot from our rifled pieces, our 11-inch solid shot
from our ships of war, and 15-inch shell from the monitors, not one
of which penetrated her ribs of iron, while near 50 shots altogether
struck her in the engagement.   The nearest approach to penetration
was from a 15-inch missile, which made a deep indentation in her
broadside, and by impaction stove through her oak backing, causing
the splinters to fly promiscuously inside.   Though underway when
this struck her, she is said to have stopped as if a magic wand had
touched her.   Her arrangement of port-shutters proved an element of
weakness.   Two of these had their system of ratchets and cogs deranged during the action, and could not be afterwards opened.   A
third (her after one) was shot away entirely,—that is to say, the pivot
on which it turned was shot off and the shutter fell to the deck, leav-

ing that port open and exposed to the hostile fire. Her rudder chains were also a most serious element of weakness with her, being carried along her deck, and covered only with a plate of half-inch iron. They were, consequently, broken early in the engagement, and her rudder was subsequently managed by means of ropes and blocks, and yet notwithstanding all these injuries, the commission of officers that surveyed the *Tennessee*, immediately after the fight, reported her " in a condition to do good service," and although captured, her resistance is a matter of great interest and importance in the new developments concerning naval warfare, and furnishes new testimony to the value of iron-clad vessels.

The *London Times*, in commenting upon this extraordinary trial, draws this conclusion; either the armor of the *Tennessee* was superior to any of the targets which represent our British iron clads, or the ordnance of the Federals is inferior to our artillery. We have already said that we do not think the former hypothesis could be maintained for a moment, and, consequently, we must close with the latter. This we do without hesitation, and we imagine that most persons acquainted with the subject would be prepared to affirm that the guns which penetrated the *Warrior* target, at Shoeburyness, would, at ten feet distance, have smashed in the sides of the *Tennessee* before the action had lasted a quarter of an hour.

Iron-clad Vessels. The Ironsides and Monitors contrasted.— The following is the substance of a Report recently made to the Secretary of the Navy by Commodore John Rodgers on the comparative merits of the Ironsides and Monitor class of vessels.

These vessels have each their peculiar defects and advantages.

In the ironsides class the hull of a wooden man-of-war, as constructed for general purposes, is clad with iron. It is true, some modification of shape and increase of size is required to meet the additional weight which she has to carry, but still in essentials she is a vessel of the ordinary model; she has the advantage of ample quarters for her crew, with free access to her deck in storms; with natural ventilation; with abundance of light; with numerous guns, giving her a rapidity of fire unattainable in a monitor, and essential in battering forts; and she is as able to carry canvas as other men-of-war.

The monitor class, as far as I know, is new. If I understand the idea, it is to cut off all the surface above the water except that which may be necessary to flotation, and to carry the guns in a revolving turret, or turrets, near the center of motion, supported upon the keel and kelsons.

The plans upon which Mr. Ericsson has worked out this idea of his may be modified by further experience, but the idea itself will be employed while iron-clad vessels are used in warfare.

It has these advantages :—

The monitor has the least possible surface to be plated, and therefore takes the least possible tonnage to float armor of a given thickness; or with a given tonnage allows the greatest possible thickness of armor, and consequently the greatest possible impenetrability. The ability to carry armor is proportionate to the tonnage, but the monitor of 844 tons has actually thicker plating than the ironsides of

3,480 tons, and than the *Warrior*, of 6,000 tons; and yet the *Iron-sides* and the *Warrior* have only the middle portion of their hulls plated, their ends being merely of wood without armor. The guns of the monitors near the center of motion are supported upon the keel and kelsons, upborne by the depth of water under them, and carried by the whole strength of the hull. In monitors, heavier guns are therefore practicable than ever can be carried in broadside out upon the ribs of a ship. In the monitors, concentration of guns and armor is the object sought. In them the plating is compressed into inches of elevation; while in the ironsides class it is extended over feet; and the comparatively numerous guns distributed over the decks of the iron-sides class are molded in a few larger ones in the turrets of the moni-tors. When the power is required in the individual guns, enough to crush and pierce the side of an adverary at a single blow, the most for-midable artillery must be employed; and 15-inch guns are the most formidable, which, so far, we have tried; but no vessels of the iron-sides class can carry these guns; and the monitors actually do carry them.

If target experiments are reliable, a shot from the 15-inch gun will crush in the sides of any vessel of the ironsides class in Europe or America. A single well-planted blow would sink either the *Warrior*, *Gloire*, *Magenta*, *Minotaur*, or *Bellerophon*. The *Dictator*, of 3,000 tons, has armor thick enough, I believe, to withstand 15-inch guns.

The objection to the monitor class, such as I have seen in use, are from fewness of guns, the lack of rapidity in fire in battering forts, or wooden vessels; the loss of accommodation from dispensing with the upper deck, or decks; the greater unhealthiness from dampness, and from confinement below in even a moderate sea; from the loss of light, and from depending upon blowers driven by steam for ventilation.

The monitors are slower than their steam power would seem to promise. In all of them the slip of their screws is excessive. This I attribute to the overhang, which if a source of strength in action, from its use as a ram, and from its protecting the propeller and rud-der, is a source of weakness and strain at sea. The overhang has the advantage of keeping the vessel very steady; she can not roll with these wing-like projections holding up her sides, nor pitch, nor send with the immense flat surface of the overhang to resist those motions; but as the monitor is slower than other vessels of like tonnage and power, it must be presumed the difference of shape makes the differ-ence of speed; and the overhang constitutes the sole difference of shape.

If ordinary vessels can endure the pitching and sending motions, it may be inferred that the monitors can endure them. If ordinary vessels can have their rams below water, so may the monitors; nor is it necessary to equality, that the rudder and propeller of the mon-itor should be better protected than those of our competitors.

The monitor model rolls very little, and is extremely easy in a sea way. In a gale of wind, it was found on board the monitor *Wee-hawken*, that while her companion, wooden corvette *Iroquois* (deemed a very perfect model), had an excessively violent motion,—so violent, indeed, that no one could stand upon her decks without the assistance of life lines,—the *Weehawken* had so little motion that a bottle of claret stood for an hour upon its narrow base on the dinner-table in the cabin, when it was put away.

I do not consider the lowness of the monitors in the water a source of unsafeness. They start to sea with sufficient buoyancy, and, by the consumption of coal and provisions, they hourly grow lighter. Anything lighter than water will float upon it; and however deeply buried, while lighter than water, it must come to the surface; but effectual means must be used to keep the vessel tight, for any considerable accumulation of water in the hull will sink her, which is true also of ships generally. The casemated vessels, — such as the ironsides, — if not safer than the monitors, are more comfortable, and therefore probably more healthy; with greater facilities for carrying canvas than the monitor class seems to admit of.

To sum up my conclusions, I think that the monitor class and the ironsides class are different weapons, each having its peculiar advantages, — both needed to an iron-clad navy, both needed in war; but that, when the monitor class measures its strength against the ironsides class, then, with vessels of equal size, the monitor class will overpower the ironsides class; and, indeed, a single monitor will capture many casemated vessels of no greater individual size or speed; and as vessels find their natural antagonists in forts, it must be considered that upon the whole the monitor principle contains the most successful elements for plating vessels for war purposes.

Admiral Porter, also, in a report made to the Department, January, 1865, on the conduct of the iron-clads in the bombardment of Fort Fisher, speaks in the highest terms of the sea-worthiness of the monitor vessels. During a gale of great violence encountered by the squadron, some of the smaller monitors, at times almost disappeared from view, but the vessels were in no danger at any time. Of the *Monadnock* (monitor), Admiral Porter writes : " She could ride out a gale at anchor in the Atlantic Ocean, and she is certainly a most perfect success so far as the hull and machinery are concerned, and is only defective in some minor details, which in the building of these vessels require the superintendence of a thorough seaman and a practical and ingenious man. The *Monadnock* is capable of crossing the ocean alone, when her compasses are once adjusted properly, and could destroy any vessel in the French or British navy. She could certainly clear any harbor on our coast of blockaders in case we were at war with a foreign power. There are four vessels in the American navy of the class of the *Monadnock*,—all ranking as second-rate iron-clads. They are built on the monitor plan, but have two turrets, in each of which will probably be placed a 15-inch gun and a 200-pounder. Their register is 1,564 tons, their length 259 feet over all, 52 feet 10 inches beam, and depth of hold 14 feet nine inches. The turrets are 21 feet in diameter. Their propellers are 11 feet six inches in diameter, and have a pitch of 24 feet. Each vessel has two screws, one on either side of the stern-post. Their draught of water, fully laden, is 12 feet.

"These vessels have laid five days under a fire from Fort Fisher, anchored less than 800 yards off, and, though fired at a great deal, they were seldom hit, and received no injury, except to boats and light matter about the decks, which were pretty well cut to pieces. Compared with the ironsides, their fire is very slow, and not at all calculated to silence heavy batteries, which require a rapid and continuous fire to drive the men from their guns ; but they are famous coadjutors in a fight, and put in the heavy blows which tell on the case-mates and bomb-proofs. The smaller class of monitors, as at present constructed, will always require the aid of a steamer to tow them and take care of them."

Admiral Porter also says he has never yet seen a vessel which came up to his ideas of what is required for offensive operations so much as the *New Ironsides*. She combines very many good qualities, the most important being the comfort with which the people on board of her live, though she would be no match for the *Monadnock* in a fight.

The American frigate " New Ironsides." — During the service of this vessel in 1863, she was struck by the shots of the enemy 241 times ; 140 of which thundered against her in the short period of two days ; but, notwithstanding, she has passed through the terrible ordeal without having sustained any serious damage, and with the loss of only one man killed. This is a most satisfactory evidence of her great powers of endurance. During the same period she discharged 4,561 rounds against the enemy.

The latest British Iron-clad.—The *London Times* gives the following description of the most approved and most formidable of the iron-clad vessels designed and in the process of construction by the British Government. The name of the vessel is the *Bellerophon*, and her builders are the well-known firm of Penn & Co. The *Times* says : —

" This vessel is in point of strength intended to be a monster among these monsters ; to be, in fact, as terrible an assailant to iron-clads as an iron-clad would be to wooden ships. The object with which this vessel is designed is, in case of another great naval war, to avoid a repetition of the long dreary work of blockading an enemy's fleet by wearisome and dangerous cruising off the mouth of harbors. The *Bellerophon* is to be a vessel of such strength and speed and tremendous weight of guns as, in case of an enemy's iron fleet running into port, she can follow them with impunity, and at long range fight them at their moorings, till she either drives them ashore or forces them out to sea. Specially built for the discharge of such duties, it is almost needless to say how carefully every point in her equipment has been considered ; and as Mr. Penn undertakes that her speed shall equal her strength, there seems to be very little doubt but that, with her impenetrable sides, and her armament of ten 300-pounders and two 600-pounders, she will be the most formidable sea-going frigate the world has yet seen. The length of this vessel is to be 300 feet, and her breadth 50 feet ; her tonnage will be 4,246 tons, her displacement 7,-053 tons ; and though carrying the heaviest armor and armament ever sent afloat, her draught will be only 21 feet forward and 26 feet aft,— less than the draught of ordinary two-deckers. The height of her lowest portsill from the water will be 9½ feet, the distance between the guns 15 feet, and the height between decks seven feet. Her midship section is smaller than that of the *Warrior*, and to that extent, therefore, she will be easier to steam and sail. She is to have four masts, — only the first square-rigged, the three others carrying immense fore-and-aft sails, a rig from which the French have got such admirable results with their iron frigates under canvass. The speed, which it is to be hoped will be attained in this vessel is an average of 15 knots, or nearly 18 miles per hour.

"The ribs and framing of the *Bellerophon* will be much the same as those of other iron frigates, with the exception that the stringer plates and diagonal bracings will all be of steel, — that is to say, of less than half the weight, and more than four times the strength, of the present system of wrought-iron fastenings. Wherever steel can be used with advantage, in point of strength and lightness, it will be adopted in the frame of this new frigate, and Mr. Reed estimated that by this method, and while making the hull infinitely stronger, he will save in weight two or three hundred tons, which can be infinitely better bestowed in increasing the thickness of the armor plating. The armor of the *Bellerophon* is to be no less than 16 inches thick, and this is to rest on 10 inches of solid teak beams. This outer protection is quite formidable enough, but what it protects is of its kind quite as strong in proportion. The inner skin consists of two plates, each of ½-inch thickness, with a stout layer of painted canvas between to deaden concussion. Outside the skin come angle-iron stringers of the tough steel. These angle-iron stringers in any metal would be of immense strength, and project from the inner skin 9½ inches and 10 inches alternately Thus they form so many longitudinal shelves, of the depth mentioned, which run from stem to stern of the ship, two under each row of plates, and in these the teak beams are laid, the longitudinal layers of the angle-irons keeping the beams up to their work and preventing the lateral splintering, while they also support the plates with their edges and prevent their bending in unfairly on the teak. The *Bellerophon* is not thus coated from end to end and over all with this tremendous armor. In the center and for 90 feet of her broadside she is thus protected, from five feet below the water line to the level of the upper deck. In this space are her guns, five 300-pounders, with one 600-pounder at each side. For the rest of her length there is only a belt of this massive armor, which goes to the same depth beneath the sea to six feet above it, so that she cannot be hit in any part where the water could enter."

Torpedo Warfare. — The earliest mention of torpedo warfare in this country is made in the published work of Robert Fulton. In October, 1805, in presence of Admiral Holloway, Sir Sidney Smith, and other British officers, near Walmer Castle, Fulton blew up a brig of 200 tons burthen, by means of torpedoes. The vessel was anchored and the torpedoes were floated under it; the clockwork attached to them having been so arranged as to explode at a given time. In August, 1807, Fulton made similar experiments in New York harbor, and blew up by torpedoes a vessel of about the same size. In 1810 he had an opportunity of explaining his system to Mr. Madison, Mr. Jefferson, and others, at the residence of his friend, Joel Barlow. During the same year Fulton published his small work entitled "Torpedo War and Submarine Explosions, &c." This little work was illustrated, and represented the several modes of using this new and novel machine. One method was to anchor the torpedoes, which were to explode when struck by a passing vessel. Another was to attach clockwork to them and to carry them in boats near the vessel to be destroyed, when the clockwork was set in motion and the torpedoes floated down the tide and under the vessel. Another method was to shoot a harpoon into the side of the vessel with a line made fast to the torpedo, which burst at the moment of contact. All of these plans were in a measure practicable at times, but there was not a sufficient degree of certainty in their operation to warrant the patronage of either Great Britain or the United States; consequently the system was neither perfected nor adopted.

The present war, which has developed so many useful appliances of naval and military science, has advanced the practice of torpedo warfare to an extent which does not yet seem to have found its limit. The Confederates have used the stationary torpedo to a considerable extent, and have destroyed or sunk some eight or ten naval vessels, including two iron-clads.

All of these casualties took place in shoal water, and most of the torpedoes in question were fired by means of a galvanic battery, worked by members of the "Confederate Torpedo Corps," located on the banks of the rivers.

The Rebels have made several attempts to destroy our war ships by means of torpedo vessels, but only one of these has ever thoroughly accomplished her work, in the sinking of the sloop-of-war *Housatonic*, off Charleston. The vessel which performed that deed, however, never returned, but sank with all on board. Similar attempts have been made upon the iron-clad frigate *New Ironsides*, and the wooden frigates *Wabash* and *Minnesota*, — the former at Charleston and the latter at Hampton Roads. Only four known attempts have been made with this kind of craft; but there is reason to believe that numerous experiments have been attempted, in which the Rebels were obliged to abandon the plan as well as the unsafe vessels built for the purpose.

After the capture of the forts in Mobile Bay, Admiral Farragut discovered, high and dry upon the beach, one of the torpedo vessels with which the Rebels designed to destroy the fleet blockading that port; but, like most of her predecessors, an accident befell her which rendered her useless. While on a trial trip one of her boilers exploded, killing nearly all of her crew, and the disaster threw a gloom over the corps which had her in charge, which fact, coupled with the difficulty of procuring another boiler, led them to abandon the project.

Until within the past year but little has been done by the United States to perfect torpedo warfare. Captain Ericsson's "devil," intended to be attached to the prow of the monitors, was a large and costly raft, to which was fixed an immense torpedo; but this invention was abandoned because its presence among a friendly fleet was of too dangerous a character to be permitted, and after an expenditure of many thousands of dollars upon the system it was cast aside.

Within the last year, however, a torpedo boat, designed and modelled by Engineer Wood of the U. S. Navy, has been constructed, and found to work better in practice than in theory. The hull is of wood, 75 feet in length, 20 feet beam, and seven feet deep, and constructed in the most substantial manner, with heavy deck beams supported by hanging knees securely bolted and fastened. The deck, two feet in thickness, is crowned two feet fore and aft, and about as much athwartships, and is now receiving an iron armor of two inches in thickness, to render it proof against shot and shell.

This vessel, called the *Stromboli*, lies very low in the water, and when in service as a torpedo boat, is further submerged by filling water-tight tanks, which bring her down so that scarcely any part of her deck is above the surface of the water. The only objects visible above the deck are the pilot-house, 38 inches in height, the smoke-stack, which is only a trifle higher, and a small ventilator which can be removed if desired. With such a small surface exposed, the risk of being met by the enemy is greatly reduced.

The general appearance of this craft is peculiar. Descending through a small hatchway, which is closed while the vessel is underway or in action, the visitor may see some curious appliances. Abaft the midships is the engine, which has a cylinder 18 inches in diameter and 18 inches stroke,—a compact yet powerful affair, working the screw at an average rate of 50 revolutions a minute, or about ten miles an hour. The boiler, situated forward, is built of extra strength, to carry a very high pressure of steam. The steering apparatus is directly underneath the little pilot-house, and so close to the commanding officer that he can give the helmsman his orders without the use of a bell, which might attract the enemy's attention. In the bow of the vessel is the torpedo machine, which, for obvious reasons, cannot now be fully described. Yet we are permitted to indicate the general plan of operation in order to give an idea of the invention.

The crew of the vessel consists of three engineer officers, one pilot and nine firemen and coal-heavers, — a force abundantly able to do all the work required of them. When a vessel is to be destroyed the torpedo craft steams boldly out, and, as she approaches her victim, she is settled in the water so as to present but little surface to the shot which may be directed at her. Nearing the doomed vessel, a torpedo, charged with from 60 to 200 pounds of powder, is placed in a "torpedo basket," which is attached to a long arm running through a stuffing-box. This basket is now inside of a water-tight box, with a lid or cover, which is opened when the torpedo is placed in position. This having been done, the cover is screwed down, the gate at the bow of the vessel is opened and the arm is run out for a distance of about 30 feet. The vessel now rapidly approaches her intended victim, and passing close alongside, the torpedo is detached from the basket, the arm is withdrawn, and at the instant desired the charge explodes, causing the instant destruction of the vessel. The torpedo vessel receives none of the shock.

The method of constructing the torpedo is a secret. It is sufficient, however, to know that this is not one of the many experiments which have failed to produce valuable results. In no instance has this invention been found deficient in power or quickness of execution. — *New York Evening Post.*

It is understood that some dozen or more of these vessels have been constructed for the U. S. Navy ; and their value has been practically tested in at least one instance ; viz : the blowing up of the Confederate iron-clad ram *Albemarle*, by Lieut. Cushing ; the ram being at the time moored to a wharf, at Plymouth, N. C.

Report of the Bureau of Naval Ordnance. — From a recent Report of the U. S. Bureau of Naval Ordnance we derive the following memoranda of interest: For broadside guns in the American navy 9, 10, and 11-inch guns and Parrott rifles, in pivot, are now used; 15-inch guns for the turrets of the monitors, and bronze howitzers and rifles for deck and boat service in shore. The armament of a first-rate ship-of-war in the American Navy is now 150-pounder rifle and one 11-inch smooth bore, in pivot, with 42 11-inch smooth, four 100-pounders, rifled, and four howitzers in broadside. The armament of vessels for other rates is in proportion. A first-class monitor carries four 15-inch guns in her turrets. The iron-plated boats on the Western rivers carry three 9-inch, four 8-inch, two 100-pounders, one 50-pounder and one 30-pounder.

The value of pivot guns over broadside, was illustrated by the fight between the *Kearsarge* and *Alabama*, where all the damage was done by the former arm. A mixed battery of both is however the most perfect.

During the past year, experiments have been quietly and systematically made with both shells and shot, from smooth bores and rifles, of all the heavier calibers. The power of the guns belonging to the navy, and in common use in the batteries of our ships, have been fairly tested against both solid and built-up plates, and the conclusion reached is wholly in favor of the guns and their solid projectiles, — the spherical shot for smooth bores being, however, immeasurably superior to the elongated rifle shot in every form. No manner or thickness of iron or steel armor that could be carried on the hulls of sea-going ships will resist the impact of solid spherical shot fired from the heaviest calibers of the navy, at close range, with appropriate charges of cannon powder. It was generally accepted as an established fact that it was impossible to cast a spherical shot of large diameter which would be *solid* throughout. It is now known, however, that it is easy to cast a 15-inch or 20-inch shot which will be perfectly sound and solid from circumference to center of figure, and one of the former has resisted, without breaking, 222 continuous blows of an, 8-ton steam hammer.

For small arms for the use of the Navy, breech-loaders are alone recommended. The following curious fact is stated in this connection, as illustrative of how much ammunition is wasted in battle, and how many muskets in the hands of incompetent or cowardly men are actually useless. On the field of Gettysburg there were 27,574 guns picked up, and of these 24,000 were found to be loaded; of these about ¼ contained two loads each, ¼ from three to ten loads each, and the balance one load each. In many of these guns from two to six balls have been found, with only one charge of powder. In some the balls have been found at the bottom of the bore with the charge of powder on top of the ball. In some, as many as six paper regulation caliber 58 cartridges have been found, the cartridges having been put in the guns without being torn or broken. 23 loads were found in one Springfield rifle-musket, each load in regular order. 22 balls and 62 buckshot, with a corresponding quantity of powder all mixed up together, were found in one percussion smooth-bore musket. In many of the smooth-bore guns, model of 1842, of Rebel make, we have found a wad of loose paper between the powder and ball, and another wad of the same kind on top of the ball, the ball having been put into the gun naked. About 6,000 of the arms were found loaded with Johnson & Dow's cartridges; many of these cartridges were about half way down in the barrels of the guns, and in many cases the ball end of the cartridge had been put into the gun first. These cartridges were found mostly in the Enfield rifle-musket. This statement constitutes one of the strongest of arguments in favor of a change to breech-loading guns. With breech-loaders it would be impossible to get in more than one charge at a time, and a man could tell at a glance whether his piece was discharged or not.

NEW GUN METAL.

A writer in the *London Times* gives some interesting particulars of a new gun metal lately invented in Austria by Baron von Rosthorn. Before giving any account of this new alloy, the writer states his opinion that the days of wrought iron are numbered, and that its place will be soon supplied by steel in some form or other. The new alloy, which has received the name of "sterrometal," from a Greek word signifying tough or firm, is composed of copper, spelter, iron, and tin, in proportions that may be slightly varied without much affecting the result. In color it resembles brass rather than gun metal; it is very close in its grain and free from porosity. It is possessed of considerable hardness, and will take a very fine polish. Several eminent Vienna engineers have tried it for the cylinders of hydraulic presses with great success. Two specimens of the alloy have been submitted to rigorous tests by the Polytechnic Institute of Vienna and the Imperial Arsenal. The proportions used in each case were the following:—

	Polytechnic Institution.	Imperial Arsenal.
Copper	55·04	57·63
Spelter	42·36	40·22
Iron	1·77	1·86
Tin	0·83	0.15
	100·000	99.86

The specimen tested at the Polytechnic Institute gave the following results per sectional inch (English): A bar prepared by simple fusion bore a weight of 27 tons. Forged red-hot it broke at 34 tons. Drawn cold, at 38 tons: the figures in the case of the specimen tried at the Imperial Arsenal being 28, 32, and 37 tons respectively; while the best English gun metal, containing ten per cent of tin and 90 per cent of copper, broke at 18 tons under similar circumstances. The specific gravity of the metal is about 8·37 when forged hot.

These results, which are official, are truly astounding when we consider that the average breaking strain of wrought iron, as given by Mr. Anderson, of Woolwich Arsenal, is only 26 tuns. The elasticity of the sterrometal is also very great. It may be stretched $\frac{1}{800}$ of its length without undergoing permanent elongation; gun metal giving only $\frac{1}{1800}$, and wrought iron $\frac{1}{1500}$. No surprise, is, therefore, felt when we are told that a tube of sterrometal is capable of resisting a pressure of 763 atmospheres, a tube of wrought iron of similar size and form giving way under 267.

New Principle in Gunnery.— The following description of an alleged new principle in Gunnery, devised by Mr. James Mackay of Liverpool, is copied from English journals:—

The principle in all rifled cannon appears to have been to allow as little windage as possible, and to make the shot fit the grooves of the piece, taking from them a rotation in its flight. Mr. Mackay, on the other hand, has conceived the plan of having the grooves so arranged that, while the shot fits closely to their outer edge, the grooves are left open for windage. By this arrangement the gas has to travel some feet further than the shot, and in doing this imparts a rapid and perfect "spin" to it. The shot are of cylindrical form, perfectly smooth, with conical heads, and cupped at the other end in proportion, so that each shot is perfectly balanced from the center of its length. Mr. Mackay in his patent also claims a peculiarity in the wadding, which is of sawdust, by which at the movement of the first ignition of the powder the elasticity of the wadding moves forward the shot slightly; the effect is that the whole of the powder is burnt, and the shock on the breech of the gun considerably lessened. Mr. Mackay has had a gun made upon this principle by the Mersey Steel and Iron Works Co. It is of wrought iron, weighs nine tons, has a bore of 8·12 inches, and in other respects corresponds with the general features of the ordinary 68-pounder. There are 12 grooves, and, as the shot do not enter these grooves, it allows of a much sharper twist than in ordinary rifled guns. The velocity has been found to be 1,640 feet a second.

The following trial has been made with this gun, against a section of a new iron-plated vessel, the *Agincourt*, now building by Laird & Co. for the British Government. The target consisted of an outer plate seven feet square and 5¾ inches thick, of rolled iron; next came nine inches of teak, then an inner plate or skin ¾ of an inch thick, then angle-iron and ribbing, and finally a backing up with timber balks and supports 18 inches thick. The plates were stated on competent authority to be the best that can be made of rolled iron. The gun was charged with 30 pounds of powder and a cast-steel shot, weighing 167 pounds. The range was 200 yards. The shot struck the target with a dull thud, a little below the bull's eye on the right, and in the very strongest part, where it was backed up by the rib of the ship's side, the angle-iron, and the timber balk. At the point of impact a perfectly circular hole was cut. The shot then powdered the teak, passed through the inner skin and the angle-iron, shattered the timber balk into fragments, and was picked up 82 yards beyond the target, together with a circular piece of the iron armor, about 80 pounds' weight, it had carried with it through the back supports. The sand showed that it had spun to the last. About 70 fragments of iron, bolts, and fragments of the inner skin and angle-iron were picked up 100 yards from the target. The shot when found was reduced from 13 inches to 11 inches in length, and increased about 1½ inch in diameter at the end which struck the target. The other end was uninjured. The whole target was forced back about six inches, and so much deranged that more shots were not fired.

The Percussion of Shot on Iron Targets. — The visitor at the scene of the experiments at Shoeburyness, in noticing the effect of the shot on the tremendous targets representing sections of the *Warrior*, the *Gloire*, and other frigates, cannot fail to observe that at the lips of every jagged metal wound there is a kind of red ulcer, the oxidization produced by the instantaneous and awful flame of the impact; while where the bolt or ball has torn its way through the tough iron, the sides of the cut are actually "blued" like gunsmith's furniture, by the same momentary and fiery heat of percussion.

Experiments on Targets of compressed Wool. — Some experiments have been made in England during the past year on the resisting properties of compressed wool to shot: Mr. Nasmyth and other authorities entertaining a confident opinion that a good thickness of wool, when pressed tight, would offer an amount of resistance to shot which, if not sufficient to keep it out altogether, was, at least, certain to be enough to justify the Government in making experimental inquiries on the subject. We do not know, says the *London Times*, even if the discovery had been successful, how it was proposed to utilize it,—how, for instance, to recoat our ironsides with 10 or 12 feet of pressed wool, or how to apply so bulky and cumbrous an appliance in any way. Fortunately there is no necessity for considering such embarrassing speculations now, inasmuch as the experiment proved the wool rather more permeable to shot than almost any other novelty that has yet been fired at. A very few words is sufficient to tell the result. The target, if we may so call it, was a wrought-iron tube, like a boiler or iron funnel, open at both ends, 10 feet in diameter and about 11 feet long. The wool part of the target was constructed by tilting this on end and filling it with wool as tightly as men could trample it down till the cylinder was full. It was then laid on its side fronting the gun, so as to present the appearance of a large white circular target or drum, 10 feet in diameter, and 11 feet thick of solid wood.

The first shot was fired from the Armstrong 100-pounder, with a 10-lb. charge, and this not only passed through the target from end to end, but buried itself in the earth behind. A second shot was fired from the 68-pounder, with the usual service charge, and this also went through, burying itself in the bank, and as a means of resistance the target was such a palpable and utter failure that even Mr. Nasmyth was satisfied with these two shots, and concurred in the uselessness of firing any more.

Firing Cannon under Water. — Some experiments on the firing of cannon under water, recently made at Portsmouth, England, are thus described : —

" A stage was erected in the harbor within the tide mark ; on this an Armstrong 110-pounder was mounted, loaded, and aimed, at low water, at a target placed also within the rise of the tide. When both gun and target were covered by the water to the depth of six feet the gun was fired by means of a tube. The targets were placed at from 20 to 25 feet from the muzzle of the gun. One was composed of piles and oak planking of a thickness of 21 inches; another consisted of the hull of an old vessel, the *Griper*, laid on a mudbank ; a third was made up of three inches in thickness of iron boiler-plates, bolted together and backed with timber. On all these the effect of shot and shell from the submerged gun was very startling. The wooden target was pierced through and through, the iron target was broken in pieces and driven into the backing, the solid shot passed right through both sides of the vessel, making a huge hole through

9*

which the water poured in torrents. A shell, with percussion fuse, burst in entering, opening up a chasm of five feet by three in the planking, shattering the ribs and bursting up the deck beams above."

New Mode of Rifling Guns.—No general principle of rifling guns seems to be recognized and practiced.

Regular and increasing twists of various pitch are used by rifle makers for guns of the same bore. Capt. T. A. Blakely, the inventor and constructor of the best guns of large caliber in Europe, has taken out a patent for the application of a new principle. It consists in rifling guns and forming projectiles in such a manner that the same power shall always act uniformly. The patentee first decides at what distance from the center of the projectiles the turning force of the spiral shall act, and the smaller the bore the nearer the center it acts. He says: "Let a circle be now drawn, with a center in the axis of the barrel, the radius of which circle is this settled distance; then form the rifling of such a shape that a line perpendicular to any point of its surface shall also be a tangent to this circle." The projectiles are formed to correspond and follow the same mathematical rules with respect to the shape of their external surfaces.

Gun-Cotton. — A committee of the French Academy, consisting of M. M. Pelouze and Maurey, appointed to consider the applicability of gun-cotton to ordnance, do not by their report at all agree with the conclusions of the Austrian or English experimenters, (see *Annual of Sci. Dis.* 1864). Contrary to the assertions made by the Austrian General Leuk, that his gun-cotton does not explode at a lower temperature than 136°, Centigrade, they affirm that all their specimens exploded or were otherwise decomposed at a temperature of 100°; and that at a temperature as low as 55°, decomposition ensued with equal certainty, but only in the course of a few hours. In one case they even obtained an explosion at 47°, which induces them to suspect that it may even be decomposed at the common temperature. Upon the whole, therefore, they do not recommend the substitution of gun-cotton for gunpowder in the French service.

Wrought-Iron Forts. — There has been recently constructed in England, for the Russian Government, a massive iron structure, which is intended to serve as a sort of shield, or outer protection to the face of a fort or rampart in the harbor of Cronstadt. Its structure is as follows:—

It is 43 feet six inches long by ten feet in hight, and is composed of wrought-iron bars of a size hitherto unattempted in "grooved rolls," 12 inches by 12 inches, rolled with a "rebate," and corresponding hollows on the opposite side, strengthened by dovetailed ribs at their back, three inches in thickness, which are attached by keys or wedges in dovetailed holes to upright beams or girders, 14 inches by 14 inches, on each side of the embrasures and at the ends, and in two equal divisions of its length, to four frames or brackets like the letter A, with one vertical side. The foundation plate on which the whole structure stands is 43 feet six inches long, two feet wide, and 3½ inches thick, rolled in one length. The total weight of the shield is about 140 tons. Each embrasure is four feet from the platform, and four feet high. In the throat. it is two feet two inches in width, cr, with the shelving of the cheeks, two feet ten inches. The military advantages of such an opening in an iron parapet of 15 inches thickness is, that the guns can be worked so as to take a greater sweep of range than is possible where the parapet is of masonry. In point of strength, an inch thickness of iron is equal to one foot thickness of stonework, so that the power of resistance of the shield in question is equivalent to that of a wall 15 feet thick. As a matter of experiment it is to be put upon the parapet of one of the outer ports at Cronstadt, but should it be found to answer expectations, it will itself take the place of the parapet, the whole metal platform being fastened by clamps and rivets into the granite rampart.

The *London Engineer* thus describes the process of rolling the immense bars of which this structure is composed. It says: As these bars were an advance upon what has been hitherto done, the result was looked forward to with some doubt, for each bar, when delivered, was to weigh six tons, to be 15 inches square, to be tongued and grooved in the rolling, and to be perfect in its soundness throughout. The furnaces were opened at three o'clock, and the immense mass of metal was drawn forth on to an iron truck, heated to a brilliancy that was almost blinding in its intense whiteness, and instantly changing the temperature of the vast factory to a scorching sulphurous heat that was insupportable. Directly it was out, workmen, shielding their faces as they best could, swept the impurities from its surface with long brooms soaked in water, but which nevertheless lit like tow the instant they came in contact with the iron, which was sparkling like a gigantic firework. It was then let down the incline to where the rollers, turned by one of the largest fly-wheels in the kingdom — more than 100 tons weight and nearly 40 feet in diameter — was waiting to crush the mass into its required form. This was the critical moment; for an instant or two the rollers failed to grip it, but at last they caught it, and the whole machinery moved slower, as amid loud cheers from the workmen they began to wind it in. As it was slowly crushed through, the refuse melted iron was squirted out in all directions, and as the mass emerged from the rollers on the other side, it lit up everything with a bright lambent flame, said to be caused by the pressure to which the bar was subjected. This was only the first roll, but it had to be passed through three times to reduce it to the proper thickness. It was not, however, as in the case of ordinary armor plates, a mere question of reduction, as these bars have to be rolled, tongued, and grooved to fit into each other. Thus in the rolling they have to overcome all the peculiar difficulties of their construction almost in two operations, which must be done while the metal is in a half melted state, or the whole is spoilt. The bars, as we have said, are 15 inches square, but each of these presents a most difficult section. In the first place, the lower part of the bar has a projecting rib, and in the upper part is a groove, corresponding in size with the rib on the lower half, so that the projection of one bar may fit into the groove of the one beneath, thus making a solid dovetailed wall of iron. Beyond these, also, is a rib at the back of the bar, formed to dovetail again into projecting masses of iron in the rear supports of the fort, and in the process of rolling all these departures from a plane and smooth surface have to be formed, and to be formed with so much accuracy that each part fits into the other without the necessity of any machine planing of surfaces. To give to the mass of metal the required section, the rollers of the mill are grooved where the raised surface is required, and sunk to produce the projecting ribs.

ENDURANCE OF HEAVY ORDNANCE.

A recent report by Gen. Gilmore, "*On the Engineer and Military Operations against the Defences of Charleston, in* 1864," furnishes some interesting information respecting the endurance of the heavy rifled ordnance recently brought into use. According to this authority, we have no guns of large caliber which will endure "with certainty 800, or even 500 rounds." The siege of Charleston was not abandoned until after 23 of the Parrott 100 and 200-pounders had burst. The famous " Swamp Angel " battery, composed of one 8-inch rifle gun, exploded at the 36th fire, blowing out the entire breech at the rear of the vent, disheartening the men, and causing a suspension of the fire on the city. For purposes of offensive war, then, we must have rifled ordnance of greater power and endurance than any yet made; and that nation which shall be the first to produce guns "strong enough, " in the language of Gen. Gilmore, "to sustain the repeated shock of at least 1,000 charges of powder, in as large quantities as can be burned with useful effect behind the projectile, and at any required elevation," must have a decided advantage over all others.

"The average number of rounds," says Gen. Gilmore, " sustained by Parrott's 100 and 200-pounders, on Morris Island, excluding those in which the bursting could be traced to the premature explosion or breaking of a shell, was 310." The system of " reinforcing " or "hooping" a gun with external hoops of steel or wrought iron, does not always answer the purpose of adding strength to the gun. On the contrary, it is often a source of weakness, " because in cast guns (whether of iron, brass, or other metal,)" as Captain Blakely remarks, " the *outside* helps but very little in restraining the explosive force of the powder tending to burst the gun, the strain not being (always) communicated to it by the intervening metal. The consequence is, that, in large guns, the inside is split, while the outside is scarcely strained. This split rapidly increases, and the gun ultimately bursts."

Gen. Gilmore says explicitly : " It is not to a want of strength in the reinforce that the premature bursting of Parrott's guns is to be attributed, for the reason that that is not where the guns generally fail. The defect has been more prominently exhibited in the cast iron." In other words, it is the hard, granulous metal itself which is at fault, and not the workmanship, which is excellent, and the only remedy for our failures is to be found in the adoption of other metals and other processes of fabrication.

In explanation of these failures, however, it is due to Mr. R. B. Parrott, the inventor and manufacturer of the guns, to state that in a letter in the Appendix, he urges that the explosions are not owing to any defect in the material or style of the guns, but to inexperience in the handling of them, and to causes of a peculiar and accidental character. He avers that, taking the extensive and repeated tests to which they have been exposed, they are an unquestionable success in every way.

Since the siege of Sebastopol the government of Great Britain has expended over $12,000,000 in experiments with wrought iron and steel, at the Royal Arsenal at Woolwich, and Elswick ; and of 3,000

Armstrong guns produced, not one, according to the testimony of Sir William Armstrong, has yet burst explosively. Whitworth has also had some success in the production of forged iron guns, although his method is defective; and Blakely in England and Krupp in Belgium are now manufacturing superior ordnance from steel. The advantages of wrought iron over cast iron consist in its greater tenacity, elasticity, and ductility, which it preserves under heavy pressure. All gun metals are said to possess a certain degree of elasticity; but the "elastic limit," in rapid firing, is always liable to be exceeded, and when this happens, cast iron, from its want of flexibility, easily cracks and crumbles. In other words, after the limit of its elasticity is overcome, any violent shock or sudden strain causes the gun to give way at once, and explode without warning; while a gun properly made of wrought iron, under similar circumstances, would only widen a little, and still be further from the point of bursting than it was before. The tensile strength of wrought iron is over 66,000 pounds to the inch, while that of the best cast iron is only about 30,000 pounds per inch.

Artillery Experiments made under the Direction of the U. S. Ordnance Department.—The *Scientific American* furnishes the following *résumé* of experiments which have been recently made with guns and targets, under the direction of the Ordnance Department of the U. S. Government. The experiments in question were all made with the 11-inch gun, of Dahlgren, with an average charge of 30 pounds of powder, an average weight of spherical cast-iron projectile equal to 165 pounds, and an average range of 80 feet.

Under the above-named conditions, an experiment was made upon a composite target of iron and India-rubber, backed with timber. The iron was outermost, and was two inches thick; the rubber came next, and was 1¾ thick; the timber was 19 inches thick, in all 22¾ inches. The target was inclined at an angle of 15°; and at the first fire the shot tore through the mass and penetrated the bank behind (a solid clay) 17 feet, being but slightly damaged in its passage.

Another experiment was tried with a 4½-inch solid scrap-iron plate, backed with 20 inches of solid oak, and the iron *faced* with rubber, four inches thick, the whole placed against a bank of solid clay; this resulted in the destruction of the target at the first fire, the charge being 30 pounds, the projectile, spherical cast iron, weighing 169 pounds, and the range 87 feet. The shot did not go entirely through the target, but penetrated the plate and rubber, and lodged in the second course of timber behind. The rubber was entirely forced off, by the violence of the concussion, and fell 15 feet forward of the target.

Still another target was made, of four 1-inch wrought-iron plates, backed by rubber four inches thick in single sheets of one inch each; the whole backed by 20 inches of solid oak. The first four inches next the timber were composed of alternate rubber and iron, two inches of each; the wrought iron was on the outer surface of the target when fired at. The whole was placed against a bank of solid clay. The charge was 30 pounds, the shot 169 pounds in weight, and the range 84 feet; at this distance, and under these conditions, the target had two clean, handsome holes bored through it,—one of which was but slightly larger than the shot itself, showing it experienced but little resistance in its passage. A repetition of the experiment, with the target inclined at an angle of 45°, produced the same result; the target being penetrated, and much more injured, than when vertical. It should have been stated, previously, that the target was 96 inches long, by 42 inches wide. In a comparative experiment, to test the value of India-rubber as a resisting agent, a target was made with four single iron plates, each one inch thick; the results, as observed by competent witnesses, did not vary materially from those obtained with rubber, and little value is attached to it as a disperser of the force of shot.

Trial of the largest British Ordnance hitherto constructed. — The following account of the most powerful gun which has as yet been constructed in Great Britain, is taken from the *London Times.* The gun is of wrought iron, with a caliber of 13½ inches, just about the same as that of Ericsson's wrought-iron guns, which are to be used in arming the *Dictator* and *Puritan* :—

"The trial," says the *Times,* "was to test the powers of the greatest gun yet forged by Sir William Armstrong, — a 600-pounder termed the 'Big Will,' against one of the thickest and most perfect plates which Messrs. Brown & Co. have as yet produced for actual armor-plating. The plate in question was no less than 11 inches in thickness,—a sample of one of many of the same enormous strength made by Messrs. Brown & Co. for the Russian Government, to plate the sea faces of some of the most important and exposed of the Cronstadt forts. According to the theory of the iron plate committee, that the strength of an iron plate increases as the square of its thickness, this 11-inch mass was equal in strength to no less than six plates of the famous *Warrior* target; yet before the experiment commenced, not the slightest doubt was entertained that the 600-pounder would utterly smash it, if fired with a 600-pound shot. The real interest of the experiment consisted in ascertaining,—first, whether the same destructive result would be gained by using the gun as a smooth-bore with a steel shot of half the weight; secondly, how the gun would stand the tremendous charge of 90 pounds of powder; and thirdly, whether the fracture of the plate would show that even Messrs. Brown could not manufacture one of 11 inches in thickness perfect throughout. These were the three points really at issue, and the solution of these was looked forward to with keen interest by all the officers on the ground. The first and only shot, we are happy to say, settled them all in the most satisfactory manner, and proved the enormous advantage of steel shot, the strength of the gun, and the excellent manufacture of the plate. The plate or slab of iron was four feet long by 3½ feet wide, and was unimpaired in its strength by a single bolt-hole or fastening. It was held up vertically against two 12-inch beams of solid oak, to which it was fastened by railway iron, passing up its face on either side. Behind it, and in support of the oak beams, was the Fairbairn target of 5-inch plates and a 1-inch inner skin, with the usual massive framework of iron rib beams. This target, however, did not support the plate to be fired at, but only the beams of oak which held it in position. There was an interval of 12 inches between the plate and the Fairbairn target, which was left purposely that the former might do its own work, if it could, unaided. The proceedings were commenced by firing two cast-iron round shot of 300 pounds' weight, levelled at 200 yards range, against a "dummy" target placed close alongside the 11-inch plate for the purpose of determining the exact degree of elevation to be given to the gun. Both these were fired with the enormous charges of 90 pounds of powder. Such charges even with 600-pounders, would not be used in actual warfare, and for experimental purposes were objectionable, as it seemed to make it almost as much an effort to destroy the gun as the target. The precise range having been ascertained, 'Big Will' was again stuffed with a sackful of powder, but, instead of a cast-iron projectile, was loaded with a steel round shot of 344 pounds' weight, and levelled against the target. This shot struck the very center of the plate with a terrific crash, at a velocity of 1,560 feet, and at one blow closed the experiments for the day. Nothing further remained to be accomplished, for the target was gone. Never, probably, has a more tremendous blow been struck by human agency. The mass of steel driven by the tremendous charge of powder must have struck the target with a power almost inconceivable, for everything went down before it. The solid oak beams behind the plate were crushed into splinters, and the plate itself hurled bodily back against the Fairbairn target and split into two pieces,—one huge piece being flung away to the right and the other to the left, and all this before the shot had time to penetrate to a greater depth than 4½ inches. The 11-inch plate, in fact, had not sufficient stability to receive the blow aimed at it; it was torn apart by the tremendous force with which it was jammed against the Fairbairn target behind, and an examination of the fracture showed that its manufacture was admirable. Fourteen feet in front of the target lay the steel shot, much flattened, and cracked, but evidently as good metal of its kind as Mr. Brown's plate itself. A close examination of the gun was next made by the Inspector of Artillery, and it was found to be wholly uninjured. Notwithstanding the use of steel round shot in a rifled gun, the grooves of the rifling remained as sharp and fine as ever, and only one feeling seemed to be entertained on the ground as to the strength of the gun and the excellence of the plate."

Construction and Trial of a new Monster Gun.—During the past year a cannon of 20-inch caliber, the largest piece of ordnance ever constructed and mounted, has been successfully cast according to the plan devised by Capt. Rodman, at the Fort Pitt foundry, Pittsburg, Pa. The amount of metal used in the casting was 160,000 pounds, and the time of cooling was upwards of two weeks. Another gun of a similar caliber, but weighing some eight tons less, was also successfully cast subsequently.

The first-named gun, which is 20 feet 3½ inches in length, and weighs 58 tons, is mounted at Fort Hamilton, New York Harbor. The carriage on which it rests is constructed wholly of iron, has an extreme length of 22 feet a hight of eight feet and eight inches, and weighs 36,000 pounds, or 18 tons. The trunnions of the gun are 18 inches in diameter. The shot intended for this enormous piece of ordnance weigh 1,080 pounds each, and are handled by machinery. The location of the gun is not in the fort, or very near to it, but amongst a tier of 15-inch guns which extends along the embankment on the bluff-front of the fort for nearly a quarter of a mile below it. Its position is such as to command the lower bay; but it may also be pointed in the direction of the city; and the Narrows are just below its mouth.

The trial of this gun, after it was mounted at Fort Hamilton, is thus described:—

It was decided, after the vent of the cannon was cleaned, to fire a charge of 50 pounds of powder. A box containing a 50 pound charge was then brought up. When lifted into the mouth of the gun, it did not occupy more than a quarter of the space. The gunners did not understand how so small a pile of powder, wrapped in cotton cloth, was to be ignited; and so this charge—which is the regular service charge of the 15-inch guns—was taken away, and a 100-pound bag of powder substituted.

Two men standing on the embankment or parapet in front of the gun, raised the charge to the mouth; a ramrod was brought forward by four men, and the charge driven home; the ramrod being used by the men as though it were a battering ram. A fuse was then inserted in the vent of the cannon, and the word was given for the crowd to retire. The report of the discharge was loud and deep, but not sharp; it was a heavy boom, not very unpleasant to the ear, but yet in its effect stunning. Volumes of smoke, resembling dark and dense clouds, rolled more than ten rods from the cannon. The recoil was very slight.

At the second discharge the gun was shotted, and a smaller charge of powder—50 pounds—was used. The bore having been carefully swabbed out with a wet sponge, and the charge carefully sent "home," the hoisting apparatus was next employed to raise the ball. Three men did this work; and after five minutes pulling at the chain, the shot was brought into position before the mouth of the cannon. The shot was held in a clamp with two arms inserted in holes in the ball, and a bar was also inserted in the shot, to aid in its management. Nearly half the shot entered the muzzle and the other part was outside. This was the point of difficulty. The question was how to release the ball. It had to be supported by main strength of the men who managed the machinery.

At this juncture Captain Rodman, who superintended the firing, directed two of the men to get under the shot and brace their shoulders against it. They at once assumed the perilous position. By dexterous management the Major took the teeth of the clamp from the ball and withdrew the bar, at the same moment starting the ball on its course in the gun.

The cannon was aimed at a spar buoy in the direction of the lower bay; there was no inclination; and at a quarter past three o'clock the signal was given for the spectators to retire. The discharge was effected by means of a friction fuse. The report was not louder than the first, owing to the lighter charge. The huge ball could be seen from the moment when it left the smoke of the powder. It struck the water at a distance of about a thousand yards from the shore. It threw up a cloud of spray, and richocheting, flew along the surface of the water for the distance of about three miles and then sank. Another shot was next fired, with a larger charge of powder, and with the gun considerably elevated. The range attained to in this instance was between four and five miles.

The Ames Wrought-Iron Rifled Gun. — In the United States, as in England and other nations of Europe, from time to time, a new type of cannon is introduced, for the purpose of more completely fulfilling the requirements of this arm of national warfare. From the history of the past, and the experience of the present century, these requirements have been thus defined: *The greatest possible accuracy of fire, range, and strength in a given weight, with the least amount of recoil.*

To obtain these results, England has had the Lancaster, Whitworth, Blakely, Somerset, and Anderson guns, with others of less pretentious caliber. The United States have had the Stockton, Dahlgren, Parrott, Sawyer, Wiard, and Rodman guns, with others of less notoriety, none of which have filled the measure of requirements of range and of strength in their fabrication, being, with few exceptions, made of cast iron. Those of wrought iron, with one or two exceptions, were of the tube and coil construction, which, from not being welded solid throughout, have failed to meet these conditions.

During the past year, however, a new description of gun, made of wrought iron, has been manufactured for the U. S. Government, by Horatio Ames, Esq., of Falls Village, Conn., which promises to be an improvement over any description of large ordnance hitherto constructed. Mr. A., about the commencement of the Rebellion, received an order from Government for a battery of 50-pounders, of wrought iron, and thereupon devoted an extensive establishment to the exclusive business of manufacturing ordnance. He conceived the idea of forging his guns solid, leaving but a small hole at the center for removing the scale or impurities worked out of the metal under the hammer. Experimental investigation he very soon saw, although an expensive school to learn in was the only one which could be relied on to remove all doubts of success in furnishing the essential requirements in forging a superior gun, which could not be burst by the usual methods of firing excessive charges of gunpowder, even though the windage was closed by rifling the gun.

The 50-pounder battery was duly completed, and, although considered perfectly successful, the guns were too small to take the place of Parrott guns before Sumter and Charleston. Another contract was therefore given in 1863 by the War Department, for a battery of 15 guns of not less than 100-pounders, capable of sustaining a charge of 25 pounds of powder.

With the latitude thus afforded, Mr. Ames at once proceeded to adapt his forges, furnaces, and machinery for guns of 7-inch caliber and 150 pound projectiles.

With a ripe experience in making and forging iron, added to the practical lessons secured in forging the 50-pounder battery, he cut loose from the trammels of precedents, and developed his own resources, which have proved quite sufficient to produce a gun from the best Salisbury iron, perfectly solid in every inch of its length and circumference, 14 feet long and 28 inches in diameter, weighing 20,000 pounds.

One of the distinctive features of this gun consists in its being molded solid throughout. The great difficulty hitherto, has been to obtain solidity around the bore of wrought-iron guns. The ordinary process of welding up the gun in ring sections from the breech to the muzzle, molds the outer surface first, leaving the forger in doubt as to the perfection of the inner welds, which no subsequent heating and hammering can perfect. By the process Mr. Ames has introduced, the section around the bore is molded first, and by each subsequent heat the molds are extended outward. The process in detail is as follows: A bar of round iron 18 feet long, ten inches diameter at one end and 14 at the other, is made to serve as the handle of the gun. Upon the larger end of this are welded one by one large bars of iron of about two feet in length, until a round mass has been formed of 30 inches in diameter, perfectly solid. This is to serve as the breech of the gun, and the end is upset by a horizontal steam hammer until it is perfectly even and true. After this the gun is built up of sections of the full size (circumference) of the gun, of about five inches in length,— the entire gun (14 feet long when completed) being composed of 30 transverse sections. These sections are made up as follows: A cylindrical block of the best refined iron is turned out seven inches long, ten inches in diameter, and with a 4-inch hole through its length. This is fitted closely into an iron band or hoop made from bars of iron six by seven inches; and this is again fitted into another band of three inches in thickness. These bands are closely welded, and as solid as the best mechanism can make them. When thus put together it will be seen that the whole forms a cylindrical section (or wheel) of 30 inches in diameter: the greater length being near the center. The hole at the center permits the impurities of the metal to be worked out from the inner rings, while being heated and hammered, while the scales which may accumulate on the outer rings, are permitted to fall outward as the weld extends towards the circumference.

The trials made with guns thus constructed, have, it is reported, been most successful. With 20 pounds of powder and 150 pounds of shell, with an elevation of 15°, a range of about four miles is attained; and with an elevation of 23¼°, a range of nearly seven miles.

Guns vs. Armor. — Mr. Fairbairn, the celebrated engineer, stated to the British Association at its last meeting that the conclusion he had arrived at from all the experiments made in England in relation to guns and armor, was "that no ship can be made to carry plates sufficient to withstand our guns, and it would probably be better to have no plating at all. We should thus have ships more lively in the water and better adapted for manœuvring and at far less cost."

English Views of Gun-Cotton.—As has been stated in a previous article in this volume, the report of the French chemists and military men, in reference to the use of gun-cotton as a substitute for gunpowder, has not been favorable; but from a Committee report, presented at the British Association, September, 1864, by Mr. Scott Russell, it appears that opposite conclusions have been arrived at by the English experimenters. Mr. Russell stated that General Hay, of the Hythe School of Musketry, had constructed a new form of cartridge suited for the Whitworth rifle; that he had found that the use of gun-cotton was cleanly, and had not the disadvantage of fouling the gun; that it had much less recoil, although the effect was the same; that one-third of the weight of charge was the equivalent proportion, and that it did not heat the gun. The General had fired at a target with gun-cotton at 500 yards. Twelve successive shots were all placed in a space one foot wide by two feet high, and the value of the practice was measured by the fact that the mean radius of deviation from the center was between nine and ten inches. Thus, therefore, the use of gun-cotton in musketry had been proved by English made gun-cotton in English rifles by an English general, to perform all that had been reported concerning the Austrian gun-cotton.

The next application of gun-cotton made during the past year was to the driving of tunnels, shafts, and drifts in connection with engineering work. It had been stated by the Committee that $\frac{1}{4}$ of the weight of charge of cotton was equal in blasting effect to gunpowder, and this had been proved in practice in a number of instances. At Wingerworth colliery, in driving a shaft through soft but solid rock, $\frac{1}{18}$ of the weight of gun-cotton as compared to gunpowder, and in the slate quarries at Llamberis, at Allan Heads, $\frac{1}{4}$ were required. At Allan Heads, in some lead mines, a tunnel was being driven seven miles long. The drift was seven feet by five in the hardest limestone. Both ends were worked with gun-cotton fired by an electric battery. The great advantage experienced was that the air was not contaminated by smoke, and that the work could be carried on more rapidly. The next application of it had been to the detaching of large masses of rock. This had been tried in several places, and it was found that one pound of gun-cotton was able to detach from 30 to 60 tons of rock.

Mr. F. A. Abel added some remarks on the chemical condition and manufacture of gun-cotton. He stated that the manufacture of it was much safer and more uniform than that of gunpowder, and when made its stability is permanent and could be relied on. He believed the Report of the French chemists against its permanency was founded on experiments made with imperfectly manufactured material. Working with large quantities during the last twelve months, he was satisfied it did possess permanence, though he stated that under certain conditions of packing and exposure to too high a temperature a slight change did take place; this he believed arose from some foreign ingredients in the cotton.

NATURAL PHILOSOPHY.

THE UNIVERSAL METAMORPHOSIS.

If a wafer be laid on a surface of polished metal, which is then breathed upon, and if, when the moisture of the breath has evaporated, the wafer be shaken off, we shall find that the whole polished surface is not as it was before, although our senses can detect no difference; for if we breathe again upon it the surface will be moist everywhere except on the spot previously sheltered by the wafer, which will now appear as a spectral image on the surface. Again and again we breathe, and the moisture evaporates, but still the spectral wafer reappears. This experiment succeeds after a lapse of many months, if the metal be carefully put aside where its surface cannot be disturbed. If a sheet of paper on which a key has been laid be exposed for some minutes to the sunshine, and then instantaneously viewed in the dark, the key being removed, a fading spectre of the key will be visible. Let this paper be put aside for many months where nothing can disturb it, and then in darkness be laid on a plate of hot metal,—the spectre of the key will again appear. In the case of bodies more highly phosphorescent than paper, the spectres of many different objects which may have been laid on it in succession will, on warming, emerge in their proper order. This is equally true of our bodies and our minds. We are involved in the universal metamorphosis. Nothing leaves us wholly as it found us. Every man we meet, every book we read, every picture or landscape we see, every word or tone we hear, mingles with our being and modifies it. There are cases on record of ignorant women, in states of insanity, uttering Greek and Hebrew phrases, which in past years they have heard their masters utter, without, of course, comprehending them. These tones had long been forgotten; the traces were so faint that, under ordinary conditions, they were invisible; but these traces were there, and in the intense light of cerebral excitement they started into prominence, just as the spectre image of the key started into sight on the application of heat. It is thus with all the influences to which we are subjected.—*Cornhill Magazine*.

CONSTITUTION OF MATTER.

Some speculative ideas by M. Graham, the master of the mint, appear in a late number of the *Philosophical Magazine*. He says: " In the condition of gas, matter is deprived of numerous and varying properties with which it appears invested when in the form of a liquid or solid. The gas exhibits only a few grand and simple features. These, again, may also be dependent upon atomic or molecular mobility. Let us imagine one kind of substance only to exist,—ponderable matter; and, further, that matter is divisible into ultimate atoms, uniform

112

in size and weight. We shall have one substance and one common atom. With the atom at rest, the uniformity of matter would be perfect; but the atom always possesses more or less motion due, it must be assumed, to a primordial impulse. This motion gives rise to volume. The more rapid this movement, the greater the space occupied by the atom, somewhat as the orbit of a planet widens with the degree of projectile velocity. Matter is thus made to differ only in being lighter or denser matter. The specific motion of an atom being inalienable, light matter is no longer convertible into heavy matter. In short, matter of different density forms different substances, different incontrovertible elements, as they have been considered." "This is not meant to be applied to the gaseous volumes which we have occasion to measure and deal with practically, but to a lower order of molecules or atoms. The gaseous molecule must itself be viewed as composed of a group or system of the above-mentioned inferior atoms, following as a unit, but similar to those which regulate its constituent atom." We must refer our readers for details and for the results of M. Graham's interesting speculations, merely adding another expression of his hypothesis: "As in the theory of light we have the alternative hypothesis of emission and undulation, so in molecular mobility the motion may be assumed to reside either in separate atoms and molecules or in a fluid medium caused to undulate. A special rate of vibration, or pulsation, originally imparted to a portion of the fluid medium enlivens that portion of matter with an individual existence and constitutes it a distinct substance or element.

THE TRANSITIONS OF MATTER.

From a discourse recently delivered before the New York Academy of Medicine, by that eminent scientist Dr. John W. Draper, we make the following interesting and suggestive extract:—

No one can devote himself to the study of physical science and especially of Chemistry without experiencing at once what might seem to be contradictory sentiments,—pride and self-humiliation. Pride, that he has been permitted to see so far as he does into the great scheme of the universe; humiliation, in recognizing how frail and insignificant he is.

What, then, are some of the latest truths that these physical senses teach? They show us how transitory, how dependent we are. There is a constant wear and tear of the human system. Particles that served the purpose of forming it accomplish their office and die, and are replaced in due succession by others. In this respect life is the result of an aggregate of deaths. The atmospheric air into which all this dismissed material eventually finds its way, is thus the cemetery of animal substance, of things that have once been organized, but that have lost their force, and lapsed into an inorganic, a lifeless state. From this inorganic, this lifeless state, such substances are destined to be recalled; for, under the influence of the rays of the sun, carbonic acid and water and ammonia are decomposed, and taking the products that arise from that operation, plants group them into organized portions again, and use them in the construction of their various parts, leaves, flowers, stems, fruits. Plants thus constitute the formative agents of the world of life. Animals are the destroyers. They

10*

organize, we consume; and thus it is that the same material oscillates back and forth, now a part of a plant, now a part of an animal, now in the air, and now in a plant again. It runs through cycle after cycle, ever returning to the point whence it set out, and ever setting out again.

We are not, then, the special or exclusive proprietors of the substance of which we are composed. Equally may the plant, and equally any animal, no matter how humble in the scale of life it may be, lay claim to it. We are bound to them and they to us by an indissoluble tie.

If that is the lesson we derive from our best knowledge of the mutations that happen to the plastic material which the hand of nature fashions into so many beautiful forms, we are brought to the same conclusion by a consideration of the physical forces with which she invigorates it,—the heat possessed by the different animal tribes, cold-blooded or hot, in their special degree, the chemical affinities and the electrical powers that preside over all the thousand combinations and decompositions perpetually occurring in the inmost recesses of the economy. "In a waterfall which maintains its place and appearance unchanged for many years, the constituent portions that have been precipitated headlong glide finally and forever away. For the transitory matter to exhibit a permanent form it is necessary that there should be a perpetual supply and also a perpetual removal. So long as the jutting ledge over which the waters rush and the broken gulf below that receives them remain unchanged, the cataract presents the same appearance. But variations in them mold it into a new shape. Its color changes with a clear or cloudy sky. The rainbow seen in its spray disappears when the beams of the sun are withdrawn. So in that collection of substance which constitutes an animal, whatever may be its position high or low in the realm of life, there is a perpetual introduction of new material and a perpetual departure of the old. It is a form rather than an individual that we see. Its permanence depends altogether on the permanence of the external conditions. If they change it also changes, and a new form is the result."

An animal is, therefore, a form, through which material substance is visibly passing, and suffering transmutation into new products. In that act of transmutation, force is disengaged. That which we call its life is the display of the manner in which the force thus disengaged is expended.

A scientific examination of animal life must include two primary facts. It must consider whence and in what manner the stream of material substance has been derived, in what manner and whither it passes away, and since force cannot be created from nothing, and is in its very nature indestructible, it must determine from what source that which is displayed by animals has been obtained, in what manner it is employed, and what disposal is made of it eventually. The force thus expended is originally derived from the sun. Plants are the intermedium for its conveyance. For the sake of obtaining it, we use them as food. And here again remarks apply similar to those we have made respecting material substance. The correlation and conservation of force holds good. The assertion of the great Spanish Mohammedan, Overroes, is confirmed by all modern science, that the sum total of force in the world is ever the same, though it is parted among myriads of individuals, who draw from a common fountain their requisite supplies.

The body that we have to-day is not the body we had yesterday; we shall change it again before to-morrow. In the course of a year a man requires a ton and a half of material—that is, nearly twenty times his own weight—to repair his wasting organs, and to discharge his vital functions. In that short space of time, the human family alone casts into the atmosphere 1,800,000,000 of tons, and we are but a little fraction of the vast aggregate of animal life which all in its proper proportion is doing the same thing.

From nature, which at this point of view presents us such an enchanting picture, let us turn to ourselves. Physiology rivals Natural Philosophy in the splendor and profound interest of its discoveries. We tremble on the brink of detecting the interior constitution of man. Will you hear me patiently while I give an example of what I mean? No event has ever taken place in the world without spontaneously leaving a recoverable impression of itself. The hand that wrote those words has cast its shadow on the paper. A century hence, if the paper should endure, that shadow might be made visible to the eye. But moralists say, "What is more transitory than a shadow?" They find in it an emblem of things of a fleeting nature. When the light, or the object that has obstructed it, is withdrawn, the shadow "fleeth away and continueth not." A sundial, that has been telling the hours of the day, presents an unblemished surface when evening comes. Each morning it is ready for its task. The traces of the past seem all to have disappeared, but in truth they still exist, buried in the marble or the metal out of which the dial is made.

They who have visited the dark rooms of photographers know very well what I mean. The portraits of our friends, or landscape views, may be hidden, and invisible to the eye, but ready to make their appearance as soon as proper means are resorted to, such as heat, or vapor of mercury, or sulphate of iron, or pyrogallic acid. Shadows are not such transitory things as men commonly suppose. In the case of photography, we happen to know the proper means for development. The fact of chief interest to us is the imperishability of the primitive impression. A spectre is concealed on a silver or glassy surface, until by our necromancy we make it come forth to the visible world. Upon the walls of our private apartments, where we think that the eye of intrusion is altogether shut out, and our retirement can never be profaned, there exist the vestiges of all our acts, silent but speaking silhouettes of whatever we have done. Can we say that among those phantoms there are not some on which we should be reluctant to have the cunning chemist try his art, and leave them, as the photographers say, fixed: some from which we should dread to hear the demand of the phantom of Endor, "Why hast thou disquieted me to bring me up?"

If men were sure that their most secret doings were at such a risk would not the world be better than it is? A sunbeam or a shadow cannot fall upon a surface, no matter of what material that surface is composed, without leaving upon it an indelible impression, and an impression, which may, by subsequent application of proper chemical agents, be made visible. In many cases we have ascertained what the appropriate agent is; our failure in others is due to the imperfection of our knowledge, and not to any impossibility in the operation. Time seems to have so little influence on these effects, that I can conceive it possible, if a new vault should hereafter be opened in the midst of an Egyptian pyramid, for us to conjure up the swarthy forms of the Pharaonic officials who were its last visitors, though forty centuries may have elapsed since their departure.

But let us see how these facts bear, in a most important manner, in the case of man.

If after the eyelids have been closed for some time, as when we first awake in the mornnig, we suddenly and steadfastly gaze at a brightly illuminated object, and then quickly close the lids again, a phantom image is perceived in the infinite darkness before us. We may satisfy ourselves that this is not a fiction of the imagination, but a reality; for many details that we had not time to examine in the momentary glance, may be contemplated at our leisure in the phantom. We may thus make out the pattern of such an object as a lace curtain hanging in the window, or the branches of a tree beyond. By degrees the image becomes less and less distinct; in a minute or two it has disappeared. It seems to have a tendency to float away in the vacancy before us. If you attempt to follow it by moving the eyeball, it suddenly vanishes.

"Now the condition that regulates the vanishing phantom-images on the retina is, that when they have declined in vigor to less than $\frac{1}{64}$ of the intensity they had while in presence of the object that formed them; they cease to disturb the sight. This principle is illustrated when a candle-flame is held opposite to the sun, or any light having more than 64 times its own brilliancy. It then ceases to be visible. The most exact of all known methods for measuring light—that by the extinction of shadows—is an application of the same principle.

"But the great fact that concerns us is this: Such a duration of impressions on the retina of the eye demonstrates that the effect of external influences on nerve vesicles is not necessarily transitory. It may continue for a long time. In this there is a correspondence to the duration, the emergence, the extinction of impressions on photographic preparations. Thus I have seen landscapes and architectural views taken in Mexico, 'developed'—as artists say—months subsequently; the images coming out, after the long voyage, in all their proper forms and in all their contrast of light and shade. The photograph had forgotten nothing. It had equally preserved the contour of the everlasting mountains and the passing smoke of a bandit fire.

"Are there then contained in the brain more permanently, as in the retina more transiently, the vestiges of impressions that have been gathered by the sensory organs? Do these constitute the basis of memory—the mind contemplating such pictures of past things and events as have been committed to her custody. In her silent galleries are there hung micrographs of the living and the dead, of scenes that we have visited, of incidents in which we have borne a part? Are these abiding impressions mere signal-marks, like the letters of a book, which impart ideas to the mind, or are they actual picture-images, inconceivably smaller than those made for us by artists, in which, by the aid of a microscope, we can see, in a space not bigger than a pin-hole a whole family group at a glance?

"The phantom-images of the retina, as I have remarked, are not perceptible in the light of day. Those that exist in the sensorium, in like manner, do not attract our attention so long as the sensory organs are in vigorous operation, and occupied with bringing new impressions in. But when these organs become weary and dull, or when we experience hours of great anxiety, or are in twilight reveries, or asleep, the latent apparitions have their vividness increased by the contrast, and obtrude themselves on the mind. For the same reason they occupy us in the delirium of fevers, and doubtless also in the solemn moments of death. During a third part of our lives we are withdrawn from external influences,—hearing, and sight, and the other senses are inactive; but the never-sleeping mind,—that pensive, that veiled enchantress, in her mysterious retirement, looks over the ambrotypes she has collected,—ambrotypes, for they are unfading impressions, —and combining them together as they chance to occur, weaves from them a web of dreams. Nature has thus introduced into our very organization a means of imparting to us suggestions on some of the most profound topics with which we can be concerned. It operates equally on the savage and on the civilized man, furnishing to both conceptions of a world in which all is unsubstantial. It marvelously extracts from the vestiges of the impressions of the past overwhelming proofs of the reality of the future, and gathering its power from what might seem a most unlikely source, it insensibly leads us—no matter who or where we may be—to a profound belief in the immortal and imperishable, from phantoms that have scarcely made their appearance before they are ready to vanish away!"

APPARATUS FOR MEASURING THE VELOCITY OF PROJECTILES.

The following is a description of an electro-ballistic apparatus, recently invented by Major Navez of the Belgium army for measuring a very small space of time, such, for instance, as a cannon-ball would take in passing over a few yards. Before we proceed to explain this interesting machine, it will be necessary to remind our readers that an electric current has the property of magnetizing soft iron, and also, to mention the peculiar principle of the pendulum. This is, that the same pendulum will always, within certain limits, perform unequal vibrations in equal times,—that is to say, that a "seconds" pendulum will always take a second to make one oscillation, whether it be raised from the perpendicular 20° or 5°. Consequently, supposing a seconds pendulum to be selected we can take the arc it describes in one vibration, and, by dividing this arc into a scale of parts, we can arrest the pendulum as it falls; and the distance it has fallen, measured into the whole length of the arc, will give the fraction of a second in which the fall took place. We see then, with what extreme minuteness we can measure time by stopping the seconds pendulum before it has fallen the $\frac{1}{1000}$ part of an arc in which it would vibrate. The electro-ballistic apparatus is used for determining the velocity of a projectile, or the rate at which a shot proceeds after it leaves the muzzle of a gun. The instrument consists of three separate parts, one of which is a principal and the others accessories. The chief part consists of a graduated arc, on which a pendulum is so adjusted that it can be arrested at any period of its oscillation, and thus denote the time it has taken to fall.   The pendulum, before an observation, is held suspended at the left extremity of the arc, by means of a piece of soft iron in the center of the bob, which is magnetized by an electric current through an electro-magnet at the point of support.   Connected with this magnet are two insulated wires, which pass away for 200 or 300 yards, and terminate by the ends being wound across an upright screen, 30 feet in front of the gun, where the ends are joined, so that the electric current is complete.   Another instrument is employed, called the conjunctor, and performs the following office : At the top of it is an electro-magnet, which is connected by wires .with the second screen, 120 feet in front of the first, i. e. 150 feet from the gun.   These wires are insulated with gutta-percha, &c., so that they may be either buried in the ground or hung on posts.   The electro-magnet in the conjunctor retains a small weight suspended over a cup of mercury.   This has a steel blade above it, with a pin so arranged that if the weight falls it presses it into the mercury.   The pendulum has an index or duplicate pendulum in rear, which is so attached to it by a light spring that it will fall and oscillate with the pendulum proper.   Behind the machine is a large electro-magnet, which has power to attract this index when magnetized.

Upon the gun being fired, the projectile cuts the wires of the first screen, and thus demagnetizes the electro-magnet which holds up the pendulum.   This latter commences to fall, and the index needle with it, along the graduated arc.   When the second, screen is cut through by the shot, the electro-magnet at the top of the conjunctor is demagnetized, and the weight falls into the mercury, pressing down the steel blade, and completes another electric circuit, which magnetizes the large magnet in the rear of the pendulum, and clamps the index needle against the scale on the arc.   The operator then reads off the scale the distance which is marked by the index, and the time thus measured is that which the shot took to pass through the screens, minus the time necessary for the weight to fall in the conjunctor, and which the operator, before commencing, finds by means of the disjunctor.   A table has been prepared which shows the time for the pendulum to fall down any arc from 0 to 150°, and only needs to be referred to for any arc through which it falls when used as above.   The time thus given has only to be divided into the distance between the screens, and the result will be the velocity of the projectile.   By this contrivance a skillful operator is able to measure pretty accurately to the $\frac{3}{1000}$ part of a second.   Such wonderful precision renders this instrument most valuable for artillery scientific purposes ; and many most important problems have been solved by its use.

PRODUCTION OF SOUND BY ELECTRICITY.

The following communication from Prof. Thomson, the well known English scientist, is published in the *London Chemical Gazette :—*

Yesterday evening, when engaged in measuring the electrostatic capacities of some specimens of insulated wire designed for submarine telegraph cables, I had occasion frequently to discharge through a galvanometer coil, a condenser consisting of two parallel plates of metal, separated by a space of air about ·007 inch across, and charged to a difference of potentials equal to that of about 800 Daniell's elements.   I remarked at an instant of discharge a sharp sound, with a very slight prolonged resonance, which seemed to come from the interior of the case containing the condenser, and which struck me as resembling a sound I had repeatedly heard before when the condenser had been overcharged and a spark passed across its air-space. But I ascertained that this sound was distinctly audible when there was no spark within the condenser, and the whole discharge took place fairly through the 2,000 yards of fine wire, constituting the galvanometer coil. I arranged the circuit so that the place where the contact was made to produce the discharge was so far from my ear that the initiating spark was inaudible; but still I heard distinctly the same sound as before from within the condenser.

Using instead of the galvanometer coil either a short wire or my own body (as in taking a shock from a Leyden phial), I still heard the sound within the condenser. The shock was imperceptible except by a very faint prick on the finger in the place of the spark, and (the direct sound of the spark being barely, if at all sensible) there was still a very audible sound, always of the same character, within the condenser, which I heard at the same instant as I felt the spark on my finger. Mr. Macfarlane could hear it distinctly standing at a distance of several yards. We watched for light within the condenser, but could see none. I have since ascertained that suddenly charging the condenser out of one of the specimens of cable charged for the purpose produces the same sound within the condenser; also that it is produced by suddenly reversing the charge of the condenser.

Thus it is distinctly proved that a plate of air emits a sound on being suddenly subjected to electric force, or on experiencing a sudden change of electric force through it. This seems a most natural result when viewed in connection with the new theory put forward by Faraday in his series regarding the part played by air or other dielectric in manifestations of electric force. It also tends to confirm the hypothesis I suggested to account for the remarkable observation made regarding lightning, when you told me of it about a year ago, and other similar observations, which I believe, have been reported, proving a sound to be heard at the instant of a flash of lightning in localities at considerable distances from any part of the line of discharge, and which by some have been supposed to demonstrate an error in the common theory of sound. I may add that Mr. Macfarlane tells me he believes he has heard, at the instant of a flash of lightning, a sound as of a heavy body striking the earth, and imagined at first that something close to him had been struck, but heard the ordinary thunder at a sensible time later.

INTERESTING ELECTRICAL PHENOMENA.

Prof. Piazzi Smyth recently sent to the British Journal of Photography a photographic picture, accompanied by the following note. On the 21st of July, I was trying the qualities of some newly-prepared dry plates by taking a window view of house-tops, and was surprised to find every chimney top surmounted by a black streak or brush; i. e. black in the negative, and therefore indicating light. Nothing of the kind was visible to the naked eye in the scene itself, as a really existent fact, nor was any similar appearance visible on the ground-glass of the camera. The appearance, therefore, did not result from any bad action of the lens, which is a very good one.

The stop employed was a small one (0·3 inch), and the definition of the developed picture was extremely sharp.   Again : the appearance could not be caused by smoke coming from the chimneys, because that would hardly have been luminous ; not $\frac{1}{10}$ of the whole chimneys could have had fires below them, and either smoke or rarefied air would have drifted with the wind, which was blowing sensibly at the time, whilst the dark rays went upward straight as arrows. Again : that the chimneys as chimneys, had nothing to do with it, was shown by a similar brush or ray appearing at the top of a certain little ventilator in the roof of one of the houses shown, and not out of the parts emitting air, but from the ornamental spike at the top.

This circumstance convinced me at the time that the phenomenon was an electrical one, invisible to the eye, but abundantly visible or sensible to the photographic camera, and the occasion was perfectly agreeable thereto ; for it was at the conclusion of a week of unusually hot, calm weather, and the sky had that morning become clouded with forms of clouds eminently electrical.   Happily the thunder-storm did not break in this neighborhood, being wafted away elsewhere ; but had it broken here, the photograph tells exactly *where* the lightning was preparing to come down ; and there is one tall iron chimney in the view, with the strongest ray of the whole above it, showing that that would certainly have been struck in preference to its neighbors, and, if unprovided with metal communication to the earth and water, would infallibly have caused mischief to the house to which it is attached.

I have sent a second plate, taken six days afterward, when east wind and rain had disposed of all the electricity that had been brewing in the air ; and it will be seen that, although it is the same view, taken with the same camera, and with the same sort of tannin dry plate, there are no electrical brushes, or black rays, surmounting the chimney pots.

ELECTRICITY FOR LIGHTING GAS.

Messrs. Cornelius & Baker of Philadelphia, have recently patented and introduced a very beautiful method of *lighting gas* by means of frictional *electricity*, arranged for use with a bracket, two portable lighters, and a table light, all being simple in arrangement and readily kept in order.

These instruments are constructed upon the principle of the electrophorus.

The electric *bracket* is arranged with a brass cup in the form of a vase, resting upon the bracket, with a connecting piece of hard rubber. This cup is lined with lamb-skin covered with silk, and contains the hard rubber electric piece, which corresponds in form to the inside of the cup. A coiled wire connects the cup with a wire attached to the burner, and terminating just above the burner.

In order to light the gas, the stop is turned, the hard rubber piece lifted partly from the cup, thus liberating the spark and lighting the gas.

The *Portable Lighter* consists of the same vase or cup, with the addition of a non-conducting handle.   When the brass cup is lifted from the electric piece, and held to the conducting wire of the burner, the gas is immediately lighted.

Another portable instrument called *Double Air-Tight Electrophorus,* consists of two metallic tubes, each closed at one end, and connecting together at the other, with a non-conducting ring of hard rubber, the inside being lined with lamb-skin. A hard rubber rod is placed within them, the length of one of the tubes, and fitting them so as to move somewhat freely from end to end. When the movable piece inside is allowed to fall to one end, and the tube is raised to the connecting wire of the burner, this piece changes its place again, falling into the tube held by the hand. The spark leaves the upper end of the tube at the same time and lights the gas.

The *Table Light Burner* consists of the same instrument, arranged upon a pivot regularly attached to the pillar light.—*Am. Gas Light Journal.*

ELECTRICAL PROPERTIES OF PYROXILINE-PAPER AND GUN-COTTON.

Prof. Johnston, of the Wesleyan University, Middletown, Conn., in a recent note to the editors of *Silliman's Journal,* calls attention to a remarkable power in pyroxiline-paper of producing positive electrical excitement in sulphur, sealing-wax, &c. His note is as follows : " We are told by writers on electricity that sulphur by friction with all other substances becomes *negatively* excited ; as cat's fur, on the other extreme, by friction with all other substances becomes excited *positively.* But a few days ago I made the discovery that sulphur by friction with paper-pyroxiline (I will call it) is excited with positive electricity, as are also sealing-wax, amber, &c. The paper is prepared in the same manner as gun-cotton, which would also in all probability be found to possess the same property."

Prof. Silliman further adds, in relation to this topic : " I have repeated and confirmed Prof. Johnston's experiment, extending it to gun-cotton. I find as he suggests that the latter substance produces the same excitement of positive electricity which is produced by the pyroxiline-paper. The most energetic effects are produced when vulcanized India-rubber is the electric. The opposite effects in this substance produced by flannel and the gun-cotton or pyroxiline-paper are very striking, and will form a good lecture-room illustration. These substances also produce powerful positive excitement in glass. It is difficult from the use of pith balls alone to determine which produces the most powerful positive excitement, glass or hard rubber, when excited by gun-cotton or pyroxiline-paper. This seeming anomaly, confounding our ordinary means of discrimination in cases of electrical excitement demands further investigation. It would appear that of negative electrics yet observed, these azotized species of cellulose are the most remarkable,—in comparison with which the most highly negative electrics hitherto known become positive."

NEW FORM OF ELECTRIC LIGHT.

Prof. Seely, of New York, has recently obtained a patent for an electric light, which is claimed to be more economical and effective than any of the methods hitherto devised. He employs the current generated by an ordinary frictional electrical machine, and obtains the light by interrupting the current. It has long been known that a very brilliant and steady light might be procured in this way, but the objection to its use is the uncertainty in the action of the frictional

11

machine. Dry air is a very poor conductor of electricity, and when a machine is excited in such an atmosphere the electricity will remain in tension for a considerable time. But moisture in the air conducts the electricity away, and when the moisture reaches a certain point the fluid is removed so rapidly that the machine will not work. Prof. Seely's invention consists in devices for making the action continuous in all weathers. This is effected by surrounding the machine with a glass case, and keeping the air within the case dry by means of chloride of calcium or other hygroscopic substance. It has been observed that when the conductor of an electric current is interrupted in a way to draw a spark across the break, the brilliancy of the spark varies with the material by which the conductor is terminated at the break. Prof. Seely is now engaged in experiments to ascertain what material will produce the most intense light.

If the apparatus works according to anticipation a cotton mill may be lighted without any current expense, except the small power required to turn the electrical machines. As in mills driven by water there is always a surplus of power during the winter months, the only time when lights are required, there would be no expense for this light except the first cost of the apparatus, which would be quite moderate. — *Scientific American.*

Fishing by the Electric Light. — An experiment has been recently made at Dunkirk, France, to use the electric light in fishing at night. The light was supplied by a pile on Bunsen's principle, composed of about 50 elements, and it succeeded tolerably well, but the employment of the pile was attended with much inconvenience. It was then determined to repeat the attempt with a magneto-electric machine. The new experiments tried at Dunkirk and Ostend had a double object — 1, to prove how the light produced by the machine would act under water; and, 2, to discover the effect the light would produce on the fish. The first object was completely accomplished, and it is now demonstrated that magneto-electric machines and the light they produce are applicable to all submarine works. In fact, this light was constant at 180 ft. under water, and it extended over a large surface. The machine, nevertheless, was placed at a distance of more than 300 ft. from the regulator of the electric light. The glass sides of the lantern remained perfectly transparent, and the quantity of coal consumed was less than if it were in the open air.

THE ELECTRIC FLY.

Mr. Charles Tomlinson communicates to the *Philosophical Journal* an interesting account of many experiments made by him with the little instrument used in connection with an electrical machine called the electric fly, or mill, or *tourniquet,* which is formed of two or more metallic radial arms, having their extremities bent at right angles and brought to a fine point. As a preliminary explanation why he has made these experiments, he gives various opinions of philosophers as to the cause of its action. After detailing its backward revolutions in the open air and under a glass vase, its inaction in rarefied air, its increased action in turpentine, benzole, and paraffine oils in both directions, and its forward motion in the air after a modification of its points, he concludes, while inclining to the opinion of Cavello as a general explanation, "that the theory of the fly requires a different expression for an aerial as compared with a liquid dielectric, its behavior is also different in air of different densities : and also when wholly and partially inclosed ; also, when the points are covered ; and even then there is a difference in action, in the presence of flame," from which we infer that its behavior is so modified by circumstances that no one expression represents the law governing its action.

ELECTRICITY IN THE TREATMENT OF HYDROPHOBIA.

The *Journal de Physique* contains a remarkable case of recovery from hydrophobia by galvanism, extracted from a "Report presented to the Academy of Turin," by Signor Eandi. A man presenting all the symptoms of hydrophobia (he had been bitten by a mad dog) was brought to Dr. Rossi, who, observing that he could not bear the sight of water, nor that even of shining bodies, provided in another room a pile consisting of 50 pairs of plates of silver and zinc, intermixed with 50 pieces of pasteboard moistened with a solution of muriate of ammonia. He employed slips of brown paper moistened, as a conductor on which the naked feet of the patient were placed, and at the moment when he opened his mouth to bite, one end of the arc was thrust into it, while the other communicated with the pile. The patient suffered a great deal from this operation, which, after several shocks, weakened him so much that he could no longer support it. Being stretched out on the floor, he was then galvanized with ease ; the operation made the sweat run from him in drops. This treatment was continued for several days, and resulted in the complete recovery of the patient. This cure, says the report, was effected in the presence of several persons. This was about 12 years ago, if I mistake not. The experiments lately made at the Hospital of Lernberg were satisfactory in so far as the application of electricity had the effect of procuring a temporary relief, though the patients were not saved thereby. Dr. Essrogen, who relates this fact in the *Zeitschrift für practische Heilkunde*, is of opinion that had the application of electricity been continued, a complete cure would have been brought about.—*Phil. Med. and Surg. Rep.*

NEW CALORIC BATTERY.

At a late meeting of the Inventor's Institute, Mr. James Dickson read an interesting paper on "Certain Inventions for inducing the Economical and Efficient Production of Voltaic Electricity for lighting Streets and other Purposes." The object of the paper was to explain the means by which electricity could be readily and economically produced. The history of Voltaic Electricity was carefully traced from the time of Volta, from whom this form of electricity took its name, to the present time, special mention being made of Grove's, Snell's, the Maynooth and other batteries, which from time to time have been looked upon as vast improvements upon their existing apparatus. The theories of Mayer & Joule were referred to, as well as the researches of Prof. Tyndall, whose "Heat as a Mode of Motion" contains so much valuable information on the subject. He considered that the rapidity of the vibration of the atoms in a conductor was exactly in proportion to its conducting power, and explained that, whilst a battery was producing light and heat, less

material was consumed than when the battery poles are directly connected with each other.   Mr. Dickson's battery was described as one of
the hot class,—the sulphuric acid was heated to 600° Fahrenheit.   He
claims, by his mode of applying heat, to be able to use iron and other
cheap metals, instead of the dear ones, zinc, copper, &c.   The relative
mobility of the atoms of an electrolite determined, he considered its force
rather than its specific gravity.   When oil of vitriol was heated to 350° Fahr.
only, the electric action is less powerful than when heated to 600° Fahr.,
probably owing to the waves being less rapid.   With the necessary percolating apparatus he was convinced that his battery would be successful
for lighthouse purposes.   He considered 15 of his cells equal to 20 ordinary cells; three of his cells are not equal to two of nitric acid cells, but
the increment in his battery was greater.   Grove's battery cost 1s. 5d.
to produce the same amount of electricity as that produced for 10 ½d.
by Dickson's.   Comparing the lighting powers, 11 ½d. with the caloric
battery, will produce the same amount of light as 1s. 5d. by Grove's.
He declared that the sulphur liberated at the negative poles could be
converted into sulphuric acid to the extent of $\frac{1}{2}\frac{2}{3}$.   The oil of vitriol
during the working of the battery, becomes combined with water, but
the acid is easily and cheaply reconcentrated.   In Snell's, Daniell's, and
Grove's battery, the sulphate of zinc cannot be recovered, whilst in his
caloric battery the recovery was not difficult.   The chairman expressed
the fear that the inventor promised so much that he was no more likely
to perform it than to obtain perpetual motion; indeed, if the invention
were not overstated, they would certainly be nearer perpetual motion
than they have ever been before.   Mr. Varley suggested that as the
principal feature in the invention appeared to be the heating of the materials, it was not impossible that it might be as great a step in advance
as the introduction of the hot-blast in the manufacture of iron : this of
course remained to be seen.—*London Mechanics' Magazine.*

ILLUSTRATIONS OF MAGNETIC ACTION.

The following is a partial report of a lecture recently delivered
before the Royal Institution of London, by Prof. Tyndall, "On some
of the Phenomena of Magnetism" :—

The Crackle of Magnetized Iron.—Here is a fine permanent magnet, competent to carry a great weight.   Here, for example, is a dish
of iron nails, which it is able to empty.   At the other side of the
table you observe another mass of metal, bent like the magnet, but
not, like it, naked.   This mass, however, is not steel, but iron, and it
is surrounded by coils of copper wire.   It is intended to illustrate
the excitement of magnetism by electricity.   At the present moment
this huge bent bar is so inert as to be incapable of carrying a single
grain of iron.   I now send an electric current through the coils that
surround it, and its power far transcends that of the steel magnet on
the other side.   It can carry 50 times the weight.   It holds a 56 lb.
weight attached to each of its poles, and it empties this large tray of
iron nails when they are brought sufficiently near it.   I interrupt the
current : the power vanishes and the nails fall.

Now the magnetized iron cannot be in all respects the same as the
unmagnetized iron.   Some change must take place among the molecules of the iron bar at the moment of magnetization.   And one

curious action which accompanies the act of magnetization I will now try to make sensible to you. Other men labored, and we are here entering into their labors. The effect I wish to make manifest was discovered by Mr. Joule, and was subsequently examined by MM. De la Rive, Wertheim, Marian, Matteucci, and Wartmann. It is this. At the moment when the current passes through the coil surrounding the electro-magnet, a clink is heard emanating from the body of the iron, and at the moment the current ceases a clink is also heard. In fact, the acts of magnetization and demagnetization so stir the atoms of the magnetized body that they, in their turn, can stir the air and send sonorous impulses to our auditory nerves.

I have said that the sounds occur at the moment of magnetization, and at the moment when magnetization ceases; hence if I can devise a means of making and breaking in quick succession the circuit through which the current flows, I can obtain an equally quick succession of sounds. I do this by means of a contact breaker which belongs to a Ruhmkorff's induction coil. Here is a monochord, and a thin bar of iron stretches from one of its bridges to the other. This bar is placed in a glass tube, which is surrounded by copper wire. I place the contact breaker in a distant room, so that you cannot hear its noise. The current is now active, and every individual in this large assembly hears something between a dry crackle and a musical sound issuing from the bar in consequence of its successive magnetization and demagnetization.

Magnetism of the Electric Current.—Hitherto we have occupied ourselves with the iron which has been acted upon by the current. Let us now devote a moment's time to the examination of the current itself. Here is a naked copper wire which is quite inert, possessing no power to attract these iron filings. I send a voltaic current through it: it immediately grapples with the filings, and holds them round it in a thick envelop. I interrupt the current, and the filings fall. Here is a compact coil of copper wire, which is overspun with cotton to prevent contact between the convolutions. At present the coil is inert; but now I send a current through it: a power of attraction is instantly developed, and you see that it is competent to empty this plate of iron nails.

Thus we have magnetic action exhibited by a body which does not contain a particle of the so-called magnetic metals. The copper wire is made magnetic by the electric current. Indeed, by means of a copper wire, through which a current flows, we may obtain all the effects of magnetism. I have here a long coil, so suspended as to be capable of free motion in a horizontal direction; it can move all round in a circle like an ordinary magnetic needle. At its ends I have placed two spirals of platinum wire, which the current will raise to brilliant incandescence. They are glowing now, and the suspended coil behaves, in all respects, like a magnetic needle. Its two ends show opposite polarities; it can be attracted, and repelled by a magnet, or by a current flowing through another coil; and it is so sensitive that the action of the earth itself is capable of setting it north and south.

Ampere's Theory.—There is an irresistible tendency to unify in the human mind; and, in accordance with our mental constitution, we desire to reduce phenomena which are so much alike to a common

11*

cause. Hence the conception of the celebrated Ampere that a magnet is simply an assemblage of electric currents. Round the atoms of a magnet Ampere supposed minute currents to circulate incessantly in parallel planes; round the atoms of common iron he also supposed them to circulate, but in all directions,—thus neutralizing each other. The act of magnetism he supposed to consist in the rendering of the molecular currents parallel to a common plane, as they are supposed to be in a permanent magnet. This is the celebrated theory of molecular currents propounded by Ampere.

The Lengthening of Iron by Magnetism.—Is it a fact that an iron bar is shortened by the act of magnetization? It is not. And here, as before, we enter into the labors of other men.

Mr. Joule was the first to prove that the bar is lengthened. Mr. Joule rendered this lengthening visible by means of a system of levers and a microscope, through which a single observer saw the action. The experiment has never, I believe, been made before a public audience, but the instrument referred to at the commencement of this lecture, will, I think, enable me to render this effect of magnetization visible to everybody present.

Before you is an iron bar, two feet long, firmly screwed into a solid block of wood. Sliding on two upright brass pillars is a portion of the instrument which you see above the iron bar. The essential parts of this section of the apparatus are, first, a vertical rod of brass, which moves freely and accurately in a long brass collar. The lower end of the brass rod rests upon the upper flat surface of the iron bar. To the top of the brass rod is attached a point of steel; and this point now presses against a plate of agate, near a pivot which forms the fulcrum of a lever. The distant end of the lever is connected by a very fine wire with an axis on which is fixed a small circular mirror. If the steel point be pushed up against the agate plate, the end of the lever is raised; the axis is thereby caused to turn, and the mirror rotates. I now cast a beam from an electric lamp upon the mirror; it is reflected in a luminous sheaf, 15 or 16 feet long, and it strikes our screen, there forming a circular patch of brilliant light. This beam is to be our index; it will move as the mirror moves, only with twice its angular velocity; and the motion of the patch of light will inform us of the lengthening and shortening of the iron bar.

I employ one battery simply to ignite the lamp. I have here a second battery to magnetize the iron bar. At present no current is passing. I make the circuit, and the bright image on the screen is suddenly displaced. It sinks a foot. I break the circuit; the bar instantly shrinks to its normal length, and the image returns to its first position. I made the experiment several times in succession; the result is always the same. Always when I magnetize, the image instantly descends, which declares the lengthening of the bar; always when I interrupt the current the image immediately rises. A little warm water projected against the bar causes the image to descend gradually. This, I believe, is the first time that this action of magnetism has been seen by a public audience.

I have employed the same apparatus in the examination of bismuth bars; and, though considerable power has been applied, I have hitherto failed to produce any sensible effect. It was at least conceivable that complementary effects might be here exhibited, and a new antithesis thus established between magnetism and diamagnetism.

No explanation of this action has, to my knowledge, been offered; and I would now beg to propose one, which seems to be sufficient. I place this large flat magnet upon the table; over it I put a paper screen, and on the screen I shake iron filings. You know the beautiful lines in which those filings arrange themselves,—lines which have become classical from the use made of them in this Institution; for they have been guiding-threads for Faraday's intelligence while exploring the most profound and intricate phenomena of magnetism. These lines indicate the direction in which a small magnetic needle sets itself when placed on any of them. The needle will always be a tangent to the magnetic curve. A little rod of iron, freely suspended, behaves exactly like the needle, and sets its longest dimension in the direction of the magnetic curve. In fact, the particles of iron filings themselves are virtually so many little rods of iron, which, when they are released from the friction of the screen by tapping, set their longest dimensions along the lines of force. Now, in this bar magnet the lines of force run along the magnet itself, and were its particles capable of free motion they also would set their longest dimensions parallel to the lines of force,—that is to say, parallel to the length of the magnet. This, then, is the explanation which I would offer of the lengthening of the bar. The bar is composed of irregular crystalline granules; and, when magnetized, these granules tend to set their longest dimensions parallel to the axis of the bar. They succeed, partially, and produce a microscopic lengthening of the bar, which, suitably magnified, has been rendered visible to you.

But can we not bring a body with movable particles within an electro-magnetic coil? We can; and I will now, in conclusion, show you an experiment devised by Mr. Grove, which bears directly upon this question, but the sight of which, I believe, has hitherto been confined to Mr. Grove himself. At all events, I am not aware of its ever having been made before a large audience. I have here a cylinder with glass ends, and it contains a muddy liquid. This muddiness is produced by the magnetic oxyde of iron which is suspended mechanically in water. Round the glass cylinder I have coiled five or six layers of covered copper wire; and here is a battery from which a current can be sent through the coil. First of all, I place the glass cylinder in the path of the beam from our electric lamp, and, by means of a lens, cast a magnified image of the end of the cylinder on the screen. That image at present possesses but feeble illumination. The light is almost extinguished by the suspended particles of magnetic oxyde. But, if what I have stated regarding the lines of force through the bar of magnetized iron be correct, the particles of the oxyde will suddenly set their longest dimensions parallel to the axis of the cylinder, and also in part set themselves end to end when the current is sent round them. More light will be thus enabled to pass; and now you observe the effect. The moment I establish the circuit the disc upon the screen becomes luminous. I interrupt the current, and gloom supervenes; I re-establish it, and we have a luminous disc once more.

ON THE MECHANICAL THEORY AND APPLICATION OF THE LAWS OF MAGNETIC INDUCTION AND ELECTRICITY.

In a paper on the above subject read before the British Association, at its last meeting, by Mr. J. B. Thomson, electricity and magnetism were considered as a force in the same way as heat and light; and electric and magnetic induction were treated in correspondence with mechanics. The summary of the author's theories is: That the phemomena called electricity and magnetism are two forms of force which may either be in conatus or in act. If in conatus, they are in a state of tension; if in act, then in a state of fluxion. Electricity is in conatus when in the static form of excitation, or when the voltaic circuit is not completed; in act, when the matter highly excited is brought in contact with matter less highly excited, or when the voltaic circuit is completed. Magnetism is in conatus when the magnetic vortical sphere is held constant by a constant electric current, or by hardened steel or magnetic iron ore, so that the earth-magnetism may flow in; in act, on its electric projection and recession, or when iron or some other paramagnetic is moved through this sphere. That electric condution is by certain molecular movements of particular portions of matter. Those wherein this movement is easily excited are called conductors, and those wherein it is with difficulty excited are called insulators. That magnetic conduction is by the symmetrical arrangement into a vortical sphere of spirals of a general medium, which pervades all matter, and holds it in that form for the time being. That particular matter wherein the sphere is easily excited is called paramagnetic, and that wherein it is with more difficulty excited is called diamagnetic. That this sphere can be fixed by means of hardened steel or magnetic iron ore: That the magnetic vortical can be excited by means of spiral currents of electricity generally, and even by a tangent to such spiral. Also it can be induced by magnetic conduction in paramagnetics. .That the magnetic force is only in a state of fluxion on the projection and recession of this sphere. That this sphere is projected in the direction of the exciting electric current, an l recedes in the opposite direction. That the electric force is induced on the projection of the magnetic vortical, and also on its recession. That, consequently, for one inducing current there are two induced currents; therefore, it would appear that by induction electric excitation is multiplied. Finally, that these inductions and conversions of force are in strict accordance with the laws of mechanical motion. In connection with the paper an induction machine was exhibited, the chief points of novelty in which appear to be these: That it is self-acting; the current of voltaic electricity which produces the induced current also drives the machine; that the machine can be so adjusted that the quantity and intensity of the induced current shall range from that of ten Daniell's cells to that of 1,000, and this without employing more than three or four cells. These are valuable properties to electricians who are engaged in experiments with electricity of high or even moderately high tension. Besides, it is applicable to any batteries whatever, having been used experimentally for telegraphy and for electrodepositing. For telegraphy through submarine and subterraneous cables there appears to have been a great objection to induction machines, or rather induction coils. The objection was, that these induction coils sent their electricity through the cables in sudden intense shocks, which injured the insulation of the cable. In this machine it is apparently a continuous flow, and no spark will jump from one electrode to the other, unless first brought in contact, as in batteries. When modified for electro-plating it is much more efficient than the ordinary battery; for though it deposits the metal more slowly on any one article, yet it deposits it much more firmly and with a better surface than the ordinary battery does, and it will deposit the same quantity on 1,000 articles at once, which enables it to deposit ten times more metal in the same time than its own exciting battery would do. The construction of the machine is apparently very simple, and will not be easily deranged or speedily worn out.

ANALYSIS OF MAGNETIC STORMS.

The first analysis of 177 magnetic storms, recently laid before the Royal Society, by the Astronomer Royal, Mr. G. B. Airy, is printed in a late number of the *Proceedings* of the Society. In regard to the physical inference to be derived from the numerical conclusions obtained from tables exhibiting the algebraic sum of fluctuations for each storm, the aggregate or mean for each year, and for seventeen years, the number of irregularities for each year and for the whole period, &c., Mr. Airy expresses his strong opinion that it is impossible to explain the disturbances by the supposition of definite galvanic currents, or definite magnets, produced in any locality whatever. He suggests that the relations of the forces found from his investigations bear a very close resemblance to what might be expected if we conceived a fluid (to which, for facility of language, the name " magnetic ether " is given) in proximity to the earth, to be subject to occasional currents produced by some action, or cessation of action, of the sun, which currents are liable to interruptions or perversions of the same kind as those in air and water. He shows that in air and water the general type of irregular disturbance is traveling circular forms, sometimes with radial currents, but more frequently with tangential currents, sometimes with increase of vertical pressure in the center, but more frequently with decrease of vertical pressure; and, in considering the phenomena which such traveling forms would present to a being over whom they traveled, he thinks that the magnetic phenomena would be in a great measure imitated. Mr. Airy recommends that observations be made at five or six observatories spread over Europe, and would prefer self-registering apparatus, provided that its zeros be duly checked by eye observations, and that the adjustments of the light give sufficient strength to the traces to make them visible in the most violent motions of the magnet.

CURIOUS MAGNETIC DISTURBANCES.

At a recent meeting of the Royal Society, Gen. Sabine brought to notice some remarkable magnetic phenomena recently brought to light by his researches, namely, the difference of direction observed in disturbances of the magnetic declination at stations in England, and others beyond the Ural Mountains. The days and hours at which the phenomena occur are, with slight exception, the same, and the movements are simultaneous, in both localities; but the direction of the magnet indicating the disturbances is directly the reverse in Eastern Siberia of the direction in England.

RESIDUAL MAGNETISM.

Dr. A. Von Waltenhofen has communicated to *Dingler's Polytechnisches Journal*, an account of a curious magnetic discovery which he has recently made. It is a well-known fact that the magnetism of an electro-magnet does not entirely disappear with the cessation of the magnetizing current. Dr. A. Von Waltenhofen has, however, observed that the amount of this residual magnetism, as it is called, is dependent upon the manner in which the current is interrupted. If this interruption takes place suddenly, the residual magnetism is much less than when it takes place gradually. A still more interesting circumstance has been observed by him, viz: that the residual magnetism obtained by suddenly breaking a very strong current, is sometimes of an opposite nature to that previously existing in the electro-magnet. This fact, which he has hitherto only noticed in very soft iron, is of great interest, inasmuch as it furnishes a new and simple proof that magnetism is not caused by the separation of two fluids, but by the motion of magnetic molecules, to which is opposed a certain amount of frictional resistance. With much ingenuity he compares the state of each magnetic molecule of the electro-magnet to that of a spring which is bent back. If the spring be suddenly released, it will return very nearly to its original position, or even go beyond it. On the other hand, if it be released gradually, it will stop at a point still further removed from its original position.

"LIQUID STEERING COMPASS" AND "MONITOR COMPASS."

Two new forms of compass recently devised by Mr. E. S. Ritchie, of Boston, have the following construction: The distinctive peculiarities of the liquid compass are an air-tight metallic case within which is placed the magnetic needle, and of such size and weight as to be of very nearly the same specific gravity as the liquid in which it is intended to float. The weight is thus removed from the pivot, and friction is almost prevented; certain modifications being introduced to provide against tilting and other emergencies occurring during the motion of the ship. The distinctive principle of the Monitor Compass is the separation of the magnet from the card or index, so that the magnet may be elevated above the sphere of disturbing attraction of the iron of the ship, while the card is brought to a convenient position to be seen by the pilot; and suspending the movable portion in a liquid so as to secure entire freedom from friction, that the needle may obey the polar force, and at the same time great steadiness is secured for the card.

New Form of Magnetic Needle.—At a recent meeting of the Manchester Philosophical Society, Mr. Joule exhibited a new form of magnetic needle for showing rapid and minute alterations of declination. It consisted of a piece of hardened and polished watch spring, an inch long, and $\frac{1}{16}$ of an inch broad suspended vertically by a filament of silk. The steel was magnetized in the direction of its breadth. He remarked that Professor Thomson had long insisted upon the advantages which would attend the use of very small bars in most magnetical investigations, and had employed excessively minute needles in his galvanometers with great success. Dr. Joule stated his intention to fit up his needle so as to be observed by light reflected from its polished surface, or otherwise, by viewing a glass pointer, attached to the bottom of the steel, through a microscope. He believed that by the latter plan he should be able to observe deflections as small as one second of an arc.

Great Electro-Magnet.—Messrs. Chester, of New York City, have recently constructed an electro-magnet of unusual size, for the New York Free Academy. It is made of the purest iron. The core is four inches in diameter; its total length is five feet. The wire wound upon it is in eight separate strands, and the aggregate weight of copper is 200 pounds. The entire weight of the magnet is 650 pounds. It is arranged either to be suspended with the faces downward, or to be placed upright on a wheeled platform. Connected with it is apparatus for diamagnetic experiments, consisting of rotating copper discs and tubes. When the magnetic force is in action the rotating disc is instantly stopped, and motion is converted into heat. The heat evolved is sufficient to cause water to boil in a copper tube.

THE TELEGRAPH AS A METEOROLOGICAL INDICATOR.

"The electric telegraph is likely to render us henceforth a service which it has not until now been known to be capable of. For some time past it has been systematically employed, to transmit to one center meteorological observations made at a great number of widely scattered points, and to transmit from that center predictions founded on these observations; but Father Secchi, the Italian *savant*, now informs us that a line of telegraph wires itself constitutes a better indicator of certain kinds of meteorological changes than any other we as yet know of. All persons at all familiar with electric telegraphy are aware that currents other than those proceeding from the batteries employed are constantly passing along all lines of telegraph wires. They are derived from either the earth or the atmosphere, and are called 'earth-currents.' They are subject to great variations, which Father Secchi and some of his friends have for some time past been carefully studying, with the result, among others, of finding that, whenever the earth-currents are more irregular than ordinary, bad weather invariably follows, the degree of their regularity of the earth-currents bearing always an exact relation to that of the storminess of the weather which they precede. We are certainly progressing as regards our power of forecasting meteorological changes."

ON PERIODIC CHANGES IN THE MAGNETIC CONDITION OF THE EARTH, AND IN THE DISTRIBUTION OF TEMPERATURE UPON ITS SURFACE.

The following is an abstract of a very curious and interesting paper recently read before the Manchester (Eng.) Philosophical Society, by Mr. Baxendall, F. R. A. S. He says:—

Considerations arising out of an investigation of the irregularities which take place in the changes of some of the variable stars, led the author some time ago to regard it as highly probable that the light of the sun, and also its magnetic and heating powers, might be subject to changes of a more complicated nature than has hitherto been supposed, and that, besides the changes which are indicated by the greater or less frequency of solar spots, other changes of a minor character, and occurring in shorter periods, might also take place.   In the hope of detecting these supposed changes, the author resolved to undertake the discussion of a series of magnetical observations, and for this purpose he selected the observations made at the Imperial Observatory of St Petersburg, the most northern station at which hourly magnetic observations have been made for any lengthened period.   Commencing, therefore, with the year 1848, the greatest and least values of the magnetic declination for every day were extracted from the observations; and, taking the differences and arranging them in order, it was found, on a careful examination, that they indicated changes of activity taking place in a period of 31 days. The daily oscillations were then arranged in a table, when it was found that out of 17 consecutive days, the amount of oscillation, on range of the magnetic needle, was *above* the mean on 13 days and below the mean on only four days; while of the remaining 14 days, the range was *below* the mean on 13 days, and above on *one* day only.   The total amount of the differences for the 17 days of maximum was $\frac{3}{10}$ per day; and for the 14 days of minimum $\frac{4}{10}$.

On proceeding to examine the observations for the succeeding years it was found that they could not be represented by a period of 31 days.   It appeared, therefore, at first sight, that the period which had been obtained for 1848 was merely accidental; but, guided partly by conclusions drawn from his variable-star investigations, and partly by the high degree of improbability that the results for 1848 could be due to mere accident, the author was led to think that the period he had found for 1848 might be variable, gradually diminishing for a series of years, and afterward gradually increasing, to diminish again when it had completed its cycle of change.   Assuming, therefore, that in every year periodic changes took place in the magnetic activity of the sun, the author proceeded to determine for each year the most probable approximate value of the period, and he obtained a series of values gradually diminishing till 1856, when the period was only about 23 days, and afterward rapidly increasing until, in 1859, it amounted to about 32 days.   A glance at these results at once suggested the idea that the variable period thus found was in some way connected with, and dependent upon, the great solar-spot period, the minimum value occurring in the year of minimum frequency of the solar spots, and the maximum values in the years when the spots were most numerous.

Several series of thermometrical observations were now examined for indications of periodical changes in the element of mean daily temperature, and it was found that they exhibited, with unexpected distinctness, changes in this element occurring also in a variable period, the range of variation being, however, somewhat less than in the case of the magnetic element, although the times of maximum and minimum were almost exactly the same.   The maximum and minimum values were respectively 31 and 23½ days,

A table is given showing the number of days included in the maximum and minimum portions of each mean period for the years 1848 to 1850, and the number of exceptional days, or those on which during the maximum part of the period the temperature was *below*, and during the minimum part *above*, the mean value. From this table it appears that out of a total number of 165 days of maximum, only 14 were exceptional; and out of a total of 164½ days of minimum, the number of exceptional days was only 16. The mean gives a ratio almost exactly as 1 to 11. Considering that the values of the period in the different years are only approximate, this result may be regarded as affording satisfactory proof of the existence of a variable period of temperature.

At St. Petersburg the average temperature of the warmer half of the period is not less than 3° greater than that of the cooler half; and as this difference of temperature is repeated at least 12 times in every year, it must necessarily exercise a powerful modifying influence over many meteorological phenomena.

Another period of change having a mean duration of rather over 18 months, is then referred to. The author was first led to it from a discussion of the Greenwich Magnetical Observations, for the years 1848 to 1859; and it has been confirmed by the results of a discussion of temperature observations, made at Brussels in Europe, and at Yakoutsk, in Asia. It is obvious that this period will, at times, interfere sensibly with the shorter one, and it is probable, that some of the cases which have been called exceptional may be due to this interference.

With regard to the probable cause of the variability of the short period the author suggests the following hypothesis: 1st. That a ring of nebulous matter exists differing in density or constitution in different parts, or several masses of such matter forming a discontinuous ring, circulating round the sun in a plane nearly coincident with the plane of the ecliptic, and at a mean distance from the sun, of about ⅓ of the radius of the earth's orbit.

2d. That the attractive force of the sun on the matter of this ring is alternately increased and diminished by the operation of the forces which produce the solar spots, being greatest at the times of minimum solar-spot frequency, and least when the spots are most numerous.

3d. The attractive force being variable, the dimensions of the ring and its period of revolution round the sun will also vary, their maximum and minimum values occurring respectively at the times of maximum and minimum solar-spot frequency.

In reference to the nature of the varying attractive force, it is not improbable that the matter of the supposed ring may be highly diamagnetic, and being much nearer to the sun than any of the known planets, of much greater bulk and lightness, and being subjected to a much higher temperature, it will be very sensibly affected by the changes which take place in the magnetic condition of the sun; and when interposed between the earth and the sun, it may act not only by reflecting and absorbing a portion of the light and heat which would otherwise reach the earth, but also by altering the direction of the lines of magnetic force. The changes of temperature at the surface of the earth will thus be due partly to differences in the amount of heat received from the sun, and partly to changes in the move-

12

ments of the great currents of the air produced by alterations in the earth's magnetic condition. If the larger part of the difference of temperature is due to the latter mode of action, we might expect that during the warmer half of the period the mean direction of the wind at any given station would be sensibly different from that during the cooler half; and also, that the epochs of maximum and minimum temperature would not be the same at all parts of the earth's surface. Both of these conclusions are borne out by the results given in the paper. Thus at St. Petersburg, in 1859, the mean direction of the wind on maximum days was S. 54° W., and on minimum days S. 73°· W. or 19° more to the west of South; and at Sitka, on the Northwest Coast of North America, in 1851, the mean direction on maximum days was S. 32° W., and on minimum days S. 56° W., the difference being 24°. As striking instances of the differences in the epochs at distant stations, it may be stated, that in 1859 the epoch of maximum at St. Petersburg corresponded precisely with the epoch of minimum at Madras; and that at Pekin, in 1851, the epoch of minimum was exactly coincident with the epoch of·maximum at Sitka.

Changes in the amount of heat received from the sun, sufficient to produce the variations of temperature observed at any given station, would no doubt affect the movements of the great currents of the atmosphere, though not to the extent indicated by the observations; but it is difficult to conceive that they could produce the differences in the epochs which are found to take place. We may therefore fairly conclude that the action of the supposed ring of nebulous matter is principally of a magnetic, and but slightly of a thermal character.

Adopting, for the present, the maximum and minimum values of the temperature period as being determined with greater accuracy than those of the magnetic period, the greatest and least values of the sidereal period of revolution of the ring will be 29·12 and 22·08 days respectively. From these numbers we find that the greatest distance of the ring from the sun is 0·185, the radius of the earth's orbit being taken as unity; the least distance, 0·154; and the mean 0·169. Taking Mr. Hind's value of the mean distance of the earth from the sun, namely, 91,328,600 miles, we have: Greatest distance of the ring, 16,921,000 miles; least distance of the ring, 14,068,000; mean distance of the ring, 15,494,500; and the range of movement to and fro in a radial direction, 2,853,000 miles. The greatest attractive force of the sun on the ring being taken as unity, the least will be 0·691. The difference is therefore nearly ⅓ of the maximum amount. It will be evident that this difference may be regarded as a measure of the forces which are concerned in the production of the solar spots.

The results of the elaborate investigations of the motions of the planet Mercury, made by Leverrier, led that accomplished mathematician to attribute a certain unexplained excess in the motion of its perihelion to the action of a disturbing body circulating round the sun within the orbit of Mercury; and, from a discussion of the probable mass of the disturbing body, he concluded that it could not be concentrated in a single planet, and that it consisted of a ring of small bodies similar to that which is known to exist between the orbits of Mars and Jupiter; and it is remarkable that the mean distance, which he seemed to regard as the most probable, is precisely that which the author has found for the ring of nebulous matter, whose existence he has assumed to account for the phenomena described in his paper. This unexpected and unlooked-for agreement between results arrived at from considerations and by methods so totally different, seems to establish the existence of this ring with quite as much certainty, as the results of the profound researches of Adams and Leverrier established the existence of Neptune before that planet had been actually seen. This ring, however, owing to its proximity to the sun, may never be seen, and, like the dark companions of Procyon and Sirius, it may only be known to us through its action on the other bodies of the system of which it forms a part. Should future researches place its existence beyond doubt, this will, it is believed, be the first instance in which the conclusions of physical astronomy have been confirmed by the results of an investigation of magnetical and meteorological phenomena. Whether, however, the hypothesis which the author has ventured to put forward be accepted or not, it is now very evident that observations of solar phenomena merit a much larger share of attention than has ever yet been devoted to them. It has long been suspected that the same causes which produce the spots on the sun's disc must in some way have an important influence on the phenomena of our own atmosphere. The facts now given, convert this suspicion into a certainty; and it is perhaps, not too much to say, that meteorology can never take rank as a true science while our knowledge of the sun remains in its present imperfect state. Moreover, there is little doubt, that many questions of high physical interest depend for their solution upon our obtaining a more intimate acquaintance than we yet possess with the operations which are going on in the great center of our system.

TELEGRAPHING BY MAGNETO-ELECTRIC MACHINES.

We copy from the *Washington Chronicle* the following communication, apparently furnished by the well-known electrician, Dr. Page:—
"The introductory report of the Patent Office for 1863 ventured upon the following anticipation: 'It is not too much to say that the days of telegraphing by the galvanic battery are numbered, and that the magneto-electric machine will erelong take its place for this as well as for many other purposes.' At that time it was well known that the magneto-electric machine was successfully working Beardslee's dial telegraph; but we witnessed, on a recent evening, the extraordinary feat of working the Morse telegraph, between Washington and New York, with one of Beardslee's little magneto-electric machines, occupying space less than a cubic foot. The correspondence was kept up over the People's Line with perfect freedom for more than an hour, and the Morse operator rattled off the messages as if he were perfectly at home. The sound of the instrument is musical, differing from that of an ordinary receiving magnet. The Commissioner's Report alludes to the firing of gunpowder through the distance of one hundred miles by means of this little machine, but on the night in question we fired gunpowder in New York, a distance of two hundred miles, and the operators there fired gunpowder in Washington with perfect ease by the same little machine used to work the telegraph. It was a perfect success, and one of the most interesting and splendid achievements of modern science. If the Atlantic

cable is ever laid, this seems the power destined to work it.   Surely, ' the days of the galvanic battery seem to be numbered.'

"The invention above referred to is thus described by Commissioner Holloway in his Report :—

"Conspicuous among the inventions which have received the sanction of letters patent is a magneto-electric telegraph, now in extensive use in the United States Army for field purposes, and elsewhere for ordinary telegraphic purposes.   This is a signal triumph in electromechanics, for by the motive power of a small magneto-electric machine, occupying less than a cubic foot, a dial or index telegraph is operated through great distances, from 5 to 200 miles, with the prospect of greater and indefinite extension.   It was found with the Atlantic telegraph, in 1858, that alternating, or to and fro currents, were indispensable to its operation, and the magneto-electric machine of the telegraph before us has the peculiar movement of normal to and fro currents in rapid succession, without any extra contrivance for their production, this condition growing out of the very arrangement of the magnetic poles and helices.   The operators for this telegraph require no training, and any person who can read can telegraph.   For the Morse telegraph two or three years of training are required.   It is not liable to piracy by tapping, as is the Morse telegraph, and may be justly regarded as the inauguration of a new era in telegraphy, by dispensing with the cumbersome, uncleanly, unhealthy, and inconstant galvanic battery as the motive power, and the introduction of a simple and economical telegraph, adapted with equal facility to domestic and public purposes.   It is not too much to say, that the days of telegraphing by the galvanic battery are numbered, and that the magneto-electric machine will erelong take its place for this, as well as for many other purposes.

"Another highly interesting development in magneto-electric science is the discovery and application of a new mode of ignition for purposes of blasting with powder.   Hitherto torpedoes and other powder blasts, fired by electricity, have depended upon the ignition of a very fine platinum wire.   When this had to be done through long circuits, or at great distances, very large and expensive galvanic batteries were required, owing to the great diminution of the quantity of electricity. It was proved by experiments made at the Capitol many years since, that 150 pairs of Grove's battery were necessary to ignite powder by the finest of platinum wires placed in the telegraph circuit between Baltimore and Washington, a distance of 40 miles.   By means of the new discovery, powder has been fired through the distance of 100 miles by means of a little magneto-electric machine, occupying less than a cubic foot.   This astonishing achievement has been accomplished by means so simple that electricians will wonder as much, if not more, than the uninitiated.   It is done by a *pencil-mark*.   The stroke of a common black-lead pencil on a block of wood is substituted for the platinum wire, and this disintegrated conductor, as it may be called, is so intensely ignited by the magneto-electric current as to set fire to the wood.

"The application of this ingenious device within a suitably-prepared cartridge, will be hailed as one of the most valuable contributions to mining and engineering operations of the present day."

PROGRESS OF TELEGRAPHIC CONSTRUCTION.

While citizens of the United States are engaged upon the great enterprise of constructing a line of telegraph to Europe via Behring's Straits and the Amoor, the British government are pushing their great project of connecting London and Calcutta with the electric wire, to a speedy conclusion. Telegraphic communication has existed for two or three years between London and Constantinople, and about the same time ago a cable was laid down through the Red Sea, between Suez and Aden, a distance of 3,000 miles, intended to complete the link between Europe and India, but it subsequently failed. Recently, however, a cable has been successfully submerged through the Persian Gulf, which with the exception of 160 miles of land line, between Diwanyeh, on the Euphrates, and the Shat-el-Arab, the western termini of the Persian Gulf cable, completes the through telegraphic communication from the Thames to the Ganges.

The distance from Constantinople to Fao, at the mouth of the Shat-el-Arab on the Persian Gulf, through which the line will pass when the Montific Arabs and the healthy season will permit its safe construction to Diwanyeh, is 1,570 miles, and passes through the following important towns, Scutari, Angora, Diarbekir, Mossul, Bagdad, and Diwanyeh. From Fao to Kurrachee, the submarine cable stretches along the bottom of the Persian Gulf for 1,300 miles, and 500 miles farther carries it across a portion of the British-Indian empire to Bombay.

The eastern terminus of the Turkish line for the receipt of messages, is at present at Bagdad, and the only communication with Fao is by way of the Tigris, by one British and two Turkish steamers, which run regularly, occupying from five to six days in the passage up the river, and 2½ down.

Another route from England to India, in connection with the Persian gulf cable, passes through Russia by way of Tiflis to Teheran, thence to Ispahan and Shiraz, and joins the cable at Bushire. As the line running through the Montific country, when completed, can scarcely be depended upon, owing to the relations existing between the tribes, who are very powerful and warlike, and the pasha of Bagdad, against whom they have risen in rebellion, the British government have contracted for the construction of a line which, effecting a considerable detour, will avoid the disturbed district completely. This wire is to pass from Bushire, on the Persian Gulf, where the cable lands before starting 170 miles further, to its terminus at Shat-el-Arab, via Kazeroor, Shiraz, Ispahan, Teheran, and Khanakeen to Bagdad, the distance between Bushire and Khanakeen being about 1,100 miles.

The Indian telegraphs, which connect together Calcutta, Bombay, Madras, Delhi, and all the principal towns in India, are now advanced eastward as far as Rangoon; and the routes thence to China and to Australia, by way of Singapore, Java, and Timor, are said to be almost entirely in comparatively shallow water, so far as the submarine part of the line is concerned, and do not otherwise offer any difficulty which should prevent instantaneous communication between London, Hong Kong, Melbourne, and Sidney.

When the Atlantic cable and the Russian line are successfully in operation, we shall have two separate routes to China and India,—to the latter via London and Constantinople, via St. Petersburg and Teheran; and to the former via Russia line from Irkoutsk in Siberia to Pekin, and via the Persian gulf cable and India. 12*

ON THE MECHANICAL PROPERTIES OF THE ATLANTIC TELEGRAPH
CABLE.

At the British Association, 1864, Mr. Fairbairn, the celebrated
English engineer and scientist, read the following paper on the above
subject :—

It appears that the Atlantic Telegraph Company, considering it
essential to the public interest that the second attempt to submerge a
telegraph cable across the Atlantic should not be left to chance, and
that a close and searching investigation should be entered upon, and
that nothing should be left undone that could be accomplished to
insure success, sought the advice of a committee composed of men of
eminence and experience in the various branches of science and engineering involved in such an undertaking to advise the Company in
the selection of a cable. For the satisfactory attainment of this
object it was considered necessary, in the first place, To determine
by direct experiment the mechanical properties of cables submitted
for submergence in deep water; 2d, To ascertain the chemical properties of the insulator, and the best means to be adopted for the
preservation and duration of the cable; and 3d, To determine the
electrical properties and conditions of the cable when immersed,
under pressure, at great depths. On the author of the paper de-
volved the duty of undertaking the first division of the inquiry, viz:
to determine, by actual experiment, the strengths, combinations,
forms, and conditions of every cable considered of suitable strength
and proportion to cross the Atlantic. A laborious series of experiments was instituted, and, in order to attain accuracy as regards the
resisting powers of each cable to a tensile strain, they were broken
by dead weights, suspended from a crab or crane, by which they could
be raised or lowered at pleasure. The weights were laid on one cwt.
at a time, and the elongations were carefully taken and recorded in
the table as each alternate $\frac{1}{4}$ cwt. was placed on the scale until it
was broken. By this process we were enabled to ascertain with
great exactitude the amount of elongation in seven ft. six in.
The result of the investigation was, the selection of the cable of
Messrs. Glass & Elliott, which stood highest in order of strength.
In this inquiry, upwards of 40 specimens of cables have been tested
in their finished state, and this might have been sufficient for the
Committee to determine the best description of cable; it was, however, deemed advisable to investigate still further, not only the cable
as a cable, but to test experimentally each separate part, in order
that every security should be afforded as to the strength and quality
of the material to be employed in the construction. With regard to
the covering wires, constituting the principal strength of the cable,
Mr. Fairbairn finds that with proper care in the selection of the material in the first instance, a judicious system of manipulation in the
second, and a rigid system of inspection of the manufacture, a wire
of homogeneous iron ·095 inches diameter can be made of strength
sufficient to sustain from 900 to 1,000 lbs., with an elongation of ·0008,
or $\frac{6.8}{10000}$ parts of an inch per unit of length. This description of
iron appears to be the most suitable for the Atlantic cable, as it combines strength with ductility, and may be produced at a comparatively

moderate cost. It was also found desirable to test the separate strands of each cable as well as the wires themselves. For this purpose a number of strands similar to those employed in the manufacture of the different cables were produced, and the tensile breaking strain and elongations carefully observed and recorded. In order to ascertain whether the length of the lay of the hemp and Manilla round the strand was of that spiral form which produced a maximum of strength, the yarn separated from the strand was also tested, and comparing the sum of the breaking strains of the wire and yarn separately, with that of the two in combination in the strand, the object by these means was approximately obtained. Another very important question arises in the construction of this cable, and that is, the strength of the core and its conducting wire, and how it is to be protected under a pressure of 7,000 lb. to 8,000 per square inch, when lodged at the bottom of the ocean. This appeared a question well entitled to consideration, and provided a properly insulated wire, of one or more strands, can, without any exterior covering, be deposited with safety at these great depths, it is obvious that the simpler the cable the better. Assuming, therefore, that gutta-percha is the most desirable material that can be employed as an insulator, it then resolves itself into the question, what additional covering and what additional strength is necessary to enable the engineer so to pay out of the ship a length of 2,600 miles, into the deepest water, as to deposit it, without strain, at the bottom of the ocean? This is the question the Committee had to solve, and for this very important object experiments were instituted. Regarding the circumstances bearing directly upon the ultimate strength of the cable, the Committee have arrived at the conclusion that the cable No. 46, composed of homogeneous wire, calculated to bear not less than from 850 lb. to 1,000 lb. per wire, with a stretch of $\frac{6}{10}$ of an inch in 50 inches, is the most suitable for the Atlantic cable. The following is the specification of No. 46 cable: The conductor consists of a copper strand of seven wires (six laid round one), each wire gauging ·048 (or No. 18 of the Birmingham wire-gauge), the entire strand gauging ·144 inch, (or No. 10 Birmingham gauge), and weighing 300 lb. per nautical mile, imbedded for solidity in the composition known as "Chatterton's Compound." The insulator consists of gutta-percha, four layers of which are laid on alternately, with four thin layers of Chatterton's compound, making a diameter of the core of ·464 inch, and a circumference of 1·392 inches. The weight of the entire insulator is 400 lb. per nautical mile. The external protection is in two parts. First, the core is surrounded with a padding of soft jute yarn, saturated with a preservative mixture. Next to this padding is the protective covering, which consists of ten solid wires of the gauge ·095 inch, drawn from homogeneous iron, each wire surrounded separately with five strands of Manilla yarn, saturated with a preservative compound; the whole of the ten strands thus formed of the hemp and iron being laid spirally round the padded core. The weight of this cable in air is 34 cwt. per nautical mile,—the weight in water is 14 cwt. per nautical mile. The breaking strain is 7 tons 15 cwt., or equal to 11 times its weight per nautical mile in water,—that is to say, if suspended perpendicularly, it would bear its own weight in 11 miles depth of water. The deepest water to be encountered between Ireland and Newfoundland is about 2,400 fathoms, and one mile being equal to 1,014 fathoms, therefore $1,014 \times 11 = 11,154$, and $2 \cdot 400 = 4 \cdot 64$: the cable having thus a strength equal to $4 \cdot 64$ times of its own vertical weight in the deepest water.

ON CELESTIAL DYNAMICS, BY DR. J. R. MAYER.

The movements of celestial bodies in an absolute vacuum would be as uniform as those of a mathematical pendulum, whereas a resisting medium pervading all space would cause the planets to move in shorter and shorter orbits, and at last to fall into the sun. Assuming such a resisting medium, these wandering celestial bodies must have on the periphery of the solar system their cradle, and in its center their grave; and however long the duration, and however great the number of their revolutions may be, as many masses will on the average in a certain time arrive at the sun as formerly in a like period of time came within his sphere of attraction. All these bodies plunge with a violent impetus into their common grave. Since no cause exists without an effect, each of these cosmical masses will, like a weight falling to the earth, produce by its percussion an amount of heat proportional to its *vis viva*.

From the idea of a sun whose attraction acts throughout space, of ponderable bodies scattered throughout the universe, and of a resisting ether, another idea necessarily follows,—that, namely, of a continual and inexhaustible generation of heat on the central body of this cosmical system. Whether such a conception be realized in our solar system,—whether in other words the wonderful and permanent evolution of light and heat be caused by the uninterrupted fall of cosmical matter into the sun,—will now be more closely examined.

The existence of matter in a primordial condition moving about in the universe, and assumed to follow the attraction of the nearest stellar system, will scarcely be denied by astronomers and physicists; for the richness of surrounding nature, as well as the aspect of the starry heavens prevents the belief that the wide space which separates our solar system from the regions governed by the other fixed stars is a vacant solitude destitute of matter. We shall leave, however, all suppositions concerning subjects so distant from us both in time and space, and confine our attention exclusively to what may be learned from the observation of the existing state of things.

Besides the 14 known planets with their 18 satellites, a great many other cosmical masses move within the space of the planetary system of which the comets deserve to be mentioned first.

Kepler's celebrated statement that "there are more comets in the heavens than fish in the ocean," is founded on the fact that, of all the comets belonging to our solar system, comparatively few can be seen by the inhabitants of the earth, and therefore the not inconsiderable number of actually observed comets obliges us, according to the rules of the calculus of probabilities, to assume the existence of a great many more beyond the sphere of our vision.

Besides planets, satellites, and comets, another class of celestial bodies exists within our solar system. These are masses which, on account of their smallness, may be considered as cosmical atoms, and which Arago has appropriately called asteroids. They, like the planets and the comets, are governed by gravity, and move in elliptical orbits round the sun. When accident brings them into the immediate neighborhood of the earth, they produce the phenomena of shooting stars and fireballs. It has been shown, by repeated observation, that on a bright night twenty minutes seldom elapse without a shooting-star being visible to an observer in any situation. At certain times these meteors are observed in astonishingly great numbers; during the great American meteoric shower, which lasted nine hours, when they were said to fall, "crowded together like snowflakes," they were estimated as at least 240,000. On the whole, the number of asteroids which come near the earth in the space of a year must be computed to be many thousands of millions.* This, without doubt, is only a small fraction of the number of asteroids that move round the sun, which number, according to the rules of the calculus of probabilities, approaches infinity.

As has been already stated, on the existence of a resisting ether it depends whether the celestial bodies, the planets, the comets, and the asteroids move at constant mean distances around the sun, or whether they are constantly approaching that central body. Scientific men do not doubt the existence of such an ether. Littrow, amongst others, expresses himself on this point as follows: "The assumption that the planets and comets move in an absolute vacuum can in no way be admitted. Even if the space between celestial bodies contained no other matter than that necessary for the existence of light (whether light be considered as emission of matter or the undulations of a universal ether), this alone is sufficient to alter the motion of the planets in the course of time and the arrangement of the whole system itself; the fall of all the planets and the comets into the sun and the destruction of the present state of the solar system must be the final result of this action."

A direct proof of the existence of such a resisting medium has been furnished by the academician Encke. He found that the comet named after him, which revolves round the sun in the short space of 1,207 days, shows a regular acceleration of its motion, in consequence of which the time of each revolution is shortened by about six hours.

From the great density and magnitude of the planets, the shortening of the diameters of their orbits proceeds, as might be expected, very slowly, and is up to the present time inappreciable. The smaller the cosmical masses are, on the contrary, other circumstances remaining the same, the faster they move towards the sun: it may therefore happen that in a space of time wherein the mean distance of the earth from the sun would diminish one meter, a small asteroid would travel more than 1,000 miles towards the central body. As cosmical masses stream from all sides in immense numbers towards the sun, it follows that they must become more and more crowded together as they approach thereto. The conjecture at once suggests itself that the zodiacal light, the nebulous light of vast dimensions which surrounds the sun, owes its origin to such closely packed asteroids.

* Compare Prof. Newton's computation of the approximate number of meteors in the August ring alone, which makes it more than 300,000,000,000,000: *Silliman's Journal*, xxxii. 461.

However it may be, this much is certain, this phenomenon is caused by matter which moves according to the same laws as the planets round the sun, and it consequently follows that the whole mass which originates the zodiacal light is continually approaching the sun and falling into it.

This light does not surround the sun uniformly on all sides; that is to say, it has not the form of a sphere, but that of a thin convex lens, the greater diameter of which is in the plane of the solar equator, and accordingly it has to an observer on our globe a pyramidal form. Such lenticular distribution of the masses in the universe is repeated in a remarkable manner in the disposition of the planets and the fixed stars.

From the great number of cometary masses and asteroids and the zodiacal light on the one hand, and the existence of a resisting ether . on the other, it necessarily follows that ponderable matter must continually be arriving on the solar surface. The effect produced by these masses evidently depends on their final velocity; and, in order to determine the latter, we shall discuss some of the elements of the theory of gravitation.

The final velocity of a weight attracted by, and moving toward, a celestial body will become greater as the hight through which the weight falls increases. This velocity, however, if it be only produced by the fall, cannot exceed a certain magnitude; it has a maximum, the value of which depends on the volume and mass of the attracting celestial body. The author then by a series of calculations, shows, that an asteroid falling into the sun, would on arriving have a motion at least as great as that of a weight falling freely to the sun from a distance great as that of the solar radius, or 96,000 geographical miles; and that the calorific effect of the percussion would equal to from 27½ to 55,000,000 of degrees of heat.

An asteroid, therefore, by its fall into the sun, develops from 4,600 to 9,200 times as much heat as would be generated by the combustion · of an equal mass of coal.

[Throughout this memoir the degrees of heat are expressed in the Centigrade scale. Unless stated to the contrary, the measures of length are given in geographical miles. A geographical mile$=\frac{1}{15}$ of degree of latitude$=1,878$ meters, and an English mile$=1,609$ meters.]

The Heat of the Sun.—The question why the planets move in curved orbits, one of the grandest of problems, was solved by Newton in consequence, it is believed, of his reflecting on the fall of an apple. This story is not improbable, for we are on the right track for the discovery of truth when once we clearly recognize that, between great and small, no qualitative but only a quantitative difference exists,—when we resist the suggestions of an ever active imagination, and look for the same laws in the greatest as well as in the smallest processes of nature. This universal range is the essence of a law of nature, and the touchstone of the correctness of human theories. We observe the fall of an apple and investigate the law which governs this phenomenon; for the earth we substitute the sun, and for the apple a planet, and thus possess ourselves of the key to the mechanics of the heavens.

As the same laws prevail in the greater as well as in the smaller processes of nature, Newton's method may be used in solving the problem of the origin of the sun's heat. We know the connection between the space through which a body falls, the velocity, the *vis viva*, and the generation of heat on the surface of this globe; if we again substitute for the earth the sun, with a mass 350,000 greater, and for a height of a few meters celestial distances, we obtain a generation of heat exceeding all terrestrial measures. And since we have sufficient reason to assume the actual existence of such mechanical processes in the heavens, we find therein the only tenable explanation of the origin of the heat of the sun.

The fact that the development of heat by mechanical means on the surface of our globe is, as a rule, not so great, and cannot be so great as the generation of the same agent by chemical means, as by combustion, follows from the laws already discussed; and this fact cannot be used as an argument against the assumption of a greater development of heat by a greater expenditure of mechanical work. It has been shown that the heat generated by a weight falling from a hight of 367 meters is only $\frac{1}{3000}$ part of the heat produced by the combustion of the same weight of coal; just as small as is the amount of heat developed by a weight moving with the not inconsiderable velocity of 85 meters in one second. But, according to the laws of mechanics, the effect is proportional to the square of the velocity; if, therefore, the weight move 100 times faster, or with a velocity of 8,500 meters in one second, it will produce a greater effect than the combustion of an equal quantity of coal.

It is true that so great a velocity cannot be obtained by human means; everyday experience, however, shows the development of high degrees of temperature by mechanical processes. In the common flint and steel, the particles of steel which are struck off are sufficiently heated to burn in air. A few blows directed by a skillful blacksmith with a sledge-hammer against a piece of cold metal may raise the temperature of the metal at the points of collision to redness. The new crank of a steamer, whilst being polished by friction, becomes red-hot, several buckets of water being required to cool it down to its ordinary temperature. When a railroad train passes with even less than its ordinary velocity along a very sharp curve of the line, sparks are observed in consequence of the friction against the rails. One of the grandest constructions for the production of motion by human art is the channel in which the wood was allowed to glide down from the steep and lofty sides of Mount Pilatus into the plain below. This wooden channel which was built about thirty years ago by the engineer Rupp, was nine English miles in length; the largest trees were shot down it from the top to the bottom of the mountain in about two minutes and a half. The momentum possessed by the trees on their escaping at their journey's end from the channel was sufficiently great to bury their thicker ends in the ground to the depth of from six to eight meters. To prevent the wood getting too hot and taking fire, water was conducted in many places into the channel.

This stupendous mechanical process, when compared with cosmical processes on the sun appears infinitely small. In the latter case it is the mass of the sun which attracts, and in place of the hight of Mount Pilatus we have distances of 100,000 and more miles; the amount of heat generated by cosmical falls is therefore at least 9,000,000 times greater than in our terrestrial example.

Rays of heat on passing through glass and other transparent bodies undergo partial absorption, which differs in degree, however, according to the temperature of the source·from which the heat is derived. Heat radiated from sources less warm than boiling water is almost completely stopped by thin plates of glass. As the temperature of a source of heat increases, its rays pass more copiously through diathermic bodies. A plate of glass, for example, weakens the rays of a red-hot substance, even when the latter is placed very close to it, much more than it does those emanating at a much greater distance from a white-hot body. If the quality of the sun's rays be examined in this respect, their diathermic energy is found to be far superior to that of all artificial sources of heat. The temperature of the focus of a concave metallic reflector in which the sun's light has been collected is only diminished from $\frac{1}{4}$ to $\frac{1}{8}$ by the interposition of a screen of glass. If the same experiment be made with an artificial and luminous source of heat, it is found that, though the focus be very hot when the screen is away, the interposition of the latter cuts off nearly all the heat; moreover, the focus will not recover its former temperature when reflector and screen are placed sufficiently near to the source of heat to make the focus appear brighter than it did in the former position without the glass screen.

The empirical law, that the diathermic energy of heat increases with the temperature of the source from which the heat is radiated, teaches us that the sun's surface must be much hotter than the most powerful process of combustion could render it.

Other methods furnish the same conclusion. · If we imagine the sun to be surrounded by a hollow sphere, it is clear that the inner surface of this sphere must receive all the heat radiated from the sun. At the distance of our globe from the sun, such a sphere would have a radius of 215 times as great, and an area 46,000 times as large, as the sun himself; those luminous and calorific rays, therefore, which meet this spherical surface at right angles retain only $\frac{1}{46000}$ part of their original intensity.

If it be further considered that our atmosphere absorbs a part of the solar rays, it is clear that the rays which reach the tropics of our earth at noonday can only possess from $\frac{100}{60000}$ to $\frac{1}{90000}$ of the power with which they started. These rays when gathered from a surface of from five to six square meters, and concentrated in an area of one square centimetre, would produce about the temperature which exists on the sun, a temperature more than sufficient to vaporize platinum, rhodium, and similar metals.

A correct theory of the origin of the sun's heat must explain the cause of such enormous temperatures. This explanation can be deduced from the foregoing statement. According to Pouillet, the temperature at which bodies appear intensely white-hot is about 1,500° C. The heat generated by the combustion of one kilogram of hydrogen is, as determined by Dulong, 34,500, and according to the more recent experiments of Grassi, 34,666, units of heat. One part of hydrogen combines with eight parts of oxygen to form water; hence one kilogram of these two gases mixed in this ratio would produce 3,850°.

Let us now compare this heat with the amount of the same agent generated by the fall of an asteroid into the sun. Without taking into account the low specific heat of such masses when compared with that of water, we find the heat developed by the asteroid to be from 7,000 to 14,000 times greater than that of the oxyhydrogen mixture. From data like these the extraordinary diathermic energy of the sun's rays, the immense radiation from his surface, and the high temperature in the focus of the reflector are easily accounted for.

The facts above mentioned show that unless we assume on the sun the existence of matter with unheard-of chemical properties as a *deus ex machinâ*, no chemical process could maintain the present high radiation of the sun; it also follows from the above results that the chemical nature of bodies which fall into the sun does not in the least affect our conclusions; the effect produced by the most inflammable substance would not differ by $\frac{1}{1000}$ part from that resulting from the fall of matter possessing but feeble chemical affinities. As the brightest artificial light appears dark in comparison with the sun's light, so the mechanical processes of the heavens throw into the shade the most powerful chemical actions.

The quality of the sun's rays, as dependent on his temperature, is of the greatest importance to mankind. If the solar heat were originated by a chemical process, and amounted near its source to a temperature of a few thousand degrees, it would be possible for the light to reach us, whilst the greater part of the more important calorific rays would be absorbed by the higher strata of our atmosphere and then returned to the universe.

In consequence of the high temperature of the sun, however, our atmosphere is highly diathermic to his rays, so that the latter reach the surface of our earth and warm it. The comparatively low temperature of the terrestrial surface is the cause why the heat cannot easily radiate back through the atmosphere into the universe. The atmosphere acts, therefore, like an envelop, which is easily pierced by the solar rays, but which offers considerable resistance to the radiant heat escaping from our earth; its action resembles that of a valve which allows a liquid to pass freely in one direction, but stops the flow in the opposite.

The action of the atmosphere is of the greatest importance as regards climate and meteorological processes. It must raise the mean temperature of the earth's surface. After the setting of the sun,—in fact, in all places where his rays do not reach the surface, the temperature of the earth would soon be as low as that of the universe if the atmosphere were removed, or if it did not exist. Even the powerful solar rays in the tropics would be unable to preserve water in its liquid state.

Between the great cold which would reign at all times and in all places, and the moderate warmth which in reality exists on our globe, intermediate temperatures may be imagined; and it is easily seen that the mean temperature would decrease if the atmosphere were to become more and more rare. Such a rarefaction of a valve-like acting atmosphere actually takes place as we ascend higher and higher above the level of the sea, and it is accordingly and necessarily accompanied by a corresponding diminution of temperature.

13

This well-known fact of the lower mean temperature of places of greater altitude has led to the strangest hypotheses. The sun's rays were not supposed to contain all the conditions for warming a body, but to set in motion the "substance" of heat contained in the earth. This "substance" of heat, cold when at rest, was attracted by the earth, and was therefore found in greater abundance near the center of the globe. This view, it was thought, explained why the warming power of the sun was so much weaker at the top of a mountain than at the bottom, and why, in spite of his immense radiation, he retained his full powers.

This belief, which especially prevails amongst imperfectly informed people, and which will scarcely succumb to correct views, is directly contradicted by the excellent experiments made by Pouillet at different altitudes with the pyrheliometer. These experiments show that, everything else being equal, the generation of heat by the solar rays is more powerful in higher altitudes than near the surface of our globe, and that consequently a portion of these rays is absorbed on their passage through the atmosphere. Why, in spite of this partial absorption, the mean temperature of low altitudes is nevertheless higher than it is in more elevated positions, is explained by the fact that the atmosphere stops to a far greater degree the calorific rays emanating from the earth than it does those from the sun.

REMARKABLE PLUMB-LINE DEFLECTION AT COWHYTHE, SCOTLAND.

The *Banffshire Journal*, Scotland, publishes the following statement respecting a curious local disturbance of the plumb-line, in the vicinity of Cowhythe, now under the process of investigation by Sir Henry James, Superintendent of the British Ordnance Survey. It says:—

Early during the present century the headland eastward of Portsoy on Cowhythe was visited by an officer of the Royal Engineers with the zenith sector, constructed for the Ordnance survey of this country by the celebrated Ramsden, and from the observations made with that instrument to determine the latitude of the trigonometrical station there, it was found that the plumb-line, instead of being vertical, was deflected northward of the zenith and southward of the earth's center fully 9″ of angular measure. This extraordinary and unexpected result was viewed with great interest by the scientific world, especially by such as were employed by their respective governments in connection with the determination of the figure of the earth; and, by way of verification, a party of the same corps, some 16 years back, furnished with a new zenith sector, designed by the present Astronomer Royal, and constructed by Troughton and Sims, visited the same spot. More observations, and to a greater number of stars, resulted in confirming the first or earlier determination, and here the matter rested, merely as a subject of occasional wonder to those concerned, till recently the Russian Engineers, in prosecution of their national survey, came upon a similar anomaly in the neighborhood of their ancient capital, Moscow. On tracing it to its limit, which they have done in a public-spirited and most creditable manner, they concluded that there is a vacuum, or a comparative vacuum, of a great many square miles in extent, under the earth's surface in that country. To give some idea of the reasoning which leads to so startling a conclusion, the reader may conceive

a wide, deep pit with a plummet suspended from its mouth at the earth's surface. The plumb-line will be vertical only when in the center of the pit (or shaft, it is called in connection with mines), because it will there be equally attracted in every direction. If carried round the side of the pit, the line will be so deflected from the vertical as to cause all the lines, if produced upwards, to meet in a point above the earth's surface; and such are the phenomena discovered by the geodetical engineers of Russia. The pit, it is true, is closed at its mouth, and no plumb-line can be let down into it, but the spirit-level, being always at right angles to the plumb-line, discloses the fact as clearly to the mind as the open pit would to the eye. Now, whether the Cowhythe deflection is to be accounted for by a comparative vacuum on the north under the Moray Firth, or by some unknown mass of extraordinary density on the south, or partly by both, is the problem to be solved, and, doubtless, it will ultimately be solved by the staff of astronomical observers and computers under Sir Henry James. The general result of the investigations thus far, may be briefly stated to be a diminution of the deflection as the observers proceed southwards, but how far it may extend is of course at present unknown.

THE BAROMETER AS AN INDICATOR OF THE EARTH'S ROTATION.

Mr. Pliny Earle Chase, in a paper recently read before the American Philosophical Society—*On the Barometer as an Indicator of the Earth's Rotation and the Sun's Distance;* sets forth the following views: The existence of daily barometric tides has been known for more than 150 years, but their cause is still a matter of dispute. It is evident that they cannot be accounted for by variations of temperature, for 1st, their regularity is not perceived until all the *known* effects of temperature have been eliminated; 2d, they occur in all climates, and at all seasons; 3d, opposite effects are produced at different times, under the same average temperature. Thus at St. Helena, the mean of three years' hourly observation gives the following average barometric heights :—

From 0^h to 12^h 28·2801 in.   From 18^h to 6^h 28·2838 in.
" 12^h to 0^h 28·2761 "   " 6^h to 18^h 28·2784 "

The upper lines evidently embrace the coolest parts of the day, and the lower lines the warmest. Dividing the day in the first method, the barometer is highest when the thermometer is highest; but in the second division the high barometer prevails during the coolest half of the day.

On account of the combined effects of the earth's rotation and revolution, each particle of air has a velocity in the direction of its orbit, varying at the equator from about 65,000 miles per hour, at noon, to 67,000 miles per hour, at midnight. The force of rotation may be readily compared with that of gravity by observing the effects produced by each in 24 hours, the interval that elapses between two successive returns of any point to the same relative position with the sun. The force of rotation producing a daily motion of 24,895 miles, and the force of terrestrial gravity a motion of 22,738,900 miles, the ratio of the former to the latter is $\frac{24895}{22738900}$, or ·00109. This ratio represents the proportionate elevation or depression of the barometer above or below its mean height that should be caused by the earth's rotation, and it corresponds very nearly with the actual disturbance at stations near the equator.

From 0h. to 6h. the air has a forward motion greater than that of the earth, so that it tends to fly away; its pressure is therefore diminished, and the mercury falls. From 6h. to 12h. the earth's motion is greatest; it therefore presses against the lagging air, and the barometer rises. From 12h. to 18h. the earth moves away from the air, and the barometer falls; while from 18h. to 24h. the increasing velocity of the air urges it against the earth, and the barometer rises.

From a relation of these forces to the power of gravitation, &c. Mr. Chase calculates what should be the daily changes in the hight of the barometer, and the results are found to correspond very closely with the changes in the barometer at St. Helena, the point nearest the equator where a long series of barometric observations have been made. From these changes in the barometric pressure he also computes the distance of the sun from the earth, and obtains results agreeing pretty nearly with those obtained by the most approved of other methods.

His conclusions also suggest that the revolution of the sun around the great Central Sun must also cause barometric fluctuations that may possibly be measured by delicate instruments and long and patient observation. The Toricellian column may thus become a valuable auxiliary in verifying or rectifying our estimates of the distances and masses of the principal heavenly bodies.

POPULAR EXPLANATION OF THE THEORY OF THE TIDES.

Mr. William Dennis, of Philadelphia, contributes to *Silliman's Journal*, March, 1864, an interesting article on the best method of presenting in a popular form the "Theory of the Tides;" from which we make the following extracts:—

After alluding to the difficulty which many persons experience, in understanding how the tides are produced, the author says: If a learner be told that the waters of the ocean are raised by the moon's attraction, his first idea, in many cases, will be that they are lifted up *by main strength*, as it were, the force of gravity being *overcome*, and having nowhere observed any similar effect of the moon's attraction, he cannot conceive how this can be. Nor will it tend in any degree to lessen his perplexity if he shall see it stated (as he may) that, according to Newton's calculations, the *disturbing* power of the moon's attraction on the surface of the earth is less than a ten millionth part of the force of gravity, and that of the sun's attraction not even half as great as it. It is therefore important to show, by a preliminary explanation, that the waters of the ocean, in their general figure and outline, are in a state of perfect equilibrium or perfectly balanced, so that, in view of this, and of their vast extent and perfect freedom of motion, they may be compared to a scale-beam in perfect equipoise, suspended in the most delicate manner, and *several thousand miles in length*. To omit this would be much the same as if one should state, in proof and illustration of the attraction of gravitation, that a weight or ball at the side of a mountain had been observed (referring to the Schehallien experiment) to be drawn towards the mountain by its attraction, leaving the learner to suppose that the weight was placed on a table or other level surface instead of being suspended by a long thread or wire.

In explaining this condition of equilibrium the most obvious course will be to refer to mere hydrostatic equilibrium, in which any portion of these waters may be regarded as exactly balanced by any other contiguous portion, each being maintained at its level by the pressure of the other which supports it ; consequently, if this pressure, be in the case of either portion, lessened or increased, *in the least degree*, that is to say, if the force of gravity, to which this pressure is due, be in any degree counteracted or added to by any other force in one of these portions and not in the other, the lighter portion will immediately give way and be buoyed up by the heavier, which will of course simultaneously sink : and this would be an explanation sufficient for the purpose. But as this statement, though true, is not the whole truth, it may be well to go a step further. The waters of the ocean do not maintain their general figure and outline under the influence of gravity alone. On the contrary, it is well known that, by the centrifugal force generated by the earth's rotation on its axis, they are kept at a higher level or greater distance from the center on other parts of the globe than at the poles, this elevation amounting at the equator where it is greatest to about 13 miles. They are therefore exactly suspended or poised between these two forces, namely, the force of gravity and the centrifugal force just mentioned, and any other force that should in the least degree add to or counteract the influence of either of these forces would at once cause a change in the figure of these waters. While therefore it is properly the hydrostatic equilibrium existing between the different portions of the waters themselves that is disturbed by the action of the forces that produce the tides, the statement just made may serve to show more clearly how far these waters are, in their normal condition, from lying as a *dead weight* in the depressions of the earth's surface that contain them.

Again, it is stated in a familiar way, that the tide on the side of the earth towards the moon is owing to the waters there being attracted by it more than the mass of the earth because they are nearer, while the tide raised at the same time on the opposite side of the earth results from the earth being drawn away from the waters there because they are more remote than the mass of the earth and are thus " left behind," or " left heaped up ;" and then we are told that, at full moon, when the attractions of the sun and moon are *opposite* in direction, they conspire to produce spring tides in the same manner as at new moon when their attractions coincide in direction. Now, as it is not easy to see how a body can be drawn away so as to leave any thing behind in two opposite directions at the same time, these statements appear quite inconsistent and are well calculated to confuse and perplex. It is therefore important and indeed indispensable to the communication of an intelligible view of this phenomenon to explain, as before remarked, the conditions and circumstances, or, to express it more definitely, the relations and dependences existing among the bodies concerned in it : a course at once so natural and so needful that it seems remarkable that it should not have been more generally and more fully adopted.

As the earth is *held* to its curved path around the sun by the attraction of that body acting in opposition to the centrifugal force generated by its rapid motion, in the same manner that a heavy ball or weight attached to the end of a cord and whirled around the head is held or restrained by the cord, we may regard it as suspended between these two forces, and if a ball be merely suspended by a cord it will be a fair illustration of its condition; the force of gravity or weight of the ball standing in place of the centrifugal force in the case of the earth, and the tension of the cord representing the restraining force of the sun's attraction which at each instant holds the earth to the place in its orbit which it occupies. But as this attraction of the sun diminishes rapidly with an increase of distance it is plain that it cannot hold *all parts* of the earth alike or equally, the nearest part being about 8,000 miles less distant than the most remote, while of course it holds *the whole as a mass* as it would hold it were it at the *mean* distance of all the parts, that is, at the distance of the center. Consequently on the nearest part or side towards the sun the attractive force being greater than the mean, there will be a small *excess* over what is sufficient to hold *this part* to its place in the orbit, and this excess acting upon the surface waters there in opposition to the force of gravity renders them specifically lighter and the exact equilibrium before described is immediately disturbed: these waters will therefore rise somewhat while those that are so situated as to be unaffected by this disturbing influence will sink simply from the *giving way* of those which having become lighter yield to their superior pressure. Again on the opposite side of the earth or that most remote from the sun, the attractive or restraining force will be less than the mean and therefore not quite equal to the centrifugal force, and here accordingly there will be an excess of this latter force: but on this side it is this centrifugal force that acts in a direction opposite to that of gravity, and this *excess* of it will consequently disturb the equilibrium of the surface waters here in precisely the same manner as in the other case.

Such is a statement of the general principle upon which the attraction of the sun (or of the moon) tends to produce a tidal elevation on two opposite sides of the earth, with intermediate depressions.

ON A NEW FORMULA FOR CALCULATING THE INITIAL PRESSURE OF STEAM.

In a communication on the above subject, made to the British Association, 1864, by Mr. R. A. Peacock, the author stated that some years ago he had occasion to attempt to calculate the probable pressure of steam at the highest known temperatures, and found, amongst other things, that between the pressures of 25 lb. per square inch and 300 lb. to the square inch, the latter being the highest pressure to which trustworthy experiments had been carried, the law of increase was, approximately: That the temperature of high-pressure steam of say 25 lb. to the square inch and upwards, increases as the $4\frac{1}{2}$ root of the pressure; and that, conversely, the pressure of the steam of say 25 lb. to the square inch and upwards, increases as the $4\frac{1}{2}$ power of the temperature. At lower pressures than about 25 lb. per square inch, a different law prevails. As it is necessary to verify the new formula by comparison with some well-known formulæ and experiments, the author has attempted to do so in a very voluminous table, and graphically in a very carefully-executed diagram. What is to be gathered from these is, that the new formula agrees with Dr. Fairbairn's experiments, from about 40 lb. to 60 lb., and very nearly with Regnault's, between 220 lb. and 336 lb.

CURIOUS APPLICATION OF AIR EXPANSION THROUGH HEAT.

It is well known that the air confined under glass, if it receive the direct rays of the sun, will become much heated, far beyond the temperature of the rays, owing to the action of the glass in absorbing these rays and conveying the absorbed heat to the air within. Prof. Mouchot, of Alençon, has made the following application of the heat thus acquired. He takes a bell of silver, very thin and covered with lampblack, and places over it two bells of glass, and exposes the whole to the rays of the sun. Two curved tubes, furnished with stopcocks, pass under the black bell, one of them to supply water when it is required, the other to give exit to the water; the latter terminating outside in an ordinary jet d'eau orifice. Being now exposed to the solar rays,—whose heat is transformed into non-luminous heat in its passage through the walls of the bells, an effect that goes on accumulating without cessation,—the air situated above the water dilates, and by its pressure causes a jet to rise, attaining sometimes in Mouchot's trials a hight of nearly 33 feet. When the water is exhausted, a screen placed before the sun will cool the interior and cause the water to return, or a new supply may be introduced through the supply-pipe. Many times the shade thrown over the apparatus by spectators caused it to stop, much to their surprise.—*Les Mondes*, Sept. 22.

EFFECT OF THE SUN ON SOIL AND AIR.

The relative heating of the soil and air by the solar rays on a high mountain and in a plain has been examined by the distinguished traveler, M. Ch. Marteus, who has reported on the subject to the Academy of Sciences at Paris. We give a few notes: A solar ray, it is said, falling on an elevated summit, should be hotter than one which, after traversing the lower and denser strata of the atmosphere, descends into a plain, since these strata necessarily absorb a notable quantity of the heat of the ray. All travelers who have ascended high mountains have been surprised at the extraordinary heat of the sun and the soil compared with the temperature of the air in the shade, or with that of the soil during the night. The observations of MM. Peltier, Bravais, and Marteus (two series, 125 in the whole), made on the Fauthorn, Switzerland, between 6 A. M. and 6 P. M., continued indifferently in fine and bad weather, give, nevertheless, for the mean temperature of the soil during the day, 11·75 per cent, that of the air being only 5·50. It became evident that heating of the soil during the day was twice that of the air; but the observers were not aware what had been the relative heating of the earth and air in the plain below during the same period. To obtain this knowledge, M. Marteus selected the summit of the Pic du Midi, in the Pyrenees, and a garden in the plain at Bagnères. By his observations, which began on Sept. 8, 1864, he obtained the following results: The mean of the temperature of the air in the shade, deduced from 20 observations at Bagnères, was 22·3; from the same on the Pic du Midi, 10·1 only. The mean temperature of the surface of the soil at Bagnères was 36·1; on the Pic, 33·8. The mean excess of the temperature of the soil over that of the air at the two stations is then as 10 : 171,—nearly double that on the mountain. These experiments put out of doubt the greater calorific power of the sun upon the mountain than upon the plain.

A NEW THERMOGRAPH.

M. Marcy has addressed to the French Academy the following description of an instrument for marking small variations of temperature: 1. The first part of this thermograph consists of a copper tube a meter in length, the interior diameter of which is capillary, not being more than ⅓ of a millimeter. It is open at one end, and soldered to a hollow copper ball at the other end. 2. The second part of the apparatus consists of a wheel resting upon knife-edges, like those of a pair of scales, whereby a very delicate oscillation may be imparted to it. The axle of the wheel carries a long vertical needle, marking the degrees on a circular scale. To the circumference of the wheel is fixed a glass tube six millimeters in diameter, and bent in conformity to the curvature of the wheel, and so situated that the middle of the tube lies vertically underneath the needle when the wheel is at rest. One of its extremities is hermetically closed, while the other is open. Now, if a little mercury be poured into this tube it will settle at the lowest point, and the interior of the tube will thus be divided into two chambers, one closed and with air confined in it, the other open. 3. Now introduce the copper tube into the glass one, giving it of course the same curvature, and so that its extremity may pass through the mercury, thus establishing a communication between the hollow copper ball and the confined chambers, and the apparatus, with a few accessory appliances, will be complete. The end of the copper tube dipping into the mercury should be varnished to prevent its being attacked by the latter metal; or better still, the end might be made of platinum. 4. To use this apparatus, put your hand to the copper ball; the warmth thus imparted to it will dilate the air it contains, and drive part of it into the confined chamber; the mercury will therefore recede, and thereby make the wheel turn round its center of gravity; the very small arc thus described will be revealed by the needle, the difference of its present position with its previous one when at rest. If, on the contrary, the copper ball be cooled, by water, for instance, the air inside will be contracted, a portion of the air of the confined chamber will rush in, and the mercury will be driven forward, the needle turning in the inverse direction. By means of this experiment very delicate physiological experiments on animal heat may be conducted.

HEAT AND FORCE.

Whenever friction is overcome, heat is produced; and the amount of heat so produced is the exact measure of the force extended in overcoming the friction. Prof. Tyndall, speaking upon the subject of "Heat considered as a Mode of Motion," says: "We usually put oil upon the surface of a hone; we grease the saw, and are careful to lubricate the axles of our railway carriages. What are we really doing in these cases? Let us get general notions first; we shall come to particulars afterwards. It is the object of the railway engineer to urge his train boldly from one place to another. He wishes to apply the force of his steam or his furnace, which gives tension to the steam to this particular purpose. It is not his interest to allow any portion of that force to be converted into another form of force which would not further the attainment of his object. He does not want his axles heated, and thence he avoids as much as possible expending his power in heating them. In fact he has obtained his force from heat, and it is not his object to reconvert the force thus obtained into its primitive form. For by every degree of temperature generated by the friction of his axle, a definite amount would be withdrawn from the urging force of his engine. There is no force lost absolutely. Could we gather up all the heat generated by the friction, and could we apply it mechanically, we should by it be able to impart to the train the precise amount of speed which it lost by the friction. Thus every one of those railway porters whom you see moving about with his can of yellow grease, and opening the little boxes which surround the carriage axles, is, without knowing it, illustrating a principle which forms the very solder of nature. In so doing he is unconsciously affirming both the convertibility and the indestructibility of force. He is practically asserting that mechanical energy may be converted into heat, and that when so converted it cannot still exist as mechanical energy, but that for every degree of heat developed, a strict and proportional equivalent of locomotive force of the engine disappears. A station is approached say at the rate of 30 or 40 miles an hour; the brake is applied, and smoke and sparks issue from the wheel on which it presses. The train is brought to rest; how? Simply by converting the entire moving force which it possessed at the moment the brake was applied, into heat."

THE COOLING OF THE EARTH AND ITS CONSEQUENCES, BY DR. J. R. MAYER.

If we assume that our globe was once in an incandescent state (as is now generally admitted), it must have lost heat at first at a very rapid rate; gradually this process became slower; and although it has not yet entirely ceased, the rate of cooling must have diminished to a comparatively small magnitude.

Two phenomena are caused by the cooling of the earth, which on account of their common origin are intimately related. The decrease of temperature, and consequent contraction of the earth's crust, must have caused frequent disturbances and revolutions on its surface, accompanied by the ejection of molten masses and the formation of protuberances: on the other hand, according to the laws of mechanics, the velocity of rotation must have increased with the diminution of the volume of the sphere, or in other words, the cooling of the earth must have shortened the length of the day. As the intensity of such disturbance and the velocity of rotation are closely connected, it is clear that the youth of our planet must have been characterized by continual violent transformations of its crust and a perceptible acceleration of the velocity of its axial rotation; while in the present time the metamorphoses of its surface are much slower, and the acceleration of its axial revolution diminished to a very small amount.

If we imagine the times when the Alps, the chain of the Andes, and the Peak of Teneriffe were upheaved from the deep, and compare with such changes the earthquakes and volcanic eruptions of historic times, we perceive in these modern transformations but weak images of the analogous processes of bygone ages.

While we are surrounded on every side by the monuments of violent volcanic convulsions, we possess no record of the velocity of the axial rotation of our planet in antediluvian times. It is of the greatest importance that we should have an exact knowledge of a change in this velocity, or in the length of the day during historic times. The investigation of this subject by the great Laplace forms a bright monument in the department of exact science.

These calculations are essentially conducted in the following manner: In the first place, the time between two eclipses of the sun, widely apart from each other, is as accurately as possible expressed in days, and from this the ratio of the time of the earth's rotation to the mean time of the moon's revolution determined. If, now, the observations of ancient astronomers be compared with those of our present time, the least alteration in the absolute length of a day may be detected by a change in this ratio, or in a disturbance in the lunar revolution. The most perfect agreement of ancient records on the movements of the moon and the planets, on the eclipses of the sun, &c. revealed to Laplace the remarkable fact that, in the course of 25 centuries, the time in which our earth revolves on its axis has not altered $\frac{1}{500}$ part of a sexagesimal second; and the length of a day therefore may be considered to have been constant during historic times. This result, as important as it was convenient for astronomy, was nevertheless of a nature to create some difficulties for the physicist. With apparently good reason it was concluded that, if the velocity of rotation had remained constant, the volume of the earth could have undergone no change. The earth completes one révolution on its axis in 86,400 sidereal seconds; it consequently appears, if this time has not altered during 2,500 years to the extent of $\frac{1}{500}$ of a second, or $\frac{1}{43000000}$ part of a day, that during this long space of time the radius of the earth also cannot have altered more than this fraction of its length. The earth's radius measures 6,369,800 meters, and therefore its length ought not to have diminished more than 15 centimeters in 25 centuries.

The diminution in volume, as a result of the cooling-process, is however, closely connected with the changes on the earth's surface. When we consider that scarcely a day passes without the occurrence of an earthquake or shock in one place or another, and that of the 300 active volcanos some are always in action, it would appear that such a lively reaction of the interior of the earth against the crust is incompatible with the constancy of its volume. This apparent discrepancy between Cordier's theory of the connection between the cooling of the earth and the reaction of the interior or the exterior parts, and Laplace's calculation showing the constancy of the length of the day, a calculation which is undoubtedly correct, has induced most scientific men to abandon Cordier's theory, and thus to deprive themselves of any tenable explanation of volcanic activity.

The continued cooling of the earth cannot be denied, for it takes place according to the laws of nature ; in this respect the earth cannot comport itself differently from any other mass, however small it be. In spite of the heat which it receives from the sun, the earth will have a tendency to cool so long as the temperature of its interior is higher than the mean temperature of its surface. Between the tropics the mean temperature produced by the sun is about 28°, and the sun

therefore is as little able to stop the cooling tendency of the earth as the moderate warmth of the air can prevent the cooling of a red-hot ball suspended in a room. Many phenomena—for instance, the melting of the glaciers near the bed on which they rest—show the uninterrupted emission of heat from the interior toward the exterior of the earth; and the question is, Has the earth in 25 centuries actually lost no more heat than that which is requisite to shorten a radius of more than 6,000,000 of meters only 15 centimeters ?

In answering this question, three points enter into our calculation: 1, the absolute amount of heat lost by the earth in a certain time, say one day; 2, the earth's capacity for heat; and 3, the coefficient of expansion of the mass of the earth. As none of these quantities can be determined by direct measurements, we are obliged to content ourselves with probable estimates; these estimates will carry the more weight the less they are formed in favor of some preconceived opinion.

Considering what is known about the expansion and contraction of solids and liquids by heat and cold, we arrive at the conclusion that for a diminution of 1° in temperature, the linear contraction of the earth cannot well be less than $\frac{1}{100000}$ part, a number which we all the more readily adopt because it has been used by Laplace, Arago, and others.

If we compare the capacity for heat of all solid and liquid bodies which have been examined, we find that, both as regards volume and weight, the capacity of water is the greatest. Even the gases come under this rule; hydrogen, however, forms an exception, it having the greatest capacity for heat of all bodies when compared with an equal weight of water. In order not to take the capacity for heat of the mass of the earth too small, we shall consider it to be equal to that of its volume of water, which, when calculated for equal weights, amounts to 0·184.

If we accept Laplace's result, that the length of a day has remained constant during the last 2,500 years, and conclude that the earth's radius has not diminished 1¼ decimeter in consequence of cooling, we are obliged to assume, according to the premises stated, that the mean temperature of our planet cannot have decreased $\frac{1}{150}$° in the same period of time. The volume of the earth amounts to 2,650,000,-000 of cubic miles. A loss of heat sufficient to cool this mass $\frac{1}{150}$° would be equal to the heat given off when the temperature of 6,150,-000 cubic miles of water decreases 1°; hence the loss for one day would be equal to 6·74 cubic miles of heat. Fourier has investigated the loss of heat sustained by the earth. Taking the observation that the temperature of the earth increases at the rate of 1° for every 30 meters as the basis of his calculations, this celebrated mathematician finds the heat which the globe loses by conduction through its crust in the space of 100 years to be capable of melting a layer of ice three meters in thickness and covering the whole surface of the globe; this corresponds in one day to 7·7 cubic miles of heat, and in 2,500 years to a decrease of 17 centimeters in the length of the radius.

According to this, the cooling of the globe would be sufficiently great to require attention when the earth's velocity of rotation is considered. At the same time it is clear that the method employed by

Fourier can bring to our knowledge only one part of the heat which is annually lost by the earth; for simple conduction through *terra firma* is not the only way by which heat escapes from our globe.

In the first place, we may make mention of the aqueous deposits of our atmosphere, which, as far as they penetrate our earth, wash away, so to speak, a portion of the heat, and thus accelerate the cooling of the globe. The whole quantity of water which falls from the atmosphere upon the land in one day, however, cannot be assumed to be much more than half a cubic mile in volume, hence the cooling effect produced by this water may be neglected in our calculation. The heat carried off by all the thermal springs in the world is very small in comparison with the quantities which we have to consider here.

Much more important is the effect produced by active volcanos. As the heat which accompanies the molten matter to the surface is derived from the store in the interior of the earth, their action must influence considerably the diminution of the earth's heat. And we have not only to consider here actual eruptions which take place in succession or simultaneously at different parts of the earth's surface, but also volcanos in a quiescent state, which continually radiate large quantities of heat abstracted from the interior of the globe. If we compare the earth to an animal body, we may regard each volcano as a place where the epidermis has been torn off, leaving the interior exposed, and thus opening a door for the escape of heat. Of the whole of the heat which passes away through these numerous outlets, too low an estimate must not be made. To have some basis for the estimation of this loss, we have to recollect that in 1783, Skaptar-Jokul, a volcano in Iceland, emitted sufficient lava in the space of six weeks to cover 60 square miles of country to an average depth of 200 meters, or, in other words, about $1\frac{1}{2}$ cubic miles of lava. The amount of heat lost by this one eruption of one volcano must, when the high temperature of the lava is considered, be estimated to be more than 1,000 cubic miles of heat; and the whole loss resulting from the action of all the volcanos amounts, therefore, in all probability, to thousands of cubic miles of heat per annum. This latter number, when added to Fourier's result, produces a sum which evidently does not agree with the assumption that the volume of our earth has remained unchanged.

In the investigation of the cooling of our globe, the influence of the water of the ocean has to be taken into account. Fourier's calculations are based on the observations of the increase of the temperature of the crust of our earth, from the surface toward the center. But $\frac{2}{3}$ of the surface of our globe are covered with water, and we cannot assume *à priori* that this large area loses heat at the same rate as the solid parts; on the contrary, various circumstances indicate that the cooling of our globe proceeds more quickly through the waters of the ocean resting on it than from the solid parts merely in contact with the atmosphere.

In the first place, we have to remark that the bottom of the ocean is, generally speaking, nearer to the store of heat in the interior of the earth than the dry land is, and hence that the temperature increases most probably in a greater ratio from the bottom of the sea toward the interior of the globe, than it does in our observations on the land. Secondly, we have to consider that the whole bottom of the sea is covered by a layer of ice-cold water, which moves constantly from the poles to the equator, and which, in its passage over sandbanks, causes, as Humboldt aptly remarks, the low temperatures which are generally observed in shallow places. That the water near the bottom of the sea, on account of its great specific heat and its low temperature, is better fitted than the atmosphere to withdraw the heat from the earth, is a point which requires no further discussion.

We have plenty of observations which prove that the earth suffers a great loss of heat through the waters of the ocean. Many investigations have demonstrated the existence of a large expanse of sea, much visited by whalers, situated between Iceland, Greenland, Norway, and Spitzbergen, and extending from latitude 76° to 80° N., and from longitude 15° E. to 15° W. of Greenwich, where the temperature was observed to be higher in the deeper water than near the surface,—an experience which neither accords with the general rule, nor agrees with the laws of hydrostatics. Franklin observed, in latitude 77° N., and longitude 12° E., that the temperature of the sea near the surface was—4°, and at a depth of 700 fathoms+6°. Fisher, in latitude 80° N. and longitude 11° E., noticed that the surface-water had a temperature of 0°, whilst at a depth of 140 fathoms it stood at +8. As sea-water, unlike pure water, does not possess a point of greatest density at some distance above the freezing-point, and as the water in latitude 80° N. is found at some depth to be warmer than water at the same depth 10° southward, we can only explain this remarkable phenomenon of an increase of temperature with an increase of depth by the existence of a source of heat at the bottom of the sea. The heat, however, which is required to warm the water at the bottom of an expanse of ocean more than 1,000 square miles in extent to a sensible degree, must amount, according to the lowest estimate, to some cubic miles of heat a day. The same phenomenon has been observed in other parts of the world, such as the west coast of Australia, the Adriatic, the Lago Maggiore, &c. Especial mention should here be made of an observation by Horner, according to whom, the lead, when hauled up from a depth varying from 80 to 100 fathoms in the mighty Gulf-stream off the coast of America, used to be hotter than boiling water.

The facts above mentioned, and some others which might be added, clearly show that the loss of heat suffered by our globe during the last 2,500 years is far too great to have been without sensible effect on the velocity of the earth's rotation. The reason why, in spite of this accelerating cause, the length of a day has nevertheless remained constant since the most ancient times, must be attributed to an opposite retarding action. This consists in the attraction of the sun and moon on the liquid parts of the earth's surface.

According to calculation the retarding pressure of the tides against the earth's rotation would cause, during the lapse of 2,500 years a sidereal day to be lengthened to the extent of $\frac{1}{16}$ of a second; as the length of a day, however, has remained constant, the cooling effect of the earth during the same period of time must have shortened the day $\frac{1}{16}$ of a second. A diminution of the earth's radius to the amount of 4½ meters in 2,500 years, and a daily loss of 200 cubic miles of heat, correspond to this effect. Hence, in the course of the last 25 centuries, the temperature of the whole mass of the earth must have decreased $\frac{1}{14}°$.

The not inconsiderable contraction of the earth resulting from such a loss of heat, agrees with the continual transformations of the earth's surface by earthquakes and volcanic eruptions; and we agree with Cordier, the industrious observer of volcanic processes, in considering these phenomena a necessary consequence of the continual cooling of an earth which is still in a molten state in its interior.

When our earth was in its youth, velocity of rotation must have increased to a very sensible degree, on account of the rapid cooling of its then very hot mass. This accelerating cause gradually diminished, and as the retarding pressure of the tidal wave remains nearly constant, the latter must finally preponderate, and the velocity of rotation therefore continually decrease. Between these two states we have a period of equilibrium, a period when the influence of the cooling and that of the tidal pressure counterbalance each other; the whole life of the earth therefore may be divided into three periods,—youth with increasing, middle age with uniform, and old age with decreasing velocity of rotation.

The time during which the two opposed influences on the rotation of the earth are in equilibrium can, strictly speaking, only be very short, inasmuch as in one moment the cooling, and in the next moment the pressure of the tides must prevail. In a physical sense, however, when measured by human standards, the influence of the cooling, and still more so that of the tidal wave, may for ages be considered constant, and there must consequently exist a period of many thousand years' duration during which these counteracting influences will appear to be equal. Within this period, a sidereal day attains its shortest length, and the velocity of the earth's rotation its maximum,—circumstances which, according to mathematical analysis, would tend to lengthen the duration of this period of the earth's existence.

The historical times of mankind are, according to Laplace's calculation, to be placed in this period. Whether we are at the present moment still near its commencement, its middle, or are approaching its conclusion, is a question which cannot be solved by our present data, and must be left to future generations.

The continual cooling of the earth cannot be without an influence on the temperature of its surface, and consequently on the climate; scientific men, led by Buffon, in fact, have advanced the supposition that the loss of heat sustained by our globe must at some time render it an unfit habitation for organic life. Such an apprehension has evidently no foundation, for the warmth of the earth's surface is even now much more dependent on the rays of the sun than on the heat which reaches us from the interior. According to Pouillet's measurements, the earth receives 8,000 cubic miles of heat a day from the sun, whereas the heat which reaches the surface from the earth's interior may be estimated at two hundred cubic miles per diem. The heat therefore obtained from the latter source every day is but small in comparison to the diurnal heat received from the sun.

If we imagine the solar radiation to be constant, and the heat we receive from the store in the interior of the earth to be cut off, we should have as a consequence various changes in the physical constitution of the surface of our globe. The temperature of hot springs would gradually sink down to the mean temperature of the earth's crust, volcanic eruptions would cease, earthquakes would no longer be felt, and the temperature of the water of the ocean would be sensibly altered in many places,—circumstances which would doubtless affect the climate in many parts of the world. Especially, it may be presumed that Western Europe, with its pleasant favorable climate, would become colder, and thus *perhaps* the seat of the power and culture of our race transferred to the milder parts of North America.

Be this as it may, for thousands of years to come we can predict no diminution of the temperature of the surface of our globe as a consequence of the cooling of its interior mass; and, so far as historic records teach, the climates, the temperatures of thermal springs, and the intensity and frequency of volcanic eruptions are now the same as they were in the far past.

It was different in prehistoric times, when for centuries the earth's surface was heated by internal fire, when mammoths lived in the now uninhabitable polar regions, and when the tree-ferns and the tropical shell-fish, whose fossil remains are now especially preserved in the coal-formation, were at home in all parts of the world.

THE INTENSITY OF SOLAR RADIATION.

The intensity of the solar radiation at different seasons of the year has been investigated by Father Secchi of the Observatory at Rome. We give some results from his paper recently printed in the *Comptes Rendus* of the Academy of Sciences at Paris. We have not space for the description of the apparatus employed, and with which he made a great number of observations during the summer, repeating them during the perfectly clear days between Nov. 22 and Dec. 8, last, when he exposed the apparatus to the solar radiation under the dome of the observatory until the temperature remained perfectly constant for a considerable time. 1. During the summer, near the meridian and near the solstice, the relative temperature varied from $14°$ to $11°$ Cent.; the mean being $12·06°$. 2. The observations continued during August gave $13°$ to $11°$: the mean $12°$. 3. Those made in November and December gave $12·5°$, $11·5°$, the mean not being sensibly changed. 4. When observing in summer, near the horizon; at an elevation of $30°$ to $34°$, he found the temperature rose only to $6·5°$. 5. The rapidity with which the blackened thermometer rose was scarcely different in summer from winter until $10°$ or $11°$; but after this limit the maximum was attained sooner in summer than in winter. The results obtained in the latter season were completely unexpected. Father Secchi thought that observing the sun at a height of about $28°$, he would find a temperature quite, or nearly equal to that which he found in summer at $32°$ of elevation, the atmospheric density being nearly the same; but it was not so. At the meridian he found nearly the same amount as in summer, although the rays traversed a thickness of atmosphere more than double, while this double thickness diminished the force of the radiation, reducing it to the half. These phenomena would be inexplicable if we did not know the absorbing power of the aqueous vapor. Father Secchi expresses his agreement with the results obtained by Prof. Tyndall, estimating its absorbing power at 60 times that of air.

MECHANICAL VALUE OF THE SUN'S HEAT UPON THE EARTH.

Mr. J. R. Mayer, well known for his researches in celestial dynamics, estimates the effect of the solar radiation in mechanical work on the total surface of the earth, as equal to 180 *billions of horse-power* per minute, or in other words, the surface of our globe receives every minute an addition of *vis viva* equivalent to this amount. A not inconsiderable portion of this enormous quantity of *vis viva* is consumed in the production of atmospheric actions, in consequence of which numerous motions are set up in the earth's atmosphere.—*Silliman's Journal.*

BREAKING ROCKS BY FIRE.

The ancient method of breaking rocks by fire has lately been revived at the Rammelsberg mine, in the Hartz Mountains. In a portable furnace about one and a half bushels of coke burn from 4 P. M. to 5 A. M., when the furnace is removed and the rock left to cool, after being sprinkled with water. About noon the face of the rock spontaneously detaches itself; and after that a further portion is broken. The effect of the fire extends to 8 inches, and with 1½ bushels of coke from 16 to 24 cwt. of ore is obtained at half the cost of the gunpowder process.

COOLING OF SOLIDS BY TENSION.

Mr. James Croll, in the *Philosophical Magazine*, directs attention to the experiments of Dr. Joule, which proved that the quantity of cold produced by the application of tension to solids was sensibly equal to the heat evolved by its removal; and further, that the thermal effects were proportional to the weight employed. The probable explanation given by Mr. Croll is this: If the molecules of a body are held together by any force, of whatever nature it may be, which prevents any further separation taking place, then the entire heat of such a body will appear as temperature; but if this binding force become lessened, so as to allow further expansion, then a portion of the heat will be lost in producing expansion. All solids, at any given temperature expand until the expansive force of their heat exactly balances the cohesive force of their molecules; after which no further expansion at the same temperature can possibly take place while the cohesive force remains unchanged. But if by some means or other the cohesive force of the molecules become reduced, then instantly the body will expand under the heat which it possesses, and of course a portion of the heat will be consumed in expansion, and a cooling effect will result.

CONDUCTION OF HEAT.

In relation to Tyndall's researches, M. L'Abbé Laborde states that he heated to redness one end of a thin iron bar so long that the other end could be held without burning. When the red end was plunged into water the other end became so hot he was compelled to drop it. The rapid compression of the hot metal, he says, is no doubt the cause of the elevation of temperature; but he asks if another cause may not be suspected: for instance, the creation of thermo-electric currents?

NOTES ON THE VARIATIONS OF DENSITY PRODUCED BY HEAT
IN MINERAL SUBSTANCES. BY DR. T. L. PHIPSON, F. C. S.

" That any mineral substance, whether crystallized or not, should
diminish in density by the action of heat, might be looked upon as a
natural consequence of dilation being produced in every case and become permanent. Such diminution of density occurs with idocrase,
Labradorite, feldspar, quartz, amphibole, pyroxene, peridote, Sam-
arshite, porcelain and glass. But Gadolinite, zircons, and yellow
obsidian augment in density from the same cause. This again may
be explained by assuming that, under the influence of a powerful heat,
these substances undergo some permanent molecular change. But in
this note I have to show that this molecular change is not permanent,
but intermittent, at least as regards the species I have examined, and
probably with all others. Such researches, while tending to elucidate
certain points of chemical geology, may likewise add something to
our present knowledge of the modes of action of heat. My experiments were undertaken to prove an interesting fact announced
formerly by Magnus,—namely, that specimens of idocrase after fusion
had diminished considerably in density without undergoing any change
of composition ; before fusion their specific gravity ranged from 3·349
to 3·45 and after fusion only 2·93 to 2·945. Having lately received
specimens of this and other minerals brought from Vesuvius, I determined upon repeating this experiment of Magnus. I found, first,
that what he stated for idocrase and for a specimen of reddish-brown
garnet was also the case with the whole family of garnets as well as
for the minerals of the idocrase groupe : secondly, that it is not necessary to melt the minerals ; it is sufficient that they should be heated
to redness without fusion, in order to occasion this change of density :
thirdly, that the diminished density thus produced by the action of a
red heat is not a permanent state, but that the specimens, in the course
of a month or less, resume their original specific gravities. These
curious results were first obtained by me with a species of lime garnet
in small yellowish crystals, exceedingly brilliant and resinous, almost
granular, fusing with difficulty to black enamel, accompanied with
very little leucite and crystallized in the second system. * * *
* * * * Specimens weighing some grammes had their specific
gravity taken with great care. They were then perfectly dried and
exposed for about a quarter of an hour to a bright red heat. When
the whole substance of the specimen was observed to have attained
this temperature, without a trace of fusion, it was allowed to cool,
and when it had arrived at the temperature of the atmosphere, its specific gravity was again taken by the same method as before. The
diminution of density being noted, the specimens were carefully dried,
enveloped in several folds of filtering paper, and put aside in a box
along with other minerals. In the course of a month it occurred to
me that it would be interesting to take the specific gravity again, in
order to ascertain whether it had not returned to its original figure,
when, to my surprise, I found that each specimen had effectively increased in density and had attained its former specific gravity. The
same experiments were made with several other minerals belonging
to the idocrase and garnet family, and always with similar results.

14*

Now, what becomes of the heat which seems to be shut up in a mineral substance for the space of a month? The substance of the mineral is dilated, the distance between its molecules is enlarged, but these molecules slowly approach each other again and in the course of some weeks resume their original positions. What induces the change, or how does it happen that the original specific gravity is not acquired immediately the substance has cooled? Will the same phenomena show itself with other families of minerals or with metallic elements? Such are the points which I propose to examine in the next place ; in the mean time the observations I have just alluded to are proof that bodies can absorb a certain amount of heat not indicated by the thermometer (which becomes latent), and that this is affected without the body undergoing a change of state : secondly, that they slowly part with this heat again until they have acquired their original densities : thirdly, so many different substances being affected by a change of density when melted or simply heated to redness and allowed to cool, it is probable this property will be found to belong, more or less, to all substances without exception."

RESEARCHES ON BOILING WATER.

Mr. William R. Grove, in a recent lecture on this subject before the Royal Institution, after defining boiling as the complete elimination of gas or air from a liquid and its transformation into vapor, expressed his conviction, founded on experiments, that water never did boil as far as we know now : what he termed an "everlasting" bubble of a gas always remaining behind. After showing, by means of the electric lamp, the phenomena accompanying boiling water in a tube,—the rising of the bubbles of air from the bottom,—he expressed his opinion that water could not boil without air. He then proceeded to describe experiments made in relation to those of Donny, who had shown that in proportion as water is deprived of air, the character of its ebullition changes, becoming more and more abrupt, boiling with sudden bursts, while between each burst the water reaches a temperature considerably above the boiling point ; to do this it was necessary to boil the water in a tube with a narrow orifice, through which the vapor issued. If the water were boiled in an open vessel it reabsorbed air, and boiled in the ordinary way. Mr. Grove illustrated the difficulty experienced in entirely expelling air or gas from water by boiling it under oil in a tube. Each bubble of steam which left the surface of the water passed through the column of oil, becoming smaller and smaller during its ascent, but it never condensed without leaving a minute bubble of gas, which would be found to be nitrogen. With the view of testing the possibility of converting an absolutely pure liquid into vapor, Mr. Grove tried bromine, but discovered in this instance that a certain quantity of oxygen occupied the space above the liquid bromine : and even sulphur and phosphorus strongly heated over a close vessel each gave off a gas. We have no space to describe Mr. Grove's experiments in relation to the decomposition of water by heat, and the mode of action in the gas-battery. He expressed his own opinion that hitherto simple boiling, in the sense of a liquid being expanded into vapor by heat, without being decomposed or having permanent gas eliminated from it, is a thing unknown. He stated that close investigations into these interesting phenomena would probably lead to most important discoveries, and expressed his regret at not having time to spare to continue his researches.

Water Boiled in Paper Vessels. — Mr. Terrill has laid before the Chemical Society of Paris, facts proving that the paper on which a layer of water is placed, may be heated to the highest temperature without being changed. He states, that the non-conductibility of the paper for heat, and the constant evaporation of the liquid through the pores of the paper, prevent the combustion of the paper and the ebullition of the water when heated in vessels of 'paper. During the experiment, there is endosmosis of the exterior gases through the pores of the paper, and hence, when the water contains metallic salts in solution, these are reduced by contact with the flame, after having traversed the paper.

ON THE PRISMATIC FORMATION OF ICE IN CERTAIN ICE CAVES AND GLACIERS.

A paper on the above subject was read at the last meeting of the British Association by Rev. G. Browne. These ice caves, he stated, were found in limestone rocks in various parts of France and Switzerland. The ice was found at depths of from 50 to 200 feet below the surface, and at altitudes varying from under 2,000, to nearly 6000 feet above the sea, and appeared in the form of columns with spreading bases formed by the freezing of water which dropped from the roof; of ice cascades supported by the sloping walls, and formed by water running into the cave from lateral fissures and in other forms. In many of these caves there was perpetual darkness; and in almost all of them a candle would burn for hours without giving any sign of the presence of a current of air. In visiting these caves, he was struck by the columnar appearance presented by the fractured side of the ice, and on examining it he found that the whole mass was composed of a vast number of prisms closely compacted. He separated the prisms at the edge with the greatest ease, and thrust them out one after the other, as one might thrust out a knot of wood from the edge of a board. The prisms reminded him of the construction of a stone wall, built without mortar, in a slaty country. The irregular stones should form a compact map, and the surface of the walls should be ground smooth. This ice resisted the effect of heat more successfully than ordinary ice.

ON THE CONDENSATION OF VAPORS ON THE SURFACE OF SOLID BODIES.

A translation of Prof. Magnus's paper on this subject appears in the *Philosophical Magazine.* Our limited space prevents us giving details of the methods of experimenting beyond the fact that the plate of the substance examined was so placed that, by means of a bellows, dry or moist air could be made to stream upon it, the change of temperature being determined by means of the thermo-electric pile and a very sensitive needle galvanometer. The Professor in conclusion, asserts, as the results of his investigations, that it has been established that the most various organic and inorganic bodies—wax, paraffin, glass, quartz, mica, gypsum, and the most dissimilar salts; also the metals, whether rough or polished, or even covered with varnish—condense on their surface aqueous vapor from the surrounding air, which has the same temperature as themselves, and, in consequence of this condensation, undergo elevation of temperature: and that when the surrounding air is changed for air containing less moisture, then a part of the previously condensed moisture should evaporate and cool the surface of the body. Results perfectly similar to those obtained with vapor of water were obtained by using vapor of alcohol, or of ether, or other vapors. Generalizing : the most various vapors condense on the surface of solid bodies in such a quantity as to cause appreciable elevation of temperature. From this it follows that, at all times, there is at the surface of solid bodies a layer of condensed vapor, which is larger or smaller according to the hygrometric state of the atmosphere. Under some conditions, this will, without doubt, exercise a by no means unimportant influence.

ON THE NATURE OF HEAT-VIBRATIONS.

Prof. Tyndall, in his researches on radiant heat, has shown that *the period* of heat-vibrations is not affected by the state of aggregation of the molecules of the heated body ; that is to say, whether the substance be in the gaseous, the liquid, or perhaps the solid condition, the tendency of its molecules to vibrate according to a given period, remains unchanged, the force of cohesion binding the molecules together, exercises no effect on the rapidity of vibration. Mr. James Croll, in a communication to the *Philosophical Magazine*, states that he has also deduced some further conclusions regarding the nature of heat-vibrations, which seem to be in a measure confirmed by the experimental results of Prof. Tyndall. One of these conclusions was that the heat-vibration does not consist in a motion of an aggregate mass of molecules, but in a motion of the individual molecules themselves. Each molecule, or rather we should say each atom, acts as if there were no other in existence but itself. Whether the atom stands by itself as in the gaseous state, or is bound to other atoms as in the liquid or the solid state, it behaves in exactly the same manner. The deeper question then suggested itself, viz : what is the nature of that mysterious motion assumed by the atom called heat ? Does it consist in excursions across centers of equilibrium external to the atom itself? It is the generally received opinion among physicists that it does. But we think that the experimental results arrived at by Prof. Tyndall, as well as some others which will presently be noticed, are entirely hostile to such an opinion. The relation of an atom to its center of equilibrium depends entirely on the state of aggregation. Now if heat-vibrations consist in excursions to and fro across these centers, then the *period* ought to be affected by the state of aggregation. The higher the *tension* of the atom in regard to the center, the more rapid ought its movement to be. This is the case in regard to the vibrations constituting sound. The harder a body becomes, or, in other words, the more firmly its molecules are bound together, the higher is the *pitch*. Two harp-chords struck with equal force will vibrate with equal force, however much they may differ in the rapidity of their vibrations. The *vis viva* of vibration depends upon the force of the stroke ; but the rapidity depends, not on the stroke, but on the tension of the cord.

That heat-vibrations do not consist in excursions of the molecules or atoms across centers of equilibrium follows also, as a necessary consequence, from the fact that the real specific heat of a body remains unchanged under all conditions. All changes in the specific heat of a body are due to differences in the amount of heat consumed in molecular work against cohesion or other forces binding the molecules together. Or, in other words, to produce in a body no other effect than a given rise of temperature requires the same amount of force, whatever may be the physical condition of the body. Whether the body be in the solid, the fluid, or the gaseous condition, the same rise of temperature always indicates the same quantity of force consumed in the simple production of the rise. Now if heat-vibrations consist in excursions of the atom to and fro across a center of equilibrium *external to itself*, as is generally supposed, then the *real* specific heat of a solid body, for example, *ought to decrease with the hardness of the body*, because an increase in the strength of the force binding the molecules together, would in such a case tend to favor the rise in the rapidity of the vibrations.

These conclusions not only afford us an insight into the hidden nature of heat-vibrations, but they also appear to cast some light on the physical constitution of the atom itself. They seem to lead to the conclusion that the ultimate atom itself is *essentially elastic*. For if heat-vibrations do not consist in excursions of the atom, then it must consist in alternate expansions and contractions of the atom itself. This again is opposed to the ordinary idea that the atom is essentially solid and impenetrable; but it favors the modern idea that matter consists of a force of resistance acting from a center.

EFFECT OF THE COLLISION OF THE MOON AND THE EARTH.

If we imagine the moon in the course of time, either in consequence of the action of a resisting medium, or from some other cause, to unite herself with our earth, two principal effects are to be discerned. A result of the collision would be, that the whole mass of the moon and the cold crust of the earth would be raised some thousands of degrees in temperature, and consequently the surface of the earth would be converted into a fiery ocean. At the same time, the velocity of the earth's axial rotation would be somewhat accelerated, and the position of its axis with regard to the heavens, and to its own surface, slightly altered. If the earth had been a cold body without axial rotation, the process of its combining with the moon would have imparted to it both heat and rotation. It is probable that such processes of combination between different parts of our globe may have repeatedly happened before the earth attained its present magnitude, and that luxuriant vegetation may have at different times been buried under the fiery debris resulting from the conflict of its now component masses.—*J R. Mayer, Silliman's Journal.*

THE DISCRIMINATION OF ORGANIC BODIES BY OPTICAL PROPERTIES.

Prof. G. G. Stokes recently delivered a lecture before the Royal Society "On the discrimination of organic bodies by their optical properties," especially by means of the apparatus of Kichhoff and Bunsen, whereby the spectrum of any substance may be produced with the greatest facility,—thus affording a test for the presence of certain substances in compounds, showing their chemical identity, &c. By means of the electric lamp and the large apparatus of the society he was able to exhibit the results of his experiments. He referred to the relation of all substances to light and to their different refractive and dispersive powers, as manifested in mixtures, pointing out how exceedingly available color is in determining the chemical character of a body. He first exhibited, by way of contrast, an impure spectrum produced by the introduction of a piece of silver in the light, and then the pure, continuous spectrum of the lamp itself. He then showed the varied action of the different rays of the pure spectrum, caused by putting in the flame a peculiar salt of copper,—some rays being cut off and others rendered opaque. He next took two bodies much alike in color,—diluted port wine and diluted blood,—and exhibited their totally different spectra. In the spectrum of blood certain rays were cut off or obscured, while two distinct red bands were manifest,—these last appeared in the spectra of several mixtures which contained blood, and even in hæmatine, an extract of that fluid. · By examining the spectrum of salts of iron it was shown that the color of the blood is not due to the presence of that mineral; it was suggested that it is probably derived from the complex nature of its crystals. Prof. S. stated that he had selected blood as a striking example of the way in which the chemical character of bodies may be tested by their relation to light.

OPTICAL PROPERTIES OF THE METALS.

M. Quincke's paper on this subject, published in the *Philosophical Magazine* is devoted to the transmission of light through thin films of metal, with especial relation to the researches of Faraday, who remarked the irregularity of the intensity and color of the light in the same metal. This, M. Quincke says, would have been attributed to the presence of holes in the plate, if Faraday had not demonstrated the property of a thin metallic film, viz: that, when placed obliquely between two crossed Nicol's prisms, it illuminates the plate and acts "just like a glass plate." This property, M. Quincke thinks, was first observed by Mr. Warren De La Rue, with regard to gold leaf, and afterwards by Faraday in thin transparent plates of platinum, palladium, rhodium, silver, copper, tin, lead, iron, zinc, and aluminum. Faraday also found that by employing rhodium, polarized light, and an arrangement of sulphate of lime plates, other colors than green could be transmitted by the gold leaf. The details given by M. Quincke in regard to his own experiments on this subject are too profound for our pages and we only give a part of his results. "Light," he says, "penetrates to an appreciable depth into the metal, and must also be reflected back from the interior; for the great difference of phase of the components of reflected light seems to be only explicable on the supposition that the reflected ray has to pass through the boundary between the metal and the medium laying adjacent to it." M. Quincke endeavored to determine directly the velocity of light through metals, and obtained the remarkable result that light travels faster through gold and silver than through a vacuum. He says, finally, that he was unable to detect any difference of phase in the components of the light which had previously passed through transparent substances such as plates of glass. "Therefore the anology between metals and transparent bodies, which Jamin has proved for refracted light, is not maintained for reflected light."

PHENOMENA PRODUCED BY REVOLVING DISCS.

Prof. Dove, some years ago, obtained a lustrous appearance by the binocular combination of geometrical figures executed in black and white, or in complementary colors ; and in 1861 Prof. D. Rood showed that *surfaces* without drawings produced the same effect, publishing his experiments in *Silliman's Journal*. The latter gentleman, in the same journal, has just published some additional experiments from which we extract the following : "A circular disc of white cardboard, nine inches in diameter, with half its surface painted of a dead black, was caused to rotate by clock-work at varying rates, while the bright light from a window fell upon it. A stereoscope, from which the ground glass had been removed, was provided with a card-board in which were cut two square apertures, at such a distance asunder that their binocular union could be easily effected, and while the disc was at rest the stereoscope was arranged so that through the right hand aperture some of the white portion of the disc was seen, and through the left-hand aperture a part of the blackened surface. On communicating rotary motion to the discs, a more or less rapid alternation of black and white was the result. It was found that with slow rates of rotation the strength of the luster was not impaired, and it was just as plainly perceptible with more rapid rates. But when the disc was made to revolve so fast that its surface seemed covered by a uniform tint of gray, and the so-called flickering had ceased, no luster, in the proper sense of the term, could be seen, the appearance being exactly that which is presented to a single eye under similar circumstances."

ON THE INVISIBILITY OF NEBULOUS MATTER.

The following communication on the above subject has been made to *Silliman's Journal*, by D. Trowbridge, Esq.

It has generally been supposed that if nebulous matter, in the proper sense of the word, or cosmical vapor, exists in the heavens, and within reach of our telescopes, it will be visible to the eye with suitable optical aid. It is proposed to show in this article, with some plausibility, that this is an erroneous idea, except in some particular cases.

Comets are the only celestial objects, whose physical constitution is approximately understood, that afford us anything like a distinct notion of what nebulous matter is. By far the greater proportion of these bodies are composed of materials so extremely rare that the solar rays can penetrate completely through the denser portion of their bodies, and the light in some cases seems to suffer scarcely any diminution in intensity. Yet these bodies, which perhaps would weigh at the surface of the earth but a few ounces, or but a few pounds, are distinctly visible with the smallest optical aid, and even, under favorable circumstances, with the naked eye. Sir John Herschel says, of this class of comets, that the most unsubstantial clouds which float in the higher regions of our atmosphere, must be looked upon as dense and massive bodies in comparison with the almost spiritual texture of these light bodies. A cloud composed of materials so rare, and whose distance from us did not exceed fifteen or twenty miles, would scarcely be visible. A comet, however, will be visible when its distance from us is many millions of miles.

What conclusion can we draw from these facts? Do they not indicate that comets do not shine wholly by reflected light? On the 3d of July, 1819, Arago made an attempt to analyze the light of comets, by applying his polariscope to the great comet of 1819. The instrument showed unmistakable signs of polarized light, and, therefore, of reflected sunlight. Similar observations on Halley's comet, in 1835, more clearly indicated the existence of polarized light. "These beautiful experiments still leave it undecided, whether, in addition to this reflected solar light, comets may not have light of their own. Even in the case of the planets, as, for instance, in Venus, an evolution of independent light seems very probable." *

"The variable intensity of light in comets cannot always be explained by the position of their orbits, and their distance from the sun."† After mentioning Arago's observations, with his polariscope, on Halley's comet, in 1835, Mr. Hind says : "Still, the variation in the intensity of light is not universally such as should follow if the comet merely reflected the sun's rays under certain permanent conditions, and we are under the necessity of looking to physical causes inherent in the body itself for an explanation of some few observations which appear irreconcilable with the theory of reflected solar light."‡ "The molecular condition of the head or nucleus, so seldom possessing a definite outline, as well as the tail of the comet, is rendered so much the more mysterious from the fact that it causes no refraction."§

I have collected these facts together to show that reflected solar light cannot completely explain, at present, all the phenomena of the light of comets. Besides the above observations, it may be added that the visibility of comets in the daytime, and even when near the sun, also indicates a light-generating process in the comet ; for otherwise we must suppose them capable of reflecting more light than the planets. Indeed, it is difficult to see how a body can maintain its gaseous or nebulous state without being kept at a high temperature, and therefore, having within itself a light-producing cause. Assuming, then, that there is a light-generating process that is active in comets, let us see what use can be made of it, and whether it will afford us any light on the subject of the visibility of nebulous matter.

It is now a well-established fact that the heads of comets contract in dimensions as they approach the sun. This was first noticed by Hevelius, but was not established till many years afterwards. What is the cause of this condensation of cometary matter as the comet approaches the sun? Whatever may be the cause of it, we know that it has a great effect on the visibility of the comet. Is it not possible that the solar rays, acting chemically or otherwise, excite in the comet those principles which cause it to send out in greater abundance, direct light? We know that a comet will increase in brightness with great rapidity as it approaches the sun ; and also decrease in brilliancy with equal rapidity in general, as it recedes from the sun, so that the fainter comets disappear in the best telescopes, when, their apparent dimensions only being considered, they ought to remain visible. The

* Cosmos, vol. 1. pp. 90, 91. Bohn's edition.   † Cosmos, vol. 1. p. 91
‡ Hind's Treatise on Comets, p. 24.   § Cosmos, vol. iv. p. 548.

dilatation of the cometary volume seems to prevent the comet from sending out much light, either reflected or direct.

Applying these principles to *nebulæ* proper, we must conclude that nebulous vapor is necessarily too diffuse, has too little density to be visible, when far removed from us. According to this, then, nebulæ can not in general be visible, unless they are considerably condensed, and perhaps actually converted into stars. It is perfectly evident that the luminosity of nebulous vapor must be very feeble, even where the light is inherent. The process of condensation only, then, can render nebulous matter visible through our telescopes. Will not this account for the fact that higher telescopic power resolves *previous* nebulæ? It is very doubtful whether our best telescopes will ever be able to bring into view any real nebulæ. According to the Nebular Hypothesis, we should not expect to find any large collection of nebulous matter in the vicinity of our system, either planetary or stellar, and ages may pass before our system, in its progress through space, will come near any of the small patches that may exist, so as to render them visible to us.

Note.—The influence of the magnetic power of the sun, may be a potent cause to render comets visible as they approach the great central luminary. It is a fact derived from observation, that the sun affects the magnetic needle, and that its period is closely connected with the period of the solar spots. It is also known that the *auroras* influence the needle; and that they are subject to the same law of periodicity as the solar spots, and thus seem to be connected with solar influence. The effect of the auroras is evidently light-producing.

ERRORS IN ASTRONOMICAL OBSERVATIONS OF PHYSIOLOGICAL ORIGIN.

A memoir on this subject, by M. Faye, has been recently read before the Academy of Sciences at Paris. In these observations the human organism no doubt attains by practice to a wonderful degree of precision; yet the eye, observing by means of a microscope, and the ear by means of a pendulum which vibrates 500 times a second will sometimes fail; and small errors in time lead to great ones in calculation. The human machine is subject to variations due to the disturbances incident to the processes of digestion and circulation, and to nervous fatigue. M. Faye proposes to substitute for the senses, or at least bring to their aid, the two great discoveries of our epoch,—photography and the electric telegraph. He was led to take up the subject in consequence of M. M. Plautamour and Hirsch detecting errors, which might be ascribed to physiological causes, in their researches to determine the difference of longitude between the observatories of Geneva and Neufchatel. The possibility of suppressing the observer has been fully demonstrated at Paris, some years ago, in experiments made under M. Faye's own direction. The process, which is of extreme simplicity in regard to the sun, becomes more delicate, but not impracticable, when applied to the stars. It consists in substituting for the eye of the observer a photographic plate, and in registering electrically the moment at which light is admitted into the dark chamber applied to the meridian glass. M. Faye thus obtained ten observations of the sun in twenty seconds.

15

THE MICROSCOPE.

It is hardly correct to say that what eyes are to the blind the microscope is to those who see. There is really no comparison between those who can not see and those who see only a little. The microscope is, in fact, an instrument which assists the sight in the same way as short-sighted persons are enabled to see more correctly than those who are long-sighted. The nearer we can place our eyes to an object and see it, the better we see. If one person sees clearly at eight inches, and another sees as plainly at six inches, the latter will see more of the object he looks at. The glasses of the microscope enable all observers to bring their eyes closer to an object when it is seen than is possible for the natural eye. Hence the great object of all microscope-makers is to construct glasses that shall enable the observer to get his eye as near as possible to the object. Twenty-five years ago it was considered the highest attainment of microscope-making, that achromatic instruments were made which would work with lenses that were brought within $\frac{1}{8}$ of an inch of the object looked at. Since then, the machinery of the microscope has been greatly improved, and one of the great microscope-making houses of London is producing object-glasses of $\frac{1}{16}$ of an inch focus. Just in proportion as these glasses are produced in working order, do new conditions of matter unfold themselves to the observer. It is hardly possible to conceive of any instrument producing more wonderful results than the microscope, which, by enabling us to see better, develops the extraordinary powers that are possessed by the human eye for adding to the facts which constitute the basis of those general laws which are the sciences of natural history and physiology.

Although the microscope reveals the minuter conditions of the existence of mineral bodies, there is a repetition in the forms of these bodies, and a resemblance between the forms seen by the naked eye and those revealed by the microscope that renders this instrument of less use in the inorganic kingdom than in the organic kingdom of nature. It is in the detection of minute forms of plants and animals, and in the unraveling of the minute structure of the organs of animals and plants, that the microscope has rendered so much service to science. A whole creation of minute plants and animals, having distinct organs and performing varied functions, has been added to our knowledge by the aid of the microscope. Let any one turn to a systematic account of the vegetable kingdom, and it will be seen that there are whole families of plants recognized as members of that kingdom whose existence can only be made out by this instrument. Such are the diatoms, the desmids, and the volvoces. Amongst the confervæ, the fungi, the fuci, are whole tribes which could only have been thus discovered. If we turn to the animal kingdom, a like series of families is there found. The rhizopods, infusorial animalcules, and other families are only known by the aid of the microscope, whilst small forms of larger groups have been abundantly demonstrated. The fascination of observing and describing new species has developed itself here, as in other departments of natural history, and hundreds, nay, even thousands, of new species of microscopic plants and animals have been discovered and described within these last 20 years.

Nor have these discoveries been the mere amusement of dilettanti philosophers. The observation of these minute forms of life has led to a more correct and satisfactory knowledge of the nature and forms of higher and more visible creations, and there are no botanists or zoologists in the present century who, like Linnæus in the last, would reject the microscope as interfering with the natural history and arrangement of those creations which are visible to the naked eye.

But the bringing to light of new forms of animal and vegetable life is perhaps the least half of what the microscope has done for science. In permitting observations to be made on the minute structure of the parts of plants and animals, it has given a deeper insight into the laws by which they exist and the nature of the special functions they are destined to perform. Let any one compare the physiology of 25 years since, as given in the manuals of that day, with what it is now. It will be seen at once how vast has been the progress made. Although Malpighi first saw blood-cells, the researches of modern microscopists have given correctness and precision to our present knowledge of that great source of animal life, the blood. It is to the start given by Schleiden, through his microscopical researches, in 1838, in the nature of vegetable cells, so ably followed by Schwann, in a series of kindred researches in animal cells, that the great science of histology owes its existence. It is in the changed nature of the cells of the living tissues that the pathologist looks for the exposition of the true nature of disease ; and although the slovenly practitioner of medicine may not be aware of the cause, the views of disease, which are modifying the practice of medicine every day, are mainly owing to the formation of more correct theories of disease under the influence of the microscope.

The history of the manufacture of this instrument is curious. Not above 25 years ago, when the London Microscopical Society was first established, it was customary for the President of that Society, in his Annual Address, to state the number of microscopes manufactured by the great houses in London in the course of the year. This practice has long been discontinued, as many houses turn out microscopes by the thousand in the course of a single year. By this demand, too, the instrument has been vastly reduced in price, and the great opticians who still manufacture microscopes that cost £100 when complete, sell instruments of great excellence at the low price of five guineas.—*London Athenæum.*

MICROSCOPIC STRUCTURE OF IRON AND STEEL.

At the British Association, 1864, Mr. H. C. Sorby exhibited "Microscopical Photographs of various kinds of Iron and Steel." He first described the manner in which the sections of iron and steel are prepared for microscopical examination. The final process consists in acting with very dilute acid on level and perfectly polished surfaces, showing no scratches, even when examined with the microscope. The acid, acting on the different constituents, or on different crystals, in a variable manner, causes the structure to be exhibited in very great perfection, by various colors or tints. He then explained the precautions required in taking enlarged photographs direct from the prepared surfaces of iron or steel, and exhibited a series photographed under his directions, illustrating the various stages in their manufacture. In the case of cast iron, the photographs show the graphite and several different compounds of iron carbon, as well as pure iron. In wrought iron, the character of the crystals and the arrangement of the slag are well seen, and the change in the constituents and in the structure, which occurs when it is converted into steel, is very striking. Other photographs show the change in structure produced by melting and hammering steel. Some meteoric irons have a structure very different from that of any of these artificial irons, as shown by another photograph. On the whole, then, when such sections are thus examined, we may see most clearly the cause of those peculiarities in physical structure which give rise to the different kinds of fracture characteristic of different sorts of iron and steel, and which are so intimately connected with those properties which make each variety more or less suitable for special purposes.

SCULPTURE BY COLORED LIGHT.

A special attraction of a recent evening assembly at the Duchess of Wellington's in London, was a peculiarly novel *al fresco* exhibition, consisting of the lighting-up under various effects of color of a number of choice works of sculpture arranged in the garden at the rear of the mansion. These works included copies of Gibson's "Venus," Thorwaldsen's ideal rendering of the same goddess, Powers's "Greek Slave," and others. The illumination of these beautiful works of art, including the foliage of the trees and shrubs amid which they were placed, was under the superintendence of Professor Pepper, who appropriated to this purpose large voltaic batteries arranged on Grove's principle, which were connected with lamps and parabolic reflectors, constructed by M. Serrin of Paris. The colors applied to this object were vivid shades of red, amber, blue, green, and white, the everchanging and floating beams of colored light on the various groups producing a most charming effect.—*London Times.*

ARTIFICIAL RAINBOW.

The *Cosmos* speaks highly of J. Duboscq's contrivance for imitating a rainbow in a French theatre. He employs an electric light made by 100 Bunsen elements. Its rays are transmitted in a parallel direction by means of a lens through a slot in the form of an arc, to a double convex lens of very short focus, from which the rays pass to a prism, and emerge with sufficient divergence to make an effective rainbow, during the ordinary illumination of the stage, on a screen 18 or 20 feet distant.

THE COLOR OF TROUT.

Mr. St. John adverts to the wonderful capability which trout possess of adapting their color to the color of the water in which they are placed. "Put a living black burn trout," he says, "into a white basin of water, and it becomes, within half an hour, of a light color. Keep the fish living in a white jar for some days and it becomes absolutely white, but put it into a dark-colored or black vessel, and although on first being placed there the white-colored fish shows most conspicuously on the black ground, in a quarter of an hour it becomes as dark-colored as the bottom of the jar, and consequently difficult to be seen."

We can entirely confirm the truth of this statement, and a striking illustration is to be found in two lochs in the northwest of Sutherlandshire, separated only by a low ridge of land. In the one—which is full of dark moss water—the trout are nearly black; in the other, where the bed of the loch is limestone, and the water so clear that you can see the bottom where it is 40 or 50 feet deep—they are almost as silvery in color as sea trout. Loch Brora, too—another loch in the same country—affords a further corroboration of the truth of Mr. St. John's observations. That loch is divided into three sheets of water, united by narrows, where the lake assumes the appearance of a river. In the upper part, where the bottom is sand and fine gravel, the trout are clear in color, with bright vermilion spots; in the central division, where the bottom is not so clean, and the water darker, they are also dark in color, and their spots are not so bright; while in the lowest division of the lake, where the bottom is very muddy, the trout are quite black and ugly, though of a larger size.—*Fraser's Magazine.*

MOTIONS OF THE EYE IN RELATION TO BINOCULAR VISION.

The motions of the eye can be compared to those of our arm. We can raise and lower the visual line, we can turn it to the left and to the right, we can bring it into every possible direction throughout a certain range—as far, at least as the connections of the eyeball permit. So far the motions of the eye are as free as those of the arm. But when we have chosen any determinate direction of the eye, can we turn the eye round the visual line as an axis as we can turn the arm round its longitudinal axis? This is a question the answer to which is connected with a curious peculiarity of our voluntary motions. Yes: there exist muscles by the action of which those rotations round the visual line can be performed. But when we ask, can we do it by any act of our will? We must answer "No." We can voluntarily turn the visual line into every possible direction, but we cannot voluntarily use the muscles of our eye in such a way as to turn it round the visual line. Whenever the direction of the visual line is fixed, the position of our eye, as far as it depends upon our will, is completely fixed and cannot be altered.

A NEW STEREOSCOPE WITHOUT LENSES.

In the *Nuovo Lincei*, M. Volpicelli describes a new stereoscope invent·d by him in April, 1854. This stereoscope is without mirrors or lenses, and consists of a rectangular horizontal box, whose proportions are as follows: hight 11 centim. (4·5 inches); depth 20 centim. (8 inches); length 62 centim. (24·8 inches). The two stereoscopic pictures are placed against the back of the box; in the front of the box two holes are bored opposite the middle of the pictures. Two diaphragms made of plates of blackened wood or card-board, of the hight of the pictures, are made to rotate around vertical axes corresponding to the front edges; and are so adjusted that they allow the right eye to see only the left picture, and the left eye the right picture. It follows that the rays by which the pictures are seen cross each other within a certain space in the middle of the box, and in this space, after a little effort, the eyes see the object in relief.

15*

If after the relief is seen the diaphragms are turned around their axes, so as to rest against the sides of the box, and no longer intercept the view—the eyes still continuing to view the picture in relief—a very interesting physiological phenomenon will be seen. There will be seen three pictures—one in the middle of the instrument, in relief, the others alongside, and by no effort of will can the middle picture be made to disappear. If the pictures be of complementary colors, they will be seen of their own colors, and the relief will be white. Those who are not accustomed to observation of optical phenomena will require some attention to see the relief at first, but it will generally be found by looking attentively at about the middle of the box. When once seen it may be recovered without any difficulty.—*Cosmos.*

DESCRIPTION OF A NEW OPTICAL INSTRUMENT CALLED THE "STEREOTROPE," BY W. T. SHAW, OF ENGLAND.

This instrument is an application of the principle of the stereoscope to that class of instruments variously termed thaumatropes, phantascopes, phenakistoscopes, &c., which depend for their results on "persistence of vision." In these instruments, as is well known, an object represented on a revolving disc, in the successive positions it assumes in performing a given revolution, is seen to execute the movement so delineated; in the stereotrope the effect of solidity is superadded, so that the object is perceived as if in motion and with an appearance of relief as in nature. The following is the manner in which I adapt to this purpose the refracting form of the stereoscope.

Having procured eight stereoscopic pictures of an object—of a steam engine for example—in the successive positions it assumes in completing a revolution, I affix them, in the order in which they were taken to an octagonal drum, which revolves on a horizontal axis beneath an ordinary lenticular stereoscope, and brings them one after another into view. Immediately beneath the lenses, and with its axis situated half an inch from the plane of sight, is fixed a solid cylinder, four inches in diameter, capable of being moved freely on its axis. This cylinder, which is called the eye-cylinder, is pierced throughout its entire length (if we except a diaphragm in the centre inserted for obvious reasons) by two apertures, of such a shape, and so situated relatively to each other, that a transverse section of the cylinder shows them as cones, with their apices pointing in opposite directions, and with their axes parallel to, and distant half an inch from, the diameter of the cylinder. Attached to the axis of the eye-cylinder is a pulley, exactly ¼ the size of a similar pulley affixed to the axis of the picture-drum, with which it is connected by means of an endless band. The eye-cylinder thus making four revolutions to one of the picture-drum, it is evident that the axes of its apertures will respectively coincide with the plane of sight four times in one complete revolution of the instrument, and that, consequently, vision will be permitted eight times or once for each picture.

The cylinder is so placed that at the time of vision the *large* ends of the apertures are next the eyes, the effect of which is that when the *small* ends pass the eyes the axes of the apertures, by reason of their eccentricity, do not coincide with the plane of sight, and vision is therefore impossible. If, however, the position of the cylin-

der be reversed end for end, vision will be possible only when the small ends are next the eyes, and the angle of the aperture will be found to subtend exactly the pencil of rays coming from a picture, which is so placed as to be bisected at right angles by the plane of sight. Hence it follows that, the former arrangement of the cylinder being reverted to, the observer looking along the upper side of the aperture will see a narrow strip extending along the top of the picture ; then, moving the cylinder on and looking along the lower side of the aperture, he will see a similar strip at the bottom of the picture ; consequently, in the intermediate positions of the aperture, the other parts of the picture will have been projected on the retinæ. The width of these strips is determined by that of the small ends of the apertures, which measure ·125 inch ; and the diameter of the large ends is 1·5 inches, the lenses being distant nine inches from the pictures. The picture-drum being caused to revolve with the requisite rapidity, the observer will see the steam engine constantly before him, its position remaining unchanged in respect of space, but its parts will appear to be in motion, and in solid relief, as in the veritable object. The stationary appearance of the pictures, notwithstanding the fact of their being in rapid motion, is brought about by causing their corresponding parts to be seen, respectively, *only* in the same part of space, and *that* for so short a time that while in view they make no sensible progression. As, however, there is an actual progression during the instant of vision, it is needful to take that fact into account, —in order that it may be reduced as far as practicable,—in regulating the diameter of the eye-cylinder, and of the apertures at their small ends.

ON ARTIFICIAL ILLUMINATION.

Prof. Frankland, in a recent lecture before the Royal Institution, London, gave the following as the conditions necessary for a good and satisfactory artificial light. In the first place, the light should contain all colors ; that is, it should be capable of showing every variety of tint which will be exposed to it. This is the case with the carbon electric light, and that of candle, oil, and gas flames, since the light from these sources contains all the colors of the spectrum. But there are many colors which the mercurial electric light is incapable of showing, since they are absent from its spectrum. It was also shown that all pure colors, except yellow, were perfectly black, when seen by the light of incandescent sodium vapor. Solar light, although in so many respects superior to artificial light, is defective as regards the showing of colors. There are certain colors which cannot be seen by solar light,—for instance, all the color which can be seen by the sodium flame is quite invisible by daylight. If a pigment could be made of such a yellow color as to be of exactly the shade of that produced by the sodium flame it would be absolutely black in solar light. But our pigments are all mixed colors, and no such pigment which thus entirely disappears in the light of the sun is known. But in addition to this tint of the sodium flame, there are hundreds of other tints which are also not present in the solar spectrum, and which are consequently invisible in daylight.

Although solar light is inferior to artificial light in the completeness of its colors, yet, in another respect—in the comparatively small amount of heat which accompanies its rays in proportion to the light itself—it is greatly superior to every sort of artificial light. The great amount of heat in our artificial lights is absolutely useless. It is nearly all intercepted by the humors of the eye.

DISCOVERY IN PHOTOMETRY.

It is the established practice in measuring the light of illuminating gas to compare the light of a five feet Argand burner with that of a spermaceti candle burning 120 grains an hour; and when the candle used burns less or more than the 120 grains it has been regarded as a matter of course that the light would vary in the same proportion. But scientific evidence recently given before the committee of the House of Lords, in England, on the bill of the Birmingham Gas Company, respecting the illuminating power of the gas supplied by the two existing companies in that town, has shown that a candle burning a large quantity of spermaceti, yields more light in proportion to the material consumed than a candle burning a small quantity. The *Journal of Gas Lighting* (London), after giving a full history of the case, remarks :—

"These experiments demonstrate that the illuminating power of burning candles increases in a greater ratio than the direct proportion of the consumption of spermaceti. It has long been known that the illuminating power of gas increases in a greater proportion than the quantity consumed, but we believe it had not been previously known that the same law operates in the combustion of candles. It is evident, from the results of the photometrical experiments with the gas supplied by the Birmingham companies, that no correct conclusions can be drawn from proportionate quantities of either the gas or spermaceti consumed, inasmuch as the amount of light is influenced by the quantity of combustible matter burned within a given time. It has been suggested that some rule may be established by which the influence on the light of the flame, produced by the relative quantities of spermaceti undergoing combustion, may be determined and allowed for. Thus, it is probable that—after the proportions have been reduced to 120 grains consumed per hour—if one per cent for each grain of spermaceti the candle may consume per hour less than 120 grains, be deducted from the indications of the photometer, and if one per cent be added to similar indications of the photometer for each grain the candle may consume more than 120 grains, the results attained would not be far from the truth. But until the subject has been further investigated it would not be safe to assume positively that such a scale of compensation would be correct. The new light which these experiments have thrown on photometry, shows the necessity for the adoption of some more certain standard of comparison than a spermaceti candle, the consumption of which it is impossible to regulate with accuracy. The Carcel lamp—which is similar to the 'moderator' lamp—is adopted generally on the Continent as the standard of comparison, and it possesses these advantages,—the consumption of oil may be regulated with the greatest nicety, while its flame approaches in luminosity that of nine candles. At the same time, it must be observed that the lamp-wick requires great attention,

and the shape and size and position of the chimney have much more influence in effecting perfect combustion than the chimney of a gas-flame. The difficulty of attaining a correct indication of the illuminating power of gas by comparison with other flames points to the adoption of the atmospheric test, invented by Professor Erdmann. By that instrument, neither photometers, nor candles, nor blackened chambers are required, the illuminating power of the gas being determined by the quantity of atmospheric air mixed with a given quantity of gas before it ceases to give white light. Such a simple method of testing the illuminating power of gas has peculiar claims to favor at the present time, as the difficulty of attaining accurate results by photometrical observations has been shown by the Birmingham experiments to be even greater than before supposed."

Increasing the Illuminating Power of Gas.—The editor of the *Sanitary Reporter* (England), in an article on testing gas, says: "The following are distinct modes of increasing the power of an argand burner consuming ordinary coal-gas: 1. Contracting the central opening to about ·45 to ·5 of an inch diameter. 2. By a perforated disc round the burner, and resting on the gallery which supports the burner. 3. By interposing a thin piece of paper or metal to contract the passage of air through the central opening. 4. By placing a little contracted cap on the top of the chimney. Now, every one of these contrivances will considerably increase the power of the argand burner. Moreover, all these contrivances act on the simple principle of diminishing the velocity of the current of atmospheric air, and thus allowing the minute particles of carbon, which the gas contains, to be longer suspended in the flame."

ON THE CHEMICAL AND PHOTOMETRICAL TESTING OF ILLUMINATING GAS.

At the last meeting of the British Association, Prof. W. B. Rogers of Boston, described the instruments and methods which have been lately adopted in the gas inspection organized by law in the State of Massachusetts, comprising the measurement as well as testing of gas. Connected with the former of these objects, an account was given of the adjustments of the standard measure for gauging gasholders,—of a universal clamp for meter-connections,—and of an appendage combining a delicate thermometer and pressure-gauge for the inlet and outlet of the meter, and by which the rate of delivery is accurately adjusted. For chemical testing, the eudiometer, consisting of a graduated tube, with cylindrical enlargement, is permanently inclosed in a wider tube full of water, which maintains the temperature nearly uniform. The mouth of the graduated tube is furnished with a hollow ground stopper, for holding the several liquid absorbents used in the successive experiments. With this apparatus it is easy to determine the percentage of carbonic acid, of illuminating hydrocarbons, of oxygen, and of carbonic oxyde; after which the hydrogen and light carbureted hydrogen are ascertained by explosion, by means of an instrument consisting mainly of two glass tubes, united below by a long loop of rubber-tube, being a modification of Frankland's apparatus. For determining the sulphur, an improved arrangement is used, in which the stream of water supplying the Liebig's condenser is made to convey a stream of air, mingled with ammonia, into the condensing tube some inches above the flame of the burning gas. To secure a larger and more constant unit of illumination than the candle commonly used, a lamp burning kerosene, with a flat wick, is employed, in which, by means of a bridge of platinum wire, the flame may be maintained of constant size, and giving a light equal to about seven candles. This is supported on a balance of peculiar construction, giving the consumption during the experiment. Prof. Rogers had found that even the small amount of carbonic acid which in some gas-works is allowed to remain in the gas produces a sensible reduction of the light. This effect, varying with the strength of the illuminating gas, was found to range from three to nearly five per cent of the illuminating power for each per cent of the impurity. 58 per cent of carbonic acid, although it did not prevent combustion, made the flame so dim as to be without effect on the photometer.

LUMINOUS AND OBSCURE RADIATIONS.

Professor Tyndall, in a paper in a recent number of the *Philosophical Magazine*, after referring to the discoveries of the Herschels and Melloni, respecting the obscure red rays of the end of the spectrum, says: Dr. Akin inferred, from the paucity of luminous rays evident to the eye, and a like paucity of extra-violet rays, as proved by the experiments of Dr. Miller, that the radiation from a flame of hydrogen must be mainly extra-red: and he concluded from this that the glowing of platinum wire in a hydrogen flame, as also the brightness of the Drummond light in the oxyhydrogen flame, was produced by a change in the period of vibration." Dr. Tyndall adds, that by a different mode of reasoning he arrived at the same conclusion. The paper referred to, contains a description of his numerous experiments demonstrating the character of the radiation from a hydrogen flame under a variety of conditions, the apparatus employed, and the results obtained. We select a few of the results. Fifty experiments on the radiant heat of a hydrogen flame make the transmission of its rays through a quantity of iodine, which is perfectly opaque to light, 100 per cent. To the radiation from a hydrogen flame the dissolved iodine is therefore perfectly transparent. It is also sensibly transparent to the radiation from solid bodies heated under incandescence, and to the obscure rays emitted by luminous bodies. Prof. Tyndall found that, dividing the radiation from a platinum wire raised to a dazzling whiteness by an electric current into 24 equal parts, one of these parts is luminous and 23 obscure; dividing the radiation from the most brilliant portion of a flame of coal-gas into 25 equal parts,—one of these parts is luminous and 24 obscure: dividing the radiation from the electric light emitted by carbon points and excited by a Grove's battery of 40 cells into 10 equal parts, one of these parts is luminous and nine obscure. We have space only for the following remarkable conclusions: "On a tolerably clear night a candle flame can be readily seen at the distance of a mile. The intensity of the electric light used by me is 650 times that of a good composite candle, and as the non-luminous radiation from the coal points which reaches the retina is equal to twice the luminous, it follows that at a common distance of a foot the energy of the invisible rays of the electric light which reach the optic nerve, but are incompetent to provoke vision, is 1,300 times that of the light of a candle. But the intensity of the candle's light at the distance of a mile is less than a 20,-000,000 of its intensity at th· distance of a foot : hence the energy which renders the candle perfectly visible a mile off would have to be multiplied by 1,300 × 20,000,000, or by 26,000,000,000, to bring it up to the intensity of that powerless radiation which the eye receives from the electric light at a good distance. Nothing, I think, could more forcibly illustrate the special relationship which subsists between the optic nerve and the oscillating periods of luminous bodies. The nerve, like a musical string, responds to the periods with which it is in accordance, while it refuses to be excited by others of vastly greater energy, which are not in unison with its own."

Opacity and Transparency.—What is the physical meaning of opacity and transparency as regards light and radiant heat? The luminous rays of the spectrum differ from the non-luminous ones, simply in period. The sensation of light is excited by waves of ether, shorter and more quickly recurrent than those which fall beyond the extreme red. But why should iodine stop the former, and allow the latter to pass? The answer to this question no doubt is, that the intercepted waves are those whose periods of recurrence coincide with the periods of oscillation possible to the atoms of the dissolved iodine. The elastic forces which separated these atoms are such as to compel them to vibrate in definite periods ; and, when these periods synchronize with those of the etheral waves, the latter are absorbed. Briefly defined, then, transparency in liquids as well as in gases, is synonymous with discord, while opacity is synonymous with accord between the periods of the waves of ether and those of the molecules of the body on which they impinge. All ordinary transparent and colorless substances owe their transparency to the discord which exists between the oscillating periods of their molecules, and those of the waves of the whole visible spectrum. The general. discord of the vibrating periods of the molecules of compound bodies with the light-giving waves of the spectrum may be inferred from the prevalence of the property of transparency in compounds, while their greater harmony with the extra-red periods, is to be inferred from their opacity to the extra-red rays. Water illustrates this transparency and opacity in the most striking manner. It is highly transparent to the luminous rays, which demonstrates the incompetency of its molecules to oscillate in the periods which excite vision. It is as highly opaque to the extra-red undulations, which proves the synchronism of its periods with those of the longer waves."—*Prof. Tyndall.*

THE PHYSICAL ASPECT OF THE SUN.

In a paper on the above subject, read before the British Association at its last meeting, the author stated that he had recently, with improved instruments, taken many occasions of scrutinizing the aspect of the sun's disc in regard to spots, faculæ, and the general porosity of the surface. For·tracing the path of a spot across the disc a Kilner eye-piece was employed with five engraved transit lines the intervals being equal to 10° in the central part of the sun's circumference. In drawing, negative eye-pieces of the ordinary kind were sometimes employed ; at others, a peculiar kind arranged by himself, with powers varying from 75 to 300 ; the best performances being usually between 100 and 200 ; the higher powers, however, being occasionally useful towards the limb of the sun. He described the bright streaks or faculæ as of diversified form and distinct outline, either entirely separate or coalescing in various ways into ridges and network. When the spots became invisible near the limb, the undulated shining ridges and folds still indicated their place, being more remarkable thereabout than elsewhere on the limb, though almost everywhere traceable in good observing weather. In a diagram made on the 29th of March last, faculæ are shown in the most brilliant parts of the sun. They appear of all magnitudes, from barely discernible, softly-gleaming spots a thousand miles long, to continuous, complicated, and heaped ridges 40,000 and more miles in length, and 1,000 to 4,000 miles and more broad. They are never regularly arched, and never found in straight bands, but always devious and minutely undulated, like clouds in the evening sky or very distant ranges of snowy mountains. When minutely studied, the ridges appear prominent in cusps and depressed into hollows. By the frequent meeting of the bright ridges, spaces of the sun's surface are included of various magnitudes, and forms somewhat corresponding to the areas and forms of the irregular spots with penumbræ. Ridges of this kind often embrace and inclose a spot, though not very closely, the spot appearing more conspicuous from the surrounding brightness; but sometimes there appears a broad white platform round the spot, and from this the white crumpled ridges pass in various directions. Towards the limb the ridges appear nearly parallel to it : further off this character is exchanged for indeterminate direction and lessened distinctness ; over the rest of the surface they are less conspicuous, but can be traced as an irregular network, more or less designated by that structure which has been designated as porosity. The faculæ preserve their shapes and position, with no visible change during a few hours of observation, and probably for much longer periods. They do not appear to project beyond the general circular outline of the sun, a circumstance which the author explains without denying that they actually do rise above the general surface, whether as clouds or mountains, to either of which they may be truly likened. In respect to porosity, the author had also devoted much time to a scrutiny of the interspaces between the faculæ towards the limb and the general surface towards the interior of the disc. Towards the interior the ground acquires more evident lights and shades, a sort of granulation difficult to analyze. Under favorable conditions for observation, there appears little or none of that tremor and internal motion described by earlier observers. What is then seen is a complicated surface of interrupted lights and the limits of which appear arched or straight or confused, according to the case; and the indeterminate union of these produces sometimes faint luminous ridges, the intervals filled up by shaded interstices and insulated patches of illuminated surface. The best resemblance to these complicated small surfaces of light and shade he had been able to procure was a disc of a particular sort of white paper placed near the eye-end of the telescope, and seen by transmitted light. Heaps of small fragments of white substances, not so uniform in figure or equal in size as rice grains, might also be suggested for comparison.

Origin of Solar Spots.—Sir John Herschel, in an article in *The Quar-*

terly Journal of Science throws out the suggestion, whether the original exciting cause of solar spots may not be found in the circulation of an elliptic ring of planetary matter, in a state of division sufficiently minute to elude telescopic vision, having a major axis such as would correspond to an average period of 11½ years, and an eccentricity such as would bring its perihelion within the region in question ; the matter of the ring being unequally distributed over its circuit with a minimum and a maximum following by an interval, somewhat less than its semi-circumference. By assuming certain conditions as to the constitution of such a ring, and the extent of deviation from an exact quantity in the periodic times of its component elements, he finds that not only the shorter period of 11½ years in the recurrence of spots first determined, but also the longer one of 56 years insisted upon by Dr. Wolf, and various other changes, are susceptible of explanation.

Chemical Action of Rays proceeding from different Parts of the Sun's Disc.—M. Secchi having shown that the heat radiated from the center of the sun is nearly double that from its borders, and that the equatorial regions are somewhat hotter than the polar, and various observers having noticed a great difference in luminosity between the center and the edge of the disc, Mr. H. E. Roscoe now reports to the Royal Society some experiments made by means of photographic paper relative to the chemical action of rays from various parts of the sun's disc. From the results of one day, it appears that the chemically active rays at the center have from three to five times the intensity of those at the edge. This difference, being greater than the difference in the heat from the same portions, is accounted for by the greater absorption effected by the solar atmosphere on the more refrangible rays. Is also appeared the chemical brightness of the south polar regions was considerably greater than that of the north polar regions, while about the equator the brightness was between that of the poles. Mr. Roscoe, in connection with Mr. Baxendell, proposes to carry out, upon the same methods, a series of observations relative to the amount of chemical brightness of the sun's disc, and hopes before long to furnish further details.

Gold in the Sun.—The observers at Kew, England, believe that they have noticed the coincidence of several bright gold lines with corresponding dark lines in the solar spectrum from which the presence of that metal may be inferred in the sun's atmosphere. If confirmed by further observations, this will be an important addition to our present knowledge.

Spectrum of Carbon.—Coal, charcoal, and the diamond cannot be vaporized by heat when isolated, yet M. Morrin, of Versailles, finding the same spectrum produced by the common gas flame, cyanogen, carbonic oxyde, carbonic acid, ascelytene, and the hydrocarbons generally, he concludes this result must be due to the only element common to all these compounds, carbon, and in a state of vapor. It follows that the theory of the candle-flame must be somewhat modified. The base of the flame, being blue, is the vapor of carbon preserved from combustion, but kept at a very high temperature by the envelop of hydrogen, the more combustible element of the gaseous carbides from the decomposition of wax, the hydrogen alone uniting

16

with the oxygen of the air. Above the blue part comes the luminous part, produced by the passage of the carbon from the gaseous to the solid state, giving out in the passage a considerable amount of heat. The black cone surrounding the wick of the candle is formed of gaseous carburets of hydrogen, which only burn in the upper part of the flame where they come in contact with oxygen. Hydrogen being not very combustible but very subtle, diffusive, and penetrating, its combustion takes place under conditions in which it would be impossible for other gaseous bodies or vapors to burn. If a candle be gently moved so that the flame may be inclined and the air allowed to come in contact with the vapor of the hydrocarbons which surround the wick, we see the hydrogen take fire, and above the flame appears the blue vapor of the carbon. The latter can only exist alone, and gives its luminous reactions when it has near it the high temperature produced by the combustion of hydrogen. When cyanogen is burnt in a current of oxygen, the high temperature produced by the interior of the flame makes the vapor of carbon intensely hot, and hence very luminous : consequently its spectrum is very luminous.

PHOTOGRAPHING NATURAL COLORS.

It has often been asserted, but never yet substantiated, that the photographic process was capable, under certain mysterious processes, of reproducing the colors of the spectrum, and not merely the gradations of black to which we are accustomed. A few years ago, an American, a Mr. Hill, startled the scientific world—at least that part of the world which knew anything about photography—by insisting that he could produce any color in the photographic image. Practically speaking, this announcement came to nothing. Now we find in Milan, something at least has been recently done for the furtherance of the idea. Suppose it be required to color the photograph of a man, in a black coat, whose hair and beard are fair, and whose figure is projected on a white background, slightly shaded off; the process of the inventor is as follows : The photograph, taken by daylight, lies in a basin of water; it is in the dark, and subsequent operations are performed by candle light. Two solutions are at hand, one, consisting of one gramme of chloride of gold and ten of acetate of soda, dissolved in 1,000 grammes of water; the other B, consisting of 20 grammes of hyposulphite of soda dissolved in 100 grammes of water. There are besides two more basins of water, and a quire of blotting paper. The photograph is taken out of the water and put between the leaves of blotting paper: it is then laid flat on a pane of glass, and the whole surface, except the face and hands, receives with a water-color brush a coating of solution B. By this means the parts subjected to the action of the gold soon change their tints into black. The photograph is then put into clean water again and left there for a few minutes, during which the operator prepares a second photograph if required. The former one being taken out, is put in solution B, where it stays for a few minutes, and is then washed and rinsed as usual. Now, as the time of immersion will influence the depth of color by successive immersions, an orange-colored cravat will be obtained in one minute, a coffee-colored great coat in five, violet-colored trousers in ten, and a black coat in 30 minutes, while the hyposulphite of soda, or solution B, gives color to the flesh and hair. Hence certain colors, though not quite the natural ones, may be obtained, which is a decided step in advance of what has been previously achieved.—*Practical Mechanic's Journal.*

PHOTO-SCULPTURE.

Every now and then, says the *London Art Journal,* we hear of " new discoveries " that turn out to be impossible, or are only the result of confused reports. We are generally, therefore, rather inclined to doubt than to believe. It is not surprising that the world should have received with a certain degree of incredulity the announcement that sculpture could be performed by means of photography. However marvelous was the discovery of photography itself, we could understand how the image of the camera obscura could leave its impression upon a chemical surface susceptible of being affected by the very light which makes it apparent to our senses. We were afterwards enabled to understand, although with more difficulty, how the stereoscope could raise two flat photographic pictures into one, presenting the illusion of relief. In fact, this seemed to us the only sculpture, or at least the only illusion of sculpture, which might possibly be the result of a process of photography, and the word photosculpture to us could not convey any other meaning; for it seemed utterly impossible that photography could transfer a block of clay or any other materials employed by sculptors, into a real plastic form. But however incredible this may appear on first consideration, we lately have had a tangible proof of the reality of a new and most extraordinary application of photography, in fact, of its capability of imparting to a block of clay the transfer in relief of the photographic image.

The inventor of this new process is M. Willème of Paris, and his establishment in that city, where the operation is practically carried out, is constructed on a large piece of ground, and includes the various reception rooms, galleries, and operating rooms necessary to carry out a photographic business on an extensive scale. The part which is devoted particularly to the photo-sculpture consists of a large circular room about 50 feet high and 40 feet in diameter, surmounted with a cupola, all of glass, to admit the greatest possible amount of light. All round the circular wall supporting the cupola are, at equal intervals, 24 round holes of about three inches in diameter, being the apertures of 24 cameræ obscuræ placed behind the wall in a kind of dark corridor surrounding the building; for we have to explain that 24 photographs of the person sitting in the center of the large round operating room are to be taken at the same moment, in order to supply the modeling apparatus with 24 different views of the person whose sculpture is to be executed. By a very simple and ingenious contrivance, the 24 cameræ obscuræ, in each of which has been placed a prepared plate, are open and shut at the same moment. The sitting is consequently as short as if only one portrait was taken, and, after a few seconds in the required fixed position, the sitter is no more wanted. His bust or his statuette will be achieved without his presence, in another part of the establishment, where the modeling is performed by the very ingenious process by which the block of clay is to take consecutively, all round, the various outlines of each of 24 photographs. This is done in the following manner: The 24 photographs are placed in their proper order, in the outer circle of a large vertical wheel, which can revolve at will merely by the impulse of the hand; so that each photograph can be placed, as long as and whenever it is necessary, before the glass of a magic lantern; and the image of this photograph is projected upon a screen of ground glass, at the distance which will give the desired dimension. The modeler, having prepared his block of clay, and placed it close to th ground glass, on a stand capable of turning upon its axis, holds in his hands an ingenious instrument known as the pantograph, and used extensively (before it was in part superseded by photography) for enlarging or reducing, or copying upon the same scale, plans and drawings, maps and diagrams. It consists of a series of bars of wood or metal, jointed together so as to form a system of "similar triangles;" one of the bars carries at its extremity a tracing point or style, and another a pen or pencil, the whole turning freely on a center carried by a third bar. When the style is guided over the outline of a drawing, the pencil moves with a perfectly similar motion over a sheet of paper placed beneath it, and so produces a perfect fac-simile of the original. Its application to photo-sculpture is as follows: Photograph No. 1 is placed in a magic lantern, and an enlarged image of it projected upon a screen. Near to this screen is a small circular table, turning upon a pivot, and divided round its circumference into 24 parts. Upon this little table is placed a block of modeler's clay, of sufficient size to allow of a bust or statuette of the required dimensions being cut from it; and between it and the screen is mounted a large pantograph, furnished at one end with the customary style or tracer, but with a sharp tool or cutter occupying the place of the pen or pencil. Photograph, pantograph, and clay block being adjusted to their proper positions, the operator carefully guides the style over the outline of the enlarged photograph, and the cutting tool, exactly following every motion of the style, cuts the clay into a profile exactly corresponding to that of the photograph, and hence exactly similar to the contour of the original model or sitter as seen from the point occupied by camera No. 1. When this is done, the next photograph is brought before the magic lantern, the block of clay is turned $\frac{1}{24}$ of the whole circle marked on its stand, another profile is imparted by the pantograph to the block of clay, and so on until the block has received all round the 24 outlines of the 24 photographs. The operation is finished as far as it relates to the employment of the photographs. The bust or the statuette produced by this means is a likeness which, although in a somewhat uneven state, no one can mistake. It is now necessary to smooth by hand, or by a tool, all the slight roughness produced by the various cuttings, and to soften down and blend the small intervals between the outlines or profiles.

This last operation requires the assistance of an artist, and is the only part of the whole process that demands any more skill than is required in the most ordinary mechanical operations. The time occupied is wonderfully short, compared with the tedious process of modeling a bust from the life, to say nothing of the disagreeable operation, often resorted to, of taking a plaster cast of the face to serve as a basis for the sculptor's work. The bust or statuette once obtained can be easily multiplied by the ordinary means in use for producing plaster images, or it may be copied into marble or bronze to suit the taste and purse of its possessor. By varying the mechanical arrangements it may be produced of colossal size, or diminished to an inch in hight. By slight modifications of the process, the portrait may be flattened to the proportions of a medallion or bas relief, or cut into a seal or die, and at the will of the operator may even be distorted to yield a grotesque figure or caricature. The editor of the *London Art Journal* describes the specimens of photo-sculpture he has examined, as well executed, and possessing, indeed, all the appearance of photographic productions, so correct were the forms and proportions, and so natural was the expression of countenance; they were, in fact, the very "carte de visite" raised in solid form. The specimens in question, represented the actor, Roger, in the character of the "Prophet," the Annamite ambassador, the Prince of Aquila, a lady sitting in a Gothic chair, a boy, a girl, and various others. There was also one medallion representing the head, half-size, of the Duc de Morny; all were very perfect in execution.

IMPROVEMENTS IN PHOTOGRAPHY.

Photographic Ghosts.—Photographers are acquainted with three or four different ways in which secondary images may appear in photographs. In the first place, when a sensitive glass plate has served its turn as a negative—as many paper positives as may be needed having been taken from it—the film of collodion or other prepared surface is removed from it, and it may then be used for a wholly new photograph. But it is found that, unless great care be used, some faint traces of the former picture still remain, and these may appear as a sort of ghostly attendant upon the figure forming the second picture. One photographer, in endeavoring to utilize an old plate which had fulfilled its duty as a negative of the late Prince Consort, could not wholly erase the image, wash or rub as he might; there was always a faint ghost of the prince accompanying any subsequent photograph taken on the same plate. Dr. Phipson relates that a friend of his received at Brussels a box of glass plates, quite new and highly polished, each wrapped in a piece of the *Independance Belge* newspaper; a lady sat for her photograph, taken on one of these plates, and both the photographer and the lady were astonished to see that her likeness was covered with printed characters, easily to be read, —the ghost of a political article in fact. In this case actinic rays had done their work before the glass was exposed to the camera. By another mode of manipulation, a photographer may produce a ghost-like effect at pleasure: a sitter is allowed to remain in the focus of the camera only half the time necessary to produce a complete photograph; he slips quickly aside, and the furniture immediately behind him is then exposed to the action of the light; as a consequence, a faint or imperfectly developed photograph of the man appears, transparent or translucent, for the furniture is visible apparently through his body or head. With a little tact, a really surprising effect may be produced in this way. As a third variety, one negative may be placed in contact with another, and a particular kind

16*

of light allowed to pass through it for a time; there results a double picture on the lower negative, one fainter than the other. It is known, moreover, to the more scientific class of photographers, that if the lens in the camera is imperfectly curved at the surfaces, spots of cloudy light may appear in the photograph, having a semi-ghostly sort of effect.—*London Photographic Journal.*

Photography and Physiology.— The following communication, which appeared in the *London Journal of Photography*, Oct. 28, 1864, is vouched for by the Editor as entirely reliable : "Some time since my wife was engaged preparing albumen paper in the silver-bath, and in a moment of abstraction pressed two of her fingers on her forehead, being at the time about to add another 'olive branch' to the family. Soon after the birth of the baby we were surprised and annoyed at noticing that the child, when in a strong light, exhibited two distinct impressions similar to silver stains before fixing; and the strangest part of the matter is that these disappear as night comes on and reappear as daylight arrives.

"These stains, although at present serving as a sort of actinometer to me, will prove a sad disfigurement to my daughter's appearance in daylight, and we much regret they were not impressed in some less conspicuous place.

I am, etc."

Wothly's Improvement in Photography —Jacob Wothly, a German photographer, has made an improvement in photographic printing which promises to be of much importance. Instead of preparing the paper, upon which the print is to be made, with albumen, he employs collodion; and, instead of the nitrate of silver as a sensitizer he uses one of the double salts of uranium. This salt is mixed with the collodion, and the only operation required is to pour the collodion upon the sheet of paper and hang it up to dry.

Concerning this discovery, the *London Times*, of October, 1864, remarks :—

"The new process which has been discovered in Germany by Herr Wothly, and from him has been named 'Wothlytype,' discards nitrate of silver, and discards albumen. For the former it uses a double salt of uranium, the name of which is at present kept secret; for the latter it uses collodion. We have explained that by the ordinary method, the paper to be printed is sized with albumen, and the surface of the albumen receives the silver preparation, which is sensitive to the light, and shows the printed image. The paper thus does not receive the image, but is, as it were, a mere bed on which lies the material that does receive it. By the substitution of collodion for albumen, a different result is reached. In the first place, the film of collodion on the paper yields a beautiful smooth surface on which to receive the image, and the result is, that pictures are printed upon it with wonderful delicacy. In the second place, the collodion, before it is washed upon the paper, is rendered sensitive by being combined with the salt of uranium. The sensitiveness, therefore, is not on the surface alone of the collodion film, it is in the film itself, and so completely passes through it, that even if it be peeled away from the paper, the image which it receives will be found on the paper beneath. The vehicle thus employed is not less superior to all others yet known for receiving the negative image on paper, than it is to all others yet known for receiving the negative image on glass. The metallic salt which combines with it has also rare merits.

"In the first place, the manipulations are very simple and easy—far more so than in the silver printing process,—and thus the labor saved is considerable. Next, the paper, when rendered sensitive for printing, or 'sensitized,' as the photographers say, keeps perfectly for two or even three weeks,—an immense boon to amateurs, who can thus have their stock of printing paper 'sensitized' for them; whereas, at present, when the paper receives the sensitive preparation, it has to be used almost immediately, and will not keep more than a day or two. Thirdly, the color and tone obtained are very various, including every shade that can be got by the ordinary silver plan; but, in addition, it has the advantage of being able to print any number of impressions of exactly the same color, and of doing away with all such difficulties as show themselves in mealiness and irregular toning. The precision of result is a great point. By the silver process, the results are never certain, and even when the print comes out perfect from the frame, the subsequent process of washing and fixing go seriously to alter it. Lastly, the permanent character of the new method is very remarkable. Nobody seems to know exactly why the old silver process gives way—whether it be on account of the albumen, or the nitrate of silver, or the hyposulphite of soda. We only know, that so many of the prints prepared by the old method fall away, that no reliance can be placed in those which seem to stand firm."

Since the publication of the above, the process has been patented in Great Britain, and made public in all its details. These are given in the specification as follows :—

To one pound of plain collodion add from $1\frac{1}{2}$ to three ounces of nitrate of uranium and from 20 to 60 grains of nitrate of silver. The paper is prepared for printing by simply pouring the above sensitized collodion upon its surface, and hanging the sheets to dry in the dark. The printing is accomplished by exposing the paper to light under the negative in the usual manner, and for about the usual time required for silvered paper; print until the desired depth is reached. It is not necessary, as in the ordinary process, to print the positive to a greater intensity of color than the fixed picture is intended to have. After printing immerse the picture in a bath of acetic acid for about ten minutes, or until that portion of the salts not acted upon by the light has been dissolved. The picture is now fixed and finished by thorough washing or rubbing with a sponge or brush, or by rinsing in pure water; then dry. Changes in the tone of the picture to suit the taste may be made before drying, by using a bath of chloride of gold, or of hyposulphite of soda.

Improvement in Photographic Printing.—An improvement in photographic printing, brought out during the past year by Mr. Joseph Swan of England, is characterized by photographers on both sides of the Atlantic as something entirely in advance, as regards results of any thing hitherto attained to. The following is substantially the process :—

" Gelatin, in combination with a salt of chromium, becomes insoluble in water after a short exposure to sunlight.   This principle is capable of application to photography in many ways, one of the most obvious of which is to attach to paper a suitable tissue, and cover it with bichromated gelatin having a pigment mixed with it ; expose this tissue to light, under a negative, and then wash away those portions of the coating not affected by the light.   The exposed parts. having become insoluble, remain attached to the paper, and so produce a picture.   The mixture of gelatin consists of one part of a solution of bichromate of ammonia (containing one part of the salt in three parts of water), two parts gelatin, one part sugar, and eight parts of water, with coloring matter added to produce the depth of tint required. The pigment used is Indian ink, either alone or mixed with indigo and carmine.

The tissue is formed by coating a plate of glass or other smooth surface, — first with collodion, and then with the colored gelatin mixture above described : the two films unite, and, when dry, may be separated in a sheet from the surface they were formed on.   By this means a pliant tissue is obtained, which may be handled like paper, and may either be used in large sheets or cut up into pieces of any convenient size.   The tissue, prepared in the manner described, corresponds with sensitive paper, and, with proper appliances, the preparation of it need not be more troublesome than the double operation of albumenizing and exciting paper in the usual way.   The tissue is much more sensitive to light than ordinary sensitive paper, and proportionately more care must be exercised to guard it from the action of light other than that which acts upon it while in the printing-frame. Like sensitive paper, too, it is better used soon after its preparation. The printing is done in the usual way, the tissue taking the place of sensitive paper, the collodionized surface being placed next the negative.   The sensitiveness of the tissue may of course be varied by varying the proportion of the components of the gelatinous part of the tissue ; but with the mixture given, the time of exposure required is only $\frac{1}{2}$ or $\frac{1}{4}$ of that which would be usually given with highly sensitive albumenized paper.

"The proper time for exposure can be determined pretty accurately, after a few trials ; for, although there is not the same means of judging of the progress of the printing as in the ordinary process, yet there is a far wider range between under and over exposure than in silver printing.   It is no exaggeration to say that you may expose one piece of tissue twice as much as another, and yet obtain a good print from both ; not perhaps quite so good as between the two extremes, but yet much more passable than would be the case with silver prints under and over exposed to the same extent.   On taking the tissue from the printing-frame the image is faintly visible, and the next step in the process is to mount the tissue, with the collodionized face down, upon a piece of paper, or any other suitable material, to act as a support during development, and sometimes to form the basis of the picture, which may, if we please, remain permanently attached to this support, or may, if thought better, be afterwards transferred. There are several ways of mounting the tissue, and several adhesive substances may be used for the purpose, such as starch or a solution of India-rubber and dammar in benzole.

After mounting, the tissue, with paper attached, is placed in water of about 100° Fahr. The water presently begins to dissolve away the non-solarized portions of the gelatin, and in a few minutes the picture is fully disclosed. It is, however, advisable not to hurry the operation, but to give the water ample time to dissolve out the bichromate. It is also advisable to change the water three or four times. Leave the prints about two hours in the water. Where the picture has been over-exposed, longer immersion and hotter water will, in a great degree, rectify the mistake. Before finally removing the prints from the water, brush their surface lightly with a broad camel-hair brush; and, after taking them out, pour a stream of water over them to remove any loosely adherent particles of foreign matter that may by accident have got attached to the surface. The prints may then be hung up to dry, and are finished by being mounted on card-board and rolled, in the usual manner.

"*Diamond Cameo*" *Photographs.*—We copy the following article describing a new style of photograph, from the *London Photographic News*. We have frequently heard the opinion expressed of late, that the "carteomania" was on the wane, that everybody had obtained his card picture, that the albums were full, and the public beginning to be sated. No doubt this is, in some quarters, to some extent true. The question has been asked, "What will be the next fashion?" In answer to this question, solar camera pictures or other enlargements, have been doubtfully mentioned. These, it is very probable, will come into increased demand: but the demand can never become a rage at all similar to that which has existed during the last few years for card pictures. The price and size at once preclude the possibility. To take the place of cards, for which the demand begins to flag, the picture must be as cheap and as easily exchanged and preserved, and at least as pretty. A novelty we have to announce more than fulfils these conditions.

This novelty, brought out by Mr. R. Window of London, under the name of the "Diamond Cameo Photograph," is of the size of an ordinary card, and contains four portraits, each giving a different view of the face. Each portrait consists of a bust about an inch long, and three-quarters of an inch wide: two are side by side in the middle of the

card, and two at the top and bottom arranged in this order 0 0. The

top and bottom generally consist of a front face view and a three-quarter face view; whilst the others consist either of two entire profiles, one of the left and one of the right side of the face, or of a profile of one side and a ⅜ view of the other; but of course, much variety in this respect is possible. But the especial peculiarity, and that which gives the cameo effect of the picture, is yet to be described: the oval containing each bust is punched into relief, so as to have a convex surface. The effect of this in giving the illusion of roundness and relief to the whole image, cannot be readily imagined by a person who has not seen it. It is difficult at first glance to believe that the features have not a special relief of their own, and the cameo effect is perfect.

Such a style of portraiture has many real charms and points of interest, besides that of novelty. Almost all the artistic difficulties which beset the photographer are got rid of. The graceful arrangement of hands and legs, and their delineation in any thing like true proportion and in good definition, cease to distract the mind. Each small head is taken with the center of the lens, and is unexceptionable in definition; and as the full aperture of the lens may be used without hesitation, the exposure is so rapid that there is no difficulty in obtaining good expressions, an end which is further aided by the entire absence of all torture in the way of arranging awkward limbs, a process so frequently fatal to a pleasant or natural expression in the face. As to the question of likeness and versimilitude, the interest of this style of picture must at once commend itself to every one.

We have not space now to enter into a detailed description of the mechanical arrangement employed in getting the best result with the least trouble. A very ingeniously-contrived dark slide has very simple movements for obtaining the four portraits in their due positions, and of the right size on the plate. When printed and mounted, the convexity of each disc is produced by means of a steel punch and an arming press, which is worked very quickly. The exquisite surface given by the face of the die to the picture, far exceeds that produced by rolling.

The general effect is that of four cameos or enamels dropped on the card.

EFFECT OF ATMOSPHERIC PRESSURE IN GUNNERY.

The French artillerists in Mexico have recently found, to their surprise, that the angle of elevation used in France for their guns, for any given range, does not afford the calculated results; and have ascertained that this is owing to the diminished pressure of the atmosphere on the Mexican plateau. It follows that cannon may serve as a kind of barometer for measuring altitudes.—*Les Mondes.*

INTERESTING BALLOON EXPERIMENT.

A small balloon constructed of goldbeater's skin, scarcely two feet in diameter, ascended from Highgate, England, on the 30th June, at 7 45 P. M., the wind blowing moderately from the N. W. A small tube fitted to the neck allowed the gas to escape as it expanded, and a paper car, filled with sand, which fell slowly through a small aperture in the bottom was attached to the balloon, in order to compensate to a certain extent for the gradual loss of gas. At 8 30 A. M., the following morning it descended near Bamberg in Bavaria. The distance is about 500 miles in a direct line, and the time occupied, allowing for the difference of longitude, as nearly as possible 12 hours.

DOES THE MOON REVOLVE ON ITS AXIS?

The following reasons may be advanced as a conclusive proof that our moon does not revolve on its axis.

If our moon revolves on its axis, then any number of moons going around the earth in the same way, each must equally turn upon its axis, and analogously if a succession of moons, performing each the same motion as the single one now does, were so closely packed as to form one continuous ring, like that of Saturn, does any astromoner claim that all the parts, forming that ring, would have a distinct axial revolution? If so, then each imaginable section of Saturn's rings must also revolve on its axis! which is an impossibility. If the connected series do not revolve on their axis, no one of them can, as the same precise principle which governs the one, controls all; this, therefore, must be considered a sufficient proof that the only centre of the moon's motion is at the centre of the planet, as are the rings to Saturn, and, like them, our moon does not revolve upon its own axis, and until cosmical laws are changed cannot do so.—*Communicated by Charles E. Townsend, Esq.*

SOUND AS A TIME MEASURE.

In a recent French work, entitled *Traité des Mécanismes*, by M. Goupilliere, we find described a curious and ingenious method of measuring time, which gives thousandth parts of a second. The description is substantially as follows: Suppose it were required to measure the exact time of the descent of the hammer of a gun-lock on the nipple. The motion is so rapid that the most delicate stop-watch is at fault. A needle might be fixed to the hammer, so as in descending to mark a curve on a blackened metal plate; but still the time would be an unknown quantity. It may, however, be measured by means of a tuning-fork, also provided with a marking-needle; then, while the former one marks the curve described by the hammer, the second needle will mark the vibrations of the fork; and as we know that they are isochronous, each of the small insinuosities thus obtained on the blackened plate will represent a fraction of time, and show how many such fractions elapsed before the fall of the hammer. To give an idea of the degree of precision which may be obtained by this process, let us suppose the normal French tuning-fork, which will perform 896 vibrations in a second; then the duration of each vibration will be $\frac{1}{896}$ of a second; and as the greatest error that can be committed cannot exceed half a vibration, the measurement will be exact to $\frac{1}{1792}$ of a second.

ON A NEW MODE OF DETERMINING THE VELOCITY OF SOUND.

The following new mode of determining the velocity of sound was proposed, by Dr. J. Stevelly, at the last meeting of the British Association.

Suppose a piece of clock-work prepared, for instance, to strike single strokes upon a bell each time the detent is set free; the detent to be under the control of an electro-magnet, which is instantly set in action by an observer, at a measured distance from the bell or other origin of sound, depressing a key, and thus completing a galvanic circuit. The observer, being furnished with a chronometer, depresses the key; the instant he hears the stroke of the bell he again depresses it; hears a second sound, and so goes on for 100 or 1,000 times, carefully noting by the chronometer the instant at which he hears the last sound of the series. A trained observer would not make a probable error of one-tenth of a second in noting the whole time occupied by the whole series; and to avoid all chance of miscounting the number of sounds in the series, the clock may be readily made to keep count of the number of strokes it makes. The whole time occupied by the entire series is made up of the following portions: 1. The time consumed in the mechanical work of the clock in producing the stroke, and of the key, from the instant the observer touches it until it has completed the circuit. 2. The personal equation of he observer. 3. The time the sound takes to travel 100 (or 1,000) times the measured distance of the origin of the sound from the observer. 4. The time the sound takes to travel 100 times (or 1,000 times, as the case may be), the measured distance. Now, the first, second, and fourth of these portions of time can be readily eliminated by repeating the same series of observations exactly (the clock being wound up at the commencement of each series exactly to the same extent); the observer, on the second occasion, placing himself at one-half, or one-fourth, or at any determined part of his previous distance from the origin of sound; or by placing himself close up to it, using the same wires for the galvanic circuit on each occasion, in order to eliminate the fourth portion. The author was not fully aware of the exact mechanism by which Prof. Piazzi Smythe discharges the cannon which he has introduced as time-signals, but he had no doubt it could be adapted to this method, and thus determine experimentally whether the velocity of sound is affected by the violence of its originating cause: a question which Mr. Earnshaw has from theory decided in the affirmative. It would, however, involve, the author supposed, the use of two cannon, each alternately to be in process of being charged while the other was at work. This, however, could be readily accomplished.

UNEQUAL POWER OF THE ORGANS OF HEARING.

In making experiments with tuning-forks by holding one to each ear at the same time, Herr Fessel, of Cologne, has discovered the ears do not possess an equal power of hearing. It appears that from numerous trials on various individuals the hearing is generally best with the right ear. A similar difference in the power of the right and left eye is also more common than is generally supposed, as the impression made on the weaker eye is absorbed or dissipated by the stronger.

NEW ANEMOMETER.

The object of a new anemometer, described at the last meeting of the British Association by Mr. C. Cator, was to obtain by the wind acting on one surface only, a daily curve of its pressure in pounds on an area of a square foot, and the number of miles traveled by it in a horizontal direction in 24 hours, or any other given time, and thence its hourly velocity. The surface upon which the wind acts, or the pressure-plate, is the base of a cone, the axis of which is horizontal, and the area of the base equal to one square foot, the object of the cone being that there shall be as little resistance as possible, and to neutralize the effect of a vacuum being formed behind it. The pressure-plate is attached to the end of a horizontal bar, and with it is moved backwards and forwards, the bar resting on friction-rollers. This is the only portion of the instrument out-of-doors and exposed to the weather. A chain attached to the horizontal bar passes down through a tube as a connection with the rest of the instrument within the building on which the anemometer is fixed. The pressure of the wind is measured by two curved levers of equal length acting against each other, their motion being in a vertical plane. At one end of the upper lever is a fixed weight, and to the opposite end of

the under one is attached the end of the connecting chain. When there is a calm, then the point of contact is at the fixed weight, and as the wind presses against the pressure-plate it causes the chain to lift up the levers, and then the point of contact moves along towards the other end, indicating the strength of the gale, the levers returning by their own weight as the pressure of the wind subsides. To the end of the under lever a string is attached, carrying a pencil to and fro along a cylinder in the direction of its length, revolving on its axis by clock-work once in 24 hours, upon which the pencil will trace, on the paper rolled round it, the pressure of the wind for 24 hours. The velocity of the wind is shown by a " gaining clock." The pencil-string attached to the end of the under lever is connected with its regulator, and is so arranged that as the wind blows more or less strongly it pulls the regulator towards the fast end, and accelerates the gaining of the clock. A counterpoise weight brings the regulator back as the pressure decreases.

INDICATIONS OF OCEANIC CURRENTS.

Capt. Belcher of the British navy, has recently published a state˜ment, respecting the information gained within the last ten years concerning the curious voyages of bottles thrown into the sea by navigators. A good many bottles cast into the sea next to the African coast, found their way to Europe. One bottle seems to have anticipated the Panama route, having traveled from the Panama Isth mus to the Irish coast. Another crossed the Atlantic from the Canaries to Nova Scotia. Three or four bottles thrown into the sea by Greenland mariners off Davis's Straits, landed on the northwest coast of Ireland. Another made a curious trip,—swam from the South Atlantic Ocean, to the west coast of Africa, passing Gibraltar, went along the Portuguese coast of France, and was finally picked up on Jersey Island. One bottle was found after 16 years' swimming, one after 14 years, and two after ten years. A few only traveled more than one year, and one only five days. This was sent off by the Captain of the *Racehorse*, on the 17th of April, in the Carribean Sea, and was found on the 22d, after having gone through three degrees of longitude (210 miles) western direction. Captain McClure of the *Investigator* threw a bottle into the sea in 1850, on his voyage to Behring's Straits. It swam 3,500 miles in 200 days, and was picked up on the Honduras coast.

NELATON'S PROBE.

In the examination of gunshot wounds by means of the probe it is often a matter of no little difficulty for the surgeon to decide whether an obstruction met with, results from the presence of a ball or from a portion of bone. This was the case in the wound of Garibaldi, the most eminent surgeons in attendance being unable to decide the question as to the presence of the ball inflicting the wound, or, assuming its presence, of its exact location. To remedy this difficulty M. Nelaton the celebrated Parisian surgeon, has invented a form of probe which is able to give the most unerring information in regard to the matter in question. The construction of this ingenious probe, which has since come into general use, is as follows: To the end of a silver wire or stem is fixed a small olive-shaped body made of unpolished china.   The mere contact or slight rubbing of this against a lead or iron surface, is sufficient to leave a mark which neither the soft parts, nor the morbid secretions of the wound can obliterate. This mark, which resembles the mark of a lead pencil on the china, thus proves the presence and the location of the metallic body in the wound without the possibility of a doubt, and the construction of the instrument may be fairly considered as one of the most ingenious of all the applications of science to the cause of surgery.

THE MASTERY OF LANGUAGES.

In a work on the "Art of speaking foreign tongues idiomatically," published during the past year in London, by Mr. S. Prendergrast, the author lays down the following propositions, which are worthy of attention.

1. Idiomatic speech may be gained by adults without going abroad. 2. Sentences may be formulated so that each lesson shall double the number of results gained [a strong assertion; think of the horseshoe problem]. 3. Acquisition of unconnected words worthless. 4. Pr liminary grammar unnecessary. 5. Speech gained by memory, not by reasoning. 6. Memory usually over-estimated; each one to ascertain his own capacity; and 7, to keep within it; and 8, not to see a word but those he is engaged on. 9. Grammar clogs the memory with imperfect recollections. 10. The beginner on the author's method will speak grammatically. 11. Children speak fluently with a small number of words, and 12, with nearly the same epitome of language all the world over. 13. A child with 200 words possesses the syntax and pronunciation. 14. Every foreign language should be epitomized for a beginner by the framing of a set of strictly practical sentences, embodying 200 of the most useful words, and comprising all the most difficult constructions. 15. By this the greatest results with the least exertion; and time for study of pronunciation. Now in this there is sense and method enough to make it clear that the writer is entitled to the attention of philologists and teachers of language. He gives illustrations on the Teloogoo and Hindoostanee. At the end of the book is an account of a machine, which is simple and ingenious, and supplies an unending power of varying exercises upon a few words. If we construct a simple sentence, and then vary its words without alteration of construction, we may, taking five words as an example, write down the following :—

This	man	is	often	cheerful
One	woman	was	never	surprised
The	master	will-be	sometimes	present
No	servant	can-be	always	watchful

Choose one word out of each column, and we have 256 grammatical possibilities; as "The man can-be often watchful." Suppose the four words in each column written on four faces of a cube, and the five cubes placed in a box of five stalls, one side of the box being of glass. By shaking and turning over the box, the visible faces of the cubes are changed at hazard, giving different verbal variations of the phrase. Mr. Long's machine has upwards of 20 words in the sentence, and the number of possible sentences is millions of millions. A teacher of language is often perplexed to give variety enough: a machine of this sort would help him and interest his pupils. And the variety is secured upon a small number of words; only 84, where the sentence is of 21 words. Mr. A. Long has also applied the principle to a machine in which the elements are musical notes, as a suggestive help in composition. Sir Walter Scott suggested that such a contrivance might be used in writing subordinate parts of novels; and Swift described the very thing as seen by Gulliver at Laputa. But the Laputans got philosophy out of the chance combination: while the author gets only exercises in grammar.

ORIGIN OF THE SIGNS + AND —.

A recent writer in the *London Athenæum*, gives the following as the origin of the signs + and —. He says: The first of these signs is a contraction of *et*. The course of transformation from its original to its present form may be clearly traced in old MSS. *Et* by degrees became &, and & became +. The origin of the second (—) is rather more singular. Most persons are aware that it was formerly the universal custom, both in writing and printing, to omit some or all of the vowels, or a syllable or two of a word, and to denote such omissions by a short dash, thus —, over the word so abbreviated. The word *minus* thus became contracted to mns, with a dash over the letters. After a time the short line itself, without the letters, was considered sufficient to imply subtraction and by common consent became so used. Hence we have now the two signs + and —.

MUSIC AS A PHYSICAL AND MORAL AGENT.

The following thoughts respecting the physical and moral agency of music are derived from an article communicated to the *Atlantic Monthly*, for February, 1865, by Gottschalk, the eminent pianist.

"Music may be objective and subjective in turn, according to the disposition in which we find ourselves at the moment of hearing it. It is objective when, affected only by the purely physical sensation of sound, we listen to it passively, and it suggests to us impressions. A march, a waltz, a flute imitating a nightingale, the chromatic scale imitating the murmuring of the wind in the "Pastoral Symphony" may be taken as examples.

"It is subjective when, under the empire of a latent impression, we discover in its general character an accordance with our own psychological state, and we assimilate it to ourselves; it is then like a mirror in which we see reflected the movements which agitate us with a fidelity all the more exact from the fact that, without being conscious of it, we ourselves are the painters of the picture which unrolls itself before our imagination. Let me explain. Play a melancholy air to a conscript thinking of his distant home; to a mother mourning the loss of a child; to a vanquished warrior; — and be assured they will all appropriate to themselves the plaintive harmonies, and fancy they detect in them the accents of their own grief.

"The fact of music is still a mystery. We know that it is composed of three principles,—air, vibration, and rhythmic symmetry. Strike an object in an exhausted receiver, and it produces no sound, because no air is there; touch a ringing glass, and the sound stops, because there is no vibration; take away the rhythm of the simplest air by changing the duration of the notes that compose it, and you render it obscure and unrecognizable, because you have destroyed its symmetry. But why, then, do not several hammers striking in cadence produce music? They certainly comply with the three conditions of air, vibration, and rhythm. Why is the accord of a third so pleasing to the ear? Why is the minor mode so suggestive of sadness? There is the mystery, — there is the unexplained phenomenon.

"We restrict ourselves to saying that music, which, like, speech, is perceived through the medium of the ear, does not, like speech, call upon the brain for an explanation of the sensation produced by the vibration on the nerves; it addresses itself to a mysterious agent within us, which is superior to intelligence, since it is independent of it, and makes us feel that which we can neither conceive nor explain.

"Let us examine the various attributes of the musical phenomenon.

"1. *Music as a Physical Agent.*—It communicates to the body shocks which agitate the members to their base. In churches, the flame of the candle oscillates to the quake of the organ. A powerful orchestra near a sheet of water ruffles its surface. A learned traveler speaks of an iron ring which swings to and fro to the sound of the Tivoli Falls. In Switzerland I excited, at will, in a poor child afflicted with a frightful nervous malady, hysterical and cataleptic crises, by playing on the minor key of E flat. The celebrated Dr. Bertier asserts that the sound of a drum gives him the colic. Certain medical men state that the sound of the trumpet quickens the pulse and induces slight perspiration. The sound of the bassoon is cold; the notes of the French horn at a distance, and of the harp, are voluptuous. The flute played softly in the middle register calms the nerves. The low notes of the piano frighten children. I once had a dog who would generally sleep on hearing music, but the moment I played in the minor key he would bark piteously. The dog of a celebrated singer whom I knew would moan bitterly, and give signs of violent suffering, the instant his mistress chanted a chromatic gamut. A certain chord produces on my own sense of hearing the same effect as the heliotrope on my sense of smell and the pineapple on my sense of taste. Rachel's voice delighted the ear by its ring before one had time to seize what was said, or appreciate the purity of her diction.

"We may affirm, then, that musical sound, rhythmical or not, agitates the whole physical economy,—quickens the pulse, incites perspiration, and produces a pleasant momentary irritation of the nervous system.

"2. *Music is a Moral Agent.*—Through the medium of the nervous system, the direct interpreter of emotion, it calls into play the higher faculties; its language is that of sentiment. Furthermore, the motives which have presided over particular musical combinations establish links between the composer and the listener. We sigh with Bellini in the finale of La Somnambula; we shudder with Weber in the sublime phantasmagoria of Der Freischutz; the mystic inspirations of Palestrina, the masses of Mozart, transport us to the celestial regions, toward which they rise like a melodious incense. Music awakens in us reminiscences, souvenirs, associations. When we have wept over a song, it ever after seems to us bathed in tears. The old man, chilled by years, may be insensible to the pathetic accents of Rossini, of Mozart; but repeat to him the simple songs of his youth, the present vanishes, and the illusions of the past come back again. I once knew an old Spanish general who detested music. One day I began to play to him my 'Siege of Saragossa' in which is introduced the ' Marcha Real' (Spanish national air), and he wept like a child. This air recalled to him the immortal defence of the heroic city, behind the falling walls of which he had fought against the French, and sounded to him, he said, like the voice of all the holy affections expressed by the word *home*. The merceuary Swiss troops, when in France and Naples, could not hear the 'Ranz Des Vaches' without being overcome by it. When from mountain to mountain the signal of revolt summoned to the cause the three insurgent Cantons, the desertions caused by this air became so frequent that the Government prohibited it. The reader will remember the comic effect produced upon the French troops in the Crimea, by the Highlanders marching to battle to the sound of the bagpipe, whose harsh piercing notes inspired these brave mountaineers with valor, by recalling to them their country and its heroic legends. Napoleon III. finds himself compelled to allow the Arab troops incorporated into his army their barbarous tam-tam music, lest they revolt. The measured beat of the drum sustains the soldier in long marches which otherwise would be insupportable. The Marseillaise contributed as much toward the republican victories of 1793, when France was invaded, as the genius of General Dumouriez.

" 3. *Music as a Complex Agent.*—It acts at once on life, on the instinct, the forces, the organism. It has a psychological action. The negroes charm serpents by whistling to them; it is said that fawns are captivated by a melodious voice; the bear is aroused with the fife; canaries and sparrows enjoy the flageolet; in the Antilles, lizards are enticed from their retreats by the whistle; spiders have an affection for fiddlers; in Switzerland, the herdsmen attach to the necks of their handsomest cows a large bell, of which they are so proud, that, while they are allowed to wear it, they march at the head of the herd; in Andalusia, the mules lose their spirit and power of endurance, if deprived of the numerous bells with which it is customary to deck these intelligent animals; in the mountains of Scotland and Switzerland, the herds pasture best to the sound of the bagpipe; and in the Oberland, cattle strayed from the herd are recalled by the notes of a trumpet.

" In conclusion : Music being a *physical agent*,—that is to say, acting on the individual without the aid of his intelligence; *a moral agent*,—that is to say reviving his memory, exciting his imagination, developing his sentiment; and *a complex agent*,—that is to say, having a physiological action on the instinct, the organism, the forces of man, —I deduce from this that it is one of the most powerful means for ennobling the mind, elevating the morals, and, above all, refining the manners. This truth is now so well recognized in Europe, that we see choral societies—Orpheon and others—multiplying as by enchantment under the powerful impulse given them by the state. I speak not simply of Germany, which is a singing nation, whose laborious, peaceful, intelligent people have in all time associated choral music as well with their labors as with their pleasures; but I may cite particularly France, which to-day counts more than eight hundred Orpheon societies, com-

17*

posed of workingmen. How many of these, who formerly dissipated their leisure time at drinking-houses now find an ennobling recreation in these associations, where the spirit of union and fraternity is engendered and developed. And if we could get at the statistics of crime, who can doubt that they would show it had diminished in proportion to the increase of these societies? In fact, men are better, the heart is in some sort purified when impregnated with the noble harmonies of a fine chorus; and it is difficult not to treat as a brother one whose voice has mingled with your own and whose heart has been united to yours in a community of pure and joyful emotions. If Orpheon societies ever become established in America, be assured that bar-rooms, the plague of the country, will cease, with revolvers and bowie-knives, to be popular institutions.

THE GREAT INDIAN CYCLONE OF 1864.

On the night of the 1st of November, 1864, a cyclone or hurricane swept over the Bay of Bengal and the adjacent coasts, which, as regards power and destructive effect, was probably the most remarkable and terrific phenomenon of the kind, which history has ever recorded. *Sixty thousand persons*, according to the official government reports, were destroyed by the immediate action on this storm, while an equal or greater number have probably died through its later and indirect influence.

"Sixty thousand persons," says the *London Times*, "was the number estimated to have been killed by the earthquake at Lisbon, on the same day of the month, a century ago. Nor was the proportionate destruction less than it was then. In the island of Saugor, out of 8,200 persons, but 1,200 have been left. The remaining 7,000 passed, in less than an hour, out of existence. All along the eastern coast of the Indian Peninsula went wind and storm, fulfilling His word. It was the time of spring tides, and under the influence of the hurricane the sea rose to an unexampled hight. Up the course of the Ganges the wave rushed, overwhelming the villages on the banks, and leaving the few who survived the flood to perish for want of food; their grain rotted and their crops were destroyed by the salt water, and they had no resource but to die. But the scene of the greatest disaster appears to have been Masulipatam, about half-way down the coast. The town lies a little to the north of one of the mouths of the Kistna, on the plain which stretches from the Kistna to the Godavery. The mud which has for ages been washed down these rivers, has formed a district little above the level of the sea. In the wet season it is overflowed by the freshets of the Kistna, and it requires at all times to be protected from the ocean by sea-walls and dikes. The Dutch, who first settled at Masulipatam, probably saw in its situation something which reminded them of Holland, and congratulated themselves that the single good anchorage on the coast was close to such a flat and fruitful plain. But the qualities which appeared to them advantages, made Masulipatam an easy prey to the storm. The Cyclone, rushing across the Bay of Bengal, fell upon the spot which was least prepared to meet it. The center of the hurricane passed within a mile of the devoted town at 10 P. M., on the 1st of November, in a night of utter darkness. Amid the storm of wind a tidal

wave 13 feet higher than the highest tide-mark surmounted sea-walls and dikes and poured over the whole of the surrounding country. For an hour the water rose and covered nearly 800 square miles of the plain, and when it retired, at 11, the work of destruction was done. The plain for 80 miles along the coast and from nine to ten miles inland had been submerged, and in one place the storm-wave had reached a spot 17 miles-from the shore. We can only feebly picture to ourselves the desolation of the scene. The low-built houses of the natives had been washed away, and those which might have reached above the wave had been blown down by the fury of the storm. The fiercest powers of the natural world were at work, and in the darkness of night there was no escape possible, whatever might have been done in the light of day. Whole villages were entirely destroyed; their inhabitants were drowned, their cattle were lost, their crops were buried beneath a thick deposit of mud and sand. To have been the sole survivor of such a calamity was, perhaps, a more cruel fate than to have perished with kinsfolk and friends. When help came from Madras, those who brought it witnessed a sight which they will not easily forget. The mud banks were full of unburied corpses in every possible attitude, combining the grotesque and the horrible. Side by side lay one whom despair had reduced to abject resignation and another whom it had driven to wild defiance. Half the town was in ruins; fallen trees, drift, the ruins of houses, and deep pools of salt water made streets and roads impassable. Huge barges had been carried into the center of the town, and masses of solid masonry had been rolled, boulder-like, distances of 60 and 70 yards. The first impression of those visiting this city of death, was sufficiently awful, but when after a while the tale of destruction was reckoned, it was seen that the first horror had fallen short of the reality. In fort and town ½ of the inhabitants had perished. One thousand were drowned in the fort and 15,000 in the town, and in the surrounding villages 20,000 more had met their death. In one Brahmin village on the outskirts of Masulipatam 70 only remained alive out of 700. For a single night, or rather for a single hour, the destroying angel had been at work, and when he finished it was as if the life of man and the life of nature had both been effaced. Beneath the sweep of his wings the prosperous plain had become desolation and the fruitful villages tenantless."

The destruction of property caused by this storm at Calcutta, and other places, was immense; and effects of the visitation must remain impressed upon the country for years.

THE FORCES IN NATURE.

The concussion of one pound of hydrogen with eight pounds of oxygen is equal, in mechanical value, to the raising of 47,000,000 pounds one foot high. I think I did not overrate matters, when I said, that the force of gravity, as exerted near the earth, was almost a vanishing quantity in comparison with these molecular forces; and bear in mind the distances which separate the atoms before combination,—distances so small as to be utterly immeasurable, still, it is in passing over these distances, that the atoms acquire a velocity sufficient to cause them to clash with the tremendous energy indicated by

the above numbers. After combination, the substance is in a state of vapor, which sinks to 212° and afterward condenses to water. In the first instance, the atoms fall together to form the compound; in the next instance, the molecules of the compound fall together to form a liquid. The mechanical value of this act can be also calculated; nine pounds of steam in falling to water, generate an amount of heat sufficient to raise $956 \times 9 = 8,614$ pounds of water 1° Fahr. Multiplying this number by 772, we have a product of 6,718,716 foot-pounds (a foot-pound is a pound raised one foot high) as the mechanical value of the mere act of condensation. The next great fall of our nine pounds of water is from the state of liquid to that of ice, and the mechanical value of this act is equal to 993,564 foot-pounds. Thus our nine pounds of water, in its origin and progress, falls down three great precipices; the first fall is equivalent to the descent of a tun weight, urged by gravity down a precipice 22,320 feet high; the second fall is equal to that of a tun down a precipice 2,900 feet high; and the third is equal to the descent of a tun down a precipice 433 feet high. I have seen the wild stone-avalanches of the Alps, which smoke and thunder down the declivities with a vehemence almost sufficient to stun the observer. I have also seen snowflakes, descending so softly as not to hurt the fragile spangles of which they were composed; yet, to produce, from aqueous vapor, a quantity of that tender material which a child could carry, demands an exertion of energy competent to gather up the shattered blocks of the largest stone-avalanche I have ever seen, and pitch them to twice the hight from which they fall.—*Tyndall on Heat.*

Bodily Work and Waste.—Every manifestation of physical force involves the metamorphosis of a certain quantity of matter. Prof. Houghton of Trinity College, Dublin, asserts, as the result of his investigations, that, in the human organism, there is a definite relation between the amount of force exerted and the amount of urea generated. The urea formed daily in a healthy man, weighing 150 pounds, fluctuates from 400 to 650 grains. Of this, 300 grains are the result of vital work; that is, of force expended in the motions of the digestive organs and the heart, and in sustaining the temperature of the body at a uniform rate. This amount exceeds all other force generated and expended in the system, and is equal to that required to raise 769 tuns one foot high. In addition to the mere act of living, the working man undergoes bodily labor equivalent to lifting 200 tuns one foot high daily, which requires the formation of 77·38 grains of urea. The force expended in two hours hard mental labor involves an expenditure of power equal to lifting 222 foot tuns, and a generation of urea weighing 86 grains. Thus we have a minimum formation of urea during 24 hours amounting to 477,38 grains, for which there is expended force equal to 969 foot tuns.

Note.—Urea is a colorless substance, which by slow evaporation crystallizes in four-sided prisms. It consists of two atoms of carbon, two of nitrogen, two of oxygen, and four of hydrogen. Its rational formula has not been definitely settled. A little more than 46 per cent by weight consists of nitrogen. It is through this important compound that nearly all the nitrogen of the exhausted tissues of the body is removed. According to Becquerel, there is an excess of

urea formed in the male sex in the ratio of 17 to 15. Although the amount depends somewhat on the nature of food, Lehmann discovered long ago that strong exercise of the bodily powers increased its excretion. Urea was first made artificially from inorganic substances by Wöhler. By the addition of two atoms of water, urea is changed to the carbonate of ammonia, and thus becomes a valuable fertilizer.

MAGNETISM OF IRON AND STEEL TURNINGS.

Iron and steel "turnings," or the long spirals resulting from the operation of turning metal in the lathe, have been discovered by M. Greiss, to possess magnetic properties. He has communicated a short paper on the subject to a late number of *Poggendorff's Annalen.* Both steel and soft iron turnings were found by him to have a very decided and permanent polarity, and to behave in all respects like ordinary magnets. He was particularly struck with the permanence of the magnetism in the case of the soft iron. His attempts to trace some connection between the direction of the spiral which the turnings assume when they leave the tool, and Ampère's law of the circulation of the currents, were only attended with partial success. He found, however, that the end of the turning at which the tool began its work was invariably a south pole; the end at which it left off, a north pole. A comparison of the strength of the magnetism in different specimens, led him to notice that the turnings whose revolutions were in the opposite direction to the motion of the hands of a watch (the observer being at the south pole) showed a much stronger magnetic power than those whose revolutions corresponded in direction with that motion.

DYNAMICAL THEORY OF ELECTRO-MAGNETISM.

Prof. Maxwell, in a late number of the Proceedings of the Royal Society, has published a "Dynamical Theory of the Electro-Magnetic Field," in which he seeks for the origin of the electro-magnetic effects in the medium surrounding the electro-magnetic bodies, and assumes that they act on each other, not immediately at a distance, but through the intervention of the medium. He considers the existence of this medium as probable, since philosophers believe that it is in such a medium the propagation of light takes place, its properties being: 1. That the motion of one part communicates motion to the parts in its neighborhood (transverse vibrations). 2. That this communication is not instantaneous, but progressive, and depends on the elasticity of the medium as compared with its density. Prof. Maxwell, after referring to the researches of Faraday, Thompson, and others, on the subject, and expressing his own opinions, defines light, according to his theory, as consisting "of alternate and opposite rapidly recurring transverse magnetic disturbances, accompanied with electric displacements; the direction of the electric displacement being at right angles to the magnetic disturbance, and both at right angles to the direction of the ray."

PHOTOGRAPHS OF THE ELECTRIC SPARK.

Prof. Rood of Columbia College, N. Y., communicates to *Silliman's Journal*, No. 114, some researches on the electric spark obtained through the aid of photography. This method consists in allowing the electric discharge to fall directly on a sensitive photographic plate, when it produces latent images of certain form, which, under the action of the developer, yield four sharp, characteristic pictures.   There is a marked difference between the positive and negative figures,—the former consisting essentially of one or more stars or rings in combination, while the latter is made up, for short discharges, of a collection of dots, or minute circles, which, by the use of a greater length of discharge, became converted into two or more thick concentric rings.

NEW ELECTRO-MAGNET.

Is it possible that our present electro-magnet is to what it might be, what the cog-wheel of the early railway engineers was to the present smooth one?   For after our electricians have for so many years been exhausting their ingenuity to accomplish a certain object, M. Du Moncel of Paris—no mean authority in such matters—comes forward and declares that the object gained by that ingenuity is worse than useless. An electro-magnet may be briefly defined to be a cylinder of iron covered with a helix of wire; very powerless is the iron if no current is passing through the wire; very powerful is it—witness the Royal Institution magnet, and the one in Paris which is covered with 20,000 ft. of wire and lifts a weight of three tons—while a current passes. We may say, therefore, that the power of the magnet depends on the wire; and it has always been considered necessary that the wire, thin or thick, according to the work to be done or the strength of the current used, must be most carefully covered with an insulated substance.   So we have wires covered with silk, with cotton, India-rubber, and varnishes of different kinds.   And this equally in the electro-magnets used for experiments as in those used for the ten thousand purposes in which electricity is now being daily employed; indeed, we may almost say that electricity works by electro-magnets.   Some time ago, M. Carlier, an electrician in Paris, asked himself the question—Is this covering necessary?   And he very properly set to work to make an electro-magnet with uncovered wire to answer the question.   M. Du Moncel, in a communication to the Paris Academy, on the 9th inst, declares that the answer thus given is so extraordinary, and the power of the uncovered electro-magnet so great, that he can scarcely believe his own experiments.   Not only can these new magnets produce all the effects of attraction of the covered ones, but the effects in some cases are more than doubled.   Let us produce M. Du Moncel's figures. A bar of iron 4½ centimeters long, and 7 millimeters in diameter, covered with a single spiral of wire 0.277 millimeters in diameter, with two small Bunsen's elements, sustained a weight of 3·9 kilogrammes; covered, it could only support 2·4 kilogrammes.   A larger magnet, covered with 12 coats of wire, held up 940 grammes; with covered wire it could only support 540 grammes.   The effects of distant attraction were even more favorable.   At a distance of one millimeter, and with a Daniell's pile of 28 elements, the weights attracted were as follows:—

Circuit.	New Magnet.	Old Magnet.
0 kilometres	83	12
10 "	12	3
20 "	4	0

The requisite condition to obtain these effects is that the different " coats " of wire shall be separated from each other by a piece of paper, and that the interior of the bobbins, whether in wood or copper, should be covered also with an isolated substance. The advantages of this system are obvious, the first being reduced cost of the magnets. Then we have greater effects, which is tantamount to a reduction of size,—and consequently another reduction of the cost. The " extra currents " being also done away with, a more prompt movement of the armatures results, and therefore greater usefulness in induction coils. In telegraphic instruments they present the additional advantage of remaining unaffected by lightning. M. Du Moncel remarks, by way of explanation—explanation is easier than prediction—I consider that in magnets of the new construction the surface of contact of the spirals between themselves represents, in fact, a linear spiral, of which the points furnish derivations. We can easily imagine that the electric flux provoked by these derivations can only be produced by furnishing a series of superposed currents circulating through all the folds of the metallic helix, by reason of the resistance to the passage from one spiral to the other. Now, if the primitive current circulating through the helix is weakened by these derivations, it is reinforced by the derived and superposed current, which, in over-exciting the pile, furnishes at last a more energetic current. Besides, it must be borne in mind that the direct current which results from the derivations, and which passes through the spirals towards the axis, ought to be derived from them, and as it is not enfeebled by its passage, it should augment the intensity of the current which flows through it." Lastly, the quantity of uncovered wire which can be used for a given magnet is greater than that of covered.

ON THE INVISIBLE RAYS OF THE ELECTRIC LIGHT.

We are so accustomed to associate the word *ray* with the idea of light, that the term dark or obscure rays stimulates the imagination by its strangeness. And such is more particularly the case when we are told that the major portion of the radiation of the sun itself is of this invisible character. This great discovery was announced 65 years ago by Sir William Herschel. Permitting a sunbeam to pass through a glass prism, he formed the colored spectrum of the solar light; and carrying a small thermometer through its various colors, he determined their heating power. He found this power to augment gradually from the violet to the red; but he also found, to his surprise, that the calorific action did not terminate where the visible spectrum ended. Placing his thermometer in the dark space beyond the red, he found the heating power there to be greater than in any part of the visible spectrum. Sir William Herschel concluded from his experiments that besides those rays which, acting separately upon the retina, produce the sensation of color, and the sum of which constitutes our ordinary sunshine, a vast outflow of perfectly invisible rays proceeds from the sun; and that, measured by the heating power, the strength or energy of these invisible rays is greater than that of all the visible rays taken together.

This result was questioned by some and confirmed by others; but, like every natural truth that can be brought to the test of experiment, the verity of Sir William Herschel's announcement was soon completely established. Forty years after the discovery of those invisible rays by his father, Sir John Herschel made them the subject of experiment. He made an arrangement which enabled him to estimate the heating power of the spectrum by its *drying* power. Wetting by a wash of alcohol paper blackened on one side, he cast his spectrum on this paper, and observed the chasing away of the moisture by the heat of the rays. His drying paper presented to him a *thermograph* of the spectrum, and showed the heating power to extend far beyond the red.

By the introduction of the thermo-electric pile Melloni created a new epoch in researches on radiant heat. This instrument enables us to examine, with a precision unattainable with ordinary thermometers, the distribution of heat in the solar spectrum. Melloni himself devoted some time to this subject. He had made the discovery that various substances, in the highest degree transparent to light, were eminently opaque to those invisible heat-rays. Pure water, for example, is a body of this kind. Only one substance did Melloni find to be equally pervious to the visible and the invisible rays, namely, transparent rock salt. And though the researches of MM. Provostaye and Desains, together with some extremely suggestive experiments executed by Mr. Balfour Stuart, show conclusively that Melloni erred in supposing rock salt to be *perfectly* transparent, it must be admitted that, in this respect, the substance approaches very near perfection.

Abandoning prisms of glass, which had been always employed previously, Melloni made use of a prism of rock salt in his experiments on the solar spectrum. He was thus enabled to prove that the ultra-red rays, discovered by Sir William Herschel, formed an invisible spectrum, at least as long as the visible one. He also found the position of maximum radiant power to lie as far on one side the red as the green light of the spectrum on the other.

Dr. Franz of Berlin subsequently examined the distribution of heat in the solar spectrum, employing for this purpose a flint-glass prism. He showed that the inaction of the ultra-red rays upon the retina did not arise from the absorption of those rays in the humors of the eye; at all events he proved that a sensible portion of the invisible rays was transmitted across the eye-ball of an ox, and reached the back of the eye. Professor Müller of Freiburg afterwards examined very fully the heat of the solar spectrum; and representing, as Sir William Herschel also had approximately done, by lines of various lengths the thermal intensity at various points, he drew a curve which expressed the calorific action of the entire spectrum.

At various intervals during the last ten years Prof. Tyndall has occupied himself with the invisible radiation of the electric light; and to the distribution of heat in its spectrum he directed attention in a recent discourse given before the Royal Institution. The instruments made use of were the electric lamp of Duboscq and the linear thermo-electric pile of Melloni. The spectrum was formed by means of lenses and prisms of pure rock-salt. It was equal in width to the length of the row of elements forming the pile, and the latter being caused to pass through its various colors in succession, and also to search the space right and left of the visible spectrum, the heat falling upon it, at every point of its march, was determined by the deflection of an extremely sensitive galvanometer.

As in the case of the solar spectrum, the heat was found to augment from the violet to the red, while in the dark space beyond the red it rose to a maximum. The position of the maximum was about as distant from the extreme red in the one direction as the green of the spectrum in the opposite one.

The augmentation of temperature beyond the red in the spectrum of the electric light is sudden and enormous. Representing the thermal intensities by lines of proportional lengths, and erecting these lines as perpendiculars at the places to which they correspond, when we pass beyond the red these perpendiculars suddenly and greatly increase in length, reach a maximum, and then fall somewhat more suddenly on the opposite side of the maximum. When the ends of the perpendiculars are united, the curve beyond the red, representing the obscure radiation, rises in a steep and massive peak, which quite dwarfs by its magnitude the radiation of the luminous portion of the spectrum.

Interposing suitable substances in the path of the beam, this peak may be in part cut away. Water, in certain thicknesses, does this very effectually. The vapor of water would do the same, and this fact enables us to account for the difference between the distribution of heat in the solar and in the electric spectrum. The comparative hight and steepness of the ultra-red peak, in the case of the electric light, are much greater than in the case of the sun. No doubt the reason is that the eminence corresponding to the position of maximum heat in the solar spectrum has been cut down by the aqueous vapor of our atmosphere. Could a solar spectrum be produced beyond the limits of the atmosphere, it would probably show as steep a mountain of invisible rays as that exhibited by the electric light, which is practically uninfluenced by atmospheric absorption.

Having thus demonstrated that a powerful flux of dark rays accompanies the bright ones of the electric light, the question arises, "Can we separate the one class of rays from the other?"

One way of doing this would be to cut off the luminous portion of the decomposed beam by an opaque screen, allowing the non-luminous portion to pass by its edge. We might then operate at pleasure upon the latter;—reflect it, refract it, concentrate it. This would be a perfectly philosophical way of detaching the light from the heat, but with our present means we could not thus obtain a quantity of heat sufficient to produce the results intended to be exhibited before the conclusion of the discourse. Another plan consists in following up a mode of experiment initiated by Sir William Herschel. He examined the transmission of solar heat through glasses of various colors, through black muslin and other substances, which intercepted a large portion of the solar light. Melloni subsequently discovered that lampblack, and also a kind of black glass, while perfectly opaque to light, transmitted a considerable quantity of radiant heat. In Prof. Tyndall's "Lectures on Heat," given at the Royal Institution in 1862, and since made public, experiments with these bodies are described. It was while conversing with his friend Mr. Warren De la Rue, in the

18

autumn of 1861, on the possibility of sifting, by absorbents, the light of a beam from its heat, that Prof. Tyndall first learned that carbon was the substance which rendered Melloni's glass opaque. This fact was of peculiar interest to him, for it and others seemed to extend to solid bodies a law which he had detected two years previously in his experiments on gases and vapors, and which showed that *elementary* gases were highly transparent, while *compound* gases were all more or less opaque—many of them, indeed, almost perfectly opaque—to invisible radiant heat. The enormous differences existing between elementary and compound gases, as regards their opacity to radiant heat, is illustrated by the following facts: For every ray intercepted in a tube four feet long, by a certain measure of air, oxygen, hydrogen, or nitrogen, transparent ammonia strikes down 7,260 rays, olefiant gas 7,950, while transparent sulphurous acid destroys 8,800.

In Prof. Tyndall's first experiments on the invisible radiation of the electric light, black glass was the substance made use of. The specimens, however, which he was able to obtain destroyed, along with the visible, a considerable portion of the invisible radiation. But the discovery of the deportment of elementary gases directed his attention to other simple substances. He examined sulphur dissolved in bisulphide of carbon, and found it almost perfectly transparent to the invisible rays. He also examined the element bromine, and found that, notwithstanding its dark color, it was eminently transparent to the ultra-red rays. Layers of this substance, for example, which entirely cut off all the light of a brilliant gas flame, transmitted its invisible radiant heat with freedom. Finally, he tried a solution of iodine in bisulphide of carbon, and arrived at the extraordinary result that a quantity of dissolved iodine sufficiently opaque to cut off the light of the mid-day sun was, within the limits of experiment, absolutely transparent to invisible radiant heat.

This then is the substance by which the invisible rays of the electric light may be almost perfectly detached from the visible ones. Concentrating by a small glass mirror, silvered in front, the rays, emitted by the carbon points of the electric lamp, we obtain a convergent cone of light. Interposing in the path of this concentrated beam a cell containing the opaque solution of iodine, the light of the cone is utterly destroyed, while its invisible rays are scarcely, if at all, meddled with. These converge to a focus, at which, though nothing can be seen even in the darkest room, the following series of effects may be produced:—

When a piece of black paper is placed in the focus, it is pierced by the invisible rays, as if a white-hot spear had been suddenly driven through it. The paper instantly blazes, without apparent contact with any thing hot.

A piece of brown paper placed at the focus soon shows a red-hot burning surface, extending over a considerable space of the paper, which finally bursts into flame.

The wood of a hat-box similarly placed, is rapidly burnt through. A pile of wood and shavings, on which the focus falls, is quickly ignited, and thus a fire may be set burning by the invisible rays.

A cigar or a pipe is immediately lighted when placed at the focus of invisible rays.

Discs of charred paper placed at the focus are raised to brilliant incandescence ; charcoal is also ignited there.

A piece of charcoal, suspended in a glass receiver full of oxygen, is set on fire at the focus, burning with the splendor exhibited by this substance in an atmosphere of oxygen. The invisible rays, though they have passed through the receiver, still retain sufficient power to render the charcoal within it red-hot.

A mixture of oxygen and hydrogen is exploded in the dark focus, through the ignition of its envelop.

A strip of blackened zinc-foil placed at the focus is pierced and inflamed by the invisible rays. By gradually drawing the strip through the focus, it may be kept blazing with its characteristic purple light for a considerable time. This experiment is particularly beautiful.

Magnesium wire, presented suitably to the focus, burns with almost intolerable brilliancy.

The effects thus far described are, in part, due to chemical action. The substances placed at the dark focus are oxydizable ones, which, when heated sufficiently, are attacked by the atmospheric oxygen, ordinary combustion being the result. But the experiments may be freed from this impurity. A thin plate of charcoal, placed *in vacuo*, is raised to incandescence at the focus of invisible rays. Chemical action is here entirely excluded. A thin plate of silver or copper, with its surface slightly tarnished by the sulphide of the metal, so as to diminish its reflective power, is raised to incandescence either *in vacuo* or in air. With sufficient battery-power and proper concentration, a plate of platinized platinum is rendered white-hot at the focus of invisible rays ; and when the incandescent platinum is looked at through a prism, its light yields a complete and brilliant spectrum. In all these cases we have, in the first place, a perfectly invisible image of the coal points formed by the mirror ; and no experiment hitherto made illustrates the identity of light and heat more forcibly than this one. When the plate of metal or of charcoal is placed at the focus, the invisible image raises it to incandescence, and thus prints itself visibly upon the plate. On drawing the coal points apart, or on causing them to approach each other, the thermograph of the points follows their motion. By cutting the plate of carbon along the boundary of the thermograph, we may obtain a second pair of coal points, of the same shape as the original ones, but turned upside down ; and thus by the rays of the one pair of coal points, which are incompetent to excite vision, we may cause a second pair to emit all the rays of the spectrum.

The ultra-red radiation of the electric light is known to consist of ethereal undulations of greater length, and slower periods of recurrence, than those which excite vision. When, therefore, those long waves impinge upon a plate of platinum, and raise it to incandescence, their period of vibration is changed. The waves emitted by the platinum are shorter, and of more rapid recurrence, than those falling upon it, the refrangibility being thereby raised, and the invisible rays rendered visible. Thirteen years ago, Prof. Stokes published the noble discovery that by the agency of sulphate of quinine, and various other substances, the ultra-violet rays of the spectrum could be rendered visible. These invisible rays of high refrangibility, impinging upon a proper medium, cause the molecules of that medium to oscillate in slower periods than those of the incident waves. In this case, therefore, the invisible rays are rendered visible by the *lowering* of their refrangibility; while in the experiments of Prof. Tyndall, the ultra-red rays are rendered visible by the *raising* of their refrangibility. To the phenomena brought to light by Prof. Stokes, the term *fluorescence* has been applied by their discoverer, and to the phenomena brought forward Prof. Tyndall proposes to apply the term *calorescence*.

It was the discovery more than three years ago, of a substance opaque to light, and almost perfectly transparent to radiant heat,—a substance which cut the visible spectrum of the electric light sharply off at the extremity of the red, and left the ultra-red radiation almost untouched, that led Prof. Tyndall to the foregoing results. They lay directly in the path of his investigation, and it was only the diversion of his attention to subjects of more immediate interest.that prevented him from reaching much earlier the point which he has now attained. On this, however, Prof. Tyndall can found no claim, and the *idea* of rendering ultra-red rays visible, though arrived at independently, does not by right belong to him. The right to a scientific idea or discovery is secured by the act of publication, and, in virtue of such an act, priority of conception as regards the conversion of heat-rays into light-rays, belongs indisputably to Dr. Akin. At the meeting of the British Association, assembled at Newcastle in 1863, he proposed three experiments by which he intended to solve this question. He afterwards became associated with an accomplished man of science, Mr. Griffith, of Oxford, and jointly with him pursued the inquiry. Two out of the three experiments proposed at Newcastle by Dr. Akin are quite impracticable. In the third it was proposed to concentrate by a large burning mirror the rays of the sun, to cut off the luminous portion of the radiation by " proper absorbents," and then to operate with the obscure rays. Dr. Akin employed in his experiments a mirror 36 inches in diameter, but he has hitherto failed to realize his idea. With a mirror four inches in diameter, the radiant source with which his researches had rendered him familiar, and a substance which he had himself discovered to filter the beam of the electric lamp, Prof. Tyndall obtained all the results above described.—*London Reader*.

EFFECT OF THE ATMOSPHERE ON LIGHT.

M. Janssen has published the result of his researches, showing the power of elective absorption which the terrestrial atmosphere exercises on light. This action, he says, is represented by fine numerous sombre rays on the spectrum of all the light, the rays of which have traversed a sufficient thickness of our atmosphere. In 1833, Sir David Brewster announced that the solar spectrum at the horizon presented new dark bands, which disappeared as the sun rose, but did not attribute their disappearance to the terrestrial atmosphere. M. Janssen, however, affirms that these bands resolve themselves into fine lines comparable to the solar rays properly so called; and that they are always visible in the spectrum, and vary only in intensity according to the hight of the sun. He finds that in the red and orange parts of the solar spectrum, the rays of terrestrial origin, are much more numerous and important than the rays of solar origin. He mentions, also, an experiment made on the Lake of Geneva, by which he determined the presence of these bands in the flame of a firwood fire at a distance of about 13 miles. This flame gave no band when examined near. M. Janssen also states, that his experiments prove that the vapor of water dissolved in air,—that is, in the state of an elastic fluid, performs an important part in the production of the phenomena; and he considers that the results of the researches of Huggins and Miller confirm his own ideas.

DURATION OF TWILIGHT AND HIGHT OF THE ATMOSPHERE.

Herr Julius Schmidt, of the Athens Observatory, communicates to *Astronomische Nachrichten* a series of observations to determine the duration of twilight, and the hight of the atmosphere. He arrives at the conclusion that the minimum hight of the atmosphere ranges from 7·5 to 10·5 geographical miles (15 to an equatorial degree?), and that it varies with the time of year, being highest in November, December, January, and lowest in May, June, July. The depression of the sun necessary for the close of twilight is not constant, the ordinary reckoning of—18° being correct only in extreme cases.

NOVEL USE OF POLARIZED LIGHT.

M. Chacornac the French astronomer states, that while recently watching small cumulus clouds that formed themselves soon after sunset, he observed them appear as bright spots seen on a dark ground, or as dark spots on a bright ground, according to whether he shut out the polarized rays, or let them reach his eye. From this it appeared that the proportion of polarized light was sufficiently great, that dark spots became luminous through the action of the *analysing* prism, and thus, passing from the condition of negative to that of positive vision,[*] could be seen further off. The region of maximum atmospheric polarization he states to be near the horizon about 78° from the sun, it there amounts to about $\frac{75}{100}$ of the total light which the atmosphere reflects. He suggests that by adding an analysing prism to the eyepiece of a telescope, distant capes at sea, and other objects, might become visible, just as he was able by such means to see alpine summits after they have been completely screened from ordinary vision by a light fog.

SIMPLIFICATION OF THE COMMON PUMP.

A modification of the ordinary suction pump has recently been patented in France, which seems, for many purposes at least, to recommend itself strongly by its simplicity, and other good qualities. The common pump consists, as is well-known, of a barrel, a piston, and two valves opening upwards; the pump to which we direct attention, of only a barrel, a solid plunger, and a single valve. The former pump is exposed to great wear and tear, and very considerable friction, from the necessity for the sucker fitting the barrel exactly; the latter is

---

[*] Negative vision is when a dark object is seen, not by its own light, but by contrast with the light surrounding it. Positive vision is when an object is visible by the light which it emits or reflects.

18*

totally free from these objections. Our readers may make an excellent model of the new pump by fitting water-tight into one end of a cylindrical glass gas chimney a piece of wood or cork, in the centre of which is an aperture, closed within the glass cylinder by a flap of leather, which will act as a simple, but tolerably water-tight valve; and selecting for the plunger a thick rod of wood that nearly fills the cylinder. To work the apparatus it is only necessary to insert the plunger in the cylinder, fill the space around it with water, and place the closed end of the cylinder in a small quantity of that fluid. When the plunger is drawn up, the valve opens, and water rushes in to supply the vacuum. When the plunger is then pushed in again, the water flows out through the upper end of the cylinder; and thus the process may be continued for any length of time. It is evident that the fluid may be made to issue from a spout or tube, if the upper end of the barrel is enlarged. The principle on which this pump produces its effect is the same as that of the common pump, but it might be supposed that, instead of water rushing up through the valve, water, and even air, would pass down from around the plunger. This, however, is not the case; and it is the most curious circumstance connected with the apparatus. It may be accounted for, however, by the capillary attraction which exists between the plunger and barrel. Experiment alone can show how large such a pump may be made, or from what depth it would cause water to ascend; but there are most probably many purposes for which it would answer well.

CURIOUS PHYSICAL EXPERIMENT.

An interesting experiment, which, though not new, is not generally known, may be performed as follows : Roll up a large card into a tube a quarter of an inch in diameter, and make the joint tight by a little sealing-wax. Then cut a disc of card two inches in diameter, make a hole through its centre exactly big enough to admit the tube. Sealing-wax the card disc on to the top of the tube so as to form a flange, taking care not to let the tube project above the surface of the disc. Cut another card disc of the same diameter, and lay it on the former, holding the tube quite upright with the disc uppermost. Blow gently through the tube, and the loose disc will be thrown off the flange. Replace it, and blow with great vehemence. The disc will then not be thrown off, but will remain close to the flange, vibrating strongly. The loose disc may then be placed on the table, and the tube with the flange downwards held very near it. On blowing violently the loose disc will spring up toward the flange and vibrate as before.

TESTING OF CHAIN CABLES.

An interesting paper on the above subject was recently read by Mr. Paget, C. E. before the Society of Arts. The average tenacity of the bars of which the links are made is stated to be 24 tons per square inch; of this 28.75 per cent is lost in the finished link, in consequence of (1) the geometrical form of the link, (2) the crushing stress undergone by the inside of the crowns, (3) the deterioration of the iron in bending, and (4)the loss of strength at the welds. As to the proper tests of the cable, Mr. Paget suggests the breaking of a portion by hydraulic pressure as affording the surest guide to the quality of the iron employed, testing the entire cable to a fixed proof strain, and finally, by blows or impacts, as specially adapted for the discovery of false welds. The apparent increase of strength of bars repeatedly broken, first exhibited in the experiments of Mr. Lloyd, is shown to be due to increase of hardness, or of the difficulty of the gliding to and fro of the particles so that whilst the resistance to purely passive loads is increased, the resistance to impulsive forces is enormously diminished at each fracture. The value of the government hydraulic test of 11·46 tons per square inch is discussed, and the permanent set under this strain is stated to be $\frac{1}{27}$ to $\frac{1}{15}$ of the length. While believing that a single application of this test does not materially injure the cable if good, Mr. Paget deprecates any attempt to make the test more severe.

PHOTOGRAPHY APPLIED TO TOPOGRAPHY.

Photography has recently been applied in France for the purpose of topography with great success. By taking photographic views of any prominent object from different points, the distance between these points being measured, it is found possible to measure distances and heights on the photographic views almost as accurately as by triangulation. By this new process, by means of 29 views taken from 18 different points in less than 60 hours, an accurate plan of the City of Grenoble and of its environs, embracing an extent of more than 20 kilometers square (12½ miles square), was executed in 60 days, which by triangulation would have taken months.

CHEMICAL SCIENCE.

ON THE NEW SYSTEM OF CHEMICAL PHILOSOPHY.

The following is an abstract of an address made by Prof. Odling, on assuming the chair of the Chemical Section of the British Association, at its last meeting, 1864. "After the great diversity, or rather antagonism, of opinion which has existed for the last dozen years or so, I am almost bound to take a somewhat prominent notice of one substantial agreement which now prevails among English chemists as to the combining proportions of the elementary bodies, and the molecular weights of their most important compounds. The present unanimity of opinion on the fundamental subject, among those who have given it their attention is, I conceive, greater then has ever been the case since Dalton published his new system of Chemical Philosophy, more than half a century ago. As yet, indeed, the unanimity of practice falls considerably short of the unanimity of belief; but even in this direction great progress is being made. As was well observed by Dr. Miller, at a previous meeting of this Association, 'Chemistry is not merely a science; it is also an art, which has introduced its nomenclature and its notation into our manufactories, and in some measure even into our daily life; hence the great difficulty of effecting a speedy change in chemical usage alike so time-honored and intimately ramified.' I propose, with your permission, to make a few remarks upon the history of this chemical reformation, more especially in connection with certain points which some of its most distinguished leaders have scarcely, I think, correctly estimated. From the time when Dalton first introduced the expression 'atomic weight,' up to the year 1842, when Gerhardt announced his views upon the molecular constitution of water, there does not seem to have been any marked difference of opinion among chemists as to the combining proportions of the principal elements. That 1 part by weight of hydrogen, united with 36 parts by weight of chlorine to form a single molecule of hydrochloric acid, and with 8 parts by weight of oxygen to form a single molecule of water, was the notion both of Berzelius and Gmelin, who may be taken as representatives of the two chief continental schools of theoretic chemistry. There was, indeed, no difference of opinion whatever between them as to the combining proportions of the three elements. Using the hydrogen scale of numbers, both chemists represented the combining proportion of hydrogen as 1, that of chlorine as 36, and that of oxygen as 8. Both, moreover, represented the molecular weight of hydrochloric acid as 37, and the molecular weight of water as 9. True it is that Berzelius professedly regarded the single combining proportions of hydrogen and chlorine as consisting each of two physical atoms; but since the two atoms of hydrogen, for instance, which constitute the one combining proportion of hydrogen, were chemically inseparable from one another, they were really tantamount to one atom only of hydrogen, and as a matter of fact were always employed by Berzelius as representing the single chemical atom of hydrogen, or its smallest actual combining proportion. Distinguishing thus between the physical atom and the combining proportion, Berzelius's recognition of the truth that equal volumes of the elementary gases contain an equal number of atoms was utterly barren. But, identifying the physical atom with the combining proportion, Gerhardt's recognition, or rather establishment, of the broader truth that equal volumes of all gases, elementary and compound, containing the same number of atoms, has been in the highest degree prolific. From Gerhardt's division of volatile bodies into a majority whose recognized molecules corresponded respectively with four volumes of vapor, and a minority, whose recognized molecules corresponded respectively with but two volumes, and from his proposal, in conjunction with Laurent, to double the molecular weights of these last, so as to make the molecules of all volatile bodies, simple and compound, correspond each with four volumes of vapor, must, I conceive, be traced the development by himself and others of the mature views of chemical philosophy which now prevail. With every respect for other authorities, I cannot join with them in regarding the indication of Gerhardt's system as an imperfect return, and its remarkable maturation in these recent days as a more complete return, to the notions of Berzelius. It is true that the elementary weights now employed, with the exception of those for some half-dozen metals, are identical with the atomic weights of Berzelius; but so different are they from his combining weights, that fully $\frac{4}{5}$ of all known compounds have to be expressed by formulæ entirely different from his,—namely, all those bodies, with but a very few exceptions, into which hydrogen, fluorine, chlorine, bromine, iodine, nitrogen, phosphorus, arsenic, boron, and the metals lithium, sodium, potassium, silver, and gold, enter as constituents. Fully admitting that the new system of atomic weights, as it now exists, is the joint product of many minds,—fully admitting that it owes its present general acceptance chiefly to the introduction of the water type by Williamson during Gerhardt's lifetime, and the recognition of diatomic metals by Wurtz, and Cannizzaro, after his decease,—and fully admitting, moreover, that some of Gerhardt's steps in the development of his unitary system were decidedly, though perhaps excusably, retrograde,—I yet look upon him as being the great founder of that modern chemical philosophy, on the general spread of which I have already ventured to congratulate the members of the Section. Prior to the time of Gerhardt's, the selection of molecular weights for different bodies, elementary or compound, had been almost a matter of hazard. Relying conjointly upon physical and chemical phenomena, he first established definite principles of selection, by pointing out the considerations upon which the determination of atomic weights must logically depend. Relying upon these principles he established his classification of the non-metallic elements into monhydrides, represented by chlorine,—dihydrides, represented by oxygen,—terhydrides, represented by nitrogen, &c.; and relying upon the same principles, but with a greatly increased knowledge of phenomena, later chemists have given to his method a development and unity, more especially as regards the metallic elements, which have secured for the new system the impregnable and acknowledged position which it at present occupies. The comparative unanimity which prevailed before the time of Gerhardt's was the unanimity of submission to authority; but the greater unanimity which now prevails is the unanimity of conviction, consequent upon an intermediate period of solitary insurrection by general disturbance and ultimate triumph. Bearing in mind how much the origin of the new system by Gerhardt, and its completion by his colleagues and disciples, owe to a correct appreciation of the harmony subsisting between chemical and physical relations, we cannot but give a hearty welcome to any large exposition of mixed chemico-physical phenomena; and whether or not we agree with all his conclusions, there can be but one opinion as to the obligation chemists are under to Prof. Kopp, of Giessen, for the great addition he has recently made to our knowledge and means of obtaining a further knowledge of what has hitherto been but a very limited subject, namely, specific heat. The agreement of chemists as to the elemental atomic weights is tantamount to an agreement among them as to the relative quantities of the different kinds of matter which shall be represented by the different elemental symbols; and this brings me to the subject of chemical notation. At one time many chemists even of considerable eminence believed and taught that Gerhardt's reformation had reference mainly to notation, and not to the association and interpretation of phenomena, and it became rather a fashion among them to declaim against the puerilities of notational questions. That the idea is of far greater importance than the mode of expressing it, is an obvious truism; but nevertheless the mode of expression has an importance of its own, as facilitating the spread of the idea, and more especially its development and procreation. It has been well asked, in what position would the science of arithmetic have been but for the substitution of Arabic for Roman numerals, the notation in which value is expressed by the change in position for that in which it is expressed mainly by the repetition of a few simple signs? It is unfortunately too true that chemical notation is at present in any thing but a satisfactory state. The much-used sign of addition is, I conceive, about the last which would be deliberately selected to represent the fine idea of chemical combination, which seems allied rather, I should say to an interpenetration than to a coarse apposition of atoms. The placing of symbols in contiguity, or simply introducing a point between them, as indicative of a sort of multiplication or involution of the one atom into the other, is, I think, far preferable; but here, as pointed out by Sir John Herschel, we violate the ordinary algebraic understanding, which assigns very different numerical value to the expressions $x\,y$ and $x \times y$ respectively. I know, indeed, that one among us has been engaged for some years past in conceiving and working out a new and strictly philosophical system of chemical notation, by means of actual formulæ, instead of mere symbols; and I am sure that I only express the general wish of the Section, when I ask Sir Benjamin Brodie not to postpone the publication of his views for a longer time than is absolutely necessary for their sufficient elaboration. In any case, however, the symbolic notation at present employed, with more or less modification of detail, must continue to have its peculiar uses as an instrument of interpretation, and it becomes therefore of importance to us to render it more precise in meaning and consistent in its application. Many of its incongruities belong to the very lowest order of convention; such, for example, as the custom of distinguishing between the representation of so-called mineral and organic compounds, one particular sequence of symbols being habitually employed in representing the compounds of carbon, and an entirely different sequence of symbols in representing the more or less analogous compounds of all other elements. Now that organic and mineral chemistry are properly regarded as forming one continuous whole,—a conclusion to which Colbe's researches on sulphureted organic bodies have largely contributed,—it is high time that such relics of the ancient superstition, that organic and mineral chemistry were essentially different from one another, should be done away with. Although during the past year the direct advance of that crucial organic chemistry, the synthesis of natural organic bodies, has not been striking; yet, on the other hand, its indirect advance has, I submit, been very considerable. Several of the artificially produced organic compounds at first thought to be identical with those of natural origin, have proved to be, as it is well known, not identical, but only isomeric therewith. Hence, *reculer pour mieux sauter*, chemists have been stepping back a little to examine more intimately the construction both of natural organic bodies and of their artificial isomers. The synthetic power having been allowed of putting the works together in almost any desired way, it is yet necessary, in order to construct some particular biological product, to first learn the way in which its constituent bricks have been naturally put together. We accordingly find that the study of isomerism, or what comes to the same thing, the study of the intimate construction of bodies, is assuming an importance never before accorded to it. Isomerism is, in fact, the chemical problem of the day; and concurrently with its rapidly advancing solution, through the varied endeavors of many *workers*, will be the advance in rational organic synthesis. It is curious to note the oscillation of opinion in reference to this subject. Twenty years ago, the molecular constitution of bodies was perceived by a special instinct, simultaneously with or even prior to the establishment of their molecular weights. Then came an interval of scepticism, when the intimate constitution of bodies was maintained to be not only unknown, but unknowable. Now, we have a period of temperate reaction, not recognizing the descried knowledge as unallowable, but only as difficult of allowment. And in this, as in many other instances, we find evidence of the healthier state of mind in which now more perhaps than ever the first principles of chemical philosophy are explored. Speculation, indeed, is not less rife, and scarcely less esteemed than formerly, but it is now seldom or never mistaken for ascertained truth. Scepticism indeed still prevails; not, however, the barren scepticism of contentment, but the fertile scepticism which aspires to greater and greater certainty of knowledge. Chemical science is advancing, I believe, not only more rapidly, but upon a surer basis than heretofore; and while, with every advance, the prospect widens before our eyes, so that we become almost alarmed at contemplating what those who come after us will have to learn, we console ourselves with the determination that their labor of unlearning shall be as little as possible—far less, we hope, than what we in our time have had to experience.

THE NEW METALS.

The new metal *Indium* found in the zinc-blend of Fryberg, by means of the spectroscope, is distinguished by having a spectrum consisting of two bright indigo-colored lines, and by its compounds tinting the colorless flame of a Bunsen burner of a violet color. Hitherto indium has only been obtained in very minute quantity from the Fryberg blende, consequently its properties and compounds have not been very carefully examined. It appears closely to resemble zinc, with which it has hitherto always been found in combination. It is, however, a softer metal, marking paper like lead; it is readily soluble in hydrochloric acid, and, heated in the open air, it oxydizes freely, yielding a white oxyd easily reducible before the deoxydizing flame of the blow-pipe. The hydrated oxyd is precipitated from its salts by potash and ammonia, but is insoluble in excess of either of these reagents; hence it is easily distinguished from both zinc and alumina. The oxyd may be separated from oxyd of iron, with which it is associated in the zinc blende by precipitating the latter with bicarbonate of soda. The precipitated sulphide is insoluble in alkalies.

Cæsium and Rubidium have recently been found to be extensively distributed, and to exist in many articles of human consumption, such as beet-root, sugar, tea, and coffee. *Thallium* has been found in many minerals in which its presence was hitherto unsuspected, and to occur also in very appreciable quantity in molasses, the yeast of wine, chicory, and even in tobacco.

A new and comparatively abundant source of these three rare metals, cæsium, rubidium, and thallium, has been discovered; the water of a spring near Frankfort, Germany, leaves on evaporation a saline residue which contains the three metals in appreciable quantity. Rubidium is a very light metal; with a white color like silver, with a yellowish shade. In contact with air it covers itself immediately with a bluish gray coating of suboxyd, is inflamed (even when in large lumps) after a few seconds, much quicker than potassium. At a temperature of 14° Fahr. it is still as soft as wax; it becomes liquid at 101-3° Fahr., and in red heat it is transformed into a greenish-blue vapor. The specific gravity of rubidium is about 1·52. It is much more electro-positive than potassium; and when thrown upon water, burns and shows a flame like that metal.

Cæsium and Tellurium.—The metal *cæsium* has hitherto been obtained only in very small quantities. To get only seven grains of its chloride Bunsen was obliged to evaporate forty tons of water; and only 0·3 per cent, of it are contained in the Lepidolite of Hebron in the United States. But it has recently been found that the mineral Pollux, which is very abundant in the island of Elba, contains 34 per cent of this metal, which had been previously mistaken for potassium.——*Tellurium* also, hitherto one of the rarest of substances, is found in considerable quantity associated with bismuth, about 15,000 feet above the level of the sea, in one of the loftiest peaks of the Andes.——The reduction of chloride of *aluminum* by means of zinc was patented in 1854, but the principle was not successfully carried out until recently. The vapor of zinc is found to reduce cobalt, nickel, and manganese with great facility.

Use and distribution of Lithium.—Lithia, the oxyd of the metal lithium, since the discovery of its wide distribution by the process of spectral analysis, has been introduced to a considerable extent into medicine, in the form of a carbonate, as an anti-acid and anti-lithic remedy. As a carbonate, it is a colorless white powder, sometimes in small crystals, soluble in 100 parts of cold water, insoluble in alcohol. It is very much like carbonate of soda in most of its properties, but is a much stronger alkali than either this or the corresponding potash salt. A mineral, termed Lepidolite, found in abundance at Hebron, Maine, has been recently shown by Mr. O. C. Allen, of the Sheffield Scientific School, New Haven, to be so rich in lithia as to justify its prospective use as a source of the carbonate for use in medicine.

Observations on the Metal Magnesium.—The spectrum of burning magnesium has been found to be particularly rich in chemical rays, and has consequently been used with success as a photographic light. Prof. Roscoe in a recent lecture before the Royal Institution stated that if the surface of burning magnesium has an apparent magnitude equal to that of the sun seen from a certain point, the chemical action effected by the magnesium on that point is equal to that produced by the sun when at an elevation of 9° 53'. And that at a zenith distance of 67° 22', the visible brightness of the sun's rays is 524·7 times that of burning magnesium, whilst its chemical brightness is only 36·6 times as great as that of the burning metal: hence the great use of the latter in photography. A thin magnesium wire produces in burning as much light as 74 stearine candles, and to continue this light for ten hours, 72 grammes—about two ounces and a half—of magnesium must be burnt, corresponding in effect to 20 pounds of stearine candles.

Economical Production of Aluminum.—M. Corbelli has discovered a new method for obtaining this metal at a very small cost. His plan is as follows:—

He takes a certain quantity of pure clay, say 100 grammes, and dissolves it in six times its weight of concentrated sulphuric, nitric, or hydrochloric acid. The solution is then allowed to stand; and afterwards decanted. The residue is first dried and then heated to 450° or 500° Centigrade; after which it is mixed with 200 grammes of prussiate of potash, which may be increased or diminished according to the quantity of silica contained in the clay. To this mixture 150 grammes of common salt are added; the whole is then put into a crucible and heated until the mixture becomes white; when cool, a button of pure aluminum is found at the bottom of the crucible.

Thallium.—At a recent meeting of the Royal Institution, Mr. Crookes, the discoverer of Thallium, exhibited an ingot of this element weighing 24 pounds. Recent chemical researches seem to indicate that Thallium ought to be included with the alkaline metals in its chemical classification.

ORIGIN OF GRAPHITE.

Iron, after remaining long buried in the earth, at last entirely decomposes, leaving a black, porous, eminently combustible residuum, known as graphite or pure carbon. M. Haidinger's report on the ferruginous masses of Kokitzan and Gotta, near Dresden, masses of uncertain origin, lends support to this general fact. One word on the formation, still so little known, of graphite (plumbago, pencil lead). The presence of graphite in granite, gneiss, and diorite, has renewed the disputes between the Neptunists and Plutonists. Graphite is well known to be nearly pure carbon, for it leaves in burning but a very small quantity of ash. Now, if these primitive crystalline rocks are of igneous formation, it is impossible to explain how graphite could coexist with silicates of protoxyd of iron without having reduced these salts; judging merely by what takes place in blast furnaces, since carbon reduces all oxyds of iron at a high temperature. It must then be admitted that granite, gneiss, and diorite, did not contain graphite when the mineral. elements of these rocks, such as mica, hornblende, and other ferrous silicates were in a state of fusion. Graphite, then, must have been subsequently introduced into these rocks,—but when, and how? Questions such as these are very difficult to answer satisfactorily. The most plausible hypothesis is that graphite has been introduced by the wet way into the crystalline rocks and substituted for one of the mineral components. Thus, in the gneiss of Passau (Bavaria), it takes the place of mica.

Graphite is frequently to be met with in granulated limestone,—a fact particularly interesting to geologists. Is limestone a product of eruption, or is it a sediment transformed by the action of heat? The presence of graphite is explicable by neither hypothesis. For at a certain temperature, which need not be very high, carbon decomposes carbonate of lime. This salt may no doubt, under · strong pressure, be heated to the melting point without losing its carbonic acid; this is a laboratory experiment often cited by the Plutonists. But it is quite a different thing with a mixture of carbon and carbonate of lime at a high temperature. If we reject the Neptunian origin of granulated limestone, we must then, as with crystalline rocks, suppose that graphite has been introduced by the wet way at a more recent period. The same remark applies to magnetic pyrites (sulphide of iron), often very rich in plumbago kerns.

Does graphite, like all carbon, belong to the organic kingdom? It is certain that anthracite, lignite, and coal, are the result of the slow decomposition of an enormous quantity of vegetables; the impressions found on them often indicate the kind of vegetables, most of them extinct, which have contributed to these carbonaceous formations. Graphite, if not formed in precisely the same way as coal and anthracite, nevertheless bears signs of an organic origin. The formation of nuclei and veins of graphite in crystalline rocks is sufficiently explained by the decomposition of carbonized hydrogen gas at a high temperature; this gas, disengaged from organic matters, and penetrating the fissures of the burning rock, would undergo decomposition into hydrogen and carbon.

It is this deposited carbon which forms graphite. If in our laboratories we do not obtain exactly the same product, it must be remembered that Nature has means at her command which escape our researches. We find it impossible to make coal from wood. The wood may be carbonized by the dry or by the wet way. In the first place the carbonization is very rapid; in the latter it is extremely slow, as is shown by the blackened points of piling sunk in water.

Finally, graphite has been found in meteorites or aerolites. Attempts have been made to explain its presence here by the continuance of these stones in soil more or less rich in carbonized principles. But with regard to newly-fallen stones, this explanation is inadmissible.

If it be maintained that graphite is an organic product, it must be admitted that in the case of newly-fallen meteorites it can proceed only from organic matters belonging to another world than our own.

In his report on Alibert graphite, M. Dumas presents some considerations on the probable origin of graphite and of the diamond. M. Despretz and others ascribe to fire the change of carbon into diamond; Newton ascribed it to the coagulation of a fatty or oily body; Liebig says the diamond is slowly. formed by processes which determine the prolonged putrefaction of a liquid body rich in carbon and in water; then, contrary to M. Despretz's method a high temperature would be unfavorable to a successful attempt. Adopting Newton's hypothesis, M. Gœppert states, in "a memoir on the solid bodies entering into the composition of the diamond, and considered with regard to their organic or inorganic origin," that he is disposed to class the diamond among the products of the decomposition of organic matters. All these hypotheses M. Dumas rejects; according to him the diamond is crystallized carbon, at the moment of its production and in the midst of a mass which has been exposed merely to the heat necessary to soften it, provided this condition is sufficiently prolonged.

Finally, M. Dumas frankly admits that nothing positive is known as to the true origin of the diamond, though the substance most allied to it, silicum, is perfectly known, and very beautiful specimens of it are obtained.

However, it is positively ascertained that the diamond and graphite have not the same origin, and that the residue of every carboniferous substance, treated at a high temperature, proves to be but a variety of graphite. The new carbon found by M. Alibert in the mines of Marinski, situated at the summit of Batougol, on the Siberian frontiers, is then a graphitoid carbon of the most beautiful kind, formed by volcanic phenomena. M. Jaquelain, after carefully comparing the external characteristics of Alibert graphite with that obtained by his process, concludes that the conditions under which they are produced must be analogous.

In fact, on comparing the texture of the two carbons, they will be found sometimes of a metallic, mirror-like lustre; at another time the surface will be of shining steel-gray, mammillated as if it had been half fused, and had passed through a pasty stage. This appearance is similar to that of oxyd of iron, nodulous, brilliant, with mammillated surface, known by the name of brown hematite. M. Jaquelain is inclined to admit that tarry and pyrogenated products, transformed in immense proportions into carbon and hydrogen, under the influence of igneous rocks, become accumulated in rents and excavations, causing an aggregation of carbon, and inducing a fusion analogous to that of carbon in retorts for lighting gas and of graphitoid carbon destined to form the pencils used for the electric light.

On this point, M. Jaquelain narrates one of his own recent experiments. On decomposing some sulphide of carbon in a porcelain tube in presence of pure copper, heated to about 3,008, sulphite of copper and graphite were formed, externally similar to natural graphite.—*Lond. Chem. News*, from *Cosmos*.

ARTIFICIAL DIAMONDS.

It has been often suggested that in default of a "Carbon-Solvent," electricity might possibly be brought to bear upon a carbonaceous solution, so as to cause the carbon to be deposited pure in a crystalline form. Starting from this point; a recent writer in the *Dublin University Magazine*, makes the following suggestions. "Diamond when fused by the heat in the open air, leaves a residue of pure carbon. Its attraction for solar light is so great that, after absorption, it is sure to give it off when placed in a dark room. Its extreme refrangibility shows it to have for its base an oily substance. It is a bad conductor of electricity, like all such substances. Suppose we take a portion of pure carbon (which is a powerful conductor of electricity), produced by burning to sooty residue a quantity of vegetable oil, say oil of origanum, which is the most inflammable; then place it in a close air-tight vessel constructed so as to admit a saturating supply of oxygen (which is a powerful conductor of electricity); then bring to bear on this intensely oxygenized piece of carbon a strong and constant electric current. While the latter produces volatilization and intense molecular aggregations, it is very possible that the union of oxygen with the carbon, under such conditions, would result in the reconstruction of diamond substance, which would take a crystallized form under the influence of the current; while the oxygen would restore to the diamond base the quality which it had lost. The instrument should be exposed constantly in the light of the sun, which exercises such influence on crystallization; and as the harder the crystals the longer the time it takes to form, the process of the experiment would of necessity be extended over several or many years."

PERMEABILITY OF IRON.

In the *Annual of Scientific Discovery* for 1864 (page 197), some curious facts showing the porosity of platinum to hydrogen, — the results of experiments by M. Deville of Paris—were given. During the past year, the same author, in a paper presented to the French Academy, announces the discovery of a similar property in iron. The experiment, proving this, is detailed by him as follows.

The great difficulty was to find a tube answering to the various conditions required for the experiment. The best iron to be found in the markets might still be open to some objection, since in point of fact it is a mere sponge flattened by a hammer, like common platinum. They succeeded at length in obtaining a tube of cast steel, containing so little carbon that it did not admit of being tempered. It was in reality rather iron than steel, and so soft that it was drawn into a tube without heating or soldering, though its sides were of a thickness of from three to four millimeters. To the ends of this tube, two other tubes of a much smaller diameter, and of copper, were soldered with silver; the whole was then introduced into an open porcelain tube, which was put into a furnace; a glass tube, luted to one end, established a communication with an apparatus generating hydrogen completely deprived of atmospheric air; while at the other end, another glass tube, bent at right angles, dipped into a mercury bath, its vertical branch being 80 centimeters long. For the space of eight or ten hours, a current of hydrogen was driven through the apparatus, which was maintained at a high temperature, so as to exhaust the action of the hydrogen on the sides of the iron tube, and to drive away all the atmospheric air, as well as the moisture contained in the tube, or likely to be produced there. This done, the communication between the iron tube and the hydrogen apparatus was cut off by melting down the glass tube by the aid of the blowpipe. No sooner was this effected, than the mercury, no longer kept down by the stream of hydrogen, yielded to the pressure of the air, and rose in the vertical glass tube to the height of 740 millimeters, or very nearly the usual barometrical hight. This would not have happened, had there not been a nearly complete vacuum in the tube the instant the supply of hydrogen was cut off. But what had become of the hydrogen supplied before? There is but one explanation possible, viz: that, notwithstanding the pressure of the atmosphere, the hydrogen had passed through the pores of the steel tube.

Additional Facts.—M. Cailletet has detailed to the French Academy some very curious additional facts bearing on the experiments of M. Deville. He says: "I passed portions of a gun-barrel through rollers till they were flattened. The ends were then welded. Thus, rectangular pieces of iron were obtained, formed of two plates in contact, and sealed at their extremities. On strongly heating one of these pieces in a furnace, the non-welded portions separated, and resumed the cylindrical form and their original volume. It could not, therefore, be doubted that the gases of the furnace had penetrated the mass of iron and distended its walls." To a similar action, M. Cailletet ascribes the cavities in large masses of forged iron ; and he states, that in the process of cementation, *acier poule* or steel with vesicles, is constantly produced; but if soft, perfectly homogeneous iron, such as can be obtained by keeping melted steel for several hours at a high temperature, be employed, it is reconstructed into steel without blisters. M. Deville remarks upon this communication, that it is "very interesting and conclusive, and he adverts to the discharge of gas from molten matter, often observed in metallurgical operations. These gases, he considers, penetrate the walls of the crucibles by endosmose, and give rise to bubbles in the metals."

Action of Porcelain and Lavas at high temperatures on Gases. Possible action of the Moon.—M. Deville, in commenting further upon the above facts, stated that his brother and M. Troost have shown that if hydrogen traverses without difficulty the walls of a porcelain tube at a high temperature, it does not do so when the tube begins to soften or vitrify. The gas is then absorbed by the vitrified surface, from whence it escapes, leaving it porous. He connects these facts with the appearance of certain lavas. He says the lavas of Vesuvius, whatever the rate of their cooling, are always crystalline, and that they disengage aqueous vapor, chlorides, sulphides, etc., as the crytallization proceeds, just as oxygen escapes from silver that takes the rocky form, or air escapes from freezing water. The crystallization of lavas he states to be accompanied by increase of density and evolution of heat. He traces a resemblance between the Campi Phlegræi and the surface of the moon, and considers that the latter may have behaved like erup-

19*

tive matter with excess of silica, which has a tendency to consolidate in a vitreous form, and imprisons gaseous matter in its solidification.

ON THE CHEAP PRODUCTION OF OXYGEN GAS.

In a recently published report of Dr. Hoffmann, of London, on the "*Chemical processes and products*" of the Great Exhibition of 1862, he notices the production and application of oxygen gas in the arts as follows : —

"Of the various processes by which oxygen gas can be produced, I think we may say that two only are now used, viz : chlorate of potash with and without manganese, and manganese alone : the latter is selected only for cheapness when a considerable quantity of the gas is required ; chlorate of potash, with manganese for facility of operation ; and chlorate of potash alone when purity is the principal object to be attained. More recently other processes have been recommended, one of which, by heating together a mixture of nitrate of soda and oxide of zinc, has been patented ; from this mixture oxygen is said to be produced at a cheaper rate than by any other method at present known. Unfortunately for the value of this discovery, the produce is contaminated with a considerable percentage of nitrogen. Mr. Kuhlman, of Lille, discovered and published an ingenious and beautiful process for the production of oxygen by means of baryta. He found that by passing a current of common air through caustic baryta, heated to dull redness, peroxyd of barium was formed, which, on an increase of temperature, is resolved into oxygen gas and caustic baryta, the latter ready again to perform its part in a similar operation. The idea naturally suggested itself that the means were now at hand for getting oxygen from the atmosphere in any quantity at a small cost. This method, although so promising, has been for the present abandoned. It was found that after a few operations, either from a molecular change or from the silica or other impurities, a sort of glass or fusion resulted on the surface, the baryta ceased to absorb oxygen, and the operation ceased."

Should this difficulty be overcome, and the process be made available for supplying oxygen at a cheap rate for manufacturing purposes, a great impulse will be given to what is termed furnace chemistry, and our power over the more refractory provinces of the mineral kingdom be proportionately increased.

As this change in the condition of the baryta in Kuhlman's process, is in the opinion of Prof. Hoffmann, physical rather than chemical, it is not unlikely that means to remedy the evil may soon be suggested.

"A cheap process for the preparation of caustic baryta, and its derivative the peroxyd of barium, would probably lead to the extensive manufacture of peroxyd of hydrogen,—a compound whose powerful bleaching and oxydizing properties would render it an invaluable adjunct in many manufacturing processes." The Report goes on to suggest many other applications where success may be expected, and adds : "Nothing, it has been well said, seems so difficult as the invention of to-morrow, nor so easy as the invention of yesterday."

OZONE AND THE ATMOSPHERE.

An important contribution to our knowledge of ozone, and its relations to the atmosphere and to electrical phenomena, has recently been made by Dr. G. Meissner of Gottingen. From an abstract of these researches, given in *Silliman's Journal*, (May and July numbers, 1864,) by Prof. S. W. Johnson, and to which we would refer our readers, we derive the following curious information respecting the formation of clouds and mists. Meissner's researches confirm the theory of the vesicular nature of mist. He has also discovered, by experiment, that while it is easy to condense moisture from any moist gas or gaseous mixture by cold or rarefaction, *it is impossible to produce a mist unless the gas is oxygen, or contains this element.* The water condensed by artificial means from pure oxygen or from the atmospheric air always exhibits the character of a cloud; that, separated from other gases or mixtures free of oxygen, always assumes directly the form of rain. Where oxygen is present, the water condenses in *vesicles;* in other cases, in *solid drops.* Meissner states, further, that air saturated with moisture gives a cloud on sudden rarefaction until the pressure is reduced to about eight inches of barometric pressure. At this levity the cloud is, however, extremely delicate and transitory, and under a less pressure no cloud could be produced. This stand of the barometer corresponds to a hight in the atmosphere, above tide-level, of 27,000 feet. According to Kämtz, the lightest and highest clouds, *cirrhi*, are formed at an average altitude of 20,000, and a greatest altitude of 24,000 feet. The densest artificial cloud is formed in the densest air, and the heaviest *cumuli* are formed within 5,000 feet from the sea-level.

THE INFLUENCE OF OZONE ON VEGETATION.

The influence of ozone on vegetation has been studied by Mr. Carey Lea, of Philadelphia, and the results reported in the *American Journal of Science.* Two sets of experiments were made. In the first, the water with which the seeds came in contact was made to contain those solid substances which are most essential to vegetation. In the second, very pure river water was used. For the first, phosphate of soda, silicate of potash, sulphate of magnesia, nitrate of lime, and sesquichloride of iron were added to water in a proportion such as to be equivalent to $\frac{8}{10}$ of one per cent of solid matter. In order to afford a just term of comparison, two vessels every way similar were filled with this prepared water, were covered with gauze, so that the gauze should rest on the surface of the water, and were placed under bell-glasses resting on glass plates. Wheat and maize grains were placed on this gauze, and beneath one bell-glass was introduced the ozone generating mixture. On the 12th day the experiment was terminated. The average hight of the wheat plants not exposed to the ozone was 10 inches, of those exposed 4 inches. The effect of ozone in checking the growth of the roots was very remarkable, especially with the wheat plants. In those not exposed to ozone the roots attained a length equal to about $\frac{1}{2}$ of the hight of the stem. In those exposed to it the roots, after starting, almost immediately ceased to grow. The strongest plant attained a hight of 6 inches, and developed 6 rootlets, averaging only $\frac{3}{16}$ of an inch in length; while those not exposed to ozone had many roots exceeding $2\frac{1}{2}$ inches. As a whole, the roots produced by the plants under the influence of ozone did not exceed $\frac{1}{15}$ of those produced in its absence, from an equal number of healthy seeds. One curious result of the almost total absence of roots was that the wheat plants were scarcely able to sustain themselves in a vertical position; the greater part of them fell over on one side. The flatness of the grains of the maize afforded these plants a better support. The presence of ozone also prevented the usual formation of mold on seeds placed in contact with air and water under a bell-glass.

The ozone used in the experiments was generated by the action of sulphuric acid upon chameleon mineral. Two or three grains of chameleon mineral were placed in a small capsule and moistened with oil of vitriol. This when placed by itself, or with a vessel of water under a bell-glass of about three litres capacity, was found to maintain a highly ozonized atmosphere for five or six days or even longer. But as the presence of vegetation would tend to destroy the ozone rapidly, it was considered expedient to renew the generating mixture every two or three days.

Pasteur has lately shown that the putrefaction and oxydation of organic bodies is effected to a very large extent by the intervention of the lowest order of vegetable organisms. That in some cases where the germs of these bodies have been carefully excluded, milk for example has been kept in the presence of atmospheric air for a year without alteration; and that when sawdust was enclosed in a flask for a month, the germs having been similarly excluded, the air still contained 16 per cent of uncombined oxygen. It therefore appears that ozone, while a highly oxydizing agent, may in some cases check putrefaction and oxydation by destroying the intermediate agencies, through which these operations are effected; a fact not without interest in connection with the alleged influence of ozone on epidemics.

Carbonic Acid.—Experiments were also made to ascertain the effect of a complete removal of carbonic acid from the atmosphere surrounding plants. The seeds were placed on gauze strained over a vessel of water, which was set in a dish containing concentrated solution of caustic soda, and the whole was covered with a bell-glass. A similar arrangement was made, exclusive of the caustic alkali, to afford a term of comparison. No appreciable difference could be observed. It is probable that seedlings, within the hight which they can attain under an ordinary bell-glass, still derive a sufficient supply of carbon from the seed. Be this as it may, the removal of carbonic acid from the atmosphere surrounding them did not interfere with their growth. Experiments made with seeds placed in an atmosphere of carbonic acid accorded with results obtained by other observers, as to total prevention of germination under circumstances otherwise favorable. The seeds, however, were found to be not in any way injured, and germinated freely on exposure to the atmosphere.

It seems probable that in those cases in which germination has been observed to take place in an atmosphere of carbonic acid gas, the exclusion of atmospheric air has not been sufficiently well maintained.

TESTS FOR OZONE.

Dr. Allnatt says: "I conclude that bibulous paper, saturated with a solution of iodide of potassium and starch or thin arrowroot, affords

the most effective tests we possess. The formula of its preparation is as follows : Take of pure white starch 1 ounce, iodide of potassium 3 drachms ; mix in a marble mortar, and add gradually 6 ounces of boiling water. The papers to be saturated with the mixture while hot, carefully dried out of contact with the external air, and preserved in close tin boxes." Mr. Lowe remarks: "Assuming that we have adopted the best tests and the most approved method of using those tests, it will be requisite to correct the readings for the velocity of air at the time, for the hight of the barometer, for temperature, and for the hygrometrical condition of the atmosphere. It must be borne in mind that if in a given time 1,000 cubic feet of air passing through the ozone-box gives a register of four, 2,000 feet passing through in the same time will give one of double that amount. Moisture can also increase or diminish the action, a very dry air or a perfectly saturated atmosphere showing a *minimum*. The lower the barometer descends, the more ozone is shown upon the tests. In very hot or very cold weather ozone is also at a *minimum*. With a west there is much more ozone than with an east wind. The *maximum* amount of ozone will occur with a moderately moist atmosphere, a temperature between 50° and 60°, a barometrical pressure under 29 inches, and a gale occurring at the same time. Before the actual amount of ozone can be ascertained, certain corrections must be applied, and until uniformity is adopted the observations cannot be made comparable. Under these circumstances, we can do little more than record much or little ozone. — *British Med. Journal*, Oct. 1864.

New Source of Ozone. — *Cosmos* mentions a process of M. Bœlger for obtaining a continuous supply of ozone. He mixes two parts by weight of finely-powdered permanganate of potash with three of sulphuric acid. A mixture of one part of the permanganate with that of the acid, is so powerful an oxydizer as to produce inflammation and explosion if brought into contact with essential oils.

THE COMPRESSION OF GASES.

An accident, through the breaking of apparatus, was reported recently by Dr. Frankland to the London Chemical Society. Being desirous of using oxygen gas under great pressure in the laboratory of the Royal Institution, he procured the apparatus made for the purpose by Natterer, of Vienna. During its use an accident occurred which fortunately led to no serious results, but which, he thought, merited the attention of chemists. We extract from the *Chemical Gazette* the following particulars given by the Professor: The apparatus consisted of two parts. On the one hand, a powerful compression-pump, worked by a crank and flywheel, which forced the oxygen or other gas into a strong cast-iron receiver, fitted with a conical screw-plug and other joints and connections of steel. The action of the pump had been maintained until 25 atmospheres of oxygen had been accumulated, when suddenly this latter part of the apparatus exploded, at the same time diffusing a shower of sparks, reminding one of the phenomena observed when iron or watch-spring was burnt in oxygen. On examining the shattered fragments of the iron receiver, it was manifest that this result had indeed happened; and it appeared that the combustion of iron was possible under the circumstances, a small quantity of oil, used as a lubricant, becoming, no doubt, in the first instance ignited, and then imparting the combustion to the iron. The whole interior surface of the iron receiver was blistered and coated with fused globules of magnetic oxyd of iron, the small tubular apertures through the screw-plug were widened to fourfold dimensions, and no less than half an inch of steel was burnt off the massive head of the apparatus. It was, perhaps, so far fortunate that a defective joint rendered it impossible to obtain more than the pressure of 25 atmospheres, under which the apparatus exploded ; for had it been augmented to 40 atmospheres, the iron must have taken fire more readily, and perhaps have been completely consumed or hurled about as red-hot bolts, endangering both life and property.   Dr. Frankland had, by a rough calculation, arrived at the conclusion that the heat developed by the union of half the contained oxygen with the iron would have been sufficient to melt the cylinder, which would then have exploded by the remaining pressure of the other half of the gas.   He concluded by referring to the possibility of applying this principle in the construction of shells, and other implements of warfare.

RESEARCHES ON THE INFLUENCE OF BAD AIR.

In a recent official report to the British Parliament on the state of the Cornwall and other mines by Dr. Angus Smith, particular notice is taken of the influence of impure air in breaking down the health and energy of the workmen.   A healthy atmosphere, says Dr. Smith, may be taken to be one with 20·9 per cent of oxygen. and ·04 per cent of carbonic acid gas.   Late in the evening in the pit of London minor theatres as much as 0·252 and 0·320 per cent of carbonic acid has · been found ; but the average of above 300 samples of air taken from the mines examined had 0·785.   Two thirds of the samples presented an atmosphere exceedingly bad, and the worst parts of the mines had only about 18·69 per cent of oxygen, and as much as 1·8 or more of carbonic acid, in one instance 2·26 per cent.   In order to test the effects of such bad air, Dr. Smith caused to be constructed a small close chamber of lead with windows sufficiently large that they might in any emergency be broken through for a way of escape.   The first trial was made by sitting down in the chamber for an hour and 40 minutes.   This produced about one per cent of carbonic acid, and the air became cheerless.   A young lady was anxious to be in the chamber when the air was such that candles would not burn.   She was not much struck by the impurity of the air on entering, although the candles were threatening to go out ; there was not quite 19 per cent of oxygen, and there was rather more than two per cent of carbonic acid.   No one had been breathing in the chamber, so that organic matter from the person was absent and that makes a great difference. She stood five minutes perfectly well, making light of the difficulty, but suddenly became white and could not come out without help.   On another occasion a still greater amount of carbonic acid was present in the chamber, but it was not accompanied with a corresponding loss of oxygen, for the gas was driven in upon pure air ; there was 20·19 per cent of oxygen, with 3·84 of carbonic acid.   Two persons got headaches instantly, and were unable to stay above seven or eight minutes. Dr. Smith stayed about 20 minutes, but felt very anxious to get out, as his movements were made with great haste, and both mind and body betrayed symptoms of feverish activity. The face was flushed, and the lungs acted more rapidly than usual. In fact there was a burning haste to live, as if life were afraid of being put out. It seems to him impossible to endure four per cent of carbonic acid for any length of time. There was a very remarkable lowering of the pulse, and as this happened regularly he puts it down as the result of poisoning with carbonic acid gas, and asks whether it may not suggest a mode of lowering the pulse in a fever. These experiments show the great mischief that must arise from the impure, unwholesome air in metalliferous mines. The men call it "thin," "poor," "dead;" the effect is slow poisoning. The explosions of gunpowder produce sulphide of potassium, the effect of which is probably like that of sulphide of hydrogen, but from its acting more slowly there is distributed over a long period that death which might ensue instantly, and so, in chemical phrase, the effect is dissolved in health, and becomes disease. Gun cotton seems to promise to perform the work of blasting with less injurious influence upon the air. In the above report, Dr. Smith touches also upon various other points of practical importance. He notices the purifying effect of rain upon the air, of which there was such a scarcity last year. Moisture with a high temperature is oppressive, but moisture with a lower temperature improves the air, and he holds that cold and moisture in such amounts as those in which they are found in Great Britain are capable of producing powerful constitutions, and that the more watery districts of the kingdom present in many instances the most healthy spots. Still, in relation to ventilation he notes that " chemical action, and with it the feelings demand a certain amount of warmth first and above all things. No function can go on without it. You may live hours, days, or years in badly ventilated places with more or less discomfort and danger, but a draught of cold air may kill like a sword. In railway carriages, and in houses also, the great instinct of man is first to be warm enough, and he is quite right. Such a universal instinct must not be sneered at."

ON THE INHALATION OF OXYGEN GAS.

In a paper on the above subject, read before the British Association 1864, by Dr. Richardson, the well-known physiological chemist, the author stated, that his experiments on the inhalation of oxygen had led him to an almost precise knowledge of the condition under which oxygen would most freely combine with blood. It had been stated in almost every modern work on physiology that oxygen inhaled in a pure form is a narcotic poison. These statements are based on the researches of Mr. Braighton, in which the late Sir Ben. Brodie, took part. The observations of Mr. Braighton, in so far as the recital of the phenomena observed by him were concerned, were strictly correct; but the inferences that had been drawn from him were nearly altogether incorrect, and were, at the best, so narrow as to be comparatively valueless. In fact, Mr. Braighton had seen but one form of oxygen inhalation. The author next stated that the influence of oxygen in inhalation was modified—1. By dilution of the oxygen; 2.

By dilution of the blood; 3. By the activity of the oxygen; 4. By the presence or absence in the blood of bodies which stop combination. On the point of dilution of oxygen, Dr. Richardson stated that a certain measure of dilution was required not because the body consumed too quickly in pure oxygen, but because neutral oxygen would not combine with the carbon of the blood unless it were diluted. In atmospheric air the dilution is just sufficient to do no more than alter combination; and the quantity of oxygen may be increased with absorption at 60° to 65° Fahr., if the oxygen is raised in amount to three parts of the gas to two of nitrogen. Beyond this, the combining power is reduced, and oxygen not absorbed. Hence animals die in the gas as it approaches the pure state; they die not by a narcotic process, but by a process of negation. On the point of dilution of the blood, the author said that blood possessing a specific gravity of 1·053 seemed to have most steady power in absorbing oxygen, as it existed in common air; by increasing the quantity of water in the blood to a limited extent, say until it lowered the blood to 1·060, the absorption of oxygen is increased to a maximum, and after that it is diminished. Below 1·055 the absorption of oxygen steadily declines. In respect to the activity of the oxygen, the most differing results are obtained according to the activity. If the oxygen be made fresh from chlorate of potassa it sustains life even in the pure form, and the activity of the functions is increased; if electric sparks are passed through the gas, or the gas be heated 100°, the same is the fact. On the other hand, if the gas is exposed to ammonia, to decomposing animal matter, or even to living animals, over and over again, it loses, even when diluted, its activity, and no longer combines with the blood. In reference to the last point, Dr. Richardson said that there were conditions of blood in which the power of absorption was limited. Alcohol, chloroform, opium, and certain alkaline products formed in the blood in disease, prevented absorption of oxygen, and death not uncommonly took place from this cause. Great increase of water did the same. After this description, Dr. Richardson added that the question had often been put, whether the inhalation of oxygen could be usefully applied in the treatment of disease. Priestley, Beddoes, Hill, and many of those who lived when oxygen was first discovered, had formed the most sanguine expectations on this point; they saw before them an elixir, if not *the* elixir vitæ. Chaptal, in speaking of the effects of oxygen in consumption, said of it: it raises hope, but, alas! it merely spreads flowers on the path to the tomb. Since then various opinions of the extremest kind have been expressed, the differences having arisen from the entire want of order that has been followed in the inquiry. One man has used pure oxygen, the other diluted; the one active, the other negative oxygen. The one has given the gas to anæmic people, whose blood is surcharged with water; the other to diabetic or choleric persons, whose blood is of high specific gravity: the one has given it heated, the other at the temperature of the day. If even a stick of phosphorus were exposed to oxygen under such varying conditions the phenomena obtained would be as variable as those which had been registered in physic regarding oxygen as a remedy. The difficulties of arriving at uniform results had been almost insurmountable from another cause, that of obtaining oxygen in a practical form for inhalation. Fortunately, this difficulty is now removed. The discovery by Mr. Robbins of a mode of evolving oxygen, by acting on peroxide of barium and bichromate of potassa with dilute sulphuric acid, had given him (Dr. Richardson) the opportunity of inventing a little apparatus for inhaling oxygen, which could be carried anywhere and used at a moment's notice. The author here exhibited and described the apparatus. It consists of two glass globes, with a double-valved - mouth-piece connected with the escape-tube of one globe. The powder containing the oxygen was placed in one globe, and dilute sulphuric acid was poured over it. The oxygen gas was evolved and passed over into the second globe, which was half-filled with water. From this, after being washed in passing through the water, the gas was inhaled. The apparatus was so arranged, that any dilution of oxygen recommended—say three parts of oxygen to two of nitrogen—could be secured; and by changing the water in the second globe, so as to have hot, or temperate, or very cold, the activity of the combination could be graduated.

French Investigations.—M. M. DeMarquay and Leconte, in a memoir, on the above subject read at a recent meeting of the Paris Academy, advocate the inhaling of oxygen in cases of diphtheritics, diabetes, and other exhausting maladies. In some cases, they say that under the influence of this gas, strength is renewed, the lost appetite returns with remarkable intensity, food being even required in the night; the pale lips are reddened; and, with these appearances of convalescence, nervous affections disappear. The gentlemen do not claim to have healed any person; but assert that at all events they have done no harm.

ON THE PHYSIOLOGICAL EFFECTS OF TOBACCO.

The following highly interesting paper, on the above subject, was read before the British Association, 1864, by Dr. B. W. Richardson, the eminent English physiologist and chemist. The author began by saying that, without being a devotee to tobacco, he had for many years often smoked. He did not come before the Section biased in any degree, as his remarks would prove; he came simply as a man of science, who had tried to comprehend the facts of the whole question, and he should put these facts forward clearly, fairly, and free from technicalities. *Products of the Combustion of Tobacco.* Some recent researches on this subject had led the author to the fact, that these products are much more complex than had been supposed. He described an apparatus which was, in fact, an automaton smoker, by which he had been enabled to have pipes of various kinds of tobacco and cigars smoked by means of a bellows; the smoke which, in the case of a man, would enter the mouth, being all caught and subjected to analysis. The results of these inquiries had led him to the determination of the following bodies as products of the combustion of tobacco: 1. Water. 2. Free carbon. 3. Ammonia. 4. Carbonic acid. 5. An alkaloidal principle, called nicotine. 6. An empyreumatic substance. 7. A resinous bitter extract. *Physical Properties of the Component Parts.* The water is in the form of vapor; the carbon in the form of minute particles, suspended in the water vapor, and giving to the eddies of smoke their blue color; the ammonia in the

20

form of gas combined with carbonic acid ; the carbonic acid gas partly free and partly in combination with ammonia.   The nicotine is a non-volatile body, an alkaloid which remains in the pipe ; the empyreumatic substance is a volatile body, having the nature of an ammonia, but the exact composition of which is as yet unknown ; it is this that gives to the smoke its peculiar odor ; it adheres very powerfully to woolen materials, and in the concentrated form is so obnoxious as almost to be intolerable.   The bitter extract is a resinous substance, of dark color, and of intensely bitter taste.   It is probably, a compound body, having an alkaloid as its base.   It is not volatile, and only leaves the pipe by being carried along the stem in the fluid form.   *Variations in different kinds of Tobacco.*   The greatest variations exist in various kinds of tobacco.   Simple tobacco, that has not undergone fermentation, yields very little free carbon, much ammonia, much carbonic acid, little water, none, or the smallest possible trace of nicotine, a very small quantity of empyreumatic vapor, and an equally small quantity of bitter extract.   Latakia tobacco yields these same products only.   Bristol's Bird's-eye yields large quantities of ammonia and very little nicotine.   Turkish yields much ammonia.   Shag tobacco yields all the products in abundance, and the same may be said of pure Havanna cigars.   Cavendish varies considerably ; some specimens which are quickly dried are nearly as simple as Latakia ; other specimens which are moist, yield all the products in great abundance.   Pigtail yields every product most abundantly.   The little Swiss cigars yield enormous quantities of ammonia, and Manillas yield very little.   *Physiological effects of the compounds named above.*   The water vapor is innocuous ; the carbon settles on the mucous membrane, and irritates the throat.   The carbonic acid is a narcotic, if it be received into the lungs : the ammonia causes dryness and biting of the mucous membrane of the throat, and increases the flow of saliva.   Absorbed into the blood it renders that fluid too thin, causing irregularity of the blood-corpuscles ; it also causes, when absorbed in large quantities, suppression of the biliary secretion and yellowness of skin ; it quickens and then reduces the action of the heart, and in young smokers, it produces nausea.   The empyreumatic substance seems to be almost negative in its effects, but it gives to the tobacco smoke its peculiar taste, and it is this substance that makes the breath of confirmed smokers so unpleasant.   Nicotine is scarcely ever imbibed by the cleanly smoker ; it affects those only who smoke cigars, by holding the cigar in the mouth, and those who smoke dirty pipes, saturated with oily matter.   Its effects, when absorbed, are very injurious ; it causes palpitation, tremor and irregular action of the heart ; tremor and unsteadiness of the muscles generally, and great prostration.   It does not, however, produce nausea or vomiting.   The bitter extract is the cause of vomiting and nausea when it is absorbed ; both it and the nicotine are always received into the mouth in solution, and produce their effects, either by direct absorption from the mouth, or by being imperceptibly swallowed and taken into the stomach.

Mode of Smoking. — The greatest difference arises from the manner of smoking.   Those who use clean, long pipes of clay, feel only the effect of the gaseous bodies and the free carbon.   Wooden pipes and pipes with glass stems are injurious.   Cigars, smoked to the end

are most injurious of all. To be safe, a cigar ought to be cast aside
as soon as it is half smoked; and every cigar ought to be smoked
from a porous tube. Cigars, indeed, are more injurious than any
form of pipe; and the best pipe is unquestionably what is commonly
called a "churchwarden," or "long clay." After the clay pipe, the
meerschaum is next wholesome. A pipe with a meerschaum bowl,
an amber mouth-piece, and a clay stem easily removable or change-
able for a half-penny, would be the *beau ideal* of a healthy pipe.
All attempts to construct pipes so as to condense the oil have
failed. To be effective they must be very large and inconvenient.
It is of no slight importance, if a man must smoke, for him to be
careful of the manner in which it is done. A man may, by practice, become habituated to a short foul pipe, but he never fails to suffer from his success in the end, nor, unless the habit of actual stupe-
faction be acquired, is any pleasurable advantage derived. What may
be called the soothing influence of tobacco is as well brought about
by a clean porous pipe, or well-made cigarette, as by any more violent
and dangerous system, while the harm that is inflicted is of an evan-
escent character.

Physiological Effects of Tobacco.—Dr. Richardson next gave his
views respecting the physiological action of tobacco, as follows: In
an adult man, who is tolerant of tobacco, moderate smoking, say to
the extent of three clean pipes of the milder forms of pure tobacco in
the twenty-four hours, does no great harm. It somewhat stops waste
and soothes, but there are times when it unsettles the digestion. To
an immoderate degree, say to six or eight pipes a day—especially if
strong tobacco and fine pipes be used—smoking unquestionably is
very injurious to the animal functions. On the heart, the symptoms
are very marked. They consist of palpitation; a sensation as though
the heart were rising upward; a feeling of breathlessness, and, in bad
cases, of severe pain through the chest, and extending through the
upper limbs. The action of the heart is intermittent, and faintness
may be experienced. Extreme smoking is also very injurious to the
organs of sense. In all inveterate, constant smokers, the pupils of the
eye are dilated, owing to the absorption of nicotine, and the vision is
impaired by strong light; but the symptom which most of all affects
the vision, is the retention of images on the retina after the eye is
withdrawn from them. Long smoking also affects the mucuous membrane of the mouth, causing over-secretion from the glands, and a
peculiar soreness of the throat, with enlargement of the tonsils, first
well described by Dr. Gibb, and since named by myself, "smoker's
sore-throat." In some persons this irritation extends into the larynx
and bronchial tube, and the free carbon of the smoke is deposited
there, giving a dark, almost jet color to the secretion. The worst
effects of moderate smoking were, he said, to be found in growing
youths, upon whom tobacco was most deleterious and injurious.

It had been urged that smoking produced cancer and consumption.
Now, in regard to consumption, there had come under his notice
cases to the total number of 361. Out of this total there were 225
persons who did not smoke, and 136 persons who did smoke or who
had smoked. Thus out of 361 consumptive persons, those who did
not smoke showed an excess of 89. Out of the total of 361, there

were 230 males and 131 females. Out of the 230 males, the number who smoked was 136; the number who did not smoke was 94. Thus, out of 230 consumptive males, the smokers showed an excess of 42. In regard to chronic bronchitis, including asthma, there came under notice cases to the total number of 475. Out of this total, there were 338 persons who did not smoke, and 137 persons who did smoke or who had smoked. Thus, out of 475 persons suffering from chronic bronchitis, those who did not smoke showed an excess of 201. Out of the total of 475, there were 249 males, and 225 females. Out of the 249 males, the number who smoked was 137, and the number who did not smoke was 112. Thus, out of 249 males suffering from chronic bronchitis, the smokers showed an excess of 25. He felt confident, therefore, that neither consumption nor bronchitis in the chronic form could be induced primarily by smoking; for while it is true that, among the men, those who smoked were the most numerous of the sufferers from both diseases, we are bound to accept this circumstance as coincidental merely.

The statements to the effect that tobacco-smoke causes specific diseases, such as insanity, epilepsy, St. Vitus dance, apoplexy, organic diseases of the heart, cancer and consumption, and chronic bronchitis, have been made without any sufficient evidence or reference to facts; all such statements are devoid of truth, and can never accomplish the object which those who offer them have in view.

That which smoking effects, either as a pleasure or a penalty, on a man, it inflicts on any national representation of the same man; and taking it all in all, stripping from the argument the puerilities and exaggerations of those who claim to be the professed antagonists of the practice, it is fair to say that, in the main, smoking is a luxury which any nation of natural habits would be better without. The luxury is not directly fatal to life, but its use conveys to the mind of the man who looks upon it calmly, the unmistakable idea of physical degradation. I do not hesitate to say that, if a community of youths of both sexes, whose progenitors were finely formed and powerful, were to be trained to the early practice of smoking, and if marriage were to be confined to the smokers, an apparently new and a physically inferior race of men and women would be bred up. Of course such an experiment is impossible as we live; for many of our fathers do not smoke, and scarcely any of our mothers, and thus, to the credit of our women chiefly, be it said, the integrity of the race is fairy preserved. With increasing knowledge we may hope that the same integrity will be further sustained; but still, the fact of what tobacco can do in its extreme action is not the less to be forgotten, for many evils are maintained because their full and worst effects are hidden from the sight. The ground on which tobacco holds so firm a footing is, that of nearly every luxury it is the least injurious. It is innocuous as compared with alcohol, it does infinitely less harm than opium; it is in no sense worse than tea; and by the side of high living, altogether contrasts most favorably. A thorough smoker may or may not be a hard drinker, but there is one thing he never is, a glutton; indeed, there is no cure for gluttony and all its train of certain and fatal evils like tobacco.

The poor savage from whom we derived tabac, found in the weed some solace to his yearning vacuous mind, and killed wearisome, lingering time. The type of the savage, extant in modern civilized life, still vacuous and indolent, finds tabac the time-killer; while the over-worked man discovers in the same agent a quietus, which his exhaustion having once tasted, rarely forgets, but asks for again and again. Thus on two sides of human nature we see the source of the demand for tobacco, and until we can equalize labor and remove the call for an artificial necessity of an artificial life, tobacco will hold its place with this credit to itself, that bad as it is, it prevents the introduction of agents that would be infinitely worse.

CURIOUS PHYSIOLOGICAL EFFECTS OF NITRITE OF AMYLE.

A paper on this subject was read at the British Association, 1864, by Dr. B. W. Richardson, the well-known English physiologist. He first described the mode of manufacture and the chemical properties of the nitrite, and then passed on to the physiological action. The first remarkable fact was that the nitrite when inhaled produced an immediate action on the heart, increasing the action of the organ more powerfully than any other known agent. As the action of the heart rises, the surface of the skin becomes red, and the face assumes a bright crimson color. A little of the nitrite was here placed on a piece of bibulous paper, and passed round to show the effect on the face; and the effect was most remarkable. causing the faces of the persons who smelt the vapor to become instantaneously flushed. Carried to an excessive degree, the nitrite excites the breathing, and produces a breathlessness like that caused by sharp running or rowing. On animals, when the agent is given in large quantities, death is produced. The author, at first thought, that the nitrite, like chloroform, would cause anæsthesia; but experiments had shown that this view was not borne out. Animals would, it is true, lose consciousness; but when such a stage was reached, great dangers resulted, owing to the slowness by which the poison was removed from the body after its absorption. On the blood the nitrite produces darkness of color, but it does not materially interfere with coagulation in the body. In the lungs it excites congestion, and in the brain slight congestion. It causes no severe spasm and no sickness. After entering into certain other details, Dr. Richardson proceeded to say that the most remarkable effect produced by the nitrite was that in the lower animals—frogs, for instance—it led to suspended animation, which could be maintained for so long as nine days with perfect after-recovery. This fact was of curious historical interest. The ancients, especially Theophrastus (Paracelsus), had stated that there was a poison which, when taken one day would not take effect until some future day. This statement, long considered as a myth, had within the present year been shown to be true by Dr. Letheby, who had discovered a poison which really produced this phenomenon. In like manner the ancients had an idea that there were medicines which would for a time suspend life.

The proceeding of Friar Laurence in giving the distilled liquor to Juliet, was based on this old fiction, or shall we not say fact? The next point discussed by Dr. Richardson had reference to the mode of action of this poison. Were the effects produced through the blood,

21*

or by the nerves direct? The speaker said that he had been led to the conclusion, from previous experiments, that all poisons were brought into action through the blood; but this very commonly accepted theory did not explain the immediate and powerful action which follows the exhibition of the minutest dose of the nitrite of amyle. He thought, therefore, that the action was immediately on the nervous system, and that such action, transferred to the filaments of nerves surrounding the arteries, paralyzed the vaso nerves, on which the heart immediately injected the vessels, causing the peculiar redness of the skin, and the other phenomenon that had been narrated. Dr. Richardson, in conclusion, said that nitrite of amyle, like to chloroform 20 years ago, was only to be considered a physiological curiosity. It might by its action suggest the cause of trance, and of what was called hysterical unconsciousness, and it might explain the mode by which certain analogous substances produced their effects on the organism. It had been suggested—naturally suggested—that in fainting, as from loss of blood or from fear, the inhalation of the nitrite of amyle might be of service. He (the author) did not, however, at the present moment recommend its use in medicine, because of the intensity of its action. This last point was at the present time under his inquiry, and he would eport further results at the next meeting of the Association.

THE EFFECTS OF ALCOHOLIC DRINKS AND TOBACCO UPON THE HEALTH.

The following curious passage relating to the effects of alcoholic drinks and tobacco upon health occurs in the sixth annual report of the Register-General for Scotland: " All classes are agreed as to the evils produced by the abuse of stimulants (alcoholic) drinks and of tobacco. But a certain class decry even the use of these, and point to the statistics as a triumphant proof of the baneful effect of such stimulants and sedatives. No such conclusion can be drawn from such statistics; and this may be proved in the most satisfactory manner. Tobacco and stimulating drinks are almost exclusively consumed by males, and by almost none under fifteen years of age. Yet we find that in every 100,000 males under fifteen years of age brain diseases cut off annually 337 persons; whereas in an equal number of females only 276 are cut off by the same disease. At the very period of life, therefore, when neither sex uses these so called obnoxious articles, the male tendency to those diseases is so much greater than it is in the female that 337 males die for every 276 females. Above fifteen years of age, when for argument's sake, we may allow the female does not consume these articles, or, at least, that the number who do is so insignificant as not to affect the general results, while the male both uses and in many cases abuses them, instead of finding that the relative proportion of male deaths from these diseases increases, we find that it rather diminishes; so that while above fifteen years of age 217 males die from these diseases in every 100,000 males, 164 females die out of a like number of females. But the subject may be viewed in a more striking light still, by taking the proportion of each sex who die from these diseases above and under fifteen years of age. By this it will be found that the relative tendency to death from these brain diseases in persons above fifteen years of age was greater in the female than the male. The only conclusion, therefore, which seems deducible from these facts appears to be that, in so far as the statistics of these deaths go, there is no evidence to prove that the consumption of alcoholic liquors (including every form, wine, beer, spirits, &c.) or of tobacco, injures the general health of the population. On the other hand, the evidence seem rather to favor the idea that the moderate use of these articles by the mass of the people so improves their health as to act as a counterpoise to the undoubtedly injurious and fatal effects to which the abuse leads in the few."

MIGRATIONS OF PHOSPHORUS.

" Large masses of phosphorus are, in the course of geological revolutions, extending over vast periods of time, restored from the organic realm of nature to the mineral kingdom by the slow process of fossilization ; whereby vegetable tissues are gradually transformed into peat, lignite, and coal, and animal tissues are petrified into coprolites, which in course of time yield crystalline apatite. After lying locked up and motionless in these forms for indefinite periods, phosphorus, by further geological movements, becomes again exposed to the action of its natural solvents, water and carbonic acid, and is thus restored to active service in the organisms of plants and lower animals, through which it passes to complete the mighty cycle of its movements into the blood and tissues of the human frame.

While circulating thus, age after age through the three kingdoms of nature, phosphorus is never for a moment free. It is throughout retained in combination with oxygen, and with the earthy or alkaline metals, for which its attraction is intense. '—*Dr. Hoffmann's Report on the Exhibition of* 1862.

MEASUREMENT OF THE CHEMICAL ACTION OF LIGHT.

Prof. H. E. Roscoe has reported to the Royal Society a method of measuring the chemical action of total daylight adapted for regular meteorological registration, and based upon a method described by Prof. Bunsen and himself in their paper on " Photometrical Measurements." It depends upon the law that equal products of the intensity of the acting light, in the times of insolation correspond, within very wide limits, to equal shades of dark tints produced upon chloride of silver of uniform sensitiveness, measured by means of a pendulum photometer. In the Society's *Proceedings*, No. 70, will be found the method of procedure, and specimens of the results obtained, and a diagram exhibiting the curves of daily chemical intensity, at Manchester, in spring, summer, autumn, and winter.

PETRIFACTION OF ANIMAL SUBSTANCES.

About 25 years ago the scientific world was surprised by an announcement of the fact that a Venetian, named Girolama Segato, had discovered a means of reducing dead bodies to a state of hardness closely approaching to that of stone, except at the joints, where he had succeeded in maintaining a certain degree of pliancy. The results obtained by Mr. Segato in this direction were altogether wonderful, and many strangers used to visit his collection at Florence, where he had settled. Nevertheless he was not encouraged at first on account of his political principles, and, secondly, because the clerical party, which were then all powerful, got up a cry of infidelity against him. His secret found no purchasers, and he died in consequence of a complaint which he had contracted in visiting some of the wildest parts of Africa. A short time after his death, the late Abbé Francesco Baldacconi, director of the Museum of Natural History at Sienna, obtained certain results which led to very strong hopes that Segato's secret might be rediscovered. Mr. Baldacconi's process consisted in steeping the anatomical specimens for several weeks in a solution of equal parts of corrosive sublimate and sal ammoniac. a mixture which by the earlier chemists was called *sal alembroth ;* and in 1844 a liver thus prepared was sent over by him to the Academy of Sciences in Paris. This specimen had acquired the consistency of steatite, or of serpentine, and was perfectly incorruptible. The Italian papers now state that a Sardinian naturalist, Prof. Marini, has rediscovered Segato's secret. His process is also kept a secret, but from the description it appears that he obtained still more remarkable results than his predecessor. He has constructed a small table entirely composed of petrified animal substances, viz: brain, blood, and gall, and having quite the appearance and consistency of breccia. His preparations are incorruptible; they preserve their natural color and will resume their original state on being immersed in water for some time.—*Silliman's Journal.*

PETTENKOFER'S PROCESS OF RESTORING PICTURES.

During the last year or more, considerable attention has been drawn to a discovery by Dr. Pettenkofer of Munich, Germany, of a method of restoring old paintings to their original beauty and freshness. The method, which has been tried with the most satisfactory results on many valuable pictures, has, however, remained a secret until within the past few months, when the discovery became protected by letters patent, in all the principal countries of Europe. From the specifications of the English patent, we derive the following memoranda. It begins by stating that the process of restoring the surface does not endanger the original state of the oil picture. It proceeds to explain that the unwelcome change which comes over varnished oil paintings after the lapse of years, is, in most cases, owing to physical and not chemical influences. Time causes the discontinuance of molecular cohesion in particular materials. The change here begins on the surface of the varnish with microscopical fissures, and this system of disintegration continues to penetrate even " through the different coats of color to the very foundation." Both the surface and the body of such a picture become intimately mixed with air, and reflect light like powdered glass, thus losing transparency like oil mingled with water or air.

The best method of rejoining the separated particles has been found to be by means of a vapor produced from spirits of wine. Dr. Pettenkofer places the picture, or pictures, in a closed case or bath, the air in which is impregnated with the fumes of alcohol at the ordinary temperature and without any application of heat. The resinous particles of the picture thereupon absorb the alcohol until they are saturated, and no longer. By this process the different separated molecules reacquire cohesion with each other, and the optical effect of the original is restored without the picture being touched, and the change is produced solely by self-action.

It is also stated that the very small quantity of alcohol that has been absorbed speedily evaporates when returned to the ordinary atmosphere, and the surface remains as clear as if newly varnished. Thus, the main principle of the patent now taken out is the *self-acting* nature of the process, being effected by means of vapor alone.

The *London Athenæum* says respecting this operation, "that its satisfactory working and results may now be openly seen and watched upon several well-known pictures in the National Gallery. The process seems to have been fairly tried, without any fear of detriment to the pictures, and the result is such as to thoroughly warrant the importance of the invention. The pictures which have thus been freshened in the National Gallery, so as to recover their almost pristine brilliancy, are, principally those of Rembrandt. It should be, however, stated, the process is understood to be only available for a resinous body like mastic varnish, and the fact of solid oil being impervious to these fumes is a satisfactory guarantee for the safety of the genuine old pictures, painted in pure oil. How it will fare with the more modern paintings, where mastic varnish was so intimately mixed up with the oil, even in the original groundwork, is a matter of some anxiety, and is likely to be the subject of a still more delicate experiment.

THE CHANGES IN DISCHARGED FIREARMS.

The changes in discharged firearms have been recently investigated by M. Decker, who states that, whatever may be the construction of the weapon, after its discharge, there is produced in its exterior and interior a modification in its physical and chemical characters varying with the progress of time. Immediately after the discharge there is formed in the interior and exterior of the gun a blackish blue deposit, the age of which may be estimated by the variations in its composition. The red spots of the gun proceed from the action of the residue of the charge on the metal, for an arm that has not been used does not rust in a moist atmosphere in the same manner as one that has been used. Variations in the quality of the powder, and in the construction of the gun, do not exercise any influence over the chemical character of the deposit resulting from the combustion of the powder. M. Decker states, that he has prosecuted his researches with especial relation to copper cannon and to gun-cotton. Thus, chemical science can detect whether a gun has been fired or not, and, to a certain extent, how long it has been so used.

ON THE UTILIZATION OF SEWAGE.

The following interesting remarks on the subject of the utilization of sewage, were submitted to the British Association at its last meeting, by Dr. H. Bird. "The London sewage was something enormous in quantity. It was collected in immense reservoirs, and then poured into the river at times when it would be swept out to sea. Thus, the whole of the sewage of London, containing important chemical constituents, was utterly wasted. He had no doubt that they should relieve the basin of the Thames completely of the sewage which fell into it from Chelsea to below London; but with regard to the utilization of the sewage, they did not see their way clearly, and on another point they were in a great difficulty.　This point was as to what was to become of the drainage of the large towns above their district, because it was impossible to join them with London, and it was idle to seek to drain Oxford by any lateral drainage that could reach the sea.　At the present time Kingston had made arrangements to pour its sewage into the Thames, but was stopped by an injunction obtained by the Conservators of the river, by which they had been taught that such nuisances could not be continued.　The question then remained, what was to be done with it? Two facts had been proved.　At Leicester, where the experiment had been carried on regardless of expense, it was proved that the deodorizing of sewage by lime would purify water and prevent it becoming a nuisance to the stream. Since then it had been proved that fish flourished there, and the herbage and fruit, which before were poisoned, had now returned to their normal condition.　This fact was also apparent, that the products which it had been thought would be sufficient to pay for these works had proved an entire failure; and except for the lime used, which was very useful for the fertilization of land, it had proved utterly useless.　The other fact was the experiment at Croydon, which certainly did appear most successful. There the river formerly was polluted by the sewage.　A farm of 40 acres was then taken; ordinary drains were cut, the sewage was turned into the land before it passed into the river, thus purifying it of its offensive ingredients, and proving of great advantage to the land."

We find the results accomplished at Croydon stated rather more fully than as above, in a recent article in the *London Times*.　"The town authorities being stopped by injunction from throwing their sewage in the river Wandle, they leased 240 acres of land at 4l. an acre, turned their sewage upon it, and relet it for 5l. an acre.　Thus they make a clear profit of 240l. a year, and enormous crops are got off the land, which serves as a pattern card, as it were, to the surrounding farmers of the value of sewage.　It should, however, be particularly stated in this connection, that Croydon is favorably situated for the distribution of its sewage, as it stands on a hight, and it can therefore be distributed by means of simple gravitation.

ON PHENIC OR CARBOLIC ACID.

The following account of phenic, or carbolic acid,— an article which from its sanitary and industrial value is yearly becoming of greater importance,—is taken from a recently published paper of Dr. Jules Lemaire of Paris.

Phenic acid ($C_{12}H_6 O,HO$) was discovered in 1834 by Runge, who has given it the name of carbolic acid.　Laurent, who studied this body, and described many of its combinations, designates it under the name of phenic and hydrate of phenyle, because he objects to place it among the acids.　Gerhardt gave it the name of phenol.　It has also received the names of phenic alcohol, of spyrol, and of salicone.　[In this country the acid is best known in trade as carbolic acid.]

It has been formed synthetically by M. Berthelot, by passing alcoholic or acetic acid vapors through a porcelain tube heated to redness. Gerhardt has obtained it from salicylic acid by the action of lime or baryta.　Stædeler has found that the urine of man, the horse, and cow, contain it in quantities easily perceivable. It exists also in commercial creasote; but it is from the oil from gas tar, which contains it in considerable quantity, that it is obtained.

Preparation.— The oil from coal tar is submitted to fractional distillation. The part which passes over between 160° and 190° is treated with a hot saturated solution of caustic potash and some powdered potash. A mass of crystals is thus obtained, which may be separated by decantation of the fluid.

When the mass is dissolved in water the solution separates into two layers, one light and oily, the other heavy and watery. The latter is separated and treated with hydrochloric acid, which sets free the carbolic acid.

The pure acid has an odor resembling creasote; the specific gravity =1·065. It is soluble to some extent in water, but is very soluble in alcohol, ether, and acetic acid, as well as in glycerine and the fixed and volatile oils. The pure acid acts energetically on the skin. A weak aqueous solution coagulates albumen and the blood, and acts as a strong antiseptic. Putrid meat and fish, fæcal matter and fermented urine instantly lose their disgusting odor, when immersed in or treated with the solution. In consequence of the supposed little solubility of carbolic acid in water, it has hitherto been chiefly employed mixed with powders, as in the case of Smith and McDougall's disinfecting powder; but the author of these papers has by careful experiments determined that the pure acid is sufficiently soluble in water for the solution to possess the power of coagulating albumen, of arresting or preventing spontaneous fermentation, and consequently of destroying infection. The saturated solution acts also on plants and the lower animals as a violent poison, though containing but five per cent of the acid. The solubility of the acid may be considerably increased by the addition of from five to ten per cent of alcohol or of acetic acid.

From the experiments which the author has made on the action of phenic acid on plants and animals, it appears that a very weak solution will instantly destroy the lowest forms of animal and vegetable life. The juices of vegetables are prevented from becoming mouldy by the addition of the smallest quantity of the acid. Herbs and shrubs watered by a stronger solution rapidly die.

The microscopic beings concerned in the production of putrefactive fermentation are as quickly destroyed by a weak solution, and the putrefaction is completely arrested. Parasitic and earth-worms also are easily killed by a solution containing ¼ per cent, or by exposure to air containing but a small proportion of the acid. A stronger solution kills the eggs of ants and earwigs, and larvæ of butterflies, caterpillars, &c.

Action on the Human Skin.—Immediately after the application of a thin coating of the pure acid, a sharp smarting is felt, which lasts about an hour. The epidermis becomes wrinkled, and in a short time the formation of a white body may be remarked wherever the acid has touched. This white coloration results from the action of the acid on albumen; it disappears by degrees, and is replaced by some congestion, which lasts about 20 days. This congestion presents all the characters of an intense inflammation, being attended with redness, heat, and swelling. If a small piece of the epidermis (which appears raised as in a blister) be stripped off, no serum escapes. The epidermis becomes detached by degrees, and when the exfoliation is complete a brown spot remains, which testifies for a long time to the energetic action of the acid. After a number of experiments on his own arms, and the arms of his friends, M. Lemaire assures us that the smarting never lasts longer than an hour. The redness of the skin endures about 20 days, but the inflammation never extends beyond the part to which the acid has been applied.

Action on the Respiratory Organs.—From experiments on mice and horses, the author concludes that the higher animals may breathe the diluted vapor of the acid for a long time without discomfort or danger.

Mode of Action.—The general fact resulting from the author's experiments is that phenic acid acts on plants and lower animals as a violent poison.

When the action of the acid on a semi-transparent leaf is examined, it is easy to prove that it coagulates albumen, and that the parenchyma and epidermis are contracted. This explains how it is that microphytes and microzoons die so quickly in its presence. All animals with a naked skin, and those which live in the water, die sooner than those which live in the air and have a solid envelop. The difference appears to result from the power of absorption, which is much greater in the former than the latter.

When frogs are placed in a saturated solution (five per cent) of the acid, the skin shrivels and becomes milky from the coagulation of the albumen. The branchiæ of fishes also become white. This coagulation of albumen led the author to suppose that the death of the animals resulted from the coagulation of their blood. To verify this supposition, he examined, under the microscope, the action of the acid on the branchiæ of the larvæ of salamanders, in which the circulation of the blood is easily seen. He then observed that, although the solution arrested the circulation instantaneously, it altered neither the form nor appearance of the blood-globules. All the change consisted in their immobility. When the blood is coagulated by mineral acids the form of the globules is changed. With carbolic acid nothing of the kind takes place. Besides this, a *post-mortem* examination of a dog and horse proved that the blood was not coagulated. Phenic acid, then, does not kill by producing coagulation of the blood! Its action on the blood-globules, however, leads M. Lemaire to think that these globules are living beings.

Insects exposed to a weak dose of the acid become asphyxiated, but they soon recover in pure air.

When a gramme or two dissolved in water is administered to a dog, the animal falls as if struck with lightning, but soon recovers again. The sudden fall the author ascribes to violent pain, and the rapidity with which it is absorbed and carried to the nervous centres. It is on the nervous system, then, that phenic acid principally acts.

COHESION FIGURES OF LIQUIDS.

In a communication made to the British Association on the above subject by Mr. C. Tomlinson, the author stated that his researches began as far back as 1861, since when he had among other results applied the principle involved to a species of chemical analysis. The principle of the examination is to place a drop of a liquid on the surface of clean water in a chemically clean glass, when a figure is produced which was characteristic of the liquid so tested, and capable of being used for its identification. The figure formed is a function of cohesion, adhesion, and diffusibility. If any one of these forces be varied the figure varies. The figures of alcohol for example on water, mercury, the fixed oils, melted lard, spermaceti, paraffin, sulphur, &c. are all different. A new set of figures is produced by allowing the drop to subside in a column of liquid instead of diffusing over its surface. These last the author calls " submersion figures of liquids." The figure of a drop of oil of lavender in a column of alcohol thus produced is singularly complicated and beautiful. The test by cohesion figures was stated by the author to be so delicate as to readily distinguish differences between oils so closely related as the oleines of beef-fat and mutton-fat, when the one was adulterated by the other.

Another series of results are obtained, not by placing a drop of the liquid on the surface of water, but by allowing the drop to sink below the surface before the figure is developed. In this way a large number of figures of great variety and beauty have been produced by allowing drops of various oils, solutions, and other liquids to subside in columns of water, spirits of wine, ether, turpentine, paraffin oil, benzol, and pyroligneous ether. For example, a solution of cochineal (from 20 to 30 grains in one fluid ounce of distilled water and filtered) forms admirable figures, in a column of water contained in a glass cylinder 11 inches high and three inches in diameter, into which about ¼ an ounce of solution of ammonia or a little alum water had been poured. If river water be used the lime is thus thrown down, so that the water should be allowed to stand a few hours before performing the experiment; or if distilled water be employed, the ammonia and the alum, by their chemical action on the cochineal, add to the beauty of the result. As soon as the drop of cochineal solution (delivered gently from a pipette) falls beneath the surface, it expands into a ring, sinks a short distance further, and then becomes poised. The more diffusive portions of the coloring matter stream upwards in a faint flame-like circular cloud; the denser portions accumulate at two opposite points of the ring, which is thus at its thinner portions bent upwards, and then drawn downwards into graceful festooned lines by the heavier portions, which form separate rings smaller than the parent ring. These rings in like manner, descend. The denser portions of coloring matter accumulate at the two opposite points, 90° from the points of attachment to the festooned lines. Each small ring is, in this case, also bent upwards, while it drops two other rings, which in their turn go through the same series of changes, until the figure becomes almost too complicated to follow. This is a very common result with a moderately weak solution of cochineal; with a stronger solution the figure undergoes some beautiful modifications. The heavier portions of the coloring matter collect not at two, but at four, six, or even seven or eight points of the ring, bending it upwards in as many curved lines, and letting drop as many rings, each of which becomes the seat of manufacture of two rings; and in this

21

polypus method of division and subdivision the coloring matter is diffused through the solution.

A more complicated figure, on the above type, is formed by allowing a drop of oil of lavender (from the end of a glass rod) gently to subside beneath the surface of spirits of wine contained in a cylindrical glass six inches high and one inch and a quarter in diameter. Oil of cubebs or of cinnamon forms good figures. The oils of turpentine and of juniper, as well as fixed oils, form flat spheroids. The appearance of the figures depends upon the solubility of the liquid employed. In some cases they are glassy or saccharine, in others chalky or milky, arising from the elaiopten of the essential oils being the first dissolved, while the stearopten is left to do the work of the figure. When a column of benzol was used, many of the essential oils formed these opaque white figures. Oil of winter-green, turpentine, camphorated spirit, oil of bitter almonds, &c. formed good figures; the fixed oils formed discs with waving edges or cup-shaped vessels, which became drawn out in descending. In a column of paraffin oil some remarkable figures were produced with absinthe, neroli, and fusel oils. With the last-named oil the drop first forms a disc bagging downwards, and this almost immediately expands upwards, swells out into a dome or cone, the ring expanding all the time; the point of the cone remains fixed in the liquid, while the lower edge becomes arched at four equidistant points, the edges of the arches beautifully fringed, and lets fall lines with drops at the ends, which form separate cones, each of which becomes arched, and lets down other lines with drops. In this way a figure is produced of great beauty, and with an architectural kind of effect which is very striking. The duration is also considerable. The texture of the figure is gauze-like and delicate. A number of figures were obtained when a column of turpentine was used; a still larger number in a column of pyroligneous ether, some of which were chalky and very persistent. A drop of water flashed into a ring, descended, and expanded in rolling on its curved axis somewhat after the manner of a bubble of phosphureted hydrogen bursting in air. In a column of ether those drops that did not immediately enter into solution formed beautiful rolling rings,—this was the case with drops of benzol and of the oils of turpentine and cajeput.

These liquid rolling rings led to an investigation of the phosphureted hydrogen rings in air, which the author thinks have not been correctly explained in our text-books. The nearest approach to a correct explanation is that given by Prof. Rogers in the *American Journal of Science* for 1858; but his explanation, which is not very precise, is embarrassed by conditions depending on the form of the orifice of the vessel from which the ring was projected, the tension of the enclosed gas, the chemical action, and, in the case of a liquid ring, the force with which the liquid is projected into a column of water, &c. Very fine liquid rings can be formed by allowing a saturated solution of common salt or of Epsom salts to drop slowly into a tall column of water from a hight of about two inches. The liquid rings thus formed roll rapidly round their curved axes, and go on expanding nearly to the bottom of the vessel before they disappear. Two ionic-like volutes are seen on either side of the rings; these are produced by the perspective of a number of rings seen through, or nearly through, each other, while at the front and back the edges of single rings only are seen.

RESEARCHES ON ACONITE.

Recent elaborate researches on the properties of aconite, the most potent perhaps of all poisons,—conducted by Messrs. S. & H. Smith, of Edinburgh, and published in the *London Pharmaceutical Journal*, have established the fact that the maximum quantity of the alkaloid, which it is possible to extract from a hundred weight of the fresh aconite-root, cannot exceed one ounce. Consequently, the *maximum* quantity of the alkaloid contained in an ounce of the tincture, as ordinarily prepared and sold, cannot exceed the ·105 of a grain, and is probably much less. M. Hertz, Professor of the Medical Faculty at Strasbourg, in an article on the subject of aconite contributed to the " *Nouveau Dictionnaire de Medecine et de Chirugie Practiques*," Paris, 1864, a work published by a committee of the leading French chemists and physicians, gives the following as a summary of our present chemical knowledge. He says, " the chemical reactions of aconitine are not yet sufficiently known to enable us to isolate it from the substance or products of the body after death."

This *résumé* of the latest information respecting this subtile poison, will be noticed with interest by many of our readers, by reason of its bearing on the celebrated case of John Hendrickson, who was tried and convicted in Albany, N. Y. in 1854, on the charge of poisoning his wife by aconite, and subsequently (in spite of the earnest remonstrances of nearly all the leading American chemists) executed. The theory of the prosecution was, that an ounce of the tincture of aconite was forcibly administered during sleep; the major part of which the deceased subsequently ejected from the stomach by vomiting. Then from a portion only of the fluids and tissues of the stomach, by means of a radically incorrect chemical treatment, it was sworn upon the trial, that about $\frac{1}{50}$ of a grain of the *pure* alkaloid was separated and extracted. And on this, and concurring medical testimony, the life of the accused was declared forfeited and taken.

The recent information relative to aconite, quoted above, fully confirms the views of the chemists who protested in 1854 against the conclusions of the jury, and further stamp this trial as one of the most disgraceful ever recorded in the history of American jurisprudence.

SUMMARY OF CHEMICAL NOVELTIES.

New Use for Gelatin.—Beautiful fancy ornaments have recently been introduced in Paris by M. Pinson, called artificial tortoise-shell, which he obtains by melting, at a moderate temperature, gelatin with a small amount of metallic salts, running the whole into molds, staining the mass with hydro-sulphate of ammonia, so as to produce an imitation of the grain of tortoise-shell. The objects so produced are then polished and ready for sale.

Cotton-seed Oil.—With the more extensive cultivation of cotton in European colonial possessions, renewed attention has been given to the subject of the oil yielded by the cotton-seed. Recent investigations show, that an oil may be obtained to the amount of from 15 to 18 per cent from cotton-seed, which is very much cheaper than linseed. The residue is nearly as valuable for fattening purposes as linseed cake.

The crude oil answers well for paints and varnishes, and makes excellent soap. The refined is considered little inferior to olive oil.

Fatty Acids for Soap and Candles.—M. Mouries, in a memoir to the French Academy, suggests a cheap and easy method of separating stearic and oleic acids and glycerine. In the ordinary state tallow is saponified with difficulty. By melting the tallow in water, containing a little soap in solution, the tallow assumes a globular state, and is then readily attacked by a small quantity of alkali. When the mixture is raised to 60° C, the alkali and glycerine quickly separate. The fatty acids are separated by placing the soap in water acidulated with sulphuric acid. The stearic acid will then crystallize, and the oleic acid can be obtained, almost colorless, with the sulphate of soda, and can then be made into soap. M Chevreul commended this process, before the Academy, as ingenious and simple.

Preparation of Essential Oils.— Mr. T. B. Groves of London suggests an exceedingly ingenious method for the separation of essential oils from watery solutions in which they exist in small quantities, such solutions being frequently produced by the distillation of aromatic herbs, etc. A proportion of olive oil is added to the aromatic solution; this is then formed into a soapy emulsion by the addition of potash. When this emulsion is destroyed by the addition of an acid, the olive oil rises to the surface, bringing with it all the aromatic oil, which may then be readily dissolved out of the fatty oil by agitation with rectified spirit.

The Volatile Constituents of Petroleum.— Mr. E. Ronalds in a recent paper before the Royal Society, Edinburgh, stated, that the gases dissolved in Pennsylvania petroleum, and which give it such a high degree of inflammability, were composed of the lower members of the marsh gas series. Gases taken from the surface of the liquid, as imported in casks from America, were shown by eudiometrical analyses to contain a mixture of nearly equal proportions of the hydrides of ethyl and propyl. The same compounds were found in the gases evolved on warming the volatile liquid: after these succeeded the hydrides of propyl and butyl, and finally there was evolved nearly pure hydride of butyl. This liquid has a spec. gr. of 0·600 at the melting point of ice, and is consequently the lightest liquid known. Its vapor density is 2·11. It is colorless, and has a sweet, agreeable odor. Alcohol at 98 p. c. dissolves between 11 and 12 times its volume of this vapor.

Liquefaction of Protoxyd of Nitrogen.—One of the most interesting objects at a recent *soirée* at the Paris Observatory consisted in the exhibition of the liquefaction of laughing gas, the protoxyd of nitrogen, by M. Bianchi. This took place at zero, Centigrade, under a pressure of thirty atmospheres, the fluid issuing in a small jet from a strong metallic reservoir. Received in a glass tube, it retained its liquid condition by reason of the depression of temperature produced by evaporation, so that mercury, being introduced, solidified and could be hammered like lead. Simultaneously, a body in the state of ignition, plunged into the atmosphere of the liquid, in which the mercury froze, burnt with a brilliant light. On pouring the protoxyd into a small platinum capsule heated to redness, the liquid was found to retain all its properties while assuming the spheroidal state, and was still able to freeze mercury contained in little glass ampulæ. Finally, the liquid protoxyd became solidified under the recipient of an air-pump, the temperature being reduced to 120° below zero, Centigrade,—the most intense cold yet obtained.

New Mode of Analysis.—The capillarity of paper as a means of analysis, as suggested by M. Schönbein, has been employed by M. Goppelsröder in the separation of coloring matters. When a band of paper is dipped into curcuma (Indian saffron) and picric acid, three distinct layers are perceived; the first formed by pure water, the second colored by picric acid, and the third by the yellow of the curcuma. If the paper be dipped into an alkaline liquid the picric layer disappears, while the curcuma remains with the brownish hue which it acquires under the circumstances. Similar experiments are produced with fuchsine, &c.

Morid's Process for recovering Writing on Paper or Parchment which has become nearly effaced.—The paper or parchment written on is first left for some time in contact with distilled water. It is then placed for five seconds in a solution of oxalic acid (1 of acid to 100 of water); next after washing it, it is put in a vessel containing a solution of gallic acid (10 grains of acid to 300 of distilled water); and finally washed again and dried. The process should be carried forward with care and promptness, that any accidental discoloration of the paper may be avoided.—*Cosmos.*

Pure Water from Lead Pipes.—Dr. Schwartz of Breslau, proposes to render lead pipes, used for water-conveyance innocuous, by filling the pipes for a short time, with a strong solution of an alkaline sulphide. A coating of insoluble sulphide of lead is thus formed, which is said to act as a perfect protecting varnish, preventing further action between the water and lead.—*Chem. News.*

New Green Color.—A prize has been awarded by the Paris Academy to M. Bouffé for a new green, which is produced by a mixture, it is said, of picric acid and the hydrous oxyd of chrome (chrome green). The new color, called by the inventor *vert naturel*, is of great beauty and brilliancy, and is suited to replace the arsenical greens often used to color wall paper from which a poisonous dust arises.

Lea's Cleaning Solution. Photographers are under great obligations to Mr. Carey Lea, of Philadelphia, for the knowledge of the following glass-cleaning preparation: Water one pint; sulphuric acid, ½ ounce; bi-chromate potash, ½ ounce. The glass plates, varnished or otherwise, are left, say 10 or 12 hours, or as much longer as desired, in this solution, and then rinsed in clean water, and wiped or rubbed dry with soft white paper. It quickly removes silver stains from the skin without any of the attendant dangers of the cyanide of potassium.

The Physical Analysis of the Human Breath.—Mr. W. F. Barrett, assistant in the Physical Laboratory of the Royal Institution, has published in the *Philosophical Magazine*, a record of some remarkable experiments on this interesting subject, made chiefly by means of the apparatus employed by Dr. Tyndall, in his researches on the absorption and radiation of heat by gaseous matter. Carefully prepared vulcanized India-rubber bags were filled with air from the lungs.—1. About half an hour after rising: 2. About ten minutes after break-

21*

fast: 3, after a brisk walk: and 4, after severe exertion. The contents are then successively allowed to enter an exhausted brass cylinder, the ends of which are stopped air-tight by plates of rock-salt. Through this cylinder the radiation from a flame of carbonic oxyd gas is passing. Immediately the breath, which has been deprived of its moisture, fills the cylinder, more than half the heat from the flame is absorbed, and this entirely by the small quantity of carbonic acid present in the expired air.· The amount of heat intercepted by the breath is, in each case accurately measured by means of a delicate thermomultiplier. The percentage of carbonic acid contained in the different specimens of breath is found by calculation and subsequent experiments, and is then compared with a chemical analysis of each specimen.

The close agreement between the methods of analysis is shown by the following numbers :—

	By physical analysis.	By chemical analysis.
Bag 1.	4·00	4·31
Bag 2.	4·66	4·56
Bag 3.	5·33	5·22

These numbers indicate the percentage of carbonic acid in breath, and show that the least amount of that gas was exhaled before breakfast.

Many other different samples of breath have been examined by Mr. Barrett; the results he has obtained prove the great delicacy of the new method of analysis in detecting small quantities of carbonic acid, or in discovering variations in the amount of this gas in the atmosphere or in the human breath. For this purpose its application in hospitals has already been suggested by eminent men.

Control of Disease by Sanitary Agencies.—At a recent meeting of the Social Science Congress, Dr. Lankester, in a paper on public health, observed that "disease and death were most expensive things to society, and when the death-rate rose above 30 in 1,000, that was a death-rate which could be controlled by human agency. This had been done in some large towns by proper attention to ventilation and drainage, and thus great benefits had been conferred upon all."

Animal Charcoal in Vegetable Poisoning.—It is well known that the infusion of coffee, tannin, camphor, vinegar, acetate of lead, fatty oils, white of eggs, &c. have been proposed in succession as antidotes to plants, or their alkaloids, belonging to the family of the papaveraceæ, and the solanaceæ. Now, Dr. Garrod prescribes animal charcoal, which, in small quantities, neutralizes, or entirely destroys, the action upon the economy of the solutions of belladonna, of stramonium, and of hyoscyamus, provided that the antidote is administered before they are absorbed. Dr. Garrod cites, in the *Bulletin de Thérapeutique* for 1858, two cases where patients had taken, by mistake, one 60 centigrammes the other 10 grammes of belladonna, and were immediately cured by the use of animal charcoal. Again, he administered to a dog a dose of aconite, which killed him promptly, while another dog of the same size, which had taken four times as much aconite, but mixed with animal charcoal, presented no symptom of poisoning. M. Garrod has remarked that animal charcoal, purified or not, acts in the same manner, and that vegetable charcoal, on the contrary, has no effect whatever upon the action of these poisons. He also believes that animal charcoal neutralizes the stupefying action of the vegetable alkaloids, as quinine, strychnine, and morphine.

Chemical Preservation of Statues.—M. Dalemagne, in a recent communication to the French Academy, is of the opinion, that coating statues, exposed to the atmosphere, with a solution of silica, is quite sufficient to insure their preservation. In proof of this, he calls attention to the circumstance that certain busts which were submitted to the process of *silicatization* ten years ago, are now in a state of perfect preservation; while others of the same age, placed under the ordinary conditions of the atmosphere, and even to which considerable attention had been paid, are now in a state of more or less marked decay. -

* * * * * * *

Kuhlmann on the Coloring Material in Minerals.—In the course of his new researches on the preservation of materials employed in building and ornamentation, this able investigator has availed himself of the new methods of analysis by the spectrum, with modifications. He expresses his belief that he has placed in the hands of chemists a sure, simple, expeditious, and safe method of analyzing the largest part of the silicious stones and a great number of natural and artificial silicates; and that he has put investigators in the right way of finding out the true cause of the color of certain stones; and finally, that he has opened up a new field of research in spectral experimentation, in analyzing by the gaseous way those minerals whose character so much depends on the nature of the solvent engaged in their formation.

Coloring Matter of the Emerald.—M. Lewy in 1858 asserted that the coloring matter of the emerald was organic and destroyed by heat. Recent researches by M. M. Wöhler and Rose seem to show, however, that the color is due to oxyd of chromium. They kept an emerald at the temperature of melted copper for an hour, and found that, although the stone became opaque, the color was not affected. They fused, however, some colorless glass with an exceedingly small quantity of oxyd of chromium, and produced a color exactly like that of the emerald. They therefore considered this substance the coloring agent, without, however, denying the presence of some organic matter.

A new Method of Extracting Gold from Auriferous Quartz, so as to obviate the necessity of employing mercury,—which is both expensive and very deleterious,—has been suggested by Prof. Crace Calvert. Finding that gold, though but slowly acted on by a solution of chlorine, is readily dissolved by that agent as it is liberated from its other combinations, or as in a nascent state, Mr. Calvert suggests that the auriferous quartz should be acted on by hydrochlorine and peroxide of manganese, when the gold is readily and completely dissolved, and is, after the separation of any copper that may be present, afterwards precipitated in a metallic form by a solution of protosulphate of iron (the green copperas of commerce).

New Method of Detecting Poisons in the Animal Economy.—Dr. Machaltee, in a paper presented to the British Association on the use of the new process of dialysis for the detection of poisons, suggested that the stomach or intestines of an animal suspected of having been poisoned by any substance capable of being dialysed, might be made to act as their own dialysers, by simply tying the openings so as to securely enclose their contents, and then plunging them into a vessel of water for some hours, when the crystalline poison, such as arsenic or strychnine, would dialyse out, and could be readily detected in the external fluid.

DYALYSIS.

The application of the researches of Prof. Graham (see *Annual Sci. Dis.* 1862, p. 197), respecting the diffusion of liquids to the purposes of practical chemistry and the arts of civilization, offers one of the most interesting examples of the eventual tendency of even the most abstract scientific investigations to become practical, and so to aid in promoting the comfort and welfare of mankind. It is almost impossible to imagine a subject offering apparently less practical advantages than does the admixture of two liquids with each other, and yet from the rigorous and scientific investigation of the phenomena of their mutual diffusion, and the laws which regulate its operation, has sprung a new method of analysis, which promises to revolutionize a very large number of chemical operations, and to introduce new methods of manufacture into the arts that will entirely subvert many existing processes.

The subject is so interesting and so novel in its practical bearings, that it is desirable to trace its gradual development from an abstract scientific truth to its present useful applications.

Mr. Graham's first experiments on the diffusion of liquids were made by means of what he terms *phial diffusion*, and they were performed as follows : Solutions of different salts, whose diffusive powers were to be examined, were prepared of equal strength, and phials of exactly the same size and shape were filled with these solutions, and then placed separately under the surface of water contained in much larger vessels, the mouths of the phials being left open. Under these circumstances it was found that a certain proportion of the heavy solution contained in the phial rose in opposition to the attraction of gravitation, and mingled with the water by which the phial was surrounded. In the case of colored solutions, this diffusion was visible to the eye, and in others it was capable of being proved by analysis. It was found, however, that the solutions of different bodies diffused themselves with very different degrees of velocity. Thus common salt diffused with twice the rapidity of Epsom salts or sugar. These, again, are doubly as diffusive as a solution of gum ; and albumen, or white of egg, in its turn, does not possess $\frac{1}{4}$ of the diffusive power of gum, nor scarcely more than $\frac{1}{20}$ of that of common salt.

These experiments were varied in different modes, by allowing the diffusion to take place under slightly varying conditions, but the same general results were obtained. The laws deduced from these phenomena are, that crystalline bodies—such as salt, sugar, niter, etc.,—are much more readily diffusible than those that are amorphous, such as gum, gelatin, albumen, solution of starch, or any substances that enter into combination with water in the same manner as the first-named bodies.

Hence, with reference to this subject, Mr. Graham arranges substances into two groups : those crystalline in character and readily diffusible in water he terms *crystalloids*; the solution of these is always free from gumminess or viscocity, is sapid, possessing in a higher or lower degree the power of affecting the nerves of taste. The other class, whose diffusive power is low, he distinguishes as *colloids*, because gelatin or glue (*colle*) may be taken as their type. The solutions of these substances have no disposition to crystallize, and in the solid form they do not possess flat surfaces, such as characterize crystals, but exhibit an irregular roundness of outline. Their solutions are always gummy when concentrated, and what is strikingly remarkable, they are all insipid or wholly tasteless. In the moist condition they are liable to undergo great changes, and solutions of them in a state of purity cannot be preserved unaltered for any length of time.

A solution of a colloid body, such as gelatin, is found to offer scarcely any impediment to the diffusion of a crystalloid throughout its entire mass. This diffusion will also take place through any soft solid with almost equal rapidity; a very familiar example of this fact is shown in the process of salting meat, in which case the rapidly diffusible crystallizable sea-salt penetrates to the interior of the flesh, which is a combination of different colloid bodies, such as fibrin, albumen, gelatin, etc.

Upon the fact that crystalloid bodies possess the power of diffusing themselves through soft solids depends the operation known as *dialysis*, and the construction of the instrument called the *dialyser*. This consists simply of a tambourine-shaped frame of gutta-percha, over which is tightly stretched a piece of parchment paper, which completes the resemblance to that musical instrument. This parchment paper is quite impervious to water, so that no passage of fluid similar to filtration can take place through it. If the dialyser be floated on the surface of pure water, and a mixed solution of a crystalloid and a colloid body be poured into it, the process termed dialysis immediately commences; all the crystalloid matter passes through the parchment paper into the water, and the colloid matter remains behind in the dialyser. As an instance of its action, let us suppose a mixed solution of sugar and gum to be poured into the dialyser, when the sugar passes through into the water below, and the gum remains behind in a pure form. If a mixture of the beautiful aniline dye known as magenta, and some burnt sugar or caramel be employed, the passage of the magenta into the pure water is readily observed, the dark-brown uncrystallizable colloid caramel remaining in the dialyser.

Other facts of great interest have been discovered as the results of these investigations. Thus it is found that by means of dialysis, we may obtain pure in solution many substances hitherto regarded as being perfectly insoluble. Amongst these may be mentioned silica, alumina, Prussian blue, peroxyd of iron, stannic acid, and numerous other bodies of a similar character.

For example, if a solution of soluble glass, which is formed by fusing silica with an excess of soda, be taken and acidified with hydrochloric acid, the acid unites with the soda, forming common salt, or chloride of sodium, the silica remaining for some time dissolved in a gelatinous or colloid form, mixed with the solution of the chloride of sodium. If, however, this mixture of gelatinous silica and common salt be placed in the dialyser, the salt rapidly diffuses itself into the water in the outer vessel, and the solution of pure silica in water remains in the dialyser.   This solution is found to have a feebly acid reaction on test paper, but not to the taste, as, being a colloid, it cannot pass through the membrane of the tongue so as to affect the nerves of taste.   The solution of silica remains for some time perfectly limpid, but eventually sets into a firm jelly.   This alteration may be brought about immediately by the presence of several substances, particularly by any earthy carbonate such as chalk.   This solution of pure silica possesses remarkable properties; it is absorbed by gelatinous tissues such as the skin of animals, in the same manner as tannin; and like it converts them into a kind of leather, which possesses the remarkable property of not putrefying when kept moist.   In the same manner a solution of pure peroxyd of iron may be obtained, by first dissolving excess of the hydrated oxyd in hydrochloric acid, and then dialysing, when a colloid solution of oxyd of iron remains, that is capable of being gelatinized like the silica.   Prussian blue, which is insoluble in pure water, is capable when recently precipitated, of being dissolved by the aid of gentle heat in a solution of $\frac{1}{4}$ of its weight of oxalic acid, when it forms the well-known permanent blue ink.   If such a solution be dialysed, the Prussian blue is, in the course of a few days, obtained in a solution in pure water, and may be rendered gelatinous by the addition of sulphate of zinc and several other metallic salts, as the solution of silica is gelatinized by the addition of carbonate of lime.

Such are a few of the many examples of these remarkable phenomena.   They are as yet of too recent discovery to have been applied to many practical purposes but a vast number of applications at once suggest themselves.   In cases of the suspected poisoning of articles of food, the poison, if a crystalloid substance like arsenic, can be readily dialysed and obtained in a pure form, however heterogeneous may be the mixture in which it is contained.   Dyeing will be greatly facilitated by steeping a fabric in a pure solution of some colloid dye, which will unite with the animal or vegetable fibre as it gelatinizes.

The purification of many drugs and the separation of different substances in the chemical arts will be rendered much easier than heretofore.   In fact, there appears scarcely a limit to the application of this principle.   Already, dialysis has thrown light upon obscure points in geology, such as the formation of flints and other silicious fossils, and it promises equally to benefit physiological research.   In fact, humble and inconspicuous as its phenomena may appear at first sight, it is probable that, in its influence on science and art, it will greatly surpass any discovery of late years.

CELESTIAL CHEMISTRY.

'The importance and marvellous character of the discoveries effected during the past year through the new method of " spectrum analysis," warrants their classification into an independent section in this yearly record of scientific discovery.

THE MOST RECENT DISCOVERIES BY SPECTRUM ANALYSIS.

In the previous volumes of the *Annual of Scientific Discovery*, (1862 ; '63 ; '64 ;) the progress of discovery effected through the beautiful process of " spectrum analysis " has been detailed at considerable length ; and in the volume for 1864, particular mention was made of the results arrived at by Messrs Huggins and Miller of England, in their examination of the sun and certain of the fixed stars. These two gentlemen, have, during the past year, continued their researches, and have announced a series of discoveries of the most extraordinary and interesting character. These discoveries may be classified under three heads, viz : Those relating to the Planetary Spectra ; to the Fixed Stars ; and to the Spectra of Nebulæ.*

The apparatus used by Messrs. Huggins and Miller is of the most ingenious and beautiful character. Without going into a detailed description of it, it may be sufficient to say that, in order to concentrate the light of such faint bodies as the stars, before admitting it into a prism, or series of prisms for refraction and dispersion in order to form a spectrum, a telescope of large size is indispensable to the observer. The telescope used by Messrs. Huggins and Miller has an object-glass of eight inches aperture and ten feet focal length, and was originally made by Mr. Alvan Clark of Massachusetts, for the Rev. W. Dawes, the well-known English astronomer. Furthermore, as a star forms only a point of light in the focus of an object-glass, this light would be drawn out by the prisms with a fine line of colored light, without sufficient breadth for affording observation of the fine lines crossing it. Some method of expanding this point of light (and in one direction only, so as to prevent unnecessary loss of light) to give the required breadth to the spectrum is therefore needed, and this has been effected by the employment of a cylindrical lens ; and the light thus spread out, is then resolved by the highly refracting prisms, into a spectral image. It has been also ascertained, that the adaptation of a small prism to the slit of the spectroscope enables the spectrum of one substance to be superposed over that of another substance ; but when it was desired, as it was absolutely necessary to do, to compare the spectrum afforded by the reflected light of the planet

---

* For the detail of these discoveries, we are mainly indebted to a report published in the *Intellectual Observer*, London, January, 1865, by Thomas W. Burr, F. R. A. S. with the concurrence of Mr. Huggins.

with the spectrum given by absolute sunlight, the difficulty of comparing the lines in the light reflected from a planet, visible only at
night with those in the light of the sun, visible only during the day,
had to be overcome. And this was accomplished by comparing the
sunlight reflected down from the atmosphere after sunset with the
light of the planet when it first became visible. In this way, the lines
in the spectra of the different planets have been compared with the
principal lines of the solar spectrum, and with those produced in the
solar spectrum by the absorptive action of the earth's atmosphere.

Observations on the Moon and the Planets.—One of the first questions which presented itself to the minds of the observers, was to test
the existence or not of an atmosphere to our satellite, the moon. On
all astronomical grounds, the evidence of no appreciable atmosphere
is very strong; but there are other points connected with the subject
which have a little contrary tendency. It is clear that the sun's light,
reflected from the lunar surface, must pass twice through the thickness of any atmosphere the moon may have before reaching us, and
judging by the effects of the rays of the sun, when at a low altitude,
traversing a length of our own atmosphere, any lines due to its existence
should be readily seen. With this view the spectrum of the moon was
carefully examined on many occasions, and while it presented a perfect
accordance with the solar spectrum, and its principal lines, nothing could
be traced that was indicative of a gaseous envelop about the moon, and
the evidence of spectrum analysis may therefore be added to the other
reasons for believing that the moon, at any rate on the side presented
to our view, has little or no atmosphere.

The planets, shining equally by light reflected from the sun, exhibit
numerous phenomena indicating the existence of atmospheres, of which
the varying belts of Jupiter and Saturn, and the diminution of light at the
edges of these planets, and Mars, and Venus, may be mentioned. The
snow and ice of Mars also could only be produced by a gaseous envelop
like our own. The examination of the spectra of the planets, by Messrs.
Huggins and Miller, has however proved, in the *first* place, that the
planetary light, as has always been assumed by modern astronomers, is reflected light from the sun, the principal lines of the solar spectrum being
easily identified in the spectra of the planets; and *secondly*, it has given
us some very interesting information respecting the existence and character
of the planetary atmospheres. Thus, in addition to the characteristic
lines of the solar spectrum, there were observed in the planetary spectra,
various new lines, indicative of the presence, in greater or less quantity,
of substances which absorb certain lines of light. And these substances,
Messrs. Huggins and Miller are inclined to think, are indicative of distinctive features of the planetary atmospheres. It should here be stated
that the spectra of the planets are not easily rendered capable of examination. The light of a planet consists of a portion of the rays radiated
from a disc, and a portion only of the light reflected from it therefore
passes through the slit of the spectroscope, and the spectrum is often exceedingly faint; while the star, being a luminous point, the whole of its
light passes in to form the spectrum.

In the case of the planet Jupiter, the light which comes to us from
this body was originally like the light which comes direct to us; but
before it reaches us it has passed through the atmosphere of Jupiter

twice and our own atmosphere once; and thus any absorptive influence in the atmospheres of the planet and of our earth would be considerable. But the light reflected from the sky when the sun is just below the horizon, having to traverse a very much greater stratum of the earth's atmosphere of high density, necessarily would experience a greater absorption than the light which reaches us through the comparatively thin stratum of the earth's atmosphere interposed between the observer and the planet; unless, therefore, the planetary atmosphere exerted an absorbent action, all the lines due to the action of the earth's atmosphere should, in the light from Jupiter, appear fainter. The results of examination showed that some were really fainter, some of equal intensity, while one was much stronger; thus indicating, that some of the gases which compose the atmosphere of Jupiter are the same as those which constitute the earth's atmosphere, but possibly existing in different proportions. The atmosphere of Mars was also found to absorb certain rays in the blue end of the spectrum in a special manner; and the loss of these is not due, moreover, to mere diminution of light, but is of such a character as to prove it to be due to some gaseous absorptive material.

With regard to Venus, although as might be expected the spectrum was of great beauty, and the principal lines of the solar spectrum were well shown, no specific atmospheric lines could be traced.

The analysis by the prism of the light of the planets, while it largely confirms the astronomical doctrine of their possessing extensive atmospheres, may, perhaps, be thought less conclusive than might have been expected, but, on the other hand, it should be remembered that, with the exception of Mars, telescopic observation shows that we are looking not directly at the bodies of the planets, but at masses of cloud suspended in their atmospheres, and reflecting the sun's light to us, and therefore such light has passed through but a very small and rarefied portion of such atmospheres, instead of through the lower and denser portions, which we know in the case of our own aerial covering, to be the principal source of the specific atmospheric lines.

The Fixed Stars.—Striking as are the results obtained by spectrum analysis when applied to the sun, moon, and planets, they sink into insignificance when compared with the revelations afforded us of the constitution of those distant bodies, the stars, and the light which is thus thrown upon their structure is conclusive as to their being of the same nature as our own sun; a result which analogy had previously indicated, but which had not been supported by any positive evidence. It might be supposed that their distance offered insuperable obstacles to such an inquiry, but spectrum analysis knows no such limits, and as long as we can obtain light of an incandescent substance from a suitable source, it matters not whether it exists within a few inches of the spectroscope, or at a distance of unnumbered millions of miles, the result being equally certain.

The difficulties of these observations from other causes are, however, according to Messrs. Huggins and Miller, very great, arising principally from the extremely few occasions when telescopic observations with a large instrument can be carried on in England, on account of the frequent atmospheric changes. The amount of work done by these gentlemen during the past two years, although at first

22

it appears small in quantity, is in reality quite remarkable, and bears testimony in a high degree to their devotion and patience as, in consequence of the few fine nights available when a star is in a good position, the mapping of spectrum of a single star completely would occupy several years.

In the spectra of all the brighter stars that have been examined, the dark lines appear to be as numerous and as fine as in the solar spectrum. No stars sufficiently bright to be observed are without lines, and therefore star differs from star only in the arrangement of the lines, and consequently in the elementary substances present; but all the stars are constructed on one and the same plan. The number of fixed stars observed by Messrs. Huggins and Miller, amounts to nearly 50; but the spectrum lines of only a few have been mapped with any degree of completeness. Among these are Aldebaran, and the bright star designated as *a* in the constellation of Orion.

Aldebaran is a star of a pale-red tint, and its spectrum is full of lines in the orange, green, and blue. We shall presently see the significance of this fact. About 70 lines were tested as regards their coincidences with metallic spectra, by direct comparison. Sixteen terrestrial elements were thus made to present their characteristic bright lines above the dark ones of the star; and sodium, magnesium, hydrogen, calcium, iron, bismuth, tellurium, antimony, and mercury, answered perfectly to the test, and proved their existence in the atmosphere of Aldebaran. Seven elements, nitrogen, cobalt, tin, lead, cadmium, lithium, and barium, gave negative evidence only. Indications of other elements were not wanting, but the observations of these fine lines were too fatiguing to the eye to be pressed further.

a Orionis has a very full spectrum. The light of the star is orange, and the lines are thickest in the red, green, and blue. About 80 lines have been measured and mapped, and 16 elementary substances tested for coincidence. With five of these, sodium magnesium, calcium, iron, and bismuth, the connection is complete and certain. Perhaps thallium also exists, but the line seen might be calcium, the apparatus not having dispersive power enough to separate the lines of the two metals at that particular point. In the case of hydrogen, nitrogen, gold, cadmium, silver, mercury, barium, and lithium, coincidence was not proved. The absence of hydrogen in the spectrum of this star and some others is a point of considerable importance, as its presence is eminently characteristic of the spectra of the sun and some 40 fixed stars, which have been examined. This observation is, moreover, especially valuable, since it proves that the lines which indicate its presence belong to the atmospheres of the luminous bodies themselves, and not, as might have been expected, to our own atmosphere.

Although a very bright star, the observations of Sirius are extremely difficult, from its low altitude in this latitude, by which it is brought within the densest and most impure part of the atmosphere. Sodium, magnesium, hydrogen, and probably iron, have been found by coincidences, and a photograph of the spectrum was obtained on wet collodion, but owing to the combined difficulties of the experiment, the lines could not be traced in the picture. If is, however, believed by the observers that further experiments will result in this important object being attained, and the facility which will then be afforded of comparison of the more refrangible and less luminous parts of the stellar spectra, when thus self-registered, with existing metallic charts, must be obvious.

Careful examinations are also in progress of α Lyræ (Vega) ; Capella ; Arcturus ; α Cygni ; Rigel ; α Andromedæ ; Regulus ; β Pegasi, and many others, from which most interesting results may be predicated.

One of the most important and interesting deductions which the observers, whose work we have been discussing, draw from their results, is connected with the origin of the colors of the stars. That there is great variety of tints among these bodies is well known ; white, yellow, and red stars are the most frequent, whilst in double stars the contrasted colors are often green or blue.* The source of the light of the stars, as well as of that of the sun, must be a solid or liquid body in a state of incandescence, as only such bodies, when raised to a high temperature, give a continuous spectrum. In the case both of the sun and stars, this continuous spectrum becomes crossed by dark bands, which are produced by the absorbing power of the constituents held in a vaporous form in the investing atmospheres. These atmospheres vary in chemical constitution according to the elements composing the star, and should the dark lines produced by the absorptive power of the vapors forming the stellar atmosphere, and which correspond to the bright lines they would form in an incandescent state, be the strongest and most numerous in the more refrangible portions of the spectrum, then the star would have a red or orange tint, because this part of the spectrum would suffer least absorption ; while, on the contrary, should the red and yellow portions have most lines, the blue and green rays would predominate in the color of the star. The frequency of the lines in the orange, green, and blue of Aldebaran's spectrum, previously pointed out, is strongly in favor of this theory, as the red is left little affected, and the other tints are subdued by the dark lines. α Orionis has the red, green, and blue rays much diminished, which produces the orange color of this star ; and β Pegasi, which much resembles α Orionis in its spectrum, has a deep yellow hue. In Sirius, which is of a brilliant white, there are no lines sufficiently intense in any particular part of the spectrum to interfere with our receiving the light in about the same proportion, as to the quantity of the different colored rays, to that which starts from the incandescent light-giving surface.

It became a matter of great interest to test this theory with respect to the double stars, which present the most marked difference in color ; but the faintness of the blue or green companions rendered the observations very difficult. Still, observations of β Cygni and α Herculis were obtained, which accord remarkably with the theory just propounded. Thus, in the bright star of β Cygni, which is light orange

* The examination of these double stars, side by side, in the spectroscope, is a matter of great difficulty, on account of their difference of size and light ; while, from their proximity, the examining instrument is liable to be sufficiently disturbed by shakes and accidents as to put one or the other out of the field of view. The labor, too, is extremely fatiguing to the eye on account of their difference in brightness.

in color, the blue and green rays are full of lines, while the few in the red and yellow are far apart; in its component, on the other hand, which is deep blue, the red and orange part of the spectrum is full of groups of fine lines that interfere with those rays and leave the blue end, which has lines few and far between, as the dominant light of the star. The colors of the components of α Herculis, which are severally reddish and green, appear to be produced in strict conformity to the same hypothesis; and although the theory cannot be considered as established by these instances, it must be regarded as exhibiting a high degree of probability, while the singular variability in the colors of stars at different times, which cannot fail to occur to our readers as not at present explained, may yet prove to be capable of some elucidation by further investigations in the same direction. Of course change in the chemical constitution of the investing atmospheres would be an obvious cause of change of color; but these latter changes are too frequent and recur with too unvarying a regularity at the known periods, to admit of such an hypothesis.

The spectrum observations have also an important bearing on the nebular hypothesis of the cosmical origin of the universe, as showing that the elementary substances must have existed in different proportions at different points of the nebulous mass, otherwise by condensation equal proportions of the elements, from the surrounding vapor, would have been collected. There is here an analogy to the manner in which the components of the earth's crust are distributed. Some of the elements are widely and universally diffused throughout animal, vegetable, and mineral matter; while others, as the rarer metals, are accumulated at particular points, and whatever the reason of this separation, the benefits to the human race caused thereby are many and obvious.

The knowledge derived from these observations has induced Messrs. Huggins and Miller to indulge in some speculations, which are so legitimate, and so ably put forward by them in their report to the Royal Society, that we can not do better than allow them to speak for themselves, especially as the report itself may not fall within the range of many of our readers.

"The closely marked connection, in similarity of plan and mode of operation, in those parts of the universe which lie within the range of experiment, and so of our more immediate knowledge, renders it not presumptuous to attempt to apply the process of reasoning from analogy to those parts of the universe which are more distant from us.

"Upon the earth we find that the innumerable individual requirements which are connected with the present state of terrestrial activity, are not met by a plan of operation distinct for each, but are effected in connection with the special modifications of a general method, embracing a wide range of analogous phenomena. If we examine living beings, the persistence of unity of plan observable amidst the multiform varieties of special adaptation of the vertebrate form of life may be cited as an example of the unity of operation referred to. In like manner, the remarkably wide range of phenomena which are shown to be reciprocally interdependent and correlative of each other, by the recent great extension of our knowledge in reference to the relation of the different varieties of forces, and their connection with molecular motion, exhibits a similar unity of operation amidst the changes of the bodies which have not life.

"The observations recorded in this report seem to afford some proof that a similar unity of operation extends through the universe as far as light enables us to have cognizance of material objects. For we may infer that the stars, while differing, the one from the other, in the kinds of matter of which they consist, are all constructed upon the same plan as our sun, and are composed of matter identical, at least in part, with the materials of our system.

"The differences which exist between the stars are of the *lower order* of differences of *particular adaptation*, or special modification, and not differences of the *higher order* of distinct *plans of structure*.

"There is, therefore, a probability that these stars, which are analogous to our sun in structure, fulfil an analogous purpose, and are, like our sun, surrounded by planets, which they by their attraction uphold, and by their radiation illuminate and energize. And if matter identical with that upon the earth exists in the stars, the same matter would also probably be present in the planets genetically connected with them, as is the case in our solar system.

"It is remarkable that the elements most widely diffused through the host of stars are some of those most closely connected with the constitution of the living organisms of our globe, including hydrogen, sodium, magnesium, and iron. Of oxygen and nitrogen we could scarcely hope to have any decisive indications, since these bodies have spectra of different orders.* These forms of elementary matter, when influenced by heat, light, and chemical force, all of which we have certain knowledge, are radiated from the stars, afford some of the most important conditions which we know to be indispensable to the existence of living organisms, such as those with which we are acquainted. On the whole, we believe that the foregoing spectrum observations on the stars contribute something towards an experimental basis, on which a conclusion, hitherto but a pure speculation, may rest, viz: that at least the brighter stars are, like our sun, upholding and energizing centres of systems of worlds adapted to be the abode of living beings."

Discoveries in Relation to the Nebulæ.—By far the most wonderful of the revelations of spectrum analysis applied to the heavenly bodies has yet to come. Encouraged by his success with the fixed stars, Mr. Huggins resolved to apply this new and potent method of research to the examination of those mysterious bodies, the Nebulæ, and this investigation was rewarded by one of the most important discoveries connected with the physical constitution of those wonderful objects, and with the cosmical origin of the universe, which we venture to think has ever been made. From the time of Sir W. Herschel, who took up Messier's scanty list of 103 Nebulæ, and increased them to 2,500, throwing out at the same time the supposition that although he had resolved nearly all those of Messier's list into clusters of stars, and discovered hundreds of other clusters, yet that there were numerous nebulæ which, from their being easily visible, and yet resisting every attempt by increased aperture or power to resolve them, must

*That is, differ entirely at different temperatures and pressures.

22*

really consist, not of stars or separate masses of condensed solid matter, but of gaseous or vaporous fluid.   He was thence led to those beautiful speculations which, enlarged and illustrated by Laplace, who showed the mathematical possibility of such an action of condensation as Sir W. Herschel required, have become widely known as the *Nebular hypothesis*, and as to the validity of which, so much controversy has been excited.   We all know, too, that of late years the tendency of telescopic observation, as conducted by the magnificent instruments of Lord Rosse, and corroborated by the splendid achromatic of Harvard University, has been to reduce the numbers of the irresolvable nebulæ; and in particular that, after the great nebula of Orion had, in parts at least, been resolved, the general impression was that the nebular hypothesis had lost all substantial evidence in its favor, and though it still might be contended that the existing systems had such an origin, yet that examples of matter in the nebulous form were not to be found in the heavens.   Still, it must not be forgotten that Lord Rosse, while resolving many of the nebulæ, had discovered others which resisted his instrumental powers, and that to many clusters there were fantastic wisps of nebulous light appended, and diffuse patches of light attached, which defied resolution, though they were evidently connected with the objects he pronounced to be starry in construction.

Among the most wonderful of the nebulous bodies are those called by Sir W. Herschel *planetary nebulæ*.   These present the appearance of small discs of uniform light, usually circular, and generally blue, or bluish green in color.   They are few in number and bright, looking, in the telescope with a low power, very much like stars out of focus. Now it was apparent to Sir W. Herschel that bodies like these, having no central condensation of light nor stellar nucleus, could not be globular clusters of stars, which necessarily would be brighter in the centre than at the edges.   A cylinder form of stars seen endways might certainly present such an appearance, or a flat disc of stars placed at right angles to our line of sight would also look like a planetary nebula; but such forms are too improbable to detain us a moment.   He therefore, came to the conclusion that these were masses of truly nebulous or vapory matter in the primal form, and presenting various stages of the process of condensation, a few points of light being visible in some, where a little solid or liquid had probably formed.   This supposition, with the addition that, at some distance from the surface the matter was sufficiently condensed to prevent light from behind penetrating it, was then sufficient to account for the existence of a uniform planetary light-giving surface.

Lord Rosse discovered an analogy between the annular nebulæ and the planetary forms, increasing the number of the former from two to seven, and showing that a nebula with a hollow center, imperfectly seen in telescopes of less aperture, might present the appearance of a planetary nebula; but the question remained one of extreme difficulty, when Mr. Huggins, in the autumn of 1864, took up the subject and attempted to bring analysis by the prism to bear upon these remarkable bodies, which seemed a class, *sui generis*, and of an order entirely different from the sun and fixed stars.

The apparatus used was essentially the same as we have described;

but the cylindrical lens was generally removed, since the nebulæ present a visible disc instead of a point when in focus. The first object attacked was 37 H. IV. Draconis, which is described by Sir J. Herschel in his latest catalogue as "very bright; pretty small; with a very small nucleus." Its color is greenish blue. Looked at with the telescope and spectrum apparatus, Mr. Huggins was astonished to find no spectrum visible, but only one short line of light in the direction which the dark lines always occupy in the spectrum. At first he suspected derangement of the apparatus, but this being found in good order, it became apparent that this celestial body differed from all others that have been examined, not in degree, but absolutely in kind; for its light was not composed of rays of different refrangibilities, but mostly of one monochromatic light only. Careful examination with a narrower slit detected a more refrangible, but much fainter bright line, and at about three times the distance another still fainter was seen. The direct comparison of these lines with those of the solar spectrum viewed through the atmosphere * was then made, and it was found that the brightest line corresponded with the strongest line due to nitrogen, and the faintest with one of the hydrogen lines, while the intermediate one was nearly, but not quite, coincident with a barium line. An excessively faint spectrum was also detected on both sides of the bright lines, which is, doubtless, due to the minute solid or liquid nucleus, and perhaps is crossed by both lines.

The significance of this discovery is invaluable. *Terrestrial* physics show us that only liquid and solid bodies give a continuous spectrum, while gases alone, when rendered luminous by heat, give out light which, after dispersion by the prism, is found to consist of certain degrees of refrangibility only, which appear as bright lines on a dark ground. Here there was clear and unimpeachable evidence, according to the present state of our knowledge, that large masses of gas exist; and these may be the nebulous matter of Herschel and Laplace; which then is no fiction, and that we may yet fairly speculate on the process of the origin of worlds from such a primal form. But other nebulæ were to be tested. A very similar planetary nebula (Σ 6), in Taurus Poniatowski, when examined, gave precisely the same bright lines, with the merest suspicion of a faint spectrum. 73 H. IV. Cygni gave the same three bright lines, with a stronger continuous spectrum than the nebula in Draco. This nebula has a distinct 11th magnitude star in the middle, which evidently produces the continuous spectrum; and this opinion was confirmed by a most crucial experiment. The cylindrical lens being removed from the apparatus, it was found that the three bright lines still remained of considerable length, corresponding to the diameter of the telescopic image of the nebula, while the faint spectrum became a narrow line, showing that the object producing it was a point in the focus of the object-glass. 51 H. IV. Sagitarii is a fainter planetary nebula, and the two brighter lines were seen, and the third by glimpses. 1 H. IV. Acquarii had the three bright lines distinct and sharp, but the indications of the faint spectrum were mere

* It should here be noted, that some of the lines crossing the solar-spectrum are due undoubtedly to the elements of our atmosphere, as oxygen, nitrogen, hydrogen, &c. It was with the lines produced by these atmospheric gaseous elements that the nebula lines were compared.

suspicions. Though brighter than the last this nebula probably contains very little matter in the liquid or solid form.

57 M. Lyræ, the well-known ring nebula, was a most interesting object. Its light is very pale, and the brightest of the three lines was the only one distinctly seen, the others being, perhaps, glimpsed, but no faint continuous spectrum whatever could be detected. The bright line was remarkable, consisting of two bright spots corresponding to sections of the ring, with a very faint connecting line. Lord Rosse had previously seen more nebulosity in the center of the ring than had been recognized by other observers; and the spectrum shows that it is full of rare nebulous matter. Another planetary nebula, 18 H. IV., but which under a power of 600 is distinctly annular, gave a fourth excessively faint line. The last object which has been examined was the celebrated Dumb-Bell Nebula, 27 M. Vulpeculæ. The light of this body after prismatic analysis remained concentrated in the strong bright line corresponding to that of nitrogen, no others being visible, nor was there any trace of a faint continuous spectrum. Various portions of this large nebula were tried, but the light, although different, in intensity, was always the same in refrangibility.

So much for the positive evidence, that these nebulæ have no resemblance whatever to any thing like stars, or clusters of stars; and this testimony is corroborated by the negative evidence obtained in the examination of a number of other bodies which are palpably of the class of clusters. For example, 92 M. Herculis, and 26 IV. Eridani, both fine clusters, gave continuous spectra as the stars do. 50 H. IV. Herculis though nebulous in the telescope, still produces a starry spectrum, showing its true character. 55 Andromedæ, which Herschel describes as a star with a nebulous atmosphere, gave a star spectrum, but no bright lines; and Lord Rosse notes that he has looked at it eight times and seen no such atmosphere, so that it is probably not a nebulous star at all. The examination of the great nebula in Andromeda is of much interest. The brightest part gave a partial though continuous spectrum, the light ceasing abruptly in the orange, and the companion 32 M. gave a similar spectrum. It would appear, therefore, that these are really clusters at the enormous and almost inconceivable distances which must be necessary so to blend the light of their constituent stars. It is, however, also possible that they may be gaseous matter so full of condensed and opaque portions as to give a continuous spectrum.

Mr Huggins remarks, "It is obvious that the nebulæ, 37 H. IV., 6Σ., 73 H. IV., 51 H. IV., 1 H. IV., 57 M., 18 H. IV., and 27 M., can no longer be regarded as aggregations of suns after the order to which our own sun and the fixed stars belong. We have in these objects to do no longer with a special modification only of our own type of suns, but find ourselves in the presence of objects possessing a distinct and peculiar plan of structure."

"In place of an incandescent solid or liquid body transmitting light of all refrangibilities through an atmosphere which intercepts by absorption a certain number of them, such as our sun appears to be, we must probably regard these objects, or at least their photo-surfaces, as enormous masses of luminous gas or vapor. For it is alone from matter in the gaseous state that light, consisting of certain definite refrangibilities only, as is the case with the light of these nebulæ, is known to be emitted."

We think our readers cannot fail to indorse this conclusion, and no one who has studied the subject and comprehends the extreme beauty of the adaptations of spectroscopic apparatus which are employed; the delicacy and care with which the observations were made, and the caution displayed in drawing conclusions only when the evidence is irrefragable, but must regard the discovery of such an analysis of the true nature of these wonderful bodies as one of the noblest additions to our knowledge which has recently been made. The speculations to which the proved existence of bodies of such enormous size, and consisting apparently of only three or four elementary substances, will give rise, are, doubtless, numerous and various in the extreme. It is singular that only one out of several nitrogen lines is seen, but Mr. Huggins has sometimes observed a difference in sharpness between this and some other bright nitrogen lines, which suggests differences in the atoms radiating the light. Again, we find the stars containing numerous elementary bodies; can it be possible that, in the process of condensation and cooling from the enormously high temperature which the nebulæ must possess, transmutation of the so-called elements may take place? Modern chemistry says "No!" but there are occasional indications that some of the so-called elementary bodies may yet be decomposed, or proved to be different forms of others. Time which has done so much will yet bring fresh wonders to light, and the powers of the spectrum analysis will be yet further exerted in the elucidation of the problems of nature. Enough for the present, that the well-matured speculations of Herschel, and the mathematical theory of Laplace, have been vindicated from the doubt under which they have been laboring, and the early nebulous condition of cosmical matter so necessary for almost all geological reasoning, proved to demonstration by the labors of the observer whose results we have detailed.

Since the above was written, Mr. Huggins has announced the discovery that the great nebula of Orion gives a spectrum indicative of gaseity. This instance, added to those of the Ring and Dumb-Bell Nebulæ, shows that resolution into points of light can no longer be accepted as a proof of a nebula being a cluster of stars.

THOUGHTS ON THE RESULTS OF SPECTRUM ANALYSIS.

If the researches through spectral analysis open to us in some degree the portals of the infinitely vast, it reconducts us by another route to the idea of unity in nature. In studying the spectrum, we at present recognize each simple body held in suspension in the flame whose rays are decomposed by the glass prism; but what is a simple body which betrays its presence, not by one bright stripe alone, but by two, three, sometimes by 60 stripes? In proportion as the spectrum increases in distinctness, the number of luminous stripes increases for each substance; shall we ever see them all? It may well be doubted. Here, then, there is a multiplicity and indeterminateness which accord but ill, it must be confessed, with the theoretic idea which we entertain of a *simple* body, a substance not compounded, always identical with itself, *substratum* of all chemical combinations. Must we admit, with some resolute spirits, that the bodies which we call simple, appear so to us only because thus far we have not succeeded in decomposing them? Should we conclude that the different simple bodies, if there are really such, are but formed of one and the same matter in different states of condensation? We thus find ourselves attracted towards the idea of unity of substance. Gas, liquid, solids, vacuum and plenum, bodies and celestial spaces, satellites, planets, suns, &c., would be but transitory forms of something eternal, the ephemeral images of something which cannot change; in the vortex of phenomena, in the eternal movement of all substance, the cosmic history everywhere shows us the future in the present, and the present in the future.—*Revue des deux mondes.*

ON THE THEORY AND APPLICATION OF SPECTRUM ANALYSIS.

We copy from the *Intellectual Observer* (London), the following remarks on the theory and application of "spectrum analysis," which may assist our readers in obtaining a clear idea of the nature of this discovery.

In the first place we would remind them, that a solar spectrum, or prismatic image of the sun, consists of a ray of sunlight, opened like a fan, and spread out so as to exhibit exquisite gradations of color, from red at one end to violet at the other. If we attempt to form a spectrum by allowing a broad mass of light to fall upon a prism, we shall only partially succeed. We shall indeed see rainbow colors, but they will be overlapped and confused. If, however, we permit the light to reach the prism through a narrow slit, and exclude extraneous rays, the confusion will be avoided, and a neat, well-defined, ribbon of parti-colored light will be obtained, in which, at certain intervals, dark lines will be observed. These lines, which would appear to a casual observer as insignificant as so many threads of a cobweb, are the hieroglyphic letters which the spectroscopist has to decipher, in accordance with the principles explained in the articles to which we have already made reference. To Sir J. Herschel belongs the credit of first pointing out that as the spectra of incandescent volatilized substances differed from each other, they might be made use of for purposes of analysis. There are only two modes in which such spectra can differ from each other, or from the solar spectrum which may be taken as a standard. Either they will afford bright lines in the place of dark lines, or dark lines in place of light ones. We have used the term *lines*, but when the breadth is considerable, *spaces* or *bands* is a better appellation.

When a glass prism acts upon a ray of light so as to give a spectrum, two distinct actions take place. First, the light ray is *refracted*, or bent out of its course; secondly, it is opened or spread out like a fan. This last action is called *dispersion*, and, like refraction, its amount varies with the substance employed in the formation of the prism.

For the detection of the metals and many other substances, a very minute examination of the spectrum is seldom required, as the spaces or bands by which their presence is indicated are conspicuously shown by any instrument that will display the chief lines of the solar spectrum. There are, however, many thousand finer lines that can be discerned if a sufficiently powerful and delicate apparatus is employed, and many lines that appear single under ordinary circumstances are found to be multiple when examined with superior means.

The size and character of the spectroscope should be regulated by the work required of it. A very small one, that can be carried in the waistcoat-pocket, will serve to indicate the presence of the most characteristic substances, or to show to the traveler whether the atmosphere—as is often the case of an afternoon and in thunder-storm weather—develops any lines of moderate magnitude that are not regularly seen. A small spectroscope, however, labors under two obvious limitations: Its prism cannot usefully receive much light; opening the slit too wide introduces confusion, as just explained, and its length must be proportioned to the size of prism, and consequently be restricted when a little one is employed. Then the telescopes attached to a small spectroscope are of small aperture and short focal length, with the consequent disadvantage of losing light, and being deficient in *separating* power. •So important is the size and focal length of the telescope, that an apparatus of four prisms and three-feet telescopes exhibits more lines than one of nine prisms furnished with two-feet telescopes. The focal length of the collimating telescope determines the apparent size of the slit. If it is short, and the curves of its glass considerable, the slit looks wider, and all the lines are spread. This action when noticed by Mr. Browning, induced him to recommend and apply telescopes of much greater focal length than had hitherto been used in spectroscope apparatus. The first requisites for a better examination of spectra will then consist in a larger prism, with telescopes of larger aperture and greater focal length. They collect more light, and are better able to separate closely adjacent lines. The larger apparatus, if equally good in its corrections and adjustment, will show the colors brighter, the lines sharper and much more numerous, and will separate or "resolve" more of the compound lines. It will also give an intelligible spectrum, with a quantity of light that a smaller instrument could not work with.

For the traveller and casual observer the small pocket form answers well. The chemist and physicist require, for many purposes, more light, a wider dispersion, and a greater resolving or separating power. For ordinary laboratory use, none of these properties are needed in excess; and a single fine prism, with two large telescopes, is amply sufficient. With this instrument the entire spectrum can be displayed at once with a magnification of 30 or 40, and a lower positive eyepiece, conveniently furnished with cross wires, enables all the principal lines in the darker part of the spectrum, as well as in the more luminous, to be seen distinctly, and their position noted down. This spectroscope, with one prism of 60°, and telescopes of an inch and a quarter clear aperture, and about 18 inches focal length, is decidedly the best in quality and form that has been produced to meet ordinary requirements; and, for common purposes, a more elaborate and complicated apparatus is not necessary, and, indeed, would not always be advantageous. The eye soon gets accustomed to the appearances of different spectra, and a momentary glance would suffice to show whether sodium, potassium, lithium, silver, etc., were absent or present. But it is necessary that the exact position of the lines or bands should be ascertained, and that means should be provided by which exact diagrams may be made. Hitherto only superior instruments, beyond the reach of ordinary students, have been furnished with these desiderata; but Mr. Browning, an optician of London, has now supplied them, in a convenient form, and at a very low price. One of the telescopes in the instrument we are describing moves over a grad-uated arc, read off to one minute by a vernier. Any line taken as a starting-point is brought into the centre of the field, so that it forms a perpendicular, cutting through the centre of the cross wires with which one eye-piece is furnished. The telescope is then clamped and the vernier read. Other lines are taken in succession, and their exact angular distance ascertained. When only moderate accuracy is needed in a diagram, a piece of paper can be ruled to a scale, and the lines laid down accordingly. Great nicety is not, however, to be obtained in this way; and Mr. Beckley, of the Kew Observatory, has suggested the plan of a "spectrograph," which Mr. Browning has carried out with great skill.

This instrument is composed of a cylinder capable of being rotated, and fixed at any point. It carries a graduated scale exactly corre-sponding with the scale of the spectroscope, so that when the cross wires of the latter instrument intersect a line, which when read off on the vernier stands at, say 10°, the cylinder can be adjusted so that a delicate metal ruler indicates the exact spot on which a line should be drawn on a slip of paper which the cylinder carries. If the next line to be mapped down is 5° distant from the first, the cylinder is moved accordingly, the ruler is again in its exact place, and the second line is drawn as correctly as the first. This instrument thus enables dia-grams to be made with precision, and a hundred observers in different parts of the world, furnished with spectroscopes and spectrographs, properly graduated, would be certain of producing diagrams capable of the exact comparison that science needs. The spectroscopes that can measure fractions of a minute can be furnished with spectrographs of proportionate delicacy.

It is often advisable to have two spectra in the field at once in or-der that their discrepancy or conformity may be ascertained by mere inspection. This is effected in a very simple way. Half the slit of the spectroscope is permitted to receive light from a source directly in front of it. The other half of the slit is covered by a small right-angled prism which prevents direct light getting in, but reflects rays that reach it at right-angles to the axis of the instrument.

For special purposes it is necessary to view and measure the posi-tion of the more delicate lines which the spectrum contains, and to separate some which look single with ordinary means. It would at first seem that the way to do this would be to employ more magnifica-tion,—to treat, in fact, the close lines as we do those on diatoms, and separate them by magnifying power. Practically this plan only ad-mits of very restricted application. Two plans are adopted to get over the difficulty,—the spectrum is made wider by greater *dispersion*, —our fan of light is spread out more; and telescopes of large aper-ture and greater focal length furnish the spectroscopist with a greater resolving or separating power, the increase of magnification being produced by the object-glasses instead of the eye-pieces.

The reader will appreciate the difference between magnifying a spectrum of given dispersion, by remembering our illustration of the *fan*. Let a fan be opened, so that a portion of the pattern painted on its spokes is concealed by overlapping. It is obvious that magni-fying the fan in this state can give us no information concerning the part which is covered up. If we open the fan still more, the conceal-ed parts will come into view. This corresponds with the additional dispersion that we must give to a spectrum that has been imperfectly spread out, in order to see the entire pattern it can show.

To spread the light out wider, a multiplicity of prisms may be em-ployed. A spectroscope constructed for Mr. Gassiot of London,— the finest instrument yet finished of its kind,—has nine prisms, about 2½ inches long, and two high, and was originally supplied with tele-scopes of two inches aperture, and two feet focal length. Two fresh telescopes have recently been made for this instrument, of 2½ inches aperture, and three feet focal length. These show many additional lines. With this instrument a very careful survey and mapping of the spectrum is being carried on, and the results will, no doubt, be the most precise and complete information concerning the number and position of the dark lines that has yet been obtained. The size of the Gassiot spectroscope enables it to give a bright image with a small allowance of light; but certain inquiries in which Mr. Huggins is en-gaged need a further extension of power in this direction, and Mr. Browning is constructing for him a monster instrument, with about half the number of prisms on Mr. Gassiot's instrument; but these prisms fully double the size of Mr. Gassiot's, and furnished with tele-scopes of four feet focal length, and proportionally large aperture. With this splendid and costly apparatus,—which has quite novel and special means for increasing the dispersion when deemed necessary,— it will be possible to obtain great separation with a minimum loss of light, so that the spectra of very feebly luminous bodies may be made out.

In these two great spectroscopes the extra separation is produced by the multiplication of glass prisms, and when these are of fine qual-ity and exquisitely wrought, the definition is the sharpest that can be obtained.

Different substances vary in their refractive and dispersive powers. Sir J. Herschel observes, "*in general*, high refractive is accom-panied by high dispersive power; but exceptions are endless, espe-cially among the precious stones, of which the diamond affords a strik-ing instance."

If the two powers had always gone together, we could have had no achromatic lenses; but happily by selecting different kinds of glass, and setting them to opposite work, we can correct all (or nearly all) the error arising from dispersion, and only neutralize a portion of the refraction. When greater dispersive power is required in a prism than ordinary glass exerts, another kind of glass may be chosen, or recourse may be had to a liquid like bisulphide of carbon, which gives a very wide spectrum. A liquid has the disadvantage that it cannot be maintained in the prismatic form except by putting it in a vessel of the required shape. Hollow prisms are accordingly made of thin glass, and filled with the fluid required. Mr. Browning has made a spectroscope of this kind for Mr. Gassiot. It consists of eleven prisms, with telescopes 2½ inches aperture and three feet focal length, and it is able to separate the principal soda lines to the extent of 3' 6", the nine glass prisms only separating them 1'. The definition is excellent while the fluid is of uniform temperature and density; but

23

becomes very bad as soon as the heat which accompanies the light ray, or arises from any other source, has disturbed its homogeneous character. This instrument is described by Mr. Gassiot in *Proceedings of the Royal Society*, No. 63. The prisms are formed with a refracting angle of 50°, and consequently eight prisms, with the usual arrangement, would " cause a ray of light to travel more than a circle." In order to employ eleven, Mr. Browning, instead of making the outer sides of each hollow prism *flat*, formed them of crown glass prisms, having a refractive angle of 6°, the angles being arranged in the contrary direction to those of the fluid prisms. These sides take off very little of the dispersive power of the bisulphide, and enable eleven prisms to be employed.

The dispersive power of glass or any other substance depends upon the different refrangibility of the different rays that make up white light. A beam of white light contains an infinite number of rays of all hues, from red to violet (besides rays invisible to man). Each ray takes its own bend on passing through the prism, and is thus more or less separated from other rays that are bent in a different degree. When this dispersive process has completely separated any ray from its companions, passing it through another prism simply *refracts* it, without any action on its color. But if a ray is imperfectly separated from adjacent rays in the scale, the further action of one or more prisms carries on the work of separation until it is complete. In a spectrum formed by slight dispersion the red, yellow, green, and blue are seen in bands that contrast strongly with each other. When the dispersion is more complete, the intermediate tints are innumerable, and one passes into the other by insensible gradations. The artistic effect of a slightly dispersed spectrum is a brilliant but violent contrast of dissimilar colors. That of the highly dispersed spectrum is a harmonious juxtaposition of all the colors in the scale.

As the human ear cannot hear all sounds, so the human eye cannot see all rays of light. There may be sounds too sharp,—consisting of vibrations too rapid,—for the ear to perceive them, and sunlight has rays which must undergo a change before our eyes can bring them to a focus. Glass absorbs many of these rays, which are highly refrangible. Quartz transmits them, and hence a prism of that substance adds them to the spectrum which it forms. If such a spectrum is received on a screen prepared with a substance called *œsculin*, obtained from the horse-chestnut, or with an alcoholic solution of stramonium, they are sufficiently altered in refrangibility to become visible, and a beautiful blue addition to the violet end of the spectrum is seen. It is very difficult to find a large quartz crystal that can be cut into a good prism, but Mr. Gassiot obtained a splendid one from Japan, and Mr. Browning worked it into a prism of 60°, with 2½-inch sides.

The different spectroscopes to which we have alluded are all constructed upon the principle of *indirect* vision. That is to say, the observer does not point the telescope straight at the light he wishes to see. It reaches him round the corner through the refraction of the prism. This plan is handy enough for fixed apparatus, but for rapid examination of the light that comes from different portions of the sky, or from radiating objects, a spectroscope of direct vision is preferable. Mr. Browning effects this by placing a dense flint glass prism of 60° between two prisms of light crown of 22°. Other opticians follow the same principle, with variations of detail. Such spectroscopes act clearly, but they lose much of the dispersive power of the chief prism. In Browning's pattern the loss is about ⅓. Although employed by Secchi and other observers, spectroscopes of this kind are by no means the best for astronomical research; though *amateurs*, who merely desire to see the principal lines which bright celestial objects afford, will probably find them adapted to their purpose.

One of the most interesting branches of spectroscope inquiry is the absorption of certain portions of the spectrum by solutions. The fluid can be put in a test tube; but for many of these experiments a *prismatic cell* is better. This consists of a rectangular glass cell, one side of which is composed of a prism. When the solution to be examined is put in the cell, it forms a fluid prism; and if the glass prism and the solution prism correspond pretty closely in refractive power, one undoes the refractive work of the other, and thus light comes straight through the combination to the slit of the collimator.

To view the spectra of gases, narrow tubes are employed, in which the gas, in a highly rarefied state, is rendered incandescent by the discharge of a Ruhmkorff's coil.

ON THE OCCULTATION OF THE SPECTRUM OF A FIXED STAR.

Mr. Huggins, in a recent communication to the Royal (Eng.) Astronomical Society, remarked that while all observations hitherto negative the existence of an atmosphere to the moon, one had occurred to him, as not yet made, which might add to the evidence on the question. This was the disappearance of the spectrum of a star when occulted by the moon's limb. It appeared to him that if the moon possessed an atmosphere, it should show itself by producing absorption bands, and also by a gradual fading of the spectrum instead of a sudden disappearance. He also thought that, supposing an atmosphere highly charged with aqueous vapor, the red rays would be least affected, and that end of the spectrum would be last to go, while a clear but dense atmosphere would, by refraction, render the blue rays most persistent. He therefore adjusted his spectrum apparatus on the star ε Piscium about three minutes before its occultation. He could not speak positively as to any extra lines being introduced by the moon's contact, the air not being in good condition, but certainly no part of the spectrum disappeared before the other, the obscuration occurring not in the direction of the length of the spectrum, but of its breadth, cutting off all the colors at the same time, and not by a process of fading, but as if an opaque screen had been slowly introduced, about $\frac{3}{10}$ of a second being occupied in the occultation. This experiment, therefore, further corroborated the general impression of the absence of any appreciable lunar atmosphere.

GEOLOGY.

ON THE RECENT PROGRESS OF GEOLOGY.

The following address, reviewing the recent progress of Geological Science, was read by Sir Charles Lyell, on taking the chair, as President of the British Association, for 1864 :—

Phenomena of Hot Springs.—Dr. Daubeny, has remarked that nearly all the most celebrated hot springs of Europe, such as those of Aix-la-Chapelle, Baden-Baden, Naples, Auverne, and the Pyrenees, have not declined in temperature since the days of the Romans ; for many of them still retain as great a heat as is tolerable to the human body, and yet when employed by the ancients they do not seem to have required to be first cooled down by artificial means. This uniformity of temperature maintained in some places for more than 2,000 years, together with the constancy in the volume of the water, which never varies with the seasons, as in ordinary springs, the identity also of the mineral ingredients which, century after century, are held by each spring in solution, are striking facts, and they tempt us irresistibly to speculate on the deep subterranean sources both of the heat and mineral matter. How long has this uniformity prevailed ? Are the springs really ancient in reference to the earth's history, or, like the course of the present rivers and the actual shape of our hills and valleys, are they only of high antiquity when contrasted with the brief space of human annals? May they not be like Vesuvius and Etna, which, although they have been adding to their flanks, in the course of the last 2,000 years, many a stream of lava and shower of ashes, were still mountains very much the same as they now are in hight and dimensions from the earliest times to which we can trace back their existence ? Yet although their foundations are tens of thousands of years old, they were laid at an era when the Mediterranean was already inhabited by the same species of marine shells as those with which it is now peopled ; so that these volcanoes must be regarded as things of yesterday in the geological calendar.

Notwithstanding the general persistency in character of mineral waters and hot springs ever since they were first known to us, we find on inquiry that some few of them, even in historical times, have been subject to great changes. These have happened during earthquakes which have been violent enough to disturb the subterranean drainage and alter the shape of the fissures up which the waters ascend. Thus during the great earthquake at Lisbon in 1755, the temperature of the spring called La Source de la Reine at Bagnères de Luchon, in the Pyrenees, was suddenly raised as much as 75° F., or changed from a cold spring to one of 122° F., a heat which it has since retained.

268

It is also recorded that the hot springs at Bagnères de Bigorre, in the same mountain-chain, became suddenly cold during a great earthquake which, in 1660, threw down several houses in that town.

It has been ascertained that the hot springs of the Pyrenees, the Alps, and many other regions are situated in lines along which the rocks have been rent, and usually where they have been displaced or "faulted." Similar dislocations in the solid crust of the earth are generally supposed to have determined the spots where active and extinct volcanoes have burst forth; for several of these often affect a linear arrangement, their position seeming to have been determined by great lines of fissure. Another connecting link between the volcano and the hot spring is recognizable in the great abundance of hot springs in regions where volcanic eruptions still occur from time to time. It is also in the same districts that the waters occasionally attain the boiling temperature, while some of the associated stufas emit steam considerably above the boiling point. But in proportion as we recede from the great centers of igneous activity, we find the thermal waters decreasing in frequency and in their average heat, while at the same time they are most conspicuous in those territories where, as in Central France or the Eifel in Germany, there are cones and craters still so perfect in their form, and streams of lava bearing such a relation to the depth and shape of the existing valleys as to indicate that the eternal fires have become dormant in comparatively recent times. If there be exceptions to this rule, it is where hot springs are met with in parts of the Alps and Pyrenees which have been violently convulsed by modern earthquakes.

To pursue still further our comparison between the hot spring and the volcano, we may regard the water of the spring as representing those vast clouds of aqueous vapor which are copiously evolved for days, sometimes for weeks, in succession, from craters during an eruption. But we shall perhaps be asked whether, when we contrast the work done by the two agents in question, there is not a marked failure of analogy in one respect,—namely, a want, in the case of the hot spring, of power to raise from great depths in the earth voluminous masses of solid matter corresponding to the heaps of scoriæ and streams of lava which the volcano pours out on the surface. To one who urges such an objection, it may be said that the quantity of solid as well as gaseous matter transferred by springs from the interior of the earth to its surface, is far more considerable than is commonly imagined. The thermal waters of Bath are far from being conspicuous among European hot springs for the quantity of mineral matter contained in them in proportion to the water which acts as a solvent; yet Prof. Ramsay has calculated that if the sulphates of lime and of soda, and the chlorides of sodium and magnesium, and the other mineral ingredients which they contain, were solidified, they would form in one year a square column nine feet in diameter, and no less than 140 feet in hight. All this matter is now quietly conveyed by a stream of limpid water, in an invisible form, to the Avon, and by the Avon to the sea; but if, instead of being thus removed, it were deposited around the orifice of eruption, like the silicious layers which encrust the circular basin of an Icelandic geyser, we should soon see a considerable cone built up, with a crater in the middle; and if the action of the spring were intermittent, so that 10 or 20 years should elapse between the periods when solid matter was emitted, or (say) an interval of three centuries, as in the case of Vesuvius between 1306 and 1631, the discharge would be on so grand a scale as to afford no mean object of comparison with the intermittent outpourings of a volcano.

The Gases evolved from Hot Springs.—Dr. Daubeny, after devoting a month to the analysis of the Bath waters in 1833, ascertained that the daily evolution of nitrogen gas amounted to no less than 250 cubic feet in volume. This gas, he remarks, is not only characteristic of hot springs, but is largely disengaged from volcanic craters during eruptions. In both cases he suggests that the nitrogen may be derived from atmospheric air, which is always dissolved in rain-water, and which, when this water penetrates the earth's crust, must be carried down to great depths, so as to reach the heated interior. When there it may be subjected to deoxydating processes, so that the nitrogen, being left in a free state, may be driven upwards by the expansive force of heat and steam, or by hydrostatic pressure. This theory has been very generally adopted, as best accounting for the constant disengagement of large bodies of nitrogen, even where the rocks through which the spring rises are crystalline and unfossiliferous. It will, however, of course be admitted, as Prof. Bischoff has pointed out, that in some places organic matter has supplied a large part of the nitrogen evolved.

Carbonic-acid gas is another of the volatilized substances discharged by the Bath waters. Dr. Gustav Bischoff, in the new edition of his valuable work on Chemical and Physical Geology, when speaking of the exhalations of this gas, remarks that they are of universal occurrence, and that they originate at great depths, becoming more abundant the deeper we penetrate. He also observes that, when the silicates which enter so largely into the composition of the oldest rocks are percolated by this gas, they must be continually decomposed, and the carbonates formed by the new combinations thence arising must often augment the volume of the altered rocks. This increase of bulk, he says, must sometimes give rise to a mechanical force of expansion capable of uplifting the incumbent crust of the earth; and the same force may act laterally so as to compress, dislocate, and tilt the strata on each side of a mass in which the new chemical changes are developed. The calculations made by this eminent German chemist, of the exact amount of distension which the origin of new mineral products may cause, by adding to the volume of the rocks, deserve the attention of geologists, as affording them aid in explaining those reiterated oscillations of level,—those risings and sinkings of land,—which have occured on so grand a scale at successive periods of the past. There are, probably, many distinct causes of such upward, downward, and lateral movements, and any new suggestion on this head is most welcome; but I believe the expansion and contraction of solid rocks, when they are alternately heated and cooled, and the fusion and subsequent consolidation of mineral masses, will continue to rank, as heretofore, as the most influential causes of such movements.

The temperature of the Bath waters varies in the different springs from 117° to 120° F. This, as before stated, is exceptionally high, when we duly allow for the great distance of Bath from the nearest region of active or recently extinct volcanoes and of violent earthquakes. The hot springs of Aix-la-Chapelle have a much higher temperature, viz: 135° F., but they are situated within 40 miles of those cones and lava-streams of the Eifel, which, though they may have spent their force ages before the earliest records of history, belong, nevertheless, to the most modern geological period. Bath is about 400 miles distant from the same part of Germany, and 440 from Auvergne,—another volcanic region, the latest eruptions of which were geologically coëval with those of the Eifel. I have little doubt that the Bath springs, like most other thermal waters, mark the site of some great convulsion and fracture which took place in the crust of the earth at some former period,—perhaps not a very remote one, geologically speaking.

Mineral Constituents of Hot Springs.—If we adopt the theory already alluded to, that the nitrogen is derived from the deoyxdation of atmospheric air carried down by rain-water, we may imagine the supply of this water to be furnished by some mountainous region, possibly a distant one, and that it descends through rents or porous rocks till it encounters some mass of heated matter by which it is converted into steam, and then driven upwards through a fissure. In its downward passage the water may derive its sulphate of lime, chloride of calcium, and other substances from the decomposition of the gypseous, saline, calcareous, and other constituents of the rocks which it permeates. The greater part of the ingredients are common to sea-water, and might suggest the theory of a marine origin; but the analysis of the Bath springs by Merck and Galloway shows that the relative proportion of the solid matter is far from agreeing with that of the sea, the chloride of magnesium being absolutely in excess, that is, 14 grains of it per gallon for 12 of common salt; whereas in sea-water there are 27 grains of salt, or chloride of sodium, to four of the chloride of magnesium. That some mineral springs, however, may derive an inexhaustible supply, through rents and porous rocks, from the leaky bed of the ocean, is by no means an unreasonable theory, especially if we believe that the contiguity of nearly all the active volcanoes to the sea is connected with the access of salt water to the subterranean foci of volcanic heat.

Prof. Roscoe, of Manchester, has been lately engaged in making a careful analysis of the Bath waters, and has discovered in them three metals which they were not previously known to contain,—namely, copper, strontium, and lithium; but he has searched in vain for cæsium and rubidium, those new metals, the existence of which has been revealed to us in the course of the last few years by what is called spectrum analysis. By this new method the presence of infinitesimal quantities, such as would have wholly escaped detection by ordinary tests, is made known to the eye by the agency of light.

Prof. Bunsen, of Heidelberg, led the way, in 1860, in the application of this new test to the hot waters of Baden-Baden and of Dürkheim in the Palatinate. He observed in the spectrum some colored lines of which he could not interpret the meaning, and had determined not to rest till he had found out what they meant. This was no easy task, for it was necessary to evaporate 50 tons of water to obtain 200 grains of what proved to be two new metals. Taken altogether, their proportion to the water was only as one to three million. He named the first cæsium, from the bluish-gray lines which it presented in the spectrum; and the second rubidium, from its two red lines. Since these successful experiments were made, thallium, so called from its green line, was discovered in 1861 by Mr. Crookes; and a fourth metal, named indium, from its indigo-colored band, was detected by Prof. Richter, of Frieberg, in Saxony, in a zinc ore of the Hartz. It is impossible not to suspect that the wonderful efficacy of some mineral springs, both cold and thermal, in curing diseases, which no artificially prepared waters have as yet been able to rival, may be connected with the presence of one or more of these elementary bodies previously unknown; and some of the newly-found ingredients, when procured in larger quantities, may furnish medical science with means of combating diseases which have hitherto baffled all human skill.

While I was pursuing my inquiries respecting the Bath waters, I learned casually that a hot spring had been discovered at a great depth, in a copper-mine near Redruth, in Cornwall, having about as high a temperature as that of the Bath waters. It seems that, in the year 1839, a level was driven from an old shaft so as to intersect a rich copper-mine at the depth of 1,350 feet from the surface. Through this metalliferous fissure, a powerful spring of hot water was observed to rise, which has continued to flow with undiminished strength ever since. At my request this water has been analysed by Prof. Miller, who finds that the quantity of solid matter is so great as to exceed by more than four times the proportion of that yielded by the Bath waters. Its composition is also in many respects very different; for it contains but little sulphate of lime, and is almost free from the salts of magnesium. It is rich in the chlorides of calcium and sodium, and it contains one of the new metals,—cæsium, never before detected in any mineral spring in England; but its peculiar characteristic is the extraordinary abundance of lithium, of which a mere trace had been found by Prof. Roscoe in the Bath waters; whereas in this Cornish hot spring this metal constitutes no less than a $\frac{1}{28}$ part of the whole of the solid contents, which, as before stated, are so voluminous.

Lithium was first made known in 1817 by Arfvedsen, who extracted it from petalite; and it was believed to be extremely rare, until Bunsen and Kirchhoff, in 1860, by means of spectrum analysis, showed that it was a most widely diffused substance, existing in minute quantities in almost all mineral waters in the sea, as well as in milk, human blood, and the ashes of some plants. It has already been used in medicine, and we may therefore hope that, now that it is obtainable in large quantities, and at a much cheaper rate than before the Wheel-Clifford hot spring was analyzed, it may become of high value.

Mr. Warington Smyth, who had already visited the Wheel-Clifford lode in 1855, re-examined it in July last, chiefly with the view of replying to several queries which I had put to him; and in spite of the stifling heat, ascertained the geological structure of the lode and the exact temperature of the water. This last he found to be 122° Fahr. at the depth of 1,350 feet; but he scarcely doubts that the thermometer would stand two or three degrees higher at a distance of 200 feet to the eastward, where the water is known to gush up more freely. The Wheel-Clifford lode is a fissure varying in width from 6 to 12 feet, one wall consisting of elvan or porphyritic granite, and the other of killas or clay-slate. Along the line of the rent, which runs east and west, there has been a slight throw or shift of the rocks. The vein-stuff is chiefly formed of cellular pyrites of copper and iron, the porous nature of which allows the hot water to percolate freely through it. It seems, however, that in the continuation upwards of the same fissure little or no metalliferous ore was deposited, but, in its place, quartz and other impermeable substances, which obstructed the course of the hot spring, so as to prevent its flowing out on the surface of the country. It has been always a favorite theory of the miners that the high temperature of this Cornish spring is due to the oxydation of the sulphurets of copper and iron, which are decomposed when air is admitted. That such oxydation must have some slight effect is undeniable; but that it materially influences the temperature of so large a body of water is out of the question. Its effect must be almost insensible; for Prof. Miller has scarcely been able to detect any sulphuric acid in the water, and a minute trace only of iron and copper in solution.

When we compare the temperature of the Bath springs, which issue at a level of less than 100 feet above the sea, with the Wheel-Clifford spring found at a depth of 1,350 feet from the surface, we must of course make allowance for the increase of heat always experienced when we descend into the interior of the earth. The difference would amount to about 20° Fahr., if we adopt the estimate deduced by Mr. Hopkins from an accurate series of observations made in the Monk-wearmouth shaft, near Durham, and in the Dukinfield shaft, near Manchester, each of them 2,000 feet in depth. In these shafts the temperature was found to rise at the rate of only 1° F. for every increase of depth of from 65 to 70 feet. But if the Wheel-Clifford spring, instead of being arrested in its upward course, had continued to rise freely through porous and loose materials so as to reach the surface, it would probably not have lost anything approaching to 20° F., since the renewed heat derived from below would have warmed the walls and contents of the lode, so as to raise their temperature above that which would naturally belong to the rocks at corresponding levels on each side of the lode. The almost entire absence of magnesium raises an obvious objection to the hypothesis of this spring deriving its waters from the sea; or if such a source be suggested for the salt and other marine products, we should be under the necessity of supposing the magnesium to be left behind in combination with some of the elements of the decomposed and altered rocks through which the thermal waters may have passed.

Hot springs are, for the most part, charged with alkaline and other highly soluble substances, and, as a rule, are barren of the precious metals, gold, silver, and copper, as well as of tin, platinum, lead, and many others; a slight trace of copper in the Bath waters being exceptional. Nevertheless, there is a strong presumption that there exists some relationship between the action of thermal waters and the filling of rents with metallic ores. The component elements of these ores may, in the first instance, rise from great depths in a state of sublimation or of solution in intensely heated water, and may then be precipitated on the walls of a fissure as soon as the ascending vapors or fluids begin to part with some of their heat. Almost everything, save the alkaline metals, silica, and certain gases, may thus be left behind long before the spring reaches the earth's surface. If this theory be adopted, it will follow that the metalliferous portion of a fissure, originally thousands of feet or fathoms deep, will never be exposed in regions accessible to the miner until it has been upheaved by a long series of convulsions, and until the higher parts of the same rent, together with its contents and the rocks which it had traversed have been removed by aqueous denudation.   Ages before such changes are accomplished, thermal and mineral springs will have ceased to act ; so that the want of identity between the mineral ingredients of hot springs and the contents of metalliferous veins, instead of militating against their intimate relationship, is in favor of both being the complementary results of one and the same natural operation.

Metamorphism of the Sedimentary Rocks.—But there are other characters in the structure of the earth's crust more mysterious in their nature than the phenomena of metalliferous veins, on which the study of hot springs has thrown light.   I allude to the metamorphism of sedimentary rocks.   Strata of various ages, many of them once full of organic remains, have been rendered partially or wholly crystalline. It is admitted on all hands that heat has been instrumental in bringing about this rearrangement of particles, which, when the metamorphism has been carried out to its fullest extent, obliterates all trace of the imbedded fossils.   But as mountain-masses many miles in length and breadth, and several thousands of feet in hight, have undergone such alteration, it has always been difficult to explain in what manner an amount of heat capable of so entirely changing the molecular condition of sedimentary masses could have come into play without utterly annihilating every sign of stratification, as well as of organic structure.

Various experiments have led to the conclusion that the minerals which enter most largely into the composition of the metamorphic rocks have not been formed by crystallizing from a state of fusion, or in the dry way, but that they have been derived from liquid solutions, or in the wet way,—a process requiring a far less intense degree of heat. Thermal springs, charged with carbonic acid and with hydro-fluoric acid, (which last is often present in small quantities), are powerful causes of decomposition and chemical reaction in rocks through which they percolate.   If, therefore, large bodies of hot water permeate mountain-masses at great depths, they may, in the course of ages, superinduce in them a crystalline structure ; and, in some cases, strata in a lower position and of older date may be comparatively unaltered, retaining their fossil remains undefaced, while newer rocks are rendered metamorphic.   This may happen where the waters, after passing upwards for thousands of feet, meet with some obstruction, as in the case of the Wheel-Clifford spring, causing the same to be laterally diverted so as to percolate the surrounding rocks.   The efficacy of such hydro-thermal action has been admirably illustrated of late years by the experiments and observations of Sénarmont, Daubrée, Delesse, Scheerer, Sorby, Sterry Hunt, and others.

The changes which Daubrée has shown to have been produced by the alkaline waters of Plombièret, in the Vosges, are more especially instructive.   These thermal waters have a temperature of 160° F., and were conveyed by the Romans to baths through long conduits or aqueducts.   The foundations of some of their works consisted of a bed of concrete, made of lime, fragments of brick, and sandstone. Through this and other masonry, the hot waters have been percolating for centuries, and have given rise to various zeolites,—apophyllite and chabazite, among others ; also to calcareous spar, arragonite, and fluor spar, together with siliceous minerals, such as opal,—all found in the interspaces of the bricks and mortar, or constituting part of their rearranged materials. The quantity of heat brought into action in this instance, in the course of 2,000 years, has, no doubt, been enormous, although the intensity of it developed at any one moment has been always inconsiderable.

The study, of late years, of the constituent parts of granite has, in like manner, led to the conclusion that their consolidation has taken place at temperatures far below those formerly supposed to be indispensable. Gustav Rose has pointed out that the quartz of granite has the specific gravity of 2·6, which characterizes silica when it is precipitated from a liquid solvent, and not that inferior density, namely, 2·3, which belongs to it when it cools, and solidifies in the dry way from a state of fusion.

But some geologists, when made aware of the intervention, on a large scale, of water, in the formation of the component minerals of the granitic and volcanic rocks, appear, of late years, to have been too much disposed to dispense with intense heat when accounting for the formation of the crystalline and unstratified rocks. As water, in a state of solid combination, enters largely into the aluminous and some other minerals, and therefore plays no small part in the composition of the earth's crust, it follows that, when rocks are melted, water must be present, independently of the supplies of rain-water and sea-water which find their way into the regions of subterranean heat. But the existence of water under great pressure affords no argument against our attributing an excessively high temperature to the mass with which it is mixed up. Still less does the point to which the melted matter must be cooled down before it consolidates or crystallizes into lava or granite, afford any test of the degree of heat which the same matter must have acquired when it was melted and made to form lakes and seas in the interior of the earth's crust.

We learn from Bunsen's experiments on the Great Geyser in Iceland, that at the depth of only 74 feet, at the bottom of the tube, a column of water may be in a state of rest, and yet possess a heat of 120° Centigrade, or 248° F. What, then, may not the temperature of such water be at the depth of a few thousand feet ? It might soon attain a white heat under pressure ; and as to lava, they who have beheld it issue, as I did in 1858, from the southwestern flanks of Vesuvius, with a surface white and glowing like that of the sun, and who have felt the scorching heat which it radiates, will form a high conception of the intense temperature of the same lava at the bottom of a vertical column several miles high, and communicating with a great reservoir of fused matter, which, if it were to begin at once to cool down, and were never to receive future accessions of heat, might require a whole geological period before it solidified. Of such slow refrigeration hot springs may be among the most effective instruments, abstracting slowly from the subterranean molten mass that heat which clouds of vapor are seen to carry off in a latent form from a volcanic

crater during an eruption, or from a lava stream during its solidification.   It is more than 40 years since Mr. Scrope, in his work on
Volcanoes, insisted on the important part which water plays in an
eruption, when intimately mixed up with the component materials
of lava, aiding, as he supposed, in giving mobility to the more solid
materials of the fluid mass.   But when advocating this igneo-aqueous
theory, he never dreamt of impugning the Huttonian doctrine as to
the intensity of heat which the production of the unstratified rocks,
those of the plutonic class especially implies.

The exact nature of the chemical changes which hydrothermal action may effect in the earth's interior will long remain obscure to us,
because the regions where they take place are inaccessible to man;
but the manner in which volcanoes have shifted their position throughout a vast series of geological epochs—becoming extinct in one region
and breaking out in another—may, perhaps, explain the increase of
heat as we descend towards the interior, without the necessity of our
appealing to an original central heat or the igneous fluidity of the
earth's nucleus.

Recent Geological Changes in the Configuration of Great Britain.—
It is already more than a quarter of a century since Sir Roderick Murchison first spoke of the Malvern Straits, meaning thereby a channel of
the sea which once separated Wales from England.   That such marine
straits really extended, at a modern period, between what are now the
estuaries of the Severn and the Dee has been lately confirmed in a satisfactory manner, by the discovery of marine shells of recent species in drift
covering the watershed which divides those estuaries.   At the time when
these shells were living, the Cotswold Hills, at the foot of which Bath city
is built, formed one of the numerous islands of an archipelago into which
England, Ireland, and Scotland were then divided.   The amount of vertical movement which would be necessary to restore such a state of the
surface as prevailed when the position of land and sea were so different
would be very great.

Nowhere in the world, according to our present information, is the evidence of upheaval, as manifested by upraised marine shells, so striking as
in Wales.   In that country Mr. Trimmer first pointed out, in 1831, the
occurrence of fossil shells in stratified drift, at the top of a hill called Moel
Tryfaen, near the Menai Straits, and not far from the base of Snowdon.
Mr. Darbishire has obtained from the same drift no less than 54 fossil
species, all of them now living either in high northern or British seas,
and 11 of them being exclusively arctic.   The whole Fauna bears testimony to a climate colder than that now experienced in these latitudes,
though not to such extreme cold as that implied by the Fauna of some
of the glacial drift of Scotland.   The shells alluded to were procured at
the extraordinary hight of 1,360 feet above the sea-level, and they demonstrate an upheaval of the bed of the sea to that amount in the time of
the living Testacea.   A considerable part of what is called the glacial epoch
had already elapsed before the shelly strata in question were deposited on
Moel Tryfaen, as we may infer from the polished and striated surfaces of
rocks on which the drift rests, and the occurrence of erratic blocks
smoothed and scratched, at the bottom of the same drift.

Cause of the Glacial Epoch.—The evidence of a period of great
cold in England and North America, in the times referred to, is now

so universally admitted by geologists, that I shall take it for granted, and briefly consider what may have been the probable causes of the refrigeration of central Europe at the era in question. One of these causes, first suggested 11 years ago by a celebrated Swiss geologist, has not, I think, received the attention which it well deserved. When I proposed, in 1833, the theory that alterations in physical geography might have given rise to those revolutions in climate which the earth's surface has experienced at successive epochs, it was objected by many that the signs of upheaval and depression were too local to account for such general changes of temperature. This objection was thought to be of peculiar weight when applied to the glacial period, because of the shortness of the time, geologically speaking, which has since transpired. But the more we examine the monuments of the ages which preceded the historical, the more decided become the proofs of a general alteration in the position, depth, and hight of seas, continents, and mountain-chains since the commencement of the glacial period. The meteorologist also has been learning of late years that the quantity of ice and snow in certain latitudes depends not merely on the hight of mountain-chains, but also on the distribution of the surrounding sea and land even to considerable distances.

M. Escher von Linth gave it as his opinion in 1852, that if it were true, as Ritter had suggested, that the great African desert, or Sahara, was submerged within the modern or post-tertiary period, that same submergence might explain why the Alpine glaciers had attained so recently those colossal dimensions which, reasoning on geological data, Venetz and Charpentier had assigned to them. Since Escher first threw out this hint, the fact that the Sahara was really covered by the sea at no distant period has been confirmed by many new proofs. The distinguished Swiss geologist himself has just returned from an exploring expedition through the eastern part of the Algerian Desert, in which he was accompanied by M. Desor, and Prof. Martins. These three experienced observers satisfied themselves, during the last winter, that the Sahara was under water during the period of the living species of Testacea. We had already learnt, in 1856, from a Memoir by M. Laurent, that sands identical with those of the nearest shores of the Mediterranean, and containing, among other recent shells, the common cockle (*Cardium edule*), extend over a vast space from west to east in the desert, being not only found on the surface, but also brought up from depths of more than 20 feet by the Artesian auger. These shells have been met with at hights of more than 900 feet above the sea-level, and on ground sunk 300 feet below it; for there are in Africa, as in Western Asia, depressions of land below the level of the sea. The same cockle has been observed still living in several salt-lakes in the Sahara; and superficial incrustations of salt in many places seem to point to the drying up by evaporation of several inland seas in certain districts.

Mr. Tristram, in his travels in 1859, traced for many miles along the southern borders of the French possessions in Africa, lines of inland sea-cliffs, with caves at their bases, and old sea-beaches forming successive terraces, in which recent shells and the casts of them were agglutinated together with sand and pebbles, the whole having the form of a conglomerate. The ancient sea appears once to have

24

stretched from the Gulf of Cabes, in Tunis, to the west coast of Africa north of Senegambia, having a width of several hundred (perhaps, where greatest, according to Mr. Tristram, 800) miles. The high lands of Barbary, including Morocco, Algeria, and Tunis, must have been separated at this period from the rest of Africa by a sea. All that we have learnt from zoölogists and botanists in regard to the present Fauna and Flora of Barbary favors this hypothesis, and seems at the same time to point to a former connection of that country with Spain, Sicily, and South Italy.

When speculating on these changes, we may call to mind that certain deposits, full of marine shells of living species, have long been known as fringing the borders of the Red Sea, and rising several hundred feet above its shores. Evidence has also been obtained that Egypt, placed between the Red Sea and the Sahara, participated in these great continental movements. This may be inferred from the old river-terraces, lately described by Messrs. Adams and Murie, which skirt the modern alluvial plains of the Nile, and rise above them to various hights, from 30 to 100 feet and upwards. In whatever direction, therefore, we look, we see grounds for assuming that a map of Africa in the glacial period would no more resemble our present maps of that continent than Europe now resembles North America. If, then, argues Escher, the Sahara was a sea in post-tertiary times, we may understand why the Alpine glaciers formerly attained such gigantic dimensions, and why they have left moraines of such magnitude on the plains of Northern Italy and the lower country of Switzerland. The Swiss peasants have a saying, when they talk of the melting of the snow, that the sun could do nothing without the Föhn, a name which they give to the well-known sirocco. This wind, after sweeping over a wide expanse of parched and burning sand in Africa, blows occasionally for days in succession across the Mediterranean, carrying with it the scorching heat of the Sahara to melt the snows of the Apennines and Alps.

M. Denzler, in a Memoir on this subject, observes that the Föhn blew tempestuously at Algiers on the 17th of July, 1841, and then, crossing the Mediterranean, reached Marseilles in six hours. In five more hours it was at Geneva and the Valais, throwing down a large extent of forest in the latter district; while in the cantons of Zurich and the Grisons it suddenly turned the leaves of many trees from green to yellow. In a few hours new-mown grass was dried and ready for the haystack; for although, in passing over the Alpine snows, the sirocco absorbs much moisture, it is still far below the point of saturation when it reaches the sub-Alpine country to the north of the great chain. MM. Escher and Denzler have both of them observed, on different occasions, that a thickness of one foot of snow has disappeared in four hours during the prevalence of this wind. No wonder, therefore, that the Föhn is much dreaded for the inundations which it sometimes causes. The snow-line of the Alps was seen by Mr. Irscher, the astronomer, from his observatory at Neufchatel, by aid of the telescope, to rise sensibly every day while this wind was blowing. Its influence is by no means confined to the summer season, for in the winter of 1852 it visited Zurich at Christmas, and in a few days all the surrounding country was stripped of its snow, even on the shadiest places and on the crests of high ridges. I feel the better able to appreciate the power of this wind from having myself witnessed in Sicily, in 1828, its effect in dissolving, in the month of November, the snows which then covered the summit and higher parts of Mount Etna. I had been told that I should be unable to ascend to the top of the highest cone till the following spring; but in 36 hours the hot breath of the sirocco stripped off from the mountain its white mantle of snow, and I ascended without difficulty.

It is well known that the number of days during which particular winds prevail, from year to year, varies considerably. Between the year 1812 and 1820 the Föhn was less felt in Switzerland than usual; and what was the consequence? All the glaciers, during those eight or nine years, increased in hight, and crept down below their former limits in their respective valleys. Many similar examples might be cited of the sensitiveness of the ice to slight variations of temperature. Capt. Godwin Austen has lately given us a description of the gigantic glaciers of the western Himalaya in those valleys where the sources of the Indus rise, between the latitudes 35° and 36° N. The highest peaks of the Karakorum range attain in that region an elevation of 28,000 feet above the sea. The glaciers, says Capt. Austen, have been advancing within the memory of the living inhabitants, so as greatly to encroach on the cultivated lands, and have so altered the climate of the adjoining valleys immediately below, that only one crop a year can now be reaped from fields which formerly yielded two crops. If such changes can be experienced in less than a century, without any perceptible modification in the physical geography of that part of Asia, what mighty effects may we not imagine the submergence of the Sahara to have produced in adding to the size of the Alpine glaciers? If between the years 1812 and 1820, a mere diminution of the number of days during which the sirocco blew could so much promote the growth and onward movement of the ice, how much greater a change would result from the total cessation of the same wind! But this would give no idea of what must have happened in the glacial period; for we can not suppose the action of the south wind to have been suspended: it was not in abeyance, but its character was entirely different, and of an opposite nature, under the altered geographical conditions above contemplated. First, instead of passing over a parched and scorching desert, between the 20th and 35th parallels of latitude, it would plentifully absorb moisture from a sea many hundreds of miles wide. Next, in its course over the Mediterranean, it would take up still more aqueous vapor; and when, after complete saturation, it struck the Alps, it would be driven up into the higher and more rarefied regions of the atmosphere. There the aërial current, as fast as it was cooled, would discharge its aqueous burden in the form of snow, so that the same wind which is now called "the devourer of ice" would become its principal feeder.

If we thus embrace Escher's theory, as accounting in no small degree for the vast size of the extinct glaciers of Switzerland and Northern Italy, we are by no means debarred from accepting at the same time Charpentier's suggestion, that the Alps in the glacial period were 2,000 or 3,000 feet higher than they are now. Such a difference in altitude may have been an auxiliary cause of the extreme cold, and seems the more probable now that we have obtained unequivocal proofs of such great oscillations of level in Wales within the period under consideration. We may also avail ourselves of another source of refrigeration which may have coincided in time with the submergence of the Sahara, namely, the diversion of the Gulf Stream from its present course. The shape of Europe and North America, or the boundaries of sea and land, departed so widely in the glacial period from those now established, that we cannot suppose the Gulf Stream to have taken at that period its present north-western course across the Atlantic. If it took some other direction, the climate of the north of Scotland would according to the calculations of Mr. Hopkins, suffer a diminution in its average annual temperature of 12° F., while that of the Alps would lose 2° F. A combination of all the conditions above enumerated would certainly be attended with so great a revolution in climate as might go far to account for the excessive cold which was developed at so modern a period in the earth's history. But even when we assume all three of them to have been simultaneously in action we have by no means exhausted all the resources which a difference in the geographical condition of the globe might supply. Thus, for example, to name only one of them, we might suppose that the hight and quantity of land near the north pole was greater at the era in question than it is now.

The vast mechanical force that ice exerted in the glacial period has been thought by some to demonstrate a want of uniformity in the amount of energy which the same natural cause may put forth at two successive epochs. But we must be careful, when thus reasoning, to bear in mind that the power of ice is here substituted for that of running water. The one becomes a mighty agent in transporting huge erratics, and in scoring, abrading, and polishing rocks; but meanwhile the other is in abeyance. When, for example, the ancient Rhone glacier conveyed its moraines from the upper to the lower end of the Lake Geneva, there was no great river, as there now is, forming a delta many miles in extent; and several hundred feet in depth, at the upper end of the lake.

Antiquity of the Glacial Epoch.—The more we study and comprehend the geographical changes of the glacial period, and the migrations of animals and plants to which it gave rise, the higher our conceptions are raised of the duration of that subdivision of time, which, though vast when measured by the succession of events comprised in it, was brief if estimated by the ordinary rules of geological classification. The glacial period was, in fact, a mere episode in one of the great epochs of the earth's history; for the inhabitants of the lands and seas, before and after the grand development of snow and ice, were nearly the same. As yet we have no satisfactory proof that man existed in Europe or elsewhere during the period of extreme cold; but our investigations on this head are still in their infancy. In an early portion of the post-glacial period it has been ascertained that man flourished in Europe; and in tracing the signs of existence, from the historical ages to those immediately antecedent, and so backward into more ancient times, we gradually approach a dissimilar geographical state of things, when the climate was colder, and when the configuration of the surface departed considerably from that which now prevails.

Archæologists are satisfied that in central Europe the age of bronze weapons preceded the Roman invasion of Switzerland; and prior to the Swiss-lake dwellings of the bronze age were those in which stone weapons alone were used. The Danish kitchen-middens seem to have been of about the same date; but what M. Lartet has called the rein-deer period of the south of France was probably anterior, and con-nected with a somewhat colder climate. Of still higher antiquity was that age of ruder implements of stone such as were buried in the fluviatile drift of Amiens and Abbeville, and which were mingled in the same gravel with the bones of extinct quadrupeds, such as the ele-phant, rhinoceros, bear, tiger, and hyena. Between the present era and that of those earliest vestiges yet discovered of our race, valleys have been deepened and widened, the course of subterranean rivers which once flowed through caverns has been changed, and many species of wild quadrupeds have disappeared. The bed of the sea, moreover, has in the same ages been lifted up, in many places hun-dreds of feet above its former level, and the outlines of many a coast entirely altered.

MM. de Verneuil and Lartet have recently found, near Madrid, fossil teeth of the African elephant, in old valley-drift, containing flint implements of the same antique type as those of Amiens and Abbe-ville. Proof of the same elephant having inhabited Sicily in the Post-pliocene and probably within the Human period had previously been brought to light by Baron Anca, during his exploration of the bone-caves of Palermo. We have now, therefore, evidence of man having coexisted in Europe with three species of elephant, two of them ex-tinct (namely, the mammoth and the *Elephas antiquus*), and a third the same as that which still survives in Africa. As to the first of these,—the mammoth,—I am aware that some writers contend that it could not have died out many tens of thousands of years before our time, because its flesh has been found preserved in ice, in Siberia, in so fresh a state as to serve as food for dogs, bears, and wolves; but this argument seems to me fallacious. Middendorf in 1843, after digging through some thickness of frozen soil in Siberia, came down upon an icy mass, in which the carcass of a mammoth was imbedded, so perfect that, among other parts, the pupil of its eye was taken out, and is now preserved in the Museum of Moscow. No one will deny that this elephant had lain for several thousand years in its icy en-velop; and if it had been left undisturbed, and the cold had gone on increasing, for myriads of centuries, we might reasonably expect that the frozen flesh might continue undecayed until a second glacial period had passed away.

When speculations on the long series of events which occurred in the glacial and postglacial periods are indulged in, the imagination is apt to take alarm at the immensity of the time required to interpret the monuments of these ages, all referable to the era of existing species. In order to abridge the number of centuries which would otherwise be indispensable, a disposition is shown by many to mag-nify the rate of change in prehistoric times, by investing the causes which have modified the animate and inanimate world with extraor-dinary and excessive energy. It is related of a great Irish orator of our day, that when he was about to contribute somewhat parsimoni-ously towards a public charity, he was persuaded by a friend to make a more liberal donation. In doing so he apologized for his first ap-parent want of generosity, by saying that his early life had been a constant struggle with scanty means, and that "they who are born to

21*

affluence cannot easily imagine how long a time it takes to get the chill of poverty out of one's bones." In like manner, we of the living generation, when called upon to make grants of thousands of centuries in order to explain the events of what is called the modern period, shrink naturally at first from making what seems so lavish an expenditure of past time. Throughout our early education we have been accustomed to such strict economy in all that relates to the chronology of the earth and its inhabitants in remote ages, so fettered have we been by old traditional beliefs, that even when our reason is convinced, and we are persuaded that we ought to make more liberal grants of time to the geologist, we feel how hard it is to get the chill of poverty out of our bones.

Recent Changes in Geological Opinions.—I will now briefly allude, in conclusion, to two points on which a gradual change of opinion has been taking place among geologists of late years. First, as to whether there has been a continuous succession of events in the organic and inorganic worlds, uninterrupted by violent and general catastrophes; and, secondly, whether clear evidence can be obtained of a period antecedent to the creation of organic beings on the earth. I am old enough to remember when geologists dogmatized on both these questions in a manner very different from that in which they would now venture to indulge. I believe that by far the greater number now incline to opposite views from those which were once most commonly entertained. On the first point it is worthy of remark that, although a belief in sudden and general convulsions has been losing ground, as also the doctrine of abrupt transitions from one set of species of animals and plants to another of a very different type, yet the whole series of the records which have been handed down to us are now more than ever regarded as fragmentary. They ought to be looked upon as more perfect, because numerous gaps have been filled up, and in the formations newly intercalated in the series we have found many missing links and various intermediate gradations between the nearest allied forms previously known in the animal and vegetable worlds. Yet the whole body of monuments which we are endeavoring to decipher appears more defective than before. For my own part, I agree with Mr. Darwin, in considering them as a mere fraction of those which have once existed, while no approach to a perfect series was ever formed originally, it having never been part of the plan of nature to leave a complete record of all her works and operations for the enlightenment of rational beings who might study them in after ages.

In reference to the other great question, of the earliest date of vital phenomena on this planet, the late discoveries in Canada have at least demonstrated that certain theories founded in Europe on mere negative evidence were altogether delusive. In the course of a geological survey, carried on under the able direction of Sir William E. Logan, it has been shown that northward of the River St. Lawrence there is a vast series of stratified and crystalline rocks of gneiss, mica-schist, quartzite, and limestone, about 40,000 feet in thickness, which have been called Laurentian. They are more ancient than the oldest fossiliferous strata of Europe, or those to which the term primordial had been rashly assigned. In the first place, the newest part of this great crystalline series is unconformable to the ancient fossiliferous or so-called primordial rocks which overlie it; so that it must have undergone disturbing movements before the latter or primordial set was formed. Then again, the older half of the Laurentian series is unconformable to the newer portion of the same. It is in this lowest and most ancient system of crystalline strata that a limestone, about 1,000 feet thick, has been observed, containing organic remains. These fossils have been examined by Dr. Dawson, of Montreal, and he has detected in them by aid of the microscope, the distinct structure of a large species of Rhizopod. Fine specimens of this fossil, called *Eozoon Canadense*, have been brought to Bath by Sir William Logan, to be exhibited to the members of the Association. We have every reason to suppose that the rocks in which these animal remains are included are of as old a date as any of the formations named Azoic in Europe, if not older, so that they precede in date rocks once supposed to have been formed before any organic beings had been created.

But I will not venture on speculations respecting "the signs of a beginning," or "the prospects of an end," of our terrestrial system,—that wide ocean of scientific conjecture on which so many theorists before my time have suffered shipwreck.

NEW FACTS RESPECTING THE ANTIQUITY OF MAN.

The search for evidence respecting the antiquity and prehistoric condition of the human race, is still prosecuted by the geologists and naturalists of Europe with the greatest zeal; and new facts of the utmost geologic and historic interest are constantly being brought to light, as the result of their researches. From the record of the past year, we have prepared the following summary of the most recent discoveries.

Cave of Bruniquel, France.—In the summer of 1863 there was opened on the estate of the Vicomte St. Jal, at Bruniquel, in the department of *Tarn et Garonne*, a cave, from which the proprietor obtained numerous specimens of remains of animals, flint instruments, bone implements, fashioned and carved by means of the flint-knives, and finally what the Vicomte believed to be human remains, all imbedded in the *breccia*.

M. St. Jal at once communicated his discovery to the French Government, and proposed a sale of the cave and contents. His communication being treated with neglect, he next applied to the British Museum. The latter was referred to Prof. Owen, who perceiving the possible value of this discovery, at once started off, and in January, 1864, personally visited the locality. After inspecting the cave and satisfying himself of its paleontological value he returned to England; and by his advice the right of exploring the cavern, with all its contents, was at once bought by the Trustees of the Museum.

Meantime, however, a somewhat curious episode occurred. The visit of Professor Owen appears to have stimulated the French authorities, and Professors Milne-Edwards and Lartet were despatched on a commission of inspection. They also recognized the value of the discovery, and presently an offer was made from the French government slightly outbidding that which Professor Owen had made, under the necessary reserve of approval by the British Museum trustees.

M. St. Jal, however, honorably adhered to his first bargain, and subsequently the contents of the cave, were exhumed and removed to London. They are understood to embrace some 1,500 fossil specimens, many of them still imbedded in the calcified mud, in which they were found beneath a coating of stalagmite. The cavern is in a Jurassic limestone, and the soil found in it is formed by the superposition of several layers, viz : first, a stalagmite deposit ; then an osseous breccia ; then black clay beds repeated several times, in the midst of which was a *pell mell* of wrought flints of all known shapes ; barbed arrow-points ; bones of carnivores, ruminants, and birds, and rounded pebbles. Mingled with these were the bones of man. About 80 per cent of the animal bones found were those of the reindeer, an animal which has not been known within the historic period south of the northern shores of the Baltic. There were besides, the bones of two species of extinct deer, a few remains of the red deer, the extinct *Bos primigenius*, the *Rhinoceros tichorinus*, and the humerus of a big bird, on which was roughly sculptured different parts of a fish. This seems to have been an amulet or ornament. Some of the other bones also were rudely carved, while most of them bear marks of having been fractured for the purpose of getting at the marrow, or making them into weapons or instruments.

At a meeting of the Royal Society, June, 1864, Prof. Owen minutely described the circumstances under which these discoveries were made, and stated that the contemporaneity of the human remains with those of the extinct and other animals with which they were associated, together with the flint and bone implements, was proved by the evidence of the plastic condition of the calcified mud of the breccia at the time of interment, by the chemical constitution of the human bones, corresponding with that of the other animal remains, and by the similarity of their position and relations in the surrounding breccia. Among the principal remains of the men of the flint period discovered in this cave he described the following :—

The hinder portion of a cranium, with several other parts of the same skeleton, which were so situated in their matrix as to indicate that the body had been interred in a crouching posture, and that, after the decomposition and dissolution of the soft parts, the skeleton had yielded to the superincumbent weight ; 2. An almost entire calvarium, which was described and compared with different types of the human skull, and which Prof. Owen showed was superior in form and capacity to the Australian type, and more closely to correspond with the Celtic type, though proportionally shorter than the modern Celtic and the form exhibited by the Celtic cranium from Engis, Switzerland ; 3. Jaws and teeth of individuals of different ages.

After noticing other smaller portions of human crania, the lower jaw and teeth of an adult, the upper and lower jaws of immature individuals were described, the characters of certain deciduous teeth being referred to. The proportions of the molars are not those of the Australian, but of other races, and especially those of ancient and modern Europeans. As in most primitive or early races in which mastication was little helped by arts of cookery, or by various and refined kinds of food, the crowns of the molars, are worn down, beyond the enamel, flat and smooth to the stumps, exposing there a central tract of osteodentine without any signs of decay.

It would thus appear that the human remains from the Bruniquel cave stand high in the scale of organization, and do not exhibit the features of an inferior or transitional type.

Exploration of Caverns in the Province of Périgord, France.— Within a comparatively recent period the existence of certain caves, rich in fossil remains, has been ascertained in the Province of Périgord, France. They occur chiefly on the banks of tributaries of the river Dordogne (which reaches the sea a little north of Bordeaux). During the past year one of these caverns, namely, that of Eyzies, was bought by Messrs. Lartet and Christy, the well-known geologists, and carefully explored.

These gentlemen divided the floor of the cave into compartments, and, with a generosity worthy of all praise, they have sent specimens of the blocks thus obtained, weighing 500 lbs. and upwards to the principal museums in Europe.

The floor of this cavern was found to consist of a compact mass of earth, charcoal, flint weapons and tools, bones, needles, &c. which have been hardened into a solid agglomerate, chiefly by the action of the calcareous droppings from the roof of the cave. This agglomerate, or breccia, as it is technically styled, formed an artificial floor to the cave of various thicknesses, from three inches to ten inches. In fact, the evidence seems complete that the cave in question was for many years the abode of an ancient people, who were accustomed to throw down, or leave upon the floor, the bones and other remnants of their feasts, very much in the manner of the Esquimaux and other savages of the present day. With these, weapons and industrial implements naturally became mingled. The animal bones found, were, as in the cave of Bruniquel, principally those of the reindeer.

At some period subsequent to the human occupancy of the cavern a flood has rushed through it, bringing in its course, and leaving in the cave, a number of boulder stones. These have been fixed to the artificial floor of breccia by the slow but unfailing mason,— the droppings from the chalk strata overhead.

Messrs. Lartet and Christy from their explorations of this cave announce the following conclusions : That a variety of the human race inhabited the caves in the region since called Périgord at the same time as the reindeer, the aurochs, and other animals which are now only found in extreme latitudes ; that this people had no knowledge of the use of metals, their only arms and tools being either of broken and unpolished flints, or of bones or horns of animals ; that they lived upon the produce of the chase and by fishing ; that they had no domesticated animal, neither dog nor cat, else some portions of the bones and sinews that have been found would have been gnawed, and some remains of the dog would have been discovered ; and that they were clothed in skins, which were sewn with bone needles and string made out of the sinews and tendons of the legs of their prey.

Exploration of a Cavern containing the Remains of Man and extinct Animals in the Pyrenees.—During the past year also Messrs. Garrigou and Martin, two French naturalists have published the result of their exploration of a cavern called *Espélugues*, situated in the Commune of Lourdes and the department of the *Hautes Pyrenees.* From their report we derive the following particulars :—

"Within the cavern, toward the entrance of the great hall, there are great numbers of large blocks of limestone lying together upon a bed of rounded stones. Among these blocks, and especially at their base, are heaps of cinders and charcoal, some fragments of which occur at different places in the general deposit of the cavern. Bones, jaws, and teeth of different Mammals were obtained, especially from the lower part of the deposit. The surface layers of the deposit, afforded us only rare fragments, and these, before commencing our second day's examination, we carefully laid aside for separate study. Quantities of cut flints, bones, and horns of various stags, worked and shaped into the form of instruments and weapons, and some carved bones, lay in confusion along with the ashes and coal.

"We will first describe the relics in the upper layer, examined by us, and then those of the lower strata."

Upper Layer.—Remains of the fox, horse, wild boar, stag, chamois, wild goat (Bouquetin), reindeer, aurochs, ox, mole, field mouse, and birds; also of a goat larger than the chamois, and a sheep of the size of a goat.

The bones of all these animals are broken like those of the Kjoekkenmodding of Denmark and of the lake habitations of Switzerland.

"Among these paleontological fragments, some, on careful examination, led us to infer that the domestication of certain animals had been in practice during the period under consideration. Among the broken bones of the surface, some had evidently been attacked by Rodents. Near by were others bearing marks of the teeth of a Carnivore (a dog, beyond doubt). Among the debris we collected, twenty centimeters below the surface, a small fragment of a rib of a Ruminant, bearing a sculptured design of fine finish, and differing in this respect from objects of the same kind found at Bruniquel."

Lower Layers.—The list of animals found in the lower beds of this cavern differ a little from the preceding. We notice the horse, the common stag, the reindeer, the aurochs, an ox somewhat smaller than the aurochs, a large sheep, two Rodents, and some bones of birds. The teeth of the horse are more abundant than those of the ox or the reindeer; but the bones of the reindeer are more numerous than those of the other Ruminants. All these bones were broken. In character and appearance the bones of the upper or surface layer differ materially from those of the lower stratum. The former are grayish white, while the latter are colored red. The former do not adhere to the tongue, and evidently contain gelatin, while the latter adhere to the tongue and contain no gelatin. In order to be sure as to the gelatin, we burned two fragments of bone on live charcoal; that taken from the surface afforded almost immediately an insupportable empyreumatic odor, and the other, taken from below, no odor at all.

Throughout the extent of the bed examined by us, even to the rolled pebbles at the surface, there are found, along with the bones, wrought flints, and also instruments and tools made of the horns of the reindeer and common stag, and of bone. More than 400 flints, most of them wrought, and coarsely so, were turned out. These may be classified as follows: (1) Knives; (2) scrapers; (3) arrow-heads roughly hewn, and sometimes having the lower extremity long for attachment to a handle; (4) wrought hatchets of small size, but of the same form with those from the diluvium of Abbeville and Amiens; (5) fragments of flint which were chipped from the instruments here described. More than 24 objects of stag horn, of reindeer horn and of wrought bones, and also one bone very coarsely sculptured, rewarded our excavations in the lower beds. The sculptured bone represents, as nearly as we can judge, a fish with ventral fins and a divided tail. The skill of the artist was inferior to that in the case before mentioned.

It appears evident to us that the inhabitants contemporary with the inferior deposits of Lourdes, had a degree of civilization nearly equal to, and yet a little below, that of the occupants of the caverns of Périgord, Bruniquel, etc.

From a review of the facts, it is plain that the age of the upper layers of the deposit in the cavern of Lourdes is not the same as that of the lower. We conclude from the presence of the Aurochs, the existence of domestic animals, the discovery of bones gnawed by dogs, the almost complete preservation of the gelatin in the bones, and their deeper color, and by the discovery of a bone finely sculptured, that the upper beds belong to an age more recent than that of the lower beds. This we would call the age of the Aurochs, with which man was contemporary. As to the lower beds, it is evident to us, from the abundant remains of the reindeer, including large quantities of its horns; from the coarseness of its wrought objects, its worked flints, and its sculpture; from the reddish brown color of the bones, and from the absence of gelatin and their adhering to the tongue, that they pertain to an epoch more ancient than the preceding. It was the age of the reindeer.

The cave of Lourdes has thus afforded the first example of the direct superposition of the beds of the two consecutive paleontological epochs of the Quaternary or Post-tertiary period.

Human Fossils from Gibraltar.—During the past year, as the result of the exploration of certain caves and fissures at Gibraltar, there has been obtained a collection of human fossils, of the most interesting and remarkable character. From two collections of cavern-breccia, forwarded to England, nearly 400 fragments of skulls have been obtained, all presenting signs of very ancient fracture, besides numerous jaw-bones. Most of these cranial fragments are too small to admit of complete cranial restoration; but Mr. Busk, the naturalist, who has the collection in charge, is of the opinion that the lower jaws may be referred to two distinct types of race. "This opinion," he says, "is strengthened by the circumstance that some of the other bones of the skeletons present very remarkable distinctive characters. Thus, among the numerous leg and thigh bones, belonging apparently to some 35 individuals, are many so singular, and as it may almost be said so monstrous in their form, as to have excited the astonishment of all anatomists who have beheld them.

Subsequently, and later in the year, the other collections of bones were received in England, obtained from the so-called Sir James Cochrane's cave at Gibraltar. Included in the first collection, was one quite perfect human cranium, except that the lower jaw properly belonging to it has been replaced by one of a different individual.

" This skull," says Mr. Busk, "as were most of the bones with which it was accompanied, was encased in a very hard gray stalagmitic crust, in some parts several inches thick, and evidently the result of very long and slow deposition. But when this was removed, the bone stood out as fresh to all appearance as if it had been carefully macerated and cleaned. It is a small, roundish, symmetrical cranium; but we have not yet so critically compared it as to allow of any definite opinion being given on the present occasion as to its nearest probable affinities. In one respect it is of extreme interest, from its being associated with several leg bones presenting the peculiar compressed form above adverted to, and among which one, from the condition of the bone itself and the exact similarity of the calcareous incrustation upon it, most probably belongs to the same individual. We thus appear to be furnished with a clue to the cranial conformation of the ' sharp-shinned ' or *platycnemic* race,—a point of considerable importance."

In the second collection, there were besides several quadrupedal bones the greater part of a human cranium, and a lower jaw not belonging to it. " This cranium," says Mr. Busk, " resembles in all essential particulars, including its great thickness, the far-famed Neanderthal skull; but, in many respects, it is of infinitely higher value than that much-disputed relic, inasmuch as it retains the entire occipital region including the hinder margin of foramen magnum, great part of the base, the whole of one temporal bone (thus giving the precise situation of the auditory opening), and nearly the entire face, including the upper jaw, with most of the much and curiously-worn teeth. As it is precisely these parts that are wanting in the Neanderthal calvarium, of which the present is, in other respects, almost an exact counterpart, the value of this cranium in the study of priscan man can not be rated too high. Its discovery also adds immensely to the scientific value of the Neanderthal specimen, if only as showing that the latter does not represent, as many have hitherto supposed, a mere individual peculiarity, but that it may have been characteristic of a race extending from the Rhine to the Pillars of Hercules. The animal bones associated with this skull, though not themselves of an extinct species, yet belong to one (*Ibex*) whose remains occur very abundantly throughout the Rock in the oldest breccia, in which are also contained those of at least one, if not of two, wholly extinct species of Rhinoceros, and of several other animals which are extinct so far as Europe is concerned."

Further Human Remains from Abbeville, France.—The alleged discovery in 1863, by M. Perthes, of a portion of a human jaw-bone, in a gravel bed (probably belonging to the drift period), and located near Abbeville, France, at a quarry known as " Moulin-Quignon," has, as our readers are doubtless well aware, excited much discussion among scientists and theologians, both in Europe and this country (see *Annual of Scientific Discovery*, 1864, p. 232). The discussions have also invested the quarry in question with great interest; and a sharp lookout has been kept ever since by naturalists in the hope of further discoveries. This hope has been at last realized. On April 24, 1864, M. Perthes and Dr. Dubois of Abbeville, found in one of the quarry beds, a portion of a human sacrum, fragments of a cranium, and human molar teeth; on the 1st of May they obtained, on digging, further remains;

and on the 11th of May, the party of exploration being increased, they turned out from a depth of about 14 feet, a human jaw-bone, nearly perfect with other bones and some cut flints. On the 7th of June, the Abbé Martin, Professor of Geology at the Seminary of St. Riquier, continued the diggings and took out from a drift bed, at a place which showed plainly by its regular stratification, that it had not been disturbed since its original deposition, a *human cranium*, the frontal bone and the parietal of which were nearly entire, and also two fragments of an upper jaw.

The number of specimens of bones thus collected from the Abbeville beds during the past year amounts to 200, and they were all found within an extent of about 130 feet. Part of these are of animals. The human remains apparently indicate a very small race of men.

Discovery of an Ancient Factory of Flint Implements.—During the past year there has been discovered near Pressigny, in the Department of *Indre-et-Loire*, in France, an ancient manufacturing place of flint implements, exceeding in interest and importance any thing of the kind before known. In a letter read to the French Academy by the Abbé Chevalier, detailing this discovery, the writer says:—

All the flint implements lie in vast quantities on the very surface of the ground; there is no walking a step without treading upon one of them. They consist of cut nuclei, tomahawks, hatchets, knives from five to six inches in length, spear heads, scrapers, and vast quantities of chips of silicious stones. They are so numerous that ploughmen, when they find them lying in front of the ploughshare, pick them up and throw them in heaps on the borders of the field. The ground has an extent of about 15 acres, and the Abbé considers the discoveries at Abbeville to be quite insignificant compared with these. A few of the articles are polished. Dr. Leueillé, the physician of the place, has had the good fortune to find a hatchet-polisher consisting of a block of sandstone about 18 inches by 12, with numerous furrows, into which the hatchets used to be inserted for the purpose of sharpening or polishing them by friction, after being previously hewn into shape.

A writer in *Galignani*, commenting on this discovery says: The question involuntarily presents itself, how it is possible that such a rich field of exploration should have remained unnoticed for so long a period, and whether the very abundance of these flint implements is not sufficient to cast a doubt upon their antiquity. The fact of flint implements having lain for thousands of years on the surface of a field, without being either noticed or picked up, or washed away or buried by the action of violent rains, is certainly much more wonderful, not to say improbable, than any of the late singular discoveries made in caverns or at certain depths below the surface of the soil.

Discovery of Fossil Stone Implements in India.—At a recent meeting of the Royal Asiatic Society of Bengal, Prof. Oldham exhibited a small collection of stone implements which had very recently been discovered by Messrs. King and Foote, of the Geological Survey of India, near Madras. These were all of the ruder forms, so well known as characterizing the flint implements which have excited so much attention within the last few years in Europe. They were all formed of dense semivitreous quartzite,—a rock which occurred in immense abundance in districts close to where these implements had

25

been found, and which formed a very good substitute for the flints of north Europe. This was the first instance in which, so far as he knew, such stone implements had been found in India *in situ*. True celts, of a totally different type and much higher finish, and in every respect identical with those found in Scotland and Ireland, had been met with in large numbers in Central India, but never actually imbedded in any deposits. They were invariably found under holy trees or in sacred places, and were objects of reverence and worship to the people, who could give no information as to the source from which they had been originally gathered together.

Those now on the table had been collected partly by himself, from a ferruginous lateritic gravel-bed, which extended irregularly over a very large area west of Madras. In places, this was at least fifteen feet below the surface, cut through by streams, and in one such place, from which some of the specimens on the table were procured, there stood an old ruined pagoda on the surface, evidencing that, at least at the time of its construction, that surface was a permanent one. This bed of gravel was in many places exposed on the surface, and had been partially denuded; and it was in such localities, where these implements had been washed out of the bed, and lay strewed on the surface, that they were found most plentifully.

Mr. Oldham remarked on the great interest attaching to such a discovery, and on the probable age of the deposit in which they occurred. Another point of interest connected with the history of such implements was the remarkable fact that while, scattered in abundance over the districts where they occurred, were noble remains of what would by many be called Druidical character-circles of large standing stones, cromlechs, kistvaens, often of large size and well preserved, all of which were traditionally referred to the Karumbers, a race of which there yet existed traces in the hills, still, all the weapons and implements of every kind found in these stone structures, were invariably of iron. No information whatever regarding these stone implements could be obtained from the peasantry, who had been quite unaware of their existence.— *Jour. of the Asiatic Society of Bengal.*

Human Fossils from Brazil.— Dr. Lund, a Danish naturalist, has recently published an account of cave explorations in Brazil. He states, that he found human fossils in eight different localities, all bearing marks of geological antiquity, intermixed with those of numerous extinct animals. In the province of Minas Geras he found human skeletons among the remains of 44 species of extinct animals, among which was a fossil horse. In a cave on the borders of a lake called Lago Santa, he again collected multifarious human bones in the same condition as those of the extinct animals, and he considers that their geological relations unite to prove that they were entombed in their present position long before the formation of the lake on whose borders the cave is situated; leaving thus no doubt of their coexistence in life and their association in death. With regard to the race to which these human fossils belong, Dr. Lund observes that the form of the skull differs in no respect from the acknowledged American type.

New Discoveries respecting the Ancient Lake Habitations of Eu-

rope.—During the past year the remains of ancient lake-habitations, similar to those heretofore discovered in Switzerland, have been found in Bavaria and Moravia. In a considerable number of lakes the piles upon which the ancient population erected their habitations are distinctly preserved; associated with fragments of rude pottery, and bones of the horse, the stag, the ox, the wild boar, and the wolf. Most of the bones have been broken, evidently for the purpose of extracting the marrow.

At Olmütz in Moravia, Prof. Jeitteles has succeeded in discovering traces of most ancient human settlements with numerous remains of animals no longer in existence. In laying pipes across a "moor"-bed, the workmen found numerous bones, teeth, and jaws of animals, together with objects of human industry in bone, stone, bronze, and iron. Gigantic teeth of the wild boar, numerous remains of the domestic pig, bones and teeth of the ur, and the domestic ox, of the old horse, stags, roes, and other ruminating animals, of the dog, and of many other big and small wild and domestic animals were dug up. The bones of the horse belong to all appearance to the extinct species of the *Equus angustidens;* the lower jaw is distinguished by two enormous corner teeth. As to the dog, the two halves of the lower jaw which were found, agree exactly in their dimensions with the proportions, stated by Rütimeyer, of the race of dogs which then lived in Switzerland. Perhaps we have here the original form of the great variety in the dog species now extant. Most of the tubular bones were split open longwise.

Prehistoric Remains from Scotland.— At a meeting of the Anthropological Society (London), Dec. 4, an interesting account was given by Mr. Laing of the exploration of some shell mounds on the coast of Scotland, near Caithness. The interesting features of these mounds, were, he said, that they resemble the "kjökkenmöddings" of Denmark, which consists of heaps of shells and bones, the refuse of the food of the men who are supposed to have lived in the prehistoric period. (For the description of the "kjökkenmöddings," see *Annual of Sci. Discovery,* 1861 and 1862.) Five mounds were opened and explored, and the results showed that the heaps had been accumulated at different periods. In the lowest stratum were found mingled with the shells of limpets and periwinkles, which appear to have constituted the principal articles of food of these ancient people, some bones of oxen, of horses and pigs, and stone implements of the rudest possible kind. Specimens were also found of the bones of a bird that has long been extinct. In continuing his explorations, Mr. Laing came to some kists consisting of slabs of stone just large enough to hold the body of a man, and inside, covered with sand, he discovered the skeletons of those who had been interred. Most of them were very short, not being more than 5 ft. 4 in. long, and in those kists no implements of any kind were found; but in two instances he discovered kists of a much larger size, the skeletons in which measured 6 ft. and 6 ft. 4 in. These were presumed to have been the chiefs of the race, and buried with one of them were fifteen stone implements, of small size and of the rudest character, exhibiting a lower degree of Art than the flint implements found with the bones of extinct animals in tertiary geological deposits. Several of

the skulls were exhibited on the table.   Mr. Laing said that the skulls
of the chieftains presented little difference from those of ancient
British skulls, but the others appeared to be of a lower type, and to
resemble, in some particulars, the skulls of negroes.   Among the
shells and bones found in the middens, there were two human jaw-
bones, one of which was the jaw-bone of a child about five years old,
which bore the marks of having been gnawed, indicating that the
child had been eaten.

Prof. Owen said the skulls differed in several essential particulars
from the form of the Ethiopian skull ; one of them might be mistaken,
from part of its configuration, for that of a negro, but the small size
of the molar teeth, the angle at which the nasal bones joined each
other, and the extent to which the parietal and alisphenoid joined,
showed that it was of a different type.   With respect to the jaw-bone
of the child, he observed that he was well acquainted with the marks
made by savages on the jaws of animals they devoured as food, and he
feared the evidence which the child's jaw afforded tended to prove
that our progenitors who inhabited Scotland at a remote period must
have been cannibals.   The dental cavity is filled with nerve pulp,
which savages relish, and the child's jaw-bone indicated that it had
been broken to extract that substance.

The Chronology of the last Geological Epoch.—The Swiss naturalists, geologists, and antiquarians have recently endeavored to make
some calculations respecting the chronology of the periods of the last
geological epoch, of which various dates have been obtained. M. Gillie-
son of Neuveville (on the Lake of Bienne), has communicated to the
Helvetic Society for Natural Philosophy at Lausanne, his geologico-
archæological researches on the marshy region situated between the
lakes of Neuchatel and Bienne, and made a chronological computation,
giving to the ancient pilework or lake-dwelling near Pont-de-Thielle,
an antiquity of about $67\frac{1}{2}$ centuries, the establishment belonging according to its remains of animals and to its other relics, to the oldest
settlements of the stone-age known in Switzerland.

All round the lake of Geneva there is to be seen a threefold system
of diluvial cones or deltas, the edges of which, turned towards the
lake, constitute a threefold séries of steps or terraces, at regular
hights of about 50, 100, and 150 feet above the present level of the
lake.   When circumstances have been favorable for their preservation,
we find all the three diluvial cones situated behind and above the
other, at the mouth of the same watercourse which formed them successively, when the lake stood first about 150, then about 100, and
lastly about 50 feet above its modern level.   Now these diluvial cones,
says M. Morlot, are posterior to the last glacial period, for they are
formed, in great part, of reworked erratic matter, and they show on
their surface no trace of erratic deposit, whilst they can frequently be
seen distinctly overlying the glacial formation.   It is the gravel-beds
of those post-glacial cones which have disclosed, near Morges on the
lake of Geneva, teeth of the *Elephas primigenius.*

From an examination of these and other evidences, M. Morlot
shows that the succession of events in the recent geological epoch has
been substantially as follows : first, a glacial period ; then a first diluvial period, without great glaciers ; then a second glacial period, of

long duration ; then a second diluvial period, without great glaciers, and to which the diluvial cones belong ; then, lastly, the modern period represented by the modern cone or delta. This succession of events, in the opinion of M. Morlot, establishes a duration of about 1,000 centuries at least for the last geological epoch, which began immediately after the retreat of the last great glaciers, which was characterized by the presence of the *Elephas primigenius* and by the appearance of man, and which ended at the beginning of the modern period, the latter having already lasted, in his opinion, about 100 centuries.

FACTS ABOUT PETROLEUM.

The development of the business of obtaining petroleum in this country has progressed during the past year with wonderful rapidity ; so much so indeed that the business itself is now recognized as one of the greatest and most lucrative branches of American industry. Respecting the origin of the petroleum, its geological relations, and its industrial applications and treatment, few facts additional to those already given in the previous volumes of the *Annual of Scientific Discovery* have been made known. Many new localities productive of oil have, however, been discovered ; and it is the opinion of some geologists who have given the subject attention, that the geographical area covered by oil-bearing rocks on the North American Continent east of the Mississippi, cannot be less than 200,000 square miles. Springs yielding petroleum in immense quantities are also reported by Prof. Silliman and others, as existing upon the Pacific coast.

We derive the following particulars respecting the present production of petroleum in the oil-districts of Pennsylvania, mainly from the correspondence of the *New York World :* —

The average depth at which oil is found by boring is from 550 to 600 feet ; in some instances, however, the wells exceed 700 feet in depth. Oil is not always obtained at once, but many of the best wells have to be pumped for days or weeks, before they commence flowing. All flowing wells, moreover, do not flow continuously, and some of the phenomena presented are highly interesting. Thus, for example, the so-called " Yankee Well " located on Cherry Run, was sunk in July, 1864, and is 606 feet deep. After being pumped two weeks, the well yielded, by pumping, from ten to twenty barrels per day. Afterwards, just as the workmen had started to pull the tubing for the purpose of improving it, oil commenced to flow without pumping, at the rate of thirty-five barrels, increasing at last to fifty barrels per day. The flow is spasmodic, lasting from five to seven minutes. The time of flow and the interval of quiet rarely vary over one or two minutes, then ceasing for about 20 minutes.

Another well, the " Gruniger," in the same district, 600 feet deep, first yielded, in September, 1864, by pumping, fifty barrels per day. It subsequently began flowing without the aid of a pump, from fifty to sixty barrels, increasing gradually to a hundred and fifty barrels per day. It is now flowing about a hundred barrels, the flow being also spasmodic, from three to five minutes duration, commencing every twelve minutes. Other wells flow once in a half hour, and some only once and for a short period in several days.

The following is a summary of the result of operations in February,

1865, in the district of Oil Creek, one of the most productive of the Pennsylvania oil localities, and embracing an area of 3,324 acres.

No. of wells down	480
No. of wells producing	189
Average daily yield, bbls.	4,325
No. of wells to be put down	542

The most noticeable aspect of an oil well are a derrick, an engine house, and many big tanks,—all very brown and oily, and all emitting an odor which, at first repulsive, is afterwards bearable, and at last becomes rather pleasant than otherwise. It the well is a pumping-well, the rattle of the engine and machinery drowns that charm which, in a flowing well, entrances the ear of the listener, viz: the luscious, spontaneous flow of the oil. An iron pipe trained from the derrick to the tank near by, conducts and delivers the precious product. Out of this pipe with a sound like the "blowing" of a whale, pulsating in greater or lesser volume according to the spasmodic force of the gas below, the brown, rich fluid rushes into tank after tank; plashing the surface of the reservoir into yellow foam, filling the atmosphere with gas that rises and wavers like the heat from a red-hot stove,—night and day unceasing,—a constant tribute of wealth to its owners. The tankage of the wells varies according to their yield. Some have tank-age for three thousand barrels. As these tanks are filled, the oil is drawn off in barrels and shipped.

The history of some of the principal wells along Oil Creek is briefly as follows :—

The "Burned" well, was completed in April, 1861, at a depth of 330 feet. On the afternoon of April 17, while the workmen were engaged in tubing, a stream of oil and gas suddenly lifted the tools out of the well and leaped above the derrick in a continuous and sick-ening volume. The engineer put out his fires, and then, with the rest of the hands, fled from the sickening odor that oppressed the air. A crowd collected, some one in which, approaching too near, suddenly ignited the gas, which went off with a terrific explosion, setting fire, of course, to the stream of oil issuing from the well. The conflagration that ensued, and which continued for four days and nights, finally destroyed the well. The lives of several persons were lost. The well has not yielded any since.

The "Brawley" well, began to flow in the summer of 1861, yielding 600 barrels per day. After flowing a year and a half, the yield began to diminish. It speedily ran down to nothing.

The "Van Slyke" well, "struck oil" in the fall of 1861, at a depth of about 500 feet, and first flowed at the rate of 600 barrels per day. It also gave out in about a year and a half.

The "Big Phillips" well struck oil in October, 1861, at a depth of 480 feet. The estimated quantity of the original flow was from 3,000 to 4,000 barrels per day. The rush of oil was so overwhelming, that it was several days before the well could be tubed; 40,000 or 50,000 barrels of oil were lost in the creek before the workmen finally got control. The well was subsequently (like every other well yielding at this period) not permitted to flow under any thing like full headway. the price of oil being so low as not to pay. The flow began to decrease about the latter part of 1862. In this year another well the "Woodford" was put down near, which tapped the same vein of oil, and assisted in diminishing the flow. The "BigPhillips" is now running at the rate of 325 barrels per day. It is believed to be the only well which began flowing without having been previously tubed.

The "Woodford" well, alluded to above, was originally a 1,500 barrel well. Its yield began to decrease in 1863, and finally ceased. Being resuscitated, it is now pumping 50 barrels per day.

The "Jones" well, put down in the latter part of 1862, within 30 feet of the "Woodford," tapped the same vein, flowing 400 barrels per day. Its flow decreased gradually until the well had to be pumped. It is now doing nothing.

The "Noble" well struck oil in April 1863. Its maximum daily yield was between 1,900 and 2,000 barrels. It flowed six months with undiminished volume, when it began to decrease. It was flowing until the 1st of February 1865 at the rate of 150 to 200 barrels per day, when an accident stopped it. This well is said to have netted its owners over $ 3,000,000.

The "Empire" well was sunk in the fall of 1861, and began flowing from 2,500 to 3,000 barrels per day. The flow continued, diminishing gradually for something over two years, when it stopped. The well lay idle about a year. In the summer of 1864, an air pump was applied, which caused the well to resume flowing lightly,—five or six barrels per day. The flow then slowly increased to 140 barrels. The well is now yielding 110 barrels per day.

Other wells have been partially resuscitated in like manner by the use of an air pump.

The average actual yield of oil in the Pennsylvania oil region is, of course, greatly exaggerated in the estimates and imaginations of most parties who have read of the subject, and heard it talked of in a general way. It is presumed by those who have most closely watched the development of the oil product from the first, that whereas the yield in 1862 was from 10,000 to 12,000 barrels per day, it is now (February, 1865,) not more than 6,000 barrels. It is probable that the former yield even exceeded the amount named, as, during 1862, all the large flowing wells then struck were prevented from running their full quantity, owing to the merely nominal price of and demand for the oil. Now, all the wells in the region are permitted and aided to deliver to their utmost capacity.

This decrease in the yield of a territory where, for more than four years, the number of oil wells has been increasing, appears at the first glance, quite inexplicable upon any other ground than that the supply of oil is becoming exhausted. Some light, however, may be gained on this subject from a brief review of the history of Pennsylvania oil production from the commencement.

The mining of petroleum began as a business in 1860, but did not prove very successful until 1861. The first well was sunk in 1859, near Titusville, Pa. It yielded some eight barrels per day. In the summer of 1861, a number of flowing wells were opened at Oil Creek. The consumption of the article was, however, very small, while the production was suddenly increased from about 150 barrels daily in February to some 2,500 barrels daily in August, and more than 6,000 barrels daily in December of the same year. The spring of 1863 was signalized by a much larger increase. The price of crude oil was reduced from 25 cents to less than one cent per gallon in the same time. But excessive cheapness forced consumption, both in this country and abroad, with unparalleled rapidity, so that, in the latter months of 1862, there occurred a large but spasmodic rise in the value of the oil. The unremunerative prices which had hitherto prevailed checked production, causing all small wells and interests to be abandoned. The year 1863 saw rising, although heavily fluctuating, prices. This state of the market continued, merging into a more even upward graduation of values, through the year 1864, when crude oil sold at one time as high as 13.50 per barrel at the wells.

The large flowing wells have generally stopped after 25 or 30 months' flow. Some few have continued with diminished volume over three years. The pumping wells have averaged about the same duration. In 1863, and until the latter part of 1864, comparatively few new wells were sunk. During this period many wells gave out and many were abandoned. Quite recently, however, it has been ascertained, that by using the air-pump, wells which had ceased to produce oil could be made to resume their yield. This fact is now established. A great many wells that were considered exhausted have been resuscitated, and are now yielding very considerable quantities of oil. The spontaneous flow of oil is undoubtedly due to a pressure of gas evolved from the petroleum greater than the pressure of the atmosphere. When this greater pressure is reduced by exhaustion to an equilibrium with the atmospheric pressure, the flow ceases until artificial pressure is applied or until a fresh accumulation of the gas causes a resumption of the flow.

" It may be safely said, then, that it is, up to this time, not the exhaustion of the oil, but the exhaustion of the gas which elevates the oil, that has produced an embarrassment to oil mining which threatened at one time to hazard its success, but which is now obviated by the application of new and efficient inventions. The many instances in which wells have been resuscitated after apparent failure have led observing oil-producers to believe that good oil lands will yield the article to an indefinite future period."

THE ROCKS IN WHICH PETROLEUM IS FOUND.

Mr. R. P. Stevens, of New York, a geological expert, contributes to the *Scientific American* the following description of the rocks in which petroleum occurs in the North American Continent. The lowest geological horizon, or stratum, in which petroleum is found of commercial importance, is in Canada, at Enniskillen, near Lake St. Clair. The oil is in the corniferous limestone. (New York nomenclature Devonian System), which is largely composed of fragments of corals, with sea shells cemented together. The cavities of these corals and sea shells are often filled with liquid bitumen, which distils from them, as can be seen in the walls of the Second Presbyterian Church, in Chicago. This limestone in the United States is in its maximum about 350 or 400 feet thick. Immediately overlying the limestone is the Marcellus shale, which is so highly charged with bitumen as to lead to great expenditures of time and money in vainly looking for coal in it. It is about 50 feet thick in Canada. These two rock formations, then, which in Canada are not over 150 feet in thickness, are the reservoirs, holding rock oil, however and whenever formed, in that country.

Ascending in the geological scale, and passing over into New York, the next stratum of rock yielding bitumen, oil and gas, is there known as the Hamilton Group, about 1,000 feet thick. The oil springs of Western New York, along the banks of its numerous lakes, are mainly in this group of rocks. They have as yet yielded oil only in small quantities for medicinal purposes. But they afford ample scope and verge for exploration.

Above this group succeed black shales, known as the Genesee Slate, 300 feet thick. The wells of Mecca, Ohio, and others of that region are most probably in this rock. Above the Genesee Slate comes in the Portage Group of slates and sandstones, 1,700 feet thick. The deeper wells of Oil Creek, Pa. will reach the sandstones of this group.

Still above lie the rocks of the Chemung Group, which are mainly composed of thin-bedded slates and limestones. In its maximum it is 3,200 feet thick, but in Western New York and Pennsylvania it is much thinner, being only about 1,000 feet thick. Much of the oil of Oil Creek is from this group; 400 and 500 feet of it are seen in the cliffs and hills of Oil Creek, the Alleghany River, and its tributaries above, and in Venango County.

Measuring the maximum development of all the rocks enumerated we find between the oil of Canada and Venango County, Pa. 6,000 to 7,000 feet of sedimentary rock, all of which bear the appearance of having been deposited in sea water. The entire group of rocks enumerated are known as the Devonian Series in England. The oil springs of Eastern Canada and New Brunswick, along the Gulf of Newfoundland, are in the upper members of this series.

Leaving for the present those portions of the United States where oil has been most successfully found, and before coming into the geological strata of the thick and heavy oils, we have on the eastern flanks of the Appalachian Mountains, in Pennsylvania and Virginia, 5,000 feet of the Catskill group of rocks. (Ponent of Prof. Rogers.) Lapping around the southern outcrop of the coal measures of Tennessee, Kentucky, and Illinois, there are 200 feet of the lower carboniferous and 3,000 feet of the middle carboniferous. (Umbral of Rogers.) A total in the aggregate, as measured in Nova Scotia and the United States, of 1,500 feet. Throughout the whole of the series oil and gas springs are found.

We now come into the true coal measures. These are divided into lower, middle, barren measures and upper, a total of the bituminous portion of 2,500 feet. The lowest member of the coal series caps the highest hills, near the mouth of Oil Creek, and lies about 600 feet above the bed of the creek, or 1,300 feet above the third sand rock, which is the most abundant oil-producing stratum. At the Kiskiminetas, Slippery Rock, Butler Co., Pa., Beaver & Smith's Ferry, oil is in the lower coal measures—800 feet thick. High up the Kiskiminetas and on the Monongahela River, oil is found in the middle coal series 1,000 feet thick. At Marietta, Ohio, and in the oil region around the strata of the upper coal are the productive series.

To conclude, then, oil is found through 24,000 feet of rocks, as measured vertically in the geological scale, and geographically from Nova Scotia to Lake St Clair, and from Virginia to Tennessee River. The geographical area, covered by the oil-bearing group of rocks in the United States, Canada, New Brunswick, and Nova Scotia, cannot be less than 200,000 square miles.

Over this area, wherever oil and gas springs are found, there we may reasonably hope for success in boring deeply for oil. But oil and gas springs are not always sure indications of subterraneous supplies of oil in their immediate vicinity, for the course the fluids may have pursued from deep depths to the surface may have been very tortuous. Neither is the absence of such springs absolute negative proof of oleaginous accumulations beneath, for in many very notable instances, such as the lower portion of Oil Creek, and at Smith's Ferry, on the Ohio River, very copious fountains were struck where no surface signs were visible.

I deduce the following practical and economical conclusions: First, Each widely-separated locality must be governed by its own laws as developed by boring and observation. Second, Each geological horizon or stratum of oil-bearing rock received its supply, not from another, but from causes operating at the time of its own deposition. Third, There is not now any reproduction of oil, but we are drawing from fountains filled of old. Fourth, No stratum of rock is so thoroughly saturated with oil as to form a subterranean sheet or belt of rocks where petroleum is surely to be found, but in frequently isolated cavities, or fissures, at various depths and of various sizes, and containing diverse grades of oils.

THE GEOLOGY OF CALIFORNIA.

From communications made to *Silliman's Journal* by Prof. J. D. Whitney, we derive the following summary of facts developed in the geological survey of California:—

In the mountains of the Sierra Nevada, abundant proofs have been obtained respecting the former existence of glaciers of great magnitude. Thousands of acres of granite retain the most exquisite glacial polish, and the existence of lateral, medial, and terminal moraines is as easily observed as in the Alps at the present day.

Perhaps the most striking result of the survey is the proof of the immense development, on the Pacific side of our continent, of rocks equivalent in age to the Upper Trias of the Alps. It is believed that this formation extends from Mexico to British Columbia: occupying a vast area, although much broken up, interrupted and covered by volcanic and eruptive rocks, and usually much metamorphosed.

Accompanying this Triassic formation in the Sierra Nevada is an extensive development of Jurassic rocks. Enough, however, have been found to justify the assertion that the sedimentary portion of the great metalliferous belt of the Pacific coast of North America is chiefly made up of rocks of Jurassic and Triassic age, with a comparatively small development of carboniferous limestone, and that these two formations are so folded together, broken up, and metamorphosed in the great chain of the Sierra Nevada, that it will be an immense labor, if indeed possible at all, to unravel its detailed structure. While we are fully justified in saying that *a large portion of the auriferous rocks of California consist of metamorphic Triassic and Jurassic strata*, we have not a particle of evidence to uphold the theory that has been so often maintained, that all, or even a portion, of the auriferous slates are older than the carboniferous, not a trace of a Devonian and Silurian fossil ever having been discovered in California, or indeed anywhere to the west of the 116th meridian. On the other hand, we are able to state, referring to the theory of the occurrence of gold being chiefly limited to "Silurian rocks, that this metal occurs in no inconsiderable quantity in metamorphic rocks belonging as high up in the series as the cretaceous.

The cretaceous formation in California is also extensive, and embraces to a great extent the coast ranges of both California and Oregon. The formation, however, so far as known, is represented on the Pacific coast by but a single member,—the upper or white chalk.

In regard to the relative ages of the different mountain chains of the Pacific coast, Prof. Whitney says:—

"There can be no doubt that the chain of the Sierra Nevada is older than the Rocky Mountain chain, or that group of chains or ranges which forms the eastern border of the great mountain region of the western side of the continent. The great mass of the Sierra was uplifted and metamorphosed after the termination of the Jurassic epoch, and prior to the deposition of the Cretaceous, for we find the last-named formation resting horizontally and unaltered on the flanks of the Sierra, all through Central California."

"We have recognized at least three distinct periods of upheaval and metamorphic action in the coast ranges. The main one was at the close of the Cretaceous epoch; the next in importance was after the deposition of the Miocene tertiary,—or, at least, of a group of strata which, for the present, may be referred to that age. The next in age is a system of east and west upheavals, which took place at the close of the Miocene; and the third is one which appears to have commenced during the later Pliocene, and to be still going on.

"It is a very interesting fact that the exterior of the coast ranges —that is to say, the mountains nearest the Pacific—are of earlier date, or older geologically, than the interior ones, or those which border the Sacramento and San Joaquin valleys. This is a repetition on a smaller scale of what has been the course of events in the formation of the whole continent, the exterior lines having been first marked out, and the interior filled up afterwards."

The vast detrital deposits on the flanks of the Sierra Nevada, where hydraulic and tunnel mining operations for gold are carried on, are of tertiary age. It has been assumed that they were of marine origin, but an examination of them has proved to the contrary, as is proved by the fact that, although frequently found to contain impressions of leaves, masses of wood and imperfect coal, and even whole buried forests, as well as the remains of land animals, and occasionally those of fresh water, not a trace of any marine production has ever been found in them.

Again, these detrital deposits are not distributed over the flanks of the Sierra in any such way as they would have been if they were the result of the action of the sea. On the contrary, there is every reason to believe that they consist of materials which have been brought

down from the mountain hights above and deposited in pre-existing
valleys: sometimes in very narrow accumulations, simple beds of
ancient rivers, and at other times in wide lake-like expansions of former watercourses; and this under the action of causes similar to those
now existing, but probably of considerably greater intensity.   The
deposition of detritus, for the most part auriferous, took place during
the later Pliocene epoch, and not as late as the drift or diluvial period,
as is abundantly proved by the character of the remains of plants and
land animals which are imbedded in it.   The deposition of this auriferous detritus was succeeded, throughout the whole extent of the
Sierra Nevada, by a tremendous outbreak of volcanic energy, during
which the auriferous gravel was covered by heavy accumulations of
volcanic sediments, ashes, pumice, and the like, finally winding up by
a general outpouring of lava, which naturally flowed from the summits
of the Sierra through the valleys, into the lake-like expansions, filling
them up and covering over the auriferous gravels, which were to remain for ages, as it were, in a hidden treasure-chamber, concealed
under hundreds of feet in thickness of an almost indestructible material.

The effect of the denudation which has taken place since these
streams of lava flowed down the mountains, has been most extraordinary.   For now, these deposits of gravel and overlying volcanic
materials, instead of occupying the depressions of the surface, are
found forming high plateaux between the present river cañons and
flat-topped ridges, known as "Table mountains," hundreds or even
thousands of feet above the present river beds.   Thus the topography
of the country is exactly the reverse of what it was at the commencement of the present geological epoch: what were once valleys are
now ridges, and the ridges of former times were where the immense cañons of the rivers flowing down the western slope of the
Sierra now are.

The Mammalian remains found in the tunnel and placer diggings of
California seem to belong to two distinct epochs.   The oldest represents the Pliocene, the other the Post-tertiary.   The former are found
under the volcanic beds, the latter in deposits which have been formed
since the period of greatest volcanic activity, and which apparently
belong to the epoch of Man.   For it appears that the facts collected
by this Survey, when fully laid before the public, will justify the assertion *that the mastodon and elephant, whose remains are so widely and
abundantly scattered through California, have been cotemporaneous
with Man in that region.*

The Highest Mountains in the United States.—A reconnoissance of
the Sierra range, between the parallels of 36° and 38°, recently undertaken by Messrs. Brewer, King, and others, shows that this portion
of the State of California, previously unexplored and unknown, contains
the greatest mass of mountains, taking width and average elevation
into consideration, which has yet been discovered within the limits of
the United States, and perhaps on the North American Continent; at
one point, within the field of view of the explorers, there were observed
five mountains of over 14,000 feet elevation; and about 50 peaks
which rose to a hight of over 13,000 feet.   The culminating point
of the Sierra Nevada in this district was, moreover, believed to be not

short of 15,000 feet above the sea level, which is considerably higher than Mt. Shasta, hitherto regarded as the most lofty peak in the United States. Prof. Whitney also states, that it is by no means impossible that some other points of the range are even yet more elevated.

These great mountains lie for the most part between the heads of King's and Kern rivers, somewhat north of the north end of Owen's lake. Between the peaks are vast snow-fields, and also numberless deep lakes, of which the most elevated are frozen. The sides of these mountains are clothed in part with a new, and as yet not named, species of pine, of a peculiar black, or bluish-green color, which color "rather augments than relieves the desolate naked aspect" of the vast masses of granite and snow.

ON THE GLACIAL EPOCH.

The following is the abstract of a lecture recently given on the above subject, before the Royal Institution, by Prof. Frankland. He referred to the fact, that in every part of the globe, indubitable evidences are found of the characteristic grinding and polishing action of ice-masses, and that a recent visit to Norway had led him to devote much attention to the examination of the causes of the formation of these mighty agents ; since modern research has led to the conclusion that the glaciers of the present time were merely the dried-up streamlets of ancient ice-rivers of enormous size, and which have evaded the valleys of the Alps, scooped out the lochs of Scotland, formed the fjords of Norway, and largely contributed features in our own mountain scenery.

Two thousand miles of coast, from Christiana to North Cape, are ice-scarred ; the rocks rarely rising above 700 feet or 800 feet ; and not presenting a sharp, rugged outline, but being polished and smooth to their summits. When, however, the Arctic Circle is approached, the scenery is changed, the hills become mountains, with peaks which have owed their immunity from the abrading influence of ice action entirely to their hight, the lower parts being smooth and polished, while the upper retain a variety of fantastic shapes. Prof. Frankland referred to the following theories, which he considered to be untenable on geological and physical grounds : 1. That the temperature of space is not uniform, and that our solar system sometimes passes through colder regions than at present. 2. That the heat emitted from the sun is subject to variations, and that the glacial epoch occurred during "a cold solar period." 3. That at one time, a different distribution of land and water had rendered the climate of certain localities colder than at present. 4. Karrutz's idea, that at the time of the glacial period the mountains were much higher than at present (Mount Blanc, for instance, was about 20,000 feet), the secondary and tertiary formation having been eroded from their summits during the glacial epoch. Prof. Frankland stated that his own theory, based upon Dr. Tyndall's researches on radiant heat and aqueous vapor, assumed the formation of glaciers to be a true process of distillation, requiring heat as much as cold for its due performance. The great natural apparatus would be the ocean as the "evaporator," the mountains being the "ice-bearers or receivers," and only in a subordinate sense the "condensers," the true "condenser" being the dry air of the upper part of the atmosphere, which permits the free radiation into space, of the heat from the aqueous

26

vapor. This theory was illustrated by experiment, the radiation of heat from aqueous vapor being proved by the galvanometer. Prof. Frankland, at some length, adduced his reasons for believing that this theory took cognizance of the following points in the history of the glacial epoch. 1. That its effects were felt over the entire globe. 2. That it occurred at a geological period. 3. That it was preceded by a period of indefinite duration, in which glacial action was entirely wanting, or very insignificant. 4. That during its continuance, atmospheric precipitation was much greater, and the hight of the snow-line considerably less than at present. 5. That it was followed by a period up to the present time—when glacial action became again insignificant,—the sole cause of the phenomena of the glacial epoch being due to the oceans, then having a higher temperature than now, and when the globe was cooling down, the land cooling more rapidly than the sea. In conclusion, Prof. Frankland expressed his opinion that the moon had also passed through a glacial epoch, and that the valleys, hills, and streaks of its surface (which were shown in a magnified photograph by the electric lamp), were not improbably due to glacial action ; adding, with reference to the apparent desolate condition of the moon, that it is probable " that a liquid ocean can only exist upon the surface of a planet so long as the latter retains a high internal temperature ; that, therefore, the moon becomes a prophetic picture of the ultimate fate awaiting our own earth, when, deprived of an external ocean, and of all but an annual rotation upon its axis, it shall revolve around the sun, an arid, lifeless wilderness, one hemisphere exposed to the perpetual glare of a cloudless sun, the other shrouded in eternal night."

THE INCREASING DESICCATION OF INNER SOUTHERN AFRICA.

A paper on the above subject was read by Mr. J. F. Wilson, at the last meeting of the British Association. A very noticeable fact has of late years attracted the attention of residents in South Africa,—namely, the gradual drying up of large tracts of country in the Trans-Gariep region. The Calabari Desert is gaining in extent, gradually swallowing up large portions of habitable country on its borders. Springs of water have diminished in their flow, and pools,—such as that at Serotli, described by Livingstone,—are now either dry or rapidly becoming so. A long list of springs and pools now gradually drying up was given by the author of the paper. The great change, however, had commenced if we may trust native traditions, long before the advent of Europeans, which are corroborated by the existence of an immense number of stumps and roots of acaciæ in tracts where now not a single living tree is to be seen. In seeking to account for this, it was necessary to dismiss from the mind all idea of cosmical changes or earthquakes, of which no trace is visible in Southern Africa. The causes lie in the physical characteristics of the country and in the customs of the inhabitants. The region drained by the Orange River is naturally arid, from the interposition of the Quathlamba Mountains between it and the Indian Ocean, whence the chief rain-clouds are derived. The prevailing winds are from the northeast. The clouds heavily laden with vapor from the Indian Ocean, are driven over Caffraria, watering these lands luxuriously : but when the moisture-bearing nimbi arrive at the summits of the mountain range which divides Caffraria from the interior country, they are not only deprived already of part of their moisture, but they meet with the rarefied air of the central plains, and consequently rise higher and evaporate into thinner vapor. There are few spots, however, which are wholly destitute of vegetation, and large trees are frequent. There is no district which does not maintain its flocks of wild animals; but the diminution of even one or two inches of rain in the year is most severely felt. The author came to the conclusion, after a careful inquiry into the geological formations of the region and the sources of springs, that much water must lie, throughout wide tracts, deep below the surface of the soil, and that the boring of artesian wells would yield a permanent supply for irrigation. But as a remedy for the growing evil, he laid particular stress on legislative enactments to check reckless felling of timber and burning of pastures, which had long been practised both by the natives and the European colonists.

Sir J. Alexander quoted instances to show how the destruction of trees led to the desiccation of countries, especially in or near the tropical zone. The protection of forests on hillsides, it was shown, had long been part of the policy of the Indian Government. Capt. Jenkins cited, as coming within his own experience, the instance of the arid territory of the Imaum of Muscat, which in a few years, owing to the wise forethought of the Imaum in extensively planting cocoa-nut and date-palms, had much increased in humidity and fertility.

ON A CHANGE IN THE PHYSICAL CONDITION OF A COUNTRY CAUSED BY ANIMALS.

In a paper read before the British Association, 1864,— on the country west of the Rocky Mountains, in British Columbia, along the line of the Thompson River,— by Dr. Cheadle and Viscount Milton, the authors stated, that a great portion of the country to the east of the mountains was noticed to have been completely changed in character by the agency of the beaver, which formerly existed here in enormous numbers. The shallow valleys were formerly traversed by rivers and chains of lakes which, dammed up along their course, at numerous points, by the work of these animals, have become a series of marshes in various stages of consolidation. So complete has this change been, that hardly a stream is found for a distance of 200 miles, with the exception of the large rivers. The animals have thus destroyed, by their own labors, the waters necessary to their existence. In the Thompson and Frazer river valleys, the travelers noticed a series of raised terraces on a grand scale. They were traced for 100 miles along the Thompson, and for about 200 miles along the Frazer river; forming three tiers on each side of the valley, each tier being of the same hight as the corresponding one on the opposite side. The lowest terrace was of great width and presented a perfectly level surface, raised some 30 or 40 feet above the water. The second was seldom more than 100 yards wide, and stood at about 50 or 60 feet above the lower one. The third lay at a hight of 400 or 500 feet above the river on the face of the inaccessible bluffs. They were all perfectly uniform and free from the rocks and boulders which encumber the present bed of the river, being composed of sand, gravel, and shale, the detritus of the neighboring mountains. The explanation of these phenomena is to be sought in the barrier of the lofty cascade chain of mountains, through which the Frazer has pierced a way lower down the valley. At a former period, the valleys of the Frazer and the Thompson seem to have been occupied by a succession of lakes, the cascade ridge then forming a barrier which dammed up this great volume of water. The highest tier of terraces would mark the level at which it then stood. Some geological convulsion caused a rent in the mountain barrier, allowing the waters to escape partially, so as to form a chain of lakes at the level of the middle terraces; and subsequently, after long periods of repose, two other similar disturbances successively deepened the cleft, and drained the waters first to the hight of the lowest terrace, and finally to their present level.

ORGANIC REMAINS IN THE LAURENTIAN ROCKS OF CANADA.

One of the most interesting of recent geological discoveries has been the detection of the remains of a protozoic animal in lower series of the Laurentian rocks of Canada, which are among the oldest of the stratified rocks which have been designated as Azoic (wanting in life). The facts relating to this discovery are substantially as follows :—

The oldest known rocks of North America, composing the Laurentian Mountains in Canada, and the Adirondacks of New York, have been divided into two unconformable groups, which have been called the Upper and Lower Laurentian respectively. In both divisions zones of limestone are known to occur, and three of these zones have been ascertained to belong to the Lower Laurentian. From one of these limestone bands, occurring at the Grand Calumet on the River Ottawa, Mr. J. McCulloch obtained, in 1858, specimens apparently of organic origin, and other specimens have also been obtained from Grenville and Burgess. These specimens consist of alternating layers of calcareous spar, and a magnesian silicate (either serpentine, white pyroxene, phyrallolite, or Loganite),—the latter minerals, instead of replacing the skeleton of the organic form, really filling up the interspaces of the calcareous fossil. Dr. Dawson of Montreal, carefully examined the laminated material, and he found it to consist of the remains of an organism which grew in large sessile patches, increasing at the surface by the addition of successive layers of chambers separated by calcareous laminæ. Slices examined microscopically showed large irregular chambers with numerous rounded extensions, and bounded by walls of variable thickness, which are studded with septal orifices irregularly disposed; the thicker parts of the walls revealed the existence of bundles of fine branching tubuli. Dr. Dawson, therefore, concludes that this ancient organism, to which he gave the name of *Eozoön Canadense*, was a Foraminifer allied to *Carpenteria* by its habits of growth, but of more complex structure, as indicated by the complicated systems of tubuli; it attained an enormous size, and by the aggregation of individuals, assumed the aspect of a coral reef. In a paper read before the (London) Geological Society, Nov. 1864, Dr. Carpenter, the eminent English microscopist and physiologist, corroborated Dr. Dawson's observations on the structure and affinities of *Eozoön*, but stated also that, as he considered the characters furnished by the intimate structure of the shell to be of primary importance, and the plan of growth to have a very subordinate value, he did not hesitate to express his belief in its affinities to *Nummulina.* Mr. Sterry Hunt also stated that the mineral silicates, occurring in the chambers, cells, and canals left vacant by the disappearance of the animal matter of the *Eozoön*, and in many cases even in the tubuli, filling up their smallest ramifications, are a white pyroxene, a pale green serpentine, and a dark green alumino-magnesian mineral, which he referred to Loganite. The calcareous septa in the last case are dolomitic, but in the other instances are composed of nearly pure carbonate of lime. Mr. Hunt then showed that the various silicates already mentioned were directly deposited in waters in the midst of which the *Eozoön* was still growing or had only recently perished, and that they penetrated, enclosed, and preserved the structure of the organisms precisely as carbonate of lime might have done; and he cites these and other facts in support of his opinion that these silicated minerals were formed, not by subsequent metamorphism in deeply buried sediments, but by reactions going on at the earth's surface.

FISH THROWN UP FROM ARTESIAN WELLS.

The statement has been frequently made of late years that with the water thrown up from many of the artesian wells, recently bored by the French in the northern district of the Sahara desert, small fish have been ejected, from depths of 150 to 200 feet. This statement, which has been generally discredited, is now, however, proved to be true; M. Desor, the eminent Swiss naturalist, who has recently returned from an exploration of the Northern Sahara, testifying to its authenticity. He states in a recent letter, that he "found the fish in the stream leading from one of the wells, at the oasis Ain-Tala, where the fish were observed when the water first rose to the surface. It is impossible that these fish should come from any where else than from out of the well, for the water stands in no communication with either basin or river. The fish belong to the family of carps, and if I am not mistaken, to the proper species of Cyprinodon. The most curious thing is that these fish, although coming from the interior of the earth, from a depth of more than 150 feet, have nothing sickly or misshapen about them; they are of a most remarkable liveliness, and, what is especially worthy of note, have fine, large, completely healthy eyes. You know that the fish and other aquatic animals which are found in the subterranean ponds of the Adelsberg Cavern in Steyermark, and in the Mammoth Cavern in Kentucky, are all blind. Their ocular organs are stunted, and often nothing is left of the eye but the optic nerve. Some naturalists therefore, have tried to classify them as a species of their own, while others maintain that every organ deprived of the opportunity to exercise its functions must necessarily degenerate at last, and become defective. But here we have a fish from the interior of the earth, with perfect eyes. How are we to account for this? I confess that this phenomenon puzzles me, yet I think I have found the key to the riddle. The subterranean basin, which feeds the artesian wells, must be of considerable dimensions, as the water springs up on a space of many square miles, wherever it is bored. Besides these artificial wells, there are ponds in several oases, especially that of Urlana, fed by rich sources, and from which real

26*

brooks spread in different directions. These ponds harbor the same little Cyprinodonts which rise in the water of the artesian wells, by which I conclude that a subterranean connection exists between the ponds and the wells. Probably they visit those ponds periodically perhaps to spawn ; this would explain why their eyes, and their forma= tion in general, show nothing abnormal.

DISCOVERY OF EMERY IN THE UNITED STATES.

It has been remarked that "a good mine of emery is worth more to a manufacturing people than many mines of gold." At a recent meeting of the Boston Society of Natural History, Dr. C. T. Jackson announced the discovery of an•apparently inexhaustible mine of emery in the town of Chester, Western Massachusetts, on the line of the Springfield and Albany railroad. For some time the existence of magnetic iron-ore was recognized in this locality, and the deposit worked to some extent, but on examination, Dr. Jackson found that the ore in question was in great part pure emery. The principal bed is in some places ten feet in thickness, and has been traced some four miles. In appearance it resembles the emery of Naxos and practical tests of it in grinding sword-blades at the Ames Manufacturing Co. at Chicopee, are said to be every way satisfactory.

MICROSCOPICAL STRUCTURE OF METEORITES.

Mr. H. C. Sorby, eminent for his application of the principles of physics in explaining geological phenomena, and his study of the microscopical structure of crystals, has turned his attention to the structure of meteorites. In a paper recently presented to the Royal Society he says that, in the first place, it is important to remark that the olivine of meteorites contains most excellent "glass cavities" similar to those in the olivine of lavas, thus proving that the material was at one time in a state of igneous fusion. The olivine also con- tains "gas cavities" like those so common in volcanic minerals, thus indicating the presence of some gas or vapor. To see these cavities distinctly, a carefully prepared thin section and a magnifying power of several hundreds are required. The vitreous substance found in the cavities is also to be met with outside and amongst the crystals, in such a manner as to show that it is the uncrystalline residue of the material in which they were formed. It is of a claret or brownish color, and possesses the characteristic structure and optical properties of artificial glasses. Some isolated portions of meteorites have also a structure very similar to that of stony lavas, where the shape and mu- tual relations of the crystals to each other proved that they were formed *in situ* on solidification. A structure is also found so remark- ably like that of consolidated volcanic ashes as to be taken for it. It would appear that after the material of the meteorites was melted, a considerable portion was broken up into small fragments, subse- quently collected together, and more or less consolidated by mechan- ical and chemical means, amongst which must be classed a segrega- tion of iron either in the metallic state or in combination with other substances. "There are," says Mr. Sorby, "certain peculiarities in physical structure which connect meteorites with volcanic rocks, and at the same time, others in which they differ most characteristically, —

facts which, I think, must be borne in mind not only in forming a conclusion as to the origin of meteorites, but also in attempting to explain volcanic action in general."

ON THE MOA, OR GIGANTIC BIRD OF NEW ZEALAND.

At a recent meeting of the Linnean Society of London, Mr. T. Allis exhibited some of the bones of the New Zealand Moa, in a most perfect state of preservation, the same having been found under a deposit of shifting sand. It had apparently been surprised whilst sitting on its young ones, the bones of which were also found with those of the parent. In the discussion which followed, Dr. Hooker suggested that the perfect condition and high state of preservation which the bones exhibited might possibly be the result of preservation in ice, similar instances being on record, but the other speakers took an entirely different view of the subject, and thought that the bird to which these enormous bones belonged had probably been living within ten years. If this conclusion be correct, it seems extraordinary that no more precise information can be obtained from the natives, a race remarkable for their intelligence; for, if so gigantic a creature were living ten years ago, it seems impossible that no more accurate information respecting it should exist than the vague and most unsatisfactory reports which have been collected by English emigrants. However, a very important point is settled in bringing the history of the bird down to the time when New Zealand was colonized by the British. It were indeed presumptuous to affirm that a moa will still be found alive; but the evidence now before us shows that such an event is any thing but impossible. In considering this subject, we must bear in mind that, being continually at war with the natives, we are debarred from that free access to the interior, and from that unrestrained exploration, which are absolutely necessary in such a case as this. The wary character of the ostrich tribe is well known: in the Great Sahara the ostrich himself is only to be discovered at an immense distance, and yet there are no intervening objects behind which he could shelter. It is very different in New Zealand: there the moa, if possessed of half the subtlety of the ostrich, might escape for years the notice of a few Europeans who have ventured to intrude on his haunts.

DISLOCATIONS OF THE EARTH'S CRUST.

Dislocations of the earth's crust of various kinds, such as elevations or depressions, are accounted for by Dr. Bischof the eminent author of the *Elements of Chemical and Physical Geology* in the following manner. "Exhalations of carbonic acid are of universal occurrence, and originate at great depths, for the deeper we penetrate the more abundant they become. Rocks occurring at such great and inaccessible depths are chiefly silicates, like the oldest of the known formations,—a fact which the volcanic eruptions of lava confirm. These silicates are decomposed by carbonic acid ascending to the surface, the decomposition being facilitated by the increase of temperature towards the interior of the earth. The products are silicate of alumina and certain carbonates, silica being displaced. When minerals or rocks combine with other substances, not only an increase of matter, but also an increase of volume takes place, provided that such combination does not involve an increase of specific gravity. On the other hand, if the latter be decreased, the volume must be increased in a still greater proportion than the matter. Such is the case when silicates are decomposed by carbonic acid. The specific gravity of the products of decomposition being below that of the undecomposed minerals, their volume must necessarily be greatly increased. If a mountain composed of silicates be supposed to exist, its upper parts being exposed to decomposition by carbonic acid and rain, then, if there be amorphous silicate of alumina in the lower parts of this mountain, and if the soluble products of decomposition (say alkaline silicates) were carried downwards by means of water, crystals of feldspar may be produced increasing the bulk of the mountain, and thus causing elevation. Not only will the upper parts be thus elevated from below, but they will also raise themselves, should their increase, through combination with water, be greater than the decrease of bulk caused by substances carried downwards. Dr. Bischof cites the slow rising of portions of the Scandinavian area, where crystalline rocks containing silicates occur, as a geological proof of the action of the cause explained above in the elevation of rock masses ; adding that, where silicates are absent, as in the south of Sweden, there has been no upheaval. Additional facts and arguments will be found in No. 78 of the *Journal of the Geological Society*, from which the foregoing notes have been selected.

✦ GEOLOGICAL SUMMARY.

Decrease of the Supply of Copper.—While the demand for copper is yearly increasing, it would appear that the supply is decreasing. The mines of England, Chili, and Cuba, all show diminished and diminishing products. Thus, in 1856, the British copper mines produced yearly 24,527 tons of metal; since which time their product has declined, till 1863, when their yield was only 14,247 tons, showing in seven years a decrease of 10,280 tons. The copper product of the United States is on the contrary, rapidly increasing.

Negative Evidence in Geology.—Many disputes in geology are founded upon the generally unwarrantable assumption that certain animals or plants could never have existed, because their remains have not been found. It is, therefore, interesting to note a modern instance, in which naturalists are without that kind of proof, furnished by a specimen, of the existence of an enormous animal, apparently not uncommon. Dr. Gray, speaking of the Physetes, or Black fish of the whalers, states in the *Annals Nat. Hist.*, "there is not a bone, nor even a fragment of a bone, nor any part which can be proved to have belonged to a specimen of this gigantic animal to be seen in any museum in Europe. This is the more remarkable, as the animal grows to the length of more than 50 feet, is mentioned under the name of the Black fish in almost all whaling voyages, and two specimens of it were examined by Sibbold, having occurred on the coast of Scotland."

Minute Geologic Evidence.—Mr. Edward Blyth has recently pointed out the existence of two very distinct forms of deposit, which are occasionally found on the teeth of fossil herbivora. By an examination of these the geologist is to some extent, enabled to determine whether an animal has been in the wild or domesticated condition. "There is a small particular or character which generally distinguishes a wild herbivorous animal from a tame one; and this is a certain incrustation of brown tartar upon the teeth." Thus deposit he did not find upon the porcine relics at the Wrekin, but he fancied, at first, that he detected it upon the teeth of the fossil bovine remains in Ireland. However, after examining the latter more carefully, he noticed a ferruginous deposit from the peat, which might easily be mistaken for the incrustation of brown tartar. "In the one case there would be traces of parasitic life under the microscope,—not so in the other case. The incrustation from the peat covered the whole tooth, at least as much of it as was not of the bony alveolus; whereas the tartar incrustation was only upon that portion of the tooth that had not been imbedded in the gum. The latter was conspicuously present in sundry teeth of *Megaceros hibernicus* and of *Cervus elaphus*." We presume that for this reason Mr. Blyth regards these species as belonging to the category of domesticated animals, but we wish the evidence was a little more convincing.—*Dublin Quarterly Journal of Science.*

Native Zinc has been discovered in a basalt from a locality near Melbourne, in Australia.

Missing Sedimentary Formations.—The *Journal* of the Geological Society has a full paper on this subject. Although it has been long known that formations are frequently absent from their places in the vertical series of sedimentary rocks (such as lias between oolite and trias, &c.) yet little notice has been taken of the fact, except mere allusions. Dr. J. J. Bigsby was therefore led to reduce to order a great deal of information on the subject, collected from the writings of the most eminent geologists. The missing formations hold a high and important place as a result of one of the constructive processes of the earth's crust, and the work is still going on. He concludes that they are among the several consequences of emergence and immersion, themselves the effect of one of the great cosmic agencies, oscillation of level, which may be gradual or paroxysmal, through all the degrees of velocity and energy. Those interested in the subject will rejoice in the details given respecting these "leaves torn out from nature's volume,"—gaps or blanks, which "by their magnitude and number, become a great feature in the earth's crust, expressive of unity of design in time and space."

Conversion of Wood into Coal under Pressure.—We have received from Mr. Robert Safely, of Cohoes, New York, an account of the conversion of a portion of the wooden step of a turbine water-wheel into a very compact coal resembling closely in texture and appearance ordinary mineral coal, along with a specimen of the coal. The step was of oak, and about ten inches through; and when taken out, the whole surface was covered with a layer of coal. The charring was a consequence of the water pipe which lubricated it becoming clogged with dirt. Mr. Safely states further, that the fall of water to which the wood was subjected when it was converted into coal, was exactly 25 feet; and as the diameter of the wheel is five feet seven inches, the pressure on the wheel would be measured by a column five feet seven inches in diameter, and 25 feet high, less what is due to the water striking the bucket at a small angle to the lane of the wheel. The gearing, wheel, shaft, etc. weigh about three tons, which would give for the pressure upon the step, if the whole weight of water was reckoned, about 20 tons. The facts exemplify the formation of coal under pressure, combined with moisture and a moderate heat, and with very slow motion.—*Silliman's Journal.*

Interesting Geological Discovery.—Another alteration in our geological charts seems likely to take place. Prof. Salter and others of England have discovered, during the past year, in the so called " Lingula Flags," (a series of rocks which lie at the base of the British Silurian System,) two new genera of trilobites and a new genus of sponge : which by reason of their specific differences from all the Silurian genera, would seem to indicate that the Lingular flags must henceforth be regarded as members of a separate formation.

Fossil Elephant of Malta.—Some exceedingly curious remains of a new species of fossil elephant, have recently been found by Dr. Leith Adams in the Island of Malta, in certain cave deposits and breccias. One of the chief points with reference to this elephant is the small size of its teeth, which, coupled with other characteristics, leaves no doubt that it was not only distinct from any living or extinct species, but that it was, as regards dimensions, a pigmy compared with them. It is supposed to have been no larger than a lion. Such specimens, together with the bones and teeth of hippopotami. which of late years have been met with in great abundance in different parts of Malta and Gozo, tend to show that these islands are but fragments of what may have been at one time an extensive continent, in all probability connected with either Europe or Africa, or both.

Great Crocodile of the Oolite.—M. A. Valenciennes recently exhibited to the French Academy a fossil crocodile tooth found in the Oolite, near Poitiers. From its size he estimated the animal to have been 100 feet long. This creature must not be confounded with the megalosaurus.

Curious Facts in Geology.—At the last meeting of the British Association, Mr. C. Moore, in some remarks on the " Geology of the southwest of England," stated, in respect to a variety of clay found in the vicinity of the town of Frome, that out of a cartload of it he had been enabled to obtain more than a million organisms, in addition to 29 types of mammalia and various kinds of reptilia. He had discovered in these beds many genera that had never been previously recognized. In these beds he had obtained over 70,000 teeth of one kind of fossil alone.

Mr. Moore produced some interesting specimens of stones which he had found in the neighborhood of Bath. These stones were about five inches in diameter, and about six or seven long, and each of them contained a specimen of some kind of fish. Indeed, he could tell by the appearance of the stone what it contained, and he would break open several to show this. He did so, and in every case the fish Mr. Moore had previously indicated was discovered ; but the most interesting specimen was the ova which contained the cuttle-fish. When Mr. Moore broke open the stone, not only was the cuttle-fish discovered, but the inky fluid—the sepia—was discovered as in a fish of the same kind that might be taken out of the sea at the present day. There was as much of it as would fill an ordinary sized ink-bottle, and Mr. Moore took a portion of it and smeared it over a piece of white paper, making it literally as black as ink. He then produced some specimens of the Ichthyosauri found in the neighborhood of Bath, and a specimen of a fish, about the size of a salmon, of six or seven pounds weight. It was so perfect in its form and appearance and shape, that but for its color, as Mr. Moore said, it might be handed by mistake to the cook to dress, and yet it must have been millions and millions of years since this fish lived and moved about in the water. In the mammal drift which entirely surrounded Bath, the remains of the mammal tribe were abundant, and Mr. Moore exhibited many specimens.

The Fossil Musk Ox.—In the valley of Oise, near Paris, Dr. Eug. Robert has found a portion of the skull of this animal,—a most interesting discovery, which has been brought under the notice of the Academy of Sciences in a memoir by M. Lartet. Here is, then, an animal now retired to North America which formerly lived in quaternary Europe. We now know that the reindeer, yet more arctic in its migrations, at the same epoch flourished at the foot of the Pyrenees, and the same may be predicted of other animals now denizens of extreme northern countries. "How," says M. Lartet, "have such changes in the geographical distribution of these animals been effected? Has it been by elective migration from their habitat? or by the progressive invasion of man? or by the gradual reduction of species, condemned to extinction, as has been the case with the great cave bear, the elephant and rhinoceros of glacial times, the great Irish elk, &c.? These questions remain to be solved, and we are still led to repeat what Stephen Geoffrey St. Hilaire said 30 years ago, 'The time of true knowledge in paleontology is not yet come.'"

Meteoric Rain.—A curious theory has been recently propounded by the eminent but somewhat eccentric scientist, Reichenbach of Vienna. He believes in the existence of a cosmical powder or dust which exists all through space, and which sometimes becomes agglomerated so as to form large and small meteorites, while, at other times, it reaches the surface of our earth in the form of impalpable powder. We know that meteorites are mainly composed of nickel, cobalt, iron, phosphorus, etc. Dr. Reichenbach went to the top of a mountain which had never been touched by spade or pickax, and collected there some dust which he analyzed, and found it to contain nickel, and cobalt, and phosphorus, and magnesia. It has often been a matter of wonder where the minute quantity of phosphorus so generally distributed on the surface of the earth came from. Mr. Reichenbach, however, claims that he has discovered it in the cosmical dust above mentioned.—*London Chemical News.*

On the Coloring of Agates.—At the British Association, 1864, Prof. Tennant gave some interesting details respecting the structure of agate and the artifices resorted to by the workmen of Oberstein in coloring the agate ornaments manufactured at that place and distributed over Europe. A large number of specimens were exhibited, not only of ornaments but of the stones, both cut and uncut, the former well adapted to show the structure. The black color is produced by steeping the specimens in oil, and then blackening them by the action of sulphuric acid.

Mr. Tennant asked Mr. Tomlinson to speak on the subject, when that gentleman gave some particulars respecting the organization of the factory at Oberstein, and remarked that the principle of colorization depended on the structure of the stones: they consisted of alternate bands of crystalline and amorphous quartz, the latter only absorbing the coloring matter, which consisted mostly of oxyd of iron. The workmen kept the pebbles in tubs of water containing the oxyd for a longer or shorter time according to the tint required; the crystalline bands remained white, the non-crystalline absorbed the color throughout. Prof. Sullivan remarked that the structure of agate illustrated beautifully the difference between *colloids* and *crystalloids*. The alkaline silicates, by repose, formed these two classes of bodies, and he had no doubt a similar action had been at work in the formation of agate.

Formation of Granite.—Dr. Percy of the London School of mines, in a recent lecture objected to the assertion of geologists that granitic rocks must have been formed by plutonic agencies; for, said he, there are certain difficulties which have always been in the way of accepting this view of the subject,—difficulties known at all events to those who have been accustomed to make experiments on the fusion of mineral substances at high temperatures. This is especially seen by examining the condition of quartz in granite; it is always found in the crystalline condition, and has invariably a specific gravity of 2·6. There is not a single instance known to the contrary. Hence there is reason to believe that the quartz could never have been fused, for the moment silica is fused, no matter in what condition it was previously, a peculiar glass-like colloidal mass is produced, having a specific gravity which never exceeds 2·3. Therefore there is good reason to conclude that granite could never have been found under the condition of a high temperature.

BOTANY.

CHLOROPHYLL.

CHLOROPHYLL, the green coloring matter in plants has been closely examined by Prof. Stokes, Sec. R. S. by the spectroscope, and in the *Proceedings of the Royal Society* he records that he finds the chlorophyll of land plants to be a mixture of four substances,—two green and two yellow,—all possessing highly distinctive optical properties. The green substances yield solutions exhibiting a strong red fluorescence; the yellow substances do not. The four substances are soluble in the same solvents, and three of them are extremely easily decomposed by acids or even acid salts,—such as binoxalate of potash; but, by proper treatment each may be obtained in a state of very approximate isolation, so far, at least, as colored substances are concerned. Prof. Stokes also examined a specimen, prepared by Prof. Harley, of viliverdia, the green substance contained in bile. supposed by Berzelius to be identical with chlorophyll, and was thereby enabled to prove that the two substances are quite distinct.

CURIOUS CONDITIONS OF VEGETATION.

In a recent communication to the Edinburgh Botanical Society, Mr. James Robertson gave a sketch of the botanical features of the Kilkee sea-cliffs. This part of the Irish coast-line is exposed to the full violence of the Atlantic winds and waves, and thus a rock 200 feet above high water is so copiously supplied with saline spray as to afford sustenance to a colony of periwinkles which fringe its summit. Notwithstanding this, the marine plants which are found at heights varying from 150 to 400 feet, and which grow in a very stunted manner, illustrate in a striking way the physiological law that if plants can do nothing else, they must produce their flowers and fruit. The flora approaches the alpine type in character, doubtless because of the peculiar external conditions.

MANNA IN THE DESERT.

Sir Roderick Murchison announces a fall of manna in Asia Minor. His informant, M. Haidinger, states that he has received a portion of this manna, which fell with a gust of rain at Charput. It is a lichen which is formed in the steppes of the Kurghis, and is often carried in these falls far to the west, across the Caspian. The grains, which are always perfectly detached, have much of the form of a raspberry or mulberry, and are found frequently to be attached, to a stony support of granite, sandstone, and lime. This manna is ground into flour, and baked into bread, and is known among the Turks by the name of *kerdertboghdasi*, which means wonder-corn or grain. It contains more than 65 per cent of oxalate of lime, and 25 of amylaceous matter.

THE DECOMPOSITION OF CARBONIC ACID GAS.

The decomposition of carbonic acid gas by the leaves of plants is the subject of a note by M. Cloez, recently laid before the Academy of Sciences at Paris. Numerous experiments have proved that plants possessed of leaves and under the influence of light assimilate carbon by the reduction of carbonic acid, giving cause to the disengagement of oxygen. The parts of the plants exposed to the light have various colors. Of these green is predominant, being the normal color of the larger plants, and, as M. Cloez asserts, should be considered as essential to the parts which decompose carbonic acid. M. Cloez maintains, in opposition to the opinion of M. M. Saussure and Corenwinder, that certain parts of the plant such as the brown, yellow, and purple leaves,—although apparently deprived of green, still retain it partially, and that it is by virtue of this part alone that they decompose carbonic acid. In vol. 57 of the *Comptes Rendus* will be found details of experiments which lead M. Cloez to affirm that leaves decompose carbonic acid under the influence of light by reason of the green matter which they contain, and that the yellow and red parts do not give rise to this decomposition.

RESPIRATION OF FRUITS AND FLOWERS.

M. Tremy, in a paper lately read before the French Academy, gives some interesting details concerning the ripening process in fruits. In the development of the latter there are three stages, which are distinguished not only by physical but chemical features. The first is that of development *par excellence*. The fruit during this stage is generally of a green color, and acts on the atmosphere in the same manner as the leaves; that is to say, it causes the decomposition of carbonic acid and the liberation of oxygen under the influence of light. In the second period, which is that of maturation, the green color of the fruit is replaced by yellow, red, or brown; the vegetable matter no longer decomposes carbonic acid but absolutely develops it by the combination of its carbon with the oxygen of the air. Slow processes of combustion take place in the cells of the pericarp, which cause the disappearance of the soluble matters usually found there, the tannin is first destroyed and the acids follow. At this stage, the fruit is eaten. The third period is that of decomposition; its final object is the destruction of the pericarp and the liberation of the seed. At this time, the air enters the cellules, and, acting in the first instance upon the sugar, it gives rise to alcoholic fermentation, marked by the disengagement of alcohol, which in operating upon the acids of the fruit gives rise to ethers, thus producing the peculiar aromas. This action, when continued, destroys the structure of the fruit and terminates in complete destruction of the tissues.

Respiration of Flowers.—The following is a *résumé* of the researches on this subject laid before the French Academy of Sciences by M. Cahous. 1. Flowers left in a limited atmosphere of common air consume oxygen and give off carbonic acid in proportions varying as they possess odor or not. 2. If the circumstances in which these flowers accomplish the phenomena be identical, the proportion of carbonic acid increases with the elevation of the temperature. 3. Generally, for flowers cut from the same plant and whose weight is equal, the quantity of carbonic acid is rather more considerable when the apparatus in which the experiment is made is exposed to light than when in extreme darkness: but in some cases there is no difference. 4. When ordinary air is replaced by pure oxygen the differences become more marked. 5. The flower beginning to develop disengages a little more carbonic acid than that which has attained its complete development: this may be due to a more energetic vital action. 6. Flowers left in an inert gas, disengage small quantities of carbonic acid. 7. The elements which constitute the flower (the pistil and the stamens) in which reside the greatest power of vitality, consume the largest quantity of oxygen and give off the largest proportion of carbonic acid.

Gases exhaled by Fruits.—M. Cahours also reports to the Academy, that he has found that the green parts of plants are not the only structures which have the power of breathing. He states that he finds that apples, oranges, and citrons, placed under bell jars containing oxygen, or this gas mixed with nitrogen, consumed oxygen, and evolved carbonic acid, the proportions being greater in diffused light than in darkness. Up to a certain point this takes place gradually, but beyond this it increases to a considerable extent, and the internal surface of the pericarp exhibits certain alterations of structure. The greater the temperature the larger will be the volume of carbonic acid exhaled. Nearly the same amount of carbonic acid is evolved during the two periods of approaching maturation and decay. But once the latter stage has been arrived at, the quantity of exhaled carbonic acid increases rapidly. The proportions of gases contained in the juices were thus estimated: The juice having been expressed was placed in vessels, and the gases expelled by ebullition. It was found in this way that carbonic acid and nitrogen are present in various proportions, but that none of the following exist in fruit juice: Oxygen, hydrogen, carbonic oxyd, carbureted hydrogen. When ripe fruit is enclosed in an atmosphere of air, it absorbs hydrogen with great rapidity, and if it is allowed to remain until it has become soft, it is found to contain a large proportion of gas rich in carbonic acid.

ZOOLOGY.

FISH PRESERVATION AND CULTURE.

To all interested in the preservation and restocking of our rivers with fish, we commend the following paper, on salmon-breeding and fish-" ways," or " ladders," read before the British Association for 1864, by the well-known English naturalist, Mr. Frank Buckland.

The author said,— Whereas the oyster is stationary, and is treated in its cultivation more like a mineral than an animal, the salmon is literally a vagabond, always on the move, and never remains long together in the same place. Upon this fact depends its preservation and multiplication, in spite of the many difficulties it has to contend with,— the greatest enemy being man. Such was the marvellous instinct which compelled the salmon to run up from the sea to the elevated ground fit for spawning, that the salmon caught at the mouth of the Rhine, and which are sold in the London market, run up that river no less than 630 miles to their spawning-ground, and, of course, 630 miles back again. Thus we may fairly conclude that a fish weighing 20 pounds has traveled in its journeys up and down the river no less than 6,000 miles. The salmon hatched in the upper waters of the Rhine are caught at Rotterdam, where there are five fishing stations : the annual produce of these fisheries is, at the lowest, 200,000 fish, which, calculated at 1s. 6d. per pound, would amount to an immense sum of money.

He had weighed a salmon in water, and out of water, and found that its specific gravity was such that it could swim through the water with the same ease as a swallow flies through the air. He then gave reasons why artifical hatching of salmon should be encouraged. First, because it might be said-the salmon did not know their own business, and were very bad nurses, for it had been calculated on excellent data, that out of one thousand young ones only one ever became human food. Salmon made their nests in the gravel one over the other, heaping up immense mounds, so that the bottom eggs would of necessity be crushed, and only those near the top ever hatch out. Secondly, there were so many enemies of the salmon, both when in the form of an egg and in the form of a young fish, that they required preservation and careful watching, like young pheasants. Several of these enemies were enumerated, and a good word said for the water ouzel, who eats *not* the salmon eggs, but the insects that come to feed

316

on the eggs. Artificial breeding had restored salmon to the Thames, for his friend Stephen Ponder, Esq. near Hampton Court, had for the last three years, in his private greenhouse, been hatching out many thousands of salmon and trout, and turned them into the Thames. The consequence is that in the shallow waters above Hampton Court, great numbers of young salmon and trout, from one to five inches long, could be seen any fine sunny morning. Any private individual might (if he could get the eggs) hatch salmon or trout with the same ease as chickens; and he explained a simple apparatus made by Mr. King, aquarium-dealer, of Portland Place, suitable for small experiments, say eight or ten thousand eggs. It had been stated that the French piscicultural establishment at Huningue, over which M. Coumes, the eminent French government engineer presided, was retrograding; but he could state that this year more than one million salmon eggs had been collected, and a large proportion distributed gratuitously all over France, and also to many parts of England. The laws for the protection of fish in France were deficient; but M. Coste had informed him that a new law would be proposed next season enabling him to shut up the fishery, and preserve the fish of any river in France for three years. The salmon laws in England afforded protection for the fish; and his friend, Mr. Ffennel, Inspector of Fisheries, was always busy in obtaining facts, which would enable him to gain knowledge on which the laws for the future should be amended and regulated. He had tried last year to obtain a hybrid between a salmon and a trout, and had been much laughed at for his pains. Still he was pleased to inform the meeting that Thomas Garett, Esq. of Clitheroe, had succeeded, not only this year, but also in previous years, and this gentleman was the first in England to obtain success in this curious experiment. M. Coste had moreover showed him, a few days since, in Paris, several specimens of hybrids between salmon and trout, and also one between the trout and the " ombre chevalier," or charr, the latter being a most curiously striped fish. M. Coste had also shown fish hatched from the eggs of a salmon *which had never been to the sea,* having been confined all its life in a freshwater pond, proving that even though salmon do not thrive without going to the sea, still they will carry eggs capable of producing young.

Upon the subject of salmon-ladders Mr. Buckland was particularly earnest, pointing out that it was not only cruel, but exceedingly shortsighted policy not to assist the salmon to get to the upper waters to lay their eggs; it was just the same as not putting a ladder to allow the hens to get up to their roosts. How could salmon be expected to get over a wall any more than a human being, unless a ladder were provided for either fish or man? And he it recollected that the ladder for the fish to ascend need not always be placed in the weir, but only at the time the fish wanted to go up. One only placed a ladder in an apple-tree when it was necessary to gather the apples, and the ladder was not left on the tree all the year round. So with the salmon-ladders. A temporary ladder might be roughly constructed with poles and boards, which would answer all the purpose, and might be removed when not wanted. The millers complained greatly of salmon-ladders, because they robbed them of the water wanted for the mill-power: but he exhibited and explained a model, a new kind of salmon-ladder,* which was to obviate the difficulties complained of by the millers. He then explained other difficulties, particularly that of finding a grating to prevent salmon swimming up mill-races, and getting injured by the mill-wheels. No grating had hitherto been invented which at the same time would prevent the salmon running up and not lead back the water on to the wheel and stop its action. Mr. Buckland concluded his instructive and at the same time amusing paper as follows: "Thus, then, I have endeavored to bring before the members of the British Association certain facts relative to two great branches of British industry,— the cultivation of the sea, and the cultivation of the rivers; the revenues derived from these both to private owners and to the public in general in the form of food, would, if put together, amount to an enormous sum, and still neither industry is as yet half developed.

In a treatise on fish-culture also recently published by Mr. Buckland, the author states, that salmon and trout carry on an average 1,000 eggs to one pound of their weight. Another important fact respecting the eggs of some fish is their great toughness, a provision, doubtless, intended to enable them to resist the crushing effect of stones and gravel in their spawning beds. In order to ascertain positively how much direct weight trout's eggs would bear, Mr. Buckland placed iron weights upon individual eggs, which did not give way until the pressure amounted to five pounds and six ounces.

In 1861, the fish-breeding establishment instituted under the auspices of Government, at Huningue, France, distributed upwards of 16,000,000 of fish-eggs, for breeding purposes over Europe. Recent authorities also declare that it is cheaper and easier to breed salmon than lambs. Salmon eggs, according to Mr. Buckland, preserve their vitality after having been imbedded in ice for the long period of 90 days; and eggs thus treated have been successfully hatched.

INFLUENCE OF MODERN CIVILIZATION ON HEALTH AND LONGEVITY.

At a recent meeting of the Association of Medical Superintendents of American Institutions for the Insane, the following remarks on the above subject were submitted by Dr. Edward Jarvis, of Massachu-

---

* This ladder is described by Mr. Buckland as follows: Two walls are constructed from the top to the foot of the weir (on its slope). Slabs of iron or stone (the stops) are then fixed at right angles into these walls, reaching about four-fifths of the way across the passage. The slots (or passages for the fish between the wall and the end of the stop) come alternately to the right and left, so that when the water runs down the ladder it describes a zigzag (or rather serpentine) course: the fish nosing about the foot of the weir, are attracted to the foot of the ladder by the current coming down it; they then make a rush through the lowermost opening into the first box or step, then into the next, and next, and so on till they get to the top. If they are tired, they can rest as long as they please in the eddies between each of the stops. It is found, however, in practice, that it does not answer to make the ascent of the ladder too easy, as, if the fish find themselves too comfortable in the eddies, they will stay there, and be liable to become a prey to poachers, as a reward for their laziness. The dimensions of a ladder for salmon which has been introduced at Teddington, England, are given as follows: Length 40ft.; width (inside the walls) 4 ft.; stops 3 ft. 3 in. long, 18 in. high, and 4 ft. apart; the slots (or openings) at the ends for the fish to go through, 9 in. wide. The total fall of the ladder is 6 ft. or 7 ft. and the incline one in seven. Up such a ladder, says Mr. Buckland, the young salmon will go with such a rush that if a man and a salmon were to start fairly from the bottom the latter would swim up to the top faster than the man could run along the wall by its side.

setts, well known for his researches on insanity. "Many believe the tone of general health is lower now than formerly; but I think it is without sufficient reason. Has there been any decrease of the vital force in the community for the last forty or one hundred years? Do civilization and progress and refinement reduce the vital power of men? Some facts show to the contrary. In 1693, the British Government issued a Tontine, to borrow millions upon the basis of certain lives upon which they were to pay annuities. Mr. Pitt issued another Tontine one hundred years afterwards in 1790, upon the same basis, and it has been found that these lives were so much longer than those a hundred years before, that the British Government were obliged to give it up. It was ruinous, so great was the increase in the duration of life in the course of a century.

' I think there are a great many deteriorating causes in civilization. A great deal of refinement refines only in the sense of attenuating life. Still, civilization has given an increase of comforts. better houses, and security against all the causes of suffering, cold and storms, greater certainty of proper food, an increase of better cooks, though these are yet bad enough. Still, cookery is better than it was in the days of our fathers, and food is more convertible into blood, and that more convertible into muscular fiber, and that fiber is more enduring than in the earlier days. The general effect of all these is to protract life, and give it greater force to resist the causes of physical and mental disease, and more power of endurance and make the number greater who will live beyond threescore and ten.

" The better health a man is in, the better are his chances of surviving the dangers of destruction. The more vital force and general health is increased, the greater is the diminution of the insane, at least from this cause. Nevertheless, it is easy to see, that whenever sickness is averted and the average longevity is increased, by better habits, more abundant and appropriate means of subsistence and protection, and wiser self-management, there may be also a larger proportion of weak constitutions that are saved from destruction by the same means. I found a proof of this a few years ago, in analyzing the bills of mortality of many nations. 1. That of a thousand children born in each country, more would survive the perils of infancy, childhood and youth, and enter on mature and responsible life, at twenty in Massachusetts, than in England, Belgium, Sweden, and some other nations. 2. That of a thousand who should survive the age of twenty, and enter on working life, more would break down in this period, and die before the age of sixty in Massachusetts, than in those nations. 3. Lastly, that of a thousand that should survive the period of labor and enter on old age at sixty, more would reach the age of eighty here than elsewhere. The explanation is this. Man may be considered as a living, working machine, which requires twenty years of the greatest skill and care to build and prepare for use, otherwise it may fall in the process of building; but when well made and of proper material, it may run forty years or longer. If the builders are rough and careless, they destroy many of their machines before they are finished, and none but those of the strongest materials can survive rough handling. But in the hands of skillful workmen, machines even of weak materials are made and finished—though from their inherent weakness, they cannot last long in doing the ordinary work put upon them. In Massachusetts, where property is so equally distributed, the comforts of home and the proper supply of food, protection, clothing, &c. are almost universal, and the people are so generally well educated, that most mothers have a certain amount of administrative wisdom, and know how to take care of the children, better than women elsewhere; more, therefore, survive the perils of infancy, and fewer weak constitutions are broken down. Massachusetts throws upon the active responsibilities of life more men of feeble constitutions, or machines made of poor material, because they are not broken down in making up. Again, in Massachusetts more people labor, and take heavy responsibilities, and more burden is thrown upon these machines, and more of them are broken down at thirty, during the working period, forty or fifty years before they have finished their work. In regard to those who survive the period of sixty, the same conditions that carried them through the perils of childhood carry them also through the discomforts and difficulties of old age, and more of them survive to extreme old age.

"I will call attention to another fact which proves the advantage of intelligence and skill in preserving infancy from destruction. I analyzed the reports of births, marriages, and mortality of England and Wales for 17 years, in order to see what connection there might be between the degree of intelligence in the domestic administration and the life of little children. I divided the countries into three classes. In the best class 31 per cent of the women, when married, signed the register with their marks, and 69 per cent could write. In the worst class 63 per cent signed their names with marks, and only 37 per cent could write. This was the only manifest difference, but it indicated a corresponding difference in general intelligence and of administrative wisdom. The second or intermediate class was omitted, and the comparison made between these extremes of education and ignorance. During these 17 years, in the first class there were 804,170 marriages, 2,935,573 births, and 443,902 deaths of children under one year. In the worst class there were 749,927 marriages, 2,853,774 births, and 541,906 deaths of infants. The first noticeable fact is the larger proportion of births to the marriages among the less intelligent than among the better-educated families. But the most interesting point is the great excess of mortality of little children in the ignorant classes, among whom about 19 per cent of all that were born died before they were a year old, while in the more intelligent countries only 15 per cent died at the same tender age. Comparing these with each other, we see that there was 25 per cent more deaths of infants in the less educated than in the better educated districts. This is a sacrifice of 111,272 to the ignorance of their mothers."

VITAL FORCE AND CONTRACTILITY.

Dr. Lionel Beale, eminent for his researches on the nervous system, thus concludes an article in the *Quarterly Journal of Microscopical Science:* "I think that every tissue or organism consists of matter that lives and matter that is formed. The first is the seat of peculiar change, *sui generis*, which never occurs in things inanimate. The second manifests phenomena which, are, properly considered, physical and chemical. The movements,—the decomposing, the formative, the analytical and synthetical power of the living matter, are due to the operation of a power, or force, or energy, which is not to be measured by the work achieved, nor to be altered or converted into other forms of force. It is a power that may be transmitted from particle to particle, and that may cease its manifestation forever. How it originated we have not the slightest knowledge. We only know now that it is always propagated from particle to particle, and that it cannot be transferred to particles at a distance. Heat is but one of the conditions under which this wonderful power manifests itself, not the power itself. Contractility is a property of muscle; contraction and elasticity are properties of fibrin, just as hardness is a property of horn, or nail, or bone, &c.; but motion, increase, formation, as manifested in germinal matter, are transmitted from particles of matter that possess them to particles of matter that do not. Muscle does not transmit its contractile property, nor yellow elastic tissue its elasticity, to matter which is void of these characteristics. Hence I distinguish the movements of germinal or living matter from the movements of muscular tissue; and surely I may correctly term them vital movements until some one proves that similar movements occur in matter which is not alive.

FACTS IN RELATION TO ENTOZOA; DANGER OF USING SEWAGE AS A FERTILIZER.

At the last meeting of the British Association, Dr. Cobbold presented in a popular manner the following important facts respecting the diffusion and action of entozoa, which name has been applied to certain minute intestinal worms. He said there was no doubt that entozoa were introduced with vegetable food. They were more likely to be taken from water-cress or other vegetables of the kind. It was necessary with all vegetables that the greatest cleanliness should be observed in preparing them for the table, and care should be taken to avoid swallowing these small molluces, which were very likely to escape observation. A great many diseases in children were, he said, charged to eating unripe fruit, but, as far as entozoa was concerned, that fear was entirely groundless; and if they should be so introduced, the chances were that the larvæ would be taken from the surface of the fruit. With regard to celery, cabbages, and all the ordinary market-garden vegetables, he said that all decomposing animal and vegetable matter contained entozoa, and the more filthy the water or liquid manure employed to secure the fertility of the garden, the more likely was a supply of entozoa to be taken with the vegetables grown upon the land. Parasitic larvæ might be found in water that was to all appearance perfectly pure; but, speaking generally, it might be inferred that fresh spring water was perfectly innocuous. Among the class introduced by water the smallest was $\frac{1}{10}$ of an inch long; it carried 30,000 eggs, and went through marvellous transformations. There was another species taken from water, the habit of which was to ensconce itself in the brain, causing death, which was invariably set down as due to cerebral disease. The way in which it reached the brain was from the coats of the stomach, through the circulating medium. There was one kind inhabiting dogs, which was

often communicated to the human being. One-sixth of all persons
who died in Iceland perished from a little creature so small that in its
larval state it could scarely be seen. If neither dog nor wolf existed
we should get rid of these species altogether. Sand and charcoal filters were of very little use. Paper filters should be employed. All
entozoa not preserved for scientific experiments should be destroyed
by fire, and under no circumstances should they be thrown aside as
harmless refuse : and he advised butchers, knackers, and others not to
throw doubtful offal to dogs frequenting their neighborhood. It was
gratifying to learn that beer, porter, and fermented drinks, were not
sources of entozoa, and were perfectly harmless. Even though impure water should have been employed, the boiling of the wort would
be alone sufficient to destroy any number of parasites. Unfermented
drinks, such as ginger beer, cider, and the like, he could not be perfectly certain about. All must depend upon the source and supply of
water. But it was satisfactory to learn that alcohol added to water
was sufficient to destroy parasitical eggs.

  Dangers of the Utilization of Sewage.—In addition to the above
remarks, Dr. Cobbold has also recently published a pamphlet in England (which has attracted no little attention), in which he predicts
the almost inevitable increase of parasitic diseases in general, if the
much talked of utilization of sewage be carried out. In respect to
one of the forms of disease which may be thus introduced, he says :
In Egypt and apparently throughout Northeastern Africa, at the Cape
of Good Hope, Natal, Mauritius, and other places, there exists a more
or less constant and formidable endemic disease, the nature of which
was first described by Drs. Griesinger and Bilharz. The disorder, or
" helminthiasis," in question is caused by a small parasite or entozoon,
which infests the bloodvessels, delighting more especially to take up
its abode in the veins connected with the liver and other abdominal
viscera ; and in these situations it gives rise to very painful symptoms,
followed, in the more advanced cases, by excessive prostration and
death. Minuter details respecting the peculiar features of the disease
itself it is here quite unnecessary for me to adduce, but I cannot proceed without a passing comment on the extraordinary prevalence of
the disease in Egypt, which may readily be realized by the fact that
out of 363 *post-mortem* examinations conducted by Dr. Griesinger,
these parasites were found in no less than 117 instances. It would,
therefore, seem that nearly ⅓ of the entire population suffer from this
parasitic malady.

  He then goes on to show that the disease in question has already
made its appearance in Great Britain, referring for corroboration to a
paper in the recently published 48th volume of the, *British Medico-
Chirurgical Transactions*. It would further appear that the disorder
is quite as prevalent at the Cape, at Natal, and in the Mauritius, as it
is in Egypt. On this he remarks :—

  " Have the kindness to observe that every colonist returning from
the Cape is liable to bring this parasitic treasure with him as a 'guest'
indeed, dwelling in his blood, and feeding on his lifestream. In the
advanced stages of the malady, the afflicted individual must frequently
evacuate the eggs and their contained embryonic larvæ, which are
thus conveyed into the ordinary receptacles of such voidings. There

let them remain, or convey them into a cesspool, and no harm follows. If deemed preferable, you may transport them, along with myriads of other human parasite eggs and larvæ into a common sewer, and thence into the sea; still entozoologically speaking, no harm follows. Here, however, let me invite you to pause; for if, without due consideration, you adopt any one of the gigantic schemes now in vogue, you will scatter these eggs far and wide; you will spread them over thousands of acres of ground; you will place the larvæ in those conditions which are known to be eminently favorable for the development of their next stage of growth; you will bring the latter in contact with land and water snails, into whose bodies they will speedily penetrate; and in short, you will place them in situations where their yet higher gradations of non-sexual growth and propagation will be arrived at. After all these changes, there is every reason to believe that they will experience no greater difficulty in gaining access to our bodies here in England than obtains in the case of those same parasites attacking our fellow-creatures, whose residence is found in Egypt, in Natal, in the Mauritius, or at the Cape. In a natural history point of view, it would not be an altogether singular result if, 20 years hence, this parasitic malady should be as prevalent in this country as it is now known to be in particular sections of the African continent. Foreseeing the possibility, not to say probability, of this contingency, am I not right, after years of long study, to raise my voice in the hope of preventing such a disaster?"

ON THE INDUCED PRODUCTION OF SUGAR IN ANIMALS BY COLD.

At a recent meeting of the Royal Society (London), Dr. Bence Jones, the eminent physiologist, read a curious paper, detailing the production of sugar in the fluids of the animal body by extreme cold, attributing its formation to deficient oxydation of the carbonaceous articles of food. For example, a grain of starch enters into the body, and is transformed into sugar; it is then acted on by oxygen, and ultimately passes out as carbonic acid and water. This is the final result of the perfect combustion; but if the oxydation stops at any stage, imperfect combustion occurs.

The combustion may be made imperfect in at least three different ways. First, by insufficient oxygen; secondly, by overwhelming fuel; thirdly, by reducing the temperature so low that chemical action is checked. From each of these causes the following scale of the combustion of starch in the body may be formed: When there is perfect combustion, then carbonic acid and water are produced. With less perfect combustion oxalic and other vegetable acids are formed. With the least possible combustion sugar results. Between perfect combustion and the most imperfect combustion,—that is, between carbonic acid and sugar,—there are probably many steps formed by many different acids; and as in a furnace one portion of the coal may be fully burnt, whilst other portions are passing through much less perfect combustion or are not burnt at all, so different portions of starch may reach different steps in the scale of combustion, and sugar, acetic acid, oxalic acid, carbonic acid, and many other acids between acetic and oxalic acid, may be simultaneously produced. From this account of the oxydation of starch, it follows that sugar should always be found

in the urine when any of the three causes mentioned reduce the oxydation in the system to its minimum. In other words, by stopping the
combustion that occurs in the body, diabetes should be produced artificially.

TEMPERATURE OF THE SEXES.

At the British Association, 1864, Dr. J. Davy gave the results of
some experiments he had made as to the relative temperature of the two
sexes. The theory of Aristotle, that a man possessed more warmth
than a woman, had been disputed; and it had been held by some, as
the result of modern research, that the temperature of woman was
slightly superior to that of men. Notwithstanding this, however,
from such observations as he had been able to make, he considered
the early opinion the more correct. Taking the average, it appeared
that the temperature of males and females was as 10·58 to 10·13. He
had more recently made some additional observations, using a thermometer of great delicacy, and taking for the purpose of his experiments six persons, three men and three women, all in good health.
The result was that the temperature in the case of the men varied between 90 and 99½, that of the women was between 97½ and 98. An
examination of other animals gave a somewhat higher temperature for
the male than the female : six fowls showing the proportion of 108·33
for the former, to 107·79 for the latter.

THE HAIRY MEN OF YESSO.

At a recent meeting of the Ethnological Society (London) a paper
descriptive of the hairy people of the island of Yesso was read by Mr.
Martin Wood. Yesso, which is inhabited in the southern portion only
by the Japanese, has an infertile soil and dreary climate. Its northern
parts are inhabited by the Mosinos, or " all hairy people " of the Japanese, who number about 100,000, and dwell principally in two large cities,
Mato-mai and Hako-dadi. These people are short, thick-set, and
muscular, but clumsy and uncouth in their movements. In appearance they are wild and repulsive, in consequence of the enormous
amount of hair with which they are covered. The hair on the scalp
forms a matted mass of gigantic size, their beards are long and thick,
growing from the greater part of the face, and the whole of their
bodies is covered with an extraordinary profusion of hair. The women
stain that part of the face which is covered by the beard in males.
The skin, when not bronzed by exposure, is somewhat paler in color
than that of the Japanese. These people, though timid from long
subjugation to the Japanese, and isolation from the rest of the world,
appear intelligent and lively. They have well-developed, prominent
foreheads, and dark, expressive eyes.

PRODUCTION OF THE SEXES AT WILL.

In the *Annual of Scientific Discovery* for 1864, a brief notice was
given of the researches and theory of Prof. Thury of Geneva, in respect
to the above interesting subject. In a memoir published by M. Thury
during the past year, he gives the following summary of his observations and deductions, which bid fair to be of special value to agri-
culturalists and stock-growers :—

1. Sex, according to Prof. Thury, depends on the degree of maturation of the ovum at the moment of its fecundation.

2. The ovum which has not attained a certain degree of maturation, if it be fecundated, produces a female ; when this degree of maturation is passed, the ovum, if fecundated, produces a male.

3. When, at the rutting-season, a single ovum separates from the ovary to descend slowly through the genital canal (as in uniparous animals), it is sufficient that the fecundation takes place at the commencement of the rutting-season to produce females, and at the end to produce males,—the turning point of the ovum occurring normally during its passage in the genital canal.

4. When several ova separate successively from the ovary during a single generative period (multiparous and oviparous animals in general), the first ova are generally the least developed, and produce females ; the last are more mature, and furnish males. But if it happens that a second generative period succeeds the first one, or if the external or organic conditions change considerably, the last ova may not attain to the superior degree of maturation, and may again furnish females. *Cœteris paribus*, the application of the principle of sexuality is less easy in the case of multiparous animals.

5. In the application of the above principles to the larger Mammalia, it is necessary that the experimenter should first of all observe the course of the phenomena of heat in the very individual upon which he proposes to act, in order that he may know exactly the duration and the signs of the rutting-season, which frequently vary in different individuals.

6. It is evident that no certain result can be expected when the signs of heat are vague or equivocal. This is scarcely ever the case in animals living in a state of freedom ; but cattle in the fattening-sheds or in the stable sometimes present this abnormal peculiarity. Such animals must be excluded from experimentation.

7. From the mode in which the law ruling the production of the sexes has been deduced, it results that this law must be general and apply to all organized beings,—that is to say, to plants, animals, and man.

It is necessary to distinguish carefully the law itself (1 and 2 of this summary), which is absolute, from the applications of it which may be made with more or less facility.

In the *Annual of Scientific Discovery* for 1864, p. 292, some statements were given of the experience of M. Cornaz, a Swiss agriculturist, in applying M. Thury's theory in cattle breeding. M. Nickles, the Paris correspondent of *Silliman's Journal* also furnishes some information bearing upon the subject. He says : "According to M. Thury, the product is always of the male sex when the fertilization of the ova occurs at complete maturity, and is always female when it takes place at a less advanced period.

There is a very simple way of solving this problem. It is to select for experiment species that come to maturity in succession, and, that during a single impregnation, fertilize the whole series of ova which detach themselves from the ovary during a period of 8, 10, 12, 15, or even 18 days. We know, indeed, that in case of the hen, a single coupling suffices for the fertilization of five, six, or even seven

28

eggs which she is about to lay and which are arranged in her ovary in the order of their maturation.   Now, in such a case, if the theory is exact, the first egg laid ought always to produce males and the others females without any possibility of the inversion of this order.   This is very near what has been observed by Messrs. Coste and Gerbe (French naturalists).

A hen, separated from the cock at the time of her first laying gave five fertile eggs in the space of eight days.   The egg laid on March 15th produced a male; that on March 17th a male; that on the 18th a female; that on the 20th a male; that on the 22d a female.   A characteristic fact in this experiment is the production of a male after a female, which ought not to have taken place according to the theory. But is it only a simple exception?   Or is it necessary to consider the fact a radical objection?   We may learn by and by on this point, from the researches in which Mr. Gerbe is now engaged.

On the occasion of the preceding note, Flourens recalled an experiment which he made 30 years ago.   Aristotle had observed that the pigeon ordinarily lays two eggs, and that, of these two eggs, one commonly produces a male and the other a female.   He wished to know which was the egg that gave the male, and which the one that produced the female.   He found that the first egg always gave the male, and the second the female.   I have repeated this experiment as many as 11 times in succession, and 11 times in succession the first egg gave the male and the second egg the female.   I have seen again that which Aristotle saw.

ZOOLOGICAL SUMMARY.

The Extinction of an Aboriginal Race.—The race of Tasmanians, or inhabitants of Van Dieman's Land, are now reduced to four individuals; an old man and three old women.   The entire race, supposed to have been from 5,000 to 7,000 in number, at the time of the first settlement of the island, has been destroyed, partly by disease, partly by drink, partly by the loss of their means of subsistence, but chiefly by violence.   They managed very early in the history of the colony to excite a profound hatred and fear among the settlers, and were hunted down without mercy.   About 1829 the last survivors were taken to Flinders Island, where they were kindly treated, but died off with astounding rapidity.   It seems probable that in half a century more there will not be one aborigine left in Australia.

Vitality of the African Race.—Dr. Livingston, in a paper read before the British Association, 1864, on his recent African explorations, stated of the African, ''that it was his opinion, that neither drink, nor disease, nor slavery can root him out of the world.   He never had any idea of the prodigious destruction of human life that takes place subsequently to the slave-hunting till he saw it; and as this has gone on for centuries it gives a wonderful idea of the vitality of the nation.''

Mortality among the Pearl Oysters.—At the last meeting of the British Association, M. Buckland, the well-known naturalist, stated that an event, which ladies would most appreciate, had taken place in Ceylon, viz: the sudden death, from unknown causes, of whole banks of the pearl-bearing oysters, the consequence of which would be that the price of pearls must be enormously increased.

Grafting Animals.—Dr. Paul Bert has published a work on the curious subject of animal grafts. He succeeded in making Siamese twins of a couple of rats, and in many other monstrosities. He exclaims, "it is a surprising spectacle to see a paw cut from one rat live, grow, finish its ossification, and regenerate its nerves, under the skin of another; and when we want a plume of feathers under the skin of a dog, what a miracle to see the interrupted vital phenomena resume their course, and the fragment of a bird receive nourishment from the blood of a mammal."—*Intellectual Observer.*

Curious Vital Statistics.—The following curious statistics appear in the Report of the Scottish Registrar-General of births, deaths, and marriages, for 1864, and illustrate the effect of town life on the human race. The officer in question says: It is a well-known fact that a residence in towns weakens the vitality of persons living there. This, as yet, has chiefly been attempted to be proved by demonstrating the much larger amount of sickness and death which annually result in a town population as compared with one residing in a rural district. But the proportion of births to the marriages, and, better still, the proportion of births to the married women at the childbearing ages, demonstrates the fact in as pointed a manner, while it is not liable to many of the objections which might be urged against the ordinary modes of proving that fact. The insular and mainland rural districts gave a result absolutely identical, only requiring 302 wives, from 15 to 45 years of age, to produce 100 children within the year; while the wives residing in the town district had their vitality so deteriorated by their town residence that it required 333 wives to produce 100 children.

Electricity and Asthma.—M. Poggioli describes to the French Academy the success which he experienced in treating asthma by electricity. He considers this remedy applicable to true asthma only, which is a nervous disorder of the respiratory apparatus, usually occurring periodically and in paroxysms, and not to asthmatic symptoms resulting from heart disease or pulmonary emphysema.

Electricity and Bright's Disease.—M. Namias has also communicated to the French Academy a case in which the obstacle to the separation of urea from the blood was removed by the application of galvanism to the loins of the patient for half an hour. Twelve of Daniell's cells were employed, and the quantity of urine and urea much increased. More albumen was also secreted, but M. Namias states that this was of small consequence compared with the benefit resulting from a greater elimination of urea.

Effects of Consanguineous Marriages.—M. Balley has called the attention of the French Academy to a remarkable result of a very singular marriage of this kind. He says, " the father and mother enjoyed good health; the father was born in lawful wedlock; the mother somewhat older, came from a foundling hospital. From this union resulted in succession four infants, stillborn; the fifth is deaf and dumb in an asylum at Rome; the sixth is a dwarf, and the seventh has not at present exhibited any peculiarity. It is now known that the individuals, so afflicted in their descendants, are brother and sister, children of the same father and mother. The girl, born before marriage, was deserted by her parents, was never reclaimed by them, and was ignorant who they were." M. Balley proposes that special inquiries should be made in deaf and dumb asylums concerning the relationship of the parents of the unfortunates. In Rome he finds out of 13 cases of persons born deaf and dumb, three were offspring of consanguineous marriages, one being connected with the deplorable story we have just cited.

Effect of open-air Exercise on Longevity.—Mr. Sargeant, of England, has recently published some remarkable facts, showing the influence of out-door occupation and exercise in lessening the rate of mortality; and that of almost all in-door occupations, long continued, in raising the rate of mortality of the classes following them.

The greater longevity of persons living in the country appears almost wholly due to the greater proportion of out-door occupation; inasmuch as shop-keepers and others following sedentary pursuits in the country have no well-marked vital superiority over the same classes in towns; whereas farm laborers, though exposed to the effects of wet, attain a greater longevity than any class of mechanics working in a confined atmosphere. Even scavengers in towns, who are exposed to very great impurities, are long-lived, owing to the vital influence of the open air in which they follow their occupation.

Acclimatization of Animals.—In a paper on this subject addressed to the British Association, 1864, by Dr. I. E. Gray, F. R. S., the author remarked, that some animals seemed to have been created with more or less of an instinctive desire to associate with man, and to become useful to him, but the number of these is very limited. It would appear as if all the animals which are possessed of this quality, and are worth domesticating have already been domesticated, and have been so from the earliest historic times. Certain French philosophers have lately taken up a notion that it was desirable to pervert the true purpose of the horse by cultivating him for food instead of work, and a society of hippophagi has been instituted with this view. Of course, under present circumstances, the flesh of the old and worn-out horses was sold for much less than the meats of well-fed ruminants, and the miserable classes in all countries were glad to obtain animal food of all kinds at a low rate, but whenever an attempt had been made to fatten horses for food it had been found that the meat could not be produced at so low a rate as that for which far better beef and mutton could be bought.

In attempting to introduce new domestic animals into some of our colonies it would be desirable not to confine themselves to European breeds but to ascertain whether some of the domestic races of Asia and Africa might not be better adapted to the climate and other conditions of the colony, although it would not be worth their while nor consistent with good policy to attempt their introduction here. Such experiments might be made in the colonies of the West Coast of Africa, for instance, where our horse, ass, oxen, sheep, goat, and even dog had greatly degenerated; where the horse and the ass live only for a very brief period, where the flesh of the ox and the sheep is described as bad and rare, and the flesh of the goat is said to be tasteless and stringy. The pig alone seems to bear the change with equanimity, and the produce of the milch pig is often sold to passengers by the mail packets and the ships on the stations, as the milk of the cow, or even the goat, is rarely to be obtained.

Improvement in the Exhibition of Osteological Collections.—Beautiful and instructive as articulated skeletons are for many purposes, they are ill adapted for the examination of some of the most important parts of the osseous system. The articular ends of the different bones of which they are composed are necessarily hidden, and a rigid comparison of one bone with another is almost impossible. The Council of the Royal College of Surgeons, London, have therefore recently proposed, that a new osteological series shall be formed at the Hunterian Museum, designed to show the principal modification in each individual element of the skeleton throughout the vertebrate series, by placing the homologous bones of a number of different animals in juxtaposition. For convenience of comparison, the specimens are all to be placed in corresponding positions, mounted on separate stands, and to each will be attached a label bearing the name of the bone and of the animal to which it belongs. It is believed that, when this series is carried out on a sufficiently extensive scale, it will afford facilities to the student of comparative osteology never before equalled, and add greatly to the real value of the College Museum to working men of science.

Researches on the Nerve Structure.—Every anatomist is now familiar with the fact that the nervous matter—the stuff which enables us to think, and makes us conscious beings—is composed of cells and fibres. By some anatomists it has been contended that certain cells and fibres are independent of each other; but Dr. L. S. Beale, in a paper recently published by the Royal Society, endeavors to prove, that in all cases the fibres are in bodily connection with cells, and that every nerve-cell has at least two fibres in connection with it. From this the author concludes that the cells and fibres of every nervous apparatus form an uninterrupted circuit.

How to detect a Real Ghost.—Every one who has pressed his eyes when shut, is more or less aware of the curious colored figures that are thus brought before the consciousness; and others are again aware that when looking into space, curiously-shaped bodies float before the eye, as though they occupied a place in space. These last, when sufficiently obvious to cause annoyance and the consultation of a doctor, have been called *muscæ volitantes*. These subjective phenomena of the eye have assumed sometimes very definite forms, and their study has enabled the physiologist to give satisfactory explanations of the supposed appearance of ghosts to persons of diseased visual apparatus. On these researches a ready means of detecting a real ghost has been discovered. All that is necessary for this purpose is, when the ghost is seen, to press the side of the eye with the finger, when, if it be not doubled, the presence of a real or objective ghost may at once be doubted.

The largest described Snake.—Mr. Speke, in his work on the discovery of the source of the Nile, thus describes the death of a snake of the *boa* species, shot by his traveling companion, Capt. Grant:—

" I shuddered as I looked upon the effects of his tremendous, dying strength. For yards around where he lay, grass and bushes and saplings, and in fact everything except the more fully grown trees, were cut clean off, as though they had been trimmed with an immense scythe. This monster, when measured, was 51 feet 2½ inches in extreme length, while round the thickest portion of its body the girth
28*

was nearly three feet, thus proving, I believe, to be the largest serpent that was ever authentically heard of."

Specific against the Bite of Serpents.—During the past year a Mr. Underwood made numerous public experiments at Melbourne, Australia, with the object of proving that he was in possession of a specific against the bites of even the most venomous serpents. He allowed himself, as well as several rabbits, to be bitten by different serpents, amongst others, the diamond snake, one of the most dangerous in Australia; neither he nor the rabbits suffered any ill effects in consequence, but the sum he asked appeared exorbitant, and the secret was accordingly not divulged. However, the *Cornwall Chronicle* asserts that the mysterious specific is no other than the *polypodium filix-mas,* or male fern. The antidote is prepared by simply infusing an ounce of the leaves of the plant nearest the root, in spirits of wine or brandy, and preserving the tincture for use in a well-stoppered bottle. If the properties of this plant are found to be really what is described, it is desirable to try whether it would counteract the poison arising from wounds made during anatomical dissections, to which so many medical men and students fall victims.

On the Larynx of the White Man and the Negro.—At the last meeting of the British Association, Dr. G. D. Gibbs, in a paper on the above subject, stated that special differences existed in the construction of the larynx of the white man and the negro, which consisted in the invariable presence of the cartilage of Wrisberg, generally absent or quite rudimentary in the white race; the obliquity of the plane of the vocal cords from within outwards, but varying in degree; and of the more or less pendent position of the ventricles, which permitted of a view of their fundus with the laryngoscope. The two latter conditions he had never seen in the white race in an examination of some 900 healthy living persons. These facts were made out from an examination of 58 negroes, including 15 *post mortem.*

SPONTANEOUS GENERATION.

In the recent proceedings of the Royal Society is inserted an account of 20 experiments relating to this question performed by Dr. G. W. Child. The substances used, were, in ten experiments, milk; and in ten, fragments of meat and water. These were in all cases placed in a bulb of glass about 2½ inches in diameter, and having two narrow and long necks. The experiments were divided into five series of four experiments each. In one series the bulbs were filled with air previously passed through a porcelain tube containing fragments of pumice-stone, and heated to vivid redness in a furnace. In the others they were filled respectively with carbonic acid, hydrogen, oxygen, and nitrogen gases. In each series two experiments were made with milk and two with meat; and each substance was boiled in one case and not boiled in the other. The joints of the apparatus were formed either by means of non-vulcanized caoutchouc tubing or India-rubber corks previously boiled in a solution of potash; and in every case, at the end of the experiment, the necks of the bulb were sealed by the lamp. The time of boiling such of the substances as were boiled varied from five to 20 minutes, and the boiling took place in the bulb, and with the stream of gas or air still passing through. The sub-

stances were always allowed to cool in the same stream of gas before
the bulbs were sealed. The microscopic examination of the contents
of the bulbs took place at various times, from three to four months
after their inclosure. In every case but one in which the substance
had not been boiled, low organisms were found apparently irrespective
of the kind of gas in which they had to exist. The case in which they
were not seen was that of meat inclosed in a tube filled with nitrogen.
This bulb burst apparently spontaneously, and its doing so may be
looked upon as a proof that in it also some change had taken place,
most likely connected with the development of organic life. Dr.
Childs concludes by saying that no definite conclusion can be drawn
from so limited a range of experiments; but it is worthy of remark
that organisms were found here under the precise circumstances in
which M. Pasteur states that they cannot and do not exist. The very
abnormal conditions under which some of these so-called organisms
are found would render it doubtful whether bacteriums, vibrios, &c.
ought to be considered as independent organisms in any higher sense
than are white blood-corpuscles, pollen grains, mucus-corpuscles, or
spermatozoa.

M. Pasteur's Conclusions respecting Spontaneous Generation.—At a
recent meeting of the Academy of Sciences, at Paris, M. Pasteur also
reverted to the controversy on this subject. In his recent memoir, he
stated, on the faith of numerous experiments, that it was always possible
to take away from any determined spot a limited, yet notable, amount of
air which has not undergone any physical or chemical change, and which
was nevertheless quite unable to provoke any alteration in an eminently
putrescible liquid. MM. Pouchet and Joly, having affirmed that this
result was erroneous, M. Pasteur defied them to prove it so. MM. Joly
and Musset, said : "If a single one of our tubes remain unaltered, we
will loyally acknowledge our defeat." And M. Pouchet also said : I declare that, on any part of the globe whence I shall take a cubic decimeter
of air, when I shall place it in contact with a putrescible liquid in a hermetically sealed tube, the latter will invariably become filled with living
organisms." In conformity with the demand of MM. Pouchet, Joly, and
Musset, accepted by M. Pasteur, the Academy has appointed a committee
composed of several of its most illustrious members.—MM. Flourens,
Dumas, Brougniart, Milne-Edwards, and Balard to repeat in its presence
the experiments, the results of which have been invoked as either
favorable or contrary to the doctrine of spontaneous generations.

ASTRONOMY AND METEOROLOGY.

NEW PLANETS AND COMETS FOR 1864.

THE discovery of three new asteroidal planets has been announced during the past year, making the whole number now recognized *eighty-two*.

The *eightieth* asteroid was discovered by Mr. Pogson of the Observatory of Madras, India. It has received the name of *Sappho*. The *eighty-first* asteroid was discovered September 30, by Mr. Tempel of Marseilles, France. It has received the name of *Terpsichore*.

The *eighty-second* asteroid was discovered November 27, by M. Luther of Bilk, Germany. It has received the name of *Alkmene*.

New Comets.— Five new comets have been discovered during the past year; but none of them exhibited any special features of interest.

Biela's Comet, which during its apparition in 1846 exhibited such remarkable phenomena,— its nucleus splitting up into two in a most mysterious manner, each component pursuing different paths,— will be with us again this year. As might have been imagined, the strange splitting up in 1846, considerably disturbed its path; but although when it was observed by Father Secchi in 1852 it was distant 6° in right ascension and 2° in declination from its predicted place, much of the deviation was due to the error of the ephemeris. The comet could not be observed at its perihelion in 1859, so that the 1865 return will be watched for by astronomers with the greatest interest.

ASTRONOMICAL SUMMARY.

Supposed fifth Satellite of Jupiter.—M. Gasparis, of the Observatory at Naples, saw, July 22, 1864, at 7.59 P.M. a black, well-defined point on the disc of the planet. In a quarter of an hour this black point, moving in the direction of the planet's rotation, disappeared, passing from the margin. M. de Gasparis asks if this is the same body that has been seen by Messrs. Long and Baxendell. M. Flammarion, in the Paris *Cosmos*, says it could not have been a little planet in conjunction with Jupiter, for in that case its motion would have been in an opposite direction, and it was not one of the four known satellites, as they were all visible. Could it, he asks, have been a fifth small satellite?

The Spectrum of Comet II, 1864.—Prof. Donati, of Florence, publishes in *Astron. Nach.* a sketch of the spectrum afforded by this comet, and he remarks that it resembles that produced by metals, the black bands being broader than the luminous.

New Relation of Periodic Times.—Mr. Finlayson, of Dover, Eng., points out the following singular proportion : The period of rotation of the earth on its axis is in the same proportion to the periodic time of the moon round the earth, as that of the period of rotation of the sun on its axis is to the periodic time of Mars round the sun.

Nebula of Eta Argûs and Southern Double Stars.—Mr. Powell, observing at Madras, confirms his own and Mr. Abbot's previous suspicions of the changes in the nebula surrounding Eta Argûs. He states that since 1860, the whole nebula has faded away very considerably, and has also altered its form ; the star now being left quite isolated, and out of the n·bulous matter altogether. It is to be remembered that the star is one of the most remarkable variabl- ones, and the phenomenon of the star and nebula varying in brightness at the same time resembles that of the disappearance of the small star and telescopic nebula of Taurus a few years since. Mr. Powell has also made some good observations on the remarkable star, Alpha Centauri, which is now at an interesting part of its orbit, as the distance is now decreasing. Gamma Coronæ Australis he finds has described 20° during the last four years.

New Nebulæ.—Mr. Lassel, the celebrated English Astronomer, who has for some time located his fine telescope in the Island of Malta, announces the discovery of nearly 200 new nebulæ during the last year.

Orbits of Binary Stars.—Prof. Kirkwood in a recent communication to *Silliman's Journal*, directs attention to the fact that the orbits of Binary Stars, so far as observed, are much more elliptical than those of the planets. Of the whole number of apparently double stars known to us, about 6,000, no less than 650 have changed their relative position. The almost circular path of planets around the sun and the extremely elliptic motions of the self-luminous stars are both accounted for by the theory of Laplace, as explained by Prof. K. For if a mass of nebulous matter in which the process of condensation has commenced, has a very slow rotation, and if instead of a *single* center of attraction, *two* distinct nuclei be formed, the consequence may be its complete separation into two bodies, while the rotation is yet so slow that the centrifugal force, as compared with centripetal, is too feeble to produce a nearly circular motion. While, therefore, orbits of small eccentricity must characterize planets formed from the abandoned equatorial rings of a condensing nebula, orbits highly elliptical may be regarded as the probable consequence of a separation in the earlier stages of its physical history.

Thoughts on the Influence of Ether in the Solar System, its Relation to the Zodiacal Light, Comets, and Seasons, and periodical Shooting-Stars.—In a communication to the American Philosophical Society by Dr. A. Wilcocks, the author advances the hypothesis that there is a constant circulation of ether induced by the heat of the sun ; that the cold ether descends near the poles of the sun, and that heated ether ascends from the sun's equator, or rather from a parallel of solar latitude just north of the equator ; that this heated current as it rises is compressed by the cold ether into a thin conical sheet ; that the ether bears with it matter capable of reflecting light, and thus causes the zodiacal light ; that the tails of the comets are lighter than the ether, and arise for that reason from the sun, except when near the poles of the sun, when they are made to descend in the vortices of descending ether, so as to present double and multiple tails; that twice in the year, in August and November, the earth plunges through the sheet of warm ether, causing a warm period in each month, the dog days and the Indian summer; and that in the middle of these two periods it causes the return of the August and November meteors.

Shute on the Companion of Sirius—M. Shute's observations on the satellite of Sirius, published during the past year, seem to support the views of Mr. Safford of Cambridge, Mass. viz: that there is no physical connection between the two stars.

Distance of Sirius.—M. Flammarion, in the *Cosmos*, speaking of this magnificent star says: "thanks to the labors of Sir John Herschel, we know that the absolute intensity of the light of Sirius has been estimated at 224 times that of the sun, and that its parallax, amounting to 0″·23, gives for its distance from the earth the probable number of 52,000,000,000 of leagues. It follows that we do not see the Sirius of to-day, but of 22 years ago; the ray of light that we receive to-day having been emitted by the star about 1840."

Comparing the Light of Stars.—In *Comptes Rendus* for the 11th of April, 1864, M. Chacornac describes a method of mounting a plane mirror so as to bring into the field of a telescope the image of one stars while the telescope receives directly the light of another. By this means the two images are brought into simultaneous view, the one of course less brilliant than it should be, through loss of light in reflection. He gives the calculations necessary to work out the comparison. Sirius he finds to be five times as bright as Arcturus. He is able to work by this method upon stars from 20° to 160° apart. When seen simultaneously, Arcturus looks orange red, and Sirius has a slight green tint.

WHAT IS KNOWN ABOUT SHOOTING-STARS.

Of shooting-stars there is an average of from five to seven visible every hour on a clear night. They are stray visitants in contradistinction to the prodigious swarms of November and August, which observation during twenty-five years has decided to be accurately returning phenomena. Arago gives a summary of the times in each month when meteors are chiefly seen; it is as follows: January. Shooting-stars are rare, 1st, to 4th, if at all. February. The ancient showers of meteors announced for this month by the chroniclers seem to have failed for the last eight or nine centuries. March. Occasionally. April. From 4th to 11th, and 17th to 25th. May. Shooting-stars are rare. June. Shooting-stars are *very* rare. July. The apparition of showers begins now to increase in number; we may expect them about July 26th to 29th. August. The well known period of 9th to 11th. September. Rare but possible from 18th to 25th. October. In the middle of the month. November. As usual from 11th to 13th, though less abundant. December. About 5th to 15th.

From this it will be seen that shooting-stars are much more numerous during the latter half of the year, when the earth is passing from summer to winter, or, in astronomical phraseology, from aphelion to perihelion. The same increase of number in the last six months of the year is observable in the appearance and fall of fire-balls and aerolites. Now by what theory can we account for this uniform return of meteors in each year?

The theory generally accepted is thus set forth by Prof. H. A. Newton, of New Haven, Conn.: which is, that there is a ring, or annulus of small bodies revolving with planetary velocity about the sun; that the bodies in question are distributed very unevenly in the ring, there being a small section of the ring where the bodies are numerous, with a few stragglers scattered along the rest of its circuit; that the earth passes through the ring every year, and each year in a new place; and that it passes through that part of the ring in which the planets are most numerous once in about 33 years. He further concludes that the period of the revolution of this ring of planets around the sun may be calculated with very great accuracy, and that it is 354·621 days,—a little less than a year.

When the bodies, composing this assumed ring, come within the limits of our atmosphere, they are rendered visible to us as shooting-stars, or fire-balls. Prof. Newton, and Mr. Alexander Herschel, have concluded independently, that shooting-stars commence at 70 miles and disappear at 50 miles above the surface of the earth. At 60 miles above the earth shooting-stars are far more frequent than at any other altitude, and they are considerably more between 40 and 80 miles above the earth than in all other elevations put together. Examples of suddenly collapsing and rekindling meteors appear to favor an hypothesis that chemical affinities, unknown at ordinary temperatures, produce in similar meteors a considerable portion of their unaccountable excess of light and heat. Prof. Newton estimates the velocity with which the November meteors arrive on the atmosphere of this earth at 20·17 miles per second, allowing for the attraction by the earth. The velocity of their passage through the air is 38·7 miles, or nearly 40 miles per second.

The periodicity and parallel divergence of all the shooting-stars from the same apex or point in the celestial sphere, can only be accounted for by the supposition of a ring, or elliptical annulus of meteors. Supposing this ellipse is crossed by the earth twice in her annual course, and that the traversing of each node occupies a day or two, we may at once account for the periodic profusion of meteors. And the parallel divergence of the stars from the same place in the heavens at each period, is exactly what would occur if the orbits of the earth and the meteoric ring intersected. In the November period, all the stars emerge from the region of *Leonis*; in August, from *Camelopardali*; the latitude of the apex is changed, but not the geometrical fact of divergence from a common source.

Father Secchi, the Roman astronomer, in a recent publication, calls attention to the small horizontal distance to which meteor appearances are limited. The cases in which this exceeds 220 kilometers are rare. The consequence of this is a curious one. At places double that distance apart it is scarcely possible that the same shooting-stars can be seen; and if we suppose the celestial vault represented by a globe 50 centimeters in diameter, we may say that the part of the sky whence the meteors proceed does not exceed the space that might be covered by a shilling.

Dr. Schmidt of the Observatory of Athens, has recently been fortunate enough to observe the explosion of a meteor by means of one of the powerful telescopes of the Athens Observatory, and the appearance which he witnessed—an incandescent shower—is entirely what would have been expected.

Our readers will bear in mind that the condition of these meteors is not one of incandescence, or ignition, while traversing space beyond the limits of our atmosphere; and it has often been wished that we might be favored with some observations of them while in the course of their interplanetary progress. This opportunity has been given within the last year to M. Heis, a European astronomer. At 8h. 31m. P. M. on the 4th of October last, as he was observing the milky way, he distinctly saw a dark mass slowly wending its way along the half-illumined sky, eclipsing the stars in its path. He was enabled to watch this strange visitant from a point situated in a 280° δ + 21° to a 291° + 18°, where it finally disappeared. How fortunate it would have been for us if another observer, as skilled as M. Heis, had also been favored with a sight of this dimmest of planets!

Prof. Newton, in a recent communication to *Silliman's Journal*, after assigning a period of about 38 years for the recurrence of the so-called "meteoric showers," thus speculates in regard to the next probable great display: If a shower occurs in 1865 (32 years after the great November display of 1833), it seems most reasonable to look for the finest appearance "in western Asia and eastern Europe; and in 1866 on the western Atlantic. The year in which we have most reason to expect a shower, is 1866, since the cycle of 33·25 years is probably to be reckoned from some date between November in 1832 and in 1833. These places and times are named with hesitation,— rather to guide observation, than as predictions. The causes alluded to above, and the possible perturbations and irregularities of structure of the group, may cause unexpected variations of time and place."

STARS THAT HAVE CHANGED THEIR COLORS.

Some additions to the catalogue of these stars are given by Mr. Jacob Ennis, in the Proceedings of the Academy of Natural Sciences at Philadelphia, based on the observations of Humboldt, Donati, Herschel, Schmidt, and others, including himself. He says, "among the 11 stars of the first magnitude, visible in this latitude, seven, according to these evidences, have undergone changes of color, and some of them more changes than one. Among the six stars of the first magnitude in the Southern Hemisphere, not visible here, two have changed their colors. And nearly all these changes have been sudden, transpiring in short periods. Moreover, none of the 11 first magnitude stars visible here are white; all are either red, yellow, green, or blue. Why has it not been made known long ago? Probably in great part, because changes in the color of stars could not be accounted for by any prevailing scientific theory. It has been rationally assumed that the stars are similar in constitution to the sun, and the sun has been encircled with a theory which affords not the least clue to any changes of color. This theory is most singularly complicated and unfortunate. It surrounds the sun, said to be dark, with an apparatus consisting of five distinct atmospheric envelops, all regularly arranged one above the other: First, a transparent envelop touching the opaque body of the sun: secondly, a fiery luminous envelop: thirdly, another transparent envelop: fourthly, another fiery luminous envelop: fifthly, a transparent envelop, surrounding all the others. Among such a number of imaginary things, there seems to be no room to imagine how changes of color could occur. Hence the mention of a change of color in a star has been regarded as anomalous', as an inconvenient fact having no relation to any popular theories and no appropriate place in the ordinary systems. Hence observations on the colors and on the changes of colors have not been stimulated, but rather repressed by this complex theory of the sun." The progress of what is termed solar and stellar chemistry will, no doubt, revive the attention of philosophers to the above-mentioned phenomena.

THE STABILITY OF THE SOLAR SYSTEM.

The doctrine of the stability of the solar system is considered by modern astronomers to be a fact established on the most satisfactory evidence. It is however, assailed by Prof. Gustav Henrichs, in an elaborate paper in the *American Journal of Science*, No. 109. He considers, in the first place, the effects of resistance, referring to the evidence of it in the case of Encke's Comet: and from his calculations deduces the following four laws : 1. That with advancing age the nearest secondary planet approaches its primary : 2. The entire system of orbits becomes closer ; 3. The regularity and symmetry disappear more and more ; and 4. That at corresponding ages similar systems must represent the same configuration. He next examines at some length the laws of density and rotation, giving the result in fifteen conclusions. We give the last two : 14. If the laws of attraction are not fully identical with those of repulsion, the created matter could already virtually contain the tangential force upon which the duration of the whole world principally depends. This is simply an instance of " throwing the first cause further back," since the translatory movement no longer needs to be considered as a direct action of the Creator, but as a design embodied and effected through some previous direct act. 15. It is probable that the force lost in resistance is converted into magnetism. " I know that some, like Brewster, will object to these and similar efforts ; yet we always feel the more deeply convinced of the glory, power, and wisdom of the Creator and governor of the universe, the more we perceive how simple his means, how grand his design, and how multiform his effects. Unlike ourselves, the Creator needs no tools, no constant effort for producing his ends. His Almighty fiat created the universe, and his hand sustains it ever since."

THEORY OF THE CONSTITUTION OF THE SUN.

The following is a *résumé* of a long memoir on this subject by M. Emile Gautier, in the *Bibliothèque Universelle,* in which he gives an account of the principal observations and theories that have been hitherto published. 1. The sun is a liquid, incandescent globe, composed of elements similar to those which enter into the composition of the earth, and probably into that of the planetary system. It exists in a state analogous to the phase of liquidity through which the earth has passed, according to the opinion generally entertained by geologists. The high temperature by which its liquidity is maintained considerably dilates its volume, and explains the feeble relative density of the globe in a state of fusion. 2. An atmosphere envelops the liquid mass, and incloses in it, in suspension, vapors or emanations of all kinds; so that its lower strata ought to be comparatively heavier than those of the terrestrial atmosphere. As the rotatory motion of the central globe cannot be supposed to be transmitted to its gaseous envelop so far as its most elevated limits with the same angular veloc- ity, the solar atmosphere is probably susceptible of exercising on the liquid surface an action analogous to that of friction. 3. The emana- tions or metallic vapors surrounding the sun, and impregnated with dust, smoke, or lava, form around it a layer of variable thickness, and present total eclipses, the appearance of red borders and protuber- ances.   4. The solar dark spots are partial solidifications of the surface, due either to cooling or to chemical action, reuniting momentarily into aggregates, salts, or oxyds, which have issued from the mass in fusion, and float on its surface. 5. The faculæ (bright spots) are the result of the appearance on the sun of very brilliant substances, endowed with radiating power. 6. The acceleration observed in the rotatory movement of the spots situated near the solar equator is the result of the exterior action of the atmospheric pressure on the liquid surface, combined with that of the interior layers of the mass in fusion. Accidental irregularities may proceed from the dis- turbance of the chemical and physical equilibrium of the various materials composing the mass.

In a paper on this same subject, recently read by Mr. Dawes to the Royal Astronomical Society, he stated that "the mottled surface of the sun can be seen with a low power." It has been variously de- scribed, and it appeared to him in many ways; but he stated that he had *not* been able to verify the appearance of the "willow leaves" described by Mr. Nasmyth. Mr. Dawes considers Sir John Her- schel's words, "the surface is like some flocculent chemical precipitate slowly settling down," to be by far the best description of the solar disc. When Mr. Dawes used a very small perforation, with an eye- piece of high powers (400 to 600), he rarely saw much change in the pores, except in the vicinity of the spots, which were rapidly expand- ing or closing, when the appearance of the surface at the margin resembled small bits of straw or thatching, interlacing in all directions. He says that with regard to the spots in the black centers, distinction ought to be made between the umbra and the nucleus. The exist- ence or absence of this black central portion may possibly determine the origin of the spots.

TEMPERATURE AND CLIMATE OF THE MOON.

Mr. James Nasmyth of England, in a recent lecture before the Royal Institution, on the above subject, dwelt on the great evidence of volcanic action in the formation of the moon's surface, and ex- pressed his own conviction that all volcanic action is of cosmical origin and as ancient as the planets themselves; the heat being essen- tially different from that of ordinary combustion, which required the presence of oxygen. The bulk or solid contents of the moon, as compared with that of the earth, is as 1 to 49. The surface of the moon, as compared with that of the earth, is as 1 to 16. On the sup- position that the moon and the earth were formed at the same period, by the condensation of nebulous matter, the rapidity of the cooling of the moon would be four times as great as that of the earth, in consequence of its greater surface as compared with its solid contents; hence the moon would have become solid long before the earth, and would offer for our contemplation an object of immense antiquity, the surface of which, from the absence of air and water, would have undergone no disintegration or change for millions of ages.

The present condition of the moon's surface seems in great part made up of craters of extinct volcanoes, some 28 miles in diameter. Some of the volcanic mountains of the moon are 28,000 feet high. These are brightly illuminated on one side by the sun; and from the absence of diffused daylight, owing to the want of an atmosphere, the further side is in shadow of intense blackness; and from the same cause, the sky, as seen from the moon, would appear perfectly dark, the stars being always visible.

The day in the moon is a fortnight in duration, and during this period the temperature on the illuminated side would probably rise to 220° Fahrenheit, or hotter than boiling water. The night would be of equal length, and during this time the heat, from the absence of aqueous vapor and atmosphere, would be radiated freely into space, and the temperature would fall to that of space, viz: to 300° below zero Fahr. The absence of air and water in the moon would render impossible the existence of animal and vegetable life corresponding to that which prevails on our globe.

The use of the moon, as a satellite of the earth, is usually regarded as being that of a luminary, but from its variable action this use must be regarded as secondary. Its value as inducing the tides and currents of the ocean is of greater importance, both as conducing to the sanitary condition of the sea, and as aiding transit in rivers, by the ebb and flow of the tide. At the conclusion of the lecture, Mr. Nasmyth illustrated the formation of the radiating cracks on the moon's surface, by congealing water in a thin glass globe hermetically sealed,—when it cracked in lines radiating from a single point,—the cracks in the moon being attributed to the contraction of its external hardened crust during the period of its rapid congelation.

GEOGRAPHY AND ANTIQUITIES.

NEW EXPEDITION TO THE NORTH POLE.

A NEW project of an expedition to reach the North Pole, has been proposed in England by Capt. Osborn, distinguished for his connection with former Arctic explorations. He proposes that his vessels shall sail in the spring of 1866, and reach Cape York in August. One vessel would then be secured in or about Cape Isabella, leaving only 25 persons in charge ; the other, with 95 men, would be pressed up the western shore in the direction of Cape Parry, taking care not to exceed a distance of 300 miles from her consort. During the same autumn, the southern ship would connect herself by *dépôts* with the northern vessel, and the northern vessel would place our *dépôts* towards the Pole, ready for spring operations. In the two following years—1867, 68—sledge and boat operations should be directed towards the Pole and over the unknown polar area ; and in 1869 the expedition would retire, thus spending only two winters and three summers in the Arctic Zone. In an address before the Royal Society, Captain Osborn pressed warmly the advantages to the physical sciences which would accrue from such an expedition. There was an area of 1,131,000 square miles around the Pole, at present a blank on our maps, and it was of the highest geographical interest to ascertain whether this space was a silent, frozen solitude, or, as some maintained, an area of lands and waters teeming with life. The ethnological problems were no less interesting, for it was extremely probable that man would be found existing much further north than was at present believed ; and his mode of existence in these regions would be very similar to that of our remote ancestors in Europe, who used flint weapons during the period when an Arctic climate prevailed over Britain and a great part of the Continent. There were also many meteorological problems of the highest interest, which could only be solved by a series of accurate observations, made by skilled persons in very high latitudes. But one of the most important services which such an expedition could render to science would be the measurement of an arc of the meridian in the Arctic zone. This great service—a measurement of 4° of the meridian—could be well performed by a party from the ship, which was proposed to be left near Cape Isabella during the summer season, while the northern expedition was on its road to the Pole. As regards the risk of polar explorations, Capt. Osborn stated, that from 1818 to 1854, England lost only two ships and 128 men out of 42 successive expeditions. Forty thousand miles had been traversed by foot parties in the search of Franklin alone, and yet not one of these parties had been ever lost. An equal amount of geographical discovery had never been accomplished on the earth's surface with so small an amount of human sacrifice. It was a superficial view that Arctic exploration had done nothing but add so many miles of unprofitable coastline to our charts. The discoveries made in the various physical sciences during these expeditions were full of practical importance. It was in the Arctic region that the clue was obtained of the laws of those mysterious currents which flow through the wastes of the ocean like two mighty rivers—the Gulf Stream and the Ice Stream. It was in Boothia that the two Rosses first reached the magnetic pole,—that central point round which revolves the mariner's compass over half the Northern hemisphere; and the mass of observations collected by our explorers on all sides of that pole had added greatly to our knowledge of the laws of magnetic declination and dip. There were two routes to be considered in a project for reaching the North Pole; the one by Spitzbergen, and the other *via* North Greenland. Hakluyt's Head, in Spitzbergen, is about 600 miles from the Pole. Sailing ships have been in this direction within 500 miles of it, and Capt. Parry on the night of July 22, 1827, stood upon floating ice exactly 435 geographical miles from the Pole. He was constrained to give up the attempt, simply because the ice was being swept faster to the south than his men could drag their boats to the north. It was the height of the Arctic summer, and the experience of the last 20 years had shown that instead of starting on such a journey in June, Parry ought to have wintered in Spitzbergen, and started for the Pole in February. The Spitzbergen route, however, has this objection—that no northern land is known on its meridian to give fixed points for the deposit of provisions. Smith's Sound, in North Greenland, would be a better starting-point. It is 120 miles nearer the Pole, and there is good ground for concluding that there is a further extension of continent or islands thence to the northward. The nature of the ice-drift tends to prove this; for it consists of icebergs, which are creatures of the land and born of glaciers. Icebergs abound in Smith's Sound, which would not have been the case had the land terminated abruptly near the Humbolt Glacier. These tell us of great lands with lofty mountains and deep valleys, retaining the moisture and snow-drift of ages, and promise that continuity of frozen seaboard needed, to enable our explorers to reach the Pole.

With respect to the distance to be traversed in going to the Pole and back, Capt. Osborn stated, that we have ample data to show that it has been frequently exceeded by our sailors over the most sterile lands yet visited in the Arctic region. In 1853, Commander M'Clintock's party made 1,220 miles in 105 days, and Captain Richards and the speaker 1,093 miles; Lieutenant Hamilton even accomplished 1,150 miles with a dog-sledge and one man. All these distances are in excess of the 964 to be traversed in going from Cape Parry to the Pole and back. Since 1853, still greater distances have been accomplished. Thus, Lieutenant Mecham marched, in 1854, 1,157 miles *in only seventy days.*

The proposed expedition has the sanction of the Royal Society.

During the past year the Swedish Diet has voted the money necessary to complete the survey for the measurement of an arc of the meridian at Spitzbergen, and there is every reason to expect that the practicability of the undertaking will be immediately settled.

RECENT GEOGRAPHICAL EXPLORATIONS.

In his address at the anniversary of the Royal Geographical Society (Eng.) for 1864, Sir R. I. Murchison, the President, stated, that of late years Russia has been the most eminent of nations in prosecuting geographical research : —

"The Geographical Society of St. Petersburg wields not only the power and influence of the Imperial Government of Russia, but receives also large grants of public money, which have enabled it to carry on simultaneous researches in the steppes near the Caspian and in the Caucasus, and also to describe the grand natural features of Central Asia, the boundaries of the Chinese Empire, and the whole river system of the mighty Amoor with its more numerous affluents. In this way serious geographical errors have been corrected, and new features laid down, by positive observations on maps; while the natural history of the animals and plants, as well as of the human inhabitants of large regions of which little was previously known, has been fully developed."

Referring to explorations in Africa, he remarked, that although much had been accomplished in late years in African exploration, " yet much remains to be done to complete a general sketch even of the geography of equatorial Africa! Is it not essential that the Victoria Nyanza of Speke, a body of water as large as Scotland, which has only been touched at a few points on its southern, western, and northern shores, should have all its shores and affluents examined? And do not the Mountains of the Moon of the same explorer invite a survey? Have we not yet to find out the source of the great Zaire or Congo, and trace that river to its mouth? And who has yet reached the sources of the mighty Niger? Again, when we cast an eye down the map southwards, are we not still in ignorance of the drainage and form of a prodigious extent of country between the Tanganyika Lake of Burton and Speke, and the Zambesi and Shiré of Livingston? Are we not at this moment most anxious to determine, by positive observation, whether there exists a great series of lakes and rivers, proceeding, from Tanganyika on the north, to Lake Nyassa on the south? And has not Livingston's very last effort been directed to this point. If Central Africa is ever to advance in civilization, and its inhabitants are to be brought into commercial relations with Europe, one of the best chances of our accomplishing it will, in my opinion, consist in rendering the great White Nile, a highway of intercourse and traffic."

ON THE EARLY MIGRATIONS OF MAN.

In a paper on the above subject read at the last meeting of the British Association by Mr. J. Crawford, the ethnologist, the author maintained that the view advocated by many writers, of extensive migrations having taken place in primitive times was entirely erroneous. To undertake migrations even on a very moderate scale, a people must have made a considerable advance in civilization. They must have learnt to produce some kind of food capable of being stored, to serve them on a long journey, and must have attained some skill in fabricating and using weapons of offence and defence. The earliest authentic records of emigrating are those of the Greeks, and they were all by sea, requiring a provision of sea-stock, ships, and some nautical experience.   There is no example of a people, considerable in number and tolerably civilized, wholly and voluntarily abandoning the country of their fathers, or even of a whole people being driven to do so by a conqueror.   The early migrations of the Malays bear a tolerably close resemblance to those of the Greeks; but when these migrations were undertaken, the Malays had acquired a certain measure of civilization.   They were a people quite equal to the enterprise of emigrating and establishing colonies.   Notwithstanding these and similar facts, some very learned writers have indulged their imaginations with the supposed migrations of such savages, fancying that the whole earth was peopled from a single starting-point, and by one race of men.   From the learned Dr. Prichard we have an example of these imaginary migrations, in the supposed peopling of the New World from the Old, the latter being fancied to have contained that spot from which the entire earth was peopled.   It is now admitted that the people who achieved this marvellous migration were in the rudest savage state, and that all their arts and acquirements, down to their very languages, were attained after their arrival in America.   It is unnecessary to show that the shortest of the sea-voyages by which these primitive tribes, could have passed from Asia to Europe would be impossible to be performed by them.   The paper concluded by a protest against the modern theory of the Indo-Germanic or Aryan migration, which the author said was founded entirely on philology run mad, and not on ethnology at all.

Prof. Rawlinson, of Oxford, combated, in a long discourse, the views of Mr. Crawford, especially with regard to the Aryan theory, which, he observed, was not a German theory, as the author of the paper asserted, but was originally propounded by our own countryman, Sir. William Jones. The speaker explained that the primitive migrations of man need not be supposed to have been undertaken by large bodies, but to have been gradual and slow.   For instance, with regard to the peopling of India by successive nations of barbarians from the northwest; this may have commenced originally by a few wanderers who finding the climate agreeable and the lands unoccupied, would remain, but, having partial communication with their compatriots left behind, would induce these, one family after another, to follow their example.   The principles of the Aryan theory rested more upon an identity of grammatical structure than on that of the vocabularies of languages.   He was inclined to believe in a single center of creation for man.   The great difficulty was in the received chronology not being sufficient to allow for the great modifications of race that had since ensued.   But we need not be bound by the chronology of Genesis, seeing that the three versions of Scriptures all differed in this respect.   He held himself at liberty to say that the true chronology had not been revealed to us.   The revelation was not meant to give us a physical history of the world, and it did not detract from the general credibility of the Bible that it should be allowed to have become corrupted on these points.

ON THE FIXITY OF THE TYPES OF MAN.

At the last meeting of the British Association, Rev. T. Farrar, in a paper on the above subject maintained that, as far as we can go back, the races of man under all zones, appear to have maintained an unalterable fixity. On the oldest Egyptian monuments we find Jews, Arabs, Negroes, Egyptians, Assyrians, and Europeans depicted with a fidelity as to color and feature hardly to be surpassed by a modern artist. It might be objected, that this fixity was due to the surrounding conditions having remained unaltered. But a glance at the map shows this objection to be invalid; for the eastern region of Asia, from 70° N. lat. to the Equator, offers every variety of temperature, yet is peopled by a single type, the Mongolian. By the side of the fair Circassian we find brown Calmucks; short, dark Lapps live side by side with tall, fair Finns. The color of the American Indian depends very little on geographical positions. In short, color is distributed over the globe in *patches, not in zones*. Europeans transplanted from the temperate to the torrid zone do not, even in the course of generations, undergo very considerable modification of type. This may be seen in the Dutch, who have lived in South Africa for 310 years, and in the descendants of the Spaniards and Portugese in South America; also in the negroes transplanted to America. Independently of this, we find races widely differing from each other, but dwelling side by side, who, so far as we know, have, from time immemorial, been affected by the same climate; such is the case with the Bosjesmen and the Kaffirs, the Fuegians and the Patagonians, the Parsees and the Hindoos. This fixity of type applies to habits as well as to corporeal features. The life of the Ishmaelite of to-day might be described in the identical terms applied to his first ancestor; and the Mongol has the same habits as in the days of Æschylus and Herodotus, or, perhaps, thousands of years before. It may be objected that a period of a few centuries is little or nothing in ethnological matters. It is, at any rate, everything, to those who, without miraculous interference, of which nothing is recorded, have not more than that period between the Deluge and the date of the oldest Egyptian monument in which to account for the appearance of, for instance, the full-grown, well-marked Nigritian type. It remains for every one who is convinced of these facts to draw from them such inferences as appear to him most truthful and logical.

In the discussion which followed, Mr. Russell stated, that he believed that the fixity of the type of races during the historical period was only one of the numerous proofs of the great antiquity of man. The results of various branches of inquiry,—geological, traditional and ethnological,—all pointed one way. He maintained that some amount of modification was known to have taken place in the descendants of one and the same race,—the European and Indian branches of the Aryan race, for example; he therefore concluded that, as two lines not exactly parallel will eventually meet if traced out, so the various races and sections of races of man must be concluded, from this known example of divergence, to have had a common origin, however remote in time that origin may have been.

ON THE SOURCES OF THE SUPPLY OF TIN FOR THE BRONZE TOOLS AND WEAPONS OF ANTIQUITY.

A paper on the above subject was read at the last meeting of the British Association by Mr. J. Crawford. Tin, as is well known is found in only a very few parts of the world, and the only localities producing it, which have reference to the question under consideration are—England, the Malayan Peninsula, and Northern China. The ore is easily reduced, and in early times was found in drift or alluvium. The tin formations of the Malayan countries are the most extensive in the world. These three sources are the only principal ones from which the nations of ancient Europe could have derived this metal. Tin would be supplied in the same manner as silk and spices, with the difference of being imported from the West as well as the East. Merchants dealing in the metal would convey it, as far as it fetched a profit, until western and eastern tin met at a central point, which may have been Egypt. All the nations west of it would be supplied with British, and all those east of it with Malayan or Chinese tin. British tin would be conveyed by land to the Channel, then, crossing it, reach France, and through France find its way to Italy, Greece, and Egypt. The author totally disbelieves, with Sir Cornwall Lewis, in the voyages of the Phœnicians to the Scilly Islands, through which they are imagined to have supplied the eastern world with Cornish tin. The voyage from the entrance of the Mediterranean would be 1,000 miles in a straight line over a stormy ocean ; a voyage very unlikely to be performed by ancient mariners, who, we know, even in the Mediterranean, only crept along the coasts, hauling their craft ashore in foul weather. Besides, the Scilly Islands, the supposed Cassitorides, afford no evidence of having ever produced tin. There is no evidence that either the Greeks or the Phœnicians ever passed the Straits of Gibraltar.

Sir C. Lyell had always wondered whence the ancients had obtained their supply of tin for the bronze articles which they manufactured in so great abundance. We have helmets and weapons of unquestionable antiquity which have just that proportion of tin and copper which is known to be the best for the purpose. Sir Henry James had recently found in the bed of the harbor of Falmouth, an ancient wrecked ingot of tin, which was of precisely that shape and weight which would adapt it as half-cargo for a horse, balanced by a similar ingot on the other side. The metal was thus conveyed along our southern coast to a favorable place for embarkation, whence the cargoes crossed the Channel and were taken overland through Gaul to the Mediterranean. The Ietis of Diodorus Siculus was St. Michael's Mount, which even now is an island at high water. There are not wanting geological signs of the great antiquity of some of the tin-works of Cornwall, for some of them are covered by marine deposits in such a manner as to show that since the time when tin was extracted, there had been a submergence and a subsequent re-elevation of the land. In those ancient times Gaul was peopled by savage tribes, and he thought it much more likely the Phœnicians then came round by sea for their cargoes of tin, than that Gaul was then sufficiently safe to be a highway for trade. Sir H. James described the ingot which he had discovered at Falmouth, and which is now in the Museum of Truro. It resembled in form an *astragalus* or knucklebone, the shape being convenient for slinging over the back of a horse, and it was important to notice that Diodorus Siculus used the term *astragali* in describing the shape of the tin-blocks brought from the Island of Ietis, which there could be no doubt was the same as St.

Michael's Mount. The ingot weighs 120 pounds, and the form of the under-surface is such as to adapt it for resting on the bottom of a boat. He believed, with Sir Charles Lyell, that in more ancient times, previous to the Roman occupation of Gaul, tin was conveyed to the Mediterranean round the coast of Gaul and Lusitania, but more recently, as Diodorus Siculus states, it was carried by land after crossing the narrow part of the channel. He did not believe that there had been any submergence and .re-elevation of the land in Cornwall, but that the marine sediment covering the mines was in existence when tin was originally worked, the ancient miners having bored through the alluvium to get at it. St. Michael's Mount was the Cassitorides of the ancients, and not the Scilly Islands, where there is not a particle of tin. The miners of the present day sometimes find bronze weapons in old tin works. It is not necessary to assume that these were imported, as there is plenty of copper in Cornwall. The speaker believed they were manufactured there, and that a vast proportion of the bronze weapons of antiquity were actually made in Cornwall and exported.

OBITUARY.

Bache, Franklin, Editor of the American Pharmacopœia.

Baikie, Dr., an African explorer.

Blanchard, Thomas, an eminent American inventor.

Bond, George P., the distinguished American astronomer.

Cappocci, M., Director of the Observatory at Naples.

Christie, Sam. H., an English physicist, formerly Secretary of the Royal Society.

Falconer, Hugh, an eminent British geologist.

Gerard, Jules, a well-known French traveler and naturalist.

Gesner, Abram, a well-known chemist of New Brunswick.

Gillis, Com. J. M., director of the National (U. S.) Observatory

Gratiolet, M., a French naturalist.

Hitchcock, Prof. Edward, the distinguished American geologist.

Holmes, Dr. Ezekiel, an American geologist and naturalist.

Maudsley, T. H., a distinguished English engineer.

McCulloch, J. M., an eminent British statistician.

Merriam, Eben, a well-known meteorologist, Brooklyn, N. Y.

Neilson, James, of England, the inventor of the "hot-blast" in iron smelting.

Normandy, Dr., an English chemist and inventor.

Pike, Benjamin, an American optician.

Plana, Baron Giovanni, the eminent Italian astronomer and mathematician.

Portlock, Maj. Gen., Chief of the British Ordnance Survey.

Pugh Evan, Ph. D., of Pennsylvania, a well-known agricultural chemist.

Roberts, Richard, an English mechanic, inventor of the slide lathe.

Rosé, Henreich, the great German chemist.

Schoolcraft, H. R., well known for his researches in reference to the American Indians.

Silliman, Benjamin, the eminent American scientist.

Speke, John Hanning, the discoverer of the source of the Nile.

Struvé, Fred, a well-known Russian astronomer.

Taylor, Prof. Wm. J., an American mineralogist and chemist.

Thomson, Dr. R. D., an eminent Scotch chemist.

Totten, Gen. Joseph G., an American military engineer.

Wagner, Dr. Rudolph, Professor of Natural Sciences in the University of Göttingen.

AMERICAN SCIENTIFIC BIBLIOGRAPHY.

1864.

Allen, H. Monograph of the Bats of North America. Smithsonian Miscellaneous Collections, No. 165.

Almanac, American Nautical for 1865, Washington Bureau of Navigation.

Almanac, National, for 1864. pp. 642. Philadelphia, G. W. Childs.

Baird, S. F. Review of American Birds in the Museum of the Smithsonian Institution. Smithsonian Mis. Collection.

Burton, Warren. The Culture of the Observing Faculties in the Family and the School. Harper & Co., N. Y.

Chapin, Ethan A. The Conservation of Gravity and Heat, with some of the Effects of these Forces on the Physical Condition of the Earth. Springfield, Mass. Pamph.

Clinton, G. W. Plants of Buffalo and its Vicinity. Pamph. Young, Lockwood, & Co., Buffalo.

Coast Survey. U. S. Report for 1862. 49 Diagrams and Charts. Washington, D. C. Pub. Doc.

Cook, Prof. J. P., Jr. Religion and Chemistry: or Proofs of God's Plan in the Atmosphere and its Elements. 8vo. pp. 348. Scribner, N. Y.

Devine, S. R. Photographic Manipulations. 12mo. pp. 98. Seely & Boltwood, N. Y.

Draper, Dr. Henry. On the Construction of a Silvered Glass Telescope, 15½ inches Aperture, and its Use in Celestial Photography. 4to. pp. 55, illus. Smithsonian Pub.

Dussauce, Prof. H. Practical Treatise on the Fabrication of Matches, Gun-Cotton, Colored Fires, &c. 12 mo. pp. 336, illus. Philadelphia. H. C. Baird.

Ede, George. The Management of Steel and Case-Hardening of Iron. D. Appleton & Co., New York.

Elliot, D. G. Monograph of the Family of the Grouse. Illus. Westermann & Co., N. Y.

Gage, Wm. L. Ritter's Comparative Geography. Translation. Phila. Lippincott & Co.

Gillis, J. M. Astronomical and Meteorological Observations made at the U. S. Naval Observatory during the Year 1862. 4to. pp. 699. Washington.

Hoffman, Dr. F. R. A Critical Review of the History of Aniline and the Aniline Colors. New York. Pamph.

Holley, A. L. Ordnance and Armor, the Principles, Fabrications, and Structure of European and American Guns; Metals for Cannon, Experiments against Armor, Notes on Gun-Cotton. 8vo. pp. 647, illus. Van Nostrand, N. Y.

Hough, G. W. Report of the Dudley Observatory, Albany, 1863. 8vo. Albany, N. Y.

Morse, E. S. Observations on the Terrestrial Pulmonifera of Maine, with Catalogue of the Fluviatile and Terrestrial Mollusca of the State. Illus. pp. 64. Portland, Maine.

Packard, A. S., Jr. Synopsis of the Bombycidae of the United States. 8vo. pp. 130. Phila.

Percy, Dr. S. R. Physiological and Chemical Observations on the Alkaloid Veratria. 8vo. pp. 87. Philadelphia. Collins.

Rafinesque, Constantine. Recent and Fossil Conchology, edited by W. G. Binney and G. W. Tryon, Jr. Illus. Baillierè, N. Y.

Report of the Commissioner of Agriculture for 1862. Public doc.

Report of the Commissioner of Patents for 1861. Public doc.

Root, M. A. The Heliographic Art, its Theory and Practice, in all its various Branches. 12mo. pp. 456. Lippincott & Co., Phila.

Safford, Truman Henry. On the Right Ascension of the Pole Star, as determined from Observations. Pamph. Cambridge, Mass.

Small, Dr. E. Anatomy and Physiology rendered attractive. Boston. Chase & Nichols.

Smiles, Samuel. Iron-workers and Tool-makers. Boston. Ticknor & Fields.

Spencer, Herbert. The Classification of the Sciences. Pamph. Appleton & Co., New York.

Stillman, Paul. The Steam Engine Indicator. Van Nostrand, N. Y.

Sullivant, W. S. Icones Muscorum: or Figures and Description of those Mosses, peculiar to Eastern North America, which have not been heretofore figured. 199 plates. pp. 216. 8vo. Cambridge. Sever & Francis.

Townsend, Howard. The Sunbeam and the Spectroscope. Pamph. Albany, N. Y. J. Munsell.

Trask, John B., Dr. Register of Earthquakes in California from 1800 to 1868. 26 pp. 8vo. San Francisco.

Tryon, G. W. Jr. American Journal of Conchology. Philadelphia (625 Market Street).

Verrill, A. E. Revision of the Polyps of the Eastern Coast of the United States. 46 pp., with plate. Boston, Mass.

Wells, David A. The Annual of Scientific Discovery for 1864. Boston. Gould & Lincoln.

Wilcocks, Dr. A. Thoughts on the Influence of Ether in the Solar System. Sherman & Co., Phila.

Winchell, A. Prof. Report on the Collections in Geology, Botany, and Zoology in the Museum of the University of Michigan. Ann Arbor Michigan.

Winslow, Dr. C. F. The Cooling Globe, or the Mechanics of Geology. Pamph. Walker, Wise & Co., Boston.

Youmans, E. L. The Correlation and Conservation of Forces. 12mo. pp. 438. D. Appleton & Co., New York.

INDEX.

𝔙aluable 𝔚orks,

PUBLISHED BY

GOULD AND LINCOLN,

59 Washington Street, Boston.

HAMILTON'S LECTURES, embracing the METAPHYSICAL and LOGICAL
COURSES; with Notes, from Original Materials, and an Appendix, containing
the Author's Latest Development of his New Logical Theory. Edited by Rev.
HENRY LONGUEVILLE MANSEL, B. D., Prof. of Moral and Metaphysical Phi-
losophy in Magdalen College, Oxford, and JOHN VEITCH, M. A., of Edinburgh.
In two royal octavo volumes, viz.,

   I. METAPHYSICAL LECTURES. Royal octavo, cloth, 3.50.

   II. LOGICAL LECTURES. Royal octavo, cloth, 3.50.

   ☞ G. & L., by a special arrangement with the family of the late Sir William Hamilton, are the
authorized, and only authorized, American publishers of this distinguished author's *matchless*
LECTURES ON METAPHYSICS AND LOGIC.
The above have already been introduced into nearly all our leading colleges.

LOOMIS' ELEMENTS OF GEOLOGY; adapted to Schools and Colleges.
With numerous Illustrations. By J. R. LOOMIS, President of Lewisburg University, Pa. 12mo, cloth, 1.25.

   "It is surpassed by no work before the American public."—*M. B. Anderson, LL. D., President
Rochester University.*

PEABODY'S CHRISTIANITY THE RELIGION OF NATURE.
Lectures delivered before the Lowell Institute in 1863, by A. P. PEABODY,
D. D., LL. D., Preacher to the University, and Plummer Professor of Christian
Morals, Harvard College. Royal 12mo, cloth, 1.50.

   A masterly production, distinguished for its acuteness and earnestness, its force of logic and fair-
ness of statement, written in a style of singular accuracy and beauty.

PALEY'S NATURAL THEOLOGY: Illustrated by forty Plates, with Selections from the Notes of Dr. Paxton, and Additional Notes, Original and
Selected, with a Vocabulary of Scientific Terms. Edited by JOHN WARK,
M. D. Improved edition, with elegant illustrations. 12mo, cloth, embossed,
1.75.

MANSEL'S PROLEGOMENA LOGICA; the Psychological Character of
Logical Processes. By HENRY LONGUEVILLE MANSEL, B. D. 12mo, cloth,
1.25.

YOUNG LADIES' CLASS BOOK: a Selection of Lessons for Reading
Prose and Verse. By EBENEZER BAILEY, A. M. Cloth, embossed, 1.25.

1

Gould and Lincoln's Publications.

HAVEN'S MENTAL PHILOSOPHY; Including the Intellect, the Sensibilities, and the Will. By JOSEPH HAVEN, Professor of Intellectual and Moral Philosophy, Chicago University. Royal 12mo, cloth, embossed, 2.00.

It is believed this work will be found preëminently distinguished for the COMPLETENESS with which it presents the whole subject.

HAVEN'S MORAL PHILOSOPHY: Including Theoretical and Practical Ethics. By JOSEPH HAVEN, D. D., late Professor of Moral and Intellectual Philosophy in Chicago University. Royal 12mo, cloth, embossed, 1.75.

It is eminently scientific in method, and thorough in discussion, and its views on unsettled questions in morals are discriminating and sound.

HOPKINS' LECTURES ON MORAL SCIENCE, delivered before the Lowell Institute, Boston, by MARK HOPKINS, D. D., President of Williams College. Royal 12mo, cloth, 1.50.

☞ An important work from the pen of one of the most profound thinkers of the age.

WAYLAND'S ELEMENTS OF MORAL SCIENCE. By FRANCIS WAYLAND, D. D., late President of Brown University. 12mo, cloth, 1.75.

WAYLAND'S MORAL SCIENCE ABRIDGED, and adapted to the use of Schools and Academies, by the Author. Half mor., 70 cts.

The same, CHEAP SCHOOL EDITION, boards, 45 cts.

WAYLAND'S ELEMENTS OF POLITICAL ECONOMY. By FRANCIS WAYLAND, D. D. 12mo, cloth, 1.75.

WAYLAND'S POLITICAL ECONOMY ABRIDGED, and adapted to the use of Schools and Academies, by the Author. Half mor., 70 cents.

All the above works by Dr. Wayland are used as text-books in most of the colleges and higher schools throughout the Union, and are highly approved.

AGASSIZ AND GOULD'S PRINCIPLES OF ZOÖLOGY; Touching the Structure, Development, Distribution, and Natural Arrangement, of the RACES OF ANIMALS, living and extinct, with numerous Illustrations. For the use of Schools and Colleges. Part I. COMPARATIVE PHYSIOLOGY. By LOUIS AGASSIZ and AUGUSTUS A. GOULD. Revised edition. 1.50.

      PART II. Systematic Zoölogy. *In preparation.*

"It is simple and elementary in its style, full in its illustrations, comprehensive in its range, yet well condensed, and brought into the narrow compass requisite for the purpose intended." — *Silliman's Journal.*

RITTER'S GEOGRAPHICAL STUDIES. Translated from the German of Carl Ritter, by Rev. W. L. GAGE. With a Sketch of the Author's Life, and a Portrait. 12mo, cloth, 1.50.

This volume contains the grand generalizations of Ritter's life-work, the Erdkunde, in eighteen volumes; his lectures on the Relations of Geography and History, and a number of important papers on Physical Geography.

PROGRESSIVE PENMANSHIP, Plain and ornamental, for the use of Schools. By N. D. GOULD, author of "Beauties of Writing," "Writing Master's Assistant," etc. In five parts, each, 20 cts.

Gould and Lincoln's Publications.

MILLER'S CRUISE OF THE BETSEY; or, a Summer Ramble among the Fossiliferous Deposits of the Hebrides. With Rambles of a Geologist; or, Ten Thousand Miles over the Fossiliferous Deposits of Scotland. 12mo, pp. 524, cloth, 1.75.

MILLER'S ESSAYS, Historical and Biographical, Political and Social, Literary and Scientific. By HUGH MILLER. With Preface by Peter Bayne. 12mo, cloth, 1.75.

MILLER'S FOOT-PRINTS OF THE CREATOR; or, the Asterolepis of Stromness, with numerous Illustrations. With a Memoir of the Author, by LOUIS AGASSIZ. 12mo, cloth, 1.75.

MILLER'S FIRST IMPRESSIONS OF ENGLAND AND ITS PEOPLE. With a fine Engraving of the Author. 12mo, cloth, 1.50.

MILLER'S HEADSHIP OF CHRIST, and the Rights of the Christian People, a Collection of Personal Portraitures, Historical and Descriptive Sketches and Essays, with the Author's celebrated Letter to Lord Brougham. By HUGH MILLER. Edited, with a Preface, by PETER BAYNE, A. M. 12mo, cloth, 1.75.

MILLER'S OLD RED SANDSTONE; or, New Walks in an Old Field. Illustrated with Plates and Geological Sections. NEW EDITION, REVISED AND MUCH ENLARGED, by the addition of new matter and new Illustrations, &c. 12mo, cloth, 1.75.

MILLER'S POPULAR GEOLOGY; With Descriptive Sketches from a Geologist's Portfolio. By HUGH MILLER. With a Resume of the Progress of Geological Science during the last two years. By MRS. MILLER. 12mo, cloth, 1.75.

MILLER'S SCHOOLS AND SCHOOLMASTERS; or, the Story of my Education. AN AUTOBIOGRAPHY. With a full-length Portrait of the Author. 12mo, 1.75.

MILLER'S TALES AND SKETCHES. Edited, with a Preface, &c., by MRS. MILLER. 12mo, 1.50.
    Among the subjects are: Recollections of Ferguson — Burns — The Salmon Fisher of Udoll — The Widow of Dunskaith — The Lykewake — Bill Whyte — The Young Surgeon — George Ross, the Scotch Agent — M'Culloch, the Mechanician — A True Story of the Life of a Scotch Merchant of the Eighteenth Century.

MILLER'S TESTIMONY OF THE ROCKS; or, Geology in its Bearings on the two Theologies, Natural and Revealed. "Thou shalt be in league with the stones of the field."— *Job.* With numerous elegant Illustrations. One volume, royal 12mo, cloth, 1.75.

HUGH MILLER'S WORKS. Ten volumes, uniform style, in an elegant box, embossed cloth, 17; library sheep, 20; half calf, 34; antique, 34.

MACAULAY ON SCOTLAND. A Critique from HUGH MILLER'S "Witness." 16mo, flexible cloth. 37 cts.

CHAMBERS' CYCLOPÆDIA OF ENGLISH LITERATURE. A Selection of the choicest productions of English Authors, from the earliest to the present time. Connected by a Critical and Biographical History. Forming two large imperial octavo volumes of 700 pages each, double-column letter press; with upwards of three hundred elegant Illustrations. Edited by ROBERT CHAMBERS. Embossed cloth, 6.50; sheep, 7.50; cloth, full gilt, 9.00; half calf, 12.00; full calf, 16.00.

This work embraces about *one thousand Authors*, chronologically arranged, and classed as poets, historians, dramatists, philosophers, metaphysicians, divines, &c., with choice selections from their writings, connected by a Biographical, Historical, and Critical Narrative: thus presenting a complete view of English Literature from the earliest to the present time. Let the reader open where he will, he cannot fail to find matter for profit and delight. The selections are gems — infinite riches in a little room; in the language of another, "A WHOLE ENGLISH LIBRARY FUSED DOWN INTO ONE CHEAP BOOK."

☞ THE AMERICAN edition of this valuable work is enriched by the addition of fine steel and mezzotint engravings of the heads of SHAKSPEARE, ADDISON, BYRON; a full-length portrait of DR. JOHNSON; and a beautiful scenic representation of OLIVER GOLDSMITH and DR. JOHNSON. These important and elegant additions, together with superior paper and binding, and other improvements, render the AMERICAN far superior to the English edition.

CHAMBERS' HOME BOOK; or, Pocket Miscellany, containing a Choice Selection of Interesting and Instructive Reading, for the Old and Young. Six volumes. 16mo, cloth, 6.00; library sheep, 7.00.

ARVINE'S CYCLOPÆDIA OF ANECDOTES OF LITERATURE AND THE FINE ARTS. Containing a copious and choice Selection of Anecdotes of the various forms of Literature, of the Arts, of Architecture, Engravings, Music, Poetry, Painting, and Sculpture, and of the most celebrated Literary Characters and Artists of different Countries and Ages, &c. By KAZLITT ARVINE, A. M., author of "Cyclopædia of Moral and Religious Anecdotes." With numerous illustrations. 725 pp. octavo, cloth, 4.00; sheep, 5.00; cloth, gilt, 6.00; half calf, 7.00.

This is unquestionably the choicest collection of *Anecdotes* ever published. It contains *three thousand and forty Anecdotes:* and such is the wonderful variety, that it will be found an almost inexhaustible fund of interest for every class of readers. The elaborate classification and Indexes must commend it especially to public speakers, to the various classes of *literary and scientific men,* to *artists, mechanics,* and *others,* as a DICTIONARY *for reference,* in relation to facts on the numberless subjects and characters introduced. There are also more than *one hundred and fifty fine Illustrations.*

BAYNE'S ESSAYS IN BIOGRAPHY AND CRITICISM. By PETER BAYNE, M. A., author of "The Christian Life, Social and Individual." Arranged in two Series, or Parts. 12mo, cloth, each, 1.75.

These volumes have been prepared and a number of the Essays written by the author expressly for his American publishers.

THE LANDING AT CAPE ANNE; or, THE CHARTER OF THE FIRST PERMANENT COLONY ON THE TERRITORY OF THE MASSACHUSETTS COMPANY. Now discovered, and first published from the ORIGINAL MANUSCRIPT, with an inquiry into its authority, and a HISTORY OF THE COLONY, 1624–1628, Roger Conant, Governor. By J. WINGATE THORNTON. 8vo, cloth, 2.50.

☞ "A rare contribution to the early history of New England."— *Journal.*